Attention and Associative Learning

Attention and Associative Learning
From Brain to Behaviour

Edited by

Chris J. Mitchell

Mike E. Le Pelley

OXFORD
UNIVERSITY PRESS

OXFORD
UNIVERSITY PRESS

Great Clarendon Street, Oxford OX2 6DP

Oxford University Press is a department of the University of Oxford.
It furthers the University's objective of excellence in research, scholarship,
and education by publishing worldwide in

Oxford New York

Auckland Cape Town Dar es Salaam Hong Kong Karachi
Kuala Lumpur Madrid Melbourne Mexico City Nairobi
New Delhi Shanghai Taipei Toronto

With offices in

Argentina Austria Brazil Chile Czech Republic France Greece
Guatemala Hungary Italy Japan Poland Portugal Singapore
South Korea Switzerland Thailand Turkey Ukraine Vietnam

Published in the United States
by Oxford University Press Inc., New York

First published 2010

British Library Cataloguing in Publication Data
Data available

Library of Congress Cataloging in Publication Data
Data available

Typeset by Glyph International, Bangalore, India
Printed in Great Britain
on acid-free paper by
CPI Antony Rowe, Chippenham, Wiltshire

ISBN 978–0–19–955053–1

10 9 8 7 6 5 4 3 2 1

Preface

Attention provides the gateway between the mass of information in the world, and the small subset of that information that we select for action, further analysis and learning. Consequently, attention is perhaps the most potent source of bias in cognition. The possibility that attention might influence what is learned (and the reverse - that what is learned might influence attention) was originally made many years ago in the context of studies of animal conditioning. This idea has really come of age, however, in the last 5-10 years. There is currently more research activity on the role of attention in learning than there has been at any previous time. This work includes analyses at the behavioral level and at the neural level, both in humans and in non-human animals. It also extends to a variety of clinical disorders.

This increase in interest in attention and learning was made especially obvious to us at the 3rd International Conference of the Australian Learning Group (ALG). The conference was held in July 2006 on Magnetic Island, just off the coast of tropical far North Queensland, Australia. A strong focus of the many excellent talks was on the role of attention in learning. Indeed, a significant proportion of the contributors to this book were delegates at that conference. We decided then that a book on the state of the art in attention and learning research would be an enormously valuable resource. This is that book.

We have summarized the contents of the book in Chapter 1, and so there is no need for further summary here. All that remains is to thank the contributors for all of their very hard work and for their patience with the many pedantic comments made by the editors. We very much hope that readers will enjoy these chapters as much as we did.

Chris Mitchell and Mike Le Pelley

Contents

Contributors

James Close
Max Planck Institute for
Evolutionary Anthropology,
Department of Developmental and
Comparative Psychology,
Leipzig, Germany

Stephen E. Denton
Department of Psychological
and Brain Sciences,
Indiana University,
Bloomington, USA

Anthony Dickinson
Department of Experimental
Psychology,
University of Cambridge,
Cambridge, UK

Anaïs M. Duffaud
INRA,
Bordeux, France

Theodora Duka
School of Psychology,
University of Sussex,
Falmer, Brighton, UK

David N. George
School of Psychology,
Cardiff University,
Cardiff , UK

Steven Graham
Functional Brain Imaging Lab,
Department of Psychology,
National University of Singapore,
Singapore

Geoffrey Hall
Department of Psychology,
University of York,
York, UK

Adam Hampshire
MRC Cognition and Brain Sciences
Unit,
Cambridge, UK

Justin A. Harris
School of Psychology,
The University of Sydney,
Sydney, Australia

Lee Hogarth
School of Psychology,
University of Nottingham,
Nottingham, UK

Peter C. Holland
Department of Psychological and
Brain Sciences,
Johns Hopkins University,
Baltimore, USA

Nathan M. Holmes
School of Psychology,
The University of Sydney,
Sydney, Australia

Robert C. Honey
School of Psychology,
Cardiff University,
Cardiff, UK

Simon Killcross
School of Psychology,
University of New South Wales,
Sydney, Australia

John K. Kruschke
Department of Psychological and Brain Sciences,
Indiana University,
Bloomington, USA

Mike E. Le Pelley
School of Psychology,
Cardiff University,
Cardiff, UK

Tzu-Ching E. Lin
School of Psychology,
Cardiff University,
Cardiff, UK

Nicholas J. Mackintosh
Department of Experimental Psychology,
University of Cambridge,
Cambridge, UK

Jean-Marie Maddux
School of Psychology,
University of New South Wales,
Sydney, Australia

Ian P. L. McLaren
School of Psychology,
University of Exeter,
Washington Singer Laboratories,
Exeter, UK

Chris J. Mitchell
School of Psychology,
University of New South Wales,
Sydney, Australia

Adrian M. Owen
MRC Cognition and Brain Sciences Unit,
Cambridge, UK

John M. Pearce
School of Psychology,
Cardiff University,
Cardiff, UK

Philip T. Quinlan
Department of Psychology,
The University of York,
York, UK

Gabriel Rodriguez
Faculty of Psychology,
University of the Basque Country,
San Sebastian, Spain

Andrew J. Wills
UK School of Psychology,
University of Exeter,
Washington Singer Laboratories,
Exeter, UK

Chapter 1

An introduction to attention and learning

Chris J. Mitchell and Mike E. Le Pelley

'Everyone knows what attention is', as William James (1890) told us. While he didn't say it, we also suspect James wouldn't disagree with the idea that 'everyone knows what learning is'. Indeed, attention and learning are two of the most studied concepts in modern experimental psychology. It should come as no surprise, then, that researchers in many psychological disciplines—cognitive, perceptual, biological, and clinical—have converged on the idea that attention and learning are not separable processes, but may interact with one another in complex ways. In this book, we have drawn together contributors from all of these disciplines, with the goal of describing this interaction, and its implications, at different levels from brain to behaviour.

The aim of this brief introductory chapter is to sketch out the shape of the book, and draw out some of the main ideas. One feature will come as no surprise to readers with even the most basic knowledge of the role of attention in learning. Nearly all of the chapters cite two specific papers. The first is by Nicholas Mackintosh (1975). The second is by John Pearce and Geoffrey Hall (1980). These two papers describe two possible mechanisms by which stimuli might change in 'salience' or 'associability' as a consequence of learning about those stimuli. Salience and associability are closely related to each other, and to the idea of attention. Salience is usually taken to refer to the degree to which a stimulus will capture attention. One determinant of salience is the physical intensity of the stimulus. Thus, a loud noise is usually expected to capture more attention than a quiet noise. Associability refers to the ease or speed with which a stimulus can be learned about. It is further assumed that, all else being equal, learning will be faster (associability will be higher) for more salient stimuli. Thus, the relationship between a loud noise and shock will be learned faster than between a quiet noise and shock (Kamin and Schaub, 1963). Although this example provides a simple demonstration of the role of attention in learning, the focus of this book is not on the physical differences that exist between stimuli, and their effect on learning. Rather, it is on the ways in which training history might affect stimulus salience, associability, or (perhaps more controversially, as we shall see in some of the chapters to follow) the attention paid to a stimulus.

Mackintosh suggested that an organism will attend more to stimuli that are good predictors of the events that follow them than to stimuli that are poor predictors of the events that follow them. The Pearce-Hall model suggests almost the reverse. According to this model, organisms will attend to stimuli only when the outcome that follows them is *not* consistently predicted. These apparently contradictory theories can accommodate a wide range of findings in the associative literature. They were originally meant to be competitors. However, many of the contributors to this volume accept that there is an element of truth to both models. Some authors have attempted to reconcile the two theories, postulating a 'hybrid' model of learning. Whatever the resolution to this ongoing debate, it is very clear that the dominance of these two theories continues to the present day.

We were very pleased, therefore, when Pearce and Mackintosh agreed to co-author a chapter for the book (Chapter 2). Perhaps surprisingly, this is the first time they have appeared together in print. The idea was that they would be well placed to provide a historical context for the chapters to follow. In their review of the findings, they find evidence to support both the Mackintosh and the Pearce-Hall model. However, they go well beyond a simple historical account, and propose a new hybrid model of learning in which associability is determined by a combination of the Mackintosh and Pearce-Hall mechanisms. Reasons why organisms should possess two attentional learning mechanisms are then tentatively suggested. This hybrid approach sees the Pearce-Hall model as describing the attention required to engage in the controlled processing necessary for learning. The Mackintosh model, on the other hand, describes the mechanism that controls attention to stimuli that have already been learned about. This mechanism helps to produce appropriate responding. This analysis has precedents in the literature, and appears again in different guises throughout the book.

Hall and Rodriguez also propose a hybrid attentional model of learning in Chapter 3. In this model, there is much greater emphasis on the role of the associability mechanism proposed by Pearce and Hall (1980). In fact the mechanism proposed by Mackintosh (1975), does not feature in the Hall-Rodriguez model. Hall and Rodriguez accept that many findings do appear consistent with the idea that predictive cues produce faster learning. However, they argue that each of these findings can be explained either by a more sophisticated application of the Pearce-Hall model, or by some other mechanism, perhaps related to differences in perceptual learning or habituation. In particular, it is suggested that predictive cues produce more vigorous responding on test because they have been protected from habituation by the outcomes that followed them in training.

In Chapter 4, Hogarth, Dickinson, and Duka present the results of their human learning experiments. Consistent with the previous two chapters, they also suggest that attention has more than one role in learning. Their approach is rather different from that taken in most animal experiments, in which attentional mechanisms are usually inferred from the examination of learning rates and conditioned responses (although see Kaye and Pearce, 1984). In Hogarth's studies, attention is examined more directly through the measurement of eye gaze. Three separable attentional processes are described: 'looking for action', 'looking for learning', and 'looking for liking'. The first two of these appear to map nicely on to the mechanisms described in Chapter 2 by Pearce and Mackintosh. Thus, 'looking for action' follows Mackintosh rules and 'looking for learning' follows Pearce-Hall rules. The third mechanism, which is new, is sensitive to the valence of the outcome with which the stimulus has been paired. Thus, attention will be maintained to stimuli that predict positive outcomes. Stimuli that predict negative outcomes might attract attention at first ('looking for action'), but will not maintain attention because they will not engage the 'looking for liking' attentional process.

This description of Chapters 2–4 makes one thing very clear. Most researchers agree that there probably is no 'unitary faculty of attention' (Hall and Rodriguez, this volume). Rather, multiple 'attentional' mechanisms or processes, which are sensitive to different aspects of the stimulus and its reinforcement history, interact to determine learning and performance. Many of the findings considered in these initial chapters relate to changes in stimulus salience (or attention) result from pairing stimuli with some outcome of significance. Of course, non-reinforced exposure to stimuli is also thought to produce changes in attention. The following two chapters focus on the possibility of changes in attention following non-reinforced stimulus exposure.

Familiar stimuli are usually thought to command fewer attentional resources than otherwise equivalent novel stimuli. One consequence of this reduction in attention is that learning occurs more slowly to familiar than novel stimuli, a phenomenon termed 'latent inhibition'. In Chapter 5, Holmes and Harris describe the theories that have been proposed to account for latent inhibition effects, which include attentional theories such as the Mackintosh (1975) and Pearce-Hall (1980) models. They point out that, although latent inhibition is often assumed to result from changes in attention, this need not be the case. Indeed, certain findings cannot easily be accounted for in attentional terms (Killcross and Balleine, 1996). Nevertheless, attentional accounts of latent inhibition remain dominant.

One interesting point made by Holmes and Harris is that Wagner's (1981) sometimes opponent process (SOP) model should be considered to be an attentional model. Wagner (1981) proposes that many learning phenomena result from capacity limits in the learning system. Indeed, this point is also touched upon by Hall and Rodriguez in Chapter 3. They point out that, consistent with SOP, the presence of a distracter stimulus will reduce learning about a target stimulus (overshadowing) in part because the target stimulus receives fewer processing resources (James and Wagner, 1980). Holmes and Harris suggest that the explanation of latent inhibition provided by SOP is also attentional. The more general issue raised by this discussion, regarding what does and what does not constitute an attentional mechanism, is addressed directly in Chapter 9.

Under some circumstances, rather than retarding learning, non-reinforced pre-exposure can actually enhance later learning. In particular, very similar stimuli (such as two Clarets) become easier to discriminate as they become more familiar – this is perceptual learning, and seems to be quite the opposite of latent inhibition. Perceptual learning has also been attributed to the operation of attentional mechanisms. In Chapter 6, McLaren, Wills, and Graham present a refinement of McLaren and Mackintosh (2000) model of perceptual learning. The new model features two mechanisms. Firstly, when two similar stimuli are presented a number of times, their common features receive twice as much exposure, and so suffer from twice as much latent inhibition, as those features that are unique to each stimulus. The relative novelty of the unique features will, therefore, enhance the relative salience of these features and allow better discrimination. However, a second, controlled attention mechanism can also produce an effect. Thus, McLaren *et al.* argue that, at a more global level, participants can better discriminate the pre-exposed stimuli only if they have learned to attend to 'this kind' of stimulus. In the example above, they must have learned to attend to Clarets *in general* in order for perceptual learning to be observed. If, by contrast, participants are encouraged to ignore the target stimuli during pre-exposure, a 'conditioned inattention' effect will instead produce a reduction in discrimination performance on test.

In these initial chapters, it is assumed that attentional mechanisms *of some kind* are in operation when we learn. Honey, Close, and Lin take a quite different approach in Chapter 7. As in the previous chapter, the focus is on perceptual learning, but following reinforced, rather than non-reinforced pre-exposure. As James (1890) pointed out, when two stimuli are followed by different outcomes during pre-exposure, discrimination performance is enhanced (see also Lawrence, 1949). This is termed acquired distinctiveness. One explanation of this finding is that, as only the unique features of the stimuli predict the two different outcomes, the organism learns to attend to those features. This is the approach taken by attentional theories such as that proposed by Mackintosh (1975). By contrast, Honey *et al.* describe a single-process connectionist model that accounts for the acquired distinctiveness effect in terms of representation development, and which has no mechanism allowing for learned changes in attention. These authors suggest that this line of reasoning could be applied to many other effects that have traditionally been taken as providing evidence for the attentional modulation of learning. This leads one to wonder whether the idea of learned changes in attention need be invoked at all in the context of associative learning.

In Chapter 8, Le Pelley takes up the challenge laid down by Honey *et al.* He argues that invoking the construct of attention in learning is useful to the extent that it describes a *set* of properties that a stimulus might possess. In other words, there is value in appealing to attention if it can be demonstrated that previous learning also influences other aspects of stimulus processing (beyond merely learning rate) that have been established as characteristic of attention in the wider cognitive psychology literature. Le Pelley cites a number of such demonstrations from studies of human learning, including attentional blink experiments, cued reaction time experiments, and eye gaze studies similar to those described by Hogarth *et al.* in Chapter 3. These findings are consistent with the idea that prior learning influences the attention paid to stimuli, but further work is needed to provide strong evidence that these learning-induced changes in attention will, in turn, affect later learning about those stimuli.

This view of attention from a cognitive psychologist's perspective continues in Chapters 9–11. In Chapter 9, Quinlan addresses the more fundamental question of what it means for a theory of learning, or an empirically observed phenomenon of learning, to be truly attentional. He argues that the concept of attention has no value unless it relates to selection among stimuli that compete for limited processing resources. This is how the term attention is understood in the human cognitive literature. Quinlan refers back to Rescorla and Wagner's (1972) point that, in most conditioning procedures, there is no reason to suppose that rats are at the limit of their cognitive capacities when learning about, for example, two stimuli each of 30 s duration—surely both stimuli can be perceived and learned about. Therefore, an attentional mechanism is unlikely to play a role in these procedures. However, Quinlan cites more recent evidence (from both rats and humans) that implicates a competition for limited resources in learning. The implication is that attention, by this definition, may play a role in learning, but might not be as pervasive as has often been assumed.

In Chapter 10, Mitchell presents some experiments in which both learning and memory are tested. He first examines associative learning in which cues and outcomes are paired in a causal judgment task. The particular focus is on blocking of learning about a target cue by the presence of a (potentially more salient) cue that is a known predictor of the outcome. Then he moves on to perceptual learning following non-reinforced pre-exposure. Mitchell's conclusion is that there is a role for attention (as defined by Quinlan in the previous chapter) in both kinds of learning. That is, in both cases, he finds evidence for competition between cues for limited processing resources. The mechanism proposed here is a very simple filter mechanism like that proposed by Broadbent (1958). Competition for access to processing resources, via the filter, results in variations in the degree to which the target stimuli are encoded in memory, and variations in the degree to which those stimuli are learned about.

In the last of the more cognitively oriented chapters, Kruschke and Denton take a Bayesian approach to the problem. Bayesian models present a major challenge to the traditional link-based models of associative learning. This approach is described briefly by Quinlan in Chapter 9 and is a close relative of the inferential approach introduced by Mitchell at the start of Chapter 10. Kruschke points out that the great virtue of Bayesian models is that they can be applied at many different levels of analysis, from learning by individual neurons (and perhaps more microscopic levels) to learning by groups of people (and perhaps more macroscopic levels). Bayesian approaches expand the theoretical landscape by opening new vistas for formally expressing notions like attention and learning. In Chapter 11, Kruschke and Denton present a 'locally Bayesian' model of learning in which Bayesian processes determine the allocation of attention to cues. A novel experiment is described, the results of which suggest that participants can learn an association between a cue and the attention paid to another cue ('in the presence of cue X, attend to cue Y'). The results also suggest that this learning of an attentional distribution may be subject to backward blocking, just as more standard cue-to-outcome associations are subject to backward blocking. It is argued that backward blocking of cue-to-attention associations of this kind support Kruschke's locally Bayesian model, and challenge traditional attentional models of learning.

The last three chapters of the book focus on the neural mechanisms underlying the interaction between attention and learning. In Chapter 12, Holland and Maddux describe their experiments investigating the effects of brain lesions on attention in rats. The idea (introduced in Chapters 2–4) that there are two attentional mechanisms, one described by the Pearce-Hall model and the other described by the Mackintosh model, is continued here. As in some of these earlier chapters, it is proposed that the Pearce-Hall model describes attention for learning, but the Mackintosh model describes attention for action. Holland and Maddux focus on associability (attention for learning), and, therefore, the Pearce-Hall model. Some very elegant lesion studies are described in which it is shown that a surprise-induced *enhancement* in associability can be disrupted by lesions of the central nucleus of the amygdala (or of certain neocortical regions to which it is connected). By contrast, an expectancy-induced *decline* in associability is disrupted by lesions to the hippocampus. It is argued that these two processes have different time courses: the occurrence of surprising outcomes produces a rapid increase in associability, whereas consistent pairings of a cue with the same outcome produce a more gradual decline in associability.

In Chapter 13, George, Duffaud, and Killcross also use results of lesion studies in rats to examine the neural mechanisms of attention. However, their focus is on attention to stimulus dimensions, and the shifting of attention between dimensions, in discrimination learning. Hampshire and Owen, in Chapter 14, use a related experimental strategy combined with functional magnetic resonance imaging (fMRI) to investigate the neural mechanisms of attention in human participants. Both research groups use experimental tasks related to the 'ID/ED' task. In this task, subjects are trained on one discrimination task and are then required to learn a second discrimination between two new stimuli. In one group, the second task can be solved by attending to the same stimulus dimension as that used to solve the first task. These subjects are said to have made an 'intradimensional shift' (the ID group). In another group, subjects are required to shift attention to a different stimulus dimension to solve the second task. These subjects are said to have made an 'extradimensional shift' (the ED group).

The ID/ED task is argued to make contact with a number of different cognitive processes, all of which are connected with attention (e.g. maintenance of attentional set and shifting from one attentional set to another). To examine these different components in isolation, George *et al.* use a novel 'optional shift' task in their rat studies, and Hampshire and Owen use a variant of the ID/ED task with humans. Both lines of research suggest that different brain regions are involved in different attentional processes. Consistent with the conclusions of many of the earlier chapters, then, the implication is that attention is not a unitary phenomenon at the neural level. Instead these results suggest that what we might label 'attention' in fact reflects the interaction of a collection of neural processes: an attentional network.

The brain areas identified in these chapters have implications beyond attentional learning. Thus, George *et al.* conclude with the intriguing idea that the brain region involved in maintenance of attentional sets is the same as that involved in the maintenance of habits in instrumental conditioning. They also suggest that there may be a link (based on common neural circuitry) between shifting of attentional sets and goal-directed instrumental behaviour. Hampshire and Owen extend their findings in a different direction, to clinical disorders such as Parkinson's disease, and obsessive compulsive disorder (OCD) as well as the cognitive deficits produced by ageing.

In summary, the chapters can be seen as addressing four main themes, with some chapters bearing on more than one of these themes. Chapters 2–7 focus on some specific theories regarding the role of attention in learning, and on the experimental evidence that allows us to choose between those theories. Chapters 7–9 address the general rationale common to all such theories (namely that attention and learning are indeed related). Chapters 8–11 look at the problem from a cognitive perspective and Chapters 12–14 focus on the neural mechanisms involved in attention and learning. We ask ourselves now, was this project successful? That is, do the ideas collected here produce a coherent whole? On the positive side, the ideas proposed by Pearce and Hall (1980) and Mackintosh (1975) appear in most of the chapters and create a common thread throughout the book. Evidence for both models is cited, and models that are a hybrid of both are suggested. This implies that most contributors agree, at least at a very general level, on what this book is about.

Another strong theme that emerges, which could be interpreted as being less positive, is that there is little agreement as to exactly what the term 'attention' means in the context of learning. Some argue that we possess a collection of attentional processes or mechanisms that have very different operating characteristics. Others argue for a narrower definition, and insist that an attentional mechanism, if it is to be classified as such, must possess certain defining features. Still others deny that the term has any useful meaning at all. But we believe that this should not be a reason for disheartenment; quite the opposite. It may be that the term attention is difficult to define. However, these arguments suggest that the question of the relationship between attention and learning is still a vibrant and relevant focus of research. Indeed, we should not be surprised if this relationship between two of the key topics in modern cognitive psychology turns out to be complex and nuanced. We think the chapters in this book will leave the reader with a thorough and up-to-date understanding of the debates surrounding this fascinating topic.

References

Broadbent, D. E. (1958). *Perception and communication*. Oxford, England: Persimmon Press.

James, J. H. & Wagner, A. R. (1980). One-trial overshadowing: Evidence of distributive processing. *Journal of Experimental Psychology: Animal Behavior Processes,* **6**, 188–205.

James, W. (1890). *Principles of psychology*. New York: Holt.

Kamin, L. J. & Schaub, R. E. (1963). Effects of conditioned stimulus intensity on the conditioned emotional response. *Journal of Comparative and Physiological Psychology*, **56**, 502–507.

Kaye, H. & Pearce, J. M. (1984). The strength of the orienting response during Pavlovian conditioning. *Journal of Experimental Psychology: Animal Behavior Processes*, **10**, 90–109.

Killcross, S. & Balleine, B. (1996). Role of primary motivation in stimulus pre-exposure effects. *Journal of Experimental Psychology: Animal Behavior Processes*, **22**, 32–42.

Lawrence, D. H. (1949). Acquired distinctiveness of cues: I. Transfer between discriminations on the basis of familiarity with the stimulus. *Journal of Experimental Psychology*, **39**, 770–784.

McLaren, I. P. L. & Mackintosh, N. J. (2000). An elemental model of associative learning: I. Latent inhibition and perceptual learning. *Animal Learning & Behavior*, **28**, 211–246.

Mackintosh, N. J. (1975). A theory of attention: Variations in the associability of stimuli with reinforcement. *Psychological Review*, **82**, 276–298.

Pearce, J. M. & Hall, G. (1980). A model for Pavlovian learning: Variations in the effectiveness of conditioned but not unconditioned stimuli. *Psychological Review*, **87**, 532–552.

Rescorla, R. A. & Wagner, A. R. (1972). A theory of Pavlovian conditioning: Variations in the effectiveness of reinforcement and nonreinforcement. In A. H. Black & W. F. Prokasy (Eds), *Classical conditioning II: Current research and theory* (pp. 64–99). New York: Appleton-Century-Crofts.

Wagner, A. R. (1981). SOP: A model of automatic memory processing in animal behavior. In N. E. Spear & R. R. Miller (Eds), *Information processing in animals: Memory mechanisms* (pp. 5–47). Hillsdale, NJ: Erlbaum.

Chapter 2

Two theories of attention: a review and a possible integration

John M. Pearce and Nicholas J. Mackintosh

During the last 30 years two theories have dominated our understanding of the relationship between attention and associative learning. One of these, proposed by Mackintosh (1975) has its roots in a tradition that originates with Krechevsky (1932) and was developed by Sutherland and Mackintosh (1971). According to this theory, correlation with reinforcement determines the amount of attention a stimulus receives. If a stimulus is better correlated with reinforcement than the other stimuli that accompany it, then attention to the stimulus will increase, and attention to the other stimuli will decrease. The second theory was proposed by Pearce and Hall (1980) and was based on their finding that stimuli that uniquely signal reinforcement lose associability (Hall and Pearce, 1979). According to this theory, stimuli that accurately predict the events that follow them will receive little attention, whereas those that inaccurately predict these events will be paid considerable attention. The fact that the theory of Pearce and Hall is based on a finding that directly contradicts the theory of Mackintosh demonstrates starkly the inherent incompatibility between these two theories.

This incompatibility between the theories forms the foundation on which the present chapter is based. In the first part, we consider whether there is sufficient evidence to justify both theoretical claims. The evidence, we argue, does indeed justify these claims, although their details may be in need of modification. In the final section, we propose one possible way in which the two theories may be reconciled.

Historical background

The potential role of attention in animal learning was first considered in the context of experiments on discrimination learning—more specifically experiments on so-called simultaneous discriminations. In a typical experiment, a rat is confronted on each trial with two stimuli, say a black and a white card, presented side by side. On some trials, black is on the left, and white on the right; on other trials, the position of the two cards is reversed. Regardless of their position, choice of the black card, but not of the white card, is rewarded. Performance usually starts at chance (50% choice of black), but, not very surprisingly, all rats will eventually choose the rewarded stimulus on every trial. The observation that suggested to Krechevsky (1932) that such learning might involve changes in attention was that although rats initially responded at chance with respect to the black and white stimuli, their choices were not random: they would be consistently responding to one particular position. One interpretation of such behaviour was that rats initially attended to the position of the stimuli rather than their brightness, discovered that this did not produce consistent reward, switched attention to brightness, and only then started learning that choice of black produced consistent reward.

This 'non-continuity theory' as it came to be called was taken up by Lashley (1942)—albeit with some misgivings, when he wrote that he was 'willing to accept the responsibility of paternity, though from a certain purposive cast in the infant's features I suspect that I am cuckold' (p. 241). In spite of these misgivings, Lashley reported the first experiment on blocking, showing that rats that had been initially trained on a size discrimination between a large and a small circle, then for 200 trials on a compound discrimination between a large triangle and a small circle, responded at chance when faced with a triangle and circle of the same size. It was as though they had learned nothing about the added shape cue, although Lashley claimed that 200 trials were normally more than sufficient to teach rats the triangle–circle discrimination.

Simultaneous discriminations can be made more complex than the simple black–white problem described above. The two stimuli shown on each trial can be made to differ not only in brightness and position, but also at the same time in size, orientation, shape, and so on. In Krechevsky's experiments, rats would consistently respond in terms of one attribute (always choose the left-hand stimulus), then another (always choose black), and then yet another (always choose horizontal). It seemed natural to say that their behaviour was controlled by only one attribute of the stimuli at a time, and hence to infer that they attended to only one attribute of the stimuli at a time. And this natural interpretation was accepted at least in part by a whole range of two-stage theories of discrimination learning (Lovejoy, 1968; Sutherland and Mackintosh, 1971; Trabasso and Bower, 1968; Zeaman and House, 1963). Although they differed greatly in details, they shared the common assumption that learning the solution to a discrimination problem involved two distinguishable processes or stages, learning to attend to the relevant stimulus dimension, and learning what values of that dimension were associated with what outcomes.

As we all know, such theories soon fell into disfavour, initially superseded by the Rescorla-Wagner (1972) model, which seemed to show that one could explain phenomena such as blocking without recourse to any concept of attention. As we shall see that remains debatable. But a more fundamental problem with these theories was that they were tied to a particular experimental paradigm, the simultaneous discrimination problem. Here it seems natural to suggest that animals must decide which attribute of the two simultaneously presented stimuli to attend to; when they choose a large black vertical rectangle on the left in preference to a small white horizontal rectangle on the right, which attribute of the stimuli is controlling their choice? Over a series of a few trials it becomes clear that it is size: they choose the larger of the two stimuli regardless of its brightness, position, or orientation. So if one attribute only is controlling their choice perhaps that is because they are attending to that attribute, and when they shift to another attribute that is because they have learned the first attribute was irrelevant, and another may be relevant.

This is indeed a natural account of how simultaneous discriminations are solved. But it is notably less natural for experiments on simple Pavlovian conditioning – even where the compound conditioned stimulus (CS) can be described as having multiple attributes. Here there is no question of the subject deciding which attribute of the CS to choose to respond to: the CS either elicits a response or it does not.[1] Moreover, as many commentators have noted, the

1 The problem for most theories of conditioning was to explain how attention to the relevant cues would increase in a Pavlovian experiment. In the instrumental case there was no problem. Consider a rat being trained on a simultaneous black–white discrimination. In the simplest model, illustrated by Lovejoy (1965), he has a certain probability of attending either to position or to brightness (where these two probabilities sum to 1.0). Given he attends to position he may choose either left or right; given attention to brightness he may choose either black or white (with these probabilities again summing to 1.0). When either an attentional response or a choice response is reinforced its probability increases; when they are not reinforced their probability decreases. In order to solve the problem, he must learn to attend to brightness rather than position, and then choose black (say) rather than white. It is easy to see how the probability of choosing black rather than white will win out. On any trial that he does happen to attend to brightness, either he chooses black and is rewarded or white and is not. In either case, the conditional probability of choosing black rather than white, given attention to brightness, increases. But as soon as the conditional probability of choosing black is greater than 0.5, it will follow that attending to brightness is more likely to be rewarded than not. And a positive feedback loop will now ensure that the more he attends to brightness, the faster the conditional probability of choosing black will increase, and the more likely attention to brightness will be reinforced.

CSs in Kamin's (1969) experiments on blocking were loud noises and bright lights that lasted for several minutes: it was hard to imagine that his rats were unable to attend to more than one aspect of the CS on any one trial. Anyway the Rescorla-Wagner model seemed to provide a simple and elegant account of blocking. Does this mean that accounts of Pavlovian conditioning can dispense with the concept of attention?

Two lines of evidence suggest that the answer is no. The first can also be traced back to studies of discrimination learning, in particular to experiments by Lawrence (1949, 1950). Lawrence did not look for evidence of systematic choice of one attribute of a complex set of stimuli rather than another or for evidence of stimulus selection effects, such as blocking or overshadowing. He studied transfer between one discrimination problem and another. Specifically, he showed that if rats were trained on one problem where the brightness of the stimuli was the key to its solution and texture was irrelevant, they would learn a second brightness discrimination faster than a group whose initial experience had been on a problem where texture was relevant and brightness irrelevant. Since his procedures were designed to ensure that any transfer observed could not be attributed to the changes in associative value of the particular stimuli used, he interpreted his results as showing that rats had learned to attend to the relevant attribute of their first problem (brightness or texture) that either facilitated or interfered with learning the second problem.

The second line of evidence came from experiments on Pavlovian conditioning and the phenomenon of latent inhibition (Lubow and Moore, 1959; Lubow, 1973). Lubow showed that unreinforced exposure to a stimulus that later serves as a CS in Pavlovian conditioning retards conditioning to it. Since such exposure will also retard subsequent inhibitory conditioning to the stimulus, it is clear that the term 'latent inhibition' is something of a misnomer, and one natural explanation is that exposure to a stimulus followed by no further consequence causes animals to stop attending to it.

The attentional interpretation of latent inhibition and of the results of experiments like those of Lawrence on discrimination learning has not gone unchallenged: latent inhibition has been explained in a variety of other ways

None of this can apply in a Pavlovian experiment – where the probability of reinforcement is dictated by the experimenter, and is wholly independent of the animal's behaviour. If trained on a Pavlovian discrimination between two auditory stimuli, A1 and A2 where A1 is always and A2 never reinforced, and both are always accompanied by an irrelevant visual stimulus V, the US will occur on 50% of trials regardless of whether he attends to auditory or visual stimuli.

The moral of this story is that theories should not be tied too closely to one particular experimental paradigm.

(Bouton, 1993; Grahame, Barnet, Gunther, and Miller, 1994; Wagner, 1981), and transfer of learning from one discrimination to another may also be explained in non-attentional terms (Hall, 1991). But such phenomena were sufficient to encourage the development of new theories that postulated changes in attention as a result of experience. Since any such theory would have to be as applicable to experiments on Pavlovian conditioning as to experiments on simultaneous discrimination learning, it was clear that they would have to be couched in terms quite different from traditional two-stage theories. As we have already suggested, and as will hardly come as a great surprise, we are agreed that two such theories need to be considered (Mackintosh, 1975; Pearce and Hall, 1980).

Mackintosh (1975)

Like Rescorla-Wagner (1972), Mackintosh's (1975) theory takes as its point of departure the basic linear operator equation from Bush and Mosteller (1951):

$$\Delta V_A = \theta(\lambda - V_A) \quad (2.1)$$

where V_A is the associative value of CS A; ΔV_A is the change in associative value of CS A on a given trial; θ is a learning rate parameter; and λ the asymptote of conditioning supported by the US. In the Rescorla-Wagner (1972) equation, of course, the V_A in brackets becomes the sum of the associative strengths of all the stimuli present on this trial; and θ is divided into two separate learning rate parameters, α_A, which is determined by the salience of the CS, and β, which is determined by properties of the US. The main change proposed by Mackintosh to the linear operator equation was that α is not a fixed function of the salience of the CS, but changes as a result of experience with the CS. The specific rule proposed sought to capture the intuition common to earlier theories of attention in discrimination learning, that subjects would learn to attend to relevant stimuli that predicted trial outcomes and ignore irrelevant stimuli that did not. So the rules for changing α were:

$$\Delta\alpha_A \text{ is positive if } |\lambda - V_A < \lambda - V_X| \quad (2.2a)$$

$$\Delta\alpha_A \text{ is negative if } |\lambda - V_A > \lambda - V_X| \quad (2.2b)$$

where V_X is the summed associative strength of all other stimuli besides A present on that trial. If $(\lambda - V_A)$ is smaller than $(\lambda - V_X)$, then A is a better predictor of the outcome of the trial than all other stimuli; if it is larger, then A is a worse predictor.

The intuition underlying this account of attention was much the same as that suggested by Lawrence (1949, 1950) in his studies on the 'acquired distinctiveness of cues', where rats trained on two consecutive discrimination problems learned the second discrimination faster if the relevant stimuli remained the same from one problem to the next than if they changed. Other studies dating from this time, on 'transfer along a continuum' (Lawrence, 1952) and the 'overtraining reversal effect' (ORE) (Reid, 1953) also suggested a plausible attentional interpretation. In the former, animals learned a difficult brightness discrimination faster if initially trained on an easier version of the problem rather than on the difficult problem from the outset. In the latter, animals learned the reversal of a brightness discrimination (i.e. black was now S^+, when white had been S^+ initially) faster after overtraining on the initial problem than after training only to criterion. On the face of it, one would expect that overtraining, by increasing the difference in associative value of the initial S^+ and S^-, should make the reversal harder. Lovejoy (1965) showed how a simple attentional theory could explain the ORE (an analysis extended by Mackintosh, 1969, to show how the theory could explain the conditions under which the ORE did and did not occur).

As already noted, these attentional interpretations did not go unchallenged. The problem was that in experiments on instrumental discrimination learning it may always be possible to appeal to the development of different response strategies that animals might adopt and which might explain the data (Hall, 1991; Siegel, 1967). One experimental paradigm whose results seemed harder to explain away in this manner was the comparison of intradimensional and extradimensional shift learning (IDS versus EDS). The basic design of such an experiment is shown in Table 2.1. Two groups are initially trained on a discrimination in which two stimuli from one dimension are relevant (A and B) and two stimuli from another dimension are irrelevant (w and x). Uppercase indicates a relevant stimulus in Stage 1, lowercase indicates one that is irrelevant. They are then shifted to a new discrimination involving additional stimuli from the previously relevant dimension (C and D) and from the previously irrelevant dimension (y and z). In an IDS, the relevant and irrelevant stimulus dimensions remain unchanged from Stage 1 to Stage 2. In an EDS, the relevant

Table 2.1 The training and test compound stimuli used to compare the effects of an intradimensional and extradimensional shift. Letters in uppercase represent stimuli from a dimension that was relevant during Stage 1; letters in lowercase represent stimuli from a dimension that was irrelevant

Stage 1	**Stage 2**	
Both groups	**IDS group**	**EDS group**
Aw+ Bw– Ax+ Bx–	Cy+ Dy– Cz+ Dz–	Cy+ Dy+ Cz– Dz–

dimension of Stage 1 becomes irrelevant in Stage 2, and the irrelevant becomes relevant. If the original training should result in more attention being paid to the stimuli belonging to the originally relevant than irrelevant dimension, then a group tested with an IDS will learn the new discrimination more readily than one tested with an EDS. Support for this prediction has been found with old world monkeys, Shepp and Schrier (1969); new world monkeys, Dias, Robbins, and Roberts (1996); rats, Shepp and Eimas (1964); and pigeons, Durlach and Mackintosh (1986); George and Pearce (1999); Mackintosh and Little (1969).

It must be admitted that this superiority of an IDS over an EDS is not always found. Failures to demonstrate this effect have been reported by Couvillon, Tennant, and Bitterman (1967) and Hall and Channell (1985). In addition, Roberts, Robbins, and Everitt (1988) have raised doubts about whether the experiments by Durlach and Mackintosh (1986), Shepp and Schrier (1969), and Shepp and Eimas (1964) provide unequivocal evidence of the IDS being superior to the EDS. In view of these problems, Dopson, Esber, and Pearce (2010) developed an alternative methodology for studying changes in attention to stimuli that are relevant and irrelevant to the solution of a discrimination (see also Pearce, Esber, George, and Haselgrove, 2008). A possible weakness with the IDS-EDS design is that the changes that take place during training are expected to generalize to the novel stimuli used for testing. If changes in attention are stimulus specific (Mackintosh, 1975), then the changes in attention to the training stimuli are unlikely to transfer fully to the test stimuli, which will make it difficult to reveal an IDS-EDS effect. As we shall see shortly, the design proposed by Dopson *et al.* overcomes this obstacle by using the same stimuli for both stages of the experiment.

Another possible weakness with the IDS-EDS design has been pointed out by Hall (1991), who suggested it might be possible to explain the IDS-EDS effect by appeal to the principles of acquired distinctiveness and equivalence, rather than to changes in attention. It has long been acknowledged that if two stimuli, A and B, are associated with different consequences, X and Y, they will be more readily discriminated than if they are both associated with the same consequence, Z (Miller, 1948). In the first stage of an IDS-EDS experiment, the two relevant stimuli, say red and yellow, are associated with different consequences, reward and no reward respectively, while the two irrelevant stimuli, say circle and square, are each associated with the same consequences, both reward and no reward. Red and yellow should therefore be more readily discriminated than circle and square and if these effects should transfer to the test stimuli, the discrimination based on an IDS will be acquired more readily than the one based on an EDS. Hall (1991) offered this explanation tentatively,

Table 2.2 The compounds that were used for the training and test stages for the experiment by Dopson et al. (2010). Stimuli A through E were from one dimension and Stimuli v through z were from another dimension. Upper case indicates the stimuli were relevant to the solution of the Stage 1 discriminations, lower case indicates they were irrelevant

Training compounds		Test compounds
Consistent group	**Mixed group**	**Both groups**
Av+ Cv–	Av+ Cv–	
Bw+ Cw–	Bw+ Cw–	
Ax+ Cx–	Ax+ Cx–	Aw+ Av– Bw–
Bx+ Cx–	Bx+ Cx–	
Dy+ Ey–	dY+ dZ–	
Dz+ Ez–	eY+ eZ–	

and it is not obvious how it can be applied successfully to a properly counterbalanced experiment.[2] Nonetheless, the point remains that acquired distinctiveness and equivalence could be responsible for the IDS-EDS effect, and it was partly in order to refute this possibility that Dopson, Esber, and Pearce (2009) conducted the following experiment.

Pigeons were trained with a set of true discriminations, e.g. Av+ Cv– involving compound stimuli composed of one relevant and one irrelevant stimulus. For a consistent group, all five stimuli that were relevant (A, B, C, D, E) belonged to one dimension, and all five that were irrelevant (v, w, x, y, z) belonged to another dimension (Table 2.2). The two dimensions were composed entirely of colours or patterns, in a counterbalanced fashion, and the two stimuli were presented in adjacent circles on a television screen behind a response key for autoshaping with pigeons. Upon the completion of this training, the birds received an Aw+ Av– Bw– discrimination, which involved one novel compound that signalled food, Aw+, and two familiar compounds that had previously signalled food but which were now followed by no food, Av– Bw–. It was anticipated that responding would remain high to Aw throughout the test discrimination. Of particular interest was the rate at which responding

[2] Suppose that red is S^+ and yellow S^- in the first stage, and blue S^+ and green S^- in the second. If there was more generalization from red to blue than to green, and from yellow to green than to blue, then the IDS would be learned rapidly. But by the same token, animals rewarded for choice of red in Stage 1, and green in Stage 2, would have difficulty with their second discrimination. By generalization, their Stage 2 S^+ would elicit a representation of no reward, and their S^- one of reward. As they started to learn the new Stage 2 contingencies, both S^+ and S^- would elicit representations of both reward and no reward.

fell off to the two non-reinforced compounds. The discrimination between Aw+ and Av– must be based on the distinctive features v and w, whereas that between Aw+ and Bw– must be based on A and B. Because v and w were previously irrelevant, and A and B were previously relevant, if the original training should result in more attention being paid to relevant than irrelevant stimuli, it follows that the former discrimination will be acquired more slowly than the latter. On the other hand, during the pretraining stage, A and B signalled the same outcome—food, and so too did v and w—food and no food—which, according to Hall (1991) will enhance generalization between A and B, and between v and w. If acquired equivalence and distinctiveness, rather than attention, determines the associability of the stimuli in the second stage of the experiment, then responding to Av and Bw will decline at the same rate.

The results from the test stage of the experiment can be seen in Figure 2.1, which portrays discrimination ratios calculated for the two component discriminations for the entire group of birds. The ratios were of the form $S^-/(S^- + S^+)$, where S^+ is the rate of responding during Aw+ and S^- is the rate during either Av or Bw. The solid line with the open circles shows the results for the Aw+ Av– discrimination, for which the two distinctive cues were originally irrelevant, and the solid line with filled circles shows the results for the Aw+ Bw– discrimination for which the two distinctive cues were originally relevant. It is evident that the discrimination based on previously relevant cues

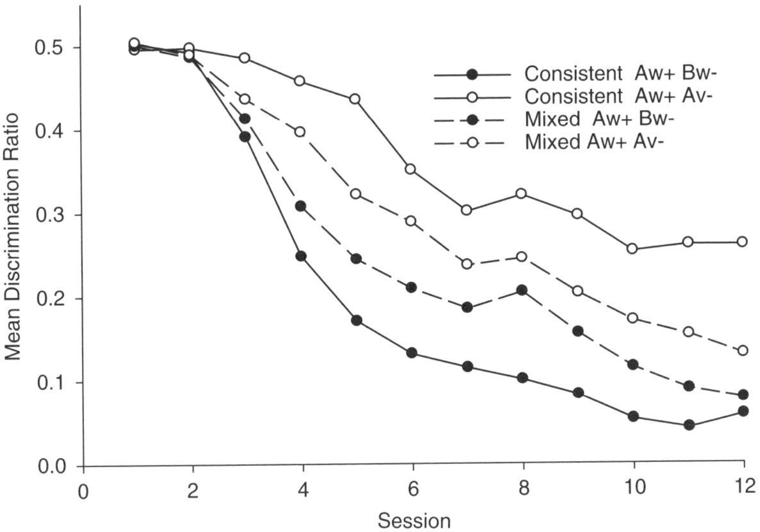

Fig. 2.1 Mean discrimination ratios for the two components of the Aw+ Av– Bw– discrimination that was given to the consistent and the mixed groups in the study by Dopson et al. (2010).

was acquired considerably more rapidly than the one based on previously irrelevant cues.

The results just described can be readily explained by assuming animals pay more attention to relevant than irrelevant stimuli, and it is hard to see how they can be explained by referring to acquired equivalence or distinctiveness. The possibility remains, however, that the results can be understood without referring to attentional processes. Gibson (1940) proposed that being required to discriminate between a pair of stimuli will sharpen the generalization gradients around them and facilitate discriminations involving those stimuli in the future. In the previous experiment, because A, B, and D signalled food, while C and E signalled the absence of food, the generalization gradients around all five stimuli would be sharpened and subsequently make it easy to discriminate between A and B during the test stage. If it is assumed that these changes to the shape of the generalization gradient are confined to the dimension to which the stimuli belong, then it would further follow that the gradients around v, w, x, y, and z would not be sharpened for two reasons: first, because all five stimuli signal the same outcome—food on half the trials; second, because they all belong to a different dimension to A through E. As a consequence, the discrimination between Aw+ and Bw– would be easier to acquire than between Aw+ and Av–.

To test this explanation, a second group of pigeons, the mixed group, was included in the above experiment. It was treated in the same way as the consistent group, except that during the initial training two of the discriminations that did not involve the test stimuli were modified. Instead of being given a Dy+ Ey– and a Dz+ Ez– discrimination, which were given to the consistent group, the mixed group received a dY+ dZ– and an eY+ eZ– discrimination. This training ensured that d and e were both irrelevant, whereas the remaining members of this dimension were relevant by either being consistently paired with food, A and B, or no food, C. According to the proposals of Gibson (1940), as a consequence of learning about the different contingencies associated with A through e the gradients around all five of them will be sharpened. The training also ensured Y and Z were both relevant by signalling the presence and absence of food respectively, whereas v, w, and x were all irrelevant. In learning which of these stimuli signalled which outcome during Stage 1, the generalization gradients around all five of them should also be sharpened. Thus if this analysis is correct, the test stage should result in the Aw+ Av– discrimination being acquired as readily as the Aw+ Bw– discrimination, and just as rapidly as the Aw+ Bw– discrimination in the consistent group.

In contrast to this prediction, the results in Figure 2.1 depicted by the dashed lines revealed that the discrimination based on the previously irrelevant cues, open circles, was acquired more slowly than the one based on the previously relevant cues, filled circles. A further problem for the proposals of Gibson (1940) is that the mixed group acquired the Aw+ Bw– discrimination more slowly than the consistent group. This outcome is puzzling because the original training should have had a similar impact on the sharpness of the generalization gradients around the test stimuli in both groups. If the mixed group failed to solve the dY+ dZ– and the eY+ eZ– training discriminations then it might be possible to understand why its results failed to conform to the predictions derived from Gibson's theory. However, the group mastered all six training discriminations in Table 2.2. Rather than sharpen generalization gradients, it would seem the original training was effective because it resulted in more attention being paid to relevant than irrelevant stimuli.

The difference between the performances of the two groups on both components of the test discrimination indicates that the associability of a stimulus is not just determined by its own relationship with reward, but also by the relationship with reward of other stimuli belonging to the same dimension. This outcome is entirely consistent with an attentional explanation for the results of the experiment. For example, Sutherland and Mackintosh (1971) talked of subjects switching in 'analyzers', where an analyzer was a system that detected variations along stimulus dimensions such as hue, brightness, orientation, shape, etc. They further proposed that the degree to which an analyzer was switched in was determined by the degree to which the stimuli from that dimension reliably signalled reinforcement. It is, however, equally possible to explain the results by saying that subjects learned to attend to, or ignore, particular features, red, yellow, vertical lines, horizontal lines, and that these attentional changes transferred to other similar stimuli. All the results from the experiment can then be explained if it is accepted that there is more generalization of a change in attention between stimuli belonging to the same than different dimensions. (Mackintosh, 1975).

On balance, the evidence favours this second explanation. The stimuli used in some IDS-EDS experiments are not readily described as varying along the sorts of stimulus dimensions described by the Sutherland and Mackintosh (1971) analyzer theory. For example, in the Dias *et al.* (1996) experiment, the two 'dimensions' were the shape of a blue polygon, and the pattern of a black line superimposed on the polygon. An experiment by Trobalon, Miguelez, McLaren, and Mackintosh (2003) provides even more convincing evidence. They trained IDS rats on two consecutive spatial discriminations in a radial maze located in a room with a variety of landmarks round the maze. In Stage 2, the rewarded arms pointed north-east and north-west. If their Stage 1 discrimination had been between south and either east (on some trials) or west (on others), they learned the Stage 2 discrimination rapidly, and faster than EDS animals who had been trained on a texture discrimination in Stage 1 (the floors of the arms were covered with rubber or sandpaper). So far, so good, and the results could be explained perfectly well by saying that the IDS animals had learned to attend to the dimension of spatial position or direction in Stage 1. However, for a second IDS group, the Stage 1 discrimination was between arms pointing north and either east or west. This group learned their Stage 2 discrimination between north-east and north-west significantly more slowly than the first IDS group, indeed slightly more slowly than the comparable EDS group. What is the explanation of this pattern of results? For the Stage 1 discrimination between north and, say, east, the relevant landmarks are those best visible from the north arm and those best visible from the east arm, and the irrelevant landmarks are those equally visible from both – that is to say, precisely those best visible from the north-east arm (the same argument obviously applies to the discrimination between north and west arms). Conversely, for the Stage 2 discrimination between north-east and north-west, the irrelevant landmarks are those visible from both arms, i.e., those in the north of the room. But these were precisely the landmarks that were relevant for the IDS group in Stage 1. In other words, on the assumption that attention is directed towards or away from particular landmarks, rather than dimensions of stimulation, IDS animals trained on the north versus east or west discrimination in Stage 1 would have learned to ignore the landmarks that became relevant in Stage 2, and to attend to the landmarks that became irrelevant.

A final strand of support for the claim that more attention is paid to stimuli that are relevant rather than irrelevant to the solution of a discrimination can be found in an experiment with humans. As we noted earlier, the most critical problem facing attempts to establish that there is significant transfer of learning to attend to, or ignore, stimuli from one problem to another, was to rule out the possibility that any transfer observed was due to specific strategies or differences in the associative value of particular stimuli. One way of achieving this would presumably be to change the nature of the reinforcing outcome from one problem to the next. But although one could no doubt change the actual reinforcer used in an animal experiment, from food to sucrose solution or to water for example, this is obviously not sufficient, since they are all appetitive reinforcers. And a change from appetitive to aversive reinforcers would bring problems of its own. But experiments with human participants can achieve what is needed. In a food allergy detection task, for example, participants are required to predict which of two possible allergic reactions a hypothetical patient will develop as a result of eating various meals. Having learned in the first stage of the experiment that Mr Smith develops allergy 1 whenever

Table 2.3 A partial summary of the design of an experiment by Le Pelley et al. (2005). Uppercase letters indicate stimuli that were relevant in Stage 1. Lowercase letters indicate stimuli that were irrelevant in Stage 1

Stage 1	Stage 2	Test
Av→1	Ax→3	AC
Bv→2	Cv→3	vx
Cx→2		
Dx→1		

he eats pumpkin pie or hamburger, and allergy 2 whenever he eats coleslaw or peas (while meals containing sausages, mashed potatoes, tomato ketchup, or green beans have no effect on his allergic reactions), participants can be asked in the second stage of the experiment to predict which combinations of foods will precipitate a quite new pair of allergic reactions. A stripped down version of the design of such an experiment by Le Pelley, Oakeshott, Wills, and McLaren (2005) is shown in Table 2.3. During Stage 1, participants were shown a list of meals that were followed by different allergic reactions. Some of the components of the meal were relevant (uppercase letters), and some were irrelevant (lowercase letters). In Stage 2, they were shown new meals, each composed of a previously relevant and irrelevant component, and each followed by a new allergic reaction. Subsequent tests to assess the effectiveness of learning in Stage 2 revealed that participants were more confident about the outcome predicted by two components if they had been relevant (AC), rather than irrelevant (vx) in Stage 1, and thus, presumably, of high rather than low associability at the outset of Stage 2. The clear implication is that learning to attend to some meals rather than others in Stage 1 transferred to the new problem of Stage 2.

The results from the experiments considered thus far are in keeping with predictions that can be derived from Mackintosh (1975). An experiment by George and Pearce (1999) indicates that at least some results from an IDS-EDS experiment lie beyond the scope of the theory as it is currently formulated. Pigeons were trained with a biconditional discrimination in which the trial outcome was indicated by two stimuli from different dimensions, rather than by individual stimuli: AX+ AY– BX– BY+. A third stimulus, P or Q, from a third dimension was added to every trial, but its presence was irrelevant to the trial outcome. Subsequent testing with new stimuli from each of the three dimensions revealed that a new biconditional discrimination was acquired more readily if the stimuli belonged to the two dimensions that were previously relevant, rather than if they belonged to one previously relevant and one previously irrelevant dimension. In the first stage of the experiment, all the stimuli were paired with food on 50% of the trials and their associabilities should have been the same if attention is governed by how well a stimulus by itself predicts a trial outcome. Instead, what appears to have determined the attention paid to the stimuli is whether they were relevant to the solution of the discrimination and it is not clear how this conclusion can be reconciled with Mackintosh (1975). The first problem is that, as it stands, the theory is unable to explain how a biconditional discrimination is solved. One solution to this shortcoming would be to assume that each compound created its own unique configural cue that functioned in much the same way as the experimental stimuli. The problem now is that Mackintosh predicts that attention to the relevant configural cues will increase while attention to all the experimental stimuli will decline. Another solution to the problem was proposed by George and Pearce (1998), but since this explanation is based on a configural theory of learning, it gains less than wholehearted support from one of the present authors.

The details of Mackintosh (1975) may be in need of modification if they are to explain the results described by George and Pearce (1999), but the conclusion that can be drawn from the experiments described thus far is clear. When animals are trained on a discrimination problem, they pay more attention to stimuli that are relevant rather than irrelevant to its solution. We now consider the evidence that points to a rather different conclusion concerning the rules that govern attention.

Pearce and Hall (1980)

The origins of the Pearce-Hall (1980) theory lie, paradoxically, in the results of an experiment that was intended to lend support to Mackintosh (1975). In order to demonstrate that attention is enhanced to stimuli that reliably predict the events that follow them, Pearce and Hall (1979) trained rats using conditioned suppression with a discrimination in which a tone was paired with shock and a tone-clicker compound was paired with nothing, T+ TC–. This treatment was expected to increase attention to T, because it was the best available predictor of shock, and increase attention to C, because it was the best available predictor for the omission of shock. These predictions were then tested by using TC to signal shock. Rather than resulting in rapid conditioning with the compound, comparison of the results with a suitable control revealed that learning about TC was rather slow. A more direct demonstration of this effect was provided in a subsequent study, again using conditioned suppression, in which a tone was first paired with a weak shock before being paired with a strong shock (Hall and Pearce, 1979). Mackintosh (1975) predicts that even though the initial training involves only a modest shock, attention to the tone will be high by the end of this training and that subsequent conditioning with the large shock should progress rapidly. But once again the opposite outcome was observed.

Pearce and Hall (1980) therefore proposed that the purpose of attention is not to encourage animals to focus on stimuli that are accurate predictors of reinforcement. Quite the opposite, if the purpose of attention is to promote rapid learning about a stimulus, then there is little point in concentrating on stimuli about which learning is complete. Rather, they proposed that attention should be directed maximally towards stimuli whose associative strength is inappropriate to the events that follow them or, in other words, which are inaccurate predictors of their consequences. When a stimulus is first presented for conditioning therefore, it will be evident that it is a poor predictor of the US and attention to the stimulus should be increased so that learning can be rapid on subsequent trials. As the stimulus becomes a better predictor of the US, attention to it may decrease and eventually cease once the US is fully predicted by the CS.

To express these ideas formally, Pearce and Hall (1980) suggested that if CS A is presented on trial n, the amount of attention, α_A paid to it on trial n+1 will be given by Equation 2.3.[3] In this equation, ΣV represents the associative strength of all the stimuli that are present on the trial, including A. The relationship between attention and learning is specified by Equation 2.4.

$$\alpha^{n+1} = |\lambda^n - \Sigma V^n| \tag{2.3}$$

$$\Delta V_A = \alpha_A \beta \lambda \tag{2.4}$$

Given these relationships, it then follows that learning about the tone when it was first paired with strong shock in the study by Hall and Pearce (1979) will progress slowly because the value of α will be close to zero once conditioning with the small shock has reached asymptote. Latent inhibition with a neutral stimulus can also be explained by these equations. Pearce and Hall (1980) assume that the attention paid to a novel stimulus is high. If the stimulus should be repeatedly presented by itself, then the value of both λ and ΣV will be zero in Equation 2.3 and attention to the stimulus will decline. As it stands, the equation makes the unrealistic prediction that one trial would be sufficient to reduce the associability of the stimulus to the lowest possible level. Pearce, Kaye, and Hall (1982) therefore proposed that changes in the value of α take place more slowly than predicted by Equation 2.3, but according to the same principles.

[3] The superscripts n and n+1 indicate the trial number and are not meant to indicate the power to which the variables should be raised.

Equation 2.3 has important implications for the changes in attention that take place during compound conditioning. If a compound should be paired with a US, then attention to each of its components will be set by how well the compound as a whole predicts the trial outcome. After extensive training with the T+ TC– discrimination employed by Pearce and Hall (1979), the trial outcome will be accurately predicted on both reinforced and non-reinforced trials and the associability of both T and C will be reduced. Excitatory conditioning with the compound would then be predicted to progress slowly during the test stage of the experiment.

A further implication of Equation 2.3 concerns the effect of partial reinforcement on the attention that is paid to a stimulus. By presenting the US after a CS on some trials, but not others, the expression $|\lambda - \Sigma V|$ will always have a positive value during a partial reinforcement schedule, no matter how many trials are given. Thus the theory predicts that whereas attention to a continuously reinforced CS will eventually be very low, attention to a partially reinforced stimulus will be sustained at a relatively high level. Several experiments have confirmed this prediction using serial conditioning (Swan and Pearce, 1988), but a more direct test of this prediction was conducted by Haselgrove, Esber, Pearce, and Jones (2010). Rats first received conditioning with four auditory stimuli, of which two were continuously paired with food, (C_1 and C_2), and two were intermittently paired with food according to a 50% schedule (P_1 and P_2). The four stimuli were each presented for the same number of trials. Upon the completion of this training, both groups were given a discrimination involving two novel compounds composed of one element that had been continuously reinforced and one that had been partially reinforced. For both groups, C_1P_1 was paired with food. The compound C_2P_1 was non-reinforced for the continuous group, and C_1P_2 was non-reinforced for the partial group. In other words, the continuous group's discrimination required them to attend to the previously continuously reinforced stimuli, while the partial group's required attention to the previously partially reinforced stimuli. If their original training resulted in more attention being paid to the stimuli that were partially rather continuously paired with food, then the partial group should learn their second problem faster than the continuous group learned theirs. The results confirmed this prediction. Figure 2.2 shows the group mean discrimination ratios for the two groups for the 12 sessions of discrimination training. The ratios were of the form $CS^+/(CS^+ + CS^-)$, where CS^+ represents the rate of responding during C_1P_1 and CS^- the rate during the non-reinforced compound. It is evident that the discrimination was acquired more readily by the partial than the continuous group.

In addition to using the associability of a stimulus as a measure of the amount of attention it is paid, other experiments have used the strength of the

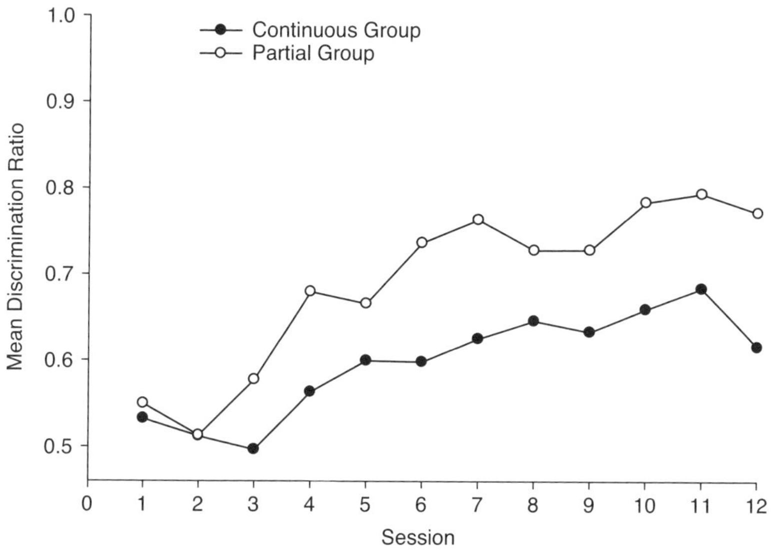

Fig. 2.2 Mean discrimination ratios for the C_1P_1+ C_2P_1- discrimination that was given to the continuous group and the C_1P_1+ C_1P_2- discrimination that was given to the partial group in the experiment by Haselgrove et al. (2010).

orienting response it elicits. Kaye and Pearce (1984) studied appetitive conditioning in rats with the illumination of a bulb in a dark chamber as the CS. In one experiment, for example, rats received serial conditioning with the sequence light-tone-food. The strength of the orienting response to the light declined to a low level in a continuous group that just received this treatment. By contrast, a partial group that received intermixed presentations of the light-tone-food sequence with the light by itself showed sustained orienting towards the light. The implication of this experiment is that the continuous group ultimately paid less attention to the light than the partial group. Further support for this conclusion comes from additional tests with the two groups in which the light was paired directly with food. Conditioning progressed more rapidly in the partial than the continuous group. Additional experiments by Swan and Pearce (1988) involved training one group of rats with the sequences light-tone-food and light-tone-nothing, and another group with light-tone-food and light-nothing. The strength of the orienting response was substantially stronger to the light for the second group than the first, which indicates that it is the accuracy with which the immediate consequences of the light can be predicted—the presence or absence of an appetitive CS—than its ultimate consequences—food—that determines the amount of attention it receives.

Hogarth, Dickinson, Austin, Brown, and Duka (2007) have demonstrated that the Pearce-Hall theory might also apply to orienting responses in humans.

Participants were shown three visual patterns that signalled a noise with a probability of 1, 0.5, or 0 and asked to predict the likelihood of the outcome during each of them. A record was taken of their eye fixations throughout the task and it was found that more time was spent attending to the pattern that signalled noise with a probability of 0.5 than at the other two patterns.

Another prediction of the theory concerns the effects of suddenly omitting a reinforcer that has consistently followed a CS. This manipulation will ensure that the CS is no longer an accurate predictor of the subsequent event and attention to it will be restored. In an experiment to test this prediction by Hall and Pearce (1982), rats first received conditioning in which a CS was paired with a weak shock. The CS was then presented for two 'surprise' trials without the US. Evidence that the surprise trials restored attention to the CS was found in a subsequent phase in which the CS was paired with a large shock. Conditioning with the large shock progressed more rapidly than for a group for which the surprise trials were omitted. Other experiments have shown a similar restoration of attention when the initial training consists of serial conditioning with the sequences light-tone-food, and light-tone-nothing which is then followed by training with the sequences light-tone-food and light-nothing. The transition from the initial phase, where the light was an accurate predictor of its immediate consequences, to the second phase, where it was an inaccurate predictor of these consequences, was found to enhance the orienting response to the light. The transition also enhanced the associability of the light, as revealed by a subsequent test when it was paired directly with food. (Wilson, Boumphrey, and Pearce, 1992).

There are, therefore, good grounds for believing that during Pavlovian conditioning attention to a CS is determined by its predictive accuracy. There are also good grounds for believing that during a simple discrimination, such as AX+ BX–, more attention will be paid to the relevant, A and B, than the irrelevant, X, features. Such a finding is clearly at odds with the Pearce-Hall (1980) theory, which predicts that attention to all three stimuli will gradually be reduced as the discrimination is solved. We will consider shortly a way in which these conflicting findings may be reconciled, but first we review briefly the analysis of blocking that is offered by the two theories of attention.

Application to blocking

An important motivation for understanding the role of attention in conditioning was to develop an alternative to the explanation offered by the Rescorla-Wagner (1972) theory for compound conditioning phenomena, such as blocking and overshadowing. Despite the very different principles on which their theories are based, both Mackintosh (1975) and Pearce and Hall (1980) make similar predictions about these phenomena, as the following discussion of the role of attention in blocking shows.

In a blocking experiment, animals first receive conditioning with a stimulus by itself, A+, before trials in which a compound of A with another stimulus is paired with the same US, AB+. Typically, responding on test trials with B by itself is weaker than if the initial training with A is omitted. According to Mackintosh (1975), on the first compound trial the associability and the associative strength of A will both be high because of the previous training. The associability of B will also be high because of its novelty. It then follows from Equation 2.1 that conditioning with B will progress normally on the first trial and, from Equation 2.2b, that the associability of B will decline after this trial and restrict any further increases in associative strength. The Pearce-Hall (1980) theory also assumes that during the first compound trial attention to B will be high, because of its novelty, and Equation 2.4 predicts that learning about this stimulus will progress normally. However, Equation 2.3 predicts that attention to B will decline after this trial and result in it gaining less associative strength than if both stimuli were novel at the start of compound conditioning. Contrary to these predictions, the Rescorla-Wagner (1972) theory predicts that blocking with B will be effective on the first trial of compound conditioning.

Tests to determine if conditioning with B on the first compound trial occurs normally have led to evidence in keeping with this outcome (Mackintosh, 1975), and against it (Balaz, Kasprow and Miller, 1982). To complicate matters further, Dickinson, Nicholas, and Mackintosh (1983) proposed that during the first compound conditioning trial, within-compound associations may develop between A and B. Blocking with B might then be effective on the first compound trial, but this effect would be compensated for through higher-order conditioning mediated by a B–A and an A–US association. Support for this explanation was found in experiments in which steps were taken to weaken the growth of within-compound associations, by presenting A and B serially with a gap between them (Dickinson *et al.*, 1983). This manipulation resulted in successful blocking even after a single trial. Thus, it seems that the two theories of attention are wrong in their prediction that blocking is due to a loss of associability by B. Instead, as the Rescorla-Wagner (1972) theory predicts, this effect occurs because the US is fully predicted by A on the first compound conditioning trial, and thereby fails to leave any associative strength to be captured by B. Rather different support for this conclusion comes from an experiment by Baxter, Gallagher, and Holland (1999) who found that lesions of the cholinergic input to the hippocampus, which were intended to disrupt the mechanism that is responsible for reducing stimulus associability, had no evident impact on blocking.

Even though blocking appears to be a consequence, at least in part, of stimuli competing for associative strength, there remain good reasons for believing that changes in attention take place during this form of compound conditioning. Two groups of rats in a study by Mackintosh and Turner (1971) received conditioning with a noise paired with a moderate shock, N+. One group then received four trials in which a noise-light compound was paired with the same shock, NL+, before both groups received four trials with the compound paired with a larger shock, NL+. Test trials with the light by itself revealed a stronger response in the group that did not receive the four trials of the noise and light paired with moderate shock, which implies that pairing the compound with the moderate shock reduced the associability of the light. It is not clear whether, in keeping with Mackintosh (1975), this loss of associability to B occurred because B was a poorer predictor of the US than A or because, in keeping with Pearce and Hall (1980) B was a component of a compound that served as an accurate predictor for the moderate shock. A related result was observed in the final stage of the blocking experiment by Baxter *et al.* (1999) that has just been mentioned. After four sessions of compound conditioning in the second stage of the experiment, conditioning trials were given with the blocked stimulus, B. Conditioning with B progressed slowly in a sham-operated control group, and rapidly in the group with impaired hippocampal function. The implication of this finding is again that attention to B was reduced in the control group during compound conditioning, and that the lesions of the cholinergic input to the hippocampus prevented this reduction from taking place.

The results of Mackintosh and Turner (1971) suggest that learning about B in a blocking task (A+ then AB+) will take place more readily if the US at the outset of compound conditioning is larger than during the training with A (see also Kamin, 1969). Dickinson, Hall, and Mackintosh (1976) extended this finding by showing that if the US should either increase or decrease in value at the outset of compound conditioning then B will gain more associative strength than if the value of the US remains unchanged. In one experiment, for example, rats first received conditioning with a clicker, which was followed immediately by a shock and then 8 s later by a second shock. One group then received the clicker with a light followed by both shocks on every trial, and another group just received the first shock after the compound. Despite, the omission of the second shock, it was the second group that demonstrated the stronger conditioned response (CR) during a test with the light by itself. This result is hard to explain with an error-correction theory such as Rescorla-Wagner (1972), which predicts that the light in the second group will become a conditioned inhibitor, but it can be explained by the two theories of attention. According to these, the surprise generated by the omission of the second shock will arrest the decline in attention to the light that would occur if the shock were present, and enable the light to enter into an association with the first shock.

It needs to be stressed that in both theories, 'attention' to a particular stimulus is at least partly defined as the *associability* of that stimulus with the outcome of a conditioning trial. A stimulus that is attended to enters into association with the trial outcome more readily than one not attended to. Mackintosh (1973) entertained the possibility that the associability of a stimulus might be specific to a particular reinforcer. Thus flavours are more readily associated with internal malaise than with shock, while lights and noises are more readily associated with shock than with malaise. Applying this idea to the case of blocking and unblocking, Dickinson and Mackintosh (1979) first replicated and extended the results of Dickinson *et al.* (1976) described above. They showed that, in both appetitive and aversive conditioning, if the value of the US predicted by A was either increased or decreased on AB trials (either by adding an unexpected second US a few seconds after the first, or by omitting a second expected US), then significant conditioning occurred to B. But they further showed that this unblocking effect only occurred if the second US was the same valence as the first. That is to say, in aversive conditioning, the addition or omission of a second shock several seconds after the first on AB trials resulted in significant conditioning to B, but the addition or omission of a food pellet some seconds after the initial shock resulted in no conditioning to B. Similarly, in appetitive conditioning, the addition or omission of a second food pellet produced significant conditioning to B, but the addition or omission of a shock after the initial food pellet US also resulted in no conditioning to B. A related finding has been reported by Le Pelley, Oakeshott, Wills, and McLaren (2005) in a study of human causal learning.

A clear implication of this discussion is that several different processes take place during blocking (see also Holland, 1997; Le Pelley, 2004; Pearce, George, and Redhead, 1998). One is based on an error-correction learning rule that will restrict learning about B once its associative strength together with that of A has reached an asymptote set by the value of the reinforcer. The other process is a loss of attention to B. This second process will lead to the stimulus entering into new associations only with difficulty, but it can be disrupted by the occurrence of a surprising event during compound conditioning. Thus, the initial aspiration of both Mackintosh (1975) and Pearce and Hall (1980) to provide a full account of the factors that govern changes in associative strength during conditioning now appears overly ambitious. Changes in attention take place during conditioning, but they are not solely responsible for determining the ultimate associative strength acquired by a CS. It thus seems that a complete theory of conditioning must take account of variations in both the processing of the CS and the US.

A unified model

It should be clear from the evidence reviewed so far that both Mackintosh (1975) and Pearce and Hall (1980) can claim substantial support, Mackintosh from studies of discrimination learning showing that attention is directed towards relevant and away from irrelevant stimuli, Pearce and Hall from studies of conditioning showing that animals stop attending to stimuli whose consequences are fully predicted, but continue to attend to partially reinforced stimuli. It is equally clear that the studies that support one theory contradict the other. The only case where they make similar predictions are studies of blocking.

What should we make of this state of affairs? We do not believe that it is possible to dismiss or somehow explain away the data supporting either theory. If that is accepted, the obvious question is whether a single, unitary theory of attention could be devised that would encompass both the data supporting Mackintosh (1975) and the data supporting Pearce and Hall (1980). That too seems rather difficult to imagine (but perhaps that merely reflects the poverty of our imagination). A rather different solution to the dilemma has been suggested by Le Pelley (2004), who has proposed a 'hybrid model' that incorporates not only the Rescorla-Wagner equation with its summed error term ($\lambda - \Sigma V$) governing changes in associative strength, but also two stimulus-specific learning rate parameters, α and σ, with α changing according to the Mackintosh rules, and σ according to Pearce and Hall. While this does indeed seem to be one way of solving the problem, there is perhaps a certain element of brute force about this solution – and also, as will appear, a certain redundancy. We should like to propose a slightly different way of incorporating both attentional theories into a single hybrid model.

The evidence of one-trial blocking, and the experiment by Baxter *et al.* (1999) described above both suggest that a complete account of blocking requires acceptance of the Rescorla-Wagner summed error term. The other reason for accepting that any theory of conditioning must incorporate such an error term is Pavlovian conditioned inhibition. After intermixed training with A+ and AB–, B becomes a conditioned inhibitor, because on AB– trials ($\lambda - \Sigma V$) is negative. If the error term for changing the value of VB was simply ($\lambda - V$B), as in the original Bush-Mosteller model, its value would be zero, and no change in VB would ever occur. Le Pelley's hybrid model, therefore, now incorporates a summed error term twice over, once in the Rescorla-Wagner equation, and a second time in the Pearce-Hall rule, expressed in Equation 2.3 above, for changing σ. Is this perhaps overkill? What would happen if we modified Equation 2.3 above for the Pearce-Hall model to read

$$\alpha_A^{n+1} = |\lambda^n - V_A^n| \tag{2.5}$$

In other words, if changes in attention to stimulus A were determined by how well it, and it alone, predicted its consequences, not by how well its consequences were predicted by other stimuli present. It seems to us that this would still capture the main intuition underlying the model—you stop attending to a stimulus to the extent that *it* predicts its consequences, and therefore there is no need to learn anything more about it. We suggest, therefore, that Equation 2.6 provides a full account of how attention influences changes in associative strength during conditioning, where σ_A represents the value of α_A as specified by Equation 2.5, and α_A is determined by Equations 2.2a and 2.2b.

$$\Delta V_A = \alpha_A \cdot \sigma_A \cdot \beta \cdot (\lambda - \Sigma V) \tag{2.6}$$

Le Pelley has argued that in a hybrid model of this sort it is necessary for the value of α to be allowed to vary between 0.05 and 1, whereas σ should be restricted to the range 0.5 to 1. The associability of stimulus A is then given by the product $\alpha_A \cdot \sigma_A$. After extensive continuous reinforcement with a single CS, it follows from Equation 2.5 that the value of σ will be close to its lowest value of 0.5 and from Equation 2.2a that α will be close to its maximum value of 1. Although this means that the associability of the CS will be relatively high, at about 0.5, it will be less than if the CS were novel, for which the associability will be close to 1, and less than if a partial reinforcement schedule had been used. In the latter case, the value of α will be high because it is the best available predictor of the US, and σ will also be high because the CS is an inaccurate predictor of its consequences. The modification is thus able to explain why conditioning in a new task with a CS that was previously consistently reinforced may progress more slowly than with either a novel CS (Hall and Pearce, 1979), or one that was partially reinforced (Kaye and Pearce, 1984; Swan and Pearce, 1988).

To appreciate the implication of these proposals for compound conditioning, we shall first consider a true discrimination of the form AX+ BX–. This treatment ensures that X is intermittently followed by food and according to Equation 2.5, the value of σ_X will remain high. However, because X is a less accurate predictor of the trial outcome than A or B, Equation 2.2b predicts that α_X will be close to zero and result in $\alpha_X \cdot \sigma_X$ also being close to zero.

Once the discrimination has been solved, the associative strength of A will be close to the asymptotic value set by the reinforcer. Equation 2.5 then predicts that σ_A will be close to its minimal value of 0.5 and Equation 2.2a predicts that α_A will be close to its maximum value of 1. Thus, the theory predicts that the discrimination will result in the associability of X being less than of A. As described earlier, this prediction has been confirmed by Dopson *et al.* (2010).

Turning now to blocking, in which conditioning with A precedes conditioning with AB. During the compound trials, Equation 2.5 predicts that σ_B will be close to 1 (because the consistently low associative strength of B will make it a poor predictor of the US), and Equation 2.2b predicts that α_B will be close to zero (because B is a poorer predictor of the US than A). The product of these values will then ensure that the associability of B is close to zero. Because A is the best available predictor of the US, α_A will be close to one and σ_A will be close to its lowest value of 0.5, so that the associability of A will then be higher than that of B. In contrast to this prediction, if associability changes during blocking were determined solely by the Pearce-Hall (1980) rule, then the associability of both A and B would be reduced to the same low level during blocking. To our knowledge, this prediction has yet to be tested.

Our proposal then is that a more parsimonious hybrid model of conditioning than that proposed by Le Pelley (2004) and discrimination learning could be achieved by making one small change to the Pearce-Hall (1980) equations. This should still allow the model to explain the data that provided unique support for the original Pearce-Hall theory, but would now attribute changes in attention during blocking and unblocking to Mackintosh (1975).

Concluding comment

The detailed analysis of blocking, as well as studies of conditioned inhibition, have shown that it is not possible to dispense with the proposal of Rescorla and Wagner (1972) rule that changes in associative strength are governed by the discrepancy ($\lambda - \Sigma V$). Once this conclusion is acknowledged then the question arises as to why animals also possess not just one, but two attentional processes. Conditioning and discrimination learning could take place successfully with the Rescorla-Wagner rule operating by itself, so what do animals gain by possessing, in addition, two attentional mechanisms?

One answer to this question can be developed by drawing a distinction between automatic and controlled processing (Schneider and Shiffrin, 1977). Controlled processing is assumed to be of limited capacity and to be essential if learning about a stimulus is to take place. Pearce and Hall (1980) argued that in view of its limited capacity, controlled processing should be devoted to stimuli about which learning is incomplete, such as those followed by unpredictable consequences. For a similar reason, controlled processing should also neglect those stimuli about which learning is complete, such as those followed by predictable consequences. Automatic processing, on the other hand, is assumed to be of unlimited capacity and its main purpose is to deal with the detection of stimuli that no longer merit controlled processing, because learning about them is complete. Once the stimuli have been detected then this form of processing is also responsible for the execution of appropriate responses. The stimuli that are most likely to be selected for this type of processing, then, are those that have proved to be reliable predictors of outcomes (Mackintosh, 1975).

Another answer to the above question sees associative learning as a means for detecting statistical regularities in the environment (Dayan, Kakade, and Montague, 2000). In line with the Pearce-Hall (1980) theory, Dayan *et al.* proposed that if a stimulus is followed by a new outcome it is statistically less likely to be a predictor for that outcome if it has a history of being consistently an accurate rather than an inaccurate predictor for a different outcome. Within this framework, it then follows that animals will pay more attention to stimuli that have been inaccurate rather than accurate predictors of their consequences. The purpose of this attention is to enable the animal to identify as rapidly and accurately as possible the predictive structure of its environment. Dayan *et al.* further proposed that animals will require another form of attention that will be important when they are confronted by more than one stimulus and must attend to one of them in order to determine how to respond. In these circumstances attention, they argue, should be directed towards the stimulus that has proved the most reliable at accurately predicting reinforcement, which is in line with Mackintosh (1975).

While these answers make it clear why the associability of a stimulus that has been an inaccurate predictor of its consequences will be high, it is not so readily apparent why a stimulus that is an accurate predictor of its consequences, and thus the one that will control behaviour, will also be of high associability. A solution to this problem is to suggest that by devoting their attention to relevant stimuli in order to achieve efficient performance, animals will inevitably be attending to them when the stimuli are used in a new learning task, and they will thus have a head start over irrelevant stimuli that are concurrently being ignored. Whatever the merits of these deliberations, the evidence we have reviewed indicates that animals possess two mechanisms of attention that operate according to different rules. Account must be taken of both of them if a complete theory of learning is to be developed.

Acknowledgements

Support for the experiments whose results are depicted in Figures 2.1 and 2.2 was provided by a grant from the UK Biotechnology and Biological Sciences Research Council.

References

Balaz, M. A., Kasprow, W. J., & Miller, R. R. (1982). Blocking with a single compound trial. *Animal Learning and Behavior,* **10**, 271–276.

Baxter, M. G., Gallagher, M., & Holland, P. C. (1999). Blocking can occur without losses in attention in rats with selective removal of hippocampal cholinergic input. *Journal of Experimental Psychology: Animal Behavior Processes,***113**, 881–890.

Bouton, M. E. (1993). Context, time and memory retrieval in the interference paradigms of Pavlovian learning. *Psychological Bulletin,* **114**, 80–99.

Bush, R. R. & Mosteller, F. (1951). A model for stimulus generalization and discrimination. *Psychological Review,* **58**, 413–423.

Couvillon, P. A., Tennant, W. A., & Bitterman, J. E. (1967). Intradimensional vs. extradimensional transfer in the discriminative learning of goldfish and pigeons. *Animal Learning and Behavior,* **4**, 197–203.

Dayan, P., Kakade, S., & Montague, P. R. (2000). Learning and selective attention. *Nature Neuroscience,* **3**, 1218–1223.

Dias, R., Robbins, T. W., & Roberts, A. C. (1996). Dissociations of affective and attentional shifting by selective lesions of prefrontal cortex. *Nature,* **380**, 69–72.

Dickinson, A., Hall, G., & Mackintosh, N. J. (1976). Surprise and the attenuation of blocking. *Journal of Experimental Psychology: Animal Behavior Processes,* **2**, 313–322.

Dickinson, A. & Mackintosh, N. J. (1979). Reinforcer specificity in enhancement of of conditioning by posttrial surprise. *Journal of Experimental Psychology: Animal Behavior Processes,* **5**, 162–177.

Dickinson, A., Nicholas, D. J., & Mackintosh, N. J. (1983). A re-examination of one-trial blocking in conditioned suppression. *Quarterly Journal of Experimental Psychology,* **35B**, 67–79.

Dopson, J., Esber, G. R., & Pearce, J. M. (2010). Differences between the associability of relevant and irrelevant stimuli. *Journal of Experimental Psychology: Animal Behavior Processes,* **36**, 258–267.

Durlach, P. J. & Mackintosh, N. J. (1986). Transfer of serial reversal learning in the pigeon. *Quarterly Journal of Experimental Psychology,* **38B**, 81–95.

George, D. N. & Pearce, J. M. (1999). Acquired distinctiveness is controlled by stimulus relevance not correlation with reward. *Journal of Experimental Psychology: Animal Behavior Processes,* **25**, 363–373.

Gibson, E. J. (1940). A systematic application of the concepts of generalization and differentiation to verbal learning. *Psychological Review,* **47**, 196–229.

Grahame, N. J., Barnet, R. C., Gunther, L. M., & Miller, R. R. (1994). Latent inhibition as a performance deficit results from CS-context associations. *Animal Learning and Behavior,* **22**, 395–408.

Hall, G. (1991). *Perceptual and Associative Learning.* Oxford: Clarendon Press.

Hall, G. & Channell, S. (1985). A comparison of intradimensional and extradimensional shift learning in pigeons. *Behavioural Processes,* **10**, 285–295.

Hall, G. & Pearce, J. M. (1979). Latent inhibition of a CS during CS-US pairings. *Journal of Experimental Psychology: Animal Behavior Processes,* **5**, 31–42.

Hall, G. & Pearce, J. M. (1982). Restoring the associability of a preexposed CS by a surprising event. *Quarterly Journal of Experimental Psychology,* **34B**, 127–140.

Haselgrove, M., Esber, G. R., Pearce, J. M., & Jones, P. M. (2010). Two kinds of attention in Pavlovian conditioning: Evidence for a hybrid model of learning. *Journal of Experimental Psychology: Animal Behavior Processes,* in press.

Hogarth, L., Dickinson, A., Austin, A., Brown, C., & Duka, T. (2007). Attention and expectation in human predictive learning: The role of uncertainty. *Quarterly Journal of Experimental Psychology,* **61**, 1658–1668.

Holland, P. C. (1997). Brain mechanisms for changes in processing of conditioned stimuli in Pavlovian conditioning: Implications for behavior theory. *Animal Learning and Behavior,* **25**, 373–399.

Kamin, L. J. (1969). Selective association and conditioning. In N. J. Mackintosh & W. K. Honig (Eds), *Fundamental Issues in Associative Learning* (pp. 42–64). Halifax: Dalhousie University Press.

Kaye, H. & Pearce. (1984). The strength of the orienting response during Pavlovian conditioning. *Journal of Experimental Psychology: Animal Behavior Processes,* **10**, 90–109.

Krechevsky, I. (1932). Hypotheses in rats. *Psychological Review,* **39**, 516–532.

Lashley, K. S. (1942). An examination of the continuity theory as applied to discrimination learning. *Journal of General Psychology,* **26**, 241–265.

Lawrence, D. H. (1949). Acquired distinctiveness of cues. I. Transfer between discriminations on the basis of familiarity with the stimulus. *Journal of Experimental Psychology,* **39**, 770–784.

Lawrence, D. H. (1950). Acquired distinctiveness of cues: II. Selective association in a constant stimulus situation. *Journal of Experimental Psychology,* **40**, 175–188.

Lawrence, D. H. (1952). The transfer of a discrimination along a continuum. *Journal of Comparative and Physiological Psychology,* **45**, 511–516.

Le Pelley, M. E. (2004). The role of associative history in models of associative learning: A selective review and a hybrid model. *Quarterly Journal of Experimental Psychology,* **57B**, 193–243.

Le Pelley, M. E., Oakeshott, S. M., Wills, A. J., & McLaren, I. P. L. (2005). The outcome specificity of learned predictiveness effects: Parallels between human causal learning and animal conditioning. *Journal of Experimental Psychology: Animal Behavior Processes,* **31**, 226–236.

Lovejoy, E. (1965). Analysis of the overlearning reversal effect. *Psychological Review,* **73**, 87–103.

Lovejoy, E. (1968). *Attention in discrimination learning.* San Francisco: Holden-Day.

Lubow, R. E. (1973). Latent inhibition. *Psychological Bulletin,* **79**, 398–407.

Lubow, R. E. & Moore, A. U. (1959). Latent inhibition: the effect of nonreinforced preexposure to the conditional stimulus. *Journal of Comparative and Physiological Psychology,* **52**, 415–419.

Mackintosh, N. J. (1969). Further analysis of the overtraining reversal effect. *Journal of Comparative and Physiological Psychology,* **67**.

Mackintosh, N. J. (1973). Stimulus selection: Learning to ignore stimuli that predict no change in reinforcement. In R. A. Hinde & J. Stevenson-Hinde (Eds), *Constraints on Learning* (pp. 75–100). London: Academic Press.

Mackintosh, N. J. (1975). A theory of attention: Variations in the associability of stimuli with reinforcement. *Psychological Review,* **82**, 276–298.

Mackintosh, N. J. & Little, L. (1969). Intradimensional and extradimensional shift learning by pigeons. *Psychonomic Science,* **14**, 5–6.

Mackintosh, N. J. & Turner, C. (1971). Blocking as a function of novelty of CS and predictability of US. *Quarterly Journal of Experimental Psychology,* **23**, 359–366.

Miller, N. E. (1948). Theory and experiment relating psychoanalytic displacements to stimulus-response generalization. *Journal of Abnormal and Social Psychology,* **43**, 155–178.

Pearce, J. M., Esber, G. R., George, D. N., & Haselgrove, M. (2008). The nature of discrimination learning in pigeons. *Learning and Behavior,* **36**, 188–199.

Pearce, J. M., George, D. N., & Redhead, E. S. (1998). The role of attention in the solution of conditional discriminations. In N. A. Schmajuk & P. C. Holland (Eds), *Occasion setting: Associative learning and cognition in animals* (pp. 249–275). Washington, DC: APA Press.

Pearce, J. M., & Hall, G. (1979). Loss of associability by a compound stimulus comprising excitatory and inhibitory elements. *Journal of Experimental Psychology: Animal Behavior Processes,* **5**, 19–30.

Pearce, J. M. & Hall, G. (1980). A model for Pavlovian learning: Variations in the effectiveness of conditioned but not unconditioned stimuli. *Psychological Review,* **87**, 532–552.

Pearce, J. M., Kaye, H., & Hall, G. (1982). Predictive accuracy and stimulus associability: Development of a model for Pavlovian conditioning. In M. L. Commons, R. J. Herrnstein & A. R. Wagner (Eds), *Quantitative analyses of behavior* (Vol. III, pp. 241–255). Cambridge, MA: Ballinger.

Reid, L. S. (1953). The development of noncontinuity behavior through continuity learning. *Journal of Experimental Psychology,* **46**, 107–112.

Rescorla, R. A. & Wagner, A. R. (1972). A theory of Pavlovian conditioning: Variations in the effectiveness of reinforcement and nonreinforcement. In A. H. Black & W. F. Prokasy (Eds), *Classical conditioning II: Current research and theory* (pp. 64–99). New York: Appleton-Century-Crofts.

Roberts, A. C., Robbins, T. W., & Everitt, B. J. (1988). The effects of intradimensional and extradimensional shifts on visual discrimination learning in humans and non-human primates. *Quarterly Journal of Experimental Psychology,* **40B**, 321–341.

Schneider, W. & Shiffrin, R. M. (1977). Controlled and automatic human information processing: I. Detection, search, and attention. *Psychological Review,* **84**, 1–66.

Shepp, B. E. & Eimas, P. D. (1964). Intradimensional and extradimensional shifts in the rat. *Journal of Comparative and Physiological Psychology,* **57**, 357–364.

Shepp, B. E. & Schrier, A. M. (1969). Consecutive intradimensional and extradimensional shifts in monkeys. *Journal of Comparative and Physiological Psychology,* **67**, 199–203.

Siegel, S. (1967). Overtraining and transfer processes. *Journal of Comparative and Physiological Psychology*, **64**, 471–477.

Sutherland, N. S. & Mackintosh, N. J. (1971). *Mechanisms of animal discrimination learning*. New York: Academic Press.

Swan, J. A. & Pearce, J. M. (1988). The orienting response as an index of stimulus associability in rats. *Journal of Experimental Psychology: Animal Behavior Processes*, **14**, 292–301.

Trabasso, T. R. & Bower, G. H. (1968). *Attention in learning: Theory and research*. New York: Wiley.

Trobalon, J. B., Miguelez, D., McLaren, I. P. L., & Mackintosh, N. J. (2003). Intradimensional and extradimensional shifts in spatial learning. *Journal of Experimental Psychology: Animal Behavior Processes*, **29**, 143–152.

Wagner, A. R. (1981). SOP: A model of automatic memory processing in animal behavior. In N. E. Spear & R. R. Miller (Eds), *Information processing in animals: Memory mechanisms* (pp. 5–47). Hillsdale, NJ.: Erlbaum.

Wilson, P. N., Boumphrey, P., & Pearce, J. M. (1992). Restoration of the orienting response to a light by a change in its predictive accuracy. *Quarterly Journal of Experimental Psychology*, **44B**, 17–36.

Zeaman, D. & House, B. J. (1963). The role of attention in retardate discrimination learning. In N. R. Ellis (Ed.), *Handbook of mental deficiency: Psychological theory and research* (pp. 378–418). New York: McGraw-Hill.

Chapter 3

Attentional learning

Geoffrey Hall and Gabriel Rodriguez

Preamble

This chapter is about *attentional learning*, and it is necessary to say something about what this phrase will be taken to mean, if confusion is to be avoided. In modern cognitive psychology, the phrase often seems to be used as a synonym for 'intentional' learning – for learning in which the participant is concentrating on the task in hand (other learning that occurs without conscious effort on the part of the subject being categorized differently, e.g. as implicit). This attempt to distinguish between forms of learning according to whether or not a faculty of attention is engaged is not our concern here. Rather we are concerned with the learning processes that determine attention itself. The mechanisms we envisage will operate both when learning is intentional and when it is not; indeed, success in specifying these mechanisms would leave us with a notion of attention quite different from that used in making the distinction. To amplify this point, it will be useful to take a historical perspective.

William James, in his famous chapter on 'attention' (in his book, *Principles of Psychology*, 1890), noted that theorists in the empiricist tradition (Locke, Mill, and so on) had little use for the notion. They were determined (to paraphrase James's account) to explain the content of consciousness in terms of the direct effects of events in the world and the associates that these events activate. They found no place for a higher-level faculty that selected some events for special treatment (no 'central executive' or 'supervisory attentional system' for them). Their intellectual descendants, the empiricists of the twentieth century (the proponents of associative learning theory), maintained this approach. Spence (1936), for example, was adamant that learning would occur to any event that impinged on the sensorium, and worked hard to explain observations that seemed to suggest that animals might learn selectively about only some aspects of the stimulus display before them.

In spite of certain sympathy for their views, James (1890) clearly felt that the empiricists were missing something. It was self-evident to him that 'millions of items of the outward order are present to my senses which never properly enter into my experience' (p. 402). He confessed to a belief (based, he said, on ethical rather than scientific considerations) that some 'spiritual force' (central executive?) was responsible for selection among these items, but he was scientist enough to allow that the evidence could be accommodated by the view that attention was a 'resultant' (effect) rather than a 'force' (or cause). Most will accept, as did James, that what he called 'immediate sensorial attention' (which might be provoked by the sudden onset of an intense stimulus) is an *effect*, to be explained in terms of the stimulating conditions. James went on to distinguish sensorial attention from a form that he referred to as 'derived attention', in which an event is held to attract attention by virtue of its association with some other interesting event. But this too, he allowed, may also be seen as an effect, in this case, of the organism's training history. He went on: 'even when attention is voluntary, it is possible to conceive of it as an effect ... The things we attend to come to us by their own laws ... The associates which bring them also fix them [as the focus of attention] by the interest which they lend' (p. 450).

Learning theorists of the late twentieth century have followed James's line. The demonstration of empirical phenomena like overshadowing and blocking (Kamin, 1969) has made clear that 'items of the outward order' may indeed impinge on the sensorium but may yet fail to command processing (as revealed by their failure to form normal associations). But these theorists have taken such demonstrations of attentional phenomena as effects to be explained, and have incorporated into their theories a range of mechanisms that attempt to do so. For the most part these mechanisms have involved associative learning processes, similar to those postulated by James's notion of derived attention. Discussion of this form of attentional learning is the central topic of the second main section of this chapter. But before turning to this discussion, it is appropriate to mention the other form of attention (immediate sensorial attention) identified by him. This too, as we shall see, is not immune to the effects of experience.

Immediate sensorial attention: effective salience and habituation

The magnitude of the unconditioned response (UR) evoked by the presentation of a simple stimulus will depend on the intensity of that stimulus (e.g. a loud noise will evoke a bigger startle response than a soft one). For purposes of theory building, we may postulate a central representation of the stimulus (a node) activated to a greater or lesser degree according to the intensity of the input, the degree of activation determining the vigour of the UR. Should the noise be accompanied by another event (say a shock), two nodes will be activated, and an association may be formed between them (the noise becoming a conditioned stimulus (CS) and the shock serving as an unconditioned stimulus (US) in traditional Pavlovian terminology). Assuming nothing but a simple contiguity rule for the time being, we may say

$$\Delta V = S \cdot \lambda \tag{3.1}$$

where ΔV represents the increment in associative strength (V) produced by this pairing, S, the level of activation in the CS node, and λ, the level of activation in the US node. Experimental studies of conditioning (see Hall, 1994, for a summary of the evidence) confirm that associative strength grows more quickly the more intense the CS and US (the higher the values of S and λ). To this extent, therefore, even the simplest imaginable theory finds a role for a form of attention by assuming that the intensity (or salience) of a stimulus will determine the extent to which it receives processing (as evidenced by its ability to evoke a response and its ability to enter into associations).

But James's concern was not primarily with the case in which a single event was presented but rather that in which an intense stimulus might command processing at the expense of other items of the outward order that might happen to present, that is, with *selective* attention. In our developing scheme, this would amount to the suggestion that activation of one node by a salient stimulus might restrict the ability of other nodes to be activated by other stimuli presented concurrently. Selectivity of this sort has played a surprisingly minor role in standard theories of learning (in contrast to the position for studies of human information processing, from Broadbent, 1958, onwards). It is, however, a basic assumption of Wagner's (1981) influential theory. Wagner assumes that there is a limit to the number of nodes that can be fully activated at one time, and that increased activity in one will suppress the ability of others to be activated even though the appropriate stimuli are present. The mechanism responsible was not specified (does it require some supervisory system that vets the activity of a whole range of nodes?) but there is experimental evidence to support the proposal. In overshadowing, the presence of a second potential CS during a conditioning trial will restrict the acquisition of associative strength by the target CS. This phenomenon is open to a range of explanations (see below) but James and Wagner (1980) were able to demonstrate that, at least in some instances, the effect occurred because of competition at the sensory/perceptual level – the level of activity in the node corresponding to the target CS (the value of S evoked by the stimulus) was depressed by the simultaneous activation of another node.

Habituation and loss of effective salience

With repeated presentation, the ability of a stimulus to evoke its UR declines. An example is provided by Figure 3.1 (top panel), which shows the results of an experiment by S. Franklin from the York laboratory. Rats lever-pressing for food received 10 presentations of a footshock over the course of five daily training sessions. The initial immediate effect of a shock (i.e. the UR to shock) was to produce a suppression of lever-pressing. The figure shows rate of lever-pressing recorded during the 10-s period following shock; at the start of training this was low, but by the final block of trials the rate had recovered to a level that was much the same as that shown in the interval between shocks. The standard account of such habituation (see, Mackintosh, 1987, for a review of the evidence) is that a failure has occurred somewhere in the chain of processes connecting activation of the stimulus node to the mechanisms responsible for organizing the response (in this case, a response that induces suppression of

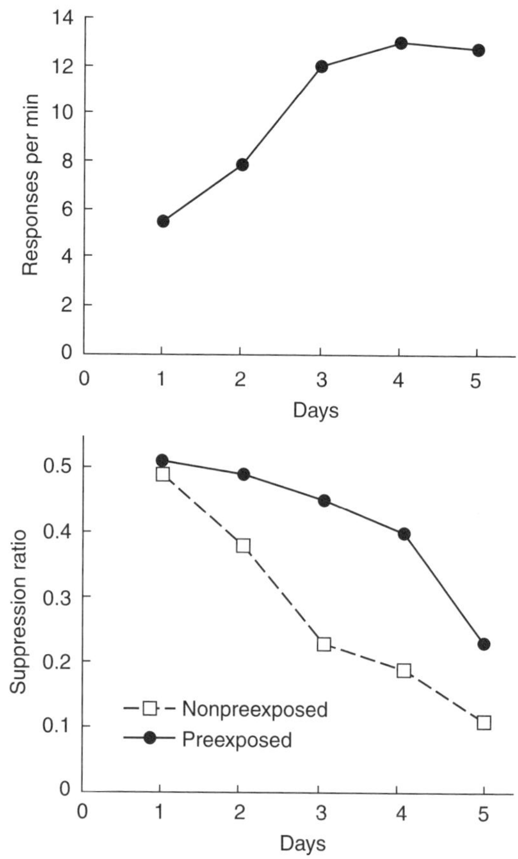

Fig. 3.1 Upper panel: Mean rates of response by rats lever-pressing for food in the 10-s period following a footshock (0.4 mA, 0.5 s). There were two shocks in each daily 40-min session, occurring 13 and 27 min after the start of the session. The lower panel shows the acquisition of conditioned suppression by these rats (the pre-exposed group) in a subsequent phase of training in which shocks continued to be presented as before, but were signalled by a 60-s light. Subjects in the non-pre-exposed group experienced shocks for the first time in this phase.

lever-pressing). There are number of theoretical options, but one possibility is that repeated direct activation of the stimulus node renders it less sensitive to stimulation, so that later presentations of the stimulus produce a lesser degree of activation than earlier presentations. If so, this means that the effective salience of the stimulus is not fixed by stimulus intensity but can change – the ability of the stimulus to govern 'immediate sensorial attention' has been modified by experience.

An implication of this interpretation is that pre-exposure should modify the ability of the stimulus to enter into association. To say that its node is less easily activated means that should the pre-exposed shock be used as a US in a subsequent conditioning procedure, the value of λ will be reduced to some extent and acquisition of associative strength, governed by Equation 3.1, will be slowed. Franklin's experiment showed just this effect in a subsequent stage of training in which shocks continued to be presented as before, but were preceded by a 60-s light signal (the CS). The lower panel of Figure 3.1 shows that the development of conditioned suppression to the light was retarded in subjects given shock pre-exposure, compared with a control group that had no previous experience of the shock. This US-pre-exposure effect has long been known, being first demonstrated in this form by Kamin (1961), who himself offered an explanation in terms of a habituation process (although later research by Randich and LoLordo, 1979, suggests that other mechanisms are also likely to have contributed to the effect).

Factors modulating habituation

This perspective, in which habituation is taken to be a learning process that reduces the effective salience of a stimulus, means that the legion of studies that has been conducted on factors that determine the course of habituation become directly relevant to our attempt to explain attentional learning. It would be impossible to review all these studies satisfactorily here, and instead we will concentrate on just one factor, the role of post-stimulus events, that turns out to be of particular importance for an understanding of attentional learning more generally.

Although the effect has not always been obtained (Mercier and Baker, 1985; Szakmary, 1977), it has frequently been observed that habituation, as measured by the decline in vigour of the UR, is prevented, or at least attenuated, when another salient and novel stimulus is presented shortly after each occurrence of the target stimulus (Green and Parker, 1975; Shanks, Preston, and Stanhope, 1986). This result has been referred to as a post-stimulus distractor effect, on the assumption that the role of the added cue is to interfere with the processing of the target stimulus that is responsible for habituation.

This interpretation is by no means secure, however, and a more neutral characterization would be that the loss of salience produced by repeated stimulus exposure is attenuated when that stimulus is reliably followed by another event. Experiments on the US-pre-exposure effect recently conducted in the York laboratory by A. Hancock are relevant to this issue.

In one of Hancock's experiments, rats received pre-exposure to a shock (there were four shocks per day over the course of five daily sessions). For the first group of subjects (the consistent group), each shock was followed by a salient event (a 60-s presentation of a noise); for the second (inconsistent) group, the noise was presented on a random half of the trials. This procedure makes it difficult to assess the UR to the shock by measuring post-shock suppression (post-shock responding is likely to be influenced by the presence, or omission, of the noise at the relevant time), but it is a simple matter to assess the effectiveness of the shock as a reinforcer in subsequent associative learning. In a further stage of training, Hancock gave all the subjects trials in which the shock was preceded by a light CS (two trials per day over six days). The results of this stage (Figure 3.2) showed that conditioned suppression to the light was established more readily in the consistent than in the inconsistent group. This outcome is in line with the conjecture that the effective salience of an event, which will normally decline with repeated presentation, will be

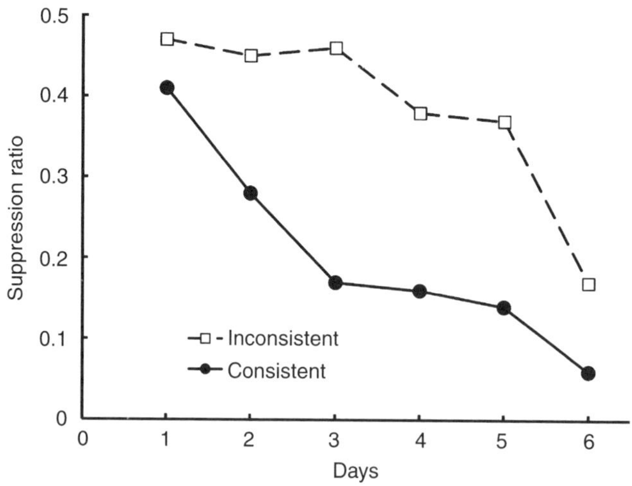

Fig. 3.2 Acquisition of conditioned suppression (group mean suppression ratios) in rats given two trials per day in which a 60-s light preceded a 0.35-mA, 0.5-s footshock. All subjects had received five pre-exposure sessions, each containing four shocks. For the consistent group, each shock was followed by a 60-s noise; for the inconsistent group, the noise followed a random half of shock presentations.

maintained when presentations are reliably followed by some other event. The significance of this observation will become apparent when we come to discuss the effects of pre-exposure to events that are used as CSs in standard conditioning experiments.

Habituation with neutral stimuli

Studies of habituation are commonly carried out with motivationally significant stimuli of the sort that are used as USs in conditioning experiments, for the very good reason that these stimuli evoke clear URs that can be readily monitored. But this does not mean that the less motivationally significant (neutral) stimuli (lights, tones, and so on) that are usually used as CSs will be free from the effects of habituation; repeated presentation of a light, say, can be assumed to bring about a reduction in effective salience just as repeated presentation of a shock does. The fact that such a pre-exposed stimulus functions rather poorly as a CS when subsequently paired with a US in a conditioning procedure (the *latent inhibition* effect) might seem to support this view—latent inhibition would thus be a simple parallel of the US-pre-exposure effect with the former resulting from a reduction in the value of S and the latter from a reduction in the value of λ. As we shall shortly see, however, there is reason to think that this salience-change process plays no more than a minor role in latent inhibition, and that other processes are primarily responsible. A preliminary indication of complications to come is found in direct studies of habituation-like effects with neutral stimuli.

Although less dramatic than the UR evoked by an event like a shock, so-called neutral stimuli may none the less evoke responses of some sort prior to any conditioning procedure. When confronted with the illumination of a light bulb in an otherwise dimly lit Skinner box, a rat will turn towards the light, rear in front of it, and approach it with his snout. This version of the UR has been referred to as an orienting response (OR), or, sometimes, the 'what-is-it?' reflex. Like other URs, its occurrence declines with repeated presentation of the stimulus. Figure 3.3 shows the results of an experiment by Kaye and Pearce (1984). Rats in the light-only group received regular presentations over 14 days of a 10-s light stimulus and the occurrence of an OR was scored at two points within the trial. Early in training, ORs were frequent, but they declined steadily over days. So far, this behaviour looks like a standard case of habituation of UR, but doubts are raised by the performance shown by other groups included in the experiment. The first group, i.e. the consistent group, received a post-stimulus event (a food pellet was presented) after each presentation of the light. That these animals showed rather more ORs over the course of training is consistent with the results we have already discussed and with the

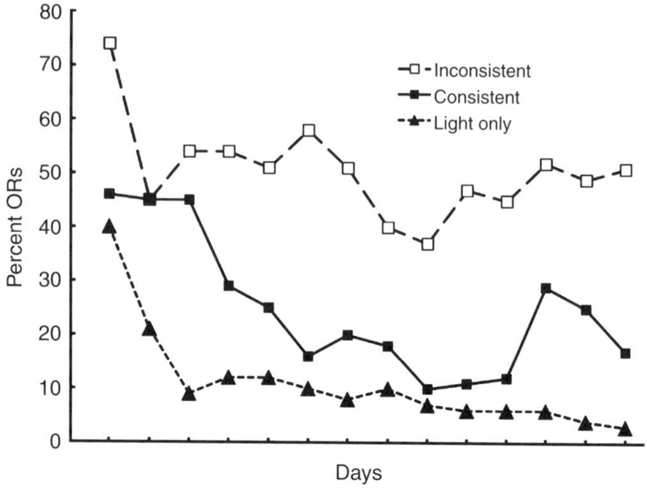

Fig. 3.3 Mean percentage of observations in which rats were scored as showing an orienting response (OR) to a light. For the consistent group, a food pellet followed every presentation of the light; for the inconsistent group, food was presented on a random half of the trials; the light-only group received no food. (Adapted from data presented by Kaye and Pearce, 1984.)

empirical generalization that the effective salience of a stimulus will be maintained when it is reliably followed by another event. But the results of the second group (the inconsistent group) constitute a challenge. For these animals the post-light event (the food pellet) was presented on a randomly chosen half of the trials; for them, the frequency of occurrence of the OR remained at a high level throughout the course of training. (See also Pearce, Wilson, and Kaye, 1988; Swan and Pearce, 1988.) This result stands in marked contrast to the conclusion, drawn above on the basis of the shock pre-exposure studies, that the effective salience of a stimulus is better maintained when it is followed reliably by some other event, than when the post-stimulus event occurs only from time to time.

Why does the OR show this pattern of behaviour? This issue was addressed by Pearce and Hall (1992) who argued that the vigour of the OR depends on two sets of mechanisms. One of these is the process that is responsible for habituation generally – repeated presentation of a light will, as for any other stimulus, bring about a reduction in the effective salience of that stimulus and, with it, a reduction in the vigour of any response it tends to evoke. The other, however, is concerned with what the stimulus in question predicts. This suggestion is not original and was put forward by Liddell (1950) in his discussion of the Pavlovian orienting reflex. According to Liddell, the occurrence of a novel stimulus will evoke not only Pavlov's 'what-is-it?' reflex, but also a 'what-happens-next?' reflex. The first of these will be subject to habituation and will decline as the animal becomes accustomed to the stimulus. The second will be evoked when the consequences of the stimulus are uncertain and thus this component of the OR will continue to be evoked when, as for the inconsistent group of Figure 3.3, the outcome of a stimulus presentation varies from trial to trial.[1]

One implication of this analysis is that the loss of the OR shown by subjects in the consistent group of Figure 3.3 should be reversible. Habituation itself is usually taken to be a one-way street (Groves and Thompson, 1970)—a stimulus that has become familiar as a result of exposure, remains so. Once habituation has occurred, there is no reason to suppose that the 'what-is-it?' reflex will play any further role, but a change in the consequences of the stimulus might be capable of restoring the 'what-happens-next?' reflex. This matter was explored in a series of experiments by Wilson, Boumphrey, and Pearce (1992); the results of one of these are shown in Figure 3.4. In this, the rats were exposed, on separate trials, to two different lights. Offset of a light was followed, on a random half of trials, by the delivery of a food pellet, but this occurred after an interval of 10 s—the immediate consequence of every light trial was the presentation of a 10-s tone. This consistency of consequence was enough to bring about a steady decline in the OR to each of the lights, as shown on the left of Figure 3.4. In the second stage of training, conditions were changed for just one of the lights (Light 1 in the figure). For Light 1, light-tone-food trials continued as before, but on the other trials the light was presented followed by no consequence. The result was an immediate increase in the frequency of occurrence of the OR, to a high level that was maintained throughout Stage 2 training. Significantly, the level of orienting to Light 2 remained at a low level. The fact that the response to Light 2 was not affected by the change of conditions in Stage 2 rules out the possibility that the increase in responding shown to Light 1 reflects a general increase in arousal produced by this change in conditions, that acted to potentiate the vigour of the OR (this is the account of dishabituation offered by Groves and Thompson, 1970). Instead, the loss and

1 It should be made clear that we are not suggesting that the rules governing the effects of pre-exposure to neutral stimuli differ from those that apply to motivationally significant stimuli; both types of stimulus are assumed to be susceptible to both the mechanisms outlined here. That the UR produced by exposure to a shock appears not to be maintained when the consequences of that shock are inconsistent may indicate simply that the response being measured is sensitive only to the habituation process and is not a component of the 'what-happens-next?' reflex.

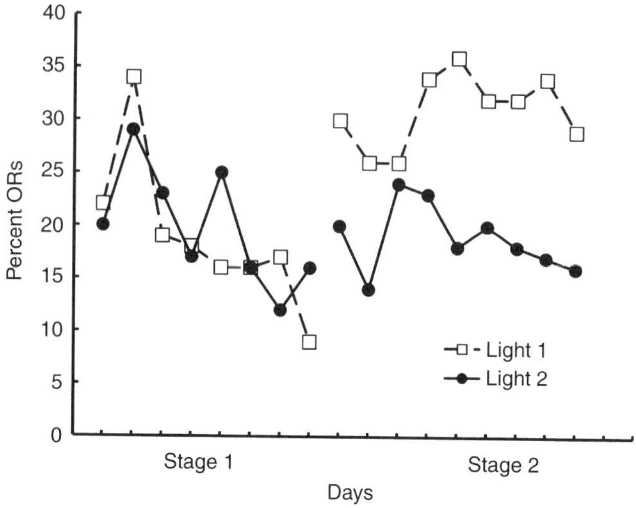

Fig. 3.4 Mean percentage of observations in which rats were scored as showing an orienting response (OR) to a light. On each trial, one or other of two spatially separated light bulbs was illuminated. In Stage 1, both lights were followed by the same consequence, a 10-s tone (itself followed by food on half the trials). In Stage 2, conditions remained the same for Light 2, but for Light 1, although light-tone-food trials continued as before, they were intermixed with light-alone trials. (From an experiment by Wilson et al., 1992.)

recovery of the OR to Light 1 does not follow the principles that govern habituation of a simple UR; rather, the OR appears to be governed by the accuracy with which the eliciting stimulus predicts its immediate consequences.

Interim conclusions

One factor that determines the attention paid to a stimulus is the intensity or salience of that stimulus. A salient stimulus will be better able to elicit its appropriate response (most obviously its UR, but presumably also any conditioned response (CR) that it comes to control by virtue of its having formed an association with some other event). And, given the principle embodied in Equation 3.1, we must assume that the ability to form associations, will be greater the more salient the stimulus, whether it be used as a CS or US.

Although the salience of a novel stimulus will be determined by its intensity, effective salience can change as a result of experience, and will decline with repeated presentations, as is evidenced by the phenomenon of habituation. The mechanism responsible for habituation remains to be specified, and a close examination of the large body of existing evidence relating to the conditions under which habituation occurs could supply the information that is needed. Our only contribution in this context has been to note that the loss of effective salience produced by repeated presentation of a stimulus appears to be retarded when that stimulus is reliably followed by another event (compared with the rapid loss that is observed when the stimulus is followed by inconsistent consequences). This observation is of particular significance given the evidence that another plausible index of the attention-getting power of a stimulus, its ability to elicit an OR, obeys quite different rules – the OR *declines* when the stimulus is consistently followed by another event but is maintained (or restored) when the immediate consequences of the stimulus vary from trial to trial. We conclude that the OR is not determined by the effective salience of the stimulus; in addition to the attentional process that reflects and determines effective salience, there is another form of attention that depends on the ability of the stimulus to predict its consequences accurately. The way in which one event can come to predict the occurrence of another is, of course, the core topic of associative learning theory and, accordingly, we turn next to an examination of the relation between associative learning and attentional learning.

Derived attention: associative learning and associability

James's second form of attention, derived attention, was taken to be an effect of association formation. He suggested that an event that is not particularly salient (and thus not likely to evoke immediate sensorial attention) may, none the less, command processing by virtue of its having formed an association with some other, more significant event. The idea has remained popular (it reappears, for example, in Mackintosh's, 1975, theory of attention) and it has a certain plausibility. Equipped with a cognitive system of limited capacity, it makes sense to give some form of priority to events of importance. Clearly a stimulus, however insignificant in itself, can be considered important if it is an accurate predictor of important events, and superior processing of such a stimulus will allow the organism to anticipate the occurrence of these important events and to respond appropriately to them. When it comes to selecting which stimulus (of the many that will be available) should control behaviour, accurate predictors deserve to be chosen.

But before the system can get round to behaving on the basis of what it has learned it first needs to learn about the relationships between stimuli and their consequences. Given the mass of available stimuli that any organism will face and the limited capacity of its processing mechanisms, it is again necessary to engage an attentional process to select the stimuli that is appropriate and necessary to learn about. What properties should a stimulus have to make it worthy of this form of attention? It seems likely that these will be different from those that determine its ability to control performance. As we have just noted, behaviour needs to be controlled by stimuli that accurately predict important consequences, but when it comes to learning, there is no need to pay attention to such stimuli, as their consequence are already known – rather, attention needs to be focussed on events, the consequences of which are uncertain or remain to be established. This analysis formed the basis of the theory to be considered next.

The Pearce-Hall model

The account of associative learning proposed by Pearce and Hall (1980) introduced (or rather, borrowed from Mackintosh, 1975) an attentional construct that was referred to as *associability*. The basic contiguity principle of Equation 3.1 was modified to become:

$$\Delta V = \alpha \cdot S \cdot \lambda \qquad (3.2)$$

where α is a parameter, varying between 0 and 1, that represents the associability of the CS in classical conditioning. The value of α for a novel stimulus was assumed to be high, but was postulated to change as a result of experience. Specifically, on trials after the first, the value of α was held to be determined by the associative learning that had occurred on the previous trial. Our interpretation of this form of attentional learning was expressed in the following equation:

$$\alpha^n = |\lambda - \Sigma V|^{n-1} \qquad (3.3)$$

Here, the value of α on trial n is taken to be determined by events occurring on the preceding trial (n–1); specifically the value of α is set to equal the absolute value of the discrepancy between the value of λ and the summed associative strength (ΣV) of all CSs that were present on that trial.[2]

This formulation implies that repeated pairings of a CS and US will generate increases in associative strength (Equation 3.2) that will rise to an asymptote as the concurrent decline in α (Equation 3.3) occurs.[3] At asymptote the value of

[2] In fact associability changes are unlikely to be as rapid as Equation 3.3 implies, and Pearce, Kaye, and Hall (1982) introduced a modification in which α was determined by a weighted average of values from a run of preceding trials. This modification does not change the principle described in the text.

[3] The introduction of ΣV into Equation 3.3 allows for cue competition effects, such as overshadowing. Thus, if two cues are conditioned as a compound, both will acquire strength (Equation 3.2). The associative strength ultimately acquired by each element of the compound will be less than λ, as conditioning will stop when their summed strength reaches λ (Equation 3.3), at which point the α value of each will be zero. This principle, with its

α will be zero. This is not to say that a fully trained CS will fail to command attention of some sort. A CS with high associative strength will evoke conditioned responding, and, to the extent that such responding depends on the effective salience of the CS (on the value of S), this too may be assumed to be high, given the evidence that the habituation process responsible for loss of salience is attenuated when presentations of a stimulus are consistently followed by some other event. That is, the ability of a CS to control responding will depend on the values of S and V. But the readiness with which a CS is learned about will be determined primarily by the value of α. Attention for learning (as opposed to the attention necessary for performance) will decline as the consequences of a given CS become established.

Negative transfer effects

Experimental results in support of this analysis come from studies of transfer of learning in simple conditioning procedures. The most obvious prediction is that when a CS has been trained to asymptote with a given reinforcer, further learning about that stimulus (as might be expected when it is paired with some new reinforcer) will be retarded – the α value of the CS will be reduced to zero by the first stage of training and a new association will be formed only when associability is restored as a result of experience of the changed conditions of the subsequent phase of training. Hall and Pearce (1979; see also Hall and Pearce, 1982; Pearce, Kaye, and Hall, 1982) demonstrated just such negative transfer in rats trained in the conditioned suppression procedure. The results of one of their experiments (Hall and Pearce, 1982) are shown in Figure 3.5.

In this experiment, rats in the group labelled T-sh/T-SH received extensive training with a tone signalling a weak electric shock, enough to establish, at asymptote, a moderate level of conditioned suppression, as shown by the isolated point on the left of the figure. The effect of this training on further learning was investigated in a second stage in which the intensity of the shock was increased. Acquisition of further suppression now became possible, but as the figure shows, this proceeded slowly. In spite of having a headstart, as a consequence of their initial training with the tone, this group learned much more slowly in Stage 2 than rats in a control condition (labelled L-sh/T-SH) for whom the tone was novel at the start of this stage. These animals had received Stage 1 training with a weak shock that was signalled, in their case, by a different stimulus, a light. At the start of Stage 2, therefore, they showed no

implication that the α values of cues trained as a compound will converge on a common value, has implications for issues to be discussed shortly. For the time being, discussion will be limited to procedures in which a single CS is used.

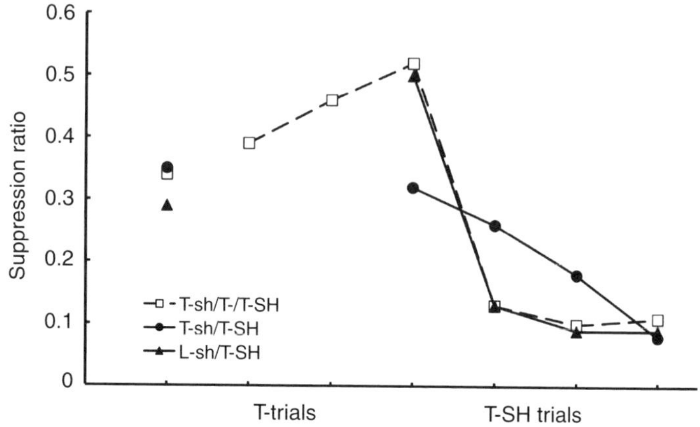

Fig. 3.5 Group mean suppression ratios for three groups of rats in the experiment by Hall and Pearce (1982). The isolated points represent the performance shown on the final day of the first phase of training in which a weak shock (sh) had been signalled by a tone (T) or a light (L). In the test phase, all subjects experienced four trials with the tone signalling a stronger shock (SH); for one of the groups pretrained with T-sh, these trials were preceded by two extinction trials in which the tone was presented alone.

suppression to the tone, but, as the figure shows, they were able to acquire it rapidly.

Our interpretation of these results, that Stage 2 learning was slow for the T-sh/T-SH group, because the associability of the tone had been reduced to zero by the first phase of training, receives support from the results obtained from a third group included in this study. These animals received identical training, having the tone followed by a weak shock in Stage 1 and by a stronger shock in Stage 2; they differed only in that two non-reinforced trials with the tone were inserted before the start of Stage 2. As might be expected, the effect of these trials (the T-trials of the figure) was to extinguish the suppression acquired in Stage 1, so that subjects in this group started Stage 2 showing no suppression to the tone. But according to the theory, the extinction trials, by establishing a discrepancy between what the tone predicts (a small shock) and what happens (no shock) should restore the value of α (Equation 3.3) and allow further learning to occur readily; and as the figure shows, this is what was observed, with the T-sh/T-/T-SH group learning just as rapidly as the group for whom the tone was novel at the start of Stage 2.

These results match those obtained from studies of the OR. As we noted, in discussing the experiment by Wilson *et al.* (1992), the OR declines when the eliciting stimulus is followed by a consistent consequence; and it is restored when that consequence is changed. The OR appears to track the value of α, as specified by the rules of the Pearce-Hall (1980) model. We also noted, in discussing the experiment by Kaye and Pearce (1984), that the OR is maintained during exposure to a stimulus, when that stimulus is followed by inconsistent consequences. This too follows from the model, as the value of α can be expected to be maintained under these circumstances. The further implication, that inconsistency in pre-exposure should alleviate the negative transfer produced by exposure in which the stimulus is followed by a consistent consequence has been tested and confirmed several times (Kaye and Pearce, 1984; Swan and Pearce, 1988; Wilson *et al.*, 1992). An instance using the conditioned suppression procedure of Hall and Pearce (1982) is presented in Figure 3.6.

In this experiment (Pearce, Kaye, and Hall, 1982), rats in the group labelled T-consistent received, as before, extensive initial training with a tone signalling a weak shock, before being trained in Stage 2 with the tone followed by a stronger shock. As before, these animals learned more slowly in Stage 2 than control subjects given Stage 1 training with a light (the L-consistent group). The new results come from groups that received Stage 1 training in which the stimulus was followed by inconsistent consequences, with the weak shock being presented on only a random half of the trials. If experience of the tone

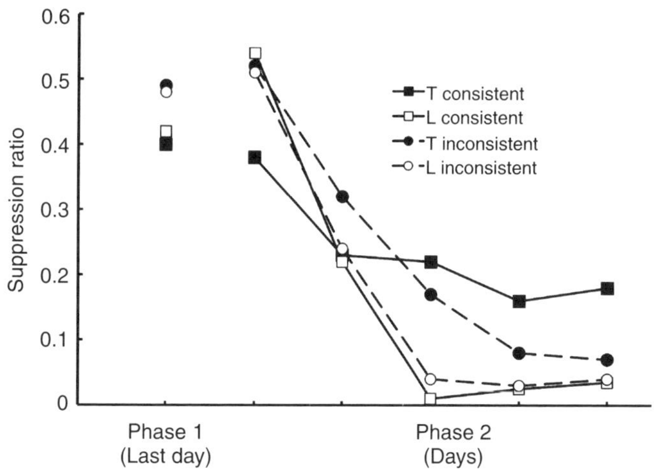

Fig. 3.6 Group mean suppression ratios for four groups of rats in the experiment by Pearce et al. (1982). The isolated points represent the performance shown on the final day of the first stage of training during which different groups had received either a tone (T) or a light (L) followed on all trials by a weak shock (the consistent groups), or by the shock on half the trials (the inconsistent groups). In Stage 2, all subjects received training in which the tone was reliably followed by a stronger shock.

with inconsistent consequences serves to maintain the associability that is lost when the consequences of the tone are consistent, the T-inconsistent group should learn more readily than the T-consistent group when trained with the tone and stronger shock in Stage 2. This was the result obtained. Experience of partial reinforcement in Stage 1 did not, in itself, influence Stage 2 performance – rats in the L-inconsistent group learned at just the same rate as those in the L-consistent group.

These results (along with a range of others, some of them summarized by Pearce and Mackintosh in Chapter 2 of this volume) firmly establish the validity of the central notion of the Pearce-Hall (1980) model. One aspect of the attention controlled by a stimulus (its associability) will decline when that stimulus reliably predicts its consequences. This may seem satisfactory but (as Pearce and Mackintosh note) a problem arises from seemingly contradictory results that have emerged from certain studies of discrimination learning. We consider these next.

Positive transfer effects

In a classic study, Lawrence (1949) trained rats on a simultaneous (choice) discrimination between two cues. When they had solved this he transferred them to a new task (a form of successive discrimination) that used the same cues but which imposed different response requirements. He found positive transfer—not at all the result to be expected on the basis of the Pearce-Hall (1980) model, which supposes that both of the cues (one followed consistently by reward, one consistently by non-reward in the first phase of training) should have suffered a loss of associability. Lawrence's result seems to suggest, rather, that the associability of the cues had been enhanced by the initial training. One response to this seemingly stark contradiction is to try to explain it away in terms of the operation of non-attentional processes. Lawrence's discrimination training procedure involved complexities not present in the simple Pavlovian paradigms that we have discussed so far; perhaps these introduce new sources of transfer that more than compensate for the loss of associability that cues are thought to have suffered. Siegel (1967) produced results favouring just this analysis, arguing that the effect observed in Lawrence's experiment might be the consequence of the transfer of particular patterns of responding acquired in the initial phase of training.

Alive to this problem, a succeeding generation of researchers in animal discrimination learning showed much ingenuity in devising a range of transfer paradigms, that were intended to ensure that any effect obtained might be unambiguously ascribed to changes in the attention governed by the pretrained stimuli rather than to direct effects produced by the associations formed in the first phase of training (Sutherland and Mackintosh, 1971; Pearce and Mackintosh, this volume). How successful they were in these efforts is still a matter for debate, given that the complexity of the designs used inevitably left scope for a range of alternative interpretations (Hall, 1991). Clear demonstrations of positive transfer in simple discrimination tasks, that cannot be readily explained away in terms of direct transfer effects, can, however, be found in experiments conducted with human subjects.

Acquired distinctiveness of cues

The two or three decades following Lawrence's (1949) experiment saw the publication of a large number of studies, using human subjects, that were designed to investigate a phenomenon often referred to as the *acquired distinctiveness of cues*. Although they differed in many details, the basic design of these studies was as follows. In the first stage of training, the subjects learned a discrimination A→1 and B→2 (where A and B represent the discriminative stimuli, and 1 and 2, different outcomes). They were then shifted to a new task involving the same stimuli, but with a new set of outcomes (A→3 and B→4). The use of human subjects allowed (as experiments in animal discrimination learning do not) flexibility in the choice of events to be used as outcomes. Commonly, those used in the first stage were verbal labels, whereas the second-stage task required the subject to make different motor responses to the two cues. In these circumstances, it is difficult to see how associations formed in the first stage could directly facilitate learning in the second stage; none the less, positive transfer was often observed. After an extensive review of all these various experiments, Hall (1991) concluded that the acquired distinctiveness effect was a reality (or at least that transfer to the test problem shown by subjects given discrimination training [A→1, B→2] in the first stage was superior to that shown by control subjects given initial non-discriminative training in which the cues were not correlated with the outcomes [A→1/2, B→1/2]).

Given this conclusion we must again face the question: Why should positive transfer be seen in these discrimination tasks when formally equivalent experiments using simple Pavlovian conditioning procedures show that a cue that is consistently followed by a given outcome will lose associability? Part of the answer appears to lie in the very fact that the experiments showing positive transfer involved discrimination between similar cues. Learning of the test discrimination, A→3, B→4, may certainly be expected to be hindered if these cues start off with low associability, but it will be facilitated by any learning process that enhances the subject's ability to tell the cues apart. There is reason to think that initial discrimination training in which the cues are reliably associated with different outcomes (i.e. A→1, B→2) recruits just such a process.

The evidence is presented in detail in Hall (1991), but the essence of the argument is as follows. Training in which each cue is followed by a different outcome will establish associations that allow each cue to activate the representation of its associate (A of 1, B of 2). A subsequent discrimination between A and B will thus involve discrimination between A plus the associatively activated representation of 1, and B plus the associatively activated representation of 2. If outcomes 1 and 2 are distinctively different, then the overall patterns of activation that must be discriminated on the test will be rendered more different than would be the case in the absence of initial discrimination training. Test performance would therefore be facilitated. By the same token, initial non-discriminative training, in which the cues will become associated with the same outcome (or outcomes), can be expected to render the cues more similar (by adding the same associatively activated common elements to each), and acquisition of the test discrimination will be retarded.

Hall, Graham, Mitchell, and Lavis (2003) have conducted a set of experiments testing a version of this interpretation of the acquired distinctiveness effect, and have confirmed its central features. They did not show, of course, that this mechanism was the sole source of the effect, and more recent work suggests that it is not.

Learned predictiveness with simple cues

After a period of quiescence, the experimental design previously known as the acquired distinctiveness of cues has recently been resurrected, and given a new name: learned predictiveness. For the most part, this new generation of studies (Le Pelley and McLaren, 2003) has used a design involving compound cues in both stages of training, an arrangement that introduces complications that will be dealt with later. We will begin by considering a simpler experiment (a study by Le Pelley, Turnbull, Reimers, and Knipe, 2009) that more closely follows the procedures used in the earlier work on this topic.

The design of the experiment is summarized in Table 3.1. In the first stage of training the subjects received training in which cues A, B, C, and D were consistently associated with others (the outcomes labelled 1 and 2 in the table); cues X and Y were associated equally often with 1 and with 2. (In the scenario employed, the cues were the names of fictional companies and the associates were colours they had used for their business cards.) In the second stage, the subjects had to learn a discrimination in which the original cues were followed by new outcomes, 3 and 4, as shown in the table (in terms of the scenario, subjects had to learn whether investment in a given company would result in a profit or loss). Acquisition of the test discrimination was found to proceed more readily for the cues A–D, the cues that had accurately predicted

Table 3.1 Experimental design: learned predictiveness with simple cues

Stage 1	**Stage 2**
A→1	A→3
B→2	B→4
C→2	C→3
D→1	D→4
X→1/2	X→3
Y→1/2	Y→4

Note: In each stage of training, all subjects experienced all trial types indicated. Letters represent cues to be learned about (names of fictional companies), associated in Stage 1 with different colours (1 and 2), and in Stage 2 with profit or loss (3 and 4). The outcome 1/2 indicates that the cue was associated equally often with each of the colours.

their associates in the first stage, than for the previously non-predictive cues, X and Y.

In its essential features, this experiment merely reproduces the result obtained in many previous demonstrations of the acquired distinctiveness and equivalence, but one aspect of the design (specifically the fact that cues, such as A and C, that were associated with different outcomes in Stage 1 are associated with the same outcome in Stage 2) rules out the associative account of acquired distinctiveness/equivalence offered for earlier studies by Hall *et al.* (2003). Le Pelley *et al.* (2009) concluded that their results should be interpreted as showing that training in which a cue is consistently followed by a given consequence leaves that cue with a high level of associability. This proposal accords with that put forward by Mackintosh in his 1975 theory of attention but runs directly contrary to the notion at the heart of the Pearce-Hall (1980) model. How can these results be reconciled with those, discussed above, that seem to confirm the validity of the latter?

One possible solution to this problem can be derived from the theory put forward by Le Pelley (2004), which endows each cue with *two* associability parameters, one of which is modified according to the rules proposed by Mackintosh (1975), whereas the other obeys the rules proposed by Pearce and Hall (1980). (Pearce and Mackintosh adopt a version of this notion in their contribution to this volume.) According to Le Pelley (2004, p235), attentional associability (the Mackintosh form) is responsible for positive transfer effects; what he refers to as salience associability (the Pearce-Hall form) is responsible for negative transfer effects. The distinction between these two forms of associability may not be wholly arbitrary and can perhaps be justified on theoretical grounds; but clearly, before accepting this multiplication of entities, we need to be certain that the results cannot be explained by a simpler model. We return, therefore, to the analysis supplied by the Pearce-Hall model; for it is not that this account has been applied to the learned predictiveness results and found wanting; rather, it has not yet been properly applied at all.

When subjects are transferred to the A→3, B→4 discrimination after initial training with A→1 and B→2, acquisition becomes possible, according to the model, because the cues no longer predict their consequences and associability will be restored. In the example of this process described above (Figure 3.5), restoration of associability was produced simply by the omission of the event that the cue had previously signalled. But in the learned predictiveness design, things are more complicated. First, the cues are followed by some quite unexpected event (i.e. 3 or 4) and the discrepancy between expectation and this outcome must be assumed to play a role in the value of α established by the change of conditions. Next, comparison is being made with a control condition in which the cues (X and Y in Table 3.1) have been followed equally often by 1 and 2. For cue A, the restoration of α will depend, in part, on the omission of the confidently expected outcome 1; for cue X, on the other hand, it will be produced by the omission of both 1 and 2, neither of which will have a strong association with the cue. In order to predict the effects to be obtained on the transfer test, it is necessary to take all these factors into account.

Figure 3.7 shows the results of a simulation, using the Pearce-Hall equations, of the changes in α, and in the strength of the association with outcome 3, of a cue that had been pretrained, either consistently followed by outcome 1, or followed equally often by 1 and 2 (the inconsistent condition of the figure). For the consistent case, the value of α after the first trial was determined both by the omission of the expected outcome 1 and by the presence of the new outcome 3; for the inconsistent cue, it was determined by the omission of both 1 and 2, and the occurrence of 3. In each case, we produced a single value for α simply by averaging those generated by computing the value of α produced by each of the associations involving that cue. At the start of this procedure, the value of α for the thoroughly trained consistent cue was zero, whereas that for the inconsistent cue had been maintained at a higher level (top panel of the figure). For both, the unexpected consequence of the first Stage 2 trial produces an increase in the value of α, which then begins to decline as the new association with outcome 3 is formed. But the increase is substantially greater for the consistent than for the inconsistent cue, that is, the surprising omission of the fully expected outcome 1 produces a greater change than the absence of the less well associated outcomes 1 and 2. The consequences for the growth in strength of the cue–outcome 3 association are shown in the lower panel of the figure; as training proceeds, the consistent cue overcomes its initial disadvantage and acquires strength more readily than does the inconsistent cue.

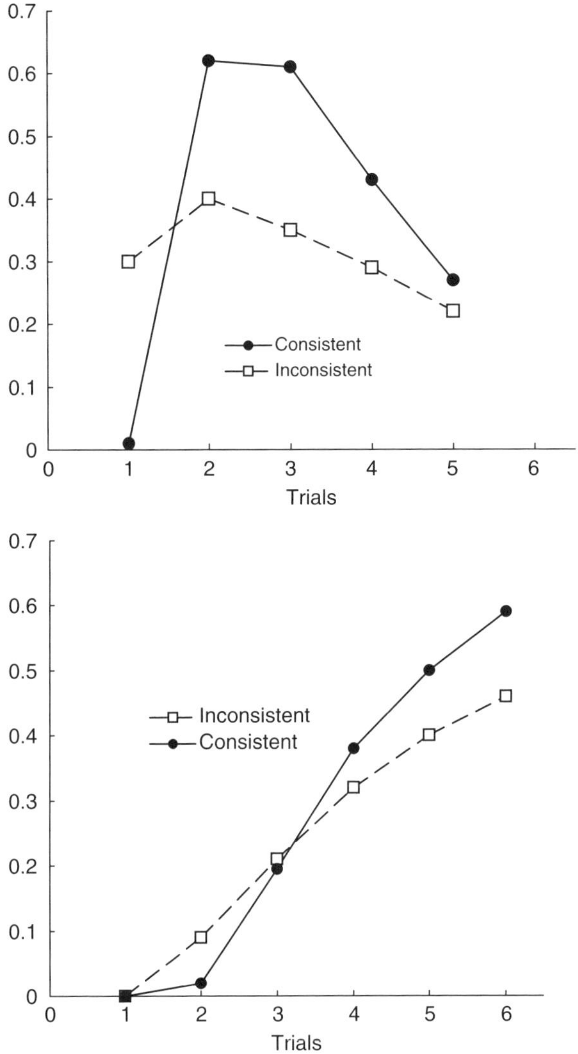

Fig. 3.7 A simulation using the Pearce-Hall (1980) model showing changes in the value of α for a cue and in the strength of its association with given outcome (O3) over six cue–O3 pairings. In the consistent condition, the cue had been followed reliably by a different outcome (O1) during a previous stage of training; in the inconsistent condition, the cue had been followed equally often by two different outcomes (O1 and O2) during pretraining. (For this simulation, the value of S was 0.5; the initial value of α was 1; the value of λ for each outcome was 0.6.)

It would be unwise to claim too much on the basis of this one simple simulation; no doubt different parameters and different assumptions (e.g. a different procedure for averaging) could produce a different pattern of results. It does demonstrate, however, that the phenomenon of learned predictiveness is not, in itself, necessarily incompatible with the assumptions of the Pearce-Hall model, and that the introduction of a second mechanism for associability change cannot be justified on the basis of the results considered so far.

Learned predictiveness with compound cues

Most recent demonstrations of the learned predictiveness effect have used an experimental design rather more complex than that just discussed. In these (Le Pelley and McLaren, 2003; Le Pelley, Oakeshott, Wills, and McLaren, 2005), the procedure has involved the presentation of compound cues in all phases of the study. Table 3.2 summarizes the basic experimental design used in these experiments. We report next a recent unpublished experiment of our own, using just this design and procedures modelled directly on those used by Le Pelley and McLaren.

In this experiment, the subjects, undergraduate students, received a first stage of training in which compound stimuli (pictures of two different fruits) were followed by a given outcome (a representation of an allergic reaction supposedly produced in a patient by consumption of these fruits). There were eight pairs of cues, and two possible outcomes. As Table 3.2 shows, some individual elements (A, B, C, and D) were reliably associated with a given outcome; others (V, W, X, and Y) were followed equally often by outcome 1

Table 3.2 Experiental design: learned predictiveness with compound cues

Stage 1	Stage 2	Test
AV→1	AX→3	AC 3? 4?
BV→2	BY→4	BD 3? 4?
AW→1	CV→3	VX 3? 4?
BW→2	DW→4	WY 3? 4?
CX→2		
DX→1		
CY→2		
DY→1		

Note: In each stage of training, all subjects experienced all trial types indicated. Each letter represents a different fruit. Pictures of two fruits were presented side by side on each trial and followed, in Stages 1 and 2, by a picture of a named negative reaction. (Stomach ache and rash were outcomes 1 and 2; headache and conjunctivitis were outcomes 3 and 4.) In the test phase, the subjects were asked to indicate on a 10-point scale, separately for outcomes 3 and 4, the likelihood that the fruits presented would produce that outcome. There were 14 presentations of each of the eight Stage 1 trial types, and four presentations of each of the four Stage 2 trial types; there were four test trials as indicated.

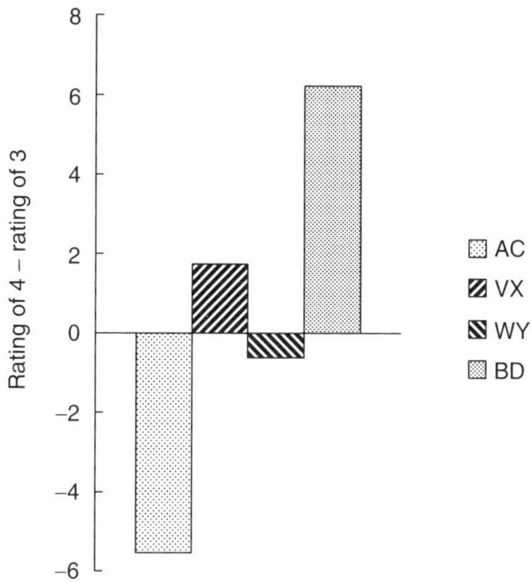

Fig. 3.8 Results for the test phase of the experiment outlined in Table 3.2. The subjects were asked to indicate on a 10-point scale, separately for outcomes 3 and 4, the likelihood of a given compound producing that outcome. Letters represent different fruits; O1 and O3 different negative reactions to them. The score given is the rating for O4 minus the rating for O3.

and by outcome 2. In the second stage of training, new compounds were created, each consisting of one previously predictive cue and one non-predictive cue (i.e. AX, BY, CV, and DW). These were associated with new and different allergic reactions, outcomes 3 and 4 (Table 3.2). In the final test phase, the subjects were asked to rate, on a 10-point scale, the likelihood that new compounds (AC, BD, VX, and WY) would produce each of the outcomes 3 and 4. The results of this test, expressed as the rating given to 4 minus that given to 3, are presented in Figure 3.8.

The score for the AC compound shows that outcome 3 was rated highly, a result to be expected, as both these cues had been paired with 3 in Stage 2. But the same was not true of the compound VX, the elements of which had also both been associated with 3 in Stage 2. Similarly, the BD compound elicited a high rating for outcome 4, whereas the WY compound did not, in spite of the fact that its constituent cues had received equivalent training in Stage 2. It will be noted that compounds that evoked high ratings consisted of elements that had accurately predicted their outcomes in Stage 1; those that evoked no consistent response on the test consisted of elements that had been poor predictors in Stage 1. These results are therefore consistent with the proposition that the learning in Stage 2 proceeded especially readily for cues that had been reliable predictors in Stage 1.

This experiment may seem no more than a rather involved replication of the positive transfer effect seen with simple cues that has just been discussed, but the use of compound cues turns out to have important theoretical implications. In discussing the positive transfer obtained with simple cues, we noted that the effect could be explained without relinquishing the Pearce–Hall principle that predictive cues lose associability. The same argument cannot apply when compound cues are used. The equation that determines the value of α (Equation 3.3, above) specifies that the associability of individual cues in a compound will be determined by the predictive power of the entire compound. This means that when A and X, for example, are trained together in Stage 2, their α levels will converge on a common value, making it difficult to predict differences in associative strength of the sort shown in Figure 3.7.[4]

Does this require us to accept that, at least in some circumstances, some aspect of the associability governed by a cue will be enhanced by training in which the cue reliably predicts a consequence? The results produced by a further group of subjects included in the experiment just described suggest not. These subjects received Stage 1 training as before, but for them Stage 2 was omitted; they thus had no opportunity to form associations between any of the cues and outcomes 3 and 4. For the test phase, they were simply told about the possible occurrence of two further allergic reactions (i.e. 3 and 4) and were asked to rate for each the likelihood that the test compound cues would elicit them. The results of this test are shown in Figure 3.9. For both outcomes, the compounds made up of cues that had been predictive in Stage 1 (AC and BD) received high ratings; the non-predictive compounds (VX and WY) received low ratings. It seems that subjects are willing to attribute the occurrence of an outcome to a previously predictive cue independently of training in which the cue and outcome are associated. This is not to say that the Stage 2 training was without effect in those subjects that received it—the selective performance shown in Figure 3.8 demonstrates that these subjects had used the opportunity to learn that A is followed by 3 and not by 4 (and so on). But the critical point is that there is no need to assume that learning in Stage 2 proceeded differently for predictive and non-predictive cues. The subjects might learn equally readily that A is followed by 3 and that X is followed by 3, but the tendency to give high ratings to previously predictive cues would result in the compound

[4] A seemingly attractive way to escape from this dilemma is to modify Equation 3.3, making the value of α for a given stimulus depend solely on its own associative strength rather than on the summed strength of all stimuli present on the trial. (Effects like overshadowing would then need to be explained in other ways.) This is just the strategy proposed, for other reasons, in the chapter by Pearce and Mackintosh. We are unwilling to adopt it, however, given the evidence from other procedures (in particular from studies of latent inhibition, see Rodriguez and Hall, 2008; Hall and Rodriguez, in press) that seems to require that Equation 3.3 retain its original form.

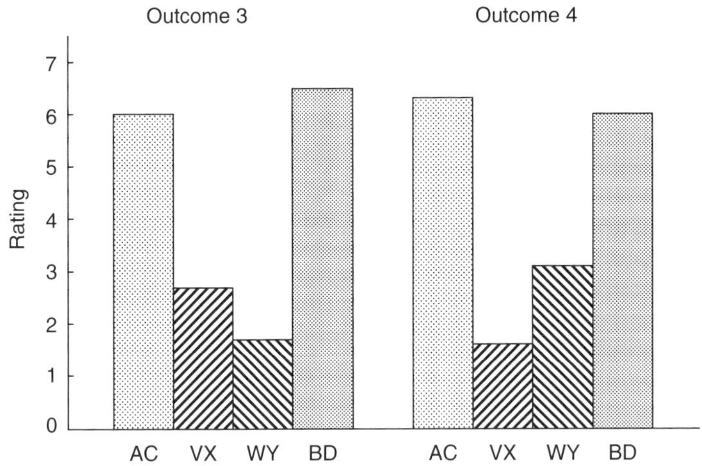

Fig. 3.9 Results for the test phase of an experiment identical to that shown in Table 3.2, but with Stage 2 omitted. The subjects were asked to indicate on a 10-point scale, separately for outcomes 3 and 4, the likelihood a given compound would produce that outcome. Letters represent different fruits; O1 and O3 different negative reactions to them.

containing A, eliciting a higher score than that elicited by the compound containing X.

It remains to explain why predictive cues should behave in this way. One possibility is that the effect is a simple consequence of generalization. After Stage 1 training a predictive cue, like cue A, will be strongly associated with one allergy; a non-predictive cue (such as X) will have weak associations with each of two allergies. Given that outcomes 3 and 4 are also allergic reactions it should be no surprise that subjects given no training with these specific outcomes are none the less willing to ascribe them to the cues trained previously. It is a simple matter to arrange parameters to ensure that the degree of generalization from one strong association will much exceed that from two weak associations, with the result that A will elicit a higher rating than X on the test. The fact that changing the nature of the outcomes between the stages (from allergies to pleasant consequences) attenuates the learned predictiveness effect (Le Pelley *et al.*, 2005) is consistent with this interpretation.

A second (not necessarily alternative) interpretation finds a role for a form of attention. Although differences in associability between the cues cannot be responsible for the differences in performance seen in Figure 3.9, it is possible that a different attentional process may be involved. In an earlier section of this chapter, we discussed how the effective salience of a stimulus can change with experience, and presented evidence that salience might be maintained when a pre-exposed cue is reliably followed by another event. The Stage 1 training given in the experimental design of Table 3.2 arranges for predictive cues to be followed reliably by a given outcome, whereas non-predictive cues (by definition) are followed by varying outcomes. Accordingly, the salience of the former can be expected to be higher than that of the latter. The salience of a cue may be assumed to influence the vigour of such responses as it evokes. Thus, even if the (generalized) strength of the association between A and outcome 3 is no higher than that of the association between X and 3, A will tend to receive a higher rating than X—the result that we obtained. (See Le Pelley, Suret, & Beesley, in press, for a further discussion and test of this general notion.)

Summary

This rather involved account can be summarized quite simply. Studies of simple Pavlovian conditioning show that the associability of a cue that is reliably followed by some another event declines as it come to predict its consequence; the associability of a cue followed by inconsistent consequences is maintained. These findings accord with the intuition that attention for the purpose of learning must be high for cues the consequences of which are unknown, but need not be expended on cues with known consequences. This notion was formalized in the Pearce-Hall (1980) model.

The fact that discrimination training with a pair of cues can sometimes produce positive transfer to a new task involving the same cues does not require any drastic revision of the model. The initial training must be assumed to reduce the associability of the pretrained cues, but the various factors that operate in these transfer experiments are capable of overcoming the deficit to be expected on these grounds. We have discussed four such factors: (1) The change in conditions that occurs when a new discrimination is introduced will lead to a restoration of associability. In some circumstances, this restoration can be shown to proceed more rapidly for cues trained initially in a discrimination task than for control cues trained in a non-discriminative procedure; (2) Discrimination training will engage the processes responsible for perceptual learning. An enhanced ability to tell the stimuli apart will produce positive transfer on a new task involving discrimination between the stimuli; (3) The associations between stimuli and outcomes that are established in the first stage of training will still be operative in the second stage. With some versions of the learned predictiveness design this will lead to positive transfer, even though the exact nature of the outcomes has been changed for the second stage; (4) Finally, discrimination training can be expected to maintain the effective salience of the pretrained cues, increasing the likelihood that they will control performance in the transfer test.

General conclusions

Attention is an everyday word used to describe phenomena that appear to be facts of everyday experience: 'Everyone knows what attention is. It is the taking possession of the mind, in clear and vivid form, of one out of what seem several simultaneously possible objects' (James, 1890, p. 403). In James's world the idea of attention as the focus of conscious awareness was central to any analysis of cognitive functioning and the apparent self-evidence of this faculty (as revealed by systematic as well as casual introspection) means that it is with us still (in concepts like the 'central executive' or the 'supervisory attentional system'). But in this, as in many things, introspection may be a poor guide to the real nature of the mechanisms involved. Experimental analysis demonstrates that the way in which an event is processed will vary according to a range of factors, which include both the intrinsic properties of that event and also the past experience of the organism.

Our own analysis suggests the need to distinguish two aspects of attention. The first is that governed by the intrinsic salience of the stimulus (usually defined in terms of its intensity). A salient stimulus will be effective in eliciting whatever response it controls, and will also be good at entering into new learning. But the effective salience of a stimulus turns out not to be fixed, and determined solely by intensity. Repeated presentation of a stimulus will produce a loss of effective salience; effective salience will be maintained when (as will be case if the stimulus is used as the CS in a conditioning procedure) presentations are reliably followed by some other event. The second form of attention we have referred to is associability. The associability of a stimulus (its ability to enter into associations) is determined by its predictive power, with stimuli that accurately predict their consequences suffering a loss of associability. These two mechanisms prove capable of accommodating the variety of experimental results reported in this chapter.

The distinction between salience and associability (unlike some other attempts to construct a hybrid theory of attention, which seem distinctly arbitrary in their assumptions) has the advantage of possessing a certain psychological plausibility. It is easy to imagine circumstances in which a weak stimulus lacking in salience needs to be learned about because it precedes the occurrence of some other event of major biological significance. Equally an event that has been established as a signal for a significant consequence need not be attended to for the purposes of learning, but needs to be able to command that aspect of attention necessary for controlling behaviour. Where does this leave the notion of a unitary faculty of attention? Is a stimulus that is powerfully controlling behaviour but which, because of its low associability, is incapable of supporting further learning, being attended to or not? Surely the answer to these questions is that the notion of 'attention' is no more than a chapter heading (or book title) that serves simply to indicate a general area, defined (if that is not too strong a word) in terms of everyday experience. Inevitably, and appropriately, scientific analysis takes us beyond this to a set of new concepts, such as salience and associability, that are tightly defined in terms of their causes and their effects.

References

Broadbent, D. E. (1958). *Perception and communication.* Oxford: Pergamon Press.

Green, K. F., & Parker, L. A. (1975). Gustatory memory: Incubation and interference. *Behavioral Biology*, **13**, 359–368.

Groves, P. M. & Thompson, R. F. (1970). Habituation: A dual-process theory. *Psychological Review,* 77, 419–450.

Hall, G. (1991). *Perceptual and associative learning* (300pp.). Oxford: Clarendon Press.

Hall, G. (1994). Pavlovian conditioning: Laws of association. In N. J. Mackintosh (Ed.), *Handbook of perception and cognition. Vol. 9: Animal learning and cognition* (pp. 15–43). San Diego, CA: Academic Press.

Hall, G., Graham, S., Mitchell, C., & Lavis, Y. (2003). Acquired equivalence and distinctiveness in human discrimination learning: Evidence for associative mediation. *Journal of Experimental Psychology: General,* **132**, 266–276.

Hall, G. & Pearce, J. M. (1979). Latent inhibition of a CS during CS-US pairings. *Journal of Experimental Psychology: Animal Behavior Processes,* **5**, 31–42.

Hall, G. & Pearce, J. M. (1982). Restoring the associability of a pre-exposed CS by a surprising event. *Quarterly Journal of Experimental Psychology,* **34B**, 127–140.

Hall, G. & Pearce, J. M. (1982). Changes in stimulus associability during conditioning: Implications for theories of acquisition. In M. L. Commons, R. J. Herrnstein, & A. R. Wagner (Eds), *Quantitative analyses of behavior, Vol. III: Acquisition* (pp. 221–239). Cambridge, MA: Ballinger.

Hall, G. & Rodriguez, G. (In press). Associative and nonassociative processes in latent inhibition: An elaboration of the Pearce-Hall model. In R. E. Lubow & I. Weiner (Eds), *Latent inhibition: Data, theories, and applications to schizophrenia.* Cambridge: Cambridge University Press.

James, J. H. & Wagner, A. R. (1980). One-trial overshadowing: Evidence of distributive processing. *Journal of Experimental Psychology: Animal Behavior Processes,* **6**, 188–205.

James, W. (1890). *Principles of psychology*. New York: Holt.

Kamin, L. J. (1961). Apparent adaptation effects in the acquisition of a conditioned emotional response. *Canadian Journal of Psychology*, **15**, 176–188.

Kamin, L. J. (1969). 'Attention-like' processes in classical conditioning. In M. R. Jones (Ed.), *Miami symposium on the prediction of behavior: Aversive stimulation* (pp. 9–33). Coral Gables, FL: University of Miami Press.

Kaye, H. & Pearce, J. M. (1984). The strength of the oreinting response during Pavlovian conditioning. *Journal of Experimental Psychology: Animal Behavior Processes*, **10**, 90–109.

Lawrence, D. H. (1949). Acquired distinctiveness of cues, I. Transfer between discriminations on the basis of familiarity with the stimulus. *Journal of Experimental Psychology*, **39**, 770–784.

Le Pelley, M. E. (2004). The role of associative history in models of associative learning: A selective review and a hybrid model. *Quarterly Journal of Experimental Psychology*, **57B**, 193–243.

Le Pelley, M. E. & McLaren, I. P. L. (2003). Learned associability and associative change in human causal learning. *Quarterly Journal of Experimental Psychology*, **56B**, 68–79.

Le Pelley, M. E., Oakeshott, S. M., Wills, A. J., & McLaren, I. P. L. (2005). The outcome specificity of learned predictiveness effects: Parallels between human causal learning and animal conditioning. *Journal of Experimental Psychology: Animal Behavior Processes*, **31**, 226–236.

Le Pelley, M. E., Suret, M. B., & Beesley, T. (In press). Learned predictiveness effects in humans: A function of learning, performance or both? *Journal of Experimental Psychology: Animal Behavior Processes*.

Le Pelley, M. E., Turnbull, M. N., Reimers, S. J., & Knipe, R. L. (2009). *Learned predictiveness effects following single-cue training in humans*. Unpublished manuscript.

Liddell, H. (1950). The role of vigilance in the development of animal neurosis. In P. H. Hoch & J. H. Zubin (Eds), *Anxiety* (pp. 183–196). New York: Hafner.

Mackintosh, N.J. (1987). Neurobiology, psychology, and habituation. *Behaviour Research and Therapy*, **12**, 81–97.

Mercier, P. & Baker, A. G. (1985). Latent inhibition, habituation, and sensory preconditioning: A test of priming in short-term memory. *Journal of Experimental Psychology: Animal Behavior Processes*, **11**, 485–501.

Pearce, J. M. & Hall, G. (1980). A model for Pavlovian learning: Variations in the effectiveness of conditioned but not of unconditioned stimuli. *Psychological Review*, **87**, 532–552.

Pearce, J. M. & Hall, G. (1992). Stimulus significance, conditionability, and the orienting response in rats. In B. A. Campbell, H. Hayne, & R. Richardson (Eds), *Attention and information processing in infants and adults: Perspectives from human and animal research* (pp. 137–160). Hillsdale, NJ: Erlbaum.

Pearce, J. M., Kaye, H., & Hall, G. (1982). Predictive accuracy and stimulus associability: Development of a model of Pavlovian learning. In M. L. Commons, R. J. Herrnstein, & A. R. Wagner (Eds), *Quantitative analyses of behavior, Vol. III: Acquisition* (pp. 241–255). Cambridge, MA: Ballinger.

Pearce, J. M., Wilson, P. N., & Kaye, H. (1988). The influence of predictive accuracy on serial conditioning in the rat. *Quarterly Journal of Experimental Psychology*, **40B**, 181–198.

Randich, A. & LoLordo, V. M. (1979). Associative and nonassociative theories of the UCS preexposure phenomenon: Implications for Pavlovian conditioning. *Psychological Bulletin,* **86**, 523–548.

Rodriguez, G. & Hall, G. (2008). Potentiation of latent inhibition. *Journal of Experimental Psychology: Animal Behavior Processes,* **34**, 352–360.

Shanks, D. R., Preston, G. C., & Stanhope, K. (1986). Effects of distractor familiarity on habituation of neophobia. *Animal Learning & Behavior,* **14**, 393–397.

Siegel, S. (1967). Overtraining and transfer processes. *Journal of Comparative and Physiological Psychology,* **64**, 471–477.

Spence, K. W. (1936). The nature of discrimination learning in animals. *Psychological Review,* **43**, 427–449.

Sutherland, N. S. & Mackintosh, N. J. (1971). *Mechanisms of animal discrimination learning.* New York: Academic Press.

Swan, J. A. & Pearce, J. M. (1988). The orienting response as an index of stimulus associability on rats. *Journal of Experimental Psychology: Animal Behavior Processes,* **14**, 292–301.

Szakmary, G. (1977). A note concerning conditioned attention theory. *Bulletin of the Psychonomic Society,* **9**, 142–144.

Wagner, A. R. (1981). SOP: A model of automatic memory processing in animal behavior. In N. E. Spear & R. R. Miller (Eds), *Information processing in animals: Memory mechanisms* (pp. 5–47). Hillsdale, NJ: Lawrence Erlbaum Associates.

Wilson, P. N., Boumphrey, P., & Pearce, J. M. (1992). Restoration of the orienting response to a light by a change in its predictive accuracy. *Quarterly Journal of Experimental Psychology,* **44B**, 17–36.

Chapter 4

Selective attention to conditioned stimuli in human discrimination learning: untangling the effects of outcome prediction, valence, arousal, and uncertainty

Lee Hogarth, Anthony Dickinson, and Theodora Duka

Introduction

Selective attention is an amalgamation of processing systems geared to select different classes of information to optimize the agent's transaction with the environment. Within selective attention, subsystems can be distinguished that select different types of stimuli. The clearest example of this can be found in perceptual psychophysics, where it has been demonstrated that a variety of 'low level' attributes of stimuli, such as colour, motion, orientation, size, etc., all drive selective attention (Wolfe and Horowitz, 2004) via at least partially segregated neural substrates (Knudsen, 2007; Yantis, 2008). The claim made in this chapter is that the 'higher level' attributes of stimuli acquired during associative learning are similarly selected for privileged processing within at least three distinct attentional systems, which appear to have partially segregated neural substrates.

Three forms of selective attention in associative learning

The idea that selective attention can be modulated by the predictive significance of stimuli has a long tradition in associative learning theory. The original theory put forward by Mackintosh (1975; see also Sutherland and Mackintosh, 1971) argued that animals attend preferentially to cues that are relatively good predictors of other events of biological importance (outcomes) such as food and water, and thereby learn more readily about relationships involving these cues. Therefore, through this attentional process the predictive history of a stimulus can inform new learning.

Subsequently, Pearce and Hall (1980) claimed that, rather than attending to reliable predictors, animals in fact attend most to stimuli that have been associated with uncertainty so that learning is directed to those stimuli for which the animal does not possess an adequate predictive mental model. According to this theory, the occurrence of an unpredicted outcome, or the absence of a predicted one, evokes a prediction error signal (surprise), which indicates that the animal does not have an adequate representation of the predictive structure of its environment and therefore needs to undertake further learning. Consequently, the animal should, in future, attend to cues that are associated with the prediction error signal in order that the animal might acquire veridical knowledge of the predictive significance of those stimuli, and so by degrees, acquire a veridical representation of the predictive structure of the environment. Once prediction is accurate, so that important outcomes can be anticipated and no error signal is evoked, there is no need to devote further learning resources to these stimuli, and attention to them declines.

The Mackintosh and Pearce-Hall theories therefore make opposing predictions concerning attention for conditioned stimuli. Mackintosh's theory suggests that attention will increase with the reliability of the predictive contingency between the stimulus and the outcome, whereas Pearce and Hall predict that attention will increase with the unreliability of the predictive contingency between the stimulus and the outcome. It is perhaps not surprising, given these opposing predictions, that much of the debate addressing these two theories has adopted an oppositional stance, where each camp has mustered evidence in favour of one or other position. However, a unified account was potentially embedded within Pearce and Hall's (1980) original formulation.

This unified account claims that there are two forms of attention in associative learning: one concerned with prediction and action, and one concerned with uncertainty and learning. More precisely, Pearce and Hall claimed that a reliable predictor commands an *'automatic'* form of attentional selection, which might today be variously labelled as fast, efficient, covert or pre-attentive, but which ultimately functions to detect predictive stimuli with maximum cognitive economy to enable rapid action selection. This automatic form of attentional selection increases with the strength of the predictive relationship between the stimulus and the outcome, and is principally involved in behavioural control. By contrast, unreliable predictive stimuli command a second form of *'controlled'* attentional selection, which may be operationalized as the maintenance of sensory focus upon the stimulus, or the holding of the stimulus in working memory (Belopolsky and Theeuwes, 2009), which facilitates the formation of knowledge about the contingency between that stimulus and subsequent outcomes. This controlled form of attentional selection increases with the unreliability of the contingency between the stimulus and the outcome and is principally involved in contingency learning. Our attentional data reviewed below tend to favour this sort of multiple systems account of selective attention in associative learning.

While the Mackintosh versus Pearce-Hall debate raged in the arena of associative learning, a tangential discussion was developing elsewhere concerning the link between attention and emotion (Vuilleumier, 2005; Vuilleumier *et al.*, 2003). The disconnection between these two debates is unwarranted, however, because whenever cues have a predictive relationship with a biologically relevant outcome they acquire affective value in their own right. Consequently, attention for predictive cues should not only vary in accordance with their associative strength and prediction error, but also, in accordance with the biological value of their associated outcome.

Research addressing the link between attention and emotion has focused to a large extent on the issue of whether attention is controlled by the arousing properties of a stimulus or its valence. The arousal dimension is considered to range from neutral to arousing (i.e. a scale from 0–1), where both appetitive and aversive cues are arousing. By contrast, the valence dimension is thought to range from appetitive at one end to aversive at the other (i.e. a scale from –1 – 0 – 1), reflecting the hedonic or affective sign of the stimulus.

Research addressing the link between attention and emotion favours the view that the early form of attentional selection equating to Pearce and Hall's automatic process is commanded in accordance with the arousing qualities of stimuli, irrespective of their valence (Brosch *et al.*, 2008; Engelmann and Pessoa, 2007; Lin and Nicolelis, 2008; Livesey *et al.*, 2009; Vogt *et al.*, 2008; Lewis *et al.*, 2007; but see Fox *et al.*, 2001; Eastwood *et al.*, 2001). Such early detection may accord with arousal, rather than valence, because it plays a critical role in the initiation of both approach and avoidance behaviour.

By contrast, following initial detection, the maintenance/avoidance of attention appears to respect the valence of the stimulus. For instance, cues associated with larger quantities of food command more attentional orienting in animals (Morris and Bouton, 2006), and increasing the incentive value of food (Mogg *et al.*, 1998) and drugs of abuse (Field *et al.*, 2004) by enforcing deprivation from these resources increases the maintenance of attention for cues associated with these resources. Finally, induction of positive mood and individual differences in positive mood state are associated with enhanced attention to reward-related cues (Tamir and Robinson, 2007).

By contrast, aversive cues command attentional avoidance following initial detection, if they are sufficiently aversive (Pflugshaupt *et al.*, 2005; Weierich *et al.*, 2008). Such attentional avoidance of aversive cues is associated with individual differences in anxiety/negative mood and exposure to stress (Beevers and Carver, 2003; Calvo and Avero, 2005; Calvo and Eysenck, 2000; Frewen *et al.*, 2008; Koster *et al.*, 2005; Morrison and O'Connor, 2008), and is thought to play a role in regulating affective state (MacLeod *et al.*, 2002).

To reconcile the fields of attention in associative learning and emotion, we propose the existence of three attentional systems, as summarized in Figure 4.1. The left column of Figure 4.1 outlines the prediction plus arousal system, which equates to Pearce and Hall's automatic detection process. This framework proposes that preferential early detection of a stimulus is jointly determined by the associative strength of the stimulus (that is, the extent to which it predicts an outcome) and the arousal value of the predicted outcome (that is, the biological importance of the outcome irrespective of whether it is appetitive or aversive). Accordingly, the left column shows early detection increasing for stimuli to the extent that they predict an appetitive or aversive outcome, but not for stimuli that predict a neutral outcome. We think that such early detection is most important for action selection. By contrast, the prediction plus valence system, outlined in the middle column of Figure 4.1, proposes that the subsequent maintenance or avoidance of attention to a stimulus is determined jointly by the associative strength of the stimulus and the appetitive/aversive valence of the outcome, which approximates the expected *utility* of the outcome[1] (Rangel *et al.*, 2008). Accordingly, the middle column shows attention being maintained to cues to the extent that they predict an appetitive outcome, avoiding cues to the extent that they predict an aversive outcome, and being unbiased for cues that predict a neutral outcome. This system may be most important for regulating affective state. Finally, the right column of Figure 4.1 outlines the uncertainty system, which equates to Pearce and Hall's controlled process. According to this framework, attention is also maintained to a stimulus to the extent that it conveys uncertainty about the probability of an outcome (prediction error), irrespective of whether the outcome is arousing (appetitive/aversive) or neutral. Accordingly, the right column shows attentional maintenance being maximal for cues with unreliable predictive relationships, compared to cues with reliable predictive

[1] In the language of decision-making, we claim that attentional maintenance/avoidance is determined by the utility of the outcome expectancy evoked by the CS, where utility is the sum of the biological value of the expected outcomes weighted by their probabilities (Rangel *et al.*, 2008).

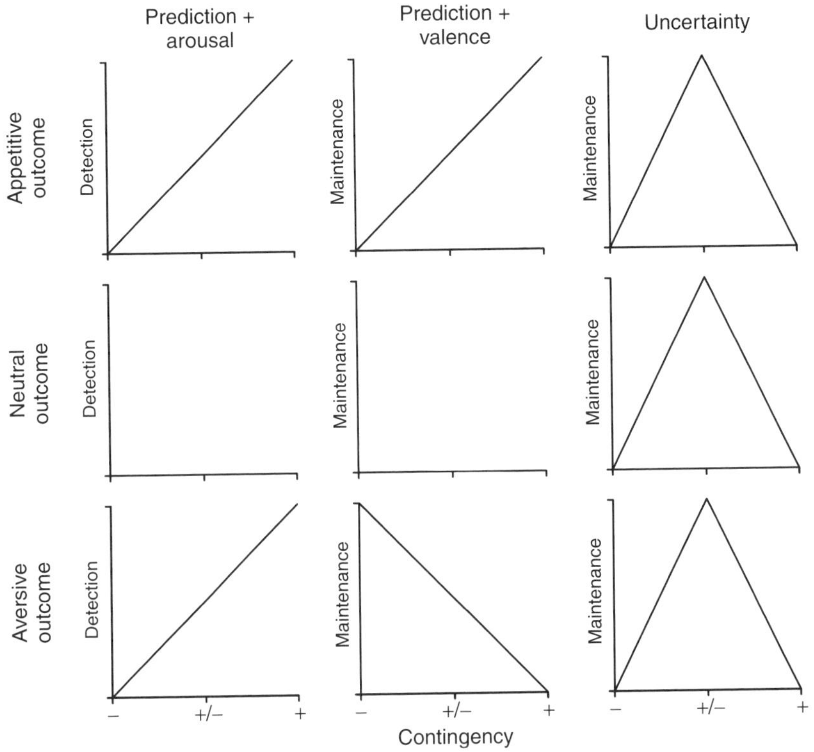

Fig. 4.1 Descriptive predictions concerning the detection and maintenance of attention to conditioned stimuli after asymptotic learning. The nine stimuli outlined differ with respect to their contingency with an outcome (no contingency –, partial contingency +/–, and full positive contingency +), and the biological value of that outcome (appetitive, neutral, aversive). Three attentional systems are proposed, which jointly govern attention to conditioned stimuli. 1. The prediction + arousal system, outlined in the left column, quickly detects stimuli to the extent that they predict arousing outcomes, which may be important for action selection. 2. The prediction + valence system, outlined in the middle column, determines the subsequent maintenance/avoidance of attention to stimuli to the extent that they predict appetitive or aversive outcomes, respectively, which may be important for regulating affective state. 3. The uncertainty system also determines the maintenance of attention to stimuli, but in accordance with the uncertainty the stimulus conveys about future outcomes (irrespective of the outcomes' arousing properties). This form of attention may be important for contingency learning. The actual observed attentional selection of conditioned stimuli should conflate these three systems, making it difficult to untangle their relative contribution behaviourally. The studies presented in this chapter have assessed only some of these 9 conditions, but overall, this work supports the existence of these three attentional systems.

or reliable non-predictive relationships, irrespective of whether the outcome is appetitive, aversive, or neutral. We think this uncertainty system is most important for learning. Finally, we believe that these three attentional systems operate concurrently, such that experimental measurement of attentional selection to some extent conflates all three. The next section outlines human discrimination learning schedules undertaken in our lab, which have served to behaviourally isolate these three attentional systems, to some extent.

Looking-for-action versus looking-for-liking

Our program of research reviewed here was originally inspired by Robinson and Berridge's (1993) incentive salience theory of addiction. This theory proposes that stimuli that are associated with addictive drugs command excessive attention, which mediates the compulsive, under-controlled nature of drug-seeking. In developing this account, Robinson and Berridge (1993) initially favoured a Pavlovian sign-tracking process (Bindra, 1978) through which drug stimuli control a strong approach response, but subsequently, their work has recognized that drug cues might also control drug-seeking through the well-established motivational impact of reward-predicting stimuli on instrumental performance (Wyvell and Berridge, 2000; Wyvell and Berridge, 2001).

To test Robinson and Berridge's (1993) proposal in humans, we established an arbitrary stimulus as a signal for when a drug-seeking response would be rewarded, so that we could measure the acquisition of an attentional bias for the stimulus and relate this attentional bias to the subjective expectancy of drug reward and the probability of performing the drug-seeking response. According to Robinson and Berridge (1993), there should be a close mapping between these measures, consistent with the role of the attentional bias in behavioural control. However, the procedure can also address Mackintosh's and Pearce-Hall's theories of attention insomuch as Mackintosh, like Robinson and Berridge (1993), predicts that attention to the predictive stimulus should monotonically increase with training, whereas Pearce-Hall anticipates most attention during learning of the stimulus–outcome contingencies, when uncertainty is greatest.

The details of the discrimination procedure are outlined in Figure 4.2. To measure the selectivity of attention, we employed the relative validity schedule developed by Wagner and colleagues, AX+, BX–, which allows two stimuli to be presented concurrently during training, with one cue signalling the availability (A) or unavailability (B) of reward in that trial, and the concurrently presented stimulus (X) being redundant (less informative) with respect to the trial outcome, therefore constituting a contextual or background stimulus

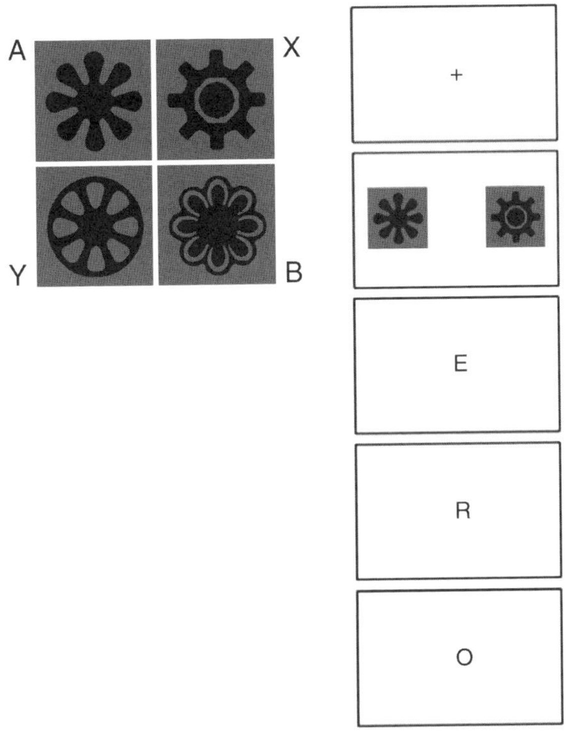

Fig. 4.2 In discrimination trainning, a fixation cross was followed by a pair of stimuli for 3 seconds during which attention was measured with an eye tracker. Participants (smokers) then reported their expectancy (E) of the tobacco win outcome by pressing a number key from 1-10. Finally, participants could perform an instrumental tobacco seeking response (R - a space bar press), which yielded a tobacco win outcome (O – 'you win ¼ of a cigarette') in AX+ and AY+ trials, or an equivalent tobacco lose outcome ('you lose ¼ of a cigarette') in BX– and BY– trials. Non responding produced no outcome. The schedule included four randomly intermixed trial types: AX+, AY+, BX–, BY–, which established stimulus A as a predictor of wins (S+), stimulus B as a predictor of equivalent losses (S–), and stimuli X and Y as redundant contextual cues that were common to both rewarded and unrewarded trials. To gain net reward, participants had to learn to perform the instrumental response more frequently in AX+ and AY+ trials (labelled A+ trials for short), than in BX– and BY– trials (labelled B- trials for short), so that wins outweighed losses. Analysis examined dwell time to the individual stimuli within the four trial types: stimulus A+, B– and the concurrently presented contextual stimuli X/Y in A trials (labelled X/Y(A)) and in B trials (labelled X/Y(B)). In addition, reward expectancy and percent trials with an instrumental response were compared across A+ trials and B– trials. The four stimuli shown were balanced in the role of A, B, X and Y.

(Wagner, 1969; Wagner *et al.*, 1968). We simply added a second contextual cue (Y) to create the schedule AX+, AY+, BX–, BY–, to match the absolute number of times all stimuli were presented, allowing us to assess attention to the informative cues A and B relative to the common contextual cues, X and Y.

The pooled results from five replications of the procedure are presented in Figure 4.3 (Hogarth *et al.*, 2006b; Hogarth *et al.*, 2008b; Hogarth *et al.*, 2007; Hogarth *et al.*, 2009). The most striking aspect of these data was that conditioned effects across the different measures were selective to participants who became aware of the stimulus–outcome contingencies, and so only data from this group are included in Figure 4.3 (awareness was classified by the participants showing a significant difference in reward expectancies between A+ and B– trials in the final block of training). This finding is consistent with the view that human conditioning is mediated by outcome expectancy (Hogarth *et al.*, 2007; Hogarth and Duka, 2006; Lovibond and Shanks, 2002) rather than by an associative architecture outside awareness (Lieberman *et al.*, 1998a; Lieberman *et al.*, 1998b; Perruchet, 1985; Perruchet *et al.*, 2006). Moreover, visual inspection of the expectancy reports of individual participants revealed a sudden differentiation between A+ and B– trials, occurring at some point in training, suggestive of sudden rule-based learning.

To determine what rules aware participants had learned, we showed them a picture of the four stimuli (Figure 4.2) and asked them the question, 'How did you decide when to press the space bar?' Some participants reported that they knew that stimulus A predicted a win and so pressed when they saw this stimulus, and that otherwise they knew that they would lose and so withheld pressing in this situation. Therefore, this group appeared to learn the identity and predictive significance of stimulus A, but not of the remaining three stimuli, and treated the absence of stimulus A as the S– condition. By contrast, other participants reporting that they knew that stimulus B predicted loss, and that they withheld responding when they saw this stimulus, and otherwise that they knew that they would win and so pressed in this situation. Therefore, this group appeared to learn the identity of stimulus B, but not of the remaining three stimuli, and treated the absence of stimulus B as the S+ condition. Finally, some participants reported knowing that stimulus A predicted a win whereas stimulus B predicted a loss, and so pressed and withheld the response when they saw these two stimuli, respectively. Therefore, this group appeared to learn the identity of both stimulus A and B. We have grouped participants in Figure 4.3 on the basis of which of these three rules they reported, to examine their differential allocation of selective attention to the stimuli.

One may wonder what differentiates participants who learned these three types of rule. The first thing to note, in this regard, is the uneven number of

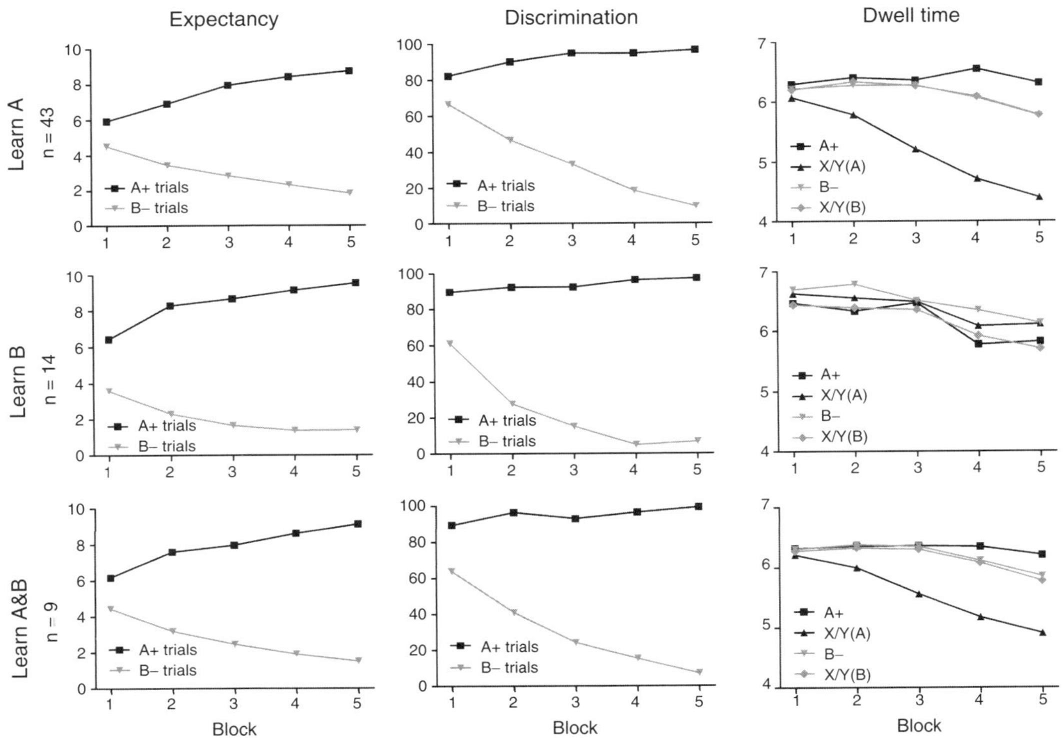

Fig. 4.3 Left column: Reward expectancy (1-10 scale) on A+ trials (that is, AX+ and AY+ trials) and B- trials (that is, BX– and BY- trials). Middle column: Discrimination (% trials with an instrumental response) between A+ trials and B– trials. Right column: Dwell time (natural logmsec) to stimulus A and B as well as the concurrently presented contextual cues X/Y in A and B trials (labelled X/Y(A) and X/Y(B), respectively). Only contingency aware participants, indexed by a significant difference in reward expectancies between A+ and B– trials in block 5, are included. Moreover, aware participants were split according to whether post experimental questioning indicated that they had learned the A=win rule (top row), the B=lose rule (middle row), or both rules (bottom row). Attention, but not expectancy or instrumental discrimination, was influenced by which rule participants used.

participants in each group (Figure 4.3, which was significant by Chi square). The smallest number of participants, who learned A&B, might be expected on the grounds of cognitive economy – why should participants explore the alternative rule when the one they are using enables asymptotic discrimination performance? The learning of the A=win vs. B=lose rules, by contrast, might have been thought a matter of chance, depending upon which was detected first. However, the uneven split between these two groups instead suggests a preference for learning the A=win rule. This preference is perhaps due to the phrasing of the expectancy question 'how likely are you to win ¼ of a cigarette' at point E in the trial sequence (Figure 4.2), which effectively prompts acquisition of the A=win rule. However, it is also possible that differential learning of these two rules is founded upon a biological trait (Frank *et al.*, 2004), but this remains to be verified.

Our concern here, however, is with the differential allocation of selective attention to stimuli depending upon which rule was learned. First of all, it should be noted that the three groups were indistinguishable with respect to the acquisition of differential reward expectancies and instrumental discrimination between A+ and B– trials. Yet the attentional performance of the three groups differed markedly. Analysis of the dwell time data shown in Figure 4.3 indicated that A-learners attended more to A than the contextual cues X/Y(A), but not to B relative to X/Y(B). By contrast, B-learners attended more to B than X/Y(B), but not more to A than X/Y(A).[2] Finally, A&B-learners showed the same pattern of attentional bias as A-learners, except their difference between A and X/Y(A) was smaller.

Perhaps the most intriguing aspect of the attentional data in Figure 4.3, is A-learners' larger bias for A over X/Y(A) than B-learners' bias for B over X/Y(B), despite the fact that these two groups were ostensibly using A and B, respectively, to control their expectancy and instrumental choice equally. There are two differences in the information conveyed by stimulus A and B for these two groups. For A-learners, stimulus A signalled that the instrumental response should be performed to obtain reward, whereas for B-learners, stimulus B signalled that the instrumental response should be withheld to avoid equivalent loss. Thus, these cues have different connections to action initiation/withholding, and are associated with outcomes with different biological

[2] In fact, this contrast between A and X/Y(A) was significant in B-learners, but it was not replicated in two subsequent studies (Figures 4.4 and 4.5) and so can be ignored as a false-positive. In addition, in B-learners, the bias for B over X/Y(B) was significantly greater than the bias for A over X/Y(A), indicating that B-learners predominately showed an attentional bias for B.

value, win/loss. The question, therefore, is whether the attentional biases seen in Figure 4.3 can be explained by looking-for-action, or, looking-for-liking.

Three observations challenge the simple link between attention and action. First, as we have noted, why was the preference for A in A-learners statistically significantly bigger than the bias for B in B-learners, when the two groups were ostensibly using these respective cues to control their performance equally? Second, why did A&B-learners show attentional selection of A but not B when they knew the relevance both cues had for behaviour? Finally, why did the preference for A in A-learners and A&B-learners increase with training, tracing the control by this stimulus over instrumental action, whereas the bias for B in B-learners remained relatively constant over blocks, failing to trace the control this stimulus exerted over instrumental action?

The alternative proposal is that attention was maintained to the extent that the stimuli had acquired reward value (i.e. in participants who were aware of the stimulus–reward contingency). This explains the large bias for A over X/Y(A) in A- and A&B-learners, compared to the small bias for B over X/Y(B) in B-learners (we'll leave aside other subtle differences in the data until later).

This idea that attention is commanded by the acquired reward value of cues, was substantiated by a subsequent modification to the design in which one key press was rewarded with tobacco in AX+ and AY+ trials, whereas a second key press was rewarded with a financially equivalent amount of money in BX+ and BY+ trials (Hogarth *et al.*, 2007, Experiment 2). Of the 11 aware participants (out of 16) in this study, five were A=tobacco-learners and six were B=money-learners (there were no A&B-learners). The results are shown in Figure 4.4. A-learners attended to A over the context, but not B, whereas B-learners showed the converse attentional bias. This finding confirms that there is a strong relationship between predictive learning and selective attention. Most critically, however, B-learners showed a larger bias for B over X/Y(B) compared to B-learners in Figure 4.3, suggesting that this bias was enhanced as a result of B being associated with a rewarding outcome.

If the attentional biases analysed so far reflect looking for liking, rather than looking for action, we should be able to dissociate this attentional bias from the control that stimuli exert over expectancy and instrumental performance. To test this proposal, we added a test phase to one of the replications included in Figure 4.3, which attempted to abolish the dwell time bias. To this end, we required participants to count visual targets that appeared amongst a rapidly alternating sequence of distracters in the centre of the screen, simultaneously during the 3-sec period of stimulus presentation, to force attention to remain in the centre rather than saccade to the peripheral location of the CS s (see Hogarth *et al.*, 2008b for details). Figure 4.5 shows the results from blocks of

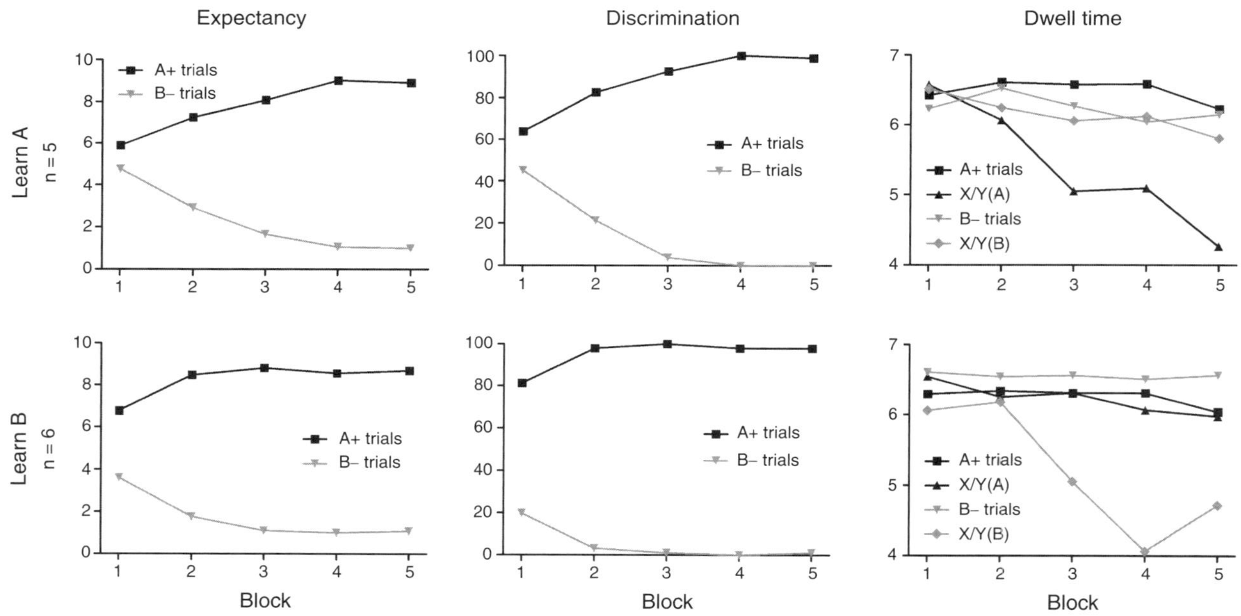

Fig. 4.4 Outcome expectancy (1=money, 10=tobacco) and instrumental discrimination (% trials with a tobacco rather than a money response) in A→tobacco vs. B→money trials, plus, dwell time (natural logmsec) to stimulus A and B relative to the concurrently presented contextual cues X/Y. Aware participants were split by whether they learned the A=tobacco or B=money rule (no one learned both rules). Again, selective attention was dependent upon which rule was acquired.

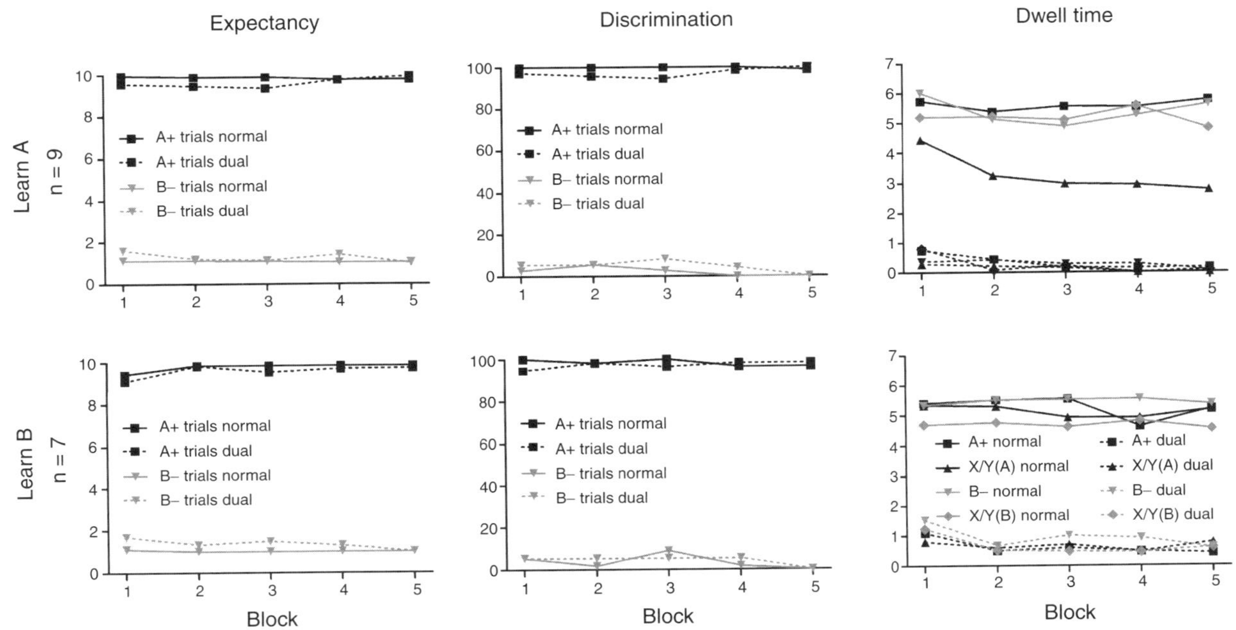

Fig. 4.5 The dual task method. Reward expectancy (1–10 scale) and instrumental discrimination (% trials with an instrumental response) between A+ and B– trials, plus, dwell time (natural logmsec) to stimulus A and B relative to the concurrently presented contextual cues X/Y. Aware participants were split according to whether they learned the A=win or B=lose rule. The results show that introducing the secondary task abolished the attentional bias for stimulus A and B in A- and B-learners, respectively, without effecting the control these stimuli exerted over expectancy and instrumental discrimination. Thus, these attentional biases were superfluous to behavioural control.

this test phase that did and did not include this secondary task (the measures are flat because they had reached asymptote by the final blocks of training). The first thing to note is that the pattern of bias seen in training continued in testing in the normal condition (without the secondary task). That is, A-learners showed a dwell time bias for A over X/Y(A), and no bias for B over X/Y(B), whereas B-learners showed the converse pattern – a bias for B over X/Y(B) and no bias for A over X/Y(A). Second, and most importantly, the inclusion of the secondary task was highly effective at abolishing attention to the peripherally located discriminative stimuli. In fact, examination of fixation count data (not shown) indicated that the discriminative stimuli were fixated in only 10% of secondary task trials. Nevertheless, despite this abolition of focal attention to stimuli, expectancy and instrumental discrimination remained fully intact in these trials. These data indicated that the dwell time biases to stimuli were unnecessary for stimuli to exert control over expectancy and instrumental performance. Indeed, these data indicate that covert detection of discriminative stimuli in the periphery of the visual field is sufficient for these stimuli to exert the same degree of control over expectancy and instrumental behaviour as when they command the maintenance of overt focal attention. Therefore, the overt maintenance of attention appears to be superfluous to behavioural control, whereas simple covert detection of stimuli appears to be sufficient for behavioural control (De Haan *et al.*, 2008 for further information on the distinction between overt and covert attention).

In a follow up study, we explored whether the 3 sec of 'dead time' during which stimuli were presented, and no action could be undertaken (Figure 4.2), allowed the superfluous attentional biases controlled by reward value to be expressed (Hogarth *et al.*, 2009). The inspiration for this study came from Premack and Collier (1966), who allowed participants to control the duration of stimulus presentation by holding down a key – known as an observing response in the operant literature (Wyckoff, 1952) – in a discrimination procedure not dissimilar to our own. Their critical finding was that observing times for stimuli paired with reward declined with training, which would be expected if attention was deployed efficiently to control instrumental behaviour, rather then increased, as might be expected if attention was controlled by the acquired reward value of cues.

The implication of Premack and Collier's (1966) finding was that the opportunity for immediate action caused participants to dispense with the overt maintenance of attention to reward cues, and instead, to employ a more economic form of stimulus detection, sufficient for expectancy and instrumental choice, but no more. To test this idea, we ran second a group alongside one of the replications included in Figure 4.3, but rather than present stimuli for a fixed 3-sec period, this group could control stimulus duration by holding down a key using a method akin to Premack and Collier (1966).

The results from the observing response group are shown in Figure 4.6 and indicate that A-learners and B-learners acquired no dwell time bias for stimulus A and B, respectively, in contrast to when stimulus presentation was fixed (Figure 4.3). Nevertheless, the control exerted by these cues over expectancy and instrumental discrimination performance was equivalent regardless of whether or not the dwell time bias was expressed, again confirming that these dwell time biases played no role in expectancy or behavioural control.

Summary: untangling arousal and valence

The foregoing data support Figure 4.1 in suggesting that the detection and maintenance of attention to conditioned stimuli are determined by the arousal and valence of the predicted outcome, respectively. With respect to the early detection of the CSs, our data clearly indicate that efficient detection, but not attentional maintenance, plays a role in the behavioural control exerted by these stimuli. In fact, in Hogarth *et al.*, (2008b) stimuli A and B were able to control expectancy and instrumental choice without being foveated on 90% of trials, indicating that parafoveal detection of these stimuli was sufficient for them to exert behavioural control. We might claim that such parafoveal detection was equal for the appetitive stimulus A and the aversive stimulus B, as predicted by the left column of Figure 4.1, from the fact that these cues controlled expectancy and instrumental choice equally in A- and B-learners. This conclusion fits with recent data showing that early detection of cues respects the arousal of those cues rather than their valence (Brosch *et al.*, 2008; Vogt *et al.*, 2008). However, the specific claim that early detection is enhanced for CSs that predict an arousing outcome is at present indirect because we currently have no way of measuring the enhancement of detection with the eye tracker.[3]

[3] One might think that the latency of the first fixation to stimulus A and B might be faster than for the contextual cues X/Y, reflecting the enhancement of early detection of cues associated with arousing outcomes. Unfortunately, however, we have found that first fixation latency was not reliably different between these cues. This measure may have been insensitive because the location of the predictive and contextual cues was randomized across trials. In the future, we may seek to measure the enhancement of early detection directly by fixing the location of stimuli, or by including alternative measures such as signal detection (Engelmann and Pessoa, 2007), EEG (Brosch *et al.*, 2008), attentional blink (Livesey *et al.*, 2009) or spatial cueing effects (Vogt *et al.*, 2008). It remains to be seen how these alternative measures might be integrated into the conditioning procedure.

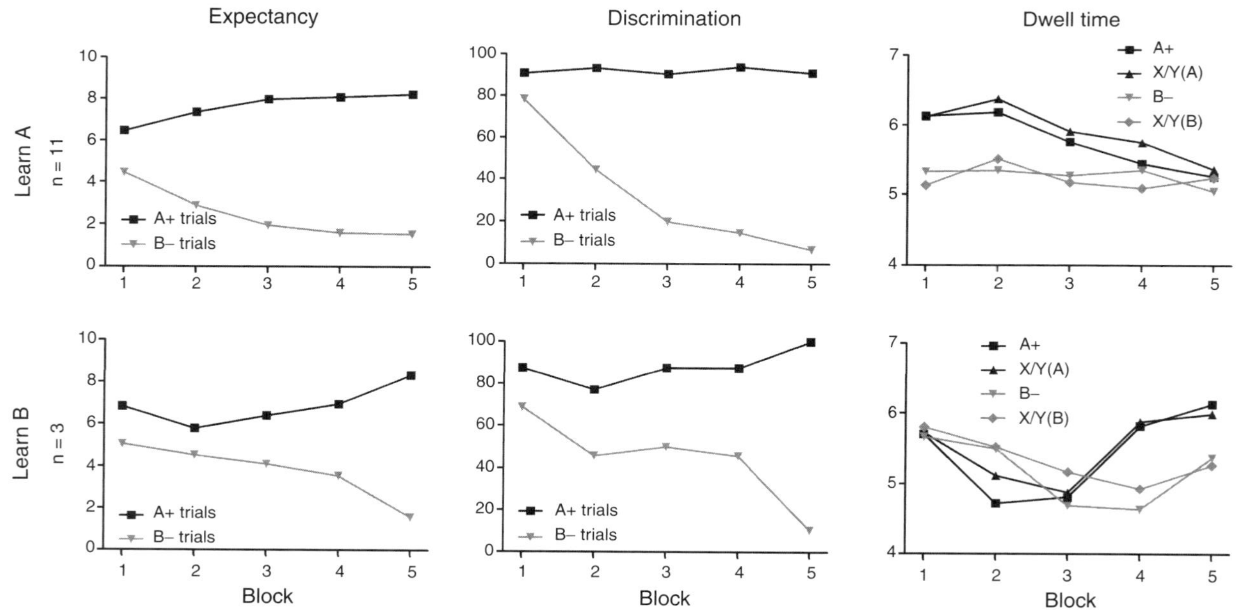

Fig. 4.6 The observing response method. Reward expectancy (1–10 scale) and instrumental discrimination (% trials with an instrumental response) between A+ and B- trials, plus, dwell time (natural logmsec) to stimulus A and B relative to the concurrently presented contextual cues X/Y. Aware participants are split according to whether they learned the A=win or B=lose rule. The results show that providing control over stimulus duration abolished the attentional bias for stimulus A and B in A- and B-learners, respectively, yet stimulus control of expectancy and instrumental performance remained unaffected.

The maintenance of attention to CSs, by contrast, was evidently determined by the valence of the predicted outcome, as anticipated by the middle column of Figure 4.1. The key finding supporting this claim was that dwell time biases were greater for the appetitive stimulus A in A-learners than for the aversive stimulus B in B-learners, despite the fact that the two cues were equally relevant for behaviour control in the two groups. These data suggest that the dwell time bias was enhanced by the prediction of the win outcome in stimulus A, compared to the prediction of the lose outcome in stimulus B. Thus, the valence of the predicted outcome appeared to determine the maintenance of attention to the CS (note that this conclusion relies on the assumption that the win and the lose outcome were equally subjectively arousing). The second key finding was that the dwell time bias for stimulus A was unnecessary for this stimulus to control expectancy and instrumental choice, consistent with the claim that this bias is linked to affective appraisal rather than behaviour control. It is important to note that although the dwell time bias for B was reduced compared to A, there was no evidence of attentional avoidance of B. Presumably, the lose outcome was not sufficiently aversive to drive avoidance, but this remains to be clarified.

The interplay of these two systems may explain the total pattern of results shown in Figure 4.3. According to this account, A-learners efficiently detected stimulus A to control instrumental choice, and subsequently, maintained gaze on stimulus A because of its acquired appetitive value (enabled because attention was not demanded elsewhere). These two forms of selection added together, creating a large dwell time bias for stimulus A relative to X/Y(A). By contrast, we propose that A&B-learners had a less specific search image for stimulus A because they also used B, or the absence of A or B, as the critical information to control instrumental choice (Plaisted and Mackintosh, 1995). Consequently, this weaker detection of A summed with the maintained bias for A, driven by the reward association, to yield a smaller overall dwell time bias for A over X/Y(A) compared to A-learners. Finally, we suggest that B-learners detected stimulus B to control instrumental choice, but did not maintain attention to this stimulus because it had no reward association. Instead, the initial detection carried over to generate a small dwell time bias compared to X/Y(B) because attention did not disengage to meet other demands (Posner *et al.*, 1980) and the aversive properties of the cue were insufficient to drive clear attentional avoidance.

Looking-for-learning

The foregoing analysis claims that a CS paired with an aversive outcome should not command a substantive dwell time bias. However, this proposal is, at first sight, contradicted by one of our published studies (Hogarth *et al.*, 2006a). In this study, the AX+, AY+, BX–, BY– design was used (outlined in Figure 4.2), but instead of reward, stimulus A signalled that a 97 dB aversive, startling white noise outcome would occur subsequently with 100% probability, and that an instrumental avoidance response would cancel this outcome with a 50% probability (to ensure that an A-noise contingency would be in force even if participants performed the avoidance response in every trial). By contrast, stimulus B signalled the absence of the aversive noise, and stimuli X/Y were contextual cues as before. This early method did not include the within-trial expectancy question, and consequently, a substantially smaller proportion of the sample became aware of the stimulus–outcome contingencies (5 out of 16), as indexed by post-experimental questioning, which also suggested that all five aware participants were A&B-learners. The important finding shown in Figure 4.7, was that these aware participants acquired a substantive dwell time bias for stimulus A over X/Y(A), but not for B over X/Y(B). At first sight, these data suggest that the aversive S+ acquired a maintained attentional bias, contradicting our claim that this bias should be selective to appetitive cues.

An alternative explanation of Figure 4.7 is that dwell time bias for stimulus A was not driven by the prediction of an arousing outcome, but by the uncertainty engaged by the this stimulus as a result of its partial contingency with the noise outcome and/or effectiveness of the avoidance response. To test this claim, we ran a modified design based upon Figure 4.2, inspired by Kaye and Pearce (1984), in which the stimulus pairs AX+, BX+/–, and CX–, were followed by the aversive noise outcome with a probability of 100%, 50%, and 0%, respectively (Hogarth *et al.*, 2008a). There was no instrumental avoidance

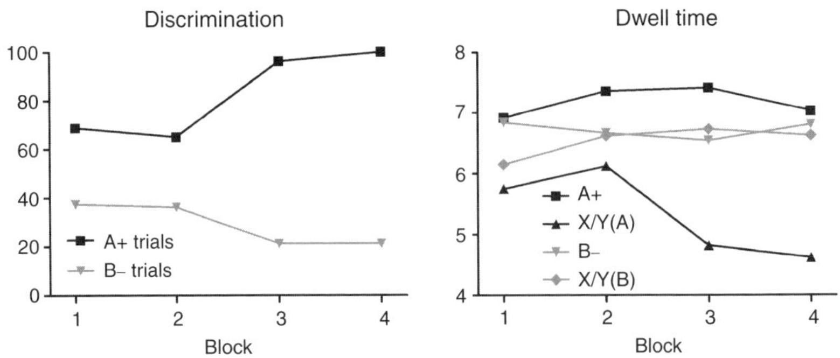

Fig. 4.7 Aversive conditioning study. Avoidance response discrimination (% trials with the avoidance response) between A+ and B– trials, plus, dwell time (natural logmsec) to stimulus A and B relative to the concurrently presented contextual cues X/Y. The five contingency aware participants included were all A&B-learners.

response, so participants' only task in the procedure was to accurately report the Pavlovian contingencies in the within-trials expectancy question, 'how likely is the loud noise', on a 1–10 scale. The top row of Figure 4.8 shows the expectancy reports of the 11 aware participants (out of 16) who showed a significant difference in their expectancy reports in the final block of training, in the direction of A>B>C, and most importantly, the dwell times for the four stimuli: A, B, C versus the concurrently presented contextual stimulus X.

The key finding was that the unreliable predictor stimulus B commanded a greater dwell time bias relative to the contextual cue X(B), than did A versus X(A) and C versus X(C). Thus, the stimulus that was associated with the greatest predictive uncertainty commanded the greatest dwell time bias. Moreover, although A and C commanded greater dwell than the contextual cue X, these biases were of equivalent magnitude, indicating that the reliable aversive predictor stimulus A commanded no greater bias than the non-predictor stimulus C. This finding confirms our claim that the prediction of an aversive outcome does not enhance the dwell time bias, in contrast to our earlier finding that the prediction of an appetitive outcome does. The reason why stimulus A and C commanded a greater dwell time than stimulus X may simply have been because X was presented in every trial, meaning that stimuli A and C had greater novelty and lower frequency than X. The implication of these findings is that the bias for stimulus A in Figure 4.6 was determined by the predictive uncertainty associated with this stimulus rather than the prediction of an arousing (aversive) outcome.

The bottom row of Figure 4.8 shows a replication of the design in which we replaced the aversive startling noise outcome with a neutral 50 dB tone, to determine whether the loss of dwell time bias for A (compared to B) was driven by attentional avoidance. The important finding was that the original effects seen in the top row were replicated with the neutral outcome, confirming that the attentional effects were determined by the differential uncertainty associated with each stimulus, rather than any affective value acquired through association with the aversive outcome.

Summary: untangling arousal, valence, and uncertainty

Our data suggest that conditioned stimuli command the three forms of attentional selection (Figure 4.1). Conditioned stimuli appear to command efficient detection to the extent that they are associated with an arousing outcome (irrespective of valence), and command the maintenance of overt attention to the extent that they are associated with an appetitive outcome. In addition to this,

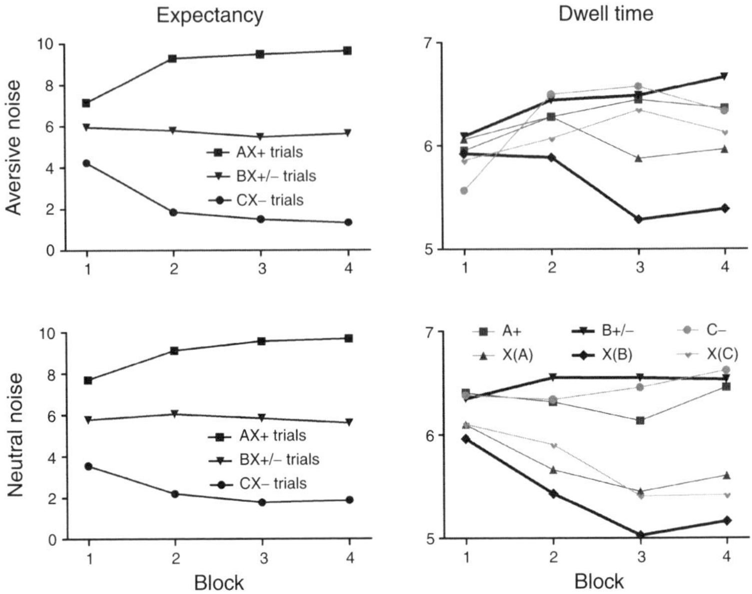

Fig. 4.8 Two studies exploring the maintenance of attention to stimuli with differential relationships to an aversive (top row) and neutral noise outcome (bottom row). Noise expectancy ratings (1–10 scale) and dwell times (natural logmsec) to a full, partial and non-predictor stimulus A, B and C, respectively, relative to a concurrently presented contextual cue X. The key result was that the dwell time bias was greatest for the partial predictor stimulus B, which was associated with the greatest uncertainty, with both the aversive and neutral outcome.

conditioned stimuli also appear to command the maintenance of overt attention to the extent that they convey uncertainty about the probability of an outcome, irrespective of whether the outcome is aversive or neutral. We propose that these three forms of attentional selection play a role in action selection, affective state, and learning, respectively.

There are several ways one might develop this work to further isolate the three attentional systems. First, further contrasts are needed of the nine conditions outlined in Figure 4.1. One gap in our analysis, for example, is that we have not assessed uncertainty effects for CSs paired with an appetitive outcome. Second, there is need to discover a measure of attention that is sensitive to the enhancement of early detection as distinct from the maintenance of attention measured by dwell time. For this purpose, we have hinted at signal detection (Engelmann and Pessoa, 2007), electroencephalogram (Brosch *et al.*, 2008), attentional blink (Livesey *et al.*, 2009) or spatial cueing (Vogt *et al.*, 2008), but the incorporation of these measures into the current procedures remains to be explored. Third, a broader range of aversive outcomes might be tested, to determine the conditions under which attentional avoidance is generated. Forth, closer analysis is required of the time course of stimulus viewing, to identify the point at which looking-for-action is superseded by looking-for-liking or looking-for-learning. Finally, direct contrasts might be made of discriminative instrumental versus Pavlovian procedures, which are otherwise yoked for cue-outcome frequency (Rescorla, 1994), to assess attentional performance when instrumental action is and is not possible. The ultimate objective of this program of work would be to isolate and dissociate the three attentional systems for application to brain imaging to contribute to a neuropsychological model of attention.

Once the appropriate parameters are established to isolate the three attentional systems, one could more clearly reassess their proposed differential role in action selection, affective state and learning. For instance, one might assess whether enhanced detection for arousing cues predicts differential behavioural control exerted by these stimuli in tests of cue competition (De Houwer and Beckers, 2002; Kruschke *et al.*, 2005). Further, one might test whether dwell time to appetitive cues, or avoidance of aversive cues is modulated by mood induction, individual affective state (Beevers and Carver, 2003; Tamir and Robinson, 2007), or post-conditioning revaluation/devaluation of the incentive value of the outcome (Holland and Straub, 1979; Hutcheson *et al.*, 2001), to explore the link between attentional maintenance and affect. Finally, one might examine whether dwell time associated with uncertainty predicts the associability of stimuli in tests of learning (Wilson *et al.*, 1992; Holland and Gallagher, 2006), although this work would have to reconcile apparent contradictory evidence that learning is sometimes superior for reliable predictors (Le Pelley, 2004; Le Pelley and McLaren, 2003). In all, this work should clarify the role of the three attentional systems in action, affect and learning.

The neural basis of attention in associative learning

One final issue concerns the neural substrates of the three attentional systems. Perhaps the most informative work addressing this issue has come from the animal behavioural neuroscience lab of Peter Holland, and this topic is discussed extensively in a separate chapter. Our aim is not to compete with this chapter, but rather, to highlight a small set of exemplary studies that appear to have isolated one of the three attentional systems in a way reminiscent of our human studies. Our purpose in highlighting the relationship between these human and animal studies is to hint at what shape a translational program of research might take to contribute to a neuropsychological theory of attention in associative learning.

Holland and colleagues recently identified a form of CS orienting that plays no role in the control that CS exert over instrumental behaviour (Groshek *et al.*, 2005; McDannald *et al.*, 2004), reminiscent of the studies outlined in Figures 4.5 and 4.6, where abolition of the dwell time bias to the CS had no impact on CS control of expectancy and instrumental performance. In these animal studies, rats learned that a 10-sec external light or noise CS was followed immediately by the availability of food in a feeding tray. In parallel with our results, rats developed an attentional bias for the conditioned stimuli, indexed by a higher frequency of orientation of the eyes or ears towards that stimulus in the early portion of its presentation, while learning to approach the food tray in response to the CS in anticipation of food delivery, in the latter portion of its presentation. The fact that attentional orientation was not necessary for reward-seeking by the rats was demonstrated by deactivation of the central nucleus of the amygdala, which abolished the attentional bias for the CS, but left intact the ability of the CS to elicit food seeking. El-Amamy and Holland (2007) recently confirmed this dissociation between the attentional bias and instrumental performance in a Pavlovian to instrumental transfer design.

These data have a striking similarity to our own (Figures 4.3, 4.5, and 4.6), in that the bias for the CS and its control of reward-seeking emerged in parallel across conditioning, yet the abolition of the attentional bias had no impact on CS control of behaviour. The question, therefore, is what caused a form of attentional bias to develop that played no functional role in behaviour? We believe that this bias reflected the looking-for-liking system, which was recruited by the prediction of the reward outcome evoked by the CS, and enabled by the fact that the CS was presented for a 10-sec period of dead time during which instrumental responding was ineffective (the implication being, that if the CS and food availability were simultaneous, as in Figure 4.6, the looking-for-action system – efficient detection – would have been unmasked in mediating instrumental responding). If this assertion is true, then by implication, the central nucleus of the amygdala is one component of the neural circuit underlying the looking-for-liking system.

Another recent experiment from Holland's lab (Maddux *et al.*, 2007) dissociated the substrates underlying the looking-for-action and looking-for-learning systems. In this study, performance of the five choice serial reaction time tasks were used to index the role of attention in guiding behavioural choice, whereas the ability of surprise (prediction error) to enhance learning was used to index the role of attention in facilitating contingency learning. This study found that lesions of the cholinergic projection from the substantiate innominata/nucleus basalis magnocellularis (SI/nBM) to the medial prefrontal cortex interfered with the role of attention in guiding behavioural choice but not in the enhancement of learning. By contrast, lesions to the cholinergic projection to the posterior parietal cortex had the converse effect – interfering with the role of attention in learning but not in behavioural control. Finally, lesions of the central nucleus of the amygdala, which is linked to the SI/nBM, interfered with both forms of attention. Collectively, therefore, the foregoing studies from Holland's lab support the notion that although the circuits underlying looking for action, liking, and learning are commonly routed through the central nucleus of the amygdala, they diverge thereafter to separate cortical projections through the SI/nBM.

Our human procedures could in the future contribute to a neuropsychological theory of attention in associative learning by first optimizing the parameters needed to behaviourally isolate the three attentional systems, as described earlier, and then transferring these methods into a magnetic resonance imaging scanner, to help elucidate the full extent of the circuits underlying each attentional system (Armony and Dolan, 2002). The animal work could then pinpoint these neuroanatomical substrates beyond the resolution of the scanner.

Acknowledgements

The preparation of this manuscript was supported by a MRC new investigator award to Lee Hogarth (G0701456).

References

Armony, J. L. & Dolan, R. J. (2002). Modulation of spatial attention by fear-conditioned stimuli: An event-related fMRI study. *Neuropsychologia,* **40**, 817–826.

Beevers, C. G. & Carver, C. S. (2003). Attentional bias and mood persistence as prospective predictors of dysphoria. *Cognitive Therapy and Research,* **27**, 619–637.

Belopolsky, A. V. & Theeuwes, J. (2009). Inhibition of saccadic eye movements to locations in spatial working memory. *Attention Perception & Psychophysics,* **71**, 620–631.

Bindra, D. (1978) How adaptive behaviour is produced: A perceptual-motivational alternative to response reinforcement, *The Behavioural and Brain Sciences,* **1**, 41–91.

Brosch, T., Sander, D., Pourtois, G., & Scherer, K. R. (2008). Beyond fear – Rapid spatial orienting toward positive emotional stimuli. *Psychological Science,* **19**, 362–370.

Calvo, M. G. & Avero, P. (2005). Time course of attentional bias to emotional scenes in anxiety: Gaze direction and duration. *Cognition & Emotion,* **19**, 433–451.

Calvo, M. G. & Eysenck, M. W. (2000). Early vigilance and late avoidance of threat processing: Repressive coping versus low/high anxiety. *Cognition & Emotion,* **14**, 763–787.

De Haan, B., Moryan, P. S., & Rorden, C. (2008). Covert orienting of attention and overt eye movements activate identical brain regions. *Brain Research,* **1204**, 102–111.

De Houwer, J. & Beckers, T. (2002). A review of recent developments in research and theories on human contingency learning. *Quarterly Journal of Experimental Psychology Section B – Comparative and Physiological Psychology,* **55**, 289–310.

Eastwood, J. D., Smilek, D., & Merikle, P. M. (2001). Differential attentional guidance by unattended faces expressing positive and negative emotion. *Perception & Psychophysics,* **63**, 1004–1013.

El-Amamy, H. & Holland, P. C. (2007). Dissociable effects of disconnecting amygdala central nucleus from the ventral tegmental area or substantia nigra on learned orienting and incentive motivation. *European Journal of Neuroscience,* **25**, 1557–1567.

Engelmann, J. B. & Pessoa, L. (2007). Motivation sharpens exogenous spatial attention. *Emotion,* **7**, 668–674.

Field, M., Mogg, K., & Bradley, B. P. (2004). Eye movements to smoking-related cues: Effects of nicotine deprivation. *Psychopharmacology,* **173**, 116–123.

Fox, E., Russo, R., Bowles, R., & Dutton, K. (2001). Do threatening stimuli draw or hold visual attention in subclinical anxiety? *Journal of Experimental Psychology – General,* **130**, 681–700.

Frank, M. J., Seeberger, L. C., & O'reilly, R. C. (2004). By carrot or by stick: Cognitive reinforcement learning in Parkinsonism. *Science,* **306**, 1940–1943.

Frewen, P. A., Dozois, D. J. A., Joanisse, M. F., & Neufeld, R. W. J. (2008). Selective attention to threat versus reward: Meta-analysis and neural-network modeling of the dot-probe task. *Clinical Psychology Review,* **28**, 307–337.

Groshek, F., Kerfoot, E., Mckenna, V., Polackwich, A. S., Gallagher, M., & Holland, P. C. (2005). Amygdala central nucleus function is necessary for learning, but not expression, of conditioned auditory orienting. *Behavioral Neuroscience,* **119**, 202–212.

Hogarth, L., Dickinson, A., Austin, A., Brown, C., & Duka, T. (2008a). Attention and expectation in human predictive learning: The role of uncertainty. *Quarterly Journal of Experimental Psychology,* **61**, 1658–1668.

Hogarth, L., Dickinson, A., & Duka, T. (2009). Detection versus sustained attention to drug cues have dissociable roles in mediating drug seeking behaviour. *Experimental and Clinical Psychopharmacology,* **17**, 21–30.

Hogarth, L., Dickinson, A., Hutton, S. B., Bamborough, H., & Duka, T. (2006a). Contingency knowledge is necessary for learned motivated behaviour in humans: Relevance for addictive behaviour. *Addiction,* **101**, 1153–1166.

Hogarth, L., Dickinson, A., Hutton, S. B., Elbers, N., & Duka, T. (2006b). Drug expectancy is necessary for stimulus control of human attention, instrumental drug-seeking behaviour and subjective pleasure. *Psychopharmacology,* **185**, 495–504.

Hogarth, L., Dickinson, A., Janowski, M., Nikitina, A., & Duka, T. (2008b). The role of attentional bias in mediating human drug seeking behaviour. *Psychopharmacology,* **201**, 29–41.

Hogarth, L., Dickinson, A., Wright, A., Kouvaraki, M., & Duka, T. (2007). The role of drug expectancy in the control of human drug seeking. *Journal of Experimental Psychology – Animal Behavior Processes,* **33**, 484–496.

Hogarth, L. & Duka, T. (2006). Human nicotine conditioning requires explicit contingency knowledge: Is addictive behaviour cognitively mediated? *Psychopharmacology,* **184**, 553–566.

Holland, P. C. & Gallagher, M. (2006). Different roles for amygdala central nucleus and substantia innominata in the surprise-induced enhancement of learning. *Journal of Neuroscience,* **26**, 3791–3797.

Holland, P. C. & Straub, J. J. (1979). Differential effects of 2 ways of devaluing the unconditioned stimulus after pavlovian appetitive conditioning. *Journal of Experimental Psychology – Animal Behavior Processes,* **5**, 65–78.

Hutcheson, D. M., Everitt, B. J., Robbins, T. W., & Dickinson, A. (2001). The role of withdrawal in heroin addiction: Enhances reward or promotes avoidance? *Nature Neuroscience,* **4**, 943–947.

Kaye, H. & Pearce, J. M. (1984). The strength of the orienting response during Pavlovian conditioning. *Journal of Experimental Psychology: Animal Behavior Processes,* **10**, 90–109.

Knudsen, E. I. (2007). Fundamental components of attention. *Annual Review of Neuroscience,* **30**, 57–78.

Koster, E. H. W., De Raedt, R., Goeleven, E., Franck, E., & Crombez, G. (2005). Mood-congruent attentional bias in dysphoria: Maintained attention to and impaired disengagement from negative information. *Emotion,* **5**, 446–455.

Kruschke, J. K., Kappenman, E. S., & Hetrick, W. P. (2005). Eye gaze and individual differences consistent with learned attention in associative blocking and highlighting. *Journal of Experimental Psychology: Learning Memory and Cognition,* **31**, 830–845.

Le Pelley, M. E. (2004). The role of associative history in models of associative learning: A selective review and a hybrid model. *Quarterly Journal of Experimental Psychology Section B – Comparative and Physiological Psychology,* **57**, 193–243.

Le Pelley, M. E. & McLaren, I. P. L. (2003). Learned associability and associative change in human causal learning. *Quarterly Journal of Experimental Psychology Section B – Comparative and Physiological Psychology,* **56**, 68–79.

Lewis, P. A., Critchley, H. D., Rotshtein, P., & Dolan, R. J. (2007). Neural correlates of processing valence and arousal in affective words. *Cerebral Cortex,* **17**, 742–748.

Lieberman, D. A., Connell, G. L., & Moos, H. F. (1998a). Reinforcement without awareness: II. Word class. *Quarterly Journal of Experimental Psychology B,* **51**, 317–335.

Lieberman, D. A., Sunnucks, W. L., & Kirk, J. D. (1998b). Reinforcement without awareness: I. Voice level. *Quarterly Journal of Experimental Psychology B,* **51**, 301–316.

Lin, S. C. & Nicolelis, M. A. L. (2008). Neuronal ensemble bursting in the basal forebrain encodes salience irrespective of valence. *Neuron,* **59**, 138–149.

Livesey, E. J., Harris, I. M., & Harris, J. A. (2009). Attentional changes during implicit learning: Signal validity protects a target stimulus from the attentional blink. *Journal of Experimental Psychology: Learning, Memory & Cognition,* **35**, 408–422.

Lovibond, P. F. & Shanks, D. R. (2002). The role of awareness in Pavlovian conditioning: Empirical evidence and theoretical implications. *Journal of Experimental Psychology – Animal Behavior Processes,* **28**, 3–26.

Mackintosh, N. J. (1975). A theory of attention: Variations in the associability of stimuli with reinforcement. *Psychological Review,* **82**, 276–298.

MacLeod, C., Rutherford, E., Campbell, L., Ebsworthy, G., & Holker, L. (2002). Selective attention and emotional vulnerability: Assessing the causal basis of their association through the experimental manipulation of attentional bias. *Journal of Abnormal Psychology,* **111**, 107–123.

Maddux, J. M., Kerfoot, E. C., Chatterjee, S., & Holland, P. C. (2007). Dissociation of attention in learning and action: Effects of lesions of the amygdala central nucleus, medial prefrontal cortex, and posterior parietal cortex. *Behavioral Neuroscience,* **121**, 63–79.

McDannald, M., Kerfoot, E., Gallagher, M., & Holland, P. C. (2004). Amygdala central nucleus function is necessary for learning but not expression of conditioned visual orienting. *European Journal of Neuroscience,* **20**, 240–248.

Mogg, K., Bradley, B. P., Hyare, H., & Lee, S. (1998). Selective attention to food-related stimuli in hunger: Are attentional biases specific to emotional and psychopathological states, or are they also found in normal drive states? *Behaviour Research and Therapy,* **36**, 227–237.

Morris, R. W. & Bouton, M. E. (2006). Effect of unconditioned stimulus magnitude on the emergence of conditioned responding. *Journal of Experimental Psychology – Animal Behavior Processes,* **32**, 371–385.

Morrison, R. & O'Connor, R. C. (2008). The robe of rumination, attentional biases and stress in psychological distress. *British Journal of Psychology,* **99**, 191–209.

Pearce, J. M. & Hall, G. (1980). A model for Pavlovian learning: Variations in the effectiveness of conditioned but not unconditioned stimuli. *Psychological Review,* **87**, 532–552.

Perruchet, P. (1985). A pitfall for the expectancy theory of human eyelid conditioning. *Pavlovian journal of biological science,* **20**, 163–170.

Perruchet, P., Cleeremans, A., & Destrebecqz, A. (2006). Dissociating the effects of automatic activation and explicit expectancy on reaction times in a simple associative learning task. *Journal of Experimental Psychology – Learning Memory and Cognition,* **32**, 955–965.

Pflugshaupt, T., Mosimann, U. P., Von Wartburg, R., Schmitt, W., Nyffeler, T., & Muri, R. M. (2005). Hypervigilance-avoidance pattern in spider phobia. *Journal of Anxiety Disorders,* **19**, 105–116.

Plaisted, K. C. & Mackintosh, N. J. (1995). Visual-search for cryptic stimuli in pigeons – implications for the search image and search rate hypotheses. *Animal Behaviour,* **50**, 1219–1232.

Posner, M., Snyder, C., & Davidson, B. (1980). Attention and the detection of signals. *Journal of Experimental Psychology: General,* **109**, 160–174.

Premack, D. & Collier, G. (1966). Duration of looking and number of brief looks as dependent variables. *Psychonomic Science,* **4**, 81–82.

Rangel, A., Camerer, C., & Montague, P. R. (2008). A framework for studying the neurobiology of value-based decision making. *Nature Reviews Neuroscience,* **9**, 545–556.

Rescorla, R. A. (1994). Control of instrumental performance by pavlovian and instrumental stimuli. *Journal of Experimental Psychology – Animal Behavior Processes,* **20**, 44–50.

Robinson, T. E. & Berridge, K. C. (1993). The neural basis of drug craving: An incentive-sensitization theory of drug addiction. *Brain Research Reviews,* **18**, 247–291.

Sutherland, N. S. & Mackintosh, N. J. (1971). Mechanisms of animal discrimination learning. New York, Academic Press.

Tamir, M. & Robinson, M. D. (2007). The happy spotlight: Positive mood and selective attention to rewarding information. *Personality and Social Psychology Bulletin,* **33**, 1124–1136.

Vogt, J., De Houwer, J., Koster, E. H. W., Van Damme, S., & Crombez, G. (2008). allocation of spatial attention to emotional stimuli depends upon arousal and not valence. *Emotion,* **8**, 880–885.

Vuilleumier, P. (2005). How brains beware: Neural mechanisms of emotional attention. *Trends in Cognitive Sciences,* **9**, 585–594.

Vuilleumier, P., Armony, J., & Dolan, R. J. (2003). Reciprocal links between emotion and attention. In Frackowiak, R. S. J., Friston, K. J., Frith, C. D., Dolan, R. J., Price, C. J., Zeki, S., Ashburner, J. T., & Penny, W. D. (Eds), *Human Brain Function (2nd edition).* San Diego, Academic Press.

Wagner, A. R. (1969). Incidental stimuli and discrimination learning. IN Gilbert, R. M., & Sutherland, N. S. (Eds), *Animal discrimination learning.* London, Academic Press.

Wagner, A. R., Logan, F. A., Haberlandt, K., & Price, T. (1968). Stimulus selection in animal discrimination learning. *Journal of Experimental Psychology,* **79**, 171–180.

Weierich, M. R., Treat, T. A., & Hollingworth, A. (2008). Theories and measurement of visual attentional processing in anxiety. *Cognition & Emotion,* **22**, 985–1018.

Wilson, P. N., Boumphrey, P., & Pearce, J. M. (1992). Restoration of the orienting response to a light by a change in its predictive accuracy. *Quarterly Journal of Experimental Psychology Section B – Comparative and Physiological Psychology,* **44B**, 17–36.

Wolfe, J. M. & Horowitz, T. S. (2004). What attributes guide the deployment of visual attention and how do they do it? *Nature Reviews Neuroscience,* **5**, 495–501.

Wyckoff, L. B. (1952). The role of the observing response in discrimination learning. Part 1. *Psychological Review,* **59**, 431–442.

Wyvell, C. L. & Berridge, K. C. (2000). Intra-accumbens amphetamine increases the conditioned incentive salience of sucrose reward: Enhancement of reward 'wanting' without enhanced 'liking' or response reinforcement. *Journal of Neuroscience,* **20**, 8122–8130.

Wyvell, C. L. & Berridge, K. C. (2001). Incentive sensitization by previous amphetamine exposure: Increased cue-triggered 'wanting' for sucrose reward. *Journal of Neuroscience,* **21**, 7831–7840.

Yantis, S. (2008). The neural basis of selective attention: Cortical sources and targets of attentional modulation. *Current Directions in Psychological Science,* **17**, 86–90.

Chapter 5

Latent inhibition

Nathan M. Holmes and Justin A. Harris

When an animal experiences repeated presentations of a stimulus on its own (i.e. in the absence of any other event) its behavioural responses to that stimulus change. One measurable change in behaviour is the habituation of unconditioned responses, such as orienting that the stimulus had previously elicited while it was still relatively novel (Thompson and Spencer, 1966). Another change is an apparent decrement in the animal's ability to learn about that stimulus. Typical demonstrations of this 'latent inhibition' (LI) effect involve tracking the acquisition of conditioned responses (CRs) to a conditioned stimulus (CS) that is followed by an unconditioned stimulus (US). LI is evident as a decrement or delay in the appearance of CRs to a CS that had been previously presented on its own. As Lubow and Moore (1959) pointed out at the time of its discovery, something must be learned during the initial non-reinforced exposures that interfere with subsequent learning about the CS or with the expression of that learning. Since then, evidence for LI has been obtained in many species, including humans, in numerous conditioning paradigms (Lubow, 1973, 1989; Lubow and Weiner, in press), and it has become one of the most intensively studied phenomena in learning over the last 50 years. Arguably its popularity derives from the apparent simplicity of the circumstances under which it is acquired—the repeated presentation of a single stimulus. The implication is that it should be easier to attain a comprehensive understanding of the mechanisms of LI than for other learning phenomena. The most popular account of LI is that non-reinforced pre-exposure produces a lasting deficit in attention to the CS. Indeed, in some quarters LI has become synonymous with changes in attention. However, as we review here, despite the large number of theoretical accounts that have been offered, none provides a completely satisfactory explanation. Rather, the available evidence indicates that LI is likely to result from more than a single process (see also Hall, 1991).

Characteristics of latent inhibition

In the 35 years since Lubow (1973) first reviewed the literature on LI, much has been discovered about the variables that affect it. Many of these variables are the same as those that affect conditioning generally.

Amount of conditioned stimulus pre-exposure

LI increases with the number of CS pre-exposures. For example, Lantz (1973) gave four groups of rats 0, 10, 30, or 60 pre-exposures to a tone, after which all rats received a single tone-shock pairing. In a subsequent test session, Lantz measured the extent to which presentation of the tone disrupted the rats' drinking. She found that the non-pre-exposed group showed the most suppression, the group given 10 pre-exposures showed modest suppression, while groups given 30 and 60 pre-exposures showed little suppression. Generally, the evidence concurs with Lubow's (1973) observation that, in experiments that used a between-subjects design to investigate LI (i.e. different groups of subjects were pre-exposed versus not pre-exposed to the CS), the deficit is most reliably obtained in groups that have received more than 16 pre-exposures to the CS.

Ayers, Philbin, Cassidy, Bellino, and Redlinger (1992) noted that previous studies investigating the relationship between LI and the amount of pre-exposure confounded the number of pre-exposures with the total pre-exposure time, so it is not clear which of these factors is most important for LI. To address this issue, they trained four groups of rats to lever-press for sucrose (Experiment 1) and, superimposed on this training, three of these groups were pre-exposed to a light. Importantly, while the number of pre-exposures varied between these groups, total pre-exposure time was the same (resulting, unavoidably, in a confound between the number of pre-exposures and the inter-stimulus interval). That is, Groups 12, 120, and 720—the numbers denoting light duration in seconds—were given 120, 12, and 2 pre-exposures per session, respectively, while Group 0 was not pre-exposed. Following pre-exposure, six light-shock conditioning sessions were superimposed on lever-press training, in which presentations of the light lasted for 120 s. Across the first three conditioning sessions, Group 0 showed more suppression than the pre-exposed groups, but the three pre-exposed groups did not differ from each other. However, in the latter three conditioning sessions, Groups 12 and 720 showed more suppression than Group 120. This difference was attributed to a generalization decrement in Groups 12 and 720 due to the difference in CS duration between pre-exposure and conditioning. Nonetheless, the more important observation was that the amount of LI was not systematically related to the substantial difference between groups in the number of CS pre-exposures or duration of each exposure, suggesting that total pre-exposure time is the most important determinant of LI.

Stimulus intensity

Rodriguez and Alonso (2002) studied the relationship between LI and stimulus intensity using rats in a conditioned taste avoidance (CTA) study. They pre-exposed two groups to a weak (0.25%) saline solution and two groups to a stronger (1%) saline solution. Two further groups were not pre-exposed. Subsequently, one group from each pair was conditioned with the weak saline solution while the other was conditioned with the stronger solution. Across nine conditioning trials, Rodriguez and Alonso found more rapid suppression of intake among rats conditioned with the stronger solution, revealing an effect of CS intensity on conditioning. Moreover, pre-exposure to the stronger solution more effectively retarded conditioning than pre-exposure to the weak solution. This was true regardless of which concentration was used for conditioning, indicating that the differential evidence for LI was not confounded with differences in the level of the aversion. Therefore, like conditioning, LI is affected by CS intensity (Schnur and Lubow, 1976).

Interval between pre-exposures

Schnur and Lubow (1976) investigated LI as a function of the interval between pre-exposures. They gave four groups of mice 40 pre-exposures to a tone. For two groups (SL and SS), the interval between pre-exposures was 10 sec, while for the other two groups (LL and LS) the interval between pre-exposures was 70 sec (S and L stand for short and long intervals). Two additional control groups (CL and CS) received non-reinforced exposure to the context at this stage. Immediately following pre-exposure (or equivalent context exposure), all groups commenced shuttle-box training where presentations of the tone signalled shock. On each trial, the tone was presented for 5 sec without shock, after which it continued with shock until the mouse crossed to the safe compartment. Groups SS, LS, and CS were trained with a short intertrial interval (ITI) of 10 sec, while Groups SL, LL, and CL were trained with a long ITI of 70 sec. Schnur and Lubow observed stronger conditioning in groups trained with the long ITI (i.e. these groups showed lower latencies and more avoidance responses), and less conditioning (stronger LI) in groups pre-exposed with the long interval between pre-exposures. There was no interaction between the two factors. Schnur and Lubow concluded that longer intervals between pre-exposures produce stronger LI, in the same way that longer intervals between CS–US pairings produce stronger conditioning (see also Lantz, 1973; but for null findings, see Crowell and Anderson, 1972; DeVietti and Barrett, 1986).

Context-specificity

One of the best established findings with respect to LI is its sensitivity to changes in the experimental context. Channell and Hall (1983) demonstrated this sensitivity using rats in a conditioned magazine approach paradigm. Rats that had been pre-exposed to a light displayed fewer magazine entries across light-food conditioning than non-pre-exposed rats, but response rates were higher among rats that were conditioned in a context different from that where they had been pre-exposed. Therefore, changing the context between pre-exposure and conditioning attenuated LI (Gordon and Weaver, 1989). Lovibond, Preston, and Mackintosh (1984) investigated whether the context-specificity of LI would be eliminated when the associative status of the experimental contexts was equated between groups that received pre-exposure and conditioning to a CS in either the same context or in different contexts. Rats were pre-exposed to a tone and a light in separate contexts before being conditioned to each stimulus. The rats showed stronger evidence of LI (i.e. poorer conditioning) when each CS was conditioned in the context where it had been pre-exposed than when each CS was conditioned in the pre-exposure context of the other CS. This demonstrates LI that is sensitive to the specific context–CS association when controlling for familiarity with the conditioning context and its association with the US. Finally, several studies have shown that the loss of LI that occurs when pre-exposure and conditioning take place in different contexts is restored in a CS-specific manner if the CS is again presented in the same context as pre-exposure (Bouton and Swartzentruber, 1989; Lovibond *et al.*, 1984; Westbrook, Jones, Bailey, and Harris, 2000). For example, Westbrook *et al.* (2000) confirmed that rats pre-exposed to a CS in one context but conditioned in another context showed more conditioned responding (i.e. less LI) than rats pre-exposed and conditioned in the same context. However, the LI lost with the context change between pre-exposure and conditioning was restored when rats were tested in the context of pre-exposure.

The influence of the context on LI is itself affected by pre-exposure to the context. Hall and Channell (1985b) reported that LI was enhanced among rats that had been repeatedly exposed to a context prior to CS pre-exposure in that context. Such context pre-exposure has also been shown to reduce the context-specificity of LI, allowing LI to be observed across shifts in context between CS pre-exposure and conditioning (McLaren, Bennett, Plaisted, Aitken, and Mackintosh, 1994). It is worth noting that McLaren *et al.* found no effect of context pre-exposure on LI among animals conditioned in the same context where the CS had been pre-exposed. Thus, it appears that the effect of context pre-exposure on generalization of LI across contexts does not simply reflect an overall increase in the amount of LI. Rather, it is possible that the increase in LI observed by Hall and Channell is due to a reduction in the context-specificity of LI following context pre-exposure. That is, the typical demonstration of LI, when a CS is pre-exposed and then conditioned in the same context, may underestimate the effect of CS pre-exposure if the introduction of the US during conditioning constitutes some form of context shift between pre-exposure and conditioning, which would attenuate LI. Context exposure in advance of CS pre-exposure may increase evidence for LI because it renders the effects of CS pre-exposure less context-specific and thus more evident during conditioning (Hall, 1991). The fact that context pre-exposure had this effect on LI in the experiments described by Hall and Channell, whereas the comparable effect was not observed in the experiments reported by McLaren *et al.*, may reflect differences in the impact of the US used in each study. That is, the shock US used by Hall and Channell may have induced a larger shift in context than the water US used by McLaren *et al.*

Delay intervals

LI is sensitive to the temporal interval between pre-exposure and conditioning, and also to the interval between conditioning and test (Aguado, Symonds, and Hall 1994; Killcross, Kiernan, Dwyer, and Westbrook, 1998; Westbrook *et al.*, 2000). In a CTA paradigm, Aguado *et al.* (1994) observed strong LI in rats that had been pre-exposed to a saccharin solution, then conditioned one day after pre-exposure, and tested for consumption of the saccharin two days after conditioning. The evidence for LI was reduced when conditioning occurred 12 days after pre-exposure, or when testing took place 12 days after conditioning. They concluded that the loss of LI depends on the length of time between pre-exposure and test. Westbrook *et al.* (2000) also showed loss of LI after a delay, and additionally demonstrated that the effect of the delay summated with the effect of a context shift on LI. They pre-exposed four groups of rats to CS1 in Context A and CS2 in Context B, before both CSs were separately paired with shock in Context C. Conditioned freezing to CS1 was then tested either in Context A where it had been pre-exposed (Groups Consistent) or in Context B where CS2 had been pre-exposed (Groups Inconsistent). Half the rats were tested 1 day after conditioning (Groups Consistent-1 and Inconsistent-1), and the remaining rats were tested 21 days after conditioning (Groups Consistent-21 and Inconsistent-21). During these sessions, the groups pre-exposed to CS1 froze less than control subjects, demonstrating LI, and the

Consistent groups froze less to CS1 than did the Inconsistent groups, demonstrating loss of LI with a context shift. LI was also lost over time, as indicated by the finding that Groups Consistent-1 and Inconsistent-1 displayed less freezing than Groups Consistent-21 and Inconsistent-21. Of particular interest, there was no interaction between context and test interval, suggesting that context change and delay had additive effects on LI. This suggests that the effect of time was not mediated via a change in recognition of the contexts. However, it must be noted that some studies have found that a delay interval between conditioning and test can enhance, rather than reduce, evidence for LI (De la Casa and Lubow, 2002; Lubow and De la Casa, 2005).

Parallels between latent inhibition and habituation

Early investigators noted the procedural similarities between LI and habituation and suggested that the two only differ with respect to the measure of stimulus effectiveness. As such, they considered that LI and habituation are underscored by common processes, and further, that LI is the result of habituation that generalizes between pre-exposure and conditioning (Ackil, Melgren, Halgren, and Frommer, 1969; Carlton and Vogel, 1967; Lantz, 1973; Schnur, 1971; Siegel, 1969). These ideas are supported by evidence that LI and habituation are sensitive to similar parametric variations. For example, both LI and habituation increase with the number of stimulus exposures, the duration of each exposure, and total exposure time (Thompson and Spencer, 1966). Schnur and Lubow (1976) noted that the effects of stimulus intensity and the interval between pre-exposures on LI were the same as their effects on habituation (Carew, Pinsker, and Kandel, 1972; Davis, 1970; Davis and Wagner, 1968; Graham, 1973; Thompson, Groves, Teyler, and Roemer, 1973; Wickelgren, 1967). That is, both LI and habituation have been found to increase with stimulus intensity and the interval between exposures when manipulation and measurement of these variables do not co-vary. Further, both LI and habituation can be disrupted by presentations of a novel stimulus (Best, Gemberling, and Johnson, 1979; Escobar, Arcediano, and Miller, 2005; Hall and Pearce, 1982; Killcross, 2001; Thompson and Spencer, 1966).

Despite the similar effects of these manipulations on LI and habituation, there is evidence that the two behavioural phenomena are determined by different mechanisms. For instance, Hall and Channell (1985a) found that changing the context after rats had been pre-exposed to a light did not affect the habituation of their orienting responses to the light (when the test context was familiar), but that the same rats showed attenuated LI when the light was later paired with food (in the test context). This result was then replicated by Hall and Honey (1989) in an experiment that assessed habituation by measuring the extent to which the pre-exposed stimulus produced unconditioned suppression of rats' lever-pressing for sucrose. Another dissociation between habituation and LI has been reported by Aguado *et al.* (1994), who found that a retention interval had different effects on LI and habituation in the CTA paradigm. A 16-day interval between pre-exposure and conditioning produced an attenuation of LI but did not reduce habituation of rats' neophobic responses to a flavour (i.e. neophobia was not reinstated). By contrast, Hall and Schachtman (1987) found that a 16-day retention interval between exposure to a light and test had the opposite effect in the conditioned suppression paradigm. They observed that habituation of rats' orienting responses to the light was disrupted after 16 days but LI that was evident (compared to a control group) when the light was trained as a CS. This same result was also obtained by Kasprow and Schachtman (1993) in the CTA paradigm. The discrepancies between these various studies are likely due to methodological differences. Whatever the source of this discrepancy, these various demonstrations that LI and habituation can be dissociated cast doubt on the claim that the two effects are determined by the same mechanism.

Parallels with extinction

Experimental extinction involves an initial phase of CS–US conditioning followed by a phase in which the CS is presented on its own—a reversal of the key stages in LI studies—and refers to the decline in conditioned responding that occurs over the latter phase. As such, Lubow and Moore (1959) noted that, in the cases of both extinction and LI, non-reinforced presentations of the CS (or the CS-to-be in the case of LI) result in reduced expression of the CR, and this persuaded them to describe LI as pre-extinction. Consistent with this view, parameters that influence LI have been found to regulate extinction in similar ways. That is, extinction has been found to increase with the number of extinction trials (Sandoz and Pham-Delegue, 2004), changes in CS duration (Haselgrove and Pearce, 2003), total extinction time (Drew, Yang, Ohyama, and Balsam, 2004; Shipley, 1974), and CS intensity (Taylor and Boakes, 2002). Furthermore, as in the case of LI, there is evidence (albeit contentious) that the interval between non-reinforced presentations of the CS influences extinction (for a review, see Cain, Blouin, and Barad, 2003).

The similarities between LI and extinction extend beyond those just described. Many studies have demonstrated that both effects are sensitive to the physical context (Bouton and Bolles, 1979; Bouton and King, 1983; Bouton and Swartzentruber, 1986, 1989; Channell and Hall, 1983; Gordon and Weaver, 1989; Hall and Minor, 1984; Harris, Jones, Bailey, and Westbrook, 2000; Lovibond *et al.*, 1984; Westbrook *et al.*, 2000). Both LI and extinction are also sensitive to the effects of time, with recovery of the CR after a delay (Aguado *et al.*, 1994; Brooks and Bouton, 1993; Hall and Minor, 1984; Killcross *et al.*, 1998; Kraemer and Spear, 1992; Rescorla and Cunningham, 1978; Westbrook *et al.*, 2000). In addition, both LI and extinction are affected by reminder treatments. In the case of extinction, presentations of the US prior to test produce reinstatement of the CR (Rescorla and Heth, 1975; see also Bouton, 1991), while a retrieval cue for extinction attenuates renewal caused by a return to the conditioning context (Brooks and Bouton, 1993). In the case of LI, presentations of the US prior to test produce a loss of LI (Kasprow, Catterson, Schachtman, and Miller, 1984), while LI is 'renewed' if pre-exposure and conditioning are conducted in different contexts and testing occurs in the context of pre-exposure (Brooks and Bouton, 1993; Bouton and Swartzentruber, 1989; Westbrook *et al.*, 2000).

Given the similar effects of parametric and procedural variations on extinction and LI (see Westbrook and Bouton, in press, for a recent discussion), some have suggested that both conditioning phenomena are produced by a set of common processes (Kraemer and Spear, 1992). For example, McSweeney and Swindell (2002) have argued that extinction is in part the result of habituation to the CS that develops during non-reinforced presentations, as has been suggested for LI. Bouton (1993, 1997) has argued that LI and extinction are both consequences of learning about non-reinforced presentations of the CS. We will discuss this account in turn when we discuss some of the many models of LI in the next section.

Models of latent inhibition

Based on the characteristics of LI reviewed above, many researchers have adopted the view that LI is the result of reduced stimulus processing, and explain the effect in terms of mechanisms that deal with attention and/or association (Le Pelley, 2004; Lubow, Weiner, and Schnur, 1981; Mackintosh, 1975; McLaren and Mackintosh, 2000; Pearce and Hall, 1980; Wagner, 1978, 1981). However, others argue that learning about pre-exposed stimuli is not impaired and that LI is the consequence of a deficit in the translation between learning and performance (Bouton, 1993, 1997; Miller and Matzel, 1988). This section provides a history and an overview of these models. The success of each model is evaluated in terms of its ability to explain several key findings reviewed in the previous section. In particular, we focus on the evidence that LI is reduced by a context change or by the passage of time, either between pre-exposure and conditioning or between conditioning and test, and that pre-exposure to the context prior to CS-pre-exposure both increases LI and makes it less context-specific.

Acquisition deficit models of latent inhibition

For decades, models of animal learning have proposed formal computations to describe putative changes in the strength (V) of CS–US associations during conditioning. The most common approach equates learning on a trial-by-trial basis with changes in associative strength (ΔV) calculated as a proportion of the arithmetic difference between the maximum associative strength supported by the US (λ) and the existing associative strength of the individual CS or of all CSs present on that trial (Bush and Mosteller, 1951; Rescorla and Wagner, 1972). In these 'error-correction' models, ΔV is constrained by multiplicative rate parameters that determine how quickly V approaches λ across trials. Thus, one simple way to allow these models to describe the learning deficits that characterize LI is to assume that pre-exposure affects one or more of these parameters, most commonly by reducing the salience or associability (α) of the stimulus. Models that take this approach are collectively referred to as 'acquisition-deficit models' since they explain LI as the result of a failure to encode the relationship between the pre-exposed stimulus and the US (Le Pelley, 2004; Lubow *et al.*, 1981; Mackintosh, 1975; McLaren and Mackintosh, 2000; Pearce and Hall, 1980; Wagner, 1978, 1981). These models are described in detail below.

Conditioned attention theory (Lubow, Weiner, and Schnur, 1981)

Conditioned attention theory (CAT, Lubow *et al.*, 1981) follows theories of selective attention (Sutherland and Mackintosh, 1971; Zeaman and House, 1963) in adopting a multiprocess view of learning where attention is conditioned to relevant stimuli, and this precedes the development of an association between them. It assumes that attention and inattention are conditioned in the same manner as Pavlovian responses, in that attention is conditioned to stimuli that are followed by environmental change and inattention is conditioned to stimuli that are not followed by environmental change. Accordingly, CAT explicitly regards LI as the consequence of conditioned inattention, and it predicts increased LI when pre-exposure involves manipulations that are known to enhance Pavlovian conditioning (i.e. any manipulation that promotes Pavlovian conditioning should, when applied during pre-exposure, promote the conditioning of inattention). Likewise, manipulations that reduce Pavlovian conditioning should, when applied to pre-exposure, decrease LI.

These predictions are partly supported in the literature. As reviewed above, LI increases with the number of pre-exposures (Lantz, 1973), intensity of the pre-exposed stimulus (Rodriguez and Alonso, 2002; Schnur and Lubow, 1976), and the interval between pre-exposures (Lantz, 1973; Schnur and Lubow,

1976)—manipulations that increase Pavlovian conditioning, and, therefore, the conditioning of inattention. Further, context pre-exposure facilitates LI (Hall and Channell, 1985b), a finding that CAT explains on the basis that conditioning of both attention and inattention is increased when stimuli are presented in a familiar context because that context receives less attention by virtue of its pre-exposure (Lubow, Rifkin, and Alec, 1976). CAT can also explain the finding that LI is attenuated when pre-exposures to a target stimulus are followed by paired presentations of a second stimulus (Lubow, Schnur, and Rifkin, 1976) because it predicts that an immediate environmental change is sufficient to offset the conditioning of inattention. However, CAT does not explicitly predict the context-specificity of LI or loss of LI over time, though it may be argued that a change of context, or the passage of time, between pre-exposure and conditioning restores attention to a pre-exposed stimulus through a generalization decrement process that produces a loss of conditioned inattention (the CR).

There is mixed support for CAT's claim that LI is decreased when pre-exposure involves manipulations that reduce Pavlovian conditioning. In support of CAT's claim, compound pre-exposure produces overshadowing of LI to the compound's elements (Honey and Hall, 1988; but see Rodriguez and Hall, 2008, for the opposite result). However, despite the fact that blocking is well known to reduce Pavlovian conditioning (Kamin, 1969), it has not been shown to attenuate LI when implemented during pre-exposure (Honey and Hall, 1988; Reed, 1995a, 1995b). Indeed, Honey and Hall (1988) found that pre-exposure to stimulus B alone prior to pre-exposure to the stimuli A and B in compound (i.e. B–, AB– pre-exposure) increased LI of A. Moreover, Reed (1995a, 1995b) used the same design and found that B–, AB– pre-exposure produced enhanced LI of A compared to a group that received pre-exposure to B alone followed by pre-exposure to A alone (Reed, Anderson, and Foster, 1999; Reed and Tsakanikos, 2002). These findings are not consistent with CAT.

Mackintosh (1975)

Mackintosh (1975) noted that theories of selective attention (Lovejoy, 1968; Sutherland and Mackintosh, 1971; Zeaman and House, 1963) assume that α is not a fixed consequence of a stimulus' physical properties (this contrasts with the treatment of α in the Rescorla-Wagner model). Mackintosh proposed that α is a function of how well a stimulus predicts its consequences: α increases if the stimulus predicts its consequences more accurately than other stimuli that are present on a conditioning trial, and α decreases if the stimulus predicts its consequences less accurately. Mackintosh argues that the size of associative change for any stimulus is determined by the discrepancy between λ and its own associative strength. According to Mackintosh, in addition to computing associative change on each trial, α of a CS changes as a consequence of the direct comparison between its predictive accuracy with that of other CSs present on that trial. Specifically, for any stimulus, A:

$$\Delta\alpha_A > 0 \text{ if } |\lambda - V_A| < |\lambda - V_X|,$$

$$\Delta\alpha_A < 0 \text{ if } |\lambda - V_A| \geq |\lambda - V_X|,$$

such that,

$$\Delta V_A = \alpha_A \times \theta \times (\lambda - V_A), \quad (5.1)$$

where θ is a general learning rate parameter, and V_X is the associative strength of all stimuli other than A that are present during conditioning of A. According to Mackintosh, LI occurs because pre-exposure to stimulus A causes α_A to decline as both A and the context equally predict non-reinforcement. Therefore, at the start of conditioning, α of the pre-exposed stimulus, A, will be lower than α of the novel stimulus, B, and hence conditioning of A will proceed more slowly than of B.

Mackintosh (1975) predicts that V_X regulates α_A during conditioning, regardless of whether the conditioning context is the same or different from the pre-exposure context. As such, the model fails to predict many of the key phenomena pertaining to LI. That is, Mackintosh does not predict the context-specificity of LI. The model also fails to give an account of how LI is facilitated by context pre-exposure.

Pearce-Hall (1980)

Like Mackintosh (1975), Pearce and Hall (1980) argued that the associability of a stimulus changes as a function of its associative strength, as well as that of its companion CSs. But, in direct contrast to the operations described by Mackintosh, the Pearce-Hall model assumes that the associability of a stimulus *declines* as a function of how accurately its consequences are predicted. Specifically, Pearce and Hall state that α is inversely related to the extent that a stimulus, or combination of stimuli, predicts some outcome. Thus, stimuli followed by consistent outcomes have low associability, while stimuli followed by inconsistent outcomes retain high associability. It should be obvious that the Pearce-Hall model stands in contrast to Mackintosh in allowing the associability of a stimulus to decline as it gains associative strength. The Pearce-Hall model attributes variations in conditioning to changes in CS effectiveness (α)

that are computed on each trial as a function of the prediction error ($\lambda - \Sigma V$). These changes are captured in the equation:

$$\alpha^n = \gamma \,|\, \lambda - V_T \,| + (1 - \gamma)\, \alpha^{n-1} \qquad (5.2)$$

where α^n is the value of α on trial n, calculated as an exponentially weighted moving average over all previous trials, γ is a scaling parameter that determines the gradient of this weighting, and V_T is the associative strength of all the stimuli that arc present on trial n (Pearce, Kaye, and Hall, 1981).

Applied to LI, the Pearce-Hall (1980) model suggests that a stimulus' associability declines during pre-exposure because it is *consistently* experienced without consequence (its outcome, nothing, is well predicted). As such, the model anticipates little learning on the first conditioning trial when the pre-exposed stimulus is paired with the nominal US, but it allows the pre-exposed stimulus' associability to gradually recover as a function of scaling parameter γ in Equation 2. This enables the Pearce-Hall model to explain how LI is affected by context shifts (Hall, 1991). Specifically, α will be slow to recover when pre-exposure and conditioning occur in the same context because changes in α are determined by a weighted average across the preceding trials. By contrast, when there is a change of context between pre-exposure and conditioning, attention to the CS may be more readily restored if trials in the original context are given little weight when computing α in the new context. However, because the Pearce-Hall model attributes LI to an acquisition deficit, it does not anticipate that evidence for LI will be recovered by a return to the pre-exposure context after conditioning. Nor does it predict that context pre-exposure attenuates the context-specificity of LI. Finally, the model does not predict that LI is increased by context pre-exposure or by pre-exposing a stimulus in compound with another already pre-exposed stimulus. This is because the prediction error during pre-exposure is the same whether the stimuli and context are novel or whether some of these stimuli are familiar and predict no outcome (in either case, $V_T = \lambda = 0$). This problem can be redressed if the Pearce-Hall model were to distinguish between the prediction of no outcome that is made by a pre-exposed stimulus versus the absence of any prediction with a novel stimulus (i.e. a novel stimulus neither predicts the outcome nor its absence; see Hall, 1991). That is, a novel stimulus or context generates a greater error than does a pre-exposed stimulus when there is no outcome. Therefore, pre-exposing a target stimulus in a familiar context, or in the presence of a pre-exposed stimulus, would generate less prediction error ($|\lambda - V_T|$) and α of the target stimulus would decline more rapidly, resulting in greater LI. A formalized description of this process has recently been presented by Hall and Rodriguez (in press). They describe how this elaborated Pearce-Hall model also explains a related finding – that pre-exposing a target stimulus in compound with a second stimulus can increase latent inhibition when the target stimulus is subsequently conditioned on its own, even though the same compound exposure during conditioning would produce overshadowing of the target stimulus (Rodriguez and Hall, 2008). According to Hall and Rodriguez, pre-exposing the two stimuli simultaneously produces more rapid learning about their consequence (no outcome), which causes a more rapid decline in α of each stimulus, and thus greater LI.

Le Pelley (2004)

Le Pelley (2004) has presented a hybrid model of CS-processing that combines aspects of both the Mackintosh (1975) and Pearce-Hall (1980) models. It uses Mackintosh's formulation to determine 'attentional associability', which essentially addresses the problem of stimulus selection, and it uses the Pearce-Hall formulation to determine 'salience associability' which specifies the amount that is learned about selected stimuli. These associability components, denoted by α_A and σ_A, respectively, are then multiplicatively combined in equations derived from extensions of Mackintosh (1975) that govern associative change.

When $R = \lambda - (\Sigma V^+ - \Sigma V^-)$ is greater than zero:

$$\Delta V_A = \alpha_A \times \sigma_A \times \beta_E \times (1 - V^+_A + V^-_A) \times | R |$$

When R is less than zero:

$$\Delta V_A = \alpha_A \times \sigma_A \times \beta_I \times (1 - V^-_A + V^+_A) \times | R | \qquad (5.3)$$

In these equations, β_E and β_I are learning rate parameters for excitatory and inhibitory learning, respectively, and V^+ and V^- refer to excitatory and inhibitory associative strength, respectively. Le Pelley allows α_A to range in value from 0.05 to 1 while σ_A only takes values in the truncated range from 0.5 to 1. This means that α has a greater capacity than σ to affect learning about a stimulus. For example, a stimulus for which α is low and σ is high will not be learned about; while a stimulus for which σ_A is low and α_A is high can still undergo a significant amount of associative change on a given conditioning episode.

Applied to LI, Le Pelley (2004) suggests that non-reinforced pre-exposure to a stimulus has no effect on α_A. This departs from Mackintosh's (1975) original contention that attention to a stimulus decreases unless it is a better predictor of some outcome (i.e. reinforcement or non-reinforcement) than other stimuli that are present. Instead, Le Pelley's account of LI is consistent with Pearce and Hall's (1980) proposal that the salience of a pre-exposed stimulus declines if it is repeatedly experienced without consequence. That is, non-reinforced pre-exposure to stimulus A reduces σ_A, which impairs stimulus A's ability to become associated with the reinforcer during conditioning. Not surprisingly, this explains many of the findings pertaining to LI in the same way as the Pearce-Hall (1980) model. However, its use of both a common error term and individual error terms for all stimuli present on a given conditioning episode potentially affords the model greater flexibility in explaining a range of other experimental data.

Wagner (1978, 1981)

Wagner's (1978) model of short term memory (STM) follows the Rescorla-Wagner (1972) model in using a summed prediction error, $\lambda - \Sigma V$, to describe changes in $V_{CS\text{–}US}$, but uses an additional prediction error, $1 - Sv$, to describe processing of the CS. That is, the STM model describes changes in $V_{CS\text{–}US}$ using a reformulation of the Rescorla-Wagner equation:

$$\Delta V = \alpha \times (l - Sv) \times \beta \times (\lambda - \Sigma V) \qquad (5.4)$$

where l captures the limited associability of the CS, and Sv refers to how well the CS is predicted by all the stimuli present on a given trial. Thus, Wagner's STM model anticipates LI because, during pre-exposure, the CS-to-be becomes readily predicted by the context, such that during conditioning, the CS is less effectively processed and changes in $V_{CS\text{–}US}$ are slow. Wagner (1981) subsequently developed further this account of both CS and US processing, but the manner by which it explains LI is essentially the same: context–CS associations interfere with CS–US conditioning by reducing CS effectiveness (i.e. associability).

Given its focus on the context as the mechanism by which CS associability is reduced, Wagner (1978, 1981) readily anticipates the evidence that LI is sensitive to manipulations of context. However, other empirical investigations into Wagner's account of LI have provided mixed results. Wagner's models predict that extinction of the context–CS association between CS pre-exposure and conditioning should reduce LI, but the evidence regarding this prediction is equivocal (Hall and Minor, 1984; Escobar, Arcediano, and Miller, 2002). Wagner also anticipates that pre-exposure to the context in advance of CS pre-exposure should reduce evidence for LI of the CS by latently inhibiting the development of context–CS associations. However, the available evidence indicates that context pre-exposure has the opposite effect, facilitating LI of the CS.

Models that regard latent inhibition as a deficit in performance

Acquisition-deficit models of LI are seriously challenged by findings that LI is diminished across a delay interval, or by presentation of a novel stimulus, between conditioning and test (Killcross, 2001; Killcross *et al.*, 1998; Kraemer and Roberts, 1984; Westbrook *et al.*, 2000). These models cannot account for such observations because they attribute LI to a deficit at the time of conditioning that obliges them to predict that the evidence for that deficit cannot change after the end of conditioning. For similar reasons, acquisition-deficit models cannot explain the effect of reminder treatments on LI, where facilitated responding to the pre-exposed stimulus (i.e. loss of LI) is observed following the presentation of a cue that was present during its conditioning. These shortcomings of acquisition-deficit models have resulted in the development of an alternative class of models that argue that LI is not due to a failure to encode the CS–US relationship during conditioning. Instead, they regard LI as the consequence of retrieval failure, consistent with Lubow and Moore's (1959) early view that pre-exposure produces a 'competing response that has become associated with the non-reinforced signal' (p417) and other early studies that discussed the possibility that LI reflects a deficit in performance (Lubow, 1965; Lubow and Siebert, 1969). In general, these models explain the effect of context shifts and reminder treatments by arguing that the passage of time and cues associated with the conditioning environment modulate the competition between different associations. There are various accounts of this performance-deficit approach to LI, some of which are described in detail below.

Comparator hypothesis

Miller and Matzel's (1988) comparator hypothesis argues that all stimuli in the conditioning environment become associated with each other. According to this hypothesis, each stimulus has a primary comparator and the extent to which it controls responding is directly related to the strength of its own 'direct' association with the US, and *inversely* related to the strength of its comparator's association with the US (the 'indirect' pathway). Consider the case of simple excitatory CS–US conditioning that occurs in some context. During an experimental session, CS–US, CS–context, and context–US associations all form as a consequence of the spatiotemporal contiguity between events, and the context becomes the primary comparator for the CS. As such, the strength of the CR on any given CS presentation is related to the extent to which the direct US activation, produced by the CS, exceeds the indirect US activation produced via CS–context and context–US links (see also Denniston, Savastano, and Miller, 2001, for the extended comparator hypothesis).

Applied to LI, the comparator hypothesis (Miller and Matzel, 1988) states that pre-exposure strengthens the association between the CS and context, and given that the context is the primary comparator for the CS, this strengthens the indirect activation of the US during conditioning (via CS–context and context–US links). This reduces the relative strength of direct US activation (CS–US). The model explains the various effects of reminder treatments and context shifts on LI by allowing retrieval of the links that mediate the indirect US representation to be either up- or down-regulated via changes in the status of the primary comparator. For example, changing the physical context between pre-exposure and conditioning reduces LI because the pre-exposure context – the primary comparator of the CS – is not associated with the US. However, this account does not explain why LI should be recovered when a post-conditioning test is conducted in the pre-exposure context, nor does it explain the effects of context pre-exposure on evidence for LI.

The comparator hypothesis also makes a unique prediction for the outcome of a design in which a pre-exposed stimulus, A, is conditioned in compound with another stimulus, B. The hypothesis assumes that A and B have the same associative strength (V) and these are greater than that of the context (i.e. $V_A = V_B > V_{context}$). However, pre-exposure to A establishes the context as A's primary comparator, while AB training establishes A as B's primary comparator. Therefore, when each CS is presented at test, V_A is high relative to its primary comparator (the context), whereas V_B is equal to its primary comparator (A). This means that the comparator hypothesis anticipates greater responding to A than B. In other words, pre-exposure to a stimulus offsets the performance deficit produced by overshadowing, while compound training offsets the performance deficit produced by latent inhibition (Denniston *et al.*, 2001). Experiments reported by Blaisdell, Bristol, Gunther, and Miller (1998) have been offered as support for these claims. However, other studies have not supported this prediction, and typically find that pre-exposure to A increases overshadowing of A by B (Carr, 1974, Holmes and Harris, 2009; Nakajima, Ka, and Imada, 1999; Nakajima and Nagaishi, 2005).

Rate estimation theory

Rate estimation theory (RET; Gallistel and Gibbon, 2000) developed from a tradition of research seeking to explain how the temporal intervals in a conditioning protocol control conditioned behaviour. This model altogether denies the existence of putative associations between CSs and USs in Pavlovian conditioning. Instead, RET suggests that during conditioning subjects accumulate a record of time during both presentations of the CS and the time between CS presentations. The accumulation of time continues across all trials in the conditioning protocol, and at the same time RET specifies that USs are also accumulated and attributed to either the CS or the background (b). Thus, RET predicts that CRs emerge when the estimated rate of reward in the presence of the CS (λ_{CS}) exceeds, by a large enough amount, the overall rate of reward ($\lambda_b + \lambda_{CS}$) in a ratio comparison [$\lambda_{CS}/(\lambda_{CS} + \lambda_b)$]. This allows RET to explain observations that CR acquisition is related to the C/T ratio, where C is the time between rewards (i.e. the cycle time) and T is the duration of the CS (i.e. the trial time) (Gibbon and Balsam, 1981).

Clearly, RET (Gallistel and Gibbon, 2000) stands in contrast to associative models in its general approach to describing the mechanisms of learning, and not surprisingly it offers a very different account of LI. RET anticipates LI on the basis that accumulated time in the pre-exposed stimulus is large at the start of the conditioning phase, thereby retarding growth of the estimation of reward in the presence of the pre-exposed CS. At the same time, accumulated time in the non-pre-exposed stimulus is zero at the start of the conditioning phase, resulting in rapid growth of the estimation of reward in the presence of the non-pre-exposed CS. Given equivalent rates of background reinforcement, RET therefore predicts that there will be less responding to a pre-exposed stimulus compared to a non-pre-exposed stimulus (i.e. disruption of the decision 'whether' to respond).

The account of LI provided by RET (Gallistel and Gibbon, 2000) fails to explain many of the characteristics of LI, including its sensitivity to changes in the physical and temporal context of pre-exposure. Because responding is determined by the ratio of λ_{CS} to λ_b, a change of context could only reduce LI (elevate responding) if it either increased λ_{CS} or reduced λ_b. Since there is no mechanism in RET by which this could occur—indeed a generalization decrement would predict a decrease in λ_{CS} or increase in λ_b—RET is left without any obvious means to account for context-specificity of LI. Moreover, it does not anticipate that context pre-exposure should facilitate LI, rather it predicts that context pre-exposure should increase conditioning (reduce LI) by reducing λ_b. Finally, the model does not predict a loss of LI with a delay between conditioning and test, because the estimations of λ_{CS} and λ_b should not change across a delay interval (unless that delay intervals were spent in the training context).

Bouton (1993, 1997)

Bouton (1993) reviewed the literature on a range of conditioning preparations, including extinction and LI, and noted that physical context switches and delay intervals influence conditioned performance in a manner that is often inconsistent with associative models. As such, he argued that reinforced and non-reinforced CS presentations result in the formation of CS–US and CS–noUS associations, respectively, and these associations compete with each other for expression. LI is attributed to proactive interference in which pre-exposure establishes CS–noUS memories that ultimately interfere with retrieval of the CS–US memories acquired during conditioning. Likewise, extinction is attributed to retroactive interference as retrieval of the CS–US memories is disrupted by the CS–noUS memories acquired during extinction. Bouton argues that retrieval of these contrasting associations is guided by contextual stimuli, including time itself, and, importantly, excitatory associations are assumed to be less sensitive to a change of context (physical or temporal) than inhibitory associations. Thus, he successfully accounts for the effects of physical context switches and delay intervals on extinction and LI. When testing occurs in either a different physical context, or after a conditioning-test delay (i.e. there is a temporal context shift), a cue for retrieval of the CS–noUS association is removed, resulting in more successful retrieval of the CS–US association, and stronger CRs. Similarly, with respect to the effect of reminder treatments, Bouton allows cues that were present during pre-exposure or extinction training to facilitate retrieval of the CS–noUS association, thereby attenuating CRs (recovering evidence for LI and extinction). Thus, these examples illustrate Bouton's view that extinction and LI can be modulated by altering the competition for retrieval of CS–US and CS–noUS associations, and hence, they show how both effects might be governed by the same processes (see Westbrook and Bouton, in press, for a recent discussion of this issue).

Several studies have shown that retrieval of excitatory CS–US associations is sensitive to context shifts following CS pre-exposure (Swartzentruber and Bouton, 1992; Westbrook *et al.*, 2000). This challenges the claim made by Bouton (1993) that CS–noUS associations are sensitive to contextual shifts but CS–US associations are not. Bouton (1997) revised his earlier proposal, arguing that it is second-learned associations that are context-dependent—an intuitive adjustment given that it is the second-learned association in both extinction and LI paradigms that produces ambiguity in what the CS predicts. Thus, much of the evidence concerning contextual control over responding in LI and extinction procedures can be accounted for if retrieval of CS–noUS associations and second-learned associations come under contextual control. However, one related finding that remains unexplained by this account is the demonstration that an excitatory CS–US association can come under contextual control following extinction of the CS (Harris *et al.*, 2000). This implies that *all* memories of the CS (CS–US and CS–noUS, whether learned first or second) are subject to some contextual control once there are contrasting memories about the association of CS with reinforcement. This conclusion could serve to resolve an outstanding discrepancy between two effects of stimulus pre-exposure. The observation that LI is sensitive to contextual change whereas habituation is not can be explained by assuming that what is learned across non-reinforced stimulus exposure initially generalizes across contexts, but this learning comes under contextual control once the stimulus is paired with reinforcement.

Models that invoke acquisition and performance deficits

Performance-deficit models of LI have considerable explanatory power owing to their flexibility in the mechanism of retrieval competition. However, these models stand to benefit from more detailed description of the underlying associative processes. Furthermore, just as acquisition-deficit models cannot explain evidence that LI is attenuated by delay intervals and reminder treatments post conditioning, there are other findings that are difficult to explain in the terms of any performance-deficit model. For example, Rescorla (1971) found that pre-exposure to a tone impaired both excitatory and inhibitory conditioning to the tone (Killcross and Balleine, 1996; Reiss and Wagner, 1972). This LI of conditioned inhibition is difficult to frame in terms of retrieval competition, such as the account developed by Bouton (1993, 1997), because this requires that the memory of non-reinforcement of the pre-exposed stimulus fails to be retrieved during a summation test, despite the fact that the pre-exposed stimulus has never been paired with reinforcement. Not surprisingly then, the vast array of findings on LI can be most successfully accommodated within the framework of models that combine aspects of both acquisition- and performance-deficit approaches to LI (Kruschke, 2001; McLaren and Mackintosh, 2000; Schmajuk, Lam, and Gray, 1996). The common feature of these models is that they incorporate a parameter that multiplicatively influences both associability (i.e. learning) and retrieval of associations (i.e. performance). They suggest that LI is the result of a partial failure to encode the CS–US relationship as well as a partial failure to retrieve whatever CS–US relationship has been encoded, and consequently, they are well placed to explain a range of experimental data pertaining to LI. These models are described in detail below.

Kruschke (2001)

Kruschke (2001) provides a more recent formulation of Mackintosh's (1975) idea that attention is shifted away from cues that are weaker predictors of their consequences compared to other stimuli that are present. Specifically, Kruschke suggests that whenever attention is directed to stimuli other than those that are predictive of the outcome (reinforcement or non-reinforcement) this generates an error, in the form of a smaller CR, because attention has been directed at stimuli that do not predict the outcome. To reduce this error, attention shifts away from non-predictive stimuli to the stimulus that is the most valid predictor of the outcome (be it reinforcement or no reinforcement). Learned changes in the associability of stimuli are quantified by a rule that minimizes the error generated at any given moment, and in this regard the model differs from that of Mackintosh in its explanation of LI. Kruschke suggests that prior to (or during) stimulus pre-exposure animals learn an association between the context and a variety of maintenance responses (i.e. general vigilance and preening, which can be regarded as equivalent to 'no response required'). When attention is then diverted to presentations of a stimulus during pre-exposure, this generates an error signal because there is an interruption to the maintenance responses yet no change in the response requirement. Under these conditions, attention shifts away from the pre-exposed stimulus to the already predictive contextual cues. This learned shift in attention away from the stimulus attenuates learning about the pre-exposed stimulus during subsequent conditioning and reduces the expression of any learning that has already occurred. Thus, Kruschke's model is similar to CAT (Lubow *et al.*, 1981) in treating 'no US' as an outcome that produces a decrease in attention to a pre-exposed stimulus. However, whereas CAT assumes that the CS–noUS association is responsible for the decrease in attention to the pre-exposed stimulus, Kruschke's model explicitly attributes the decrease in α_A to a blocking of the A-'noUS' association by the context during pre-exposure.

Kruschke (2001) explains the context-sensitivity of LI in a similar way to the explanation offered by CAT: a change of context between pre-exposure and conditioning provokes a generalization decrement that attenuates the learned shift in attention away from the pre-exposed stimulus. The loss of LI over time can be similarly explained as decay ('forgetting') of the learned shift in attention away from the CS. Kruschke also explicitly predicts that context pre-exposure increases LI (Hall and Channell, 1985b) on the basis that this allows for asymptotic conditioning of 'maintenance responses', thereby increasing the error generated when attention is shifted to the pre-exposed stimulus. However, the model would not predict that context pre-exposure attenuates the context-specificity of LI, as reported by McLaren *et al.* (1994).

McLaren and Mackintosh (2000)

Most of the models described above explain LI as due to changes in processing of the CS, either as a consequence of how reliably it signals its outcome, or how well its own occurrence or its outcome is signalled by other stimuli such as the context. But beyond this, these models treat the CS as a discrete event. McLaren and Mackintosh (2000) present a model that provides a more detailed description of the representations of the stimuli themselves, considering them to be composed of multiple elemental units. This level of description has provided new opportunities for considering mechanisms that might contribute to LI.

McLaren and Mackintosh (2000) assume that stimuli are represented by sets of elements that receive external and/or internal input when the relevant stimulus features are sampled. When a subject samples a particular feature, this causes a burst of external input to its representative element. At the same time, internal input to an individual element varies as a function of how well that element is predicted at any given moment. The discrepancy between an element's external input and its internal input determines its 'salience modulation', such that a large discrepancy results in a large boost to the element's activation. The activation strength of a CS element determines its associability, α, as well as the strength with which its activation spreads to US elements following conditioning. Therefore, as a stimulus becomes familiar, its elements receive stronger internal input and so receive a smaller boost to their activity. As a result, the stimulus' associability declines, as does its control over conditioned responding. In other words, for McLaren and Mackintosh, LI is both a decline in the associability of the pre-exposed stimulus and a decrement in conditioned responding to the CS.

McLaren and Mackintosh (2000) argue that elements are at their most salient and most associable level when the stimulus is novel since attention to the relevant features results in maximum external input and zero internal input. As a result, these elements become associated with each other, and further presentations of the stimulus increase the strength of associations between its concurrently active elements (known as 'unitization'). At the same time, the elements of the context also become associated with the elements of the stimulus. Thus both the associations between elements of the stimulus itself and the associations between the context and stimulus contribute to increasing the internal input to the stimulus elements and reducing their salience and associability. Because this modulation of salience and associability can be driven by both within-stimulus associations and context–stimulus associations, the McLaren-Mackintosh model anticipates that LI can be both context-specific and context-independent. For example, if a stimulus is pre-exposed in a novel context, strong context-stimulus associations will be acquired during pre-exposure, and the decline in the stimulus' salience and associability will depend on its being conditioned and tested in that context. That is, LI will be sensitive to a change in context prior to conditioning or test. However, if the context is pre-exposed in advance of stimulus pre-exposure, the context's own associability will be reduced at the time of stimulus pre-exposure due to strong internal input between the elements of the context (the context will have become unitized). As a result, stimulus pre-exposure will produce strong within-stimulus associations but relatively weak context-stimulus associations, and the decline in associability and salience of the stimulus' elements will generalize readily across contexts, as observed empirically by McLaren *et al.* (1994).

Schmajuk, Lam, and Gray (1996)

Schmajuk *et al.*'s (1996) model (SLG) consists of five distinct systems that depend on moment-to-moment fluctuations in stimulus processing. According to the model, the memory trace initiated by presenting a stimulus or its associate determines subsequent changes in attention, associative strength, expected outcomes, and novelty. These changes generate feedback and behavioural output in the form of both orienting and conditioned responses. Specifically, in SLG, the presentation of a CS activates a short-term memory trace, τ_{CS}, which in turn activates a representation of the CS (X_{CS}) into intermediate memory. The strength of X_{CS} is proportional to the strength of τ_{CS} plus activation of X_{CS} from other cues associated with the CS, with this combined input being multiplied by attention. Attention is affected by novelty, which is calculated as the absolute value of the discrepancy between the average observed and average predicted values of each stimulus in the current trial (i.e. when all events are well predicted, novelty is low). Attention to a CS (z_{CS}) is determined by the extent to which activation of X_{CS} coincides with novelty. This means that z_{CS} increases (to a maximum of +1) if a stimulus is presented or predicted under conditions where novelty is high, and decreases (to a minimum of −1) if it is presented or predicted under conditions where novelty is low. This is sometimes referred to as conditioned attention, and indeed, the function of z_{CS} in the model is consistent with that envisaged by Lubow *et al.* (1981).

According to SLG, the CS–US association is determined by the overlap of X_{CS} with presentation of the US, and the change in the CS–US association is proportional to the discrepancy between the observed and predicted values of the US (as described by Rescorla and Wagner, 1972). Indeed, like Le Pelley (2004), SLG describes learning as the product of two error terms: a common error term and a CS-specific error term. However, the SLG model is unique in its use of the construct novelty. Because novelty becomes associated with the stimulus trace, τ_{CS}, via conditioned attention, z_{CS}, it modulates the amplitude of the stimulus representation, X_{CS}. Because X_{CS} controls both the acquisition and retrieval of associations, such that larger values of X_{CS} produce faster learning and retrieve CS–US associations more strongly, attention can affect both rate of learning and performance of CRs.

The primary motivation for the SLG model was to develop a framework that adequately explained the many phenomena associated with LI (Schmajuk *et al.*, 1996). According to the model, LI occurs as a consequence of low environment novelty during pre-exposure that results in decreased attention (reduced z_{CS}) to the pre-exposed stimulus. This decreased attention affects activation of the stimulus representation, $X_{CS,}$ and the magnitude of LI thus depends on the time needed to re-establish X_{CS} by recovering z_{CS} during conditioning. Expressed differently, SLG proposes that attention to a stimulus declines, and thus the representation of the stimulus is depressed, because the stimulus is experienced under circumstances in which total environmental novelty is low (novelty is low because the stimulus is successfully predicted by both the context and itself). Because X_{CS} controls both the storage and retrieval of V_{CS-US}, LI is a failure of both acquisition and performance. Therefore, this allows the model to anticipate effects like the context-sensitivity of LI, because a context change increases novelty, which in turn increases attention, thus enabling more effective conditioning as well as stronger performance of CRs. Likewise, if a long delay is imposed between pre-exposure and conditioning, or between conditioning and test, the return to the context would be computed as relatively novel (e.g. the animal is out of the habit of being trained each day). This increase in novelty, and resultant recovery of attention, would explain the loss of LI across a delay. Further, exposure to the context prior to CS pre-exposure will accelerate the decline in attention to the CS because the increased familiarity of the context will reduce total environmental novelty.

Conclusions

The year 2009 marked 50 years since publication of the first demonstration that extensive exposure to a stimulus prior to conditioning retards the development of conditioned responding to that stimulus (Lubow and Moore, 1959). Since then, a great deal of empirical evidence has been amassed pertaining to the characteristics of this LI effect, and numerous theories have been constructed to explain the phenomenon. As reviewed in this chapter, some accounts have attributed LI to information learned during pre-exposure that interferes with retrieval of the CS–US association (Bouton, 1993, 1997; Miller and Matzel, 1988). However, a decline in attention to the pre-exposed stimulus has proved to be the most popular construct invoked to explain LI. This decline has been attributed to learning about the stimulus across pre-exposure, but the content of this learning differs between different theoretical accounts. Thus, LI has been attributed to: learning that the stimulus predicts nothing (Lubow *et al.*, 1981); learning that the stimulus is no better than the context in predicting the outcome (Kruschke, 2001; Mackintosh, 1975); learning that the stimulus' outcome is well predicted (Pearce and Hall, 1980; Le Pelley, 2004); learning to predict the stimulus itself (McLaren and Mackintosh, 2000; Wagner, 1978, 1981); and learning that the stimulus is associated with low environmental novelty (Schmajuk *et al.*, 1996). In each case, the loss of attention to the pre-exposed stimulus affects its processing in such a way as to retard subsequent learning during conditioning. An important feature of this mechanism is that it anticipates an effect of pre-exposure on any learning, and therefore explains why pre-exposure impairs both excitatory and inhibitory conditioning to a CS.

Two characteristics of LI have proved important in distinguishing between different accounts of LI. One is the evidence that LI is sensitive to changes in the physical or temporal context, such that LI is lost across a delay between pre-exposure and conditioning or when the CS is conditioned in a context different from that in which it was pre-exposed. To explain these effects, models that attribute LI to a decline in attention have suggested that a change in context or the passage of time can restore attention to the pre-exposed stimulus. The restoration of attention is attributed to a generalization decrement in conditioned inattention (Kruschke, 2001; Lubow *et al.*, 1981), or occurs because context–CS associations are responsible for the CS-processing deficit that causes LI (McLaren and Mackintosh, 2000; Wagner, 1978, 1981) or because the change in context (or passage of time) reinstates environmental novelty and thereby restores attention to the pre-exposed stimulus (Schmajuk *et al.*, 1996). The second characteristic of LI to be explained comes from demonstrations that LI is reduced across a delay between conditioning and test presentations of the CS, and that LI can be restored after conditioning by cues associated with pre-exposure. The fact that LI is sensitive to these post-conditioning manipulations indicates that LI is, at least in part, a deficit in responding to the CS, rather than being purely a learning deficit. While this evidence of a performance deficit is well captured by models that describe LI in those precise terms (Bouton, 1993; Miller and Matzel, 1988), it is also anticipated by some attention-based models (Kruschke, 2001; McLaren and Mackintosh, 2000;

Schmajuk *et al.*, 1996) in which the loss of attention affects the CS's ability to both acquire and retrieve the CS–US association. There is, however, one further property of LI, not discussed earlier, that cannot be accommodated so easily by current attention-based accounts.

Motivational state and latent inhibition

Killcross and Balleine (1996) investigated the extent to which LI is influenced by a subject's motivational state during pre-exposure. They pre-exposed rats to two auditory stimuli (S1 and S2) on alternate days: the rats were hungry during pre-exposure to S1 and thirsty during pre-exposure to S2. Next, both stimuli were conditioned with a food reinforcer for some rats and with a fluid reinforcer for other rats. During this conditioning phase, the rats were hungry and thirsty. Despite the fact that both stimuli were pre-exposed, the rats conditioned with food responded more to S2 than S1 during conditioning, while the rats conditioned with fluid responded more to S1 than S2. That is, rats were more impaired in learning the CS–food association for the stimulus that had been pre-exposed when they were hungry, and were more impaired in learning the CS–fluid association for the stimulus that had been pre-exposed when they were thirsty. Killcross and Balleine suggested that during pre-exposure the animals learned an association between the pre-exposed stimulus and their current motivational state, and that subsequent learning about a stimulus is impaired if it has been pre-exposed in a motivational state for which the US at conditioning is relevant, but not if it has been pre-exposed in a motivational state for which the US at conditioning is irrelevant. They tested the latter part of this claim in a second experiment. As in their first experiment, rats were pre-exposed to S1 while hungry and S2 while thirsty, before being conditioned with S1 and S2 using either food or fluid. However, unlike the previous experiment, the rats also received conditioning with a third stimulus, S3, which was entirely novel. This provided the opportunity to test whether either stimulus suffered LI. As in their previous experiment, conditioning proceeded more slowly for the stimulus pre-exposed in the motivational state that was relevant to the US compared to both other stimuli. Indeed, the novel stimulus and the stimulus pre-exposed in an irrelevant motivational state conditioned at the same rate. Thus, Killcross and Balleine argued that the difference in learning about the pre-exposed stimuli represented the full magnitude of LI, and that 'pre-exposure to a stimulus per se has little or no impact on the associability of that stimulus' (p37).

Kilcross and Balleine's findings indicate that at least some of what is learned during pre-exposure includes information about the motivational state in which the stimulus was pre-exposed and its relevance to the US in subsequent conditioning. This is important because, for accounts that attribute LI to a loss of attention, whatever effect motivational state may have on changes in attention to a stimulus during pre-exposure, those changes cannot interfere with learning or performance in a way that is selective for the type of US used during conditioning. Rather, the strong implication of this finding is that pre-exposure to a stimulus while hungry promotes learning that the pre-exposed stimulus has no relationship to food, and pre-exposure while thirsty promotes learning that the pre-exposed stimulus has no relationship to fluid. Clearly this implication is much more in keeping with associative interference accounts of LI (e.g. Bouton), and may well confirm Hall's (1991) conclusion that LI reflects a combination of associative interference and changes in attention to the pre-exposed CS. Nonetheless, even those accounts are troubled by the additional finding, reported by Killcross and Balleine, that motivational state during pre-exposure had the same effect on evidence for LI during subsequent inhibitory conditioning. That is, inhibitory conditioning to a CS was retarded if the CS had been pre-exposed while the rat was in a motivational state (hunger or thirst) relevant to the US (food or fluid) used during feature-negative training. Therefore, pre-exposure while hungry did not establish a CS–no food association, and pre-exposure while thirsty did not establish a CS–no water association. Rather, during pre-exposure, it appears that animals learn that a stimulus is unrelated to the type of reinforcement that is relevant to their current motivational state. This conclusion raises new questions about the nature of such learning, and its applicability to other paradigms in which there is no comparable motivational drive affecting learning (e.g. fear conditioning to a CS paired with shock).

We noted at the start of this chapter that the basic LI effect seems, on the surface, to be a very simple phenomenon, with the implication that it should be relatively easy to elucidate the mechanism underlying it. In contrast, the results reported by Killcross and Balleine provide a further demonstration that, even after 50 years, LI remains a problem for learning theorists, resistant to explanation in terms of a single, simple mechanism. Clearly progress has been made in understanding LI, but work remains to be done.

References

Ackil, J. E., Melgren, R. L., Halgren, C., & Frommer, G. P. (1969). Effects of CS preexposures on avoidance learning in rats with hippocampal lesions. *Journal of Comparative and Physiological Psychology*, **69**(4), 739–747.

Aguado, L., Symonds, M., & Hall, G. (1994). Interval between preexposure and test determines the magnitude of latent inhibition: Implications for an interference account. *Animal Learning and Behavior*, **22**, 188–194.

Ayers, J. J. B., Philbin, D., Cassidy, S., Bellino, L., & Redlinger, E. (1992). Some parameters of latent inhibition. *Learning and Motivation*, **23**, 269–287.

Best, M. R., Gemberling, G. A., & Johnson, P. E. (1979). Disrupting the conditioned stimulus preexposure effect in flavor-aversion learning: Effects of interoceptive distractor manipulations. *Journal of Experimental Psychology: Animal Behavior Processes*, **5**, 321–334.

Blaisdell, A. P., Bristol, A. S., Gunther, L. M., & Miller, R. R. (1998). Overshadowing and latent inhibition counteract each other: Support for the comparator hypothesis. *Journal of Experimental Psychology: Animal Behavior Processes*, **24**, 335–351.

Bouton, M. E. (1991). Context and retrieval in extinction and in other examples of interference in simple associative learning. In L. Dachowski & C. F. Flaherty (Eds), *Current topics in animal learning: Brain, emotion, and cognition* (pp 25–53). Hillsdale, NJ: Erlbaum.

Bouton, M. E. (1993). Context, time, and memory retrieval in the interference paradigms of Pavlovian learning. *Psychological Bulletin*, **114**, 80–99.

Bouton, M. E. (1997). Signals for whether versus when an event will occur. In Bouton, M. E. & Fanselow, M. S. (Eds), *Learning, motivation, and cognition: The functional behaviorism of Robert C. Bolles* (pp. 385–409). American Psychological Association. Washington.

Bouton, M. E. & Bolles, R. C. (1979). Contextual control of the extinction of conditioned fear. *Learning and Motivation*, **10**, 445–466.

Bouton, M. E. & King, D. A. (1983). Contextual control of the extinction of conditioned fear: Tests for the associative value of the context. *Journal of Experimental Psychology: Animal Behavior Processes*, **9**, 248–265.

Bouton, M. E. & Swartzentruber, D. (1986). Analysis of the associative and occasion-setting properties of contexts participating in a Pavlovian discrimination. *Journal of Experimental Psychology: Animal Behavior Processes*, **12**, 333–350.

Bouton, M. E. & Swartzentruber, D. (1989). Slow reacquisition following extinction: Coding, encoding, and retrieval mechanisms. *Journal of Experimental Psychology: Animal Behavior Processes*, **15**, 43–53.

Brooks, D. C. & Bouton, M. E. (1993). A retrieval cue for extinction attenuates spontaneous recovery. *Journal of Experimental Psychology: Animal Behavior Processes*, **19**, 77–89.

Bush, R. R. & Mosteller, F. (1951). A mathematical model for simple learning. *Psychological Review*, **58**, 313–323.

Cain, C. K., Blouin, A. M., & Barad, M. (2003). Temporally massed CS presentations generate more fear extinction than spaced presentations. *Journal of Experimental Psychology: Animal Behavior Processes*, **29**, 323–333.

Carew, T. J., Pinsker, H. M., & Kandel, E. R. (1972). Long term habituation of a defensive withdrawal reflex in aplysia. *Science*, **175**, 451–453.

Carr, A. F. (1974). Latent inhibition and overshadowing in conditioned emotional response conditioning with rats. *Journal of Comparative and Physiological Psychology*, **86**, 718–723.

Carlton, P. L. & Vogel, J. R. (1967). Habituation and conditioning. *Journal of Comparative and Physiological Psychology*, **63**(2), 348–351.

Channell, S. & Hall, G. (1983). Contextual effects in latent inhibition with an appetitive conditioning procedure. *Animal Learning & Behavior*, **11**, 67–74.

Crowell, C. R. & Anderson, D. C. (1972). Variations in intensity, interstimulus interval, and interval between preconditioning CS exposures and conditioning with rats. *Journal of Comparative and Physiological Psychology*, **79**(2), 291–298.

Davis, M. (1970). Effects of interstimulus interval length and variability on startle-response habituation in the rat. *Journal of Comparative and Physiological Psychology*, **72**(2), 177–192.

Davis, M. & Wagner, A. R. (1968). Startle responsiveness after habituation to different intensities of tone. *Psychonomic Science*, **12**, 337–338.

De la Casa, L. G. & Lubow, R. E. (2002). An empirical analysis of the super-latent inhibition effect. *Animal Learning and Behavior*, **30**, 112–120.

Denniston, J. C., Savastano, H. I., & Miller, R. R. (2001). The extended comparator hypothesis: Learning by contiguity, responding by relative strength. In R. R. Mowrer & S. B. Klein (Eds), *Handbook of contemporary learning* (pp 65–117). Mahwah, NJ: Lawrence Erlbaum Associates, Inc.

DeVietti, T. L. & Barrett, O. V. (1986). Latent inhibition: No effect of intertribal interval of the preexposure trials. *Bulletin of the Psychonomic Society*, **24**(6), 453–455.

Drew, M. R., Yang, C., Ohyama, T., & Balsam, P. D. (2004). Temporal specificity of extinction in autoshaping. *Journal of Experimental Psychology: Animal Behavior Processes*, **30**, 163–176.

Escobar, M., Arcediano, F., & Miller, R. R. (2002). Latent inhibition and contextual associations. *Journal of Experimental Psychology: Animal Behavior Processes*, **28**, 123–136.

Escobar, M., Arcediano, F., & Miller, R. R. (2005). Disruption of latent inhibition by interpolation of task irrelevant stimulation between preexposure and conditioning. *Learning and Behavior*, **33**(3), 371–385.

Gallistel, C. R. & Gibbon, J. (2000). Time, rate, and conditioning. *Psychological Review*, **107**, **2**, 289–344.

Gibbon, J. & Balsam, P. D. (1981). The spread of association in time. In C. Locurto, H. S. Terrace, & J. Gibbon (Eds), *Autoshaping and conditioning theory* (pp. 285–308). New York: Academic Press.

Gordon, W. C. & Weaver, M. S. (1989). Cue-induced transfer of CS preexposure effects across contexts. *Animal Learning and Behavior*, **17**, 409–417.

Graham, F. K. (1973). Habituation and dishabituation of responses innervated by the autonomic nervous system. In H. V. S. Peeke & M. J. Herz (Eds), *Habituation: Behavioral Studies* (Vol. 1). New York: Academic Press, 1973.

Hall, G. (1991). *Perceptual and associative learning*. New York: Oxford University Press.

Hall, G. & Channell, S. (1985a). Differential effects of contextual change on latent inhibition and on the habituation of an orienting response. *Journal of Experimental Psychology: Animal Behavior Processes*, **11**, 470–481.

Hall, G. & Channell, S. (1985b). Latent inhibition and conditioning after preexposure to the training context. *Learning and Motivation*, **16**, 381–397.

Hall, G. & Honey, R. C. (1989). Contextual effects in conditioning, latent inhibition, and habituation: Associative and retrieval functions of contextual cues. *Journal of Experimental Psychology: Animal Behavior Processes*, **15**, 232–241.

Hall, G. & Minor, H. (1984). A search for context-stimulus associations in latent inhibition. *Quarterly Journal of Experimental Psychology*, **36B**, 145–169.

Hall, G. & Pearce, J. M. (1982). Restoring the associability of a pre-exposed CS by a surprising event. *Quarterly Journal of Experimental Psychology*, **34B**, 127–140.

Hall, G. & Rodriguez, G. (in press). Associative and nonassociative processes in latent inhibition: An elaboration of the Pearce-Hall model. In: R. E. Lubow & I. Weiner (Eds), *Latent inhibition: Data, theories, and applications to schizophrenia.* New York: Cambridge University Press.

Hall, G. & Schachtman, T. R. (1987). Differential effects of a retention interval on latent inhibition and the habituation of an orienting response. *Animal Learning and Behavior*, **15**, 76–82.

Harris, J. A., Jones, M. L., Bailey, G. K., & Westbrook, R. F. (2000). Contextual control over conditioned responding in an extinction paradigm. *Journal of Experimental Psychology: Animal Behavior Processes*, **26**, 174–185.

Haselgrove, M. & Pearce, J. M. (2003). Facilitation of extinction by an increase or a decrease in trial duration. *Journal of Experimental Psychology: Animal Behavior Processes*, **29**, 153–166.

Holmes, N. M. & Harris, J. A. (2009). The loss of latent inhibition across compound conditioning. *Journal of Experimental Psychology: Animal Behavior Processes*, **35**, 328–339.

Honey, R. C. & Hall, G. (1988). Overshadowing and blocking procedures in latent inhibition. *Quarterly Journal of Experimental Psychology*, **40B**, 163–186.

Kamin, L. J. (1969). Predictability, surprise, attention, and conditioning. In B. A. Campbell & R. M. Church (Eds), *Punishment and Aversive Behavior* (pp. 276–296). New York: Appleton-Century-Crofts

Kasprow, W. J., Catterson, D., Schachtman, T. R., & Miller, R. R. (1984). Attenuation of latent inhibition by post-acquisition reminder. *Quarterly Journal of Experimental Psychology*, **36B**, 53–63.

Kasprow, W. J. & Schachtman, T. R. (1993). Differential effects of distractor stimuli and the interval between flavor exposures on neophobia and latent inhibition. *Psychological Record*, **43**(1), 25–37.

Killcross, S. (2001). Loss of latent inhibition in conditioned taste aversion following exposure to a novel flavour before test. *Quarterly Journal of Experimental Psychology*, **54B**, 271–288.

Killcross, S. & Balleine, B. (1996). Role of primary motivation in stimulus preexposure effects. *Journal of Experimental Psychology: Animal Behavior Processes*, **22**, 32–42.

Killcross, A. S., Kiernan, M. J., Dwyer, D., & Westbrook, R. F. (1998). Effects of retention interval on latent inhibition and perceptual learning. *Quarterly Journal of Experimental Psychology*, **51B**, 59–74.

Kraemer, P. J. & Roberts, W. A. (1984). The influence of flavor preexposure and test interval on conditioned taste aversions in the rat. *Learning and Motivation*, **15**, 259–278.

Kraemer, P. J. & Spear, N. E. (1992). The effect of nonreinforced stimulus exposure on the strength of a conditioned taste aversion as a function of retention interval: Do latent inhibition and extinction involve a shared process? *Animal Learning and Behavior*, **20**, 1–7.

Kruschke, J. K. (2001). Toward a unified model of attention in associative learning. *Journal of Mathematical Psychology*, **45**, 812–863.

Lantz, A. E. (1973). Effect of number of trials, interstimulus interval, and dishabituation during CS habituation on subsequent conditioning in a CER paradigm. *Animal Learning and Behavior*, **1**, 273–277.

Le Pelley, M. E. (2004). The role of associative history in models of associative learning: A selective review and hybrid model. *Quarterly Journal of Experimental Psychology*, **57B**, 193–243.

Lovejoy, E. (1968). *Attention in discrimination learning*. San Francisco: Holden-Day.

Lovibond, P. F., Preston, G. C., & Mackintosh, N. J. (1984). Context specificity of conditioning, extinction, and latent inhibition. *Journal of Experimental Psychology: Animal Behavior Processes*, **10**, 360–375.

Lubow, R. E. (1965). Latent inhibition: Effects of frequency of nonreinforced preexposure of the CS. *Journal of Comparative and Physiological Psychology*, **60**(3), 454–457.

Lubow, R. E. (1973). Latent inhibition. *Psychological Bulletin*, **79**, 398–407.

Lubow, R. E. (1989). *Latent inhibition and conditioned attention theory*. Cambridge University Press.

Lubow, R. E. & De la Casa, L. G. (2005). Time-induced super-latent inhibition is dependent on the distinctiveness of the retention-interval context from the other experimental contexts. *Learning and Motivation*, **36**, 322–330.

Lubow, R. E. & Moore, A. U. (1959). Latent inhibition: The effect of non-reinforced pre-exposure to the conditional stimulus. *Journal of Comparative and Physiological Psychology*, **52**, 415–419.

Lubow, R. E., Rifkin, B., & Alec, M. (1976). The context effect: The relationship between stimulus preexposure and environmental preexposure determines subsequent learning. *Journal of Experimental Psychology: Animal Behavior Processes*, **2**, 38–47.

Lubow, R. E., Schnur, P., & Rifkin, B. (1976) Latent inhibition and conditioned attention theory. *Journal of Experimental Psychology: Animal Behavior Processes*, **2**, 163–174.

Lubow, R. E. & Siebert, L. (1969). Latent inhibition within the CER paradigm. *Journal of Comparative and Physiological Psychology*, **68**(1), 136–138.

Lubow, R. E. & Weiner, I. (in press). *Latent Inhibition: Data, theories, and applications to schizophrenia*. New York: Cambridge University Press.

Lubow, R. E., Weiner, I., & Schnur, P. (1981). Conditioned attention theory. In G. H. Bower (Ed.), *The psychology of learning and motivation* (Vol. 15, pp. 1–49). San Diego, CA: Academic Press.

McLaren, I. P. L., Bennett, C. H., Plaisted, K. C., Aitken, M. R. F., & Mackintosh, N. J. (1994). Latent inhibition, context specificity, and context familiarity. *Quarterly Journal of Experimental Psychology*, **47B**, 387–400.

McLaren, I. P. L. & Mackintosh, N. J. (2000). An elemental model of associative learning: I. Latent inhibition and perceptual learning. *Animal Learning and Behavior*, **28**, 211–246.

McSweeney, F. K. & Swindell, S. (2002). Common processes may contribute to extinction and habituation. *Journal of General Psychology*, **129**(4), 364–400.

Miller, R. R. & Matzel, L. D. (1988). The comparator hypothesis: A response rule for the expression of associations. In G. H. Bower (Ed.), *The psychology of learning and motivation* (Vol. 22, pp. 51–92). San Diego, CA: Academic Press.

Nakajima, S., Ka, H., & Imada, H. (1999). Summation of overshadowing and latent inhibition in rats' conditioned taste aversion: scapegoat technique works for familiar meals. *Appetite*, **33**, 299–307.

Nakajima, S. & Nagaishi, T. (2005). Summation of latent inhibition and overshadowing in a generalized bait shyness paradigm of rats. *Behavioural Processes*, **69**, 369–377.

Pearce, J. M. & Hall, G. (1980). A model for Pavlovian learning: Variations in the effectiveness of conditioned but not unconditioned stimuli. *Psychological Review*, **87**, 532–552.

Pearce, J. M., Kaye, H. & Hall, G. (1981). Predictive accuracy and stimulus associability. In M. L. Commons, R. J. Herrnstein, & A. R. Wagner (Eds), *Quantitative Analyses of Behavior: Acquisition* (Vol. 3). Cambridge, MA: Ballinger.

Reed, P. (1995a). Enhanced latent inhibition following pre-exposure. *Quarterly Journal of Experimental Psychology*, **48B**, 32–45.

Reed, P. (1995b). Compound stimulus preexposure effects in an appetitive conditioning procedure. *Learning and Motivation*, **26**, 1–10.

Reed, P., Anderson, E., & Foster, C. (1999). Modality of stimulus effects in compound preexposure procedures: Associative influences in enhanced latent inhibition. *Learning and Motivation*, **30**, 35–52.

Reed, P. & Tsakanikos, E. (2002). The influence of a distractor during compound preexposure on latent inhibition. *Animal Learning and Behavior*, **30**, 121–131.

Reiss, S. & Wagner, A. R. (1972). CS habituation produces a latent inhibition effect but no active conditioned inhibition. *Learning and Motivation*, **3**, 237–245.

Rescorla, R. A. (1971). Summation and retardation tests of latent inhibition. *Journal of Comparative and Physiological Psychology*, **75**(1), 77–81.

Rescorla, R. A. & Cunningham, C. L. (1978). Recovery of the US representation over time during extinction. *Learning and Motivation*, **9**, 373–391.

Rescorla, R. A. & Heth, C. D. (1975). Reinstatement of fear to an extinguished conditioned stimulus. *Journal of Experimental Psychology: Animal Behavior Processes*, **1**, 88–96.

Rescorla, R. A. & Wagner, A. R. (1972). A theory of Pavlovian conditioning: Variations in the effectiveness of reinforcement and nonreinforcement. In A. R. Black & W. F. Prokasky (Eds), *Classical conditioning II* (pp. 64–99). New York: Appleton-Century-Crofts.

Rodriguez, G. & Alonso, G. (2002). Latent inhibition as a function of CS intensity in taste aversion learning. *Behavioral Processes*, **60**, 61–67.

Rodriguez, G. & Hall, G. (2008). Potentiation of latent inhibition. *Journal of Experimental Psychology: Animal Behavior Processes*, **34**, 352–360.

Sandoz, J. & Pham-Delegue, M. (2004). Spontaneous recovery after extinction of the conditioned proboscis extension response in honeybees. *Learning and Memory*, **11**(5), 586–597.

Schmajuk, N. A., Lam, Y., & Gray, J. A. (1996). Latent inhibition: A neural network approach. *Journal of Experimental Psychology: Animal Behavior Processes*, **22**, 321–349.

Schnur, P. (1971). Selective attention: Effect of element preexposure on compound conditioning in rats. *Journal of Comparative and Physiological Psychology*, **76**(1), 123–130.

Schnur, P. & Lubow, R. E. (1976). Latent inhibition: The effects of ITI and CS intensity during pre-exposure. *Learning and Motivation*, **7**, 540–550.

Shipley, R. H. (1974). Extinction of conditioned fear in rats as a function of several parameters of CS exposure. *Journal of Comparative and Physiological Psychology*, **87**(4), 699–707.

Siegel, S. (1969). Effect of CS habituation on eyelid conditioning. *Journal of Comparative and Physiological Psychology*, **68**(2), 245–248.

Sutherland, N. S. & Mackintosh, N. J. (1971). *Mechanisms of animal discrimination learning*. New York: Academic Press.

Swartzentruber, D. & Bouton, M. E. (1992). Context sensitivity of conditioned suppression following preexposure to the conditioned stimulus. *Animal Learning and Behavior*, **20**, 97–103.

Taylor, K. M. & Boakes, R. A. (2002). Extinction of conditioned taste aversions: Effects of concentration and overshadowing. *Quarterly Journal of Experimental Psychology*, **55B**, 213–239.

Thompson, R. F., Groves, P. M., Teyler, T. J., & Roemer, R. A. (1973). A dual-process theory of habituation: Theory and behavior. In H. V. S. Peeke & M. J. Herz (Eds), *Habituation: Behavioral Studies* (Vol. 1). New York: Academic Press, 1973.

Thompson, R. F. & Spencer, W. A. (1966). Habituation: A model phenomenon for the study of neuronal substrates of behavior. *Psychological Review*, **73**, 16–43.

Wagner, A. R. (1978). Expectancies and the priming of STM. In: S. H. Hulse, H. Fowler, & W. K. Honig (*Eds*), *Cognitive processes in animal behavior* (pp. 177–209). Hillsdale, NJ: Lawrence Erlbaum Associates, Inc.

Wagner, A. R. (1981). SOP: A model of automatic memory processing in animal behaviour. In N. E. Spear & R. R. Miller (Eds), *Information processing in animals: Memory mechanisms* (pp. 5–47). Hillsdale, NJ: Lawrence Erlbaum Associates, Inc.

Westbrook, R. F. & Bouton, M. E. (in press). Latent inhibition and extinction: Their signature phenomena and the role of prediction error. In: R. Lubow and I. Weiner (Eds), *Latent Inhibition: Data, theories, and applications to schizophrenia*. New York: Cambridge University Press.

Westbrook, R. F., Jones, M. L., Bailey, G. K., & Harris, J. A. (2000). Contextual control over conditioned responding in a latent inhibition paradigm. *Journal of Experimental Psychology: Animal Behavior Processes*, **26**, 157–173.

Wickelgren, B. G. (1967). Habituation of spinal interneurons. *Journal of Neurophysiology*, *30* (6), 1424–1438.

Zeaman, D. & House, B. J. (1963). The role of attention in retardate discrimination learning. In N. R. Ellis (Ed.), *Handbook of mental deficiency: Psychological theory and research*. New York: McGraw-Hill.

Chapter 6

Attention and perceptual learning

Ian P. L. McLaren, Andrew J. Wills, and Steven Graham

Perceptual learning as a phenomenon

We are all experts. Each one of us is able to effortlessly distinguish between a large number of people that we encounter in our everyday lives. When considered as stimuli in the abstract this is a difficult discrimination task as the stimuli are all rather similar to one another, yet we can identify an individual in a moment with an accuracy that would put a supercomputer to shame. We will argue that this particular expertise comes about because we are very experienced with the class of stimuli in question (in this case, faces), and that it is simply a more commonplace example of a type of expertise that we can study in twitchers (experts in the identification of birds), field botanists (experts in plant identification in a particular habitat), and dog show judges (experts in fine discriminations betweens dogs drawn from the same class such as gundogs; as reported in Diamond and Carey, 1986). We can also manipulate experience with stimuli in the laboratory and show that an enhanced ability to discriminate between stimuli is a consequence of the right kind of experience with the right kind of stimuli (McLaren, Leevers, and Mackintosh 1994; McLaren, 1997; Lavis and Mitchell, 2006; Mundy, Honey, and Dwyer, 2007). This phenomenon goes by the name of perceptual learning, and many people's first reaction to it is to make the claim that experience helps one learn what aspects of the stimulus to attend to. Perceptual learning, in its broadest sense, can be understood to be any enhancement of learning to a stimulus as a consequence of experience with that stimulus. Thus the proposal would be that perceptual learning is a consequence of the allocation of attention based on past experience with a particular stimulus type. This assertion is a natural (and plausible) response to the data, but is it the correct line to take? The question addressed in this chapter is whether perceptual learning phenomena can be explained by appealing to mechanisms that control attention (we will conclude that in some cases they can) or whether there is a need to appeal to other mechanisms as well (we hope to show that there is). Starting with some examples of what might be considered perceptual learning phenomena taken from our early work, we go on to discuss them in the context of current research on perceptual learning, with an emphasis on analyzing the possible role that attention might play in producing these effects. We will focus on perceptual learning in humans, but will allow ourselves to appeal to evidence from infrahuman studies where appropriate.

Enhanced acquisition of a discrimination after stimulus exposure

The general idea of the experiments reported here was to have human participants learn discriminations in much the same circumstances as an animal (such as the rat) might. In the test or discrimination phase, a pair of stimuli would be presented side by side on a visual display with the arbitrarily designated 'positive' stimulus equally often on the left or right. Participants were allowed to choose one of the stimuli by means of a keypress, and received immediate feedback as to the correctness of the choice. One problem with perceptual learning experiments is the need to pre-expose participants to stimuli in such a way as to guarantee that they attend to the stimuli, but receive no information specific to the discrimination problem presented after the pre-exposure phase (otherwise the procedure would be one of pre-training rather than pre-exposure). In the first two experiments, we will consider exploiting the fact that we were carrying out a series of experiments on delayed matching of visual stimuli in which participants were exposed to 'pattern' stimuli and 'masks' over a substantial number of trials. The pattern stimuli were the experimental items in the delayed matching task: participants had to decide if a probe was the same as, or different from, a prime presented a few seconds before the probe. The masks intervened between prime and probe. Neither of the methods of exposure to these stimuli relates to the discrimination learning task used in the experiments reported in this chapter, and so we exploited this fact by 'piggy-backing' perceptual learning experiments onto the delayed matching sessions.

The stimuli used in Experiment 1 were quasi-random dot patterns generated with certain constraints in operation to favour the formation of interesting, but difficult to describe, blobs or clumps of dots. Examples are shown in the top panel of Figure 6.1. This type of stimulus was used because it had little or no linguistic component, but was nevertheless complex and detailed. Each participant saw four different pairs of stimuli in this experiment; two of the pairs had been extensively pre-exposed (exposure to each stimulus was more than 96 sec and less than 152 sec), while the other two (control) pairs were taken from the stimuli to which another participant was pre-exposed, and so were novel for this participant.

Fig. 6.1 Top panel: Examples of the dot pattern stimuli used in Experiment 1. Bottom panel: Examples of the chequerboard stimuli used in Experiment 2.

As previously indicated, in the test or discrimination phase, a pair of stimuli would be presented side by side on a VDU with the arbitrarily designated 'positive' stimulus equally often on the left or right. Participants were allowed to choose one of the stimuli by means of a keypress, and received immediate feedback as to the correctness of the choice. The feedback given was either 'correct' displayed in the centre of the screen or 'error' and a beep if the wrong stimulus was chosen. It was emphasized to the participants that the designation of one member of a stimulus pair as 'correct' was arbitrary and this designation was consistent within the experiment, and that members of the pair would always be presented together but with either member equally often to the left or right of the other. Summary feedback on the number of errors and the mean correct reaction time was given at the end of each block. The results for the accuracy measure (our main dependent variable) for the pre-exposed and non-pre-exposed discriminations are shown in the top panel of Figure 6.2. Statistical analysis confirmed that the effect of pre-exposure was significant, $F(1,18) = 8.26$, $p < 0.01$, with performance on the pre-exposed stimuli superior to controls. Latencies were in line with the error data, with time to respond significantly longer for the novel stimuli.

What have we learned from this simple experiment? It is possible to conclude that experience with the stimuli used here facilitated the subsequent

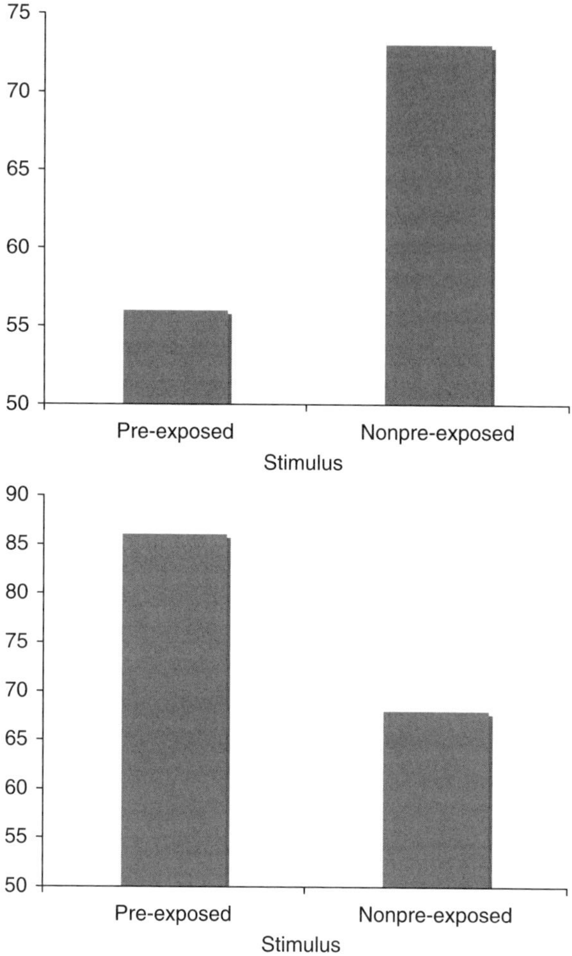

Fig. 6.2 Top panel: Results of Experiment 1 for the dot pattern stimuli. Chance performance = 50%. Bottom panel: Results of Experiment 2 for the chequerboard stimuli. Chance performance = 50%. In both cases, the non-pre-exposed control stimuli were also used as experimental (pre-exposed) stimuli for a different participant, so that stimuli were counterbalanced across conditions.

acquisition of a discrimination involving those stimuli. We should acknowledge at once that the type of pre-exposure to the stimuli given here is not that most commonly employed in typical perceptual learning experiments nowadays. The use of a paradigm that would have encouraged participants to try and differentiate between the stimuli (a prerequisite to successfully making the same/different judgement that was required of them on each trial) would be considered suspect in that it contains an element of pre-training on the discrimination that follows. Nevertheless, the learning enhancement effect demonstrated in this experiment was, to our knowledge, the first of its kind at the time when it was conducted. The more typical result in the previous research had no effect of pre-exposure with adults and older children unless special procedures were used. Lubow, Caspy, and Schnur (1982) reported no effect on discrimination learning with simple pre-exposure, and Lubow, Alek, and Arzy (1975) found no effect of pre-exposure on simple learning. Pre-exposure in children resulted in a retardation in learning, a phenomenon termed the stimulus familiarization effect by Cantor (1969) who reviewed a number of studies on this point (Kaniel and Lubow, 1986). The same result (i.e. a retardation in acquisition of the discrimination) can be obtained in adults or older children if pre-exposure takes place using an 'incidental learning' procedure (Lubow *et al.*, 1982; Ginton, Urca, and Lubow, 1975), which involved pre-exposing the stimuli as an irrelevant component of some other task. The only experiment to have produced an enhancement in discrimination learning after stimulus pre-exposure was one by Lubow, Rifkin, and Alek (1976) with five-year-olds, where enhanced discrimination occurred after a change of context. Even in this study, if discrimination learning took place in the same context as pre-exposure (as it does here) then acquisition was significantly retarded compared to controls.

The results taken from the literature on stimulus pre-exposure at the time, then, suggested that first of all, the enhancement in discrimination learning observed here was unusual, and secondly, that if stimuli had instead been pre-exposed using an incidental learning procedure then a retardation in discrimination learning might have been expected. We shall defer any explanation of these results until we have presented the next experiment in which a set of eight stimuli unique to each participant were used as masks in the delayed matching task. This experiment naturally follows on from Experiment 1 and will enable us to make contact with the literature on incidental pre-exposure. The stimuli used in this experiment were somewhat different from the dot patterns used in Experiment 1, as they had to be easily discriminable from them to avoid participants erroneously responding to them, and played no role in the experiment other than that of masking the dot pattern stimuli.

Retarded acquisition of a discrimination after stimulus exposure

The design of this experiment was exactly as for Experiment 1, as were the procedures used in it. The only difference was in the stimuli used and the method of pre-exposure. Examples of the stimuli used in Experiment 2 are shown in the bottom panel of Figure 6.1. These 16 × 16 (where each square is 4 × 4 pixels) chequerboard-type stimuli were generated as follows. Stimuli were generated at random for each participant by making the probability that a square would be black 0.5, then two more were generated by changing a randomly designated square (i.e. one of the 16) in each of the 16 rows. This gave pairs of very similar stimuli (as shown in the example) for each participant. Control stimuli were taken from those used as experimental stimuli by another participant. Pre-exposure was accomplished by using these stimuli as masks in the delayed matching reaction time task described earlier. The masks were quite easily discriminated from the dot patterns, having a coarser grain to their features, and there was every reason for the participant to fixate on the masks because the test pattern on that delayed matching trial would soon appear in the same place. Total exposure for each mask was 72 sec over 72 separate presentations, half of which occurred in the same session as this experiment and just prior to it, with the other half taking place in an earlier session on the previous day.

The results of this study were quite different from those of Experiment 1 and are shown in the bottom panel of Figure 6.2. Statistical analysis confirmed that the effect of pre-exposure was significant with the pre-exposed stimuli discriminated worse than the novel pair, $F(1,19) = 7.66$, $p < 0.025$. Reaction times showed a similar pattern. Thus pre-exposure now resulted in slower learning. Why is there this difference between the results of our two experiments? Clearly the type of pre-exposure given is a key factor. We have already discussed how the pre-exposure regime in Experiment 1 provided an incentive for participants to learn to tell the stimuli in that experiment apart. The pre-exposure technique in Experiment 2 does no such thing; instead its incidental nature would, if anything, provide some incentive for participants to ignore these stimuli as they focussed on the ones that mattered (the dot patterns) during that phase of the experiment. Thus one general class of explanation of these results can be identified as being attentional in nature. It proposes that participants learn to attend, or not to attend, to the stimuli according to the type of pre-exposure given. Effectively, this raises or lowers stimulus salience, thus enhancing or retarding learning to these stimuli. Detailed models that fall into this class would be the conditioned attention theory of Lubow, Weiner, and Schnur (1981), later refined by Lubow (1989), and the models dealing with negative priming introduced by Tipper (1985). Although the processes involved in negative priming were once thought to operate on a much shorter time scale, we now know that this does not have to be the case (Treisman and DeSchepper, 1996; Grison, Tipper, and Hewitt, 2005). If we adopt a Lubowian terminology for the moment, the general idea here is that stimuli can have attention conditioned to them—such that stimuli to which one is deliberately paying attention gradually become able to elicit an attentional response automatically (and hence can enter into learning more effectively), whereas stimuli that the participant is trying to ignore can instead come to suffer from conditioned inattention such that they automatically elicit the response of being ignored, resulting in slower learning to these stimuli.

Thus, in Experiment 1 participants needed to pay attention to the dot patterns, and over time this became an automatic response for the dot patterns they were trained with (but not to just *any* stimulus that was a dot pattern, at least, not to the same extent, as the results with the control stimuli show). The outcome would be that these patterns then elicited attention when encountered in a subsequent discrimination, and this would lead to faster acquisition of the discrimination. In Experiment 2, however, the stimuli were masks, and the response conditioned to them was to ignore them. Thus, when these stimuli were used in the final discrimination task the attentional response to them was to lower their salience, and this led to slower acquisition. One key aspect of these results is that they are stimulus specific: that is, only the stimuli experienced by the participants in the experiment demonstrate the full effect. It is not possible to explain these findings by reference to changes in some general level of attention to all stimuli encountered subsequently as this would predict no difference in acquisition to the discrimination between experimental stimuli and controls. Hence, the notion of some general gating of stimulus input that varies in the course of experience is not sufficient to explain the results that we have considered so far.

This analysis is further supported by a series of experiments performed by Graham and McLaren (1998) in which participants had to attend to one set of chequerboard patterns in order to classify them as members of one of two possible groups, while ignoring other chequerboard patterns onscreen (that they nevertheless had to look at). After this phase (Phase 1), they were then required to learn discriminations of exactly the type used here (Phase 2) between pairs of patterns they had either been attending to or ignoring. The result was that they showed faster acquisition than to control pairs for the attended-to patterns, but slower acquisition (relative to controls) to the patterns they had been ignoring during pre-exposure. Importantly, Graham and McLaren were able to go one step further, and show that a similar result was obtained even if the to-be-discriminated patterns used in Phase 2 were small distortions of the patterns pre-exposed in Phase 1 (this technique is further elaborated when considering Experiment 3 shortly). The result would not be expected on the basis of theories that explain perceptual learning effects in terms of latent inhibition (LI), as these theories would predict that the features of incidentally exposed stimuli would accrue LI, and that small changes to these stimuli would then stand out, which in turn would aid discrimination based on these distortions. This latter result, which is the opposite of the effect observed by Graham and McLaren, has been obtained in experiments using simple pre-exposure in animals other than humans (Gibson, Walk, Pick, and Tighe, 1958; Forgus, 1958a, 1958b), in particular in a very similar experiment using chequerboard stimuli with pigeons (Aitken, Bennett, McLaren, and Mackintosh, 1996). It is at this point, then, that we part company with Lubow—who proposes that his conditioned attention mechanism can also serve as a model of LI in infrahumans. Instead, we feel that this result makes it all the more likely that what we have here is not some effect analogous to LI in animals, but rather a phenomenon that derives from attentional processes that make the transition from intentional control to automatic allocation in the course of experience with these stimuli. The argument would then be that the distortions of the pre-exposed stimuli were small enough to allow generalization of the conditioned attention (or inattention) to them—leading to the same results as before (more on this later as well).

This analysis prompts us to ask, 'Are all the effects of previous experience with stimuli due to conditioned attention or inattention to those stimuli?' Our answer will be 'no'—there are perceptual learning phenomena that do not admit of this explanation and also effects whereby experience with certain stimuli retard learning to a stimulus in a way that cannot be explained by appealing to attention. To prove this assertion, however, we will need to consider more complex pre-exposure paradigms. The basic approach to be used is illustrated in Experiment 3.

Perceptual learning and categorization

Experiment 3 examined the effect of category learning on the ability to discriminate both between two categories and within a given category. The experiment consisted of two phases. In the first, the participants learnt to categorize stimuli into two categories. In the second, they learnt discriminations as in Experiments 1 and 2, using category exemplars and category prototypes as the stimuli.

The stimuli used were of the same type as the masks used in the delayed matching task in Experiment 2, but were generated separately for each participant and were not used as masks. Two base stimuli were generated randomly as before. These 'prototypes' were used to define two categories by generating a set of exemplars for each category by adding noise to the base patterns. The technique for adding noise involved changing whole horizontal lines

Fig. 6.3 Example stimuli from Experiment 3. The lower pair of stimuli are example prototypes, and the upper pair are minimal distortions (used as test exemplars) of the lower right-hand prototype.

of blocks by replacing that line with another randomly generated one. This was done stochastically, with the probability of a line replaced being 0.39 so that on average 6.25 lines were changed. This resulted in considerable distortion of the base stimulus. Examples of the base stimuli and exemplars are shown in Figure 6.3.

The lower pair of stimuli are example prototypes, and the upper pair are minimal distortions of the lower right hand prototype or base pattern. This kind of exemplar is used in the discrimination task that follows on from the category learning phase of this experiment, but the exemplars used in categorization training were much more distorted than the exemplars shown here. As many exemplars as were necessary for a given participant were generated online during the course of the experiment.

Participants were told that once they pressed the space bar a constant stream of stimuli would appear on screen, and their task was to sort these stimuli into two categories. They were to do this by pressing one of two keys and would receive immediate feedback as to the correctness of their response. If they did not respond within a few seconds (4.25 s) they would be timed out. The participants were warned that the task would be quite difficult initially, as the stimuli would vary considerably and some would be quite ambiguous. Nevertheless the stimuli belonging to a given category would tend to share features in common, though the variability would be such that no particular feature would be a reliable index of category membership. For this reason, they were encouraged to scan the stimulus before making a decision; speed of response was relatively unimportant, the need for accuracy was emphasized. This was further sharpened by telling them that after a certain minimum number of trials had been completed this phase of the experiment would end 'when they were doing well enough'. In fact, at least 50 trials were required and the criterion required to finish was six correct responses in a row, which must include the last response made. Once the participant initiated the experiment, trials were continuous. Stimuli were presented singly, with 1 sec allowed for feedback and a 1-sec pause before the next stimulus came on screen, during which a fixation stimulus was displayed. No summary feedback was presented when the session terminated.

Five minutes after they had completed the categorization phase, participants progressed to the discrimination phase of the experiment. The procedure for the discrimination task was exactly as in Experiments 1 and 2, with the following changes in stimuli and design. For each participant the 'pre-exposed' stimuli were the two base patterns from that participant's categorization phase, and two new exemplars (from one category) that were generated so as to be very similar both to one another and to the prototype for their category. This was achieved by making the probability of altering a line only one-sixteenth, so that only one line is expected to change. Checks were run to ensure that the resulting exemplars were not in fact the same. The effect of all this was to produce one pair of stimuli that were moderately similar (the two base stimuli) and one pair that were very similar but discriminable. Examples of two base stimuli and two exemplars used in this task were shown in the figure earlier. Control, non-pre-exposed stimuli were taken from another participant so that all stimuli were used in the same way in both the pre-exposed and non-pre-exposed conditions, but for different participants.

One participant was unable to complete the categorization phase of the experiment and did not go on to the discrimination task. The overall mean for the number of trials to criterion during this categorization phase was 68.9 with a standard error of 4.3. Our measure of how well participants can categorize the stimuli is given by the number of correct categorizations divided by the total number of trials attempted by a given participant expressed as a percentage. The last six correct trials were excluded from this analysis, so that a null hypothesis of 50% correct could be assumed to apply. Overall the mean percentage correct was 62.4 with a standard error of 2.3. The accuracy data for each of the four conditions during the final, discrimination phase of the experiment is shown in Figure 6.4.

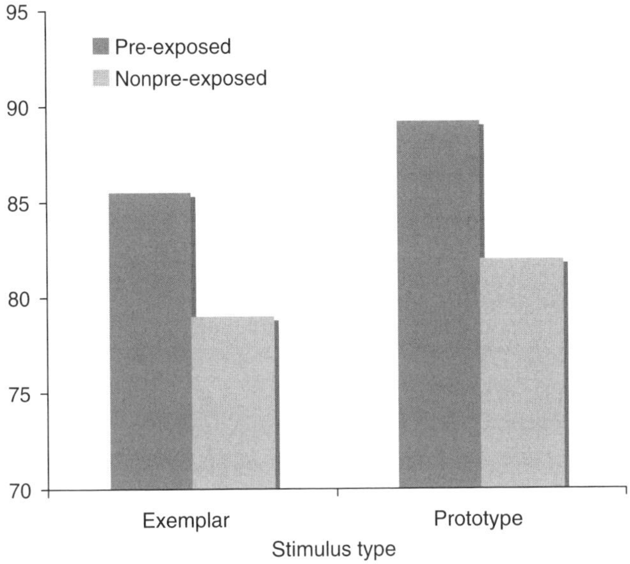

Fig. 6.4 Results of the test phase involving the base patterns (prototypes) and test exemplars in Experiment 3. Darker bars give the results for the pre-exposed stimuli, lighter bars for the controls that were also used as the experimental stimuli for another participant. Chance performance = 50%.

The graph indicates that pre-exposure resulted in faster acquisition of the discrimination to a roughly equal extent for both stimulus types, and that the prototypes were somewhat easier to discriminate than the exemplars. Analysis of variance revealed a significant effect of pre-exposure, $F(1, 22) = 3.13$, p (one-tailed)[1] < 0.05. Pre-exposure facilitated acquisition of the discrimination roughly equally for both stimulus types and there was a similar pattern in the latency to respond.

The results presented here demonstrate that learning to categorize stimuli that are appropriately characterized as distortions of a prototype enhances the discriminability between the prototypes for the two categories involved *and* between two novel exemplars drawn from one of the categories. As neither the prototypes nor the exemplars used in the test discrimination were shown during training, this extends the results of Experiment 1 considerably. Putting this difference to one side for the moment, the pre-exposure regime for the prototypes is perhaps closest to that used in Experiment 1, as in both cases the

[1] A one-tail test because the effect was predicted on the basis of theory (see later) and other experimental work is not considered in this chapter.

stimuli (dot patterns in Experiment 1, chequerboard category exemplars in Experiment 3) have to be distinguished from one another either to make a same/different decision (Experiment 1) or to allocate the exemplar to the appropriate category (Experiment 3). If this is necessary for attention to accrue to the stimuli then we might expect attention to become conditioned to the two categories of stimuli used for each participant and then this would be elicited by the prototypes during discrimination training (as in some sense they are the 'best' exemplars of each category by virtue of their similarity to the set of pre-exposed exemplars) and lead to enhanced acquisition. This account obviously requires some mechanism for generalizing conditioned attention between category exemplars to be successful. What that mechanism might be is further constrained by the result obtained with the exemplar discrimination. This was that a discrimination between two very similar exemplars drawn from the same category was acquired more rapidly if that category was familiar. First of all note that in this case, there is now no incentive for participants to have previously tried to distinguish between the exemplars that belonged to one category during training, so the implicit requirements in play during pre-exposure were somewhat different for these stimuli and if we are to appeal to the same attentional mechanisms to explain the effect then we must take this into account. But perhaps the strongest inference that can be made on the grounds of this result would be that generalization of conditioned attention must be driven by a whole stimulus comparison rather than operating on a feature by feature basis. The argument is that if attention is allocated to individual features of stimuli, then those features that best discriminated between the two categories will be the ones that have attention conditioned to them. These will be the prototypical features (which would help explain enhanced discrimination of the prototypes). But the exemplars created for the test discrimination have not been seen before, and they differ only on features on which they also differ from the prototype. Put another way, they are very similar, and this similarity is because they both have a very large number of prototypical features. If these features elicit an attentional response, this will make discrimination more difficult, as the participant will be preferentially attending to the features that are the same for the two stimuli rather than those on which they differ. Not a recipe for successful discrimination.

In fact this argument can also be deployed when considering the results of the final experiment in Graham and McLaren (1998). In that experiment, distortions similar to those used to make the exemplars here were performed on a base pattern that had previously been incidentally exposed, to create two stimuli that subsequently had to be discriminated. If conditioned inattention had been to the features of the base pattern, then the distortions, that is, the changed features in the two variants that had to be discriminated would have been relatively salient and this would have helped discrimination. The fact that all the features common to the two stimuli would have been ignored would also have been helpful in acquiring the discrimination, and this would not easily have produced the retardation in acquisition relative to controls that was the result of that experiment.

Our conclusion, then, has to be that generalization takes place on a 'whole stimulus' basis if we wish to continue with our conditioned attention/inattention account of the phenomena considered to date. With this proviso, the results of Experiment 3 can perhaps be accommodated and we have yet to find circumstances in which the conditioned attention approach to changes in learning as a consequence of experience with stimuli has difficulties in explaining the results. This, however, will change when we consider the next variation on this design.

Perceptual learning, categorization, and inversion

McLaren (1997) was able to demonstrate one of the perceptual learning effects commonly found in face recognition, but using quite different stimuli that had not been encountered prior to the experiment. In typical face recognition experiments, discrimination performance with upright faces is much better than with inverted faces and this difference is significantly bigger for faces than for other stimuli such as houses (Yin, 1969). McLaren (1997) was able to show that this type of effect can also be induced in the laboratory using chequerboards of the type considered in Experiment 3. Two categories were generated by creating prototypes and then adding noise to them to create exemplars of each category. Participants were trained on these categories until they were able to classify the stimuli successfully as in Experiment 3, and then transferred to a test discrimination, which this time involved pairs of stimuli that were similar exemplars drawn from one category. Four pairs were used concurrently as before, two experimental and two control pairs taken from another participant's experimental stimuli. The two experimental pairs were in one case two upright exemplars of one of the categories that had not yet been seen by the participant, and in the other case two inverted (rotated through 180 degrees) exemplars from the same category (also unseen to that point). The question asked in this experiment was how inversion would interact with the perceptual learning effect that was expected to follow from the experience with the categories prior to learning these discriminations. One very appealing feature of this experiment was that an inverted chequerboard is still a chequerboard, thus minimizing any cues the participants might have access to with regard to the experimental manipulation that was in play. In the case of inverted faces, you know immediately that you are dealing with an upside down face and this may alter the way you go about dealing with it. In the case of the chequerboards, this was less likely to be an issue.

The results were clear and strongly supported the notion that the face inversion effect is, at least in part, a perceptual learning phenomenon. Performance on the upright familiar exemplars was significantly better than on the inverted familiar exemplars (an inversion effect, see the left side of the left panel of Figure 6.5), and was also significantly better than on controls (shown in the right panel of Figure 6.5), replicating the effect of better discrimination within a category contingent on pre-exposure to that category. In addition, the inversion effect for the familiar exemplars was significantly greater than any such effect in the controls (in fact there wasn't even a hint of one there). This result is an analogue of the face inversion effect and can also be explained by our attentional mechanism for perceptual learning. We simply have to assume that attention is conditioned to the upright exemplars that participants are trained on and generalizes to other novel exemplars during test, but that inversion renders the resultant chequerboards sufficiently unfamiliar to prevent this generalization occurring. The analogy to the face inversion effect could not be considered complete, however, until it was possible to show that other types of stimuli did not generate this effect even though participants were familiarized with them. Recall that part of the face inversion effect result is that the difference in performance in a recognition task between upright and inverted faces is much bigger than for other types of stimuli such as houses. The problem

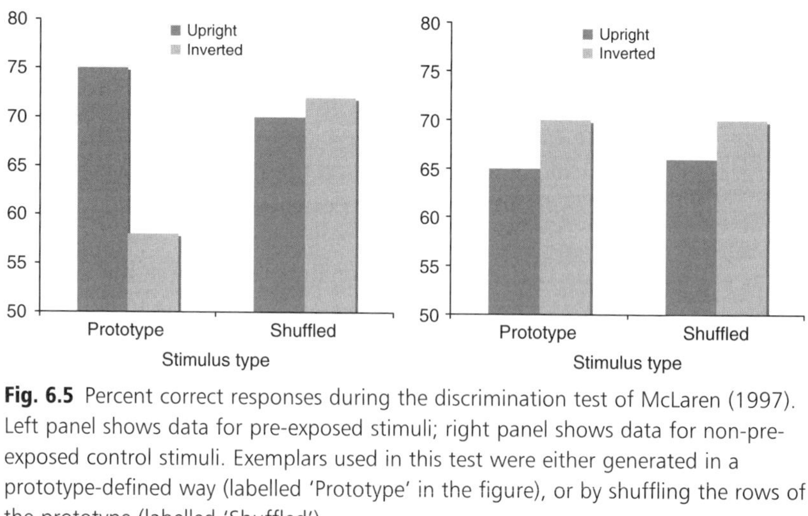

Fig. 6.5 Percent correct responses during the discrimination test of McLaren (1997). Left panel shows data for pre-exposed stimuli; right panel shows data for non-pre-exposed control stimuli. Exemplars used in this test were either generated in a prototype-defined way (labelled 'Prototype' in the figure), or by shuffling the rows of the prototype (labelled 'Shuffled').

here was to come up with a chequerboard stimulus that could play the role of the image of a house the same way that the exemplars drawn from a prototype-defined category had played the role of faces in this experiment. The solution adopted was to construct exemplars from base patterns by shuffling or permuting rows of squares as units rather than adding noise at random. Thus, after generating a base pattern, the first exemplar simply shuffled, at random, the 16 rows that made up the base pattern. Additional exemplars were generated in the same way, with a random permutation of all the rows in the chequerboard stimulus to create the exemplar. This produces a category with a quite different structure to the prototype-defined ones previously used. There is now no 'special' exemplar (this would be the prototype itself in the prototype-defined category); all exemplars have equal status, even the base pattern, and averaging all the exemplars generated would not result in the base pattern as was the case when adding random noise to generate exemplars. This technique also promised to generate categories that could still be learned and this did indeed turn out to be the case. Using the same procedures as before participants were able to learn to categorize these stimuli (two categories were used) in a mean of 76 trials with a mean percentage correct of 64.2%. These were slightly better, but entirely comparable results to those obtained with prototype-defined stimuli in this experiment (and very similar to those in Experiment 3), and there were no significant differences in categorization between the two groups trained on the different stimulus types. The key results, however, are those from the discrimination test after categorization training. The results are also shown in Figure 6.5.

There was no inversion effect in this case (right side of left panel of figure), no perceptual learning effect either and there was an interaction between these results and the results with the prototype-defined stimuli, which forces the conclusion that the inversion effect was contingent not just on familiarity with the stimuli that made up the category concerned, but also on the category being prototype-defined, i.e. possessing a certain stimulus structure. It is this role for stimulus structure in generating the perceptual learning effect that conditioned attention theories of perceptual learning cannot explain. If attention is conditioned during the categorization phase, then this should apply equally well whether the category is prototype-defined or created by row permutation, given that both categories are equally easy to learn. Taking this last point, the learning data show no significant differences and a slight numerical advantage in this case for the shuffled stimuli. Post categorization tests showed that upright shuffled exemplars were classified at 70% accuracy and inverted ones at 59% accuracy with upright prototype-defined exemplars at 66% and inverted ones at 59%. All these results are above chance, and while performance on the upright stimuli is significantly better than for the inverted stimuli (as might be expected, note that the inverted shuffled stimuli will be rather different to the upright shuffled stimuli because of the left/right reversal contingent on being rotated by 180 degrees), there is no effect of category type, and no interaction with this factor. Clearly, just as for the prototype-defined category, participants can detect the similarity between shuffled exemplars that belong to the same category (as it is this similarity on which categorization must be based). Given this, it is hard to explain why a conditioned attention mechanism would not predict exactly the same pattern of effects for the shuffled stimuli as for the prototype-defined stimuli, since in each case attention should generalize from the trained exemplars to the similar exemplars encountered in the discrimination test. But this is very much not what is observed. We are forced to search for some alternative mechanism to explain the perceptual learning effects found here, and to re-evaluate the role of attention in perceptual learning.

Perceptual learning as a consequence of latent inhibition

In fact, the experiments just reported were motivated by a quite different theory of perceptual learning, one based on a model of LI first proposed by McLaren, Kaye, and Mackintosh (1989) and subsequently developed in McLaren and Mackintosh (2000, 2002). In this model, LI is considered to be caused by a reduction in stimulus salience due to the lower activation of units representing the features of stimuli, which itself is a consequence of the associations that have formed between these units in the course of experience. The more reliable and more frequent the co-occurrence of certain features in a stimulus, the more the units representing those features become associated. This then lowers their activation, making them slower to form new associations.

This model can explain how familiarization with a prototype-defined category can lead to better discrimination of exemplars taken from that category. Exposure to exemplars of the category leads to strong associations forming between units representing prototypical features of that category as they will co-occur reliably. This will lead to a reduction in the activation of the units representing the prototypical features, which are exactly those features that tend to be shared by exemplars drawn from that category. It will be the non-prototypical features of an exemplar (those introduced by the addition of noise) that will be relatively more salient as they will not suffer from LI in the same way. As these features can be used to differentiate between exemplars, the prediction of enhanced discrimination between exemplars drawn from a familiar prototype-defined category follows.

But the real strength of this account is that it can explain why the same result would not be expected in the case of a category that is not defined by a prototype but instead has the structure of our shuffled stimuli. In this case, there are no prototypical features shared by most exemplars that are represented by units that then lose salience as a result of association formation. Most of the features of an exemplar drawn from a category with this structure will tend to be relatively unpredicted and hence salient. As a consequence, this mechanism cannot operate and confer any benefit contingent on familiarity with the category that will reduce the perceived similarity between two exemplars. Thus, perceptual learning will be weak or non-existent and this will undermine any inversion effect that relies on it. The reader may object that if there are no shared prototypical features, then how is it that our participants are able to discriminate successfully between categories? Surely there must be some set of features held in common by the exemplars of a particular category that makes classification possible? There may well be; one example that comes readily to mind is the overall luminance of the stimuli. If one category happens to have more black squares than the other – or even more black squares on the left than the other category does – then this holistic attribute of the stimuli will enable reliable categorization and units representing it may come to suffer LI. But the more local features of any exemplar, due to a particular arrangement of squares, will not accrue much by way of LI, and it is these local features that will be needed to discriminate between exemplars belonging to the same category. Many of these features will be shared (by chance) by any given pair of exemplars and these common features will be as salient as the unique features that will make acquisition of the discrimination between them difficult.

The perceptual learning that accrues as a result of experience with a category defined by a prototype may not be explicable by means of conditioned attention then. The attentional account cannot be rescued by shifting to a modified version whereby attention is conditioned to individual features rather than the stimulus as a whole, because, as we have already seen, this would lead to the prediction of retarded rather than speeded acquisition in many cases. It would be the units representing prototypical features that would elicit attention the most strongly and this would tend to make a discrimination between category members more difficult rather than easier. The same argument applies to Graham and McLaren's (1998) finding (though in this case to give the converse result) as here conditioned inattention to units representing the features of the pre-exposed base patterns would, when distortions are introduced, mean that units still representing the remaining original features would be less salient, the units representing the distortions more salient, and so discrimination on the basis of the distortions would be enhanced. We must acknowledge, however, that our LI-based mechanism for perceptual learning has no way of explaining the basic conditioned inattention result in Experiment 2 or in Graham and McLaren (1998). Some attempt can be made to appeal to salience reduction and to postulate that this is severe in the case where incidental pre-exposure is used, but the inevitable consequence of deploying a theory that operates at an elemental or feature-based level is that, given the initial requirement to explain the retarded learning consequent on incidental pre-exposure, when noise or distortions of some kind are introduced the prediction is that these distortions are relatively salient and that discrimination in the sort of scenario employed by Graham and McLaren will be facilitated. As this is clearly not the case, we are left with the need to acknowledge that a conditioned inattention explanation of these results is required, and if this is allowed then it would seem odd to deny that conditioned attention could play at least a part in the results of Experiments 1 and 3 (in the latter experiment particularly for the discrimination between the prototypes of the two categories, as the requirement during familiarization is to distinguish between the categories defined by these prototypes). The requirement would seem to be for two classes of theory here, one operating at an elemental level (LI) and one at a whole stimulus or configural level (attention).

Latent inhibition in humans

Before we can feel entirely secure in this conclusion, however, it would be as well to give further consideration to how these two classes of mechanism might complement one another. In particular, given that one of them is a theory of LI, we must discuss LI in humans and the somewhat vexed question of why it is so hard to find simple, straightforward evidence of LI in humans. Note here that we are not directly addressing the question of whether LI can be demonstrated in humans. This is an interesting question in its own right, and there have been reports of such an effect in a variety of conditioning preparations (Schnur and Ksir, 1969; Surwit and Poser, 1974; Siddle, Remington, and Churchill, 1985; Klosterhalfen, Kellermann, Stockhorst, Wolf, Kirschbaum, Hall, and Enck, 2005), but it is not, perhaps, the most interesting question to ask. The problem for the elemental theory of LI put forward by McLaren, Kaye, and Mackintosh (1989) and others like it was always that when applied to humans it seemed to suggest that if they were simply pre-exposed to a stimulus, then had to learn about that stimulus, the consequence should be that learning would be slow relative to control stimuli. This has been known to be the case for infrahumans since the seminal work of Lubow and Moore (1959) and has proven a straightforward and reliable phenomenon to demonstrate, but has by comparison been an elusive target for human studies. One proposal (Lubow, 1989) had been that incidental pre-exposure is required to reveal LI in humans, which would fit well with Experiment 2 and some of Graham and McLaren (1998) but cannot survive the finding that distortions of incidentally pre-exposed stimuli are still learned about more slowly than controls, which is quite unlike the result typically found with infrahumans (see Hall, 1980 for a review of early evidence on this point, and it is reinforced by the results of Aitken *et al.*, 1996). The question is, then, why LI in humans should prove so difficult to demonstrate if it is the case that it plays a key role in producing perceptual learning phenomena that are, by comparison, readily observable? The answer we shall offer to this conundrum is that it is a consequence of the fact that both classes of mechanism, those based on LI and attention respectively, are typically operating in studies in which stimuli are pre-exposed, and that the effects of one mechanism (based on conditioned attention) often conceals at least some of the impact of the other (based on LI).

Consider the most basic type of pre-exposure to a stimulus. A human participant is repeatedly shown a stimulus on a screen, let's say it's a chequerboard pattern to be both specific and topical. After some time they enter a new phase in which they have to learn that, when this pattern is shown on screen, if they press a key they will receive a monetary reward. This is as close to a typical LI experiment in infrahumans as one can come without employing more specialist conditioning preparations (eyeblink, electrodermal, and induced nausea would be examples of these). If a thirsty rat is pre-exposed to a tone in an operant chamber then trained that the tone signals water delivery it will learn this relationship more slowly than non-pre-exposed controls (McLaren, Bennett, Plaisted, Aitken, and Mackintosh, 1994), so why should we not expect a similar effect here with our human participants? Our explanation is that during pre-exposure attention was conditioned to the pre-exposed stimulus at the same time as LI of the elements making up that stimulus also took place. In contrast to conditioned inattention, which will occur as a result of repeated attempts to ignore stimuli, we see conditioned attention occurring in these circumstances as a result of repeatedly paying attention to stimuli because participants assume that they will be relevant later. In combination, these two effects could produce almost any result, but in terms of simple learning to the stimulus they clearly act in opposition to one another making little detectable impact on learning a not unlikely result. If instead we now consider the case where two rather similar chequerboard patterns are pre-exposed, before our participant is trained to discriminate between them, then the analysis is the same but the expected outcome is rather different. The effects of LI will be to reduce the salience of the common elements shared by the two stimuli rather more than the elements unique to a particular stimulus, since these common elements, being present in both stimuli, will be exposed twice as often (and hence will be subject to twice as much LI) as the unique elements, which by definition only occur in one stimulus. The effects of conditioned attention will be to raise the salience of all the elements in each stimulus, which will leave the differential effects of LI on the shared and unique features of the stimuli unaltered. The prediction is now quite clear, discrimination between the two stimuli should be enhanced as their representations have been fine-tuned to make them more discriminable without incurring much by way of a 'latent inhibition penalty'. The two mechanisms that are invoked by stimulus pre-exposure have here combined to produce perceptual learning in a sophisticated fashion that improves on what each mechanism on its own would be capable of.

A similar analysis follows for pre-exposure leading to conditioned inattention. Incidental exposure to our stimulus will produce a combination of LI and conditioned inattention that clearly predicts that simple learning will be slower to this stimulus. The case of discrimination between two similar and incidentally pre-exposed stimuli is a more ambiguous scenario, with the differential effects of LI to some extent opposing the effects of overall LI and conditioned inattention, but the expectation will be for the overall loss in salience to quite often outweigh the differential effects of LI.

Reverse perceptual learning

Armed with this hypothesis about the effects of pre-exposure being mediated by two different classes of mechanism, one elemental and resulting in LI, one holistic and operating by means of conditioned attention, we can now ask if it is possible to find circumstances where, without using special conditioning procedures (which have a somewhat controversial status with regard to what actually is learned when they are used) or incidental pre-exposure (which is likely to invoke conditioned inattention and so confound our results), it will be possible to demonstrate retarded acquisition as a consequence of pre-exposure in humans? In fact, it is possible to find a set of circumstances where this type of effect should manifest in human experiments using simple pre-exposure, but they are quite restrictive and unlikely to occur in the normal run of things. This, in itself is taken to be good, in that it indicates that the combination of mechanisms for attention and LI is very robust in preventing what might be seen as the undesirable consequences of LI affecting the general rate of learning, while maintaining its utility as a mechanism for producing perceptual learning.

One requirement for obtaining poorer learning as a consequence of simple pre-exposure is to use stimuli that do not benefit from the differential LI of common elements. We can achieve this by using the shuffled stimuli from McLaren (1997). But recall that in that experiment there was no evidence of retarded learning to the shuffled stimuli, it was more that they did not benefit from the perceptual learning effect that accrued to the prototype-based stimuli. We will return to this point shortly, but the conclusion we reached was that we also needed to find a task that involves stimuli that vary from trial to trial. The particular paradigm that meets these requirements is given in Wills, Suret, and McLaren (2004) (see also Wills and McLaren, 1998; Wills and McLaren, 2002). In this paradigm, pre-exposure to the stimuli is given by means of a running recognition task. Stimuli are shown one at a time to a participant who has to decide if it is the first (new) or second (old) time in the block that that particular stimulus has been seen. The pre-exposed stimuli were drawn from two categories, with the exemplars shown generated by shuffling or permuting the rows of a base pattern as before. After this pre-exposure phase, the test phase was not the type of discrimination experiment used in the other studies discussed here. Instead, this phase involved participants learning to categorize stimuli from the two categories that had been pre-exposed, with the categorization task being performed in exactly the way used to provide pre-exposure in our earlier experiments. A separate control group was also run on this test phase after experience of running recognition using quite different stimuli. The dependent measure in this experiment was mean number of trials to criterion during the categorization test phase, with criterion being a run of six consecutive correct responses. Mean number of trials to criterion was higher (42) in the pre-exposed group, than in the non-pre-exposed control group (21). Statistical analysis showed that this difference was significant, $F(1, 20) = 4.67$, $p < 0.05$ Thus pre-exposure via a running recognition task, which can hardly be classified as incidental pre-exposure, increases the number of trials taken to learn to successfully categorize the shuffled stimuli. In order to check that this result was genuinely a result of the stimulus structure of these categories and not an inevitable consequence of our procedures, another condition using exemplars from prototype-defined categories was also run (i.e. running recognition followed by categorization training). This gave the opposite pattern of results, with pre-exposure now leading to faster acquisition (i.e. fewer trials to criterion) as expected, and there was a significant interaction between the effects of pre-exposure and stimulus type used in the experiment, $F(1, 40) = 8.66$, $p < 0.01$. Thus, we have strong evidence that simple exposure to the shuffled stimuli can retard learning involving them, in this case, learning to classify them as members of one category or another.

Having obtained this result, we can now ask why it follows from the analysis presented in this chapter. The key to understanding this lies in the fact that the LI mechanism is operating on the shuffled stimuli, and that as a consequence it will modulate the relative salience of some features of these stimuli considerably. The full analysis of what happens in this experiment is complex, but a simple thought experiment will make the general idea clear. Imagine for a moment that the two base patterns that are used to generate the category exemplars differ in the number of black and white squares that occur in a given column. Perhaps the third column from the left has many black squares in Base Pattern 1, but rather few in Base Pattern 2. This feature of these stimuli will be invariant under the row shuffling transformation, and as a consequence of experience with these stimuli we assume that participants learn that the chance of a white square in this column is rather low for the stimulus set defined by Base Pattern 1, but rather high for the set defined by Base Pattern 2. By this we do not mean that the participants have learned to categorize the stimuli at this stage during pre-exposure (since running recognition does not require the participants to categorize the stimuli), but merely that other features present in the stimuli predict that the squares in the third column will be black in the case of stimuli from Category 1 and white in the case of stimuli from Category 2. Now, when the participant moves onto the categorization phase they will be attempting to learn which key to press to any given stimulus by trial and error. Any learning that takes place will tend to involve the most salient features of the stimuli on screen, and we can ask what these will be for the third column of our hypothetical stimuli. For members of Category 1 where a black square will be expected in any position in this column it will be the few white squares that have been shuffled into position that will be most salient, the majority black squares less so. The converse will apply to Category 2. Hence, a white square in the third column will tend to be associated to Category 1 membership, and a black square to Category 2 membership. But, in fact, the opposite contingency is in force, and a black square is predictive of this exemplar being a member of Category 1. Recall that the position of the minority colour squares will change from exemplar to exemplar, so it is only the general contingency between colour of square and category that will prove to be reliable over time in this task, and this will eventually lead to acquisition, but the counteracting effect of stimulus salience will slow this process and retard acquisition of the discrimination between these categories compared to non-pre-exposed control categories. Hence, the retardation observed can be said to be a consequence of the LI mechanism operating under conditions of simple exposure, but it relies on differential LI in this case emphasizing the wrong features to aid discrimination, rather than the right ones as in the case of prototype-defined categories. As such, it may perhaps be better to consider it as more a case of reverse perceptual learning rather than LI per se. Note also how this explanation relies on the stimuli changing from trial to trial in this particular task. If instead we had used our conventional discrimination design taking two exemplars of one of the familiar categories, then the salient features of each (the unexpected squares in a column) could have been exploited to speed acquisition.

Perceptual learning and attention: a model and some conclusions

There is one more topic to discuss before we can summarize with some concluding remarks about attention and perceptual learning, and that is to address the issue of what a model that combined LI and conditioned attention might look like. Figure 6.6 gives one possible instantiation of the ideas contained in this chapter.

In essence, this is the McLaren, Kaye, and Mackintosh (1989) model with a configural module added that can detect when certain combinations of stimulus elements or features occur and so can recognize that a particular stimulus is present. This configural representation then has connections that can gate input to the associative module that represents stimulus features. If attention is being paid to the stimulus then these connections are strengthened

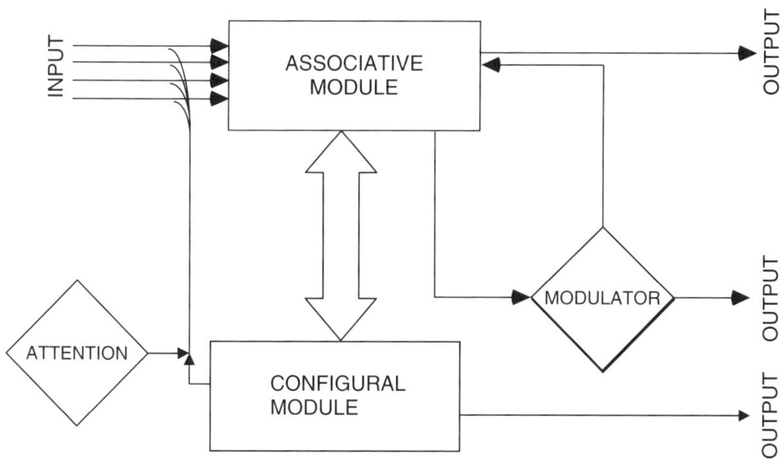

Fig. 6.6 A combined elemental latent inhibition and configural conditioned attention model of stimulus representation and development. The associative module employs elemental representations and is modulated to produce latent inhibition as a result of pre-exposure. These representations feed into a configural module that recognises whole stimuli and can condition attention or inattention on this basis.

enhancing input to the associative module, if the stimulus is being ignored then these connections can become negative and suppress input to the associative module. This process of raising or lowering attention is, in itself a controlled and active one, which can be flexibly determined by the individual, but the connections themselves persist over time, such that a stimulus that has been repeatedly attended to will elicit attention when presented again because there will be strong positive weights from its configural representation (which will be activated by presentation of the stimulus) gating stimulus input. Equally, a stimulus that has been ignored in the past will have developed strong negative weights from its configural representation that will suppress stimulus input when it is presented again (other things being equal). It is important to note that the configural module, which serves the purpose of recognizing specific stimuli with some history of a given level of attention being paid to them, must be set up so that once a configural unit is activated its effect in gating stimulus input is general and not just confined to the features of the stimulus that activated it. If this were not the case then the effect of conditioned attention to stimuli that were small distortions of previously experienced stimuli would be incorrect – and would lead to elemental-type results. Instead a stimulus sufficiently similar to one that has some past history of conditioned attention or inattention will partially activate the appropriate configural unit, which must then gate stimulus input for that entire stimulus to some extent. This will ensure that conditioned attention will generalize in the correct fashion to complement elemental LI. The requirement that the stimulus be sufficiently similar will prevent this effect generalizing to control stimuli in the experiments reported here.

We must, of course, acknowledge that the proposed model leaves many questions unanswered, and, indeed, there are many issues to do with the relationship between attention and perceptual learning that have not been resolved in the course of this discussion. We believe that we have made a powerful case that there is a role for attention to play in perceptual learning in humans. The data seem to require that there be two separate mechanisms active during preexposure, one elemental and modulating unit salience on the basis of how predicted that unit is by others concurrently active, while the other is configural in nature and captures the history of controlled and flexibly allocated attention to a given stimulus, but we have not been able to provide unequivocal proof for the positive effects of conditioned attention. Instead, we have had to rely on the somewhat stronger evidence for conditioned inattention and argue that it would be rather strange if inattention could be conditioned and attention could not. The reader might argue that simple priming phenomena (e.g. repetition priming) provide the necessary evidence for this conjecture, but it would be better if there were evidence from the perceptual learning domain that supported the notion of conditioned attention unconfounded by other possible explanations such as those provided by the differential LI of common elements mechanism. We think it likely that the results of Experiment 1 are due, in part at least, to conditioned attention, but fall short of being able to prove that this is the case.

We have not considered other models of perceptual learning (Goldstone, 1998) and other theories of LI (Pearce and Hall, 1980) in this treatment. Our reason for this is that we wished to explore how attention and LI might be integrated into a single model without entering into arguments about which model of perceptual learning or LI was the best. Obviously the type of model of perceptual learning or LI one starts with will constrain any attempt to incorporate attentional factors into the model and probably change the nature of the final hybrid system, but we are happy to leave this exercise to the authors of the various models currently under development with the proviso that they will have to rise to the challenge provided by the data presented in this chapter. We have also not considered the strand of research on human (and infrahuman) associative learning that makes the case for variation in the attention paid to stimuli as a consequence of past associative history (Mackintosh, 1975; Lochman and Wills, 2003; Le Pelley and McLaren, 2003; Le Pelley, Oakeshott, Wills, and McLaren, 2005). Again, our reason is that this would have diluted our focus on the issue at hand (which is more the effects of pre-exposure than pre-training), but we acknowledge that this research points towards the role that attention may play in parameterizing associative learning. We certainly believe that the role of attention in representation development as a consequence of stimulus pre-exposure is a topic that is worthy of a great deal more study than has so far been the case, and look forward to a coming together in the next few years of conventional research on attention and the parallel strand of research on perceptual learning in humans and infrahumans that increasingly seems to contain hints of convergence with that on attentional processes. The models that emerge from that collision may be the first mature models of human representation development that are both rooted in research on infrahumans yet also have the capacity to model human abilities that go beyond the merely associative and take us into the realm where association and cognition interact to produce truly complex behaviours.

References

Aitken, M. R. F., Bennett, C. H., McLaren, I. P. L., & Mackintosh, N. J. (1996). Perceptual differentiation during categorization learning by pigeons. *Journal of Experimental Psychology: Animal Behavior Processes*, 22, 43–50.

Cantor, G. N. (1969). Stimulus familiarisation effect and the change effect in children's motor task behaviour. *Psychological Bulletin*, **71**, 2, 144–160

Diamond, R. & Carey, S. (1986). Why faces are and are not special: An effect of expertise. *Journal of Experimental Psychology: General*, **115**, 107–117

Forgus, R. H. (1958a). The effect of different kinds of form preexposure on form discrimination learning. *Journal of Comparative and Physiological Psychology*, **51**, 75–78.

Forgus, R. H. (1958b). The interaction between form preexposure and test requirements in determining form discrimination. *Journal of Comparative and Physiological Psychology*, **51**, 588–91.

Gibson, E. J., Walk, R. D., Pick, H. L., & Tighe, T. J. (1958). The effect of prolonged exposure to visual patterns on learning to discriminate similar and different patterns.

Ginton, A., Urca, G., & Lubow, R. E. (1975). T he effects of preexposure to a non-attended stimulus on subsequent learning: Latent inhibition in adults. *Bulletin of the Psychonomic Society*, **5**, 5–8.

Goldstone, R. L. (1998). Perceptual learning. *Annual Review of Psychology*, **49**, 585–612.

Graham, S. & McLaren, I. P. L. (1998). Retardation in human discrimination learning as a consequence of preexposure: Latent inhibition or negative priming? *Quarterly Journal of Experimental Psychology*, **51B**, 155–172.

Grison, S., Tipper, S. P., & Hewitt, O. (2005). Long-term negative priming: Support for retrieval of prior attentional processes. *Quarterly Journal of Experimental Psychology*, **58A**.

Hall, G. (1980). Exposure learning in animals. *Psychological Bulletin*, **88**, 535–50.

Kaniel, S. & Lubow, R. E. (1986). Latent inhibition: A developmental study. *British Journal of Developmental Psychology*, **4**, 367–375

Klosterhalfen, S., Kellermann, S., Stockhorst, U., Wolf, J., Kirschbaum, C., Hall, G., & Enck, P. (2005). Latent inhibition of rotation-chair induced nausea in healthy male and female volunteers. *Psychosomatic Medicine*, **67**, 335–340.

Lavis Y. & Mitchell C. (2006). Effects of preexposure on stimulus discrimination: An investigation of the mechanisms responsible for human perceptual learning. *Quarterly Journal of Experimental Psychology*, **59**, 2083–2101.

Le Pelley, M. E. & McLaren, I. P. L. (2003). Learned associability and associative change in human causal learning. *Quarterly Journal of Experimental Psychology*, **56B**, 56–67.

Le Pelley, M. E., Oakeshott, S. M., Wills, A. J., & McLaren, I. P. L. (2005). The outcome-specificity of learned predictiveness effects: Parallels between human causal learning and animal conditioning. Journal of Experimental Psychology: *Animal Behavior Processes*, **31**(2), 226–236.

Lochmann, T., & Wills, A. J. (2003). Predictive history in an allergy prediction task. In F. Schmalhofer, R. M. Young, & G. Katz (Eds), *Proceedings of EuroCogSci 03* (pp. 217–222). Mahwah, NJ: Erlbaum.

Lubow, R. E. (1989). *Latent inhibition and conditioned attention theory*. Cambridge, UK: Cambridge University Press.

Lubow, R. E., Alek, M., & Arzy, J. (1975). Behavioural decrement following stimulus preexposure: Effects of number of preexposures, presence of a second stimulus, and interstimulus interval in children and adults. *Journal of Experimental Psychology: Animal Behaviour Processes*, **104**, 2, 178–188.

Lubow, R. E., Caspy, T., & Schnur, P. (1982). Latent inhibition and learned helplessness in children: Similarities and differences. *Journal of Experimental Child Psychology*, **34**, 231–256.

Lubow, R. E., Rifkin, B., & Alek, M. (1976). The context effect: The relationship between stimulus preexposure and environmental preexposure determines subsequent learning. *Journal of Experimental Psychology: Animal Behaviour Processes*, **1**, 38–47.

Lubow, R. E. & Moore, A. U. (1959). Latent inhibition: The effect of non-reinforced preexposure to the conditioned stimulus. *Journal of Comparative and Physiological Psychology*, **52**, 415–419.

Lubow, R. E., Weiner, M., & Schnur, P. (1981). Conditioned attention theory. In G. H. Bower (Ed.), *The psychology of learning and motivation* (Vol. 15, pp. 1–49). New York: Academic Press.

Mackintosh, N. J. (1975). A theory of attention: Variations in the associability of stimuli with reinforcement. *Psychological Review*, **82**, 276–298.

McLaren, I. P. L. (1997).Categorisation and perceptual learning: An analogue of the face inversion effect. *Quarterly Journal of Experimental Psychology*, **50A**, 257–273.

McLaren, I. P. L., Bennett, C., Plaisted, K., Aitken, M., & Mackintosh, N. J. (1994). Latent inhibition, context specificity, and context familiarity. *Quarterly Journal of Experimental Psychology*, **47B**, 387–400.

McLaren, I. P. L., Kaye, H., & Mackintosh, N. J. (1989). An associative theory of the representation of stimuli: Applications to perceptual learning and latent inhibition. In R. G. M. Morris (Ed.), *Parallel distributed processing – Implications for psychology and neurobiology* (pp. 102–133). Oxford: Oxford University Press.

McLaren, I. P. L., Leevers, H. L., & Mackintosh, N. J. (1994). Recognition, categorisation and perceptual learning. In C. Umilta & M. Moscovitch (Eds), *Attention & Performance XV*. Cambridge, MA: MIT Press.

McLaren, I. P. L. & Mackintosh, N. J. (2000). An elemental model of associative learning: I. Latent inhibition and perceptual learning. *Animal Learning & Behavior*, **38**(3), 211–246.

McLaren, I. P. L. & Mackintosh, N. J. (2002).Associative learning and elemental representation: II. Generalization and discrimination. *Animal Learning & Behavior*, **30**(3), 177–200.

Mundy, M. E., Honey, R. C., & Dwyer, D. M. (2007). Simultaneous presentation of similar stimuli produces perceptual learning in human picture processing. *Journal of Experimental Psychology – Animal Behavior Processes*, **33**, 124–138.

Pearce, J. M. & Hall, G. (1980). A model for Pavlovian learning: Variations in the effectiveness of conditioned but not of unconditioned stimuli. *Psychological Review*, **87**, 532–552.

Schnur, P. & Ksir, C. J. (1969). Latent inhibition in human eyelid conditioning. *Journal of Experimental Psychology*, **80**, 388–389.

Siddle, D. A. T., Remington, B., & Churchill, M. (1985). Effects of conditioned stimulus pre-exposure on human electrodermal conditioning. *Biological Psychology*, **20**, 113–127.

Surwit, R. S. & Poser, E. G. (1974). Latent inhibition in the conditioned electrodermal response. *Journal of Comparative and Physiological Psychology*, **86**, 543–548.

Tipper, S. P. (1985). The negative priming effect: Inhibitory priming by ignored objects. *Quarterly Journal of Experimental Psychology*, **37A**, 571–590.

Treisman, A. & DeSchepper, B. (1996). Object tokens, attention, and visual memory. In T. Inui & J. L. McClelland (Eds), *Attention & performance XVI* (pp. 15–46). Cambridge, MA: MIT Press.

Wills, A. J. & McLaren, I. P. L. (1998). Perceptual learning and free classification. *Quarterly Journal of Experimental Psychology*, **51B**.

Wills, A. J. & McLaren, I. P. L. (2002). Frequency, predictability and salience. Unpublished manuscript, www.willslab.co.uk.

Wills, A. J., Suret, M. B., & McLaren, I. P. L. (2004). The role of category structure in determining the effects of stimulus pre-exposure on categorisation accuracy. *Quarterly Journal of Experimental Psychology*, **57B**, 79–88.

Yin, R. K. (1969). Looking at upside-down faces. *Journal of Experimental Psychology*, **81**, 141–145.

Chapter 7

Acquired distinctiveness and equivalence: a synthesis

Robert C. Honey, James Close, and Tzu-Ching E. Lin

Introduction

Pavlov (1927) is widely credited as providing the first formal demonstration of stimulus generalization, when he observed that dogs given pairings of one tone with food showed conditioned salivation not only to that tone, but also to other tones of a similar frequency (for a review and analysis of stimulus generalization, see Mackintosh, 1974). Theoretical accounts of stimulus generalization share the assumption that stimuli activate sets of elements, and that while some of these elements are uniquely activated by the specific stimulus presented during training, others are commonly activated by both the training stimulus and other test stimuli (e.g. Atkinson and Estes, 1963; McLaren and Mackintosh, 2000, 2002; Pearce, 1994; Rescorla, 1976). According to such accounts, similarity and its behavioural sequelae reflect the proportion of common elements that a training and test stimulus activate. This popular account has been challenged by demonstrations of the acquired distinctiveness and equivalence of cues.

Acquired changes in stimulus distinctiveness

Lawrence's (1949) claim that stimuli or cues acquire distinctiveness as a result of discrimination training was based on the following finding: Rats given discrimination training with one set of stimuli acquired a second discrimination, involving the same stimuli but different response requirements, more readily than rats for whom the first discrimination involved different stimuli. This pattern of results is not readily interpreted in terms of the direct transfer of responding acquired during the first discrimination, through associative learning, to the second discrimination. Instead, the results have often been taken to suggest that discrimination training increases attention paid to the critical stimuli, with these increases in effective stimulus intensity producing concomitant increases in the rate at which they are learnt about (e.g. Mackintosh, 1975). This interpretation has received support from other findings involving the transfer between discrimination learning problems (e.g. the intra-dimensional shift versus extra-dimensional shift advantage; see George and Pearce, 1999; Shepp and Eimas, 1964; Mackintosh and Little, 1969; Oswald *et al.*, 2001). In fact, the intradimensional shift (IDS)/extradimensinal shift (EDS) effect has occupied a special place in the history of animal learning theory since Mackintosh (1974) noted that it represented. 'Perhaps the best evidence that transfer between discrimination problems may be based partly on increases in attention to relevant dimensions and decreases in attention to irrelevant dimensions' (Mackintosh, 1974, p. 597). We shall return to the IDS/EDS effect later on.

One of the contentions of this chapter is that it might be unnecessary to appeal to a second process of attentional modulation, as it is usually conceived, in order to explain transfer effects of the type described in the preceding paragraph. Rather, we consider a complementary analysis of the way in which cues might acquire distinctiveness during discrimination training. This analysis is based on the proposition that discrimination training, in which two stimuli predict different outcomes, results in an increase the discriminability of those stimuli; and on the complementary proposition that training in which two stimuli predict the same outcome results in decrease in their discriminability. In contrast to the suggestion that demonstrations of the acquired distinctiveness of cues require one to invoke two processes (association and attention), we offer a purely associative analysis in which changes in distinctiveness are brought about by the operation of simple associative processes within a connectionist network. As will become evident, in some ways, this analysis can be considered to implement components of two-process theories of learning, but it does so without recourse to a second process of learning (i.e. attention).

Acquired distinctiveness/equivalence in a simple conditioning procedure

The suggestion that the effective similarity of stimuli changes during discrimination training receives support from experiments that have assessed stimulus generalization after discrimination training. For example, in an unpublished study taken from Melissa Allman's doctoral thesis (Allman, 2004), rats first received training in which the separate presentation of two stimuli (A and B; e.g. two experimental contexts distinguished by their visual properties) predicted the same outcome (food), whereas the separate presentation of two other stimuli (C and D; a second pair of contexts) both predicted a different outcome (no food; see upper panel of Table 7.1). The rats acquired this simple discrimination, and then received a fear conditioning procedure in which A was paired with mild footshock and C was not. This revaluation procedure

Table 7.1 Experimental designs I

Training	**Revaluation**	**Test**
Acquired distinctiveness/equivalence in a simple conditioning procedure		
A→food		
B→food	A→shock	B
C→no food	C→no shock	D
D→no food		
Acquired distinctiveness/equivalence in a configural discrimination procedure		
AX→food, AY→no food		
BX→food, BY→no food	A→shock	B
CX→no food, CY→food	C→no shock	D
DX→no food, DY→food		
Interleaved training on two configural discriminations		
Both groups	Group Congruent:	Group Incongruent:
AX→food, AY→no food	AV→food, AW→no food	AV→food, AW→no food
BX→food, BY→no food	BV→food, BW→no food	BV→no food, BW→food
CX→no food, CY→food	CV→no food, CW→food	CV→no food, CW→food
DX→no food, DY→food	DV→no food, DW→food	DV→food, DW→no food

resulted in significantly more generalized fear to B than to D. Similarly, when C was paired with shock and A was not, rats showed greater generalized fear to D than B (see also, for example, Honey and Hall, 1989a; for parallel results in humans, see e.g. Grice and Davis, 1958). One simple account for such acquired changes in distinctiveness is that when stimuli (A and D) predict different outcomes (e.g. A→food and D→no food) the memories of A and D become more distinct, and this limits the subsequent generalization of fear between them; whereas, when stimuli predict the same outcome (e.g. A→food and B→food) the memories of A and B become less distinct or more similar, thereby enhancing generalization between them. This analysis seems plausible, but it is clearly in need of more detailed specification, and the next sections we evaluate several attempts to provide such specification.

An elemental associative analysis

One popular analysis that has been offered for the acquired distinctiveness and equivalence of cues has its origins in the writings of William James (1890; see also, Hall, 1996; Hull, 1939; Miller and Dollard, 1941). He supposed that when two stimuli (burgundy and claret in his colourful example, A and D in ours) are paired with different outcomes (e.g. A→food and D→no food) they will come to evoke different associates (the memories of food and no food), and these associatively provoked elements will add to the unique elements that are activated by the presentation of A and D. And by simple extension, when two stimuli (e.g. A and B) are paired with the same outcome, they will come to evoke the same associate (e.g. the memory of food), and this associatively provoked element will add to the common elements activated by the presentation of A and B. Under such conditions, when A is later paired with shock, there should be greater generalization to B (which evokes the same associate as A) than to D (which does not; see for example, Honey and Hall, 1989a). This analysis is undermined by recent results that have adopted more complex experimental designs.

Acquired distinctiveness/equivalence in a configural discrimination procedure

The associative analysis presented above has the virtue of simplicity, and it is perhaps for this reason that it has retained an enduring popularity in one form or another (see Hall, 1996). However, the results of recent studies cannot be explained by this associative analysis and instead provide support for alternative, connectionist accounts: these accounts assume that there is a more subtle and interesting interaction between the process of representing stimuli and linking these representations to the outcomes that they predict.

Honey and Watt (1998) gave rats a configural discrimination in which four compounds were paired with food (AX, BX, CY, and DY) and four were paired with no food (CX, DX, AY, and BY; see central panel of Table 7.1). After configural discrimination training, A was paired with footshock and C was not. This revaluation treatment resulted in B eliciting greater generalized fear than D (see for additional examples, Honey and Watt, 1999; Ward-Robinson and Honey, 2000; see also Delamater, 1998). This is an interesting finding because, taken together with other evidence, it cannot be explained in terms of the associative analysis offered by James (1890) or by successive, elemental associative analyses (e.g. Honey and Hall, 1989a; Hull, 1939; Miller and Dollard, 1941). Thus, in the procedure used by Honey and Watt (1998), each of the four stimuli between which stimulus generalization was assessed (A, B, C, and D) had been paired equally often with food and no food, and with X and Y. Consequently, there are no grounds for supposing that the associates that A–D provoke, as a result of appetitive training, could have served as a basis for the differential generalization of fear between them. So, how did configural discrimination training alter the amount of generalization that occurred between A and the test stimuli, B and D?

An extended configural analysis

One account for the results reported by Honey and Watt (1998, 1999; see also, Ward-Robinson and Honey, 2000) can be derived from an extension to a configural analysis of learning. For example, Pearce (1994) supposed that the pattern of stimulation (e.g. AX) presented on a given trial activates a set of input units (A and X) that become linked to a configural unit (which we can label *ax*), and this unit in turn becomes linked to the output unit activated by the outcome that AX precedes (e.g. food). In and of itself, such an analysis cannot provide an account for Honey and Watt's (1998) observations. According to Pearce (1994), the first stage of configural discrimination training will result in each of the eight patterns (AX, BX, CX, DX, AY, BY, CY, DY) becoming linked to their own configural units, which are linked to the outcomes that follow these patterns. There is no basis upon which these configural units could mediate greater generalization of fear between A and B than between A and D: Presentation of A is likely to activate configural units (*ax* and *ay*) that are as similar to those activated by B (i.e. *bx* and *by*) as to those activated by D (i.e. *dx* and *dy*).

In order for a configural analysis to provide an explanation for the fact that there was greater generalization between A and B than between A and D in the study by Honey and Watt (1998), it is necessary to extend the nature of what is encoded on a given trial. Specifically, it is necessary to assume that the pattern of stimulation (e.g. A and X), together with some component of the outcome of the trial (e.g. the evoked representation of food, *f*, or no food, *nf*), are both encoded (see Honey and Watt, 1998, p. 333; Rescorla, 1991, p. 21; see also, Ludvig and Koop, 2008). If rats acquire extended configural representations of this type, then the configural units activated by A and B (e.g. *axf* and *bxf*, respectively) will be more similar to one another than those activated by A and D (e.g. *axf* and *dxnf*). This difference in similarity could provide an account for the fact that the generalization of fear is more marked between A and B than between A and D. However, this extended configural analysis cannot explain results reported by Honey and Ward-Robinson (2001).

In one experiment by Honey and Ward-Robinson (2001), all rats received the same configural discrimination that was given to rats by Honey and Watt (1998) in which A, B, C and D were presented with two auditory stimuli (X and Y); however, rats were also given a second set of configural training trials involving A, B, C and D, and two visual stimuli (V and W; see lower panel of Table 7.1). Days on which rats received configural discrimination involving the auditory stimuli were interleaved with days on which they received the discrimination involving visual stimuli. For group Congruent, separate presentations of A and B with V predicted food, and presentations of A and B with W predicted no food (i.e. AV→food, BV→food, AW→no food, BW→no food); whereas, separate presentations of C and D with V and W predicted the complementary outcomes (i.e. CV→no food, DV→no food, CW→food,

DW→food). For group Incongruent, presentations of A and D with V predicted food, and presentations of A and D with W predicted no food (i.e. AV→food, DV→food, AW→no food, DW→no food); whereas when B and C were presented with V and W, the complementary outcomes were presented (i.e. BV→no food, CV→no food, BW→food, CW→food).

According to the extended configural account, discrimination learning should proceed equally readily in groups Congruent and Incongruent. This prediction is based on the fact that the (extended) configural representations formed during the discriminations given to group Congruent will be as similar to one another as those formed during the discriminations given to group Incongruent. This fact reflects three features of the discriminations given to the two groups: First, each of the compounds presented in the auditory discrimination (i.e. AX, BX, CX, DX, AY, BY, CY, and DY) differs from those presented in the visual discriminations, because either X or Y has been replaced with either V or W (i.e. AV, BV, CV, DV, AW, BW, CW, and DW). Second, each compound from the auditory discrimination (e.g. AX) shares one component (e.g. A) with another compound (e.g. AY) from the auditory discrimination and two compounds (e.g. AV and AW) from both visual discriminations. Finally, these shared components (e.g. A) are part of compounds in the auditory and visual discriminations that are equally likely to be followed by food as they are to be followed by no food. These three features mean that the set of configural representations that develop during the auditory discrimination (i.e. *axf*, *bxf*, *cxnf*, *dxnf*, *aynf*, *bynf*, *cyf*, and *dyf*) are as similar to those that develop during the visual discrimination for group Congruent (i.e. *avf*, *bvf*, *cvnf*, *dvnf*, *awnf*, *bwnf*, *cwf*, and *dwf*) as they are to those that develop during the visual discrimination for group Incongruent (i.e. *avf*, *bwf*, *cvnf*, *dwnf*, *awnf*, *bvnf*, *cwf*, and *dvf*).

As we have noted, the foregoing configural analysis predicts that there should be no difference in the rates at which the Congruent and Incongruent groups acquired the discriminations, but Honey and Ward-Robinson (2001) observed that rats in group Congruent acquired the discriminations involving auditory and visual stimuli more readily than did rats in group Incongruent. This is not an isolated observation. A formally equivalent congruence effect has also been demonstrated in pigeons (e.g. Zentall *et al.*, 1991) and in humans (Delamater and Joseph, 2000; Hodder *et al.*, 2003). Thus, both an extended elemental analysis and an extended configural analysis fail to provide a fully satisfactory account of the acquired changes in stimulus distinctiveness. This conclusion forced us to consider an alternative, connectionist analysis, in which changes in distinctiveness play a more integral part in the process of discrimination learning: Within this analysis, discrimination learning involves an interplay between learning about the stimuli and the outcomes that they predict.

Connectionist analyses

Connectionist networks have frequently been used as a way of modelling aspects of learning, memory and perception, and the interaction between these processes. For example, a connectionist or neural network for Pavlovian conditioning might consist of: a set of dedicated *input* and *output* units, and a layer of intervening or *hidden* units that lie between these input and output units. While the input and output units become active upon presentation of specific stimuli (e.g. the presentation of a tone of a given frequency or the delivery of food, respectively), the hidden units are not activated by any particular stimulus at the outset of training. Rather, it is often assumed that the input-to-hidden layer links are initially weak and random, but these links change as a consequence of experience. Consequently, a given pattern of stimulation (e.g. AX) and other similar patterns (e.g. BX, CX, and DX) will tend to activate the same hidden unit or units at the outset of a discrimination, but as training proceeds, the hidden-layer units become tuned to respond to specific patterns of activity across the input layer. This process of tuning is achieved through changing the strengths of the links between the input and hidden units.

One feature of some of these connectionist networks, which makes them very interesting in the present context, is the effect that training has on the input-to-hidden layer links: When two similar patterns of input (e.g. those provoked by AX and DX) predict different outcomes, they are more likely to come to activate different hidden units than when two patterns (e.g. AX and BX) predict the same outcome, in which case they will be more likely to come to activate the same hidden unit. These properties, sometimes called *predictive differentiation* and *redundancy compression* (see, for example, Gluck and Myers, 1993; see also, Goldstone, 1998; Maki, 1993; Maki and Abunaswass, 1991), allow connectionist networks to provide one form of analysis for acquired changes in stimulus distinctiveness. An evaluation, application, and development of this analysis forms the basis of the remainder of this chapter.

We will first present an informal application of this analysis to the results of Honey and Watt (1998). Remember, in this procedure, rats received the following trial types: AX→food, BX→food, CX→no food, DX→no food, AY→no food, BY→no food, CY→food, DY→food (see central panel of Table 7.1 for experimental design). The idea that when similar compounds (e.g. AX and BX) are followed by the same outcome (e.g. food), the input units that they activate (*a*, *b*, and *x*) become linked to the same hidden unit (*abx*), but when similar compounds (e.g. AX and DX) are followed by different outcomes, they become linked to different hidden units, predicts that four units will be created during appetitive training: *abx*, *cdx*, *aby*, and *cdy*. Under these conditions, when A was later paired with shock, *abx* and/or *aby* would become active and linked to a representation of shock. Consequently, presentations of B will be more likely to provoke fear than D, because B will activate the configural units *abx* and *aby*, and D will not. This analysis also provides a ready explanation for the results of Honey and Ward-Robinson (2001): briefly, for rats in the congruent condition, the groupings of A with B (and of C with D) are consistent across the two kinds of discrimination, but for rats in the incongruent condition, this is not the case (for further discussion, see Honey and Ward-Robinson, 2001).

Clearly, there are many ways to implement the general ideas presented in the previous paragraph – some more complex and less penetrable than others. Our approach has been to use, what we regard to be, the simplest network that will characterize the results of interest here. Of course, this empirically constrained simplicity is all very well, but it inevitably transpires that the resulting network is too simple even within the limited domain to which it is being applied here, (principally, studies involving conditioning in nonhuman animals). However, the network represents a starting position.

Figure 7.1 shows the pattern of connections within a neural network that develop, given the assumptions unpacked below, during the configural training given to rats by Honey and Watt (1998). The critical component of the network that allows synthetic hidden units (i.e. *abx*, *aby*, *cdx*, *cdy*) to develop is feedback from the output units to the hidden layer units. This feedback operates via simple reciprocal links that also form as a result of training. In general terms, these links allow the accuracy with which the outcome of a trial is predicted, on the basis of propagation of activity from the input units through the hidden units to the outcome units, to influence which of the hidden units is selected to be learnt about on a given trial. In particular, simulations by D.N. George show that synthetic units (e.g. *abx*) will develop if the activity that the presentation of an outcome (e.g. food) has on its corresponding outcome unit is allowed to provide feedback to the hidden layer, and influence the selection of which hidden unit wins the competition to be learnt about on that trial. We will now illustrate how this feedback results in the development of the critical synthetic units.

Some critical details

In the simulations, the network initially receives a pattern of input across the input layer (e.g. A and X) and generates a prediction (or performance) based

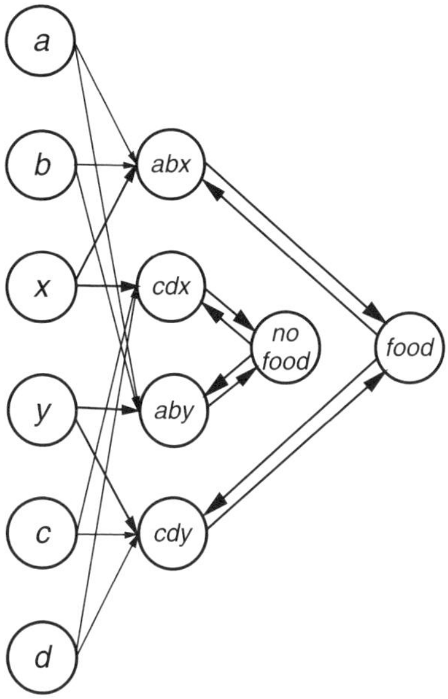

Fig. 7.1 A connectionist network in which: input units (*a*, *b*, *c*, *d*, *x*, and *y*) activated by similar compound stimuli (e.g. AX and DX) that have been followed by different outcomes (food and no food, respectively) have become linked to different hidden-layer units (e.g. *abx* and *cdx*); whereas similar compound stimuli (e.g. AX and BX) that have been followed by the same outcome (e.g. food) have become linked to the same hidden-layer unit (e.g. *abx*; adapted from Allman et al., 2004).

on (i) the hidden unit that wins an initial competition to be selected and (ii) the output unit that this unit activates (*food* or *no food*). Briefly, the probability that a given hidden unit will be selected as the winner upon presentation of an input pattern, depends upon the (weighted) activity that it receives from the active input units: the greater the activity that a hidden unit receives relative to other units, the more likely it is to be selected as the winner. Once the outcome is presented, this selection process is repeated with the influence of the now active output unit included; this influence on the hidden layer is mediated by the output-to-hidden layer links. At this point, changes are made to the strength of links (using Hebbian learning principles[1]; Hebb, 1949; Stent, 1973) between: the input units (*a*, *b*, *c*, *d*, *x*, or *y*) activated by the stimuli presented on that trial (A, B, C, D, X, or Y) and the resulting winning hidden unit; and to the reciprocal links between the winning hidden unit and the output unit (*food* or *no food*) activated by the outcome of the trial (food or no food). The pattern of connections that develops within the network becomes more

[1] The use of simple Hebbian learning principles might seem to be contraindicated by selective learning phenomena like blocking (Kamin, 1968); however, adopting a more complex analysis of, for example, the types of activation of the units (e.g. Wagner, 1981) allows simple Hebbian learning to generate these selective learning phenomena (cf. Honey, 2000).

like that caricatured in Figure 7.1 as the number of hidden units that are initially available increases (e.g. from 4 to 16).

To give a concrete example of how this process produces the desired groupings, imagine first that on Trial 1, AX is paired with food. The presentation of AX will result in a hidden unit (*ax*) being recruited, and then the input-to-hidden layer (*a*→*ax* and *x*→*ax*) links and the reciprocal links between *ax* and the food output unit (*ax*→*food*, and *food*→*ax*) will be strengthened upon presentation of food. Imagine now that either BX or DX is presented on Trial 2. Both compounds will have a tendency to result in the *ax* hidden unit being selected by virtue of the *x*→*ax* link that was strengthened on Trial 1. However, once the outcomes are delivered following presentation of BX (i.e. food) and DX (i.e. no food), the *ax* hidden unit is more likely to be selected as the 'winner' and focus for (further) learning on the BX trial than on the DX trial. When food is delivered after BX, it will provide an additional source of activation to *ax* (via the *food*→*ax* link), but this will not be the case when no food is presented after DX: links between the *no food* output unit and the hidden layer units have not been changed as a consequence of the AX→food trial. Consequently, when BX is followed by food on Trial 2, the winning hidden unit is likely to remain *ax* and there will be strengthening of the *b*→*ax* link. This will result in all three of the input units activated by AX and BX becoming linked to the same, *abx* hidden unit. However, the same process of assimilation is less likely to operate on a trial in which DX is followed by no food, because *ax* is less likely to remain the winning unit when no food follows the presentation of DX, and under these conditions, there will be no strengthening of the *d*→*ax* link. This analysis is based upon several assumptions (some more critical than others), but even presented at this relatively sparse level of detail, it should be apparent that it makes a number of interesting predictions. In the next section, we review our investigations of whether these predictions are borne out.

Ambiguous test compounds

According to the analysis being considered, changes in stimulus distinctiveness solely reflect changes in the input-hidden-layer links that result in different input patterns becoming more or less likely to activate the same hidden layer units: Increases in distinctiveness reflect the fact that when two similar patterns have predicted different outcomes (e.g. AX and DX in Honey and Watt, 1998), they will have come to activate different hidden-layer units. Reductions in distinctiveness reflect the fact that when two stimuli have predicted the same outcome (e.g. AX and BX) they will have come to activate the same hidden-layer unit. Through these changes, animals will, in some sense, perceive two stimuli that share the capacity to activate the same hidden unit as being more similar to one another than two stimuli that activate different hidden units. One obvious prediction that follows from this analysis concerns the consequence of presenting different kinds of ambiguous compounds once the hypothetical structure depicted in Figure 7.1 is in place. In short, combining the unique components (e.g. A and B) of two equivalently trained compound stimuli (e.g. AX and BX) will result in dual activation of a shared hidden unit (e.g. *abx* or *aby*), whereas combining the unique components (e.g. A and D) of two stimuli that have been paired with different outcomes (e.g. AX and DX) will provide a single source of activation to *abx*, *aby*, *cdx*, and *cdy* (see upper panel of Table 7.2).

The behavioural consequences of the difference in hidden-layer activity described in the preceding paragraph depend upon the specific assumptions that one makes about the characteristics of the hidden units. If one assumes, for example, that (i) one hidden unit will become fully active at any point in time, and the conventional assumption that (ii) the output of this unit is a sigmoidal function of the input that it receives (e.g. Rumelhart *et al.*, 1986), then presentation of AB will strongly activate either *abx* or *aby*. In turn, *abx* or *aby* will strongly activate either the food output unit or the no food output unit, respectively. Given the fact that *abx* is linked to the food output unit whereas *aby* is linked to the no food unit (see Figure 7.1), the behavioural

Table 7.2 Experimental designs II

Training	**Test**	
Ambiguous test compounds		
AX→food, AY→no food		
BX→food, BY→no food	AB/CD	
CX→no food, CY→food	AD/BC	
DX→no food, DY→food		
Training	**Revaluation**	**Test**
Contextual modulation of similarity		
AX→food, AY→food		
BX→food, BY→no food	B→shock	AX, CX
CX→no food, CY→no food	D→no shock	AY, CY
DX→no food, DY→food		
Training	**Test**	
Selection by feedback		
AX→food, AY→no food	food→AB	
BX→food, BY→no food	food→AD	
CX→no food, CY→food	no food→CD	
DX→no food, DY→food	no food→BC	

consequences will be that, at a given point in time, some rats will respond at a high rate and others at a low rate. That is, there should be a great deal of variability in response rates when rats are presented with AB that reflects whether *abx* or *aby* wins the competition (and affects behaviour) at a given point in time. The situation just described is analogous to a human faced with two equally valid interpretations of an ambiguous figure (e.g. a Necker cube), where the two interpretations compete with one another, and the ambiguous figure is interpreted first in one way and then the other.

In contrast, the presentation of AD will provide a single source of activation to *abx*, *aby*, *cdx*, and *cdy*, and once a winner is determined, this should be relatively less successful at affecting activity in the food or no food output units; either because it takes a greater amount of time to determine the winner, or because the output of the winning unit is dependent on the activation that it has received. In summary, our connectionist analysis predicts greater variability on AB (and CD) trials than on AD (and BC) trials.

Honey and Ward-Robinson (2002) observed that while the mean level of responding on AB and AD trials was relatively similar, the variability in the level of responding was significantly greater on AB trials than on AD trials (for a parallel finding in humans, see Hodder *et al.* 2004). Moreover, unpublished data from the same experiment revealed that individual rats showed greater variability in responding across time during, for example, AB trials than during AD trials. One obvious interpretation of this finding is that the hidden unit that is activated by the ambiguous compound, AB, was oscillating between *abx* and *aby* across time in an analogous way to how the interpretation of a Necker cube is bistable across time. Further evidence consistent with this analysis has been reported by Allman *et al.* (2004; see also, Allman and Honey, 2006).

Contextual modulation of similarity

The connectionist approach to acquired changes in stimulus distinctiveness/equivalence makes a further intriguing prediction. Imagine that the network (and rats) received training in which separate presentations of AX and BX are paired with food, CX and DX are paired with no food, AY and DY are paired with food, and BY and CY are paired with no food (see central panel of Table 7.2). According to the theoretical analysis that we have been considering, this training should result in a network with four configural units: *abx*, *cdx*, *ady*, and *bcy*. That is, A should be grouped with B, and C should be grouped with D, when these stimuli are accompanied by X, whereas A should be grouped with D, and B should be grouped with C, when these same stimuli are presented with Y. To assess this prediction, after receiving the appetitive training

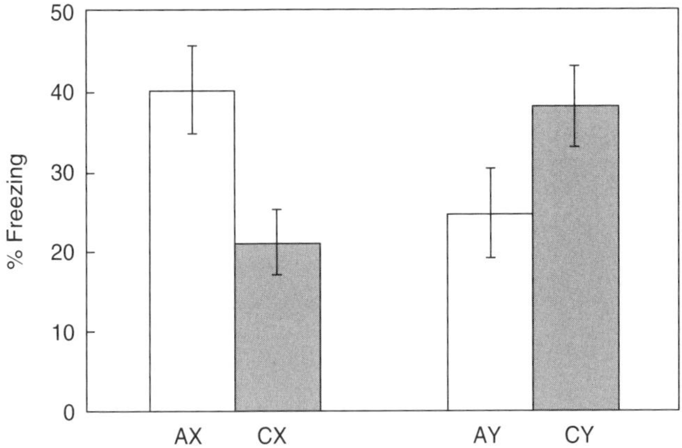

Fig. 7.2 Mean percentages of time freezing during A and C (±SEM) as a function of whether they were presented with X or Y (for experimental design, see centre panel of Table 7.2; adapted from Close et al., 2009).

trials described above, Close *et al.* (2009) gave rats conditioning trials in which B was paired with shock and D was not. The presentation of B should activate *abx* and/or *bcy* during the revaluation procedure, which should result in them becoming linked to shock. Based upon the connectionist analysis outlined previously, the test compounds that provide dual sources of activation to either *abx* or *bcy* should be more likely to elicit fear than the test compounds that provide only a single source of activation to them. Accordingly, AX, which strongly activates *abx*, should elicit more fear than CX, which weakly activates *abx* and *cby*; and CY, which strongly activates *bcy*, should elicit more fear than AY, which weakly activates *bcy* and *abx*. This was exactly the pattern of results observed by Close *et al.* (2009; see Figure 7.2). This dramatic modulation of the generalization of fear to A and C, brought about by the presence of X or Y, is entirely consistent with the connectionist analysis of acquired changes in stimulus distinctiveness. Moreover, this finding in rats resonates with the observation that in humans similarity judgements are influenced by the context (X or Y in Close *et al.*, 2009) in which those judgments are made (see Barsalou, 1982; Medin, *et al.* 1993; Tversky and Gati, 1978). For example, a flashlight and a rope are considered dissimilar to one another until they are presented in the context '*taken on camping trips*'.

Selection by feedback

Within the connectionist account being considered, the outcome of a trial plays a significant role in determining whether the hidden unit that has been selected on the basis of the propagation of activation from the input to the hidden layer should be retained to serve as the focus for leaning on that trial, or whether another hidden unit should be selected instead. To use a gambling metaphor, the outcome of a trial determines whether the network should *stick* with the hidden unit that has been selected on the basis of the input pattern, or *twist* to a different hidden unit based on the outcome that is presented. The network is more likely to stick when the prediction that is generated on the basis of the input pattern is accurate compared to when it is not. The role of the outcome in determining which hidden unit is chosen (from those that could be selected) has been examined in an outcome priming procedure developed by Honey and Ward-Robinson (2002; see also, Honey and Watt, 1998).

Once the presumed pattern of connections shown in Figure 7.1 had been acquired, rats received a treatment designed to activate the food output unit and then received test trials with AB and AD (see lower panel of Table 7.2). As we have already noted, these ambiguous compounds ordinarily provoke similar mean levels of conditioned responding. However, when rats were given a food prime immediately before the test trials, AB elicited more responding than AD. This finding indicates the food prime resolves which of the two rival interpretations of AB (i.e., *abx* or *aby*) should win the competition to influence performance. In this case, the food prime results in *abx* winning (because it has received input from *a*, *b* and *food*) and it can then (re)activate the food outcome unit. Presumably, the food prime also influences which of the hidden units (i.e. *abx*, *aby*, *cdx*, and *cdy*) weakly activated by AD wins, but this influence is less marked than it is for AB. A formally equivalent analysis applies to the effects of activating the *no food* unit immediately before the presentation of CD or CB. In this case, the predicted pattern of results, and that observed by Honey and Ward-Robinson (2002), is that CD should provoke less responding than CB (see also, Honey and Watt, 1998).

Configural learning without changes in distinctiveness

As we have just noted, the feedback process that operates between the output and hidden layers plays a critical role in producing changes in stimulus distinctiveness (e.g. Honey and Ward-Robinson, 2001, 2002; Honey and Watt, 1998, 1999). Indeed, without this feedback process, the network would become akin to a simple configural network, like that developed by Pearce (1994); where similar patterns (e.g. AX and BX or AX and DX) might well be more likely to activate the same hidden units than would quite different patterns (e.g. AX and BY or AX and DY), but in which the effective similarity of the patterns would not be influenced by whether those patterns predicted different outcomes or the same outcome. This form of network would be capable of learning a configural discrimination, but this process of learning would not result in changes in stimulus distinctiveness. In fact, such a dissociation has been observed in rats with lesions of the enthorhinal cortex in a procedure that was analogous to that developed by Honey and Watt (1998).

Rats that had received excitotoxic lesions of the enthorhinal cortex or hippocampus acquired the appetitive configural discrimination (depicted in the centre panel of Table 7.1) as readily as sham-operated controls rats. After an appetitive revaluation procedure involving A and C (A→food and C→no food; cf. Ward-Robinson and Honey, 2000), control rats and those with lesions of the hippocampus showed greater generalization to B than to D. That is, both groups showed an acquired distinctiveness/equivalence effect. However, this effect was not observed in the group of rats with lesions of the enthorhinal cortex: after the revaluation procedure involving A and C, these rats showed equivalent generalization to B and D (see Coutureau *et al.*, 2002; see also, Iordanova *et al.*, 2007).

The obvious interpretation of the pattern of results in rats with lesions of the enthorhinal cortex was that configural learning was occurring without changes in stimulus distinctiveness. That is, patterns of input were both being represented (e.g. by activating different hidden units) and associated with the appropriate outcomes, but this process was not accompanied by changes in the likelihood that the inputs would be grouped according to the outcomes that they predicted. This interpretation received further support from a more detailed analysis of data from the first stage of configural training in Coutureau *et al.* (2002; see also Iordanova *et al.*, 2007). Thus, although rats with lesions of the enthorhinal cortex acquired the original configural discrimination as readily as the other groups, there was evidence that the way in which the configural discrimination was acquired differed from these groups. Examination of the correlations between the configural discrimination scores involving the contexts that should activate the same configural units (e.g. A and B) revealed that they were closely coupled (i.e. correlated) in the sham-operated control rats and rats with hippocampus lesions, but not in rats with enthorhinal cortex lesions. This pattern of correlations is precisely what one would anticipate if the effective similarity of A and B (and C and D) was greater in the sham-operated and hippocampal rats than in those with lesions of the enthorhinal cortex (see Coutureau *et al.*, 2002; see also, Iordanova *et al.*, 2007).

Changes in distinctiveness assessed using an IDS/EDS procedure

Oswald *et al.* (2001) have conducted another study with rats to examine the influence of lesions to the enthorhinal cortex on a second instance of acquired distinctiveness. In this case, the behavioural finding of interest was the observation that transfer between two discriminations is better when the same dimension remains relevant (an IDS) than when the dimensions that are relevant change across discriminations (an EDS; e.g. George and Pearce, 1999; Mackintosh and Little, 1969; Shepp and Eimas, 1964). The procedure used by Oswald *et al.* (2001) was analogous to that developed by George and Pearce (1999; see also, Kruschke, 1996). Rats with enthorhinal cortex lesions acquired the configural discriminations in the first and second stages of training perfectly readily. However, while there was an IDS/EDS effect in control rats, there was no evidence of this effect in rats with lesions of the enthorhinal cortex.

The fact that lesions of the enthorhinal cortex abolished the IDS/EDS effect and the acquired distinctiveness/equivalence effect (which has been the focus of interest here; cf. Coutureau *et al.*, 2002) is consistent with the proposition that these two effects have a common origin. It will be recalled that the IDS/EDS effect has most often been taken to reflect the operation of attentional processes (cf. Mackintosh, 1974, p. 597). In contrast, we suppose that the IDS/EDS effect, like the acquired distinctiveness/equivalence effect, reflects the tuning of input-to-hidden layer links brought about through a process of feedback from the outcome-to-hidden unit links. We have already applied this analysis to the acquired distinctiveness/equivalence of cues and now apply it to a simple IDS/EDS effect.

A connectionist analysis of the IDS/EDS effect

Oswald *et al.* (2001, pp. 846–848) proposed that the grouping of patterns resulting from the operation of a process of acquired equivalence paved the way for the network to 'tune in' to the more 'predictive' components of equivalent patterns and to 'tune out' their less predictive components. This idea can be illustrated with reference to the simple situation in which the input units (*a*, *b*, and *x*) activated by two similar patterns (AX and BX) have become linked to the same hidden unit (*abx*) as a result of predicting the same outcome (e.g., food); whereas the inputs (*a*, *b*, and *y*) activated by AY and BY have become linked to *aby* as a result of predicting no food. This is the situation that should arise during the first stage of a simple IDS/EDS experiment, where X and Y represent the stimuli from a relevant dimension, and A and B represent stimuli from an irrelevant dimension. That is, hidden units *abx* and *aby* should develop as a result of the following trial types: AX→food, BX→food, AY→no food, and BY→no food. It should be immediately evident that input unit *x* will have a stronger link to *abx*, and *y* will have a stronger link to *aby*, than will either *a* or *b*: There are a greater number of *x*→*abx* and *y*→*aby* pairings than there are *a*→*abx or b*→*abx* and *a*→*aby or b*→*aby* pairings. Moreover, repeated activation of *abx* by AX (without accompanying input from *b*) and BX (without input from *a*) will reduce the *b*→*abx* and *a*→*abx* links, respectively; similarly, repeated activation of *aby* by AY (without accompanying input from *b*) and by BY (without input from *a*) will reduce the *b*→*aby* and *a*→*aby* links, respectively. That is, the strengthening of the *a*→*abx* and *b*→*abx* links, and of *a*→*aby* and *b*→*aby* links, will be constrained by the operation of an anti-Hebbian learning process (cf. Stent, 1973; see also, Bateson and Horn, 1994). The result will be that the relevant stimuli (X and Y) and stimuli similar to them (V and W), will exert a greater influence on the hidden-layer unit (in this case *abx* and *aby*) than will the irrelevant stimuli (A and B) and stimuli similar to them (C and D).[2]

Now, if one assumes that the discrimination learning trials described in the previous paragraph have left the irrelevant dimension (A, B, C, and D) with little or no capacity to activate the hidden layer units (*abx* and *aby*), it becomes a relatively simple matter to appreciate why a discrimination involving an IDS will be acquired more readily than one that involves an EDS. In an IDS, the stimuli from the formerly relevant dimension (V and W) will strongly activate both *abx* and *aby*, while those from the present but irrelevant dimension (C and D) will not. On each trial, links between the input units uniquely activated by V and W (i.e. *v* and *w*) and *abx* or *aby* will be changed through the Hebbian and anti-Hebbian learning processes described above. For example, consider a trial in which V is paired with food and *abx* wins the competition to be learnt about. This trial will result in both the strengthening of the *v*→*abx* link (through Hebbian learning) and the weakening of the *w*→*abx* link (through anti-Hebbian learning); the remaining links (*v*→*aby* and *w*→*aby*) will be unchanged. These changes will result in correct performance when V is encountered next (because V consistently predicts food, and *v*→*abx*→*food* is greater than *v*→*aby*→*no food*). They will also result in correct performance when W is encountered on a nonreinforced trial (because *w*→*aby*→*no food* is greater than *w*→*abx*→*food*). In an EDS, V and W will again strongly activate *abx* and *aby*, and C and D will not. However, the same changes in the links between *v*, *w*, and *abx* on a trial in which V is paired with food will not result

[2] For the sake of simplicity, we have restricted our analysis by assuming that each of the components of the various trials (e.g., A, B, and X) activates a single input unit; but we recognize that each component is likely to activate many input units (cf. Atkinson and Estes, 1962). Once it is assumed that A and B (for example) activate common input units, then the fate of these common units will be equivalent to the fate of X; similarly, the fates of the unique input units activated by A and B will be equivalent to those described for A and B. That is, the common input units that both A and B activate will gain greater control over a shared hidden-layer unit than will the inputs that they uniquely activate.

in accurate performance when V (or W) is next encountered (because V and W are not consistently reinforced or nonreinforced). Importantly, it should be noted that the analysis outlined above still holds when links are concurrently changed (i.e. increased) between the input units activated by C and D (*c* and *d*) and the hidden layer units (*abx* and *aby*).

The analysis of the IDS/EDS effect described above does not require us to appeal to a process of attentional modulation and is consistent with our connectionist analysis of the effects of training on stimulus distinctiveness (e.g. Honey and Watt, 1998). As we have mentioned, this analysis receives support from the finding that lesions of the enthorhinal cortex disrupt both effects. One issue that still remains concerns how the dissociation between configural learning (normal in rats with such lesions) and acquired distinctiveness effects (abolished by the same lesions) should be explained. An obvious locus within our network that could result in such a dissociation is the feedback process that operates between the outcome units and hidden-layer units: As previously noted, although this process is central to generating acquired changes in stimulus distinctiveness/equivalence, it is not required to explain the acquisition of a configural discrimination (cf. Pearce, 1994). If lesions to the enthorhinal cortex disrupted this feedback process, then configural learning could proceed in the absence of changes in stimulus distinctiveness (see George, 2010, this volume, for a detailed analysis of the neural mechanisms involved in acquired distinctiveness).

Further development and application

Among a number of outstanding issues, two that merit consideration here are a conundrum concerning how patterning discriminations are solved and the issue of how simple unsupervised exposure to patterns of stimulation results in a change in their distinctiveness. We will address these issues in turn.

Acquired distinctiveness/equivalence in patterning discriminations

In negative patterning, while the presentation of either one stimulus (A) or another (B) signals one outcome (e.g. the delivery of food), the presentation of both stimuli together (AB) signals a different outcome (e.g. the absence of that outcome, or no food). Configural models of the kind developed by Pearce (1994) suppose that the presentation of A, B, and AB results in the input units that they excite becoming linked to corresponding configural units that code for whether A and B have either been presented alone (and activate *a* and *b* configural units, respectively), or together (and activate an *ab* unit). The configural units *a*, *b*, and *ab* are, in turn, linked to (outcome) units activated by the presentation of either food or no food (cf. Konorski, 1967; see also, Honey and Ward-Robinson, 2002; Honey and Watt, 1998) or become connected by excitatory (*a* and *b*) and inhibitory (*ab*) links to food (cf. Pearce, 1994; Rescorla and Wagner, 1972). Support for this form of analysis can be derived from the results of studies by Redhead and Pearce (1995; see also, Williams *et al.*, 2002, 2004). However, this analysis seems, if not contrary to, then certainly inconsistent with the spirit of the connectionist analysis developed herein: The thrust of this chapter is that stimulus distinctiveness and equivalence are brought about within a network in which (similar) stimuli that predict different outcomes come to activate different hidden units, and stimuli that predict the same outcome (e.g. A and B in a patterning discrimination) come to activate the same hidden unit. So, how can the principles just outlined be squared with the fact that animals can acquire patterning discriminations?

One could argue that when A and B are quite different, as they often are in patterning discriminations, then there will be no initial tendency for them to activate the same hidden unit, and the fact that they are both paired with the same outcome will not result in them becoming more likely to do so (cf. Delamater, 1998; Honey and Watt, 1998). This is an unsatisfactory position to adopt: rats can acquire patterning discriminations in which a common element (X) is explicitly added to each of the trial types (i.e. AX→food, BX→food, ABX→no food), albeit rather slowly (see Redhead and Pearce, 1995; Rescorla, 1972). So, how could rats solve patterning problems in a way that retains the principle that when stimuli are followed by the same outcome they come to address the same hidden unit? The suggestion that because A and B (or AX and BX) predict the same outcome (e.g. food) in a patterning discrimination they should come to activate the same hidden unit (let us call it *a/b*) has attendant problems. For example, there is nothing in what has been written thus far that would lead one to expect that when A or B are presented such an *a/b* unit will activate one outcome unit (i.e. food), but when AB is presented this unit will activate a different outcome unit (i.e. no food). Similarly, even if the *a/b* unit was linked to one outcome (e.g. food) and a further hidden unit (*ab*) was linked to a different outcome (e.g. no food), it is not immediately obvious why separate presentations of A or B should be more likely to activate the *a/b* than the *ab* unit, but that the reverse should be the case when the AB compound is presented. However, there is an elegant solution to this conundrum that was devised by Christopher Grand in his doctoral thesis (Grand, 2007) in the form of the *dual node model.*

The dual node model is depicted in the upper panels of Figure 7.3. This model has an *ab* unit that becomes active upon presentation of A and B together, but does not become fully active when either A or B are presented alone; it also has

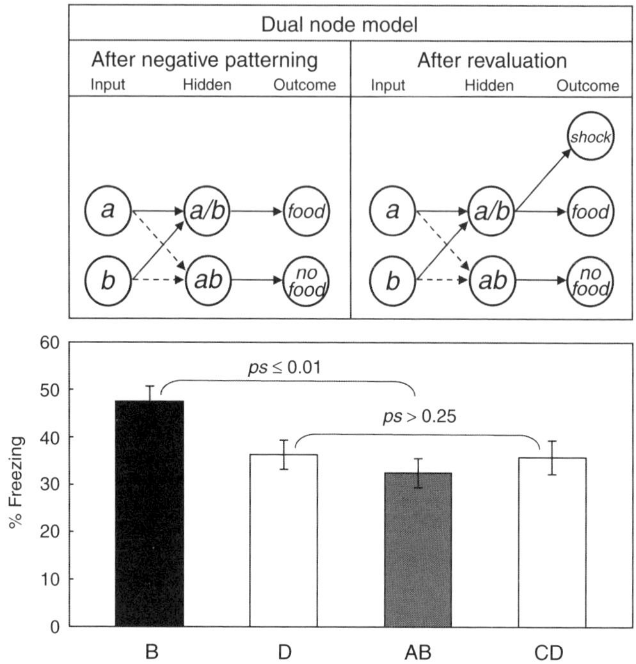

Fig. 7.3 Upper panel: Illustration of the state of a novel connectionist network after negative patterning training (left) and the consequences, for the network, of pairing stimulus A with shock after patterning training (right). Lower panel: Mean percentages of time freezing (±SEM) during B, D, AB, and CD (for experimental design, see upper panel of Table 7.3; adapted from Grand and Honey, 2008).

a second type of unit (*a/b*) whose activation profile is the opposite to that just described: the *a/b* unit becomes active upon presentation of either A or B alone and does not become fully active when A and B are presented together. According to the dual node model, negative patterning is solved by the presentation of A with B activating *ab*, which is linked to no food, and the presentation of A or B activating *a/b*, which is linked to food (see left upper panel of Figure 7.3). The way in which the nonreinforced AB compound and its reinforced components, A or B, become linked to their respective *ab* or *a/b* unit involves the same feedback processes that have been described above, and for which there is direct evidence (cf. Honey and Ward-Robinson, 2002; Honey and Watt, 1998). Although this second type of unit might seem contrived, there is some indirect evidence to support it from, for example, single-cell recording studies in macaques. Specifically, there is a large population of cortical visual neurons that have an analogous property to hypothetical *a/b* units: they

Table 7.3 Experimental designs III

Training	**Revaluation**	**Test**
Acquired distinctiveness/equivalence in patterning discriminations		
A→food, B→food, AB→no food	A→shock	B, AB
C→no food, D→no food, CD→food	C→no shock	D, CD
Preexposure	**Configural learning**	**Test**
Configural preconditioning		
AB	AX→food, AY→no food	BX, BY
CD	CX→no food, CY→food	DX, DY

supersaturate at high contrast rather than exhibiting saturation. This means that at high contrast their firing decreases rather than plateaus (Peirce, 2007).

Grand and Honey (2008) have assessed the analysis described in the previous paragraph in a series of experiments with rats. The general logic behind the experiments was straightforward: Once rats had acquired a patterning discrimination (e.g. A→food, B→food, AB→no food), they received revaluation trials on which A was paired with shock (see upper panel of Table 7.3). According to the connectionist model in which there are two types of hidden layer units (e.g. *a/b* and *ab*), pairing A with shock should result in the *a/b* unit, but not the *ab* unit, becoming linked to an outcome unit activated by shock (see right upper panel of Figure 7.3). Under these conditions, presenting B alone should also be capable of activating the shock output unit and eliciting fear, because it too will activate the *a/b* unit. However, presenting the compound AB should not activate the shock output unit as it will activate the *ab* unit. This is precisely the result observed by Grand and Honey (2008; see lower panel of Figure 7.3). Moreover, B also elicited greater generalized fear than a control stimulus, D, which had originally been trained in a positive patterning discrimination, and a compound stimulus (CD) that had been paired with the same outcome as B (in this case food).[3] The dual node connectionist network uniquely predicts this pattern of results. The introduction of different types of hidden unit might strike some as an awkward development, lacking parsimony. It is certainly an idea that raises theoretical issues that will need, at a future date, to be addressed. However, it is worth repeating that there is

[3] In fact, the design was counterbalanced, so that half of the rats received the assignment of stimulus pairs (A and B, C and D) to patterning discrimination (negative or positive) shown in the upper panel of Table 7.3, whereas the remainder received the reverse (i.e. A and B were the designated stimuli for positive patterning, and C and D were the stimuli for negative patterning).

independent evidence to support this theoretical analysis from studies of real, as opposed to artificial, neural networks (e.g. Peirce, 2007).

Exposure learning and configural learning

The main focus of this chapter has been on the changes in stimulus distinctiveness that are a product of training in which stimuli are paired with outcomes that have motivational significance. Our theoretical analysis of these changes has been based upon the neural network depicted in Figure 7.1. Although one might suppose that the hidden-layer units within such a network might be especially likely to be recruited when motivationally significant stimuli are involved, there is, in fact, evidence that is consistent with the involvement of this network during exposure to neutral stimuli. For example, there are demonstrations of the acquired distinctiveness/equivalence of cues that have employed a formally equivalent design to that used by Honey and Hall (1989a; see upper panel of Table 7.1), but in which the roles of food and no food are replaced by the presence or absence of a (relatively) neutral stimulus (see Honey and Hall, 1991). Also, animals can learn configural discriminations in which all of the components are neutral stimuli (see Iordanova *et al.*, 2008; cf. Honey *et al.*, 2010). In a similar vein, Lin and Honey (2010) have recently demonstrated that simple preexposure to compound stimuli (e.g. AB and CD) allows subsequent configural learning involving A and C (i.e. AX→food, AY→no food, CX→no food, CY→food) to transfer to novel compounds involving B and D (i.e. BX and DY elicit more conditioned responding than do BY and CX; see lower panel of Table 7.3). This *configural preconditioning* effect suggests that input units activated by B and D become assimilated into the hidden units recruited during configural learning (see also, Allman and Honey, 2006). Taken together, these observations suggest that our theoretical analysis is applicable to simple, exposure learning effects.

Another well-established consequence of exposure to two similar compounds (AX and BX) is that it reduces the extent to which conditioned responding established to AX generalizes to BX (e.g. Honey and Hall, 1989b), and increases the rate at which a discrimination between AX and BX is acquired (e.g. Gibson and Walk, 1956). In the terms of this chapter, familiarity with stimuli can enhance their distinctiveness. A thorough review of the literature concerning such *perceptual learning* effects is beyond the scope of the current chapter (see, for a review and analysis, Hall, 1991; McLaren and Mackintosh, 2000), but the possibility that such effects, like those under scrutiny in this chapter, could be captured within a shared neural network merits further consideration.

One way in which stimulus exposure might influence stimulus distinctiveness is by modifying the strengths of links between the input units (e.g. *a* and *b* in Figure 7.1). Changes in these links might then alter which input units are linked to the hidden-layer units during later learning involving AX and BX (cf. Allman and Honey, 2006; Lin and Honey, 2010). For example, McLaren *et al.* (1989) have argued that alternating exposure to AX and BX might result in the development of inhibitory links between the unique elements of these compounds (i.e. A and B; see Dwyer and Mackintosh, 2002; Honey *et al.*, 1994; Mundy *et al.*, 2006). McLaren *et al.* (1989) suggested that these links would counteract any tendency for B to become active when AX is presented, or A to become active when BX is presented – tendencies that would result from the formation of A–X and B–X associations. If such inhibitory links were to form between *a* and *b* in the network shown in Figure 7.1, then they would similarly counteract any tendency for *b* to become assimilated into the hidden unit activated on an AX trial, or *a* to become assimilated into the hidden unit activated on a BX trial: Such assimilation might be expected on the basis of the strengthening of a link involving the input unit activated by the common element (*x*) and a hidden layer unit.

An alternative possibility is that stimulus exposure influences the pattern of links between the input units and hidden-layer units (cf. Allman and Honey 2006). For example, repeated exposure to X during intermixed exposure to AX and BX might result in (short-term) adaptation or habituation in the *x* input unit which could (1) reduce the likelihood that AX and BX would be drawn into same hidden unit (see Honey and Bateson, 1996; Mundy *et al.*, 2007, 2009; see also Mitchell *et al.* 2008), or (2) increase the likelihood that *a* and *b* will be linked to different hidden layer units. There is indirect evidence, from the studies of perceptual learning cited above, that is consistent with both of these analyses of how simple exposure might influence the patterns of activation within the kind of neural network depicted in Figure 7.1.

Concluding comments

The central thesis of this chapter is that the modulation of stimulus distinctiveness can be best understood in terms of a relatively simple neural network that operates according to penetrable principles: where experience shapes the patterns of connections between sensory input and a layer of hidden units within the network. We submit that these changes to input-to-hidden layer links occur as the result of simple exposure to patterns of stimulation, but that the nature of these changes is influenced by a process of local feedback that is based upon the accuracy with which the outcome of a given trial is predicted (see also, Le Pelley, 2010). The evidence that we have adduced in support of this analysis comes from a variety of sources, and we have argued that this evidence is difficult to interpret in terms of simpler associative analyses. Moreover, our connectionist analysis obviates the need to supplement associative processes with other processes, such as attention, to explain how cues gain and lose distinctiveness. Perhaps, then, it is time to retreat from invoking a family of such attentional processes (cf. Pearce and Mackintosh, 2010, this volume) and to instead give greater consideration to whether the available evidence requires us to appeal to anything more than associative processes operating within a relatively simple connectionist architecture.

Acknowledgements

The authors thank the BBSRC (UK) for funding the research upon which parts of this chapter are based. We are also indebted to Chris Mitchell, Dave George, and Mike Le Pelley for providing comments on a draft of this chapter.

References

Allman, M. J. (2004). *Analysis of the nature of the representations that mediate acquired equivalence and distinctiveness*. PhD thesis, Cardiff University.

Allman, M. J. & Honey, R. C. (2005). Associative change in connectionist networks: An addendum. *Journal of Experimental Psychology: Animal Behavior Processes*, **31**, 363–367.

Allman, M. J. & Honey, R. C. (2006). Transfer of configural learning between the components of a preexposed stimulus compound: Implications for elemental and configural models of learning. *Journal of Experimental Psychology: Animal Behavior Processes*, **32**, 307–313.

Allman, M. J. Ward-Robinson, J., & Honey, R. C. (2004). Associative change in the representations acquired during conditional discriminations: Further analysis of the nature of conditional learning. *Journal of Experimental Psychology: Animal Behavior Processes*, **30**, 118–128.

Atkinson, R. C. & Estes, W. K. (1963). Stimulus sampling theory, in R. D. Luce, R. R. Bush, and E. Galanter (Eds) *Handbook of mathematical psychology: Vol. 2*, pp. 121–268. New York: Wiley.

Barsalou, L. W. (1982). Context-independent and context-dependent information in concepts. *Memory & Cognition*, **10**, 82–93.

Bateson, P. & Horn, G. (1994). Imprinting and recognition memory: a neural net model. *Animal Behaviour*, **48**, 695–715.

Close, J. Hahn, U., & Honey, R. C. (2009). Contextual modulation of similarity in the rat. *Journal of Experimental Psychology: Animal Behavior Processes*, **35**, 509–515.

Coutureau, E. Killcross, A. S. Good, M. Marshall, V. J. Ward-Robinson, J., & Honey, R. C. (2002). Acquired equivalence and distinctiveness of cues: II. Neural manipulations and their implications. *Journal of Experimental Psychology: Animal Behavior Processes*, **28**, 388–396.

Delamater, A. R. (1998). Associative mediational processes in the acquired equivalence and distictiveness of cues. *Journal of Experimental Psychology: Animal Behavior Processes,* **24**, 467–482.

Delamater, A. R. & Joseph, P. (2000). Common coding in symbolic matching tasks in humans: Training with a common consequence or antecedent. *Quarterly Journal of Experimental Psychology*, **53B**, 255–273.

Dwyer, D. M. & Mackintosh, N. J. (2002). Perceptual learning: Alternating exposure to two compound flavours creates inhibitory associations between their unique features. *Animal Learning & Behavior,* **30**, 201–207.

George, D. N. (2009). Neural correlates of attentional set, in C. J. Mitchell and M. E. Le Pelley (Ed.) *Attention and learning,* this volume. Oxford: Oxford University Press.

George, D. N. & Pearce, J. M. (1999). Acquired distinctiveness is controlled by stimulus relevance not correlation with reward. *Journal of Experimental Psychology: Animal Behavior Processes*, **25**, 363–373.

Gibson, E. J. & Walk, R. D. (1956). The effect of prolonged exposure to visually presented patterns on learning to discriminate them. *Journal of Comparative and Physiological Psychology*, **49**, 239–242.

Gluck, M. A. & Myers, C. E. (1993). Hippocampal mediation of stimulus representation: A computational theory. *Hippocampus*, **3**, 491–516.

Goldstone, R. L. (1998). Perceptual learning. *Annual Review of Psychology*, **49**, 585–610.

Grand, C. S. (2007). *Perceptual and functional categorisation in associative learning.* PhD thesis, Cardiff University.

Grand, C. S. & Honey, R. C. (2008). Solving XOR. *Journal of Experimental Psychology: Animal Behavior Processes*, **34**, 486–493.

Grice, G. R. & Davis, J. D. (1958). Mediated stimulus equivalence and distinctiveness in human conditioning. *Journal of Experimental Psychology*, **55**, 565–571.

Hall, G. (1991). *Perceptual and associative learning.* Oxford, England: Clarendon

Hall, G. (1996). Learning about associatively activated representations: Implications for acquired equivalence and perceptual learning. *Animal Learning and Behavior*, **24**, 233–255.

Hebb, D. O. (1949). *The organization of behavior.* New York: John Wiley & Sons Inc.

Hodder, K. I. George, D. N. Killcross, A. S. & Honey, R. C. (2003). Representational blending in human conditional learning: Implications for associative theory. *Quarterly Journal of Experimental Psychology*, **56**, 223–238.

Honey, R. C. (2000). The Experimental Psychology Society Prize Lecture: Associative priming in Pavlovian conditioning. *Quarterly Journal of Experimental Psychology*, **53B**, 1–23.

Honey, R. C. & Bateson, P. (1996). Stimulus comparison and perceptual learning: Further evidence and evaluation from an imprinting procedure. *Quarterly Journal of Experimental Psychology*, **49B**, 259–269.

Honey, R. C. Bateson, P., & Horn, G. (1994). The role of stimulus comparison in perceptual learning: An investigation with the domestic chick. *Quarterly Journal of Experimental Psychology*, **47B**, 83–103.

Honey, R. C. & Hall, G. (1989a). Acquired equivalence and distinctiveness of cues. *Journal of Experimental Psychology: Animal Behavior Processes*, **16**, 178–184.

Honey, R. C. & Hall, G. (1989b). Enhanced discriminability and reduced associability following flavor preexposure. *Learning and Motivation*, **20**, 262–277.

Honey, R. C. & Hall, G. (1991). Acquired equivalence and distinctiveness of cues using a sensory preconditioning procedure. *Quarterly Journal of Experimental Psychology*, **43B**, 121–135.

Honey, R. C., Iordanova, M., & Good, M. (2010). Latent inhibition and habituation: Evaluation of an associative analysis, in R.E. Lubow and I. Weiner (Eds) *Latent inhibition: Cognition, Neuroscience, and Applications to Schizophrenia*, pp. 163–182. Cambridge: Cambridge University Press.

Honey, R. C. & Ward-Robinson, J. (2001). Transfer between contextual conditional discriminations: An examination of how stimulus conjunctions are represented. *Journal of Experimental Psychology: Animal Behavior Processes*, **27**, 196–205.

Honey, R. C. & Ward-Robinson, J. (2002). Acquired equivalence and distinctiveness of cues: I. Exploring a neural network approach. *Journal of Experimental Psychology: Animal Behavior Processes*, **28**, 378–387.

Honey, R. C. & Watt, A. (1998). Acquired relational equivalence: Implications for the nature of associative structures. *Journal of Experimental Psychology: Animal Behavior Processes*, **24**, 325–334.

Honey, R. C. & Watt, A. (1999). Acquired relational equivalence between contexts and features. *Journal of Experimental Psychology: Animal Behavior Processes*, **25**, 324–333.

Hull, C. L. (1939). The problem of stimulus equivalence in behavior theory. *Psychological Review*, **46**, 9–30.

Iordanova, M. Good, M. & Honey, R. C. (2008). Configural learning without reinforcement: Integrated memories for what, where and when. *Quarterly Journal of Experimental Psychology*, **61**, 1785–1792.

Iordanova, M. Killcross, A. S. & Honey, R. C. (2007). Role of the medial prefrontal cortex in the acquired distinctiveness and equivalence of cues. *Behavioral Neuroscience*, **121**, 1431–1436.

Kamin, L. J. (1968). Attention-like processes in classical conditioning, in M. R. Jones (Ed.) *Miami symposium on the prediction of behavior: Aversive stimulation*, pp. 9–32. Coral Gables, FL: University of Miami Press.

James, W. (1890). *The principles of psychology*. New York: Holt.

Konorski, J. (1967). *Integrative activity of the brain: An interdisciplinary approach*. Chicago, IL: University of Chicago Press.

Kruschke, J. K. (1996). Dimensional relevance shifts in category learning. *Connection Science*, **8**, 225–247.

Lawrence, D. H. (1949). Acquired distinctiveness of cues: I. Transfer between discriminations on the basis of familiarity with the stimulus. *Journal of Experimental Psychology*, **39**, 770–784.

Le Pelley, M. E. (2010). Attention and human associative learning, in C. J. Mitchell and M. E. Le Pelley (Eds) *Attention and learning*, this volume. Oxford: Oxford University Press.

Lin, T. E. & Honey, R. C. (2010). Analysis of the content of configural representations: The role of associatively evoked and trace memories. *Journal of Experimental Psychology: Animal Behavior Processes* (under review).

Ludvig, E. A. & Koop, A. (2008). Learning to generalize through predictive representations: A computational model of mediated conditioning, in *From Animals to Animats 10: Proceedings of Simulation of Adaptive Behavior (SAB-08)*, pp. 342–351.

Mackintosh, N. J. (1974). *The psychology of animal learning*. London: Academic Press.

Mackintosh, N. J. (1975). A theory of attention: Variations in the associability of stimuli with reinforcement. *Psychological Review*, **82**, 276–298.

Mackintosh, N. J. and Little, L. (1969). Intradimensional and extradimensional shift learning by pigeons. *Psychonomic Science*, **14**, 5–6.

Maki, W. S. (1993). From elementary associations to animal cognition: Connectionist models of discrimination learning, in T. R. Zentall (Ed.) *Animal cognition: A tribute to Donald A. Riley*, pp. 293–312. Hillsdale, NJ: Erlbaum.

Maki, W. S. & Abunawass, A. M. (1991). A connectionist approach to conditional discriminations: Learning, short-term memory, and attention, in M. L. Commons, S. Grossberg and J. E. R. Staddon (Eds) *Quantitative analysis of behavior: Neural network models of conditioning and action*, pp. 241–278. Hillsdale, NJ: Erlbaum.

McLaren, I. P. L. Kaye, H. & Mackintosh, N. J. (1989). An associative theory of the representation of stimuli: Applications to perceptual learning and latent inhibition, in R. G. M. Morris (Ed.) *Parallel distributed processing: Implications for psychology and neurobiology*, pp. 102–130. Oxford: Clarendon.

McLaren, I. P. L. & Mackintosh, N. J. (2000). An elemental model of associative learning: I. Latent inhibition and perceptual learning. *Animal Learning & Behavior*, **28**, 211–246.

McLaren, I. P. L. & Mackintosh, N. J. (2002). Associative learning and elemental representation: II. Generalization and discrimination. *Animal Learning & Behavior*, **30**, 177–200.

Medin, D. L. Goldstone, R. L. & Gentner, D. (1993). Respects for similarity. *Psychological Review*, **100**, 254–278.

Mitchell, C. J. Nash, S. & Hall, G. (2008). The intermixed-blocked effect in human perceptual learning is not the consequence of trial spacing. *Journal of Experimental Psychology: Learning Memory & Cognition*, **34**, 237–242.

Miller, N. E. & Dollard, J. (1941). *Social learning and imitation*. London: Kegan Paul, Trench, Trubner & Co.

Mundy, M. E. Dwyer, D. M. & Honey, R. C. (2006). Inhibitory associations contribute to perceptual learning in humans. *Journal of Experimental Psychology: Animal Behavior Processes*, **32**, 178–184.

Mundy, M. E. Honey, R. C. & Dwyer, D. M. (2007). Simultaneous presentation of similar stimuli produces perceptual learning in human picture processing. *Journal of Experimental Psychology: Animal Behavior Processes*, **33**, 124–138.

Mundy, M. E. Honey, R. C. & Dwyer, D. M. (2009). Superior discrimination between similar stimuli after simultaneous exposure. *Quarterly Journal of Experimental Psychology*, **62**, 18–25.

Oswald, C. J. P. Yee, B. K. Bannerman, D. B. Rawlins, J. N. P. Good, M. & Honey, R. C. (2001). Involvement of the entorhinal cortex in a process of attentional modulation: Evidence from a novel variant of an IDS/EDS procedure. *Behavioral Neuroscience*, **115**, 841–849.

Pavlov, I. P. (1927). *Conditioned Reflexes*. London: Oxford University Press.

Pearce, J. M. (1994). Similarity and discrimination: A selective review and a connectionist model. *Psychological Review*, **101**, 587–607.

Pearce, J. M. & Mackintosh, N. J. (2010). Two theories of attention: A review and possible integration, in C. J. Mitchell and M. E. Le Pelley (Eds) *Attention and Learning*, this volume. Oxford: Oxford University Press.

Peirce, J. W. (2007). The potential importance of saturating and supersaturating contrast response functions in visual cortex. *Journal of Vision*, 7, 1–10.

Redhead, E. S. & Pearce, J. M. (1995). Stimulus salience and negative patterning. *Quarterly Journal of Experimental Psychology*, **48B**, 67–83.

Rescorla, R. A. (1972). 'Configural' conditioning in discrete-trial bar pressing. *Journal of Comparative and Physiological Psychology*, **79**, 307–317.

Rescorla, R. A. (1976). Stimulus generalization: Some predictions from a model of Pavlovian conditioning. *Journal of Experimental Psychology: Animal Behavior Processes*, **2**, 88–96.

Rescorla, R. A. (1991). Associative relations in instrumental learning: The eighteenth Bartlett memorial lecture. *Quarterly Journal of Experimental Psychology*, **43B**, 1–23.

Rescorla, R. A., & Wagner, A. R. (1972). A theory of Pavlovian conditioning: Variations in the effectiveness of reinforcement and nonreinforcement, in A.H. Black and W.F. Prokasy (Eds), *Classical conditioning II: Current research and theory*, pp. 64–99. New York: Appleton-Century-Crofts.

Rumelhart, D. E. Hinton, G. E. & Williams, R. J. (1986). Learning internal representations by error propagation, in D. E. Rumelhart and J. L. McLelland (Eds) *Parallel distributed processing: Explorations in the microstructure of cognition: Vol. 1. Foundations*, pp. 318–362. Cambridge, MA: MIT Press.

Shepp, E. M. & Eimas, P. D. (1964). Intradimensional and extradimensional shifts in the rat. *Journal of Comparative and Physiological Psychology*, **57**, 357–361.

Stent, G. S. (1973). A physiological mechanism for Hebb's postulate of learning. *Proceedings of the National Academy of Sciences, USA*, **70**, 997–1003.

Tversky, A. & Gati, I. (1978). Studies of Similarity, in E. Rosch and B.B. Lloyd (Eds) *Cognition and categorization*, pp. 79–98. Hillsdale: Erlbaum.

Ward-Robinson, J. & Honey, R. C. (2000). A novel contextual dimension for use with an operant chamber: From simple to hierarchical forms of learning. *Journal of Experimental Psychology: Animal Behavior Processes*, **26**, 358–363.

Williams, D. A. Dumont, J- L. & Mehta, R. (2004). Conditions favoring superconditioning of irrelevant conditioned stimuli. *Journal of Experimental Psychology: Animal Behavior Processes*, **30**, 148–159.

Williams, D. A. Mehta, R. Poworoznyk, T. M. Orihel, J. S. George, D. N. & Pearce, J. M. (2002). Acquisition of superexcitatory properties by an irrelevant background stimulus. *Journal of Experimental Psychology: Animal Behavior Processes*, **28**, 284–297.

Zentall, T. R. Steirn, J. N. Sherburne, L. M. & Urcuioli, P. J. (1991). Common coding in pigeons assessed through partial versus total reversals of many-to-one conditional and simple discriminations. *Journal of Experimental Psychology: Animal Behavior Processes*, **17**, 194–201.

Chapter 8

Attention and human associative learning

Mike E. Le Pelley

Attention provides the gateway between the mass of information in the real world and the relatively tiny subset of such information we select for further analysis or action. As such, attention is perhaps the most potent source of bias in human cognition: the action taken, or decision made, in a given situation will largely be determined by which of the available stimuli are selected for processing. If we walk into a bank and our attention is drawn to an advertising poster, we might start considering whether this new low-rate mortgage is suitable for us; if, on the other hand, our attention is drawn to the balaclava-clad man with a gun at the counter, we may be more inclined to leave and call the police. Consequently, if we are to understand human behaviour, then we must first understand the factors that determine which stimuli will be selected under a given set of circumstances.

Much of the research related to this issue described in the cognitive psychology literature has focused on the 'intrinsic' properties of stimuli, demonstrating that attentional selection can be driven by the perceptual and emotional properties of a stimulus. For example, a stimulus is more likely to capture attention if it is highly perceptually salient (e.g. if it has an abrupt onset, or a bright colour: Folk, Remington, and Johnston, 1992), or if it is 'emotionally relevant': negative mood states (such as those caused by anxiety or depression) bias attention towards threatening information (MacLeod, Mathews, and Tata, 1986), while positive mood states bias attention to desirable, rewarding stimuli (Tamir and Robinson, 2007). A second line of research has instead examined the ability of other events to modulate attention to stimuli. For example, the influence of attention to a stimulus persists for longer if selection of that stimulus is highly rewarded than if it is only weakly rewarded (Della Libera and Chelazzi, 2006).

While the studies described above have considered the effects of stimulus and reward properties on attentional selection in isolation, research on animal conditioning and (more recently) human learning indicates that we should also perhaps consider them in combination. The results of these studies are consistent with the idea that attentional selection of a stimulus is influenced by learning about its *predictive validity* (PV), i.e. its ability to predict the occurrence of events of significance (such as rewards). That is, the likelihood of selection of a particular 'cue' stimulus seems to be influenced by learning about the relationship between that cue and the outcome that follows it.

This possibility is illustrated by an experiment by Le Pelley and McLaren (2003), the design of which is shown in Table 8.1. Participants, playing the role of an allergist, examined the effects of various foods on fictitious patients. On each training trial they were told the contents of a meal eaten by the patient, and were asked to predict the type of allergic reaction (e.g. nausea) that the patient would suffer after eating that meal, with immediate corrective feedback. Letters A–Y refer to different cues and o1 to o4 to different outcomes, e.g. 'AV-o1' indicates that cues A and V were presented together, and that the correct outcome prediction was outcome o1.

In Stage 1, participants learnt about the effects of foods on 'Mr. X'. During this stage, cues A–D were predictive: they predicted the outcome on each trial (A and D were consistently paired with o1; B and C with o2). Cues V–Y were nonpredictive, being followed equally often by o1 and o2. Over several blocks of Stage 1 training, participants learnt to predict the correct outcome on each trial.

At the outset of Stage 2, participants were told that they would now learn about a new patient, Mr. Y, who suffered from different reactions compared to Mr. X. During this stage, compounds of a previously-predictive and previously-nonpredictive cue were paired with novel outcomes o3 and o4. The objective statistical contingency between previously-predictive cues (A–D) and Stage 2 outcomes is identical to that between previously-nonpredictive (V–Y) cues and those same outcomes. For example, both A and X are paired with o3 an equal number of times, on exactly the same trials. Despite this objective

Table 8.1 Design of Le Pelley and McLaren (2003)

Stage 1	Stage 2	Test
AV–o1	AX–o3	AC
AW–o1	BY–o4	BD
BV–o2	CV–o3	VX
BW–o2	DW–o4	WY
CX–o2		
CY–o2		
DX–o1		
DY–o1		

equivalence, in a final test, participants rated compounds AC and BD as significantly more predictive of outcomes o3 and o4, respectively, than were compounds VX and WY. This implies that, during Stage 2, participants had learnt cue–outcome associations more rapidly for previously-predictive cues than for previously-nonpredictive cues.

This finding is certainly consistent with the suggestion that attention is influenced by learning. Indeed, it follows naturally from certain 'attentional' theories of associative learning (e.g. Kruschke, 2001; Mackintosh, 1975; Sutherland and Mackintosh, 1971). Such theories propose that, to some extent, attention can act at a cue-specific level (i.e. people might pay different amounts of attention to different cues, even if those cues are presented simultaneously), and that this attention is determined by the learnt PV of a cue. Specifically, these theories propose that cues experienced as having a high PV will, other things being equal, capture more attention than those experienced as having low PV.[1]

This idea can be applied to Le Pelley and McLaren's study. During Stage 1, participants will learn that the predictive cues A–D have higher PV than the nonpredictive cues V–Y. Consequently, the attentional theories described above suggest that participants will learn to attend more strongly to cues A–D than to cues V–Y. The second main assumption of these attentional theories is that cues that are attended more strongly will be learnt about more rapidly in future. This assumption allows such theories to account for the more rapid Stage 2 learning about cues A–D (which will be strongly attended following Stage 1) than cues V–Y (which will be weakly attended).

Attentional theories of learning have typically drawn their support from studies that are conceptually similar to that of Le Pelley and McLaren. These studies generally involve a pretraining phase in which certain cues are established as having higher PV than others, which is followed by a critical training phase that assesses the rate of novel learning about these different cues. Any difference in learning rate between high-PV and low-PV cues during this latter training phase is then taken as evidence for a difference in attention to these cues, with more attention presumed to result in faster learning. Many studies conducted along these lines in both animals (e.g. Bennett, Wills, Oakeshott,

1 Other attentional theories of associative learning, developed on the basis of animal studies, take a very different view of the relationship between PV and attention (e.g. Pearce and Hall, 1980). However, empirical evidence from human learning studies typically supports the general approach offered by the Mackintosh and Kruschke models, while being inconsistent with the view taken by Pearce and Hall (but see Hogarth, Dickinson, Austin, Brown, and Duka, 2008). Therefore discussion in this chapter will focus solely on the former approach.

and Mackintosh, 2000; Mackintosh and Little, 1969; Oswald *et al.*, 2001; Shepp and Schrier, 1969; see Le Pelley, 2004, for a review) and humans (e.g. Beesley and Le Pelley, 2010; Bonardi, Graham, Hall, and Mitchell, 2005; Kruschke, 1996; Owen, Roberts, Polkey, Sahakian, and Robbins, 1991) have produced results consistent with the suggestion that attention is greater to high-PV cues than to low-PV cues.

Consistent with the view advanced earlier of attention as a potent source of bias in behaviour, all of these findings that have been taken as support for attentional theories demonstrate learning that is not statistically normative. For example, in Le Pelley and McLaren's study, the objective cue–outcome relationships are equal for all cues, and yet participants learn more rapidly about some cues (those previously experienced as having high PV) than others. Attentional theories account for this bias in learning via a proposed interaction between attention and learning. Moreover, the bias in learning generated by differences in previously-learnt PV could potentially influence many aspects of human behaviour. For example, Le Pelley *et al.* (2010) have recently demonstrated that prior experience of membership of social groups as being predictive or nonpredictive of neutral attributes (e.g. the typical height of members) influences the rate at which participants subsequently form evaluative attitudes regarding those groups based on experience of group members performing evaluatively-positive behaviours (e.g. 'visiting a sick friend in hospital') or evaluatively-negative behaviours (e.g. 'vandalizing a phone box'). A model based on Mackintosh's (1975) attentional theory was shown to provide a good account of this influence of prior predictiveness on the rate of attitude formation.

Moreover, this influence of PV on novel learning seems to operate at a relatively automatic level. Beesley and Le Pelley (2010) have examined the influence of previously-learnt PV in sequence learning, using the serial reaction time (SRT) task. In this task, participants are instructed to respond to the location of a single moving target. While participants are not explicitly informed of the fact, the target's movements are governed by a sequence. Learning of this sequence manifests as a decrease in reaction times (RTs) following movements of the target which obey the sequence as opposed to RTs following movements which do not obey the sequence (unsequenced movements).

During Stage 1, appearance of the target in certain 'good predictor' locations predicted with high probability where it would appear next. Appearance of the target in other, 'poor predictor' locations was less predictive of where it would appear next. During Stage 2, locations entered into new predictive relationships such that both previously-good predictor and previously-poor predictor locations now predicted movement of the target to new locations.

Crucially, during Stage 2, all locations (regardless of whether they had been good and poor predictors in Stage 1) were equally good predictors of where the target would move next. Stage 2 followed on seamlessly from Stage 1, and the experimental context remained unchanged between Stages 1 and 2 – the possible target locations were constant across both – such that participants received no explicit indication that the sequence had changed. In fact, participants' subsequent verbal reports suggested that none of them noticed this change in the sequence between the two phases. Nevertheless, we found a significant advantage in learning of the new Stage 2 relationships for locations that had been good predictors in Stage 1 over those that had been poor predictors (see Figure 8.1).

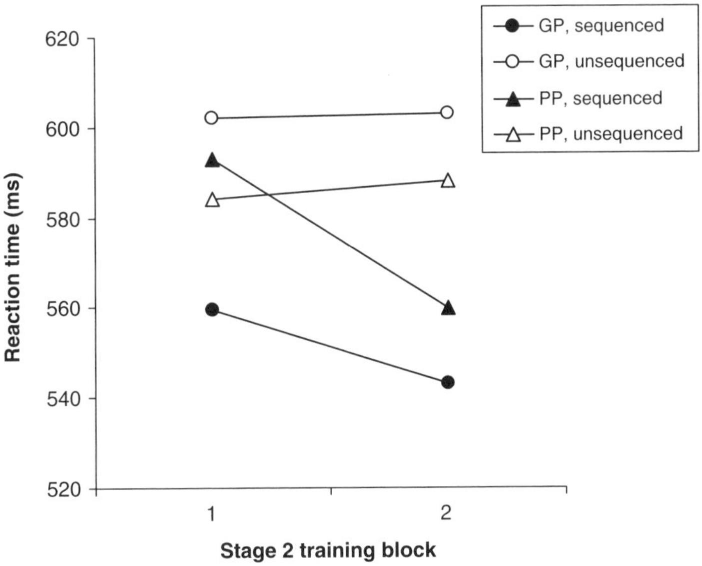

Fig. 8.1 Reaction times (RTs) to movements of the target in Beesley and Le Pelley's (2010) serial reaction time task. 'GP, sequenced' refers to RTs following predictable movements of the target from locations that were good predictors in Stage 1; 'GP, unsequenced' refers to RTs following unpredictable movements of the target from these same locations. 'PP, sequenced' and 'PP, unsequenced' refer to equivalent RTs following movements from locations that were poor predictors in Stage 1. Sequence learning is defined as the extent to which RTs following sequenced (predictable) movements are faster than following unsequenced (unpredictable movements). The difference between sequenced and unsequenced RTs (and hence learning) is significantly greater for movements following good predictor locations than poor predictor locations. Beesley, T. & Le Pelley, M. E. (in press). The effect of predictive history on the learning of sub-sequence contingencies. *Quarterly Journal of Experimental Psychology*. Printed with permission from Taylor & Francis Ltd. (http://www.informaworld.com).

It is generally accepted that learning in the SRT task is incidental (see Cleeremans, Destrebecqz, and Boyer, 1998), in that there is no instruction to participants to learn or requirement for them to do so: they are asked to respond to, rather than predict, the outcome on each trial, such that the task can be performed with perfect accuracy in the absence of any learning. Thus the instructions provide participants with no reason to engage in strategic, hypothesis-testing processes, or to intentionally exploit any explicit knowledge of the cue–outcome contingencies that they may possess (and post-experimental tests of participants' awareness of these contingencies indicate that they possess very little explicit knowledge). The observation of an influence of PV on novel learning under such conditions therefore implies that this influence need not result from the operation of higher-level reasoning processes (as suggested by De Houwer, Beckers, and Vandorpe, 2005), but rather that it can have a more automatic, lower-level basis.

In further support of this idea, Le Pelley *et al.* (2010) have demonstrated that the biasing influence of PV on formation of evaluative attitudes regarding social groups, mentioned earlier, is abolished by a manipulation designed to increase the ease of reasoning, namely presenting all contingency information to participants in a summary form, rather than requiring them to learn this information on the basis of trial-by-trial experience. Participants received exactly the same contingency information as in the trial-by-trial case described above (i.e. that some groups were predictive of clothing colour while others were nonpredictive, and that some groups were paired with a majority of positive behaviours while others were paired with a majority of negative behaviours). However, in this latter experiment, they had explicit access to all of this information, which would be required to make a reasoned judgment, at the time of making that judgment. Previous studies have demonstrated that providing such summary information increases the ease of reasoning (Arkes and Harkness, 1983; Ward and Jenkins, 1965). Nevertheless, this manipulation eliminated the biasing influence of PV on attitude formation (see Le Pelley, Oakeshott, and McLaren, 2005, for a similar example). The implication is that the root of this bias is not in reasoning, but instead in more automatic, lower-level processes, such that any manipulation that increases participants' reliance on reasoning will decrease the magnitude of the bias observed.

Regardless of the 'cognitive level' at which these effects are best interpreted (low-level automatic processes or high-level reasoning), given the amount of supporting evidence, it seems safe to conclude that the rate of novel learning about a cue in humans (and animals) is influenced by the previously-experienced PV of that cue. What is perhaps more contentious is the claim that this influence of PV on learning reflects the operation of attention. In other words, does the learning advantage for high-PV cues really reflect greater attention to these cues? After all, the putative relationship between attention and learning – an idea that is central to attentional theories of learning – has been invoked only to account for the kind of learning experiments described above. There is little external confirmation from the cognitive psychology literature that this PV effect is really a consequence of attention.

This issue is made more pertinent by alternative accounts of such effects that do not appeal to an interaction between attention and learning. For example, Oswald *et al.* (2001; see also Honey, Close and Lin, 2010, this volume) suggested that the influence of PV might instead reflect a process of representation development. Specifically, in their model the sensory units representing high-PV cues are better-able to activate units in a hidden layer that mediate learning about relationships between cues and outcomes. It is then supposed that, the more strongly a cue's sensory unit is represented in this hidden layer, the more rapidly that cue can enter into a new cue–outcome relationship. Honey *et al.* have argued that this is a nonattentional account, since the model makes no explicit mention of a separate attentional mechanism that interacts with the learning system. That is, there is no suggestion of a distinct, cue-specific attentional factor that modulates the rate of learning about a cue. Instead, this view suggests that the influence of PV is simply an emergent property of a nonlinear learning system in which the 'functional' representation of a cue (in the hidden layer) is determined by prior learning about that cue.[2]

Why does it matter exactly how PV exerts its influence on learning? This issue is clearly of interest from a theoretical point of view, given that attention and learning are two of the most important topics in modern cognitive psychology. Attention controls the gateway to cognition, and learning allows us to predict, manipulate, and control our environment. It seems plausible that there might be some level of interaction between these systems, but the evidence cited above is equivocal on this issue. In more practical terms, deficits in selective attention have been implicated in several types of mental disorder, most notably schizophrenia (Braff, 1993; Elvevåg and Goldberg, 2000) and attention deficit hyperactivity disorder (Shue and Douglas, 1992). An understanding of

2 Of course, a die-hard supporter of attentional learning theories could feasibly argue that the strength with which a cue is represented in the hidden layer corresponds to attention to that cue. However, while Honey *et al.*'s account predicts that high-PV cues will be learnt about more rapidly than low-PV cues, it does not explicitly anticipate that PV will influence the other aspects of cue processing, discussed later, that are held to be characteristic of attention (e.g. overt and covert orienting, susceptibility to attentional blink, neural markers etc.). Consequently it seems reasonable to characterize this account of the PV effect as non-attentional.

exactly how attention might influence, and be influenced by, other aspects of cognition such as learning potentially brings us closer to understanding the causes and implications of aspects of these mental disorders.

There are two critical assumptions made by attentional theories of the influence of PV on learning that set them apart from alternative accounts of this bias. These assumptions were mentioned in passing earlier in the discussion and are repeated here:

Assumption 1: Differences in PV give rise to differences in attention to cues.
Assumption 2: Differences in attention to cues, caused by differences in PV, give rise to differences in subsequent learning about cues.

Note that it is quite possible for Assumption 1 to be true while Assumption 2 is false: differences in PV could produce differences in the attention paid to cues, but the difference in the rate of learning about these cues observed empirically may have another, non-attentional source. (It is not possible for Assumption 2 to be true while Assumption 1 is false, given that Assumption 1 is built into Assumption 2.) These two assumptions, as expressed here, specify an intricate interaction between attention and learning; each influences, and is influenced by, the other. In the remainder of this chapter we will examine the empirical evidence relating to each of these assumptions in turn.

Testing Assumption 1: does learning influence attention?

Assumption 1 can be paraphrased as the idea that 'learning influences attention'. Recall that, in Le Pelley and McLaren's (2003) study, participants learnt more rapidly in Stage 2 about cues (e.g. A) that had previously been established as having high PV than those (e.g. X) previously established as having low PV. Assumption 1 suggests that, during Stage 1 of Le Pelley and McLaren's (2003) experiment, participants' learning about the different PV of cues A and X causes them to come to pay more attention to the former than to the latter.

The studies cited earlier that have been taken as support for attentional theories provide, at best, very indirect support for Assumption 1: on the basis of an observed difference in learning during Stage 2, we infer that there was a difference in attention to the cues involved, and further infer that this difference arose as a result of the difference in PV of these cues during Stage 1. Clearly a better approach would be to take a direct measure of attention to cues that differ in PV during Stage 1.

The problem with this approach is that there is no 'direct' measure of attention. Attention is a theoretical construct invoked by cognitive psychologists to explain various empirical phenomena: it is a process, rather than an independently observable entity. However, all is not lost! For, while we cannot directly measure attention, we can measure its effects. Indeed, given that the theoretical construct of attention has only been invoked in order to account for such effects, it is in some sense *defined by* these effects: if a particular manipulation produces the set of effects that are characteristic of attention, then we can say that this manipulation must be influencing attention.

Hence, if our aim is to establish that the 'attention' influenced by PV is the same property as that studied by cognitive psychologists, then our argument must rely on a weight of evidence. Consider effects E_1, E_2, E_3, and E_4, which have been externally validated in the cognitive psychology literature as being characteristic of attention. Suppose now that we observe that PV influences effect E_1. This would be relatively weak evidence on which to base the idea that attentional processes are at work – it is presumably possible that other, non-attentional processes might also give rise to effect E_1. That is, while E_1 might be characteristic of attention, it is most likely not perfectly predictive of attention and exclusive with regard to all other cognitive processes (just as the relationship between PV and learning observed empirically is also open to non-attentional interpretations, e.g. Honey *et al.*, 2010). If, on the other hand, we observe that PV influences all of E_1, E_2, E_3, and E_4, then we may be more confident that this really is a consequence of attention, since it is unlikely that another process would map onto all of these disparate effects. And the more attention-characteristic effects that we observe to be related to PV, the greater becomes our confidence in a true relationship between PV and attention. We will return to this idea of a 'weight of evidence' argument for a relationship between PV and attention throughout this chapter. For now, we will consider the weight of evidence relating to Assumption 1.

Responses are faster to events occurring in attended locations

It is well-established that people are faster to respond to events that occur in locations to which they are paying attention. This is the basis of the spatial cueing task, developed by Posner and colleagues (Posner, 1980; Posner, Nissen, and Ogden, 1978) to measure shifts of visual attention. Participants are required to respond to a peripherally presented target, which is preceded by a 'cue' directing participants to expect this target to appear in a certain location. It is typically found that targets appearing at cued locations are detected more rapidly than those at uncued (and hence unexpected) locations.

This characteristic of attention also underlies the dot probe task, which has been ussed to demonstrate attentional bias towards threatening information

(MacLeod *et al.*, 1986). On each trial of a typical dot probe task, two stimuli appear briefly, one on either side of a screen. On critical trials one of these stimuli is threatening (e.g. a threat-related word such as 'death', or an angry face), while the other is emotionally neutral. When the stimulus pair disappears, a dot appears in the location previously occupied by one of the stimuli, and participants are asked to respond to this dot as rapidly as possible. It is typically found that anxious individuals respond more rapidly when the dot appears in the location previously occupied by the threatening stimulus than the location previously occupied by the neutral stimulus. This finding has been used to argue for an automatic attentional bias towards threatening material in these individuals.

Recent experiments using a variant of the dot probe task have indicated that people show a similar automatic attentional bias towards high-PV, as opposed to low-PV, cues (Le Pelley, in preparation). On each trial of an initial categorization phase, two stimuli appeared: a green square (which could take one of two slightly different shades of green) and a set of oblique lines (which could take one of two slightly different orientations). Participants categorized this stimulus pair into one of two categories, with immediate corrective feedback provided on each trial. For half of the participants, the shade of green predicted category membership and the orientation of the lines was nonpredictive. Thus, if Gre1 and Gre2 represent the two shades of green, and Ori1 and Ori2 represent the two orientations, stimulus pair (Gre1, Ori1) and (Gre1, Ori2) would belong to category 1, and pairs (Gre2, Ori1) and (Gre2, Ori2) would belong to category 2. For the remaining participants, the orientation of the lines was predictive of category membership and shade of green was nonpredictive.

A subsequent test phase used the dot probe procedure to assess whether learning about the differential predictiveness of the cues with regard to category membership produced a bias in attention towards predictive cues and away from nonpredictive cues. On each trial a central fixation cross appeared – participants had earlier been strongly cautioned to maintain fixation throughout the trial. A pair of stimuli (again a green square and set of oblique lines) was then presented for 150 ms on either side of fixation. These stimuli then disappeared, and after 200ms a triangular probe could appear in the location formerly occupied by one of them. This probe was equally likely to appear in either location; participants' task was to respond to the appearance of the triangle as rapidly as possible by pressing a single key (yielding a simple RT), and to withhold responses on occasional catch trials when no triangle appeared.

Figure 8.2 shows RTs to the probe across four cycles of categorization training followed by test. RTs were significantly shorter when the probe appeared in

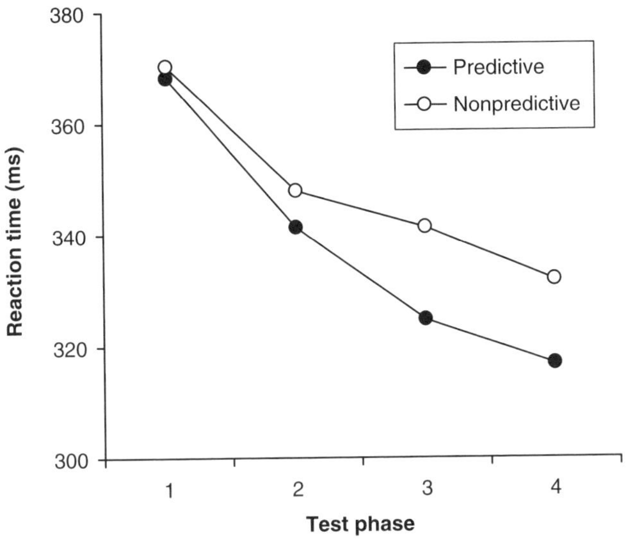

Fig. 8.2 Simple reaction times (RTs) to the triangle probe across four test phases (each preceded by a phase of categorization training) in Le Pelley's (in preparation) study. RTs to the probe were significantly shorter when it appeared in the location previously occupied by the cue that was predictive during categorization training than when it appeared in the location occupied by the cue that was nonpredictive during categorization training. There was a tendency for this RT difference to increase across test phases, i.e. with greater experience of the categorization task and hence more opportunity for learning.

the location previously occupied by the predictive cue than when it appeared in the location occupied by the nonpredictive cue. Given that increased processing speed (in terms of more rapid detection of and/or response to targets) is characteristic of an attended location, these data imply that high-PV cues capture attention, and hence support Assumption 1. Notably these findings suggest that the influence of PV on attentional capture can be relatively automatic: participants display a bias towards the location occupied by the previously-predictive cue, despite the fact that the probe is equally likely to appear in either location such that this shift of attention is non-optimal.

Attended stimuli are protected from the attentional blink

The attentional blink refers to the observation that, when presented with a rapid sequence of visual stimuli appearing in the same location, identification of the second of two targets is often impaired if it appears 200–500 ms after presentation of the first target. The attentional blink is widely assumed to reflect attentional limitations during encoding that restrict perceptual awareness of targets (Raymond, Shapiro, and Arnell, 1992). Consistent with this interpretation, it has been shown that the attentional blink is reduced for targets that are higher in perceptual salience (e.g. letters among numbers, Chun and Potter, 1995), emotional salience (e.g. negatively valenced words, Anderson and Phelps, 2001), or semantic salience (e.g. one's own name, Shapiro, Caldwell, and Sorensen, 1997), and which are hence more likely to capture attention.

In further support of Assumption 1, Livesey, Harris and Harris (2009) have recently demonstrated that high-PV targets are protected from the attentional blink. Livesey *et al.* used an attentional blink task in which on each trial participants had to detect two targets in a rapidly presented sequence of letters. However, in a departure from the standard attentional blink task, immediately after presentation of each sequence of letters, a cue appeared instructing participants to make a left or right keypress response as rapidly as possible. Once they had made this cued response, participants had to report the two targets that had appeared in the letter sequence (as normal for an attentional blink task). While participants were not explicitly informed of the fact, the appearance of a certain item (labelled Tp) as the second target in the letter sequence predicted which cued response would be required on that trial, while another second-target item (Tnp) was nonpredictive of which cued response would be required. Thus Tp had high PV with respect to this cued response task, while Tnp had low PV.

On early trials of this task, the critical items Tp or Tnp appeared in the letter sequence some time after the first target, such that they would not be subject to the attentional blink. Participants were able to learn about the predictive relationship between presentation of Tp in the letter sequence and the cued response that would be required immediately after that letter sequence. This learning was evident in that, after experience of many trials, cued responses following sequences containing Tp were significantly faster than those following sequences containing Tnp.

After many such trials (i.e. once this predictive relationship had been learnt), participants were presented with letter sequences in which Tp or Tnp followed very shortly after the first target and hence would normally be subject to the attentional blink. Crucially, detection of Tp in these letter sequences was significantly better than detection of Tnp. In other words, detection of Tp was less impaired by the attentional blink than was detection of

Tnp, supporting the suggestion that PV influences the attentional resources devoted to a stimulus.

Eye gaze and attention

One of the most obvious features of visual attention is that it tends to coincide with where our eyes are looking. It is, of course, possible to make 'covert' shifts of attention that are not accompanied by eye movements (e.g. Posner, 1980; and the 'dot probe' study described above, in which attentional effects were observed despite participants maintaining central fixation throughout each trial). Nevertheless, eye movements and attentional shifts are generally tightly coupled (Deubel and Schneider, 1996), especially when dealing with relatively complex stimuli such as words.

In recent work, we have examined the relationship between PV and overt attention as indexed by eye gaze (Le Pelley, Beesley, and Griffiths, in preparation). This study used Le Pelley and McLaren's design (Table 8.1) in a more abstract categorization scenario, where the cues were nonsense words (e.g. 'Slatorion', 'Forditic') and participants had to predict the particular sound (e.g. a splash or a squeak) that would follow each pair of words.

Figure 8.3A shows the distribution of participants' eye gaze across the course of Stage 1 training. The two cues presented on each trial appeared in well-separated locations on the left and right of the screen. Gaze location was

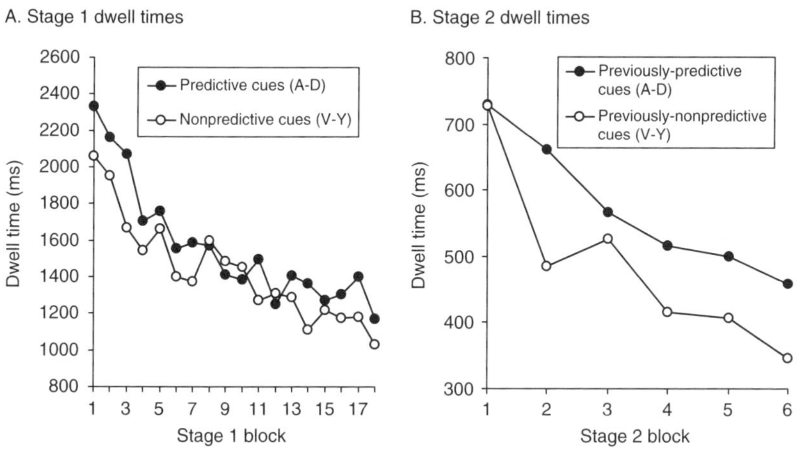

Fig. 8.3 Data from Le Pelley, Beesley, and Griffiths's (in preparation) eye tracking study, using the design shown in Table 8.1. Panel A: Dwell times for predictive and non-predictive cues during Stage 1. Panel B: Dwell times for previously-predictive and previously-nonpredictive cues during Stage 2.

sampled every 20 ms, and dwell on a cue was defined as a recording of gaze within a relatively small region surrounding the position of each cue on the screen. Dwell time was then summed across the period from stimulus onset to the point at which participants made a prediction response. This summed dwell time was significantly greater to the predictive cue presented on each Stage 1 trial (e.g. A on AV–o1 trials; see Table 8.1) than to the nonpredictive cue (in this case V). Thus it is clear that PV influences the overt attention to cues in this task (see also Beesley and LePelley, in press; Kruschke, Kappenman, and Hetrick, 2005; Wills, Lavric, Croft, and Hodgson, 2007).

Puzzlingly, using a rather different design, Hogarth, Dickinson, Austin, Brown, and Duka (2008; see also Hogarth, Dickinson, and Duka, 2009, this volume) demonstrated a bias in eye gaze towards nonpredictive cues, relative to predictive cues – the opposite of the effect discussed above. The reason for this discrepancy is not entirely clear, but there are several candidates arising from differences in procedure. For example, in Hogarth *et al.'s* study, the predictive and nonpredictive cues were not presented together on the same trial and hence the comparison was indirect; moreover trials were considerably longer, and the analysed eye gaze data included the post-response period while participants were waiting for feedback (in our study, the eye gaze data were purely pre-response). In any case, Hogarth *et al.'s* findings are still consistent with Assumption 1 that PV influences the attention paid to cues, albeit in a different way to that observed in our own study.

Electrophysiological markers of selective attention

Previous studies have identified several electrophysiological 'markers' of selective attention; such markers are examples of event-related potentials (ERPs). When participants are instructed to attend to a particular spatial location, the magnitudes of three ERP components (the P1, posterior N1, and anterior N1, each of which is temporally well-defined) elicited by stimuli appearing at that location are significantly greater than for stimuli appearing at an unattended location (Hillyard and Anllo-Vento, 1998). Similarly, N1 magnitude is enhanced for attended target stimuli defined in terms of form or colour when these stimuli must be discriminated from distractors (Vogel and Luck, 2000). Selection of stimuli on the basis of colour or shape is also associated with a broad negative ERP termed 'selection negativity' (Hillyard and Anllo-Vento, 1998). If PV influences attention to cues, then we might expect to see differences in the magnitude of these ERP markers elicited by high-PV and low-PV cues.

This idea has recently been tested by Wills *et al.* (2007), using the design shown in Table 8.2. Cues A–Y were represented by abstract shapes; participants were told that these were cell bodies present in patients' blood. Their aim

Table 8.2 Design of Wills et al. (2007)

Stage 1	Stage 2	Stage 3
A+	AX+	X?
B-	BY+	Y?
I-	IJ-	A+
		B-
		AX+
		BY+

A.J. Wills, A. Lavric, G.S. Croft, and T.L. Hodgson, 'Predictive Learning, Prediction Errors, and Attention: Evidence from Event-related Potentials, and Eye Tracking', *Journal of Cognitive Neuroscience*, 19:5 (May, 2007), pp. 843–854.

was to predict whether each patient suffered from 'Jominy Fever' on the basis of these cell bodies; a '+' symbol in Table 8.2 indicates that a patient with that combination of cell bodies suffered from Jominy Fever, a '–' symbol indicates that they did not.

The critical comparison relates to cues X and Y. Following Stage 2, cue X should have low PV. This is because pretraining of A alone as a predictor of fever in Stage 1 means that the occurrence of fever on Stage 2 AX+ trials is already well-predicted, and hence learning about X will be blocked (Dickinson, Shanks, and Evenden, 1984; Kamin, 1968). In contrast, Y should develop high PV. Pretraining of B as nonpredictive of fever in Stage 1 will ensure that the occurrence of fever on Stage 2 BY+ trials is surprising and hence will support learning of a Y→fever association. During Stage 3, in addition to reminders of all of the earlier trial types, cues X and Y were presented individually (while participants were still required to make predictions of the outcome that would follow these cues, they were not given corrective feedback on these trials). Consistent with the suggestion of a difference in PV between X and Y, the mean proportion of 'fever' responses to X was significantly lower than to Y on these trials. And most importantly, Wills *et al.* observed corresponding differences in the ERP markers of selective attention elicited by these cues. Specifically, Y elicited a larger anterior N1 component than did X, and also demonstrated a selection negativity relative to X. Once again, this demonstration that an attentional marker is influenced by PV provides support for Assumption 1.

In summary, then, the available data from a range of preparations are consistent with Assumption 1 – differences in PV really do seem to give rise to differences in attention, in the way that 'attention' is generally understood by cognitive psychologists. While the relation between PV and any one of the empirical features discussed above may potentially be open to alternative interpretations when considered in isolation, the weight of evidence across a range of characteristic effects of attention presents a more compelling case.

Attention and limited capacity

Before moving on to consider the evidence relating to Assumption 2, a brief aside is warranted on the nature of the attentional effects observed in the preceding studies. Cognitive psychologists typically assume that selective attention has a limited capacity, such that if attention to one stimulus increases, then attention to other stimuli must necessarily decrease; the *inverse hypothesis*. Indeed, Quinlan (2010, this volume) argues that limited capacity is a defining characteristic of attention; if a particular theory does not invoke a limited capacity, or if a particular empirical effect is incompatible with the existence of a limited capacity system, then that theory/effect is not attentional in nature.

In contrast, certain 'attentional' models of associative learning do not suggest a limited capacity; for example, Mackintosh's (1975) theory does not instantiate the inverse hypothesis, and hence would not be considered a truly attentional theory under Quinlan's approach. That said, however, it is perfectly possible to generate a model in which PV influences stimulus processing in a way that follows the general spirit of Mackintosh's model (with processing increased for high-PV cues and decreased for low-PV cues), but which is subject to the inverse hypothesis; Kruschke (2001) and Sutherland and Mackintosh (1971) provide examples.

Moreover, none of the studies described above are inconsistent with the idea that the influence of PV on stimulus processing follows the inverse hypothesis. For example, the results of Le Pelley's (in preparation) dot probe studies could be described in terms of (i) an increase in processing of high-PV cues with no decrease in processing of low-PV cues, (ii) a decrease in processing of low-PV cues with no increase in processing of high-PV cues, or (iii) an increase in processing of high-PV cues with a corresponding decrease in processing of low-PV cues. Possibility (i) would not be compatible with a limited capacity system, but possibilities (ii) and (iii) certainly are compatible, in that neither of these latter possibilities requires an overall increase in the amount of attention that is being allocated. Consequently, even if we accept the suggestion that limited capacity is a defining feature of selective attention, the extant studies relating to the influence of PV on stimulus processing can still be interpreted as 'attentional' effects even under this more restricted definition.

Testing Assumption 2: does attention influence learning?

On the surface, the answer to the question of whether attention influences learning is self-evident: of course it must! Suppose that, during one of the learning experiments discussed earlier, a particular participant were to spend his time staring out of the laboratory window and entirely ignoring the information flashing by on the computer screen in front of him. We can be quite confident that this participant would show no evidence of any learning in a final test as a consequence of his inattention.

However, the situation is a little more complicated than this. Merely to ask whether attention influences learning is to paraphrase Assumption 2, which states that 'Differences in attention to cues, *caused by differences in PV*, give rise to differences in subsequent learning about cues'. That is, attentional theories of learning (Kruschke, 2001; Le Pelley, 2004; Mackintosh, 1975; Pearce and Hall, 1980) assume that it is the same parameter that is determined by the prior PV of a stimulus, which itself influences the rate of subsequent learning about that stimulus. For example, the explanation offered by the Mackintosh (1975) model for the effect of prior predictiveness observed by Le Pelley and McLaren (2003) relies on the PV of cues established in Stage 1 influencing a particular parameter (α), which itself modulates the rate of novel learning about those cues in Stage 2. And the theme of this chapter is whether this single α parameter really reflects attention.

The evidence presented earlier indicates that Assumption 1 may be correct, i.e. that PV does influence attention. If attention is a unitary construct, then Assumption 2 must follow naturally. To see why this is the case, imagine that there is only one type of attention, i.e. a single 'pool' of resources that can be influenced by, and can in turn influence, other aspects of cognition. In that case, the reduction in attention experienced by a low-PV cue (as evidenced by the studies relating to Assumption 1) would be in some sense equivalent to our hypothetical participant staring out of the window. That is, the reduction in attention caused by low PV would result in a depletion of the same pool of resources as the reduction in attention caused by staring out of the window, since there is only one such pool. And since we already know, from the example of staring out of the window, that a depletion of this pool can influence learning, then it follows that a depletion caused by any means, including via the effect of PV, can also influence learning.

The problem is that attention may well *not* be a unitary construct. For example, in this volume, Hogarth, Dickinson, and Duka (2010, this volume) make a persuasive case for selective attention being an 'amalgamation of processing systems'. Hence it is possible that a cue having low PV influences a different pool of resources from that influenced by a participant staring out of the window, in which case the reduction in learning caused by the latter tells us nothing about the whether the former will also have an effect on learning. Consequently our analysis of Assumption 2 will be restricted to cases in which the original deficit in attention was caused by differences in PV, as envisaged by attentional models of learning. And we shall see that there is, in fact, rather little existing evidence to suggest that differences in attention wrought by differences in prior PV exert any influence on the rate of subsequent learning about cues.

Eye gaze and attention revisited: a longitudinal analysis

In the discussion of Assumption 1 above, I mentioned a study by Le Pelley, Beesley, and Griffiths (in preparation), in which we recorded participants' eye gaze as they carried out a categorization task based on the experimental design used by Le Pelley and McLaren (2003; Table 8.1). Consistent with Assumption 1, while participants learnt about the differential PV of the cues during Stage 1, dwell time was significantly greater to predictive cues than to nonpredictive cues (Figure 8.3A).

But what of the data relating to Stage 2? Prior behavioural studies (e.g. Le Pelley and McLaren, 2003) anticipate that participants will learn more rapidly about previously-predictive cues (A–D) than previously-nonpredictive cues (V–Y) during Stage 2, and this was the result we observed. Prediction ratings were obtained in a final test phase, to a question of the form 'how likely is it that [sound o3 or sound o4] will follow the words P and Q?', where P and Q refer to a particular pair of cues (AC, BD, VX, or WY; see Table 8.1). Participants rated compounds AC and BD as significantly more predictive of outcomes o3 and o4, respectively, than were compounds VX and WY.

Attentional theories of learning (e.g. Kruschke, 2001; Mackintosh, 1975) suggest that this difference in learning is a consequence of differences in attention to the cues during Stage 2 (which itself arises as a result of differences in the PV of these cues during Stage 1). Hence these theories anticipate greater dwell time to previously-predictive cues than to previously-nonpredictive cues during Stage 2, on the assumption that eye gaze provides a valid index of attention. Figure 8.3B shows that, consistent with this prediction, dwell time was indeed greater for previously-predictive cues than for previously-nonpredictive cues during Stage 2. Recall that the objective, statistical cue–outcome contingency is equal for all cues during Stage 2; hence these findings clearly demonstrate a biased distribution of attention during the critical learning phase.

Up to this point, these data are consistent with attentional accounts of the biased learning during Stage 2. However, one further aspect of these results does not agree so well with this account. Attentional theories suggest that it is a difference in attention to cues (arising as a result of Stage 1 training) that drives differences in learning about the perceived PV of these cues during Stage 2; this is the essence of Assumption 2. Consequently, these theories anticipate that a difference in attention to previously-predictive and -nonpredictive cues will *precede* a difference in learning about those cues. Indeed, the unequal attentional distribution should be present from the outset of Stage 2 (given that it carries over from Stage 1), while a difference in learning should emerge only later.

Unfortunately our data do not allow us to identify the point at which unequal *learning* about previously-predictive and previously-nonpredictive cues first emerges, since the only point of comparison for these cues is during the final test phase. Even so, the dwell time data in Figure 8.3B do not bode particularly well for Assumption 2. It is quite clear that dwell times for previously-predictive and previously-nonpredictive cues are very similar in the first block of Stage 2, with an unequal distribution emerging only later, once there has been an opportunity for learning.

On the face of it, then, these data are more consistent with an account in which the unequal learning to previously-predictive and previously-nonpredictive cues is caused by some factor other than attention. This factor would promote learning about the previously-predictive cues relative to the previously-nonpredictive cues from the outset of Stage 2. It is then to be expected that, as a consequence of this difference in learning rate to previously-predictive and -nonpredictive cues, a difference in dwell time to these cues will emerge as Stage 2 continues; from the discussion of Assumption 1 above we already know that differences in learning can drive differences in attention. Thus while it is clear that differences in PV produce differences in attention during Stage 1, it is not so clear that it is these differences in attention that produce differences in learning (and hence in the perceived PV of cues) during Stage 2.

While these data are problematic for Assumption 2, this conclusion should be approached with a degree of caution. For one thing, it relies on a null effect; the failure to observe differential dwell time during the first block of Stage 2. That said, this is a consistent pattern that we have observed in a number of replications of this study. However, it is possible that the context change occurring between Stages 1 and 2, when participants receive further instructions introducing the new outcomes o3 and o4, introduces additional processes that mask differences in attention to cues during this first block. That is, this context change might, for whatever reason, encourage participants to orient equally to all cues at first, but as Stage 2 proceeds and participants realize that the task is procedurally very similar to what has come before, the unequal attentional distribution may emerge and drive differences in learning. Without an online measure allowing us to establish definitively that the difference in learning precedes a difference in attention, it is impossible to rule out such an interpretation. The problem is compounded, of course, by the fact that the possibility of covert attention means that eye gaze cannot provide a perfect, unambiguous measure of attention (Wright and Ward, 2008).

Finally, it is important to note that while attentional theories anticipate that a difference in attention will precede any difference in learning about the cues involved, observing such an effect would not provide unequivocal support for attentional theories. Even if we had observed a difference in attention (as measured by dwell time) to high- and low-PV cues at the very beginning of Stage 2, prior to any difference in learning about those cues, we could still not be sure that it is this difference in attention that has *caused* the difference in learning about those cues. It remains quite possible that the difference in learning is the product of some other, nonattentional mechanism. This problem is inherent in any attempt to test Assumption 2 using a correlative technique, i.e. an approach that takes separate measurements of attention (as assessed by eye gaze, EEG, susceptibility to attentional blink, etc.) and learning, and demonstrates that the two go hand-in-hand.

Attention, learning, and schizotypy

A potentially more fruitful line of attack would be to use an experimental approach to test Assumption 2. Suppose that there exists a manipulation that will reduce the extent to which a person is able to use selective attention. If this manipulation also reduces the influence of PV on subsequent learning, this would support the suggestion that the influence of PV on learning is via attention. In fact, this 'manipulation' need not be a manipulation in the traditional sense. For example, perhaps we could find a group of people who have a natural deficit in their ability to deploy attention. If the unequal learning observed as a consequence of a difference in prior PV is caused by attention (i.e. if Assumption 2 is correct), then this group should show a relatively weak influence of PV on learning.

Individuals with schizophrenia could potentially form such a group. It is now relatively well-established that schizophrenia patients are impaired in their ability to direct attention appropriately, as assessed across a wide range of cognitive tasks (for reviews, see Braff, 1993; Elvevåg and Goldberg, 2000). For example, Wang *et al.* (2005; see also Gooding, Braun, and Studer, 2006) used a flanker task, in which participants had to respond to the direction (left/right) in which a central target arrow pointed, when that arrow could be flanked by additional arrows pointing in the same direction as the target (congruent flankers) or in the opposite direction (incongruent flankers). On these incongruent trials, correct responding requires attentional selection; the target must be selected from the flankers, and the response conflict caused by the presence of the flankers must be suppressed. Healthy participants typically respond faster on congruent trials than incongruent trials, demonstrating a cost of this requirement for selection. However, schizophrenia patients showed a significantly larger flanker interference effect than healthy controls, indicating an impairment in attentional selection (or 'executive attention' to use Wang *et al.'s* terminology). That is, schizophrenia patients were less able to inhibit attention to the irrelevant flankers; they were more distracted by irrelevant information.

Related evidence comes from studies of the negative priming effect, wherein healthy participants are slower to name a target that has previously been ignored as a distractor (Tipper, 1985). The negative priming effect is typically attributed to inhibition of attention to previously-rejected information (Tipper, Weaver, and Milliken, 1995). Consistent with the suggestion that schizophrenia patients are impaired in their ability to inhibit attention to irrelevant information, several studies have demonstrated reduced negative priming in these individuals (see Peters *et al.*, 2000, for a review).

Hence, if Assumption 2 is correct, we might expect a reduced influence of prior PV on novel learning in patients with schizophrenia. There are problems with conducting such a test, however, not least because of variation in the participant sample due to differences in disease chronicity, nature, and severity of symptoms at the time of testing, and medication state, all of which (it has been claimed) have led to conflicting results in previous, related studies (e.g. see Gray and Snowden, 2005). In order to avoid such confounds, an alternative approach has been to examine individual differences in the general population under the assumption that the features of psychotic disorders such as schizophrenia lie on a continuum of 'schizotypy' and hence might be observed to a greater or lesser extent in healthy people (Claridge, 1997). This assumption has been bolstered by studies demonstrating that high schizotypes do indeed resemble individuals with schizophrenia on a number of information processing correlates (e.g. Baruch, Hemsley, and Gray, 1988; Broks, 1984; Lenzenweger and Korfine, 1994; Linney, Peters, and Ayton, 1998). Most importantly for the current argument, high schizotypes demonstrate attentional impairments similar to those observed in schizophrenia patients (e.g. Obiols, Garcia-Domingo, de Trincheria, and Domenech, 1993; Peters, Pickering, and Hemsley, 1994; Steel, Hemsley, and Pickering, 2002; Williams, 1995).

With this support in mind, we recently examined the relationship between schizotypy and the influence of prior PV on novel learning (Le Pelley, Schmidt-Hansen, Harris, Lunter, and Morris, 2010). In addition to completing the learning task shown in Table 8.1, participants completed the Oxford-Liverpool Inventory of Feelings and Experiences (O-LIFE: Mason, Claridge, and Jackson,

1995), a 160-item questionnaire assessing schizotypal traits on four subscales. Of particular interest was the 'unusual experiences' (UnEx) subscale, which examines deviant perceptual and cognitive experiences and relates to the positive symptom cluster of schizophrenia; previous research identifies this factor in particular as associated with attentional abnormalities both in high schizotypes (e.g. Evans, Gray, and Snowden, 2007; Steel *et al.*, 2002; Williams, 1995) and schizophrenia patients (Peters *et al.*, 2000). While participants scoring low on the UnEx scale showed a large influence of prior PV on novel learning (with greater learning about previously-predictive cues than previously-nonpredictive cues during Stage 2), this influence was significantly smaller in participants scoring high on the UnEx scale; indeed, these latter participants showed approximately equal learning about all cues in Stage 2 (Figure 8.4).[3]

This finding is consistent with an attentional account of the influence of PV on learning. We know from the existing literature that high schizotypes are impaired in their ability to use selective attention to ignore irrelevant stimuli. Hence it is natural to view the reduced influence of PV in these individuals as being a further reflection of an attentional deficit. That is, if the effect of prior PV on novel learning depends on an unequal distribution of attention to cues (i.e. if Assumption 2 is correct), then it is to be expected that people who are impaired in learning this unequal distribution of attention will show a reduced effect of prior PV.

Of course, the support for Assumption 2 provided by this study is very indirect; it relies on the assumptions that (i) schizotypy is associated with an attentional deficit, and (ii) it is this deficit in particular that underlies the reduced PV effect observed in high schizotypes. To the extent that either of these is incorrect, support for Assumption 2 is undermined. For example, an alternative interpretation of the reduced PV effect in high schizotypes would be that these individuals are more sensitive to the change in context between Stages 1 and 2 than are low schizotypes. The occurrence of a PV effect in this experiment relies on what is learnt in Stage 1 transferring to influence learning in Stage 2. If, for whatever reason, high schizotypes are less likely to apply what was learnt earlier to the new context of Stage 2, then we should expect a reduced PV effect, although attention need not be implicated.

[3] Why might a deficit in the appropriate allocation of attention during learning be particularly related to the positive dimension of schizotypy/schizophrenia? One possibility is that such a deficit could predispose people towards forming associations between nonpredictive, and hence unrelated, stimuli, and these associations may, ultimately, form the basis of a delusion, one of the major positive symptoms of schizophrenia.

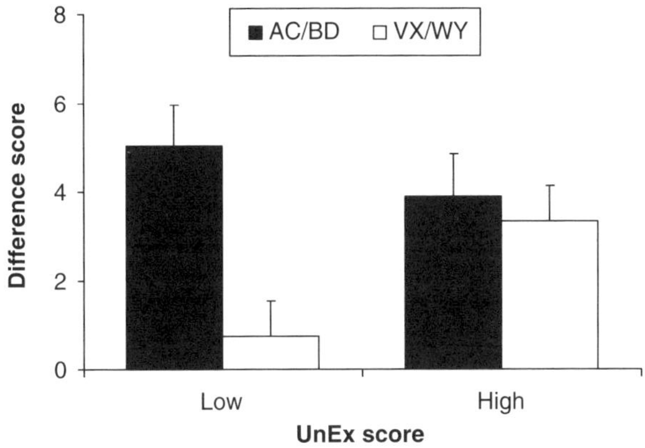

Fig. 8.4 Schizotypy-dependent variation in the influence of prior PV on novel learning (Le Pelley et al., 2010). 'Low' schizotypy refers to participants with Unusual Experiences scores lying below the lower tertile; 'high' refers to participants with scores above the upper tertile. The dependent variable is a difference score computed for each compound by taking each participant's rating of that compound regarding the outcome with which its elements were paired during Stage 2, and subtracting from that the rating for the same compound regarding the Stage 2 outcome with which its elements were not paired. For example, the difference score for compound AC was calculated by taking the rating for AC with respect to o3 (as A and C were paired with o3 during Stage 2), and subtracting from that the rating for AC with respect to o4 (as A and C were not paired with o4). Difference scores provide a measure of selective learning; the extent to which a compound is perceived as predicting the outcome with which it was paired more strongly than it does other outcomes. Higher scores (maximum=10) indicate better learning. (Copyright M. E. Le Pelley 2010).
Reprinted from Psychiatry Research, (in press), Le Pelley, M.E., Schmidt-Hansen, M., Harris, N.J., Lunter, C.M., & Morris, C.S., Disentangling the attentional deficit in schizophrenia: Pointers from schizotypy (2010), with permission from Elsevier.

Where next for Assumption 2?

While the support for Assumption 2 from this study of schizotypy is clearly equivocal, this is not to say that the general approach is without merit. We can return to the idea of a 'weight of evidence' argument similar to that used in the discussion of Assumption 1. Suppose we have several distinct manipulations, all of which have been demonstrated to alter people's ability to deploy selective attention (or several distinct populations of people, all of whom have been demonstrated to differ in their ability to deploy selective attention). Schizotypy provides one such 'manipulation', but many others are possible.

For example, participants in a negative mood have been shown to be more selective in their attentional allocation than those in a positive mood (Rowe, Hirsh, and Anderson, 2007), so a mood induction procedure would be another candidate. Yet another possibility would be administration of ketamine, which is thought to impair selective attention (Oranje *et al.*, 2000).

Suppose further that each one of these manipulations is demonstrated to modulate the influence of PV on learning; those manipulations that have been externally verified as impairing selective attention reduce the influence of PV on learning, while those manipulations verified as enhancing the selectivity of attention increase the influence of PV on learning. Of course, each of these manipulations might also influence aspects of cognition other than attention, so none of these effects on PV considered in isolation would constitute strong evidence for an attentional account of this phenomenon. But if the manipulations are sufficiently varied, such that an influence on attention is their one common theme, then many such demonstrations would provide a strong weight of evidence in support of an attentional account of the effect of PV on learning.

Concluding comments

To reiterate, the two assumptions that are central to attentional models of learning are:

Assumption 1: Differences in PV give rise to differences in attention to cues.
Assumption 2: Differences in attention to cues, caused by differences in PV, give rise to differences in subsequent learning about cues.

The problem in evaluating these assumptions is that no single effect or experimental manipulation is perfectly characteristic of the operation of attention to the exclusion of all other cognitive processes. Consequently, in both cases evaluation comes down to considering the weight of evidence, across a range of effects or manipulations, that bears on the relationship between PV and learning expressed in each of these assumptions.

With regard to Assumption 1 at least, this weight of evidence already provides a compelling case. That is, evidence from a wide range of studies provides clear support for the idea that one parameter that changes with learning about the PV of cues bears many of the hallmarks of attention, as the concept is understood by cognitive psychologists.

In contrast, the evidence relating to Assumption 2 is currently less clear-cut. This is not to say that this assumption is incorrect (and hence that attentional models of learning are fundamentally flawed), merely that the existing evidence does not allow us to come to a firm conclusion on this issue. In some sense, it would be surprising if Assumption 2 were *not* correct; why have a system in which PV guides attention, if the resulting attentional distribution has no further influence on behaviour? And future learning seems as likely a candidate as any to be a point of influence of that attentional system.

So, relative to Assumption 1, there is simply less evidence currently available that is relevant to the evaluation of Assumption 2. But, as for Assumption 1, a weight of evidence from a number of studies using different attentional manipulations could potentially make a forceful case for support. The influence of schizotypy on the PV effect provides one such piece of evidence; gathering the remainder remains a task for the future.

Acknowledgements

The author thanks the ESRC (UK) for funding the research upon which parts of this chapter are based, and Tom Beesley, Rob Honey, and Chris Mitchell for reading a previous draft. Much of this chapter was written while the author was a Visiting Fellow at the University of New South Wales.

References

Anderson, A. K. & Phelps, E. A. (2001). Lesions of the human amygdala impair enhanced perception of emotionally salient events. *Nature,* **411**, 305–309.

Arkes, H. R. & Harkness, A. R. (1983). Estimates of contingency between two dichotomous variables. *Journal of Experimental Psychology: General,* **112**.

Baruch, I., Hemsley, D. R., & Gray, J. A. (1988). Latent inhibition and 'psychotic proneness' in normal subjects. *Personality and Individual Differences,* **9**, 777–783.

Beesley, T. & Le Pelley, M. E. (2010). The effect of predictive history on the learning of sub-sequence contingencies. *Quarterly Journal of Experimental Psychology,* **63**, 108–135.

Beesley, T. & Le Pelley, M. E. (in press). The impact of blocking on attention and associability in human learning. *Journal of Experimental Psychology: Animal Behavior Processes.*

Bennett, C. H., Wills, S. J., Oakeshott, S. M., & Mackintosh, N.J. (2000). Is the context specificity of latent inhibition a sufficient explanation of learned irrelevance? *Quarterly Journal of Experimental Psychology,* **53B**, 239–253.

Bonardi, C., Graham, S., Hall, G., & Mitchell, C. J. (2005). Acquired distinctiveness and equivalence in human discrimination learning: Evidence for an attentional process. *Psychonomic Bulletin and Review,* **12**, 88–92.

Braff, D. L. (1993). Information processing and attention dysfunctions in schizophrenia. *Schizophrenia Bulletin,* **19**, 233–259.

Broks, P. (1984). Schizotypy and hemisphere function: II. Performance asymmetry on a verbal divided visual field task. *Personality and Individual Differences,* **5**, 649–656.

Chun, M. M. & Potter, M. C. (1995). A two-stage model for multiple target detection in RSVP. *Journal of Experimental Psychology: Human Perception and Performance,* **21**, 109–127.

Claridge, G. (1997). *Schizotypy: Implications for illness and health.* New York: Oxford University Press.

Cleeremans, A., Destrebecqz, A., & Boyer, M. (1998). Implicit learning: News from the front. *Trends in Cognitive Sciences*, **2**, 406–416.

De Houwer, J., Beckers, T., & Vandorpe, S. (2005). Evidence for the role of higher order reasoning processes in cue competition and other learning phenomena. *Learning and Behavior,* **33**, 239–249.

Della Libera, C. & Chelazzi, L. (2006). Visual selective attention and the effects of monetary rewards. *Psychological Science,* **17**, 222–227.

Deubel, H. & Schneider, W. X. (1996). Saccade target selection and object recognition: Evidence for a common attentional mechanism. *Vision Research,* **36**, 1827–1837.

Dickinson, A., Shanks, D.R., & Evenden, J.L. (1984). Judgement of act-outcome contingency: The role of selective attribution. *Quarterly Journal of Experimental Psychology,* **36A**, 29–50.

Elvevåg, B. & Goldberg, T. E. (2000). Cognitive impairment in schizophrenia is the core of the disorder. *Critical Reviews in Neurobiology,* **14**, 1–21.

Evans, L. H., Gray, N. S., & Snowden, R. J. (2007). A new continuous within-participants latent inhibition task: Examining associations with schizotypy dimensions, smoking status and gender. *Biological Psychology,* **74**, 365–373.

Folk, C. L., Remington, R. W., & Johnston, J. C. (1992). Involuntary covert orienting is contingent on attentional control settings. *Journal of Experimental Psychology: Human Perception and Performance,* **18**, 1030–1044.

Gooding, D. C., Braun, J. G., & Studer, J. A. (2006). Attentional network task performance in patients with schizophrenia-spectrum disorders: Evidence of a specific deficit. *Schizophrenia Research,* **88**, 169–178.

Gray, N. S. & Snowden, R. J. (2005). The relevance of irrelevance to schizophrenia. *Neuroscience and Biobehavioral Reviews,* **29**, 989–999.

Hillyard, S. A. & Anllo-Vento, L. (1998). Event-related brain potentials in the study of visual selective attention. *Proceedings of the National Academy of Sciences of the United States of America,* **95**, 781–787.

Hogarth, L., Dickinson, A., Austin, A., Brown, C., & Duka, T. (2008). Attention and expectation in human predictive learning: The role of uncertainty. *Quarterly Journal of Experimental Psychology,* **61**, 1658–1668.

Hogarth, L., Dickinson, A., & Duka, T. (2010). Selective attention to conditioned stimuli in human discrimination learning: Untangling the effect of outcome prediction, value and uncertainty. In C. J. Mitchell and M. E. Le Pelley (Eds), *Attention and Learning* (this volume). Oxford: Oxford University Press.

Honey, R. C., Close, J., & Lin, E. (2010). Acquired distinctiveness and equivalence: A synthesis. In C. J. Mitchell and M. E. Le Pelley (Eds), *Attention and Learning* (this volume). Oxford: Oxford University Press.

Kamin, L. J. (1968). Attention-like processes in classical conditioning. In M. R. Jones (Ed.), *Miami symposium on the prediction of behavior: Aversive stimulation* (pp. 9–32). Coral Gables, FL: University of Miami Press.

Kruschke, J. K. (1996). Dimensional relevance shifts in category learning. *Connection Science,* **8**, 225–247.

Kruschke, J. K. (2001). Towards a unified model of attention in associative learning. *Journal of Mathematical Psychology,* **45**, 812–863.

Kruschke, J. K., Kappenman, E. S., & Hetrick, W. P. (2005). Eye gaze and individual differences consistent with learned attention in associative blocking and highlighting. *Journal of Experimental Psychology: Learning, Memory, and Cognition,* **31**, 830–845.

Le Pelley, M. E. (2004). The role of associative history in models of associative learning: A selective review and a hybrid model. *Quarterly Journal of Experimental Psychology,* **57B**, 193–243.

Le Pelley, M. E. (in preparation). Learned predictiveness influences attentional capture in humans.

Le Pelley, M E., Beesley, T., & Griffiths, O. (in preparation). Overt attention and predictiveness in human associative learning.

Le Pelley, M E. & McLaren, I. P. L. (2003). Learned associability and associative change in human causal learning. *Quarterly Journal of Experimental Psychology,* **56B**, 68–79.

Le Pelley, M. E., Oakeshott, S. M., & McLaren, I. P. L. (2005). Blocking and unblocking in human causal learning. *Journal of Experimental Psychology: Animal Behavior Processes,* **31**, 56–70.

Le Pelley, M. E., Reimers, S. J., Calvini, G., Spears, R., Beesley, T., & Murphy, R. A. (2010). Stereotype formation: Biased by association. *Journal of Experimental Psychology: General,* **139**, 138–161.

Le Pelley, M.E., Schmidt-Hansen, M., Harris, N. J., Lunter, C. M., & Morris, C. S. (2010). Disentangling the attentional deficit in schizophrenia: Pointers from schizotypy. *Psychiatry Research,* **176**.

Lenzenweger, M. F., and Korfine, L. (1994). Perceptual aberrations, schizotypy, and the Wisconsin Card Sorting Test. *Schizophrenia Bulletin,* **20**, 345–357.

Linney, Y. M., Peters, E. R., & Ayton, P. (1998). Reasoning biases in delusion-prone individuals. *British Journal of Clinical Psychology,* **37**, 285–302.

Livesey, E. J., Harris, I. M., & Harris, J. A. (2009). Attentional changes during implicit learning: Signal validity protects a target stimulus from the attentional blink. *Journal of Experimental Psychology: Learning, Memory, and Cognition,* **35**, 408–422.

Mackintosh, N. J. (1975). A theory of attention: Variations in the associability of stimuli with reinforcement. *Psychological Review,* **82**, 276–298.

Mackintosh, N. J. & Little, L. (1969). Intradimensional and extradimensional shift learning by pigeons. *Psychonomic Science,* **14**, 5–6.

MacLeod, C., Mathews, A., & Tata, P. (1986). Attentional bias in emotional disorders. *Journal of Abnormal Psychology,* **95**, 15–20.

Mason, O., Claridge, G., & Jackson, M. (1995). New scales for the assessment of schizotypy. *Personality and Individual Differences,* **18**, 7–13.

Obiols, J. E., Garcia-Domingo, M., de Trincheria, I., & Domenech, E. (1993). Psychometric schizotypy and sustained attention in young males. *Personality and Individual Differences,* **14**, 381–384.

Oranje, B., van Berckel, B. N., Kemner, C., van Ree, J. M., Kahn, R. S., & Verbaten, M. N. (2000). The effects of a sub-anaesthetic dose of ketamine on human selective attention. *Neuropsychopharmacology,* **22**, 293–302.

Oswald, C. J. P., Yee, B. K., Rawlins, J. N. P., Bannerman, D. B., Good, M., & Honey, R. C. (2001). Involvement of the entorhinal cortex in a process of attentional modulation: Evidence from a novel variant of an IDS/EDS procedure. *Behavioral Neuroscience,* **115**, 841–849.

Owen, A. M., Roberts, A. C., Polkey, C. E., Sahakian, B. J., & Robbins, T. W. (1991). Extra-dimensional versus intra-dimensional set shifting performance following frontal-lobe excisions, temporal-lobe excisions or amygdalo-hippocampectomy in man. *Neuropsychologia,* **29**, 993–1006.

Pearce, J. M., and Hall, G. (1980). A model for Pavlovian conditioning: Variations in the effectiveness of conditioned but not of unconditioned stimuli. *Psychological Review,* **87**, 532–552.

Peters, E. R., Pickering, A. D., & Hemsley, D. R. (1994). 'Cognitive inhibition' and positive symptomatology in schizotypy. *British Journal of Clinical Psychology,* **33**, 33–48.

Peters, E. R., Pickering, A. D., Kent, A., Glasper, A., Irani, M., David, A. S., *et al.* (2000). The relationship between cognitive inhibition and psychotic symptoms. *Journal of Abnormal Psychology,* **109**, 386–395.

Posner, M. I. (1980). Orienting of attention. *Quarterly Journal of Experimental Psychology,* **32**, 3–25.

Posner, M. I., Nissen, M. J., & Ogden, W. C. (1978). Attended and unattended processing modes: The role of set for spatial location. In H. L. Pick and I. J. Saltzman (Eds), *Modes of perceiving and processing information.* (pp. 137–157). Hillsdale, NJ: Erlbaum.

Quinlan, P. T. (2010). On the use of the term 'attention'. In C. J. Mitchell and M. E. Le Pelley (Eds), *Attention and Learning* (this volume). Oxford: Oxford University Press.

Raymond, J. E., Shapiro, K. L., & Arnell, K. M. (1992). Temporary suppression of visual processing in an RSVP task: An attentional blink? *Journal of Experimental Psychology: Human Perception and Performance, 18.*

Rowe, G., Hirsh, J. B., & Anderson, A. K. (2007). Positive affect increases the breadth of attentional selection. *Proceedings of the National Academy of Sciences of the United States of America,* **104**, 383–388.

Shapiro, K. L., Caldwell, J., & Sorensen, R. E. (1997). Personal names and the attentional blink: A visual 'cocktail party' effect. *Journal of Experimental Psychology: Human Perception and Performance,* **23**, 504–514.

Shepp, B. E. & Schrier, A. M. (1969). Consecutive intradimensional and extradimensional shifts in monkeys. *Journal of Comparative and Physiological Psychology,* **67**, 199–203.

Shue, K. L. & Douglas, V. I. (1992). Attention deficit hyperactivity disorder and the frontal lobe syndrome. *Brain and Cognition,* **20**, 104–124.

Steel, C., Hemsley, D. R., & Pickering, A. D. (2002). Distractor cueing effects on choice reaction time and their relationship with schizotypal personality. *British Journal of Clinical Psychology,* **41**, 143–156.

Sutherland, N. S. & Mackintosh, N. J. (1971). *Mechanisms of animal discrimination learning.* New York: Academic Press.

Tamir, M. & Robinson, M. D. (2007). The happy spotlight: Positive mood and selective attention to rewarding information. *Personality and Social Psychology Bulletin,* **33**, 1124–1136.

Tipper, S. P. (1985). The negative priming effect: Inhibitory priming by ignored objects. *Quarterly Journal of Experimental Psychology,* **37A**, 571–590.

Tipper, S. P., Weaver, B., & Milliken, B. (1995). Spatial negative priming without mismatching: Comment on Park and Kanwisher (1994). *Journal of Experimental Psychology: Human Perception and Performance,* **21**, 1220–1229.

Vogel, E. K. & Luck, S. J. (2000). The visual N1 component as an index of a discrimination process. *Psychophysiology,* **37**, 190–203.

Wang, K., Fan, J., Dong, Y., Wang, C.-Q., Lee, T. M. C., & Posner, M. I. (2005). Selective impairment of attentional networks of orienting and executive control in schizophrenia. *Schizophrenia Research,* **78**, 235–241.

Ward, W. D. & Jenkins, H. M. (1965). The display of information and the judgment of contingency. *Canadian Journal of Psychology,* **19**, 231–241.

Williams, L. (1995). Further evidence for a multidimensional personality disposition to schizophrenia in terms of cognitive inhibition. *British Journal of Clinical Psychology,* **34**, 193–213.

Wills, A. J., Lavric, A., Croft, G. S., & Hodgson, T. L. (2007). Predictive learning, prediction errors, and attention: Evidence for event-related potentials and eye-tracking. *Journal of Cognitive Neuroscience,* **19**, 843–854.

Wright, R. D. & Ward, L. M. (2008). *Orienting of attention.* New York: Oxford University Press.

Chapter 9

On the use of the term 'attention'

Philip T. Quinlan

My experience is what I agree to attend to.
(*James*, 1890/1981, p. 380)

What I intend to do in this chapter is to examine the term 'attention' and provide some important examples of how it has been used in the experimental psychology literature. The aims are (i) to show how the term has been applied in different areas, (ii) to try to work out whether there is a useful explanatory construct that is being discussed in the different areas, and, in particular, (iii) to focus on how attention has been used as an explanatory concept in theories of learning. In covering this material, a particular framework for thinking about attention is advanced, namely, stimulus selection as a consequence of some form of processing constraint. As a consequence, the chapter rests on a, perhaps, wishful aspiration that the framework will prove helpful in deciding about whether any theory of learning necessarily implicates attentional processes.

A typical opening gambit in any discussion on attention is to include the following quote from William James: 'Everyone knows what attention is. It is the taking possession by the mind, in clear and vivid form, of one out of what seem several simultaneously possible objects or trains of thought' (1890/1981, p. 381). This tends to ward off any further penetrating questioning on the grounds that everyone knows what attention is so how could the questioner not grasp the simplicity of it all? However, if we are to make any progress in understanding, then it is only right to probe further. Intuitively James tells us everything we need to know, yet if we are to examine the explanatory nature of that which we call 'attention', then we will need to go further.[1]

From 1890 we move, with perhaps undue haste, to 1971. This is the year that Sutherland and Mackintosh (1971) published their seminal monograph on

[1] For nothing more than expository convenience, a somewhat lazy distinction will be drawn between 'humans' and 'animals'. Unless otherwise stated, the term 'animals' will be used to refer to non-human vertebrates and, as is the norm in the 'animal' literature, specifically the behaviour of rats and pigeons will be key.

discrimination learning. Central to their account of discrimination learning is a model of attention. A primary ambition was to 'show that evidence collected by ourselves and others *proves* that selective attention plays an important role in animal learning.' (p. 21; emphasis added). This is a bold (perhaps rash) statement and we are going to need some further help if we are to make sense of it. A starting point is the acceptance that not everything that confronts an animal has a controlling influence on its behaviour. A distinction is made between the important aspects of the environment and the irrelevant aspects: 'important' in the sense that these are the aspects of the environment that act as effective predictors of future events. The selected stuff is the important stuff – the stuff that can be used to predict the future and the animal should take it into account if it is to behave adaptively. Distinguishing between the important and the irrelevant, in theory, implies that, in practice, the animal selects out the important from the irrelevant. In functional terms, this is defined in terms of some form of act of selection. From this sample of evidence arriving at the senses, only a sub-sample is selected. This form of selection critically underpins the notion of attention.

In answer to the question 'what is this form of selection useful for?' the reply is it is the basis of the animal's ability to make successful predictions. Therefore it is useful to draw a distinction between prediction over what will happen next and prediction over what to do next (Allport, Tipper, and Chmiel, 1985). Both forms of prediction are important. For instance, the appearance of rain clouds leads to the prediction that rain will shortly follow. In addition, the presence of rain clouds leads to the prediction of rain and the necessity of finding shelter. In adopting this latter sense of prediction, we have a view of attention defined in terms of something known as 'selection for action' (Allport *et al.*, 1985). The important stuff is selected and it is this that determines future actions. In contrast, the irrelevant stuff is discarded or ignored.

A further common assumption is that such selection is a necessary by-product of the fact that the brain is limited in its capacity (Broadbent, 1958; Mackintosh, 1965). There are the now classic statements (such as Allport's, 1989) that the fundamental 'purpose of attentional mechanisms is to protect the brain's limited capacity system (or systems) from informational overload' (p. 633). The idea is that the brain can only process effectively a sub-set of the evidence that is presented to the senses at any one time. To get a better grip on these ideas, Carrasco (2006) has brought the arguments right up-to-date in the following manner. She wrote: 'Given that the amount of overall energy consumption available to the brain is constant, the average discharge rate in active neurons will determine the number of neurons that can be active at any time' (p. 34). Such so called 'bioenergentic limitations' therefore provide, in concrete terms, the neurophysiological basis for the brain's limited capacity. The basic idea is that there is only a certain amount of neural energy to go around at any one time and, because of this limitation on processing, there is the necessity for selective attention. Rather than randomly discard the right amount at each moment, the assumption is that there is a process by which certain aspects of the environment are selected and certain others are discarded. The act of selection is taken to be an *attentional process*.

An overarching framework for thinking therefore is provided by the claim that attentional selection takes place because the brain is unable to deal with everything it is confronted with at a given moment in time. What this seems to suggest is that attentional processes will be most evident when the brain is overloaded. However, the arguments can be a little more slippery if the following is accepted. Although attentional selection is a by-product of limitations of the processing system, it is also taken to be ongoing even in conditions where the system is not overloaded. When reading this book in a quiet room presumably, the main focus is with the text being read rather than the ambient temperature of the room. The text is selected and the temperature is ignored. Intuitively, this kind of selection is made more apparent when attempting to read this book in a busy bus station, but the assumption is that attentional selection is working even when the system is not overloaded.

Such commonsense notions do have some important consequences (as we will see) because it is typically (but not exclusively) the case that in the human literature, attentional processes are studied when the system is pushed to its limits. Stimuli are presented at or below the threshold such that they are physically degraded, masked, briefly presented, etc. Alternatively, more than one task is undertaken at a time. Notably therefore, from an historical point of view, our understanding of attention has come about from experiments in which performance is at the margins (see Quinlan and Dyson, 2008, Chapter 8). This gives rise to two possibilities. One is that performance at the margins is qualitatively different from performance under normal circumstances. The other is that it is not. The implicit assumption, however, is that it is not and the experimental evidence is taken to provide a window on attentional processes that happen normally on a moment-by-moment basis.

Such concerns have been touched upon in the animal literature and they do indeed carry some force. Some theorists (e.g., Rescorla and Wagner, 1972) have questioned the utility of any theory of learning that implicates attentional processes that is itself derived from a consideration of performance in very simple tasks. The central point is that although attentional processes may be operating, they are unlikely to be the primary determiners of performance in very simple tasks. To take an example from the human literature, a visual lexical decision task is where a printed string of letters is presented on a trial and the subject has to decide as quickly and as accurately as possible whether the string constitutes a word. Now, of course, the subject must attend to the string, but selective attention is not the primary driver of performance in such a task. Of main interest is the fact that performance varies across different sorts of letter strings. For instance, subjects respond more quickly and accurately to common than rare words. However, given that the subjects are attending equally to both sorts of strings, accounts of performance do not depend on appeals to selective attention in any critical way. We will return to these points as the discussion proceeds. Nonetheless, it is worth pointing out, at the outset, that some of the difficulties that have arisen in coming to terms with attention in the animal literature may well be due to attempting to build theories of learning based on assumptions about attentional processes from situations in which such processes play only a marginal role.

To return to Sutherland and Mackintosh (1971), in setting the scene for their text, they began with what they termed a 'two-process theory'. Namely, 'discrimination in animal learning involves two processes: learning to which aspects of the stimulus to attend and learning what responses to attach to the relevant aspects of the stimulus situation' (p. 21). For present purposes, what is significant about this statement is that it very clearly sets the discussion of attention in the context of learning. What the animal learns about is, in part, determined by what it attends to. This is a crucial point and lies at the heart of the difference between 'attention' as used in the human literature and 'attention' as used in the animal literature. Although there are cases where the 'attention' is used as an explanatory construct in the literature on human learning (see Shanks, 2005), it is much more usual to find the term being used in a variety of contexts that have nothing to do with learning. This stands in contrast with much of the animal work because animal learning theorists have attempted to define attention in terms of implications for learning. Such an idea is exemplified in the following quote from Mackintosh (1975, p. 294): 'the probability of attending to a stimulus determines the probability of learning about that stimulus'.

On the face of it therefore, the term 'attention' is being used for very different purposes in the non-human and human literature. On the one hand in animal experiments, it is performance in learning tasks that is studied. The interesting stimuli are the ones that are defined relative to how they have been correlated with reinforcement in the past (see Mackintosh, 1975, p. 278). On the other hand, in human experiments, past experience is not necessarily key. In classic cases, what matters more is the current intentions of the subject. For instance, the subject is instructed to hear out and report the message in the right ear whilst trying to ignore the message in the left (cf. Cherry, 1953).

Here part of the difference in emphasis reflects the fact that we may distinguish *stimulus factors* from *subject factors*—a distinction that maps onto the difference between so-called *exogenous* and *endogenous* attentional factors (Klein and Shore, 2000; Posner, 1980). Exogenous factors relate to the physical characteristics of the stimulus such as loudness of the tone and brightness of light etc. Such characteristics reflect the attention-getting aspects of the stimulus and the implication is that there is an involuntary attentional component: the subject cannot help but attend to the stimulus (think of what happens when the fire alarm goes off). In contrast, endogenous factors refer to psychological processes that are independent of any external stimulus. The subject's intentions fall into this category. The associated implication is that there is a corresponding voluntary attentional component. Within the human literature, it has been accepted (without dissent) that attentional selection can be active in the sense that some form of intention is at play. Sentiments of a similar nature are included in James' briefer quote that precedes the main text: 'My experience is what I agree to attend to'. The important idea here is that to attend to something in this way involves an element of choice—not only can I agree to attend to something but I can also ignore it if I so choose.

Within the context provided by the pages of this book, it would be perhaps folly to pursue these ideas about 'intention' further. I have yet to find mention of them in literature on animal learning upon which this chapter is based. Nonetheless, it would be a basic error to attempt to castigate animal learning theorists on the grounds that they have completely ignored endogenous factors in their accounts of attention. It is clear that they have been acutely aware of the difference between stimulus and subjective factors. As Mackintosh (1975, p. 278) was at pains to point out, both the physical characteristics of a stimulus (such as its intensity or modality) and the subject's (past) experience must be taken into account (see also Dickinson, 1980, p. 125). The fact remains though, that insofar as subjective factors are taken into account, these can be explained simply by recourse to a detailed record of the preconditions and consequences of the previous exposures of the stimulus to the subject. Appalled cognitive psychologists may decide to stop reading here.

This introductory section can be brought to a close by outlining how the ensuing material unfolds. In the first half of the chapter, I try to convey how the language and concepts of attention have been used in the human literature. The aim here is to expose the sorts of theoretical ideas that have been advanced to explain attention and attentional processes. This section ends with a summary (and personal view) of the key points to emerge. Having established a framework for thinking about attention, the intention is then to see whether such a framework is useful in trying to understand learning. Consequently the second half of the chapter focuses on theories of animal learning that implicate 'the language and concepts of attention'.

The study of attention in humans

Foundational is the idea that the use of the term 'attention' implies stimulus selection because of some sort of processing constraint. It will probably come as no surprise that within the human experimental literature such ideas are typically discussed in functional terms within the framework of some form of abstract information processing model. Historically, the discussion of putative attentional mechanisms has been addressed at an abstract, functional level with little regard for the possible underlying neurophysiological substrate. As discussion proceeds however, it will become apparent that much recent work has attempted to bridge the gap between the functional and the physical. Nowadays, and perhaps regrettably, focus is with neural mechanisms.

If we take Broadbent's (1958) filter model as a starting point, this encapsulates everything that needs to be known about early selection models of attention. It is a paradigm case of an information processing model. Within the model, we can draw a rough division between an early feature registration stage of processing and a subsequent more detailed analysis of the input. All aspects of information stimulation at the sensorium are captured initially in a very brief short-term memory store. The filter operates as a means to select from this store aspects of the stimulation that are, in some sense, important. The filter is set to select aspects of the stimulation on the basis of one of the indefinite physical characteristics of the stimulus. For instance, select the red items. This privileged sensory representation (the important stuff) is then subject to further analysis. Stimulus identification is a crucial objective of these further processes. Everything that is not so selected because of a mismatch between the setting of the filter and nature of the stimulus remains in the short-term store. Unless the filter setting is changed to accommodate the remaining information in the store, it decays and will be lost.

There are both structural and processing constraints in the model. For instance, a structural constraint is located after the filter. Located immediately after the filter is a structural bottleneck such that strict limits are set on the amount of stimulus information that can be dealt with at any one time. A corresponding processing constraint reflects decay in the short-term store (as just mentioned)—unless information from the store is passed on by the filter, or it is refreshed by a process of rehearsal, it decays away. The rate of decay contributes to the limit that an individual can deal with in the current stimulus situation—the quicker information in the store decays the more rapidly can the uptake of new information take place.

The contrary late-selection accounts of attention are based on the assumption that any bottleneck exists not prior to stimulus identification but after this. A critical quote here is that 'all sensory messages which impinge upon the organism are perceptually analyzed at the highest level.' (Deutsch and Deutsch, 1963; p. 85). Now the constraints that apply are more concerned with choosing which signals are remembered and/or acted upon.

Both sorts of models honour the notion that attentional mechanisms are necessary because of constraints in the brain's inability to deal with all of the sensory stimulation at any one moment in time. A choice has to be made about what to respond to, and this is reflected in the setting of the filter. The setting of the filter defines what is attended to. In both early and late filter models there is the assumption that ignored information (i.e., the filtered-out, ignored stuff) is simply discarded and plays no further role in influencing the subject's behaviour. However, if we delve further into the issues we can ask about what other sorts of attentional processes there might be. One way to proceed is to consider what the differences are between selected and ignored stimuli. We need to clarify what is meant by attending to something. What are the consequences of attending to this and ignoring that?

Attention construed as changes in the signal-to-noise ratio

One very useful way of thinking about these issues is in terms of signal-to-noise ratio. Introspection dictates that the clarity of the attended is more acute than is the clarity of the unattended. This is self-evident when reading a page of printed text. The letters of the current word are plain to see and those several degrees away in the visual periphery are indistinguishable. More generally, it has been claimed that the same is true of attention in all modalities—the clarity of the attended is greater than that of the ignored. Opinions differ as to what this might actually mean in terms of the underlying attentional operations. As a consequence, let us proceed in theory-neutral terms and assume that the signal-to-noise ratio is greater for attended than unattended stimuli. How might this come about?

In the traditional early filter model, the difference between attended and unattended is down to the operation of the filter. The filter determines the current contents of consciousness—there are no gradations of clarity. According to Deutsch and Deutsch (1963), the signals selected as being important are those that the organism is aware of. However, there are many vexed issues and, more recently, some progress has been made on the particular issue of *signal-to-noise enhancement*.

For an appreciation of the basic ideas, we will turn to the work of Carrasco and colleagues (here the central reference is to the recent review by Carrasco, 2006). An initial point of interest is how closely the ideas about changes in the signal-to-noise ratio are linked to neuronal processing. In the work under consideration, the functional ideas are discussed in terms of underlying neurophysiological processes. For instance, and to reiterate, Carrasco defended the ideas about limited resources in terms of the actual amount of work done (in terms of energy expended) by the brain. First we assume that neuronal activity consumes energy: there is a metabolic cost associated with neuronal activity. If we also assume that such energy is associated with a finite resource then the conclusion is that 'the average discharge rate in active neurons will determine the number of neurons that can be active at any time' (p. 34). This argument provides the basis for attentional selection and the idea that, at the psychological level, there are clear constraints on the amount of sensory information that the organism can deal with at any one moment.

Cast in these terms, the implication is that at the neural level there is competition for a finite resource. If neural centre *x* is demanding to be in a highly active state, the implication is that some other neural centre *y* will suffer as a consequence. For Carrasco (2006), the particular area of interest is with the operation of the visual system and the attentional constraints that apply in vision. The basic conclusion of this work is that 'neural activity increases at attended locations and decreases at unattended locations' (p. 35): there are both costs and benefits in attending to something. The signal-to-noise ratio is enhanced at the location of the thing that is attended. Concomitant with this is that the signal-to-noise ratio is diminished at competing unattended locations.

Upon reflection though, it is, perhaps important to treat the benefits and costs as separate possibilities. For instance, it is quite possible to think in terms of the focus of attention as being shorthand for enhancement of the signal at a particular location. Whether we also need to posit a concomitant decrease in the signal-to-noise ratio for unattended locations is an additional empirical issue. Cast thus the argument is reminiscent of whether or not inhibition is a necessary construct (MacLeod, Dodd, Sheard, Wilson and Bibi, 2003)—maybe changes in excitation are sufficient? Answers to these particular issues (in the context of visual processing, at least) are provided in the spatial cueing studies undertaken by Carrasco and colleagues.

Fundamental to this work is something known as the *spatial cueing paradigm* (Posner, 1980). In this context, the basic understanding is that the focus of visual attention (i.e., the direction of attention in space) can be altered by providing spatial cues. Simply put, the focus of attention can be orientated in space by the presentation of an alerting visual event (or cue) at a so-called *cued location*. The literature on spatial cueing is immense, but all that needs to be appreciated here is that given the right sorts of cues and the right sorts of timings, there is very good evidence that the focus of visual attention can be controlled by external events. Given there is such a huge number of experiments on spatial cueing, there is a wealth of evidence that supports the basic idea that visual attention can be moved around the visual field either by the will of the subject or the presence of effective cues (see previous discussion of the difference between endogenous and exogenous attentional processes.) The experiments under discussion were primarily concerned with the attention-getting (exogenous) properties of peripheral visual cues.

Figure 9.1 provides a schematic of the basic cueing task and the sorts of displays as described by Carrasco, Ling, and Read (2004). The thrust of the work was to examine the degree to which spatial cueing can influence the fidelity of stimulus encoding when attention is cued to a particular spatial locale.

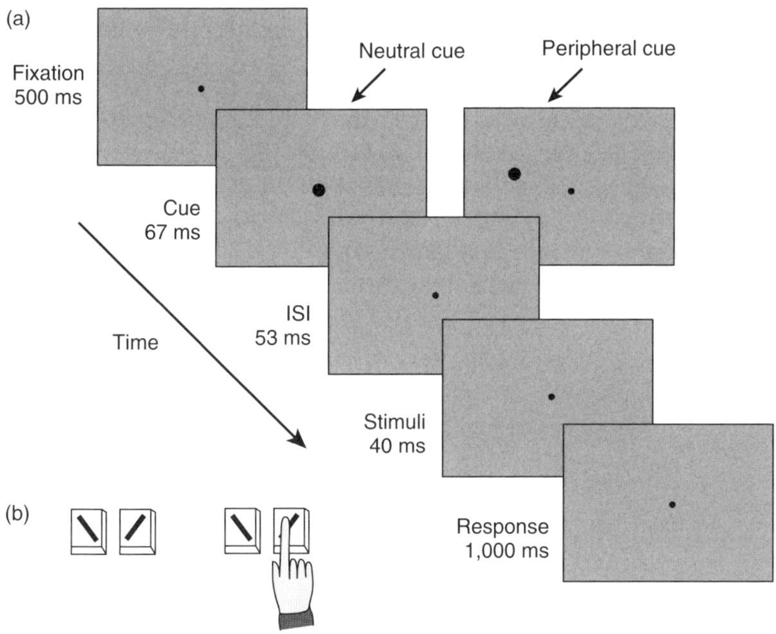

Fig. 9.1 (A) The sequence of events on a trial as reported by Carrasco et al. (2004). (B) The response keys arrangement used in the experiment. The subject had to decide which of the two patches was the brighter and then decide the orientation of the grating. Reprinted by permission from Macmillan Publishers Ltd. Figure 1, p. 309 from Carrasco, M., Ling, S., and Read, S. (2004). Attention alters appearance. *Nature Neuroscience*, **7**, 308–313.

Is there any evidence for signal-to-noise enhancement at cued locations? On a given trial, the subject fixated a central spot on a computer screen. Following this, a cue was presented: the *neutral cue* was simply a larger spot presented at the centre of the screen and the *peripheral cue* was a larger spot presented either to the right or the left of fixation. Following a brief representation of the central spot, two patches of oriented gratings were presented to the right and left of fixation, respectively. The subject now had to indicate (i) which of the two patches was of the higher contrast (appeared to be more distinct from the grey background) and (ii) what the orientation of the grating was (either sloping to the left or sloping to the right). One of the patches was known as the standard and was always presented at the same near-threshold level of contrast. The contrast of the other test patch was varied. The main index of performance was the percentage of responses indicating that the test patch was the more distinct and these measures were analysed both as a function of the actual contrast of the test patch and the nature of the cue.

The basic motivation in undertaking such an experiment was to demonstrate what the consequences of orienting visual attention actually are. In this regard, performance in the neutral cue condition is critical because it provides a baseline condition in which attention is maintained at the central location. Performance in this condition reflects performance in which attention is not directed systematically at either cued location. More particularly, Carrasco stated that the expectation is that in the neutral condition, the point at which the test and standard patch are indistinguishable (the point of subjective equality) should correspond to the point at which the test and standard patches are physically identical.

Two forms of directed cueing were examined in this experiment. On valid trials the peripheral cue was presented at the same location as the ensuing test patch, whereas on invalid trials, the cue was presented at the location of the standard patch. In both cases, subjects were instructed to judge the test patch regardless of where the cue was located. A critical point, here is that the location of the cue was *uninformative* or, more exactly, uncorrelated with the position of the test patch. Hence there can be no sense in which responses directed to the position of the cue could be systematically related to correct responding. Remember the task was to judge the contrast of the test patch not its position.

One central issue now was with how performance across the various cueing conditions would vary. A *cueing benefit* is where performance on valid trials is better than on neutral trials and a corresponding *cueing cost* is where performance on invalid trials is worse on invalid trials than neutral trials. As probably can be imagined, depending on which papers are consulted, various patterns of performance have been reported in cueing literature. In theory-neutral terms though, it is simple to see how cueing benefits may arise through valid cueing. The focus of attention is directed by the cue to the location of the ensuing test patch. We can then ask how judgements about the patch are affected by the prior presentation of the cue. A straightforward expectation is that if the cue is able to direct the focus of attention and the role of attention is to improve the signal-to-noise ratio at the focus, then performance on valid trials should be better than performance on neutral trials. This is essentially what Carrasco *et al.* (2004) reported.

More critically though, emphasis was placed on comparing the estimates of subjective equality across the valid and neutral conditions. Here it was found that the point of subjective equality had shifted such that a lower contrast test patch was judged to be equivalent to the standard patch. So when the subject's focus of attention was cued validly to the location of the test patch, this patch was judged to be of a discernible higher contrast than it actually was. This particular result was taken to support the idea of signal enhancement, namely, 'that attention directly improves the quality of the stimulus representation' (Carrasco, 2006, p. 37). The effect was one in which the contrast sensitivity was enhanced at the location of the cue (for a converging but different set of supporting evidence for signal enhancement see Dayan and Zemel, 1999). In summary, here is evidence of directed attention improving the signal-to-noise ratio. What these data do not, however, reveal is whether there is a concomitant decrease in signal-to-noise ratio at locations outside the focus of attention.

As a consequence, and following a related rationale, comparisons between the neutral and invalid trials were now undertaken. The comparisons revealed that, generally speaking, performance was worse on invalid trials than it was on neutral trials. On invalid trials, it was found that the point of subjective equality for the test patches was shifted, but in a direction indicating poorer stimulus resolution. Now the test patch needed to be of a physically higher contrast than the standard in order for it to be judged to be equivalent to it. The contrast of the test patch appeared to be less than it actually was on invalid trials. On these grounds (see also Pestilli and Carrasco, 2005), it was argued that, in addition to the signal enhancement that operates within the focus of attention, there is a corresponding external noise reduction that occurs. More particularly, attention acts 'by actively suppressing the strength of representation for areas outside (of the focus)' (p. 36; text in parentheses added). By this view, there is more to attention than signal-to-noise enhancement: signals presented outside the current focus of attention are also essentially inhibited.

It would be disingenuous not to note that the nature of such cueing effects is short-lasting. In the experiments reported, the delay between the onset of the cue and that of the imperative stimuli was 120 ms and the effects had dissipated when this was increased to 500 ms. Therefore, the relevance of this to the more typical animal learning experiment could, rightfully, be called into question. However, the effects do reflect on the sorts of attentional mechanisms that have been identified and the issues are foundational: The neural apparatus appears to both enhance the attended signal and inhibit the processing of ignored signals. Further evidence for this conclusion comes from other data interpreted in terms of the *biased competition* view of attentional processes in the brain, and it is to this that we now turn.

Attention as biased competition

It is typical to cast the issues in terms of the historical clash between early and late selection theorists with the middle ground being occupied by the conclusion that attentional constraints most probably exist at various stages or loci throughout the processing system (Allport, 1989). However, a slightly different take on the issues arises from consideration of different theoretical perspectives. For instance, there is relatively good evidence for the idea that perceptual processing can be characterized in general terms as being constituted by an initial rather crude stage of analysis that is then followed by a more detailed scrutiny of the sensory evidence (Broadbent, 1977; Navon, 2003; see Quinlan and Dyson, 2008, Chapter 5, for a more thorough appraisal of these ideas). Such ideas are typically discussed in terms of an initial bottom-up (stimulus driven) stage of processing followed by a subsequent top-down (knowledge driven) stage. Again most of the theorizing has taken place in terms of the operation of visual information processing but in abstract terms, there is no reason to think that the framework does not have a more general application. By this view, the notion of a structural filter is too simple and a more appropriate approach is to think in terms of different sorts of processing constraints. Indeed it is the interplay of both stimulus-driven and knowledge-driven factors that is central to the theory of *biased competition*.

According to the biased competition view, following immediately on from the presentation of a particular visual scene, some form of object parsing takes place such that the sensory evidence is packaged into object-sized chunks (how this may actually take place remains unspecified). Once such object parsing has occurred though, competition for attentional resources may begin. Critically the nature of this competition can be biased both by (i) 'bottom-up neural mechanisms' (an intense signal will accrue more resources than a less intense signal) and (ii) 'top-down mechanisms that select objects of relevance to current behavior' (Desimone and Duncan, 1995, p. 216: the exogenous/endogenous distinction reappears). By way of explanation, consider the case where the subject is instructed to find an item of a particular type in a visual scene (e.g. find the green A) and because of this a mental template that describes the item (i.e. green A) is borne in mind. Competition for attentional resources can therefore be biased (in a top-down fashion) towards the object features that are defined within the template, that is, green things and 'A's. As Driver and Frackowiak (2001) pointed out, a critical claim is that top-down biasing can take place prior to the onset of the stimulus. In this sense, certain neural pathways can be primed such that relevant stimuli are prioritized when the stimulus array is presented. For instance, the primary focus of attention is set up to be with the green items: when the scene is presented, search through the green items first.

Data in support of the biased competition view appeared in a study involving single electrode recordings of cells in the inferotemporal cortex of the monkey brain (Chelazzi, Duncan, Miller and Desimone, 1998; see also Duncan, 2006). Such cells are known to be particularly sensitive to visual pattern information. In pre-testing, cells were identified, each of which preferentially responded to a particular kind of visual pattern. Line drawings of common objects were used. For each cell, a good stimulus, a poor stimulus, and a neutral stimulus were identified. Responding to the good stimulus was strong, weak for the poor stimulus, and there was no particular response requirement for the neutral stimulus (i.e., in most cases, the responses were intermediate relative to those defined for the good and poor stimuli).

The task was simple and involved presenting a central fixation point (for 700 ms). Next a cue was presented at fixation (for 300 ms; the cue was either the good, poor, or neutral stimulus for the cell being currently recorded), there was a brief delay in which the central fixation point was represented and then a so-called search display was presented. (We will simply consider the cases where each search display contained either a single picture or two pictures.) During pre-training, the monkey had been taught to make a directed eye movement to the cued object, but only if it was present in the search display. If the cued object was not present, then the monkey had to maintain central fixation.

On target present trials, the search display contained the cued item and on target absent trials, the cued item was not present. Performance on target absent trials was assessed when the cue was the neutral stimulus but never occurred in the search display. Under these circumstances, the neutral cue did not instil a bias towards either the good or poor stimulus. Consider performance on the target absent trials, when the neutral stimulus acted as the cue, but the monkeys had to maintain central fixation. Cells fired vigorously when the search display contained only the good stimulus and they were essentially silent when the display contained the poor stimulus. When both good and poor items were present, the cells fired at an intermediate level. This pattern of results was taken to show that the presence of the poor stimulus had a suppressive effect on the cell's responses to the good stimulus. The cell's responses triggered by the presence of the good stimulus were modulated downwards by the presence of the poor stimulus in the search display when neither stimulus was the target of a directed eye movement.

Additional evidence for such competition was also found on target present trials. Consider first performance for trials in which single item displays were presented. In these cases, both the cue and target were the same. As expected, cells' responsiveness was largest when the good stimulus was presented and essentially flat when the poor stimulus was presented. The crucial data though relate to cases where both good and poor stimuli were present in a two-item search display. When the good stimulus was cued, the cell responded vigorously when the display was presented initially. However, the cell's initial response was substantially below that shown when only the good stimulus was present in the display on its own. Nevertheless, responding gradually climbed to the levels seen when the good stimulus was presented as the target in single-item displays. What this overall pattern was taken to suggest was that several stimuli can compete for resources: responding to the good stimulus was initially muted when the poor stimulus was also present. Through a process of competition though, the activation of the irrelevant poor stimulus was gradually suppressed and the cell eventually and preferentially fired to the good stimulus. From this sort of data (see Duncan, 2006 for a more extensive review) emerges the biased competition view of how attentional processes actually operate in the brain. Indeed the argument by extension is what is true of the brain cell is true of the brain.

So what can we conclude about attentional processes in humans?

The basic ideas behind biased competition accord well with the claim that when attention is deployed, attended signals are enhanced, and non-attended signals are inhibited. The data, so far reviewed, essentially rule out the idea that attention implies *merely* signal enhancement. Indeed, in taking the behavioural work of Carrasco and colleagues together with the data from the neuroscience community (i.e., the evidence that supports the biased competition view), there is an emerging consensus on what sorts of things are implied in discussions of attention.

(i) There is the notion of finite resources and, as we have seen, at a functional level, the discussion revolves around the notion of some sort of abstract mental energy that is constant and may be in short supply. Such ideas have been bolstered by equating limitations in mental energy with constraints that apply to metabolic activity in the brain.

(ii) The notion that there is only one sort of attentional constraint (such as a single selective filter) is no longer given credence. As Pashler (1998) has cogently argued, if we are to attain a proper understanding of how attention operates, it is most appropriate to think in terms of both structural limitations (exemplified by filtering mechanisms) and capacity limitations (such as finite processing resources). A perhaps unfortunate consequence of accepting this, is the view from neuroscience, namely, that there is a myriad of different sorts of constraints that apply throughout the processing system. Generally though, the notion of biased competition provides a very useful framework for thinking about how attentional processes operate: attended signals are enhanced and non-attended signals are inhibited.

(iii) Regardless of how such issues are ultimately resolved, there is also clear agreement that there are both constraints that arise because of the nature of the stimulus and different constraints that arise because of the subject. It is both useful and sensible to distinguish exogenous attentional factors associated with the stimulus from endogenous factors associated with the mental state of the subject. If subjects are told to listen to and report back the verbal message delivered to the right and not the left ear, to large measure (Wood and Cowan, 1995), they can do this.

Attention and animal learning

Some of the ideas embodied in the biased competition view have been explored in the animal learning literature although the connection until now (as far as I know) has not been made. For example, Pearce, George, and Redhead (1998) were concerned with how attention may be implicated in pattern discrimination learning. The basic research question was, 'To what degree, if any, is learning about relevant cues impaired by the concurrent presentation of irrelevant cues that nevertheless demand attention?' Their experiments addressed the issue of how competition for attention amongst a set of plausible cues for learning a *particular* pattern discrimination problem might operate.[2]

The basic preparation used by Pearce *et al.* (1998, Experiment 2) was autoshaping with pigeons using a negative patterning discrimination. Food

[2] In perceptual psychology the term 'cue' is used to refer to either an object or the property of an object such as its colour. Here the term is used interchangeably with 'conditional stimulus' (i.e., CS).

was delivered following A and following B but not after the joint presentation of A and B (i.e., A+, B+, AB0). The incidental cue C was also present in some cases (i.e., AC+, BC+, ABC0). The stimulus displays contained many small randomly positioned rectangles. A, B, and C were defined, respectively, relative to a particular colour of rectangle (e.g., A referred to red rectangles). Three groups of animals were tested.

In *Group Simple* the standard feature-negative regime was used, that is, A+, B+, and AB0. In *Group Common* the procedure used for Group Simple was embellished with the presentation of C on every trial, that is, AC+, BC+, and ABC0. Finally in *Group Continuous*, training was as for Group Simple but the C rectangles were presented continuously. Only the presentation of the A and B rectangles was intermittent. Comparisons involving Groups Common and Continuous were central. The reasoning was as follows. For Group Common, C would, in a sense, act as a competitor cue with A and B for attention. Given the assumption of a finite attentional resource, A and B would receive less attention, if attention to C increases. However, the reverse would be true for Group Continuous, if attention to C wanes over the course of the experiment. Indeed given that C remained on throughout the training period for Group Continuous, then there is no sense in which it could act as a particularly useful signal for reward. As it turned out, the results were consistent with this general line of reasoning; learning was fastest for Group Simple, slowest for Group Common, and intermediate for Group Continuous. Pearce *et al.* drew the conclusion that, essentially, C lost its attentional competitive edge for Group Continuous when it failed to signal reward in any systematic way.

The reinvigoration of the inverse hypothesis?

Pearce *et al.* (1998) went on to examine these ideas in more detail and we will return to their efforts shortly, but, it is interesting to note that the data from this experiment can be considered alongside the previous evidence concerning biased competition. Here the connection is via something that Mackintosh (1975) referred to as the 'inverse hypothesis'. According to this hypothesis, CSs, in a sense, compete such that there exists a trade-off: 'stimuli compete for attention, so that an increase in attention to one set of stimuli will necessarily involve a decrease in attention to some other set of stimuli' (p. 281). As a consequence, an increase in the associability of one CS will be offset by a decrease in the associabilities of the alternative CSs. For Mackintosh (1975), the term 'associability' refers to the ease with which a CS becomes associated with reinforcement.

We need to tread particularly carefully here because now there is a blurring in the use of the terms 'attention' and 'associability'. Although Mackintosh (1975) examined the assumption that 'the probability of attending to a stimulus determines the probability of learning about that stimulus', the eventual theory concerned explaining changes in associability of stimuli with reinforcement (p. 294). So in discussing the inverse hypothesis, the phrase 'an increase in attention to one set of stimuli' is understood in terms of an increase in associability to those set of stimuli. In adopting this position, Mackintosh (1975), in his extensive review of the then extant data, was unable to find unequivocal support for the inverse hypothesis. The favoured interpretation was that changes in associability for different stimuli are independent. In contrast to this, the data from the Pearce *et al.* (1998) experiment (Experiment 2) indicate that the amount of attention paid to A and that paid to B varied according to the presence and nature of C. The case for the demise of the inverse hypothesis should perhaps be re-visited?

Clearly further work on the inverse hypothesis is needed, but Pearce *et al.* ran a subsequent experiment that also speaks on the basic issues. Now the performance of a Group Common was examined alongside two further groups. In Group C0 in addition to the AC+, BC+, and ABC0 trials, C was presented alone on a large number of occasions, but it was not rewarded. In contrast for Group C+, the C presentations were followed by reward. In general terms, the rationale was as follows. For Group C+, the additional reward C trials in a sense alert the animal to the utility of C as a signal for reward, hence the animal should pay more attention to C when it is present. As a consequence and on the assumption of biased competition, this will mean that the animals will attend less to A and B in the ABC0 compound hence their learning will be retarded relative to Group C0.

The elegance of the reasoning is noteworthy, however, the data failed to provide strong empirical support. Relative to Group Common, discrimination learning for both Group C0 and C+ was facilitated to the same degree. So the mere presentation of trials containing C alone regardless of reward was sufficient to facilitate the discrimination learning relative to the case in which there were no such presentations of C. As consequence, the data were re-interpreted in terms of a principle central to the Pearce and Hall theory of learning (1980). According to this view, a stimulus will lose its ability to engage attention as the animal learns what the actual consequents of the stimulus are. In this regard, the performance of Groups C+ and C0 is understandable because, for both groups, C loses its allure as a result of its overfamiliarity.

Attention and the Pearce and Hall model

It is perhaps unsurprising that in discussing their experiments Pearce and colleagues implicated processes that were originally developed in the context of the Pearce and Hall (1980) model of learning. Central to the Pearce and Hall model is an acceptance of limited processing resources; there is a limited capacity information processing device (cf. Wagner, 1978). In the model, learning about an association between a given CS and US is predicated on the claim that representations for both enter into the central limited capacity processor. Unless both the CS and US are represented within the central processor, no learning about the relations between the two occur. Moreover, whereas it is inevitable that the US will enter the processor, the probability of the CS entering the processor is given by its current level of associability. According to the theory, 'stimuli that fully predict their consequences will be denied access to the processor' (Pearce and Hall, 1980; p. 538). In contrast, stimuli that have been followed by unexpected consequences in the recent past will most likely gain access to the processor.

Given our initial exploration of the term 'attention', it is quite acceptable to label this as a model of attentional processing on the grounds that there is stimulus selection because of limited access to a finite resource. Stimuli compete for some form of limited capacity resource, namely, the operations carried out within the central processor. The model formalizes how it is that access to the processor is gauged by something known as *associability*. The theory states that the change in associability of a given stimulus (A) on a particular conditioning trial is given by:

$$\Delta V_A = S_A \alpha_A \lambda \tag{9.1}$$

The S parameter refers to the intensity of the CS. This is a physical variable sometimes referred to as 'salience' (e.g., the brightness of a light). The α parameter is the associability of the stimulus defined below and the λ parameter is the intensity of the US (i.e., the amount of reinforcement).

The current level of associability of a given stimulus (A) is given by:

$$\alpha_A^n = \left|\lambda^{n-1} - V_T^{n-1}\right| \tag{9.2}$$

where n refers to the current trial hence $n - 1$ refers to the immediately previous trial. The notation is perhaps a little confusing. The n and $n - 1$ are not exponents but merely indicate the trial as either current (i.e., n) or immediately previous (i.e., $n - 1$). The λ parameter is as before but now the V term refers to 'the aggregate associate strength of all stimuli present on the immediately previous trial'. As Equation (9.2) shows the current level of associability reflects the difference between the intensity of the US and the degree to which that US was predicted on the previous trial.[3] Nonetheless, when a CS_A is reliably paired with a US, V_A increases accordingly and α_A declines to zero.

[3] Although there seems to be an undue fixation on the previous trial, it was acknowledged at the time and in more recent discussions it has been emphasized (Hall, 2007;

Fundamentally, the theory embodies the idea that CSs that are followed by unexpected outcomes are learnt about more quickly than are CSs that are reliable predictors of outcomes. As Dickinson (1980) remarked, the associability of the CS is determined by its past predictive power. Learning only determines when a stimulus is not a consistent predictor of consequent events.

Attention and associability

The main focus in the animal learning literature has been with the conditions by which changes in associability take place. Such changes in associability have been further analysed by Le Pelley (2004). What is at stake in this particular context is the problem of how best to resolve the conflicting evidence regarding 'surprisingness'. On the one hand, there are claims associated mainly with Mackintosh (1975) that 'attention to a stimulus will increase if it is the best available predictor of reinforcement' (Pearce and Bouton, 2001; p. 117). On the other hand, there are the claims mainly associated with Pearce and Hall (1980) that 'the associability of a stimulus is higher when it is an inaccurate than an accurate predictor of the events that follow it' (Pearce and Bouton, 2001; p. 118). The idea here is that attention to such a stimulus is 'restored only when unexpected consequences occur' (Hall, 2007; see also Swan and Pearce, 1988).

For Le Pelley (2004), the simplest way to address this seeming paradox is by positing two forms of associability, namely, 'attentional associability' (inherited from Mackintosh, 1975) and 'salience associability' (inherited from the Pearce and Hall model (1980). The basis of this manoeuvre is the following. It is stated that 'the overtraining reversal effect, intradimensional shift advantage, and learned irrelevance all support an approach wherein good predictors of an outcome maintain a high associability' (p. 226). Such evidence is foundational to the Mackintosh (1975) account and leads to the notion of attentional associability. Then there is the other evidence such as Hall–Pearce negative transfer (Hall and Pearce, 1979) and the fact that better learning accrues to CSs that have surprising outcomes (Swan and Pearce, 1988). This leads to the conclusion that 'poor predictors maintain a higher associability than good predictors' (Le Pelley, 2004; p. 226) and the consequent motivation for salience associability. Incorporating separate parameters for both forms of associability in a hybrid model appears to provide additional explanatory power to that associated with the models that contain either parameter alone (see Le Pelley, 2004).

Pearce, Kaye, and Hall, 1982) that more gradual changes can be accommodated if performance over an extended preceding sequence of trials is considered.

The overriding concern now though is whether it is appropriate to discuss changes in associability as being changes in attention. Indeed it seems that Le Pelley (2004) is inclined to the view that 'attentional associability' is truly attentional in that it is an index of which stimuli should be picked out and learnt about.[4] In contrast, 'salience associability' is an index of how much should be learnt about those stimuli that are picked out. Contra Pearce and Hall (1980), there is, apparently, no implication by Le Pelley (2004) of attentional processes in discussion of salience associability. It will, no doubt, turn out that more complex models are needed, but currently there appears to be little consensus. Moreover, some of the issues may boil down to concerns about terminology, but further clarity is desperately needed.

'Attention' without resource limitations

Dayan, Kakade, and Read Montague (2000) have provided a quite distinctive take on the basic issues. They focussed on the problems that the animal faces in a classical conditioning situation in which there is a variety of stimuli to attend to but only a subset is systematically related with reward. How does the animal learn which cues are relevant to reward? Moreover, the situation is likely to be relatively complex because the stimulus–reward contingencies may change over time. The animal must be able to adapt to such changes if it is going to be able to predict reward successfully in a nonstable environment. By this view, the animal must be able to build up a statistical model of the past environment in such a way that it is able to make successful predictions about the environment in the future. It must make statistical inferences about the future based on its past experience.

According to Dayan *et al.* (2000, p. 1218), one form of attentional selection relates to 'how learning should be competitively allocated among stimuli', this is, essentially, the basic issue that underpins discussions of attention by theorists of animal learning (e.g., Mackintosh, 1975; Pearce and Hall, 1980; Rescorla and Wagner, 1972). The second form of so-called 'attentional' selection relates to deciding which prediction about outcomes to make on the basis of competing cues. Both of these ideas were explored within the framework of connectionist modelling (see Quinlan, 1991, for a review), but there is not space here to consider these ideas in detail.

[4] This is an interesting step to take and perhaps not one that Mackintosh (1975) would be too comfortable with. In 1975 he was at pains to point out that the changes in associability he was discussing reflected 'the associability of stimuli with reinforcement… There is no implication that changes in α correspond to changes in perception.' (p. 294).

In broad strokes, it is assumed that each of the predictions that the animals make comes with an index of uncertainty. If the pairing of A with a high reward has been consistent in the past then the prediction about A being a signal for high reward now comes with a low level of uncertainty. Each prediction of a particular outcome given a CS (e.g., A leads to a high reward) is associated with an index of uncertainty known as prediction error. The size of the prediction error is indexed by the difference between the actual reward and the predicted reward. Correct predictions are therefore associated with a low prediction error. More critically, the size of the prediction error directly reflects the amount of learning. Quite simply, learning takes place following surprising outcomes (cf. Pearce and Hall, 1980).

To take an example from the paper, various coloured lights are presented over time and rewards of different magnitudes (various numbers of food pellets) are also delivered. In some cases more than one light is presented concurrently and following the ensuing reward, the associabilities of the various lights are changed in a competitive fashion. The associability of the stimulus linked with the most uncertain prediction is changed the most. There is no sense in this account in which changes in associability are determined by past success or failure of the CSs for some limited capacity attentional resource. Changes in the associability of given CSs are, essentially, determined by the degree to which they have failed to predict reward correctly.

The term 'uncertainty' in the account refers, in a sense, to the importance of a given prediction and this determines how well competing predictions are learnt. Predictions with low levels of uncertainty are most easily established. In contrast, 'unreliability' refers to the degree with which any given prediction is chosen and acted upon in preference to all other competing predictions when multiple cues are presented. Consider the case where a CS has been a reliable predictor, but now the environment is ambiguous. For instance, assume that a green light has typically not been rewarded but has occasionally been followed by 2 pellets. Assume also that typically a red light has been followed by one pellet. On these grounds, the prediction of a 1 pellet reward following a red light is more reliable than the prediction of 2 pellets following a green light. As a consequence, the prediction of the reward is weighted towards 1 pellet rather 2 pellets when both lights occur concurrently. Dayan *et al.* (2000) outlined a formal method that takes into account the individual reliabilities of the various cues in generating a prediction following multiple cues. Indeed they went so far as to state that competition between the cues in generating a prediction could be construed as another form of 'selective attention … not induced by any resource constraint, but as a normative consequence of a natural statistical model of prediction' (p. 1221).

Winding up

It is time to wind up and try to pull together something sensible from this somewhat untidy collection of thoughts. From my outsider's point of view, it is clear that there are significant issues in the animal learning literature over how best to deal with 'attention'. Primarily there are issues over the use of language. What is the best way to deploy language such 'attention', 'selection', 'limited capacity', 'attentional resources', and 'attentional processes'? Such labels are used freely, and with few if any feelings of awkwardness or soul searching by those whose interests lie with humans. Moreover, given the size of the human literature on 'attention', this kind of language is apparently useful. For the animal theorists though, there are real concerns over whether this acts as a smokescreen that conceals a lack of explanatory rigour.

How best to proceed? Perhaps progress can be made if we return to Broadbent (1958) and accept that attentional concepts make most sense when defined against some form of processing constraint such as a limited capacity resource. Given such a finite resource, then it is to be accepted that only a subset of the possible environmental stimulation can effectively control an animal's behaviour. It is therefore sensible, by this view, to describe the animal's behaviour in terms of stimulus selection: there is a sensible distinction to be drawn between the attended and the unattended and this distinction does have consequences for learning.

For this kind of definition to be useful, the notion of the processing constraint comes to the fore. Understanding selection rests on understanding the nature of the processing constraint. For instance, in the original Pearce and Hall (1980) model, much was made of the limited capacity processor, that is, a central assumption was that both CS and US must enter the central processor in order for learning about relations between the two to take place. An associated assumption was that the probability that a given CS enters the central processor is given by its associability. By the current view, this model implicates attentional processes because it rests on assumptions about stimulus selection and the constraint of the limited capacity resource that characterizes the nature of the central processor.

A corollary of this definition is that, without stimulus selection, because of some form of processing constraint, such as a limited capacity resource, there are clear cases where reference to attention ought not to be made. In this regard, the example of the work by Dayan *et al.* (2000) is important. Their discussion of learning explicitly avoids mention of competition for any form of limited capacity resource. On these grounds, there seems little point in discussing these sorts of changes in attentional because these have misleading connotations.

In the current context, a basic idea is that it is only sensible to use the vocabulary of attention in discussing changes in associability if the implication of selection because of a processing constraint is accepted. We can adopt a rather general definition of constraint. For instance, consider the situation in which the animal looks in one direction rather than in a different direction. Looking in the one direction rules out looking in a different direction at the same time (for a literal linking of looking and learning, see Matsuka and Corter, 2008). This notion of constraint is clearly defined in terms of the animal's anatomical make up: the eyes can only look in one direction at once but, by the present view, any form of constraint that demands some form of stimulus selection invites the use of attentional constructs as explanatory tools. Fundamental is the idea that the consequences of stimulus selection because of a processing constraint are that (i) not all stimuli that are presented to animal are taken into account by the animal, (ii) the selected stuff receives privileged processing, and (iii) the unselected stuff receives less processing than would otherwise occur. There is both stimulus excitation (for attended CSs) and stimulus inhibition (for unattended CSs). Unless these core concepts are central to the behaviour under discussion then appeals to the language of attention may prove to be distracting.

The issue now is: can we more generally account for the various learning phenomena without implicating attention? Is it really appropriate (or more critically, necessary) to rely on notions of attention to account for changes in the effectiveness of a stimulus for learning? Hall (2007) has recently revisited the S and α parameters in the original Pearce and Hall (1980) account. Consider S, the salience parameter (i.e., the physical intensity of the CS), first. Although S, for any given CS, was fixed in the original Pearce and Hall (1980) equations, Hall (2007) discussed the possibility that this theoretical constraint could be relaxed and the associated parameter may be allowed to vary. Despite the unchanging nature of the physical stimulus, the animal may well habituate to a repeated CS and this may be realized as a reduction in S linked to that stimulus. Hall (2007) went on to discuss such issues in a little more detail but here the main concern is whether there is really any need to discuss such effects in terms of attention? We may talk in terms of the stimulus losing its allure and the animal losing interest in it, but is this form of talk really helping? As Rescorla and Wagner (1972, p. 95) pointed out, such a use of language may be nothing more than a 'redescription of the data'.

Aside from the S parameter, the major effort has been in attempting to understand changes in the α parameter. As is probably clear, the major theories of learning have concentrated on explicating these. Nevertheless, we should ask whether there is a need to invoke the language of attention to discuss the corresponding changes of the associability of a stimulus with reinforcement (cf. Mackintosh, 1975; p. 294). The response here is that, yes we do if the basic explanatory constructs are selection because of some form of processing constraint. If such changes are better explained by other means (cf. Dayan *et al.*, 2000), then reliance on the notion of attention is obviated.

In drawing the chapter to a close, we return to a quote by Mackintosh (1975): 'the probability of attending to a stimulus determines the probability of learning about the stimulus' (p. 294). In other words, to learn about a CS, the animal must attend to it. A difficulty with this is that various ideas have been conflated: the processes of attentional selection have been conflated with learning. For instance, the selection of a CS is determined by salience and/or associability that themselves are taken to drive learning. A different approach would be to separate out factors concerning stimulus selection from those to do with learning. We need to be clear in separating out which stimuli are selected, from how learning about those stimuli progresses.[5] A worry though is that issues concerning stimulus selection may be of no consequence because the testing conditions are such that the capacity limits of the animal are not being exceeded (cf. Rescorla and Wagner, 1972; p. 94). Appeals couched in the language of attention may therefore be misplaced. If the capacity limitations of the animal are not exceeded, then explanations of learning need not implicate attentional mechanisms. The animal has no problem in individuating the possibly relevant stimuli: it is quite able to identify the nature of tone, light, shock etc. The real problems reside in learning about the relations between these stimuli and the contingent outcomes. If all the possibly relevant stimuli can be processed in this way, then it would be a mistake to conflate attention with learning.

This line of argument invites a possibly unfortunate conclusion, namely, that because attention serves no useful purpose in our current understanding of animal learning preparations, it is an inherently useless construct. Here we may return to James (1981). In discussing the impression of changing the focus of attention at will (now I am drinking my tea and thinking of the cricket score, next I return to the text on the screen in front of me), James discussed the possibility that such an impression conveys a false sense of the actuality. The changes in the focus of concentration are simple accompaniments to more microscopic changes carried out at a neural level. In his words, 'Thus the notion that an effort in attending is an original faculty, a force additional to the others of which the brain and mind are the seat, may be an abject superstition.

[5] This sort of manoeuvre has been attempted by Le Pelley (2004) but it remains to be seen just how successful it will turn out to be.

Attention may have to go, like many a faculty once deemed essential, like many a verbal phantom … It may be an excrescence on Psychology' (p. 428).

Some may be tempted to conclude that we should remove attention from all of our theories of behaviour. Against this though is the view, outlined here, that there is a coherent set of ideas that coalesce around stimulus selection as a consequence of some form of processing constraint. There is a coherent set of core concepts that make sense within this proscribed framework for thinking. Of course, whether any such ideas need play a pivotal role in attempts to understand the acquisition of CS/US relations in typical animal learning experiments remains to be established.

Acknowledgements

Any conceptual errors are mine but many more would have been committed had it not been for discussions held with Pearce and Hall, respectively. I thank both John and Geoff for their generous help.

References

Allport, D. A. (1989). Visual attention. In M. I. Posner (Ed.), *Foundations of cognitive science* (pp. 631–682). Cambridge, MA: The MIT Press.

Allport, D. A., Tipper, S. P., & Chmiel, N. R. J. (1985). Perceptual integration and post-categorical filtering. In M. I. Posner & O. S. M. Marin (Eds), *Attention and performance, XI* (pp. 107–132). Hillsdale, NJ: Erlbaum.

Broadbent, D. E. (1958). *Perception and communication*. Oxford: Persimmon Press.

Broadbent, D. E. (1977). The hidden preattentive processes. *American Psychologist,* **32**, 109–118.

Carrasco, M. (2006). Covert attention increases contrast sensitivity: psychophysical, neurophysiological and neuroimaging studies. In S. Martinez-Conde, S. Macknik, L. Martinez, A. Jose-Manuel & P. Tse (Eds), *Progress in brain research* (Vol. 154, pp. 33–70). Amsterdam: Elsevier B. V.

Carrasco, M., Ling, S., & Read, S. (2004). Attention alters appearance. *Nature Neuroscience,* 7, 308–313.

Chelazzi, L., Duncan, J., Miller, E. K., & Desimone, R. (1998). Responses of neurons in inferior temporal cortex during memory-guided visual search. *Journal of Neurophysiology,* **80**, 2918–2940.

Cherry, E. C. (1953). Some experiments on the recognition of speech, with one and two ears. *Journal of the Acoustical Society of America,* **26**, 554–559.

Dayan, P., Kakade, S., & Read Montague, P. (2000). Learning and selective attention. *Nature Neuroscience,* **3**, 1218–1223.

Dayan, P. & Zemel, R. S. (1999). Statistical models and sensory attention. *International Conference on Artificial Neural Networks,* **2**, 1017–1022.

Desimone, R. & Duncan, J. (1995). Neural mechanisms of selective visual attention. *Annual Review of Psychology,* **18**, 193–122.

Deutsch, J. A. & Deutsch, D. (1963). Attention: Some theoretical considerations. *Psychological Review,* **70**, 80–90.

Dickinson, A. (1980). *Contemporary animal learning theory.* Cambridge: Cambridge University Press.

Driver, J. & Frackowiak, R. S. J. (2001). Neurobiological measures of human selective attention. *Neuropsychologia,* **39**, 1257–1262.

Duncan, J. (2006). Brain mechanisms of attention. *The Quarterly Journal of Experimental Psychology,* **59**, 2–27.

Hall, G. (2007). Learned changes in stimulus representations (A personal history). *The Spanish Journal of Psychology,* **10**, 218–229.

Hall, G. & Pearce, J. M. (1979). Latent inhibition of a CS during CS – US pairings. *Journal of Experimental Psychology: Animal Behavior Processes,* **5**, 31–42.

James, W. (1981). *The principles of psychology. Volume I.* Cambridge, MA: Harvard University Press.

Klein, R. M. & Shore, D. I. (2000). Relations among modes of visual orienting. In S. Monsell & J. Driver (Eds), *Attention and performance XVIII: Control of cognitive processes* (pp. 195–208). Cambridge, MA: The MIT Press.

Le Pelley, M. E. (2004). The role of associative history in models of associative learning: A selective review and a hybrid model. *The Quarterly Journal of Experimental Psychology,* **57B**, 193–243.

Mackintosh, N. J. (1965). Selective attention in animal discrimination learning. *Psychological Bulletin,* **64**, 124–150.

Mackintosh, N. J. (1975). A theory of attention; Variations in the associability of stimuli with reinforcement. *Psychological Review,* **82**, 276–298.

MacLeod, C. M., Dodd, M. D., Sheard, E. D., Wilson, D. E., & Bibi, U. (2003). In opposition to inhibition. *The Psychology of learning and motivation,* **43**, 163–214.

Matsuka, T. & Corter, J. E. (2008). Observed attention allocation processes in category learning. *The Quarterly Journal of Experimental Psychology,* **61**, 1067–1097.

Navon, D. (2003). What does a compound letter tell the psychologist's mind? *Acta Psychologica,* **114**, 273–309.

Pashler, H. E. (1998). *The psychology of attention.* Cambridge, MA: The MIT Press.

Pearce, J. M. & Bouton, M. E. (2001). Theories of associative learning in animals. *Annual Review of Psychology,* **52**, 111–139.

Pearce, J. M., George, D. N., & Redhead, E. S. (1998). The role of attention in the solution of conditional discriminations. In N. A. Schmajuk & P. C. Holland (Eds), *Occasion setting. Associative learning and cognition in animals* (pp. 249–275). Washington, DC: APA.

Pearce, J. M. & Hall, G. (1980). A model of Pavlovian learning: Variations in the effectiveness of conditioned but not of unconditioned stimuli. *Psychological Review,* **87**, 532–552.

Pearce, J. M., Kaye, H., & Hall, G. (1982). Predictive accuracy and stimulus associability: Development of a model of Pavlovian learning. In M. L. Commons, R. J. Hernstein & A. R. Wagner (Eds), *Quantitative analysis of behavior: Acquisition.* Cambridge, MA: Ballinger.

Pestilli, F. & Carrasco, M. (2005). Attention enhances contrast sensitivity at cued and impairs it at uncued locations. *Vision Research,* **45**, 1867–1875.

Posner, M. I. (1980). Orienting of attention. *Quarterly Journal of Experimental Psychology*, **32**, 3–25.

Quinlan, P. T. (1991). *Connectionism and psychology. A psychological perspective on new connectionist research.* Hemel Hempstead: Harvester Wheatsheaf.

Quinlan, P. T. & Dyson, B. J. (2008). *Cognitive psychology.* Harlow, England: Pearson.

Rescorla, R. A. & Wagner, A. R. (1972). A theory of Pavlovian conditioning: Variations in the effectiveness of reinforcement and nonreinforcement. In A. H. Black & W. F. Prokasy (Eds), *Classical conditioning II: Current research and theory* (pp. 64–99). New York, NY: Appleton-Century-Crofts.

Shanks, D. R. (2005). Implicit learning. In K. Lamberts & R. L. Goldstone (Eds), *Handbook of cognition* (pp. 202–220). London, England: Sage.

Sutherland, N. S. & Mackintosh, N. J. (1971). *Mechanisms of animal discrimination learning.* New York: Academic Press.

Swan, J. A. & Pearce, J. M. (1988). The orienting response as an index of stimulus associability on rats. *Journal of Experimental Psychology: Animal behavior processes*, **4**, 292–301.

Wagner, A. R. (1978). Expectancies and the priming of STM. In S. H. Hulse, H. Fowler & W. K. Honig (Eds), *Cognitive processes in animal behavior* (pp. 177–210). Hillsdale, NJ: Erlbaum.

Wood, N. L. & Cowan, N. (1995). The cocktail party phenomenon revisited: Attention and memory in the classic selective listening procedure of Cherry (1953). *Journal of Experimental Psychology: General*, **124**, 243–262.

Chapter 10

Attention and memory in human learning

Chris J. Mitchell

Human learning and memory are areas of psychology usually investigated by different researchers who publish in different journals, present at different conferences, and speak quite different theoretical languages. This is something of a puzzle, especially given that learning theorists and memory theorists often postulate apparently similar psychological mechanisms to explain the phenomena they observe. For example, at the heart of most contemporary associative learning theories lies some notion of selective attention (Mackintosh, 1975), or the idea that processing resources are limited (Pearce and Hall, 1980; Wagner, 1981). These ideas are also central to memory theory (e.g. Baddeley, 1990). It would be hardly surprising, therefore, if parallels were found between the phenomena observed in learning and those observed in memory.

In the present chapter, I shall describe some recent experiments in my laboratory designed to investigate the relationship between attention, memory, and learning. A central assumption of most associative theories is that learning involves the encoding of a link between two representations in memory. For example, Pavlov's dogs learned to associate a ringing bell with food; after many bell–food pairings, they salivated on hearing the tone even in the absence of food. In Pavlovian conditioning of this kind, it is usually assumed that a link forms between the mental representations of the bell and the food, such that presentation of the bell alone activates, via the link, the representation of food. It is the activation of the representation of food that produces salivation. In the first section of the chapter, experiments are described that seek evidence for this link mechanism in humans. In the subsequent sections of the chapter, the focus is on attention and memory, and their effects on both associative learning and perceptual learning. I argue that one very simple (and not especially novel) way to interpret the data from both of these lines of research is to suppose that there are limits to our processing resources for which simultaneously presented stimuli compete. The processing resources devoted to a target stimulus will be determined by the salience of the other stimuli present.

The processing that a stimulus receives will, in turn, at least to some extent, determine two things: the degree to which the stimulus is encoded in memory and the degree to which participants learn about that stimulus.

Encoding of cue–outcome links in human associative learning

The bell–food link, in the example of Pavlovian conditioning described above, can be thought of as a form of memory (see e.g. Pearce and Hall, 1980; Wagner, 1981). Thus, the strength of the link determines the degree to which the memory of the food is activated by the presentation of the bell. This, in turn, determines the strength of the salivation conditioned response (CR) observed on test. This same link-based mechanism has also been proposed to be one determinant of the way people arrive at judgements of cue–outcome causality. On this view, when a cue is judged to cause an outcome, it is at least to some extent because a link has formed between the representations of the cue and the outcome in memory. In a typical causal judgement experiment, a participant might be told, on a number of occasions (experimental trials), that a fictitious Mr. X ate cabbage (the cue) and developed an allergic reaction (the outcome). Participants will then judge cabbage to be a cause of Mr. X's allergic reaction. According to the link-based account, participants arrive at this belief as a consequence of the link that has formed between the representations of cabbage and the allergic reaction. In fact, causal learning is now the most studied form of associative learning in humans (Dickinson, Shanks, and Evenden, 1984; Dickinson, 2001) and it will be the focus of much of the present chapter.

An alternative to the link-based approach is the idea that associative learning is the consequence of highly flexible and controlled propositional reasoning processes. For example, in tone–shock conditioning, a series of tone–shock pairings support the inference that the tone is a signal of the shock. When the tone is then presented on test, the belief that the tone signals shock leads to an expectation that the shock will be delivered. This expectation of shock then leads to anxiety and increased skin conductance (the CR). Causal learning is explained in a very straightforward way by this account; beliefs about causal relationships (judgements of causality) result from participants reasoning about those relationships.

The data confirm that participants can be very flexible in the way they learn associative relationships. This observation lends support to the propositional/inferential view, and weakens the case for a simple link-formation mechanism. For example, associative learning is affected by rules that the participants have learned prior to pairings of the target events (e.g., Mitchell, Killedar, and Lovibond, 2005; Shanks and Darby, 1998). It is also affected by what can be logically deduced from the learning scenario (e.g. Beckers, De Houwer, Pineno, and Miller, 2005; De Houwer, Beckers, and Glautier, 2002; Lovibond, Been, Mitchell, Bouton, and Frohardt, 2003; Mitchell, Lovibond, and Condoleon, 2005; Mitchell and Lovibond, 2002). Thus, learning appears, in many cases, to rely on the same complex analytical abilities that we use to solve cryptic crosswords and murder mysteries.

These findings lend support to an inferential view of learning. They do not, however, rule out the possibility that some learning phenomena result from variations in the degree to which cue–outcome links are encoded in memory. In what remains of this section, I will present some causal learning experiments designed to test the straightforward prediction of the link-based mechanism, that causal judgements reflect the strength of a cue–outcome link. The aim of these experiments is to provide a more direct measure of the strength of the hypothesized link than that provided by causal judgements or CRs. Thus, following training of various cue–outcome relationships, participants were presented with a cue and asked whether they could remember the outcome that had followed this cue in training. A strong link should allow the cue to activate the representation of the outcome, and participants will then correctly identify that outcome. If it is assumed that this memory measure is an index of link strength, then the hypothesis can be tested that link strength also determines causal judgements. On this view, the conditions under which good outcome memory is demonstrated should be the same conditions as those under which high causal ratings are given. Evidence for dissociation between outcome memory and causal ratings would suggest that the causal ratings are not the consequence of link formation. The experiments implement some of the most important phenomena in learning. The first is blocking (Kamin, 1969).

In a blocking design implemented in the allergist task described above, a cue such as apple (cue A) is followed by the allergic reaction in the first phase (A+). In the second phase, a compound of apple and, for example, banana (AB) is followed by the allergic reaction (AB+). The commonly observed result is that little is learned about cue B (e.g. Chapman and Robbins, 1990; Shanks, 1985). The associative interpretation is that the presence of cue A in Phase 2 results in a failure to form a B-outcome link. Although blocking seems very simply described in terms of failure to encode a cue–outcome link, inferential accounts are equally straightforward. Participants may process both the cue and outcome very well in blocking (and encode the pairings in memory), but nevertheless infer that B is non-causal. Thus, participants might reason that, because cues A and B together cause the outcome to occur with the same intensity and probability as does cue A alone, then cue B is not a cause of the outcome. Indeed, blocking is usually strongest when B can be deduced to be non-causal (e.g. De Houwer *et al*, 2002; Mitchell and Lovibond, 2002).

In order to test whether participants have failed to encode a B-outcome memory, my colleagues and I have used a modified causal learning procedure in which three different outcomes are used (see also Le Pelley, Oakeshott, and McLaren, 2005 for a similar approach). The blocking design (A+ and then AB+) is implemented three times, once with each outcome. For example, blocking might be implemented with three allergic reaction outcomes—rash, nausea, and dizziness (outcomes 1, 2, and 3 respectively). In Phase 1, participants learn that apple (cue A1) leads to rash (outcome 1). They also learn that almond (A2) leads to nausea (outcome 2) and that apricot (A3) leads to dizziness (outcome 3). In Phase 2, apple and banana (the A1B1 compound) lead to rash. Two further compounds, almond and butter (A2B2) and apricot and beef (A3B3) lead to nausea and dizziness (outcomes 2 and 3), respectively.

On test, two questions can be addressed. Firstly, to what extent are the B cues attributed causal strength? For this, participants are presented with each cue in turn and asked to say the degree to which that cue caused an allergic reaction *of any kind* in Mr. X. Secondly, and more importantly, are participants able to remember which outcome followed the B cues (banana, butter and beef) in training? For this, participants are presented with a cue and asked to choose which of the three allergic reactions—rash, nausea, and dizziness—it was paired with in training. This second memory test addresses one of the central assumptions of associative learning theory, that blocking is the consequence of a failure to encode a B-outcome link in memory. A failure to remember on test which outcome followed banana (B1) in training would lend support to the associative view.

Mitchell, Lovibond, Minard, and Lavis (2006) conducted an experiment similar to that described above. The blocked cues B1–3 were compared to overshadowing cues C1–3 and D1–3 that were trained in compound in Phase 2 (CD+), and which had not been presented in Phase 1. We observed the usual blocking effect on the causal judgement measure; the B cues were given lower ratings than the overshadowing control cues. More interestingly, participants were less able to correctly identify the outcomes that had been paired with the blocked cues B1–3 than they were the outcomes paired with the control cues. It would appear that pretraining with cues A1–3 in Phase 1 reduced the degree to which the B-outcome pairings were encoded in memory. This is exactly the result predicted by the associative account.

We have also observed extinction and latent inhibition in a similar task. In an extinction design, pairings of A and the outcome (A+) in Phase 1 are followed by A-no outcome presentations (A-) in Phase 2. Extinction (low responding to A on test) is usually assumed to reflect a failure to retrieve the A-outcome link formed in Phase 1, as a consequence of interference from the A-no outcome trials (e.g. Bouton, 1993; Rosas and Callejas-Aguilera, 2006). Latent inhibition is similar to extinction but the phases are reversed (A- then A+ trials are given). The result is the same; ratings of A on test are reduced by A- training (e.g. Escobar, Arcediano and Miller, 2003; Lubow and Moore, 1959). There are many explanations of latent inhibition (see Holmes and Harris, this volume). A very common one is that A- training in Phase 1 produces a decline in attention to cue A. This results in a failure to form an A-outcome link in Phase 2.

In our recent study of extinction (Scully and Mitchell, 2008), exemplars of cue A were paired with different allergic reaction outcomes (e.g. A1 was paired with outcome 1). They were then followed by A in the absence of any outcome in Phase 2. In the latent inhibition study, the phases were reversed (Mitchell and Scully, in preparation). On test, just as in the blocking study described above, participants were asked to give a causal rating for each cue and to identify the exact outcome with which each exemplar was paired in training (the memory measure). Scully and Mitchell (2008) observed extinction on both the causal judgement and the memory measure. Furthermore, there was a moderate correlation between the level of extinction (the difference between the extinguished and control cues) shown by each participant on the two measures. Thus, lower causal judgements were given to the A cues by participants who were unable to recall the cue–outcome pairings. Mitchell and Scully (in preparation) observed a very similar pattern of results in their study of latent inhibition; lower causal ratings and poorer memory performance were observed to the preexposed cues than to the controls. Again, there was a moderate correlation between the level of latent inhibition observed on the two measures.

The findings described above are very promising for the associative view. Some of the most important phenomena in learning do appear to reflect, at least in part, the degree to which participants can remember cue–outcome pairings. These variations in the ability to recall the specific outcome paired with a cue might reflect the strength of a link between representations of the cue and outcome. For example, the ability to remember that the cue 'apple' was followed by 'rash' may reflect the strength of an apple–rash link. This is, of course, not the only way to model this memory performance. Failure to remember the outcome paired with a cue may reflect a failure to encode or retrieve an episodic memory of the cue–outcome pairing. This would be consistent with early verbal learning research by, for example, Bilodeau and Schlosberg (1951; see Slamecka and Ceraso, 1960 for review). However, if one were to compare a strictly inferential account, in which memory for events is assumed to be perfect, to an associative account in which variations in link strength (memory) are responsible for the variations in causal judgements, the data support the associative account. At the very least, a simple inferential account would need some additional memory mechanism to account for the present data.

Not all of our findings, however, are consistent with the associative view. It is possible to demonstrate strong dissociations between outcome recall and causal judgements. Mitchell, Lovibond, and Gan (2005) used the procedure described above to investigate cue competition. One condition was similar to a blocking design, but used a single phase procedure; AB+ trials were intermixed with A+ trials. A second condition was a protection from overshadowing design in which CD+ trials were intermixed with C- trials. In this experiment (unlike those described above), the food cues were not randomly assigned to their roles in the experimental design. The cues presented in compound (e.g. AB) were already related to one another. Thus, cues A1 and B1 might be 'fish and chips', cues A2 and B2 might be 'peaches and cream'. In other words, strong 'within compound associations' existed between the members of each pair.

On test, Mitchell *et al.* (2005) observed cue competition in the causal ratings; cue B was given a lower causal rating than cue D. This is consistent with the idea that A+ training prevented the formation of a link between B and the outcome on AB+ trials (blocking). Alternatively, or in addition, it could be argued that C- training increased the strength of the D-outcome link formed on CD+ trials (protection from overshadowing). The memory measure, however, showed that these causal ratings were not based on the degree to which the cues could activate the outcome representations. In fact, outcome recall showed the opposite pattern to that seen in the causal judgements. Participants were better able to recall the outcomes paired with B cues than those paired with D cues; a form of 'augmentation' (Batsell, Paschall, Gleason and Batson, 2001) was observed. In this memory test, the B cues appeared to have inherited associative strength from their partner A. Thus, participants knew which outcome had followed A from the many A+ training trials, and they also knew that B had been presented with A because A and B (e.g. 'fish and chips') were already linked in memory. When presented with B on test, participants could then combine these two memories to produce the correct response to cue B. Memory for the outcome paired with the D cues was poor because their partners, the C cues, were not given additional pairings with the outcome.

It is a straightforward matter to explain either the causal judgement result or the memory result in terms of associative links. A weak B-outcome link following A+/AB+ training is due to cue competition. This can be explained in terms of the Rescorla-Wagner model (see below). A strong B-outcome link following the same training is due to the inheritance of associative strength by B from A, as a consequence of a within-compound association (e.g. Rescorla and Cunningham, 1978). But this experiment shows that causal judgements are not a direct reflection of link strength. The target cues that appeared to activate the outcome representation most strongly (the B cues) were judged least causal.

In an experiment with a similar rationale, Mitchell, Livesey, and Lovibond (2007) investigated conditioned inhibition. Thus, participants were given A+ trials intermixed with AB- trials. Again, more than one outcome was used; for example, pairings of A1 with outcome 1 were intermixed with presentations of A1B1 in the absence of any allergic reaction outcome (A1B1- trials). Inhibition by B1 of outcome 1 was demonstrated in causal ratings. However, a categorization task showed clearly that B1 was very easily categorized with outcome 1; critically, it was more easily categorized with outcome 1 than with outcome 2. This second result indicates the existence of an *excitatory* link between B1 and outcome 1. One might argue that it is unsurprising that B1 should be more easily categorized with outcome 1 (O1) than outcome 2 (O2); inhibition training of this kind might generate a 'B–no O1' link (see Konorski, 1967). If so, then B1 is related to O1 – it explicitly predicts the absence of O1 – but it is quite unrelated to O2. This might explain why B1 was more easily categorized with O1 than O2. However, the way in which B1 is related to O1 is important. The B-no outcome link, if it is to produce inhibition of O1 in causal ratings, should also prevent participants from learning to put B1 and O1 together in a categorization task. In other words, the categorization task is a retardation test of inhibition, and B1 failed to inhibit O1 on this task. This result is similar to that of Mitchell *et al.* (2005) study; causal ratings of the cue were dissociated from the ease with which participants were able to put the cue and outcome together.

In summary, the two experiments just described provide evidence that causal judgements are not entirely driven by memories for the cue-outcome pairings. However, there is evidence from blocking, extinction, and latent inhibition experiments to suggest that failures to encode and retrieve memories of cue–outcome pairings may make an important contribution to causal judgements. What is not yet known is the nature of the mechanism that produced these failures. In the following section, I shall focus on some recent experiments conducted in my laboratory that investigate the mechanism responsible for the memory failures observed in blocking. These experiments evaluate what will seem to many cognitive psychologists as the most obvious explanation of the blocking effect. This is the idea that blocking might be the consequence of divided attention. That is, participants fail to encode the B–outcome relationship, and indeed may fail to encode cue B itself, because they focus more of their attentional resources on the important, predictive cue A.

The role of divided attention in blocking

The blocking effect is usually taken to suggest that participants failed to encode a B–outcome memory (although other explanations have been proposed, e.g. Miller and Matzel, 1988). There are two distinct kinds of associative model that predict this encoding failure. On AB+ trials in phase 2, either the unsurprising outcome (because it was predicted by the A cue) was not processed (Rescorla and Wagner, 1972; Wagner, 1981) or the B cue itself was not processed (Mackintosh, 1975; Pearce and Hall, 1980). Models that attribute variations in responding to variations in cue processing are generally termed attentional models; in blocking, because cue A predicts the outcome, less attention is paid to the redundant cue B. Griffiths and Mitchell (2008) examined the second of these possibilities in a modified version of the allergist task described above. The task was designed to measure both learning of the cue–outcome relationship and encoding of the cues in memory. A straightforward prediction of the idea that the presence of cue A reduces processing of cue B is that participants will not only fail to learn about cue B, but might also fail to encode cue B in memory.[1] Griffiths and Mitchell (2008) tested this prediction.

In Griffiths and Mitchell's experiments, categories of foods, rather than individual foods, played the role of cues. For example, meats (category A) might cause an allergic reaction in Mr. X in the first phase of training. Thus, one exemplar of the category meat would be presented on each A+ trial in Phase 1. For example, on the first A+ trial, Mr. X might eat lamb and suffer an allergic reaction. On the second A+ trial, he might eat beef and then suffer the allergic reaction. Across trials, participants could infer that meat in general (category A) caused an allergic reaction in Mr. X. No specific food was presented more than once in training. In the critical trials of Phase 2, two foods were presented, one from category A (meats) and one from category B (e.g. vegetables). Just as in category A, a different exemplar of category B (vegetables) was presented on each trial.

[1] This prediction could be argued not to follow from a strict interpretation of either the Mackintosh (1975) or the Pearce-Hall (1980) model. The main point here, though, is that the prediction is consistent with the intuition on which the two models are based.

On test, participants were asked to give causal ratings to two individual exemplars of each category, one which had been presented in training (an old exemplar) and one which had not been presented in training (a new exemplar). Blocking was observed; lower ratings were given to the exemplars of category B than to a standard overshadowing control condition D (which was trained in compound with another novel category, C, in Phase 2). The old/new status of the test exemplars of the B category had no impact on the size of this blocking effect. That is, blocking was observed at the category level. In addition to causal ratings, participants were tested for their memory for the individual category exemplars presented in training. Participants were presented with all of the foods from each category on test, as well as new foods from those categories that had not been presented in training (foils). Participants showed poorer recognition performance for the exemplars of the B category than of the D category. That is, a blocking effect was observed with respect to the encoding of the cues in memory.

The most straightforward explanation for this finding is that, on AB+ trials, as a result of the presence of the pretrained A, little attention was paid to cue B. This reduced both learning about category B, and memory for the exemplars of this category. This idea has something in common with the model proposed by Mackintosh (1975). He suggested that attention is paid to the best predictor of the outcome on any given training trial. Attention to all other cues present will decline. Cue A is a better predictor than is B on the very first AB+ trial in Phase 2. Therefore, attention to B will decline after that first training trial. Perhaps this is why little is learned about B and exemplars of B are poorly encoded in memory.

One feature of the results observed in the category-based blocking procedure, however, seems inconsistent with an account in which predictive cues gain more attention (as suggested by Mackintosh, 1975). Griffiths and Mitchell (2008) found that, as a category became a better predictor of the outcome, exemplars of that category were more poorly encoded in memory. Thus, for example, memory for exemplars of category A in the blocking design was not especially good. More decisively, in Experiment 3, Griffiths and Mitchell found that if a category changed status part way through training (from causal to non-causal or vice versa), later presented exemplars of that category were better recognized on test, than if the category consistently predicted the allergic reaction throughout training. Although the idea that poor predictors might be better encoded in memory is inconsistent with the Mackintosh (1975) model, it is consistent with another attentional learning theory. Pearce and Hall (1980) proposed that more attention is paid to cues when their outcomes are surprising. If the status of the category of foods changes half way through training, then the outcome will be surprising and more attention will be paid to cues on those trials. This can be expected to produce better encoding in memory of exemplars of inconsistent predictor categories. It also explains why exemplars of the highly predictive category A in the blocking task were not especially well remembered.

Thus, the data appear to favour an approach based on the Pearce–Hall model over one based on Mackintosh (1975). However, with an additional (and reasonably uncontroversial) assumption, the Mackintosh (1975) model provides an account of the data described above. Take the failure to remember exemplars of predictive categories. Participants learn, over a number of trials, that, for example, meat will be followed by an allergic reaction in Mr. X. The meat category is common to all meat exemplars such as lamb and beef. According to Mackintosh (1975), when pork is presented on a later trial, the category membership of this exemplar (which is highly predictive of the outcome) will command a great deal of attention. This may reduce processing of the unique features of this exemplar. It is precisely these unique features that are needed for pork to be correctly judged 'old' in the recognition test. In other words, in predictive categories, category membership (e.g. meat) might attract attention, and prevent (or block) encoding of the unique stimulus features of the exemplar (e.g. pork) in memory.

If it is assumed that category membership can block encoding of unique stimulus features, then Mackintosh (1975) and the Pearce–Hall model make the same predictions with respect to the memory measure used by Griffiths and Mitchell (2008). That is, if one of the categories present is a good predictor, then little attention will be paid to any of the exemplar-specific features present. This includes features of the exemplars of the predictive category (e.g. pork in the example above) as well as any other exemplars presented. Although the two theories now make the same predictions with respect to memory for each cue, they make different predictions with respect to causal judgements. One result that is often taken to be decisive in this debate (but see Hall and Rodriguez, this volume) comes from Le Pelley and McLaren's (2003) very elegant learned predictiveness design. In Phase 1, of this experiment, two cues are presented on each trial, only one of which is predictive of one of two outcomes (e.g. nausea and dizziness). The other cue presented is paired with both outcomes equally often across the trials in Phase 1. In Phase 2, new compounds of one predictive and one non-predictive cue from Phase 1 are paired with one of two new outcomes (e.g. headache and itchiness). In this second phase, both cues are equally (and perfectly) predictive of the outcome with which they are paired. Le Pelley and McLaren (2003) found that the cues that were predictive in Phase 1 were learned about more readily in Phase 2. This suggests that participants learned to attend to the predictive cues in Phase 1 (as anticipated by Mackintosh, 1975), and this learning transferred to Phase 2. Griffiths and Mitchell (2008) observed the same result in their category-based procedure.

The causal judgement results presented here lend support to the idea that predictive cues command greater attention than do nonpredictive cues. These biases in attention then influence later learning about those cues (see also Griffiths and Le Pelley, 2009; Mitchell, Harris, Westbrook, and Griffiths, 2008; Bonardi, Graham, Hall, and Mitchell, 2005). Importantly, in Griffiths and Mitchell's experiments, it is the category (not the specific food presented on any given trial) that is predictive. Therefore, it is the category that is hypothesized to control attention in this task. A focus of attentional resources on category A in the blocking design provides an account of the performance observed on the memory task; participants' attention was focused away from the specific details of the exemplars of both the A and the B cue.

I have argued that Griffiths and Mitchell's (2008) data are consistent with the idea that participants fail to notice cue B on AB+ trials of a blocking design, because their attention is focused on A. This is a very low-level, almost perceptual account of blocking, in which a failure to learn is the consequence of competition for limited processing resources. In other words, a truly attentional mechanism is implicated (see Quinlan, this volume). This analysis would fit nicely with another claim (Le Pelley *et al.*, 2005), that the attentional mechanism in operation in associative learning is automatic. Thus, predictive cues command attention in a manner that is quite outside of the participants' control, and is independent of inferential reasoning processes. However, the data presented above are not inconsistent with a quite different, inferential approach. Thus, in Phase 2 of a blocking design, participants may first reason that cue B is non-causal (and, indeed, that the specific exemplars presented are irrelevant). As a consequence, they may devote fewer resources to encoding cue B, and all other exemplar details in memory. Encoding of episodic memories is seen as an active, elaborative process (e.g. Craik and Lockhardt, 1972; Craik and Tulving, 1975). Therefore, given that the task here is to predict the outcome on a given trial, one should expect the inferences participants draw about the predictive nature of the stimuli to affect encoding and later recognition of those stimuli. We have tested this hypothesis in the blocking design.

Is biased attention in blocking inference-based?

We used the same approach as Lovibond *et al.* (2003) to test for inferential processes in category-based blocking (Griffiths and Mitchell, 2009). Thus, prior to blocking training, participants were shown the effect of two causal cues presented (eaten by Mr. X) together. In the additive group, participants were shown that when two causal foods are consumed in one meal, Mr. X develops a stronger than usual allergic reaction. The outcome is said to be additive because the two causal foods combined to produce an outcome of greater magnitude. Under these circumstances, blocking (low ratings of B) can be inferred from A+/AB+ training. This is because, given that A is causal, if B were also causal, then a larger than usual outcome would be expected to be observed on presentation of the AB compound. Because only the standard allergic reaction is observed on AB+ trials, B can be reasoned not to be causal.

In a second, non-additive group, participants were shown in pretraining that when two causal cues are presented together, they produce an outcome of similar magnitude to that produced by a single cause. Given this cue-combination rule, when A and B are presented together, the standard outcome can be expected whether B is causal or not. Thus, AB+ trials are uninformative as to the causal status of B. In sum, blocking is a logical inference given additive but not given non-additive cue combination rules. These additive and non-additive cue combination rules are known to have profound effects on the levels of blocking observed in causal judgement experiments (e.g. Lovibond *et al.*, 2003; see also De Houwer *et al*, 2002) and electrodermal conditioning (Mitchell and Lovibond, 2002). Blocking is either weaker or not observed at all when non-additive combination rules are given.

These rules may not, however, apply in the same way to the category-based procedure used by Griffiths and Mitchell (2008). Dickinson (2001) and Le Pelley *et al.* (2005) have argued that the automatic associative link mechanism is best revealed when the inferential system is unable to operate. One such situation is when the task is too complex to allow inferences to be drawn. One feature of the category-based causal judgement task is that it places a very heavy cognitive load on the participant. Every trial features one or two novel cues, and, before any cue–outcome learning can take place, participants must infer the identity of the food categories from the exemplars presented. Griffiths and Mitchell (2009) manipulated participants' assumptions about cue additivity through pretraining in a category-based causal learning task with a blocking design. An interesting pattern of results emerged.

Overall, just as in Griffiths and Mitchell (2008), participants showed a blocking effect in both causal ratings and memory. However, the additivity manipulation appeared to produce, if anything, the opposite effect to that observed in previous experiments. In causal ratings, the additivity manipulation did not significantly alter the strength of the blocking effect (no interaction between pretraining and blocking was observed). Furthermore, follow-up tests revealed significant blocking in the non-additive, but not in the additive group; if anything, this is the reverse of the usual pattern. In the memory test, the pattern was similar except that, on this measure, additivity pretraining produced significantly weaker blocking than non-additivity pretraining.

The results of Griffiths and Mitchell's (2009) experiment present a problem for inferential theories of learning. In contrast to previous results, blocking was observed only when blocking was *not* a logical inference. This might suggest the operation of a low-level associative mechanism. However, the observation that the additivity pretraining had an effect of any kind is also a problem for a more low-level attentional mechanism. The data pattern is complex, and a detailed analysis is not possible here. However, Griffiths and Mitchell argued that the data were broadly consistent with the following hypothesis. It is important first to point out that, for the blocked category B, both causal ratings and recognition performance were low in both groups. Thus, the first part of Griffiths and Mitchell's explanation was that little attention was paid to cue B by participants in either group. This is consistent with the operation of a low-level mechanism that reduces attentional resources to cues that appear in the presence of a good predictor of the outcome (e.g. Mackintosh, 1975).

Effects of the additive and non-additive rules were seen in differences in the causal ratings and memory for the overshadowed control cue D. In particular, a post-hoc analysis revealed that cue D was given a lower causal rating in the additive than in the non-additive group (similar, but much smaller, differences have been seen in our previous studies of additivity; Lovibond *et al.*, 2003; Mitchell and Lovibond, 2002). The second part of the argument, therefore, relates to the effect of additivity training on the ratings of the overshadowed cue D (trained in compound with cue C). The compound CD produced an outcome of standard magnitude (CD+). On this basis, ratings of cue D should be lower for additive than for non-additive participants. For additive participants, only cue C *or* cue D can be causal, not both. If both cues C and D were causal, the CD compound would have produced a larger outcome (CD++). Cue D is causal in one of these two scenarios. For non-additive participants, it is possible that *both* C and D are causal, or that only one of C or D is causal. Cue D is causal in two out of three of these scenarios. Simply on the basis of the number of hypothetical scenarios in which cue D is causal, D will be rated higher by the non-additive than by the additive group of participants. If participants reason in this way about cue D, and if cue B is not subject to inferential reasoning because it is filtered out by the low-level attentional mechanism, then the difference between B and D (blocking) can be expected to be greater in the non-additive group.

The above analysis is consistent with the idea that blocking is, at least to some extent, a product of a low-level attentional/associative mechanism such as that described by Mackintosh (1975). Thus, predictive cues (A) reduce the associability of less predictive cues (B) when the two types of cues are trained in compound (AB+). However, although the data are consistent with this view, other explanations are possible. It may be that participants used inferential reasoning (rather than a low-level associative mechanism) to learn the A–outcome relationship in Phase 1. Because cue A allows participants to make correct outcome predictions (it reliably predicts an allergic reaction), it may have increased in salience. Thus, inferential reasoning in Phase 1 may have produced the attentional bias towards cue A, and therefore, in Phase 2, biased attention away from cue B. It is well established that when attention is divided (in this case between cues A and B), memory is impaired (e.g. Murdock, 1965; Baddeley, Lewis, Eldridge, and Thomson, 1984). Thus, Griffiths and Mitchell's (2008, 2009) data relating to encoding of cue B allow an explanation either in terms of a low-level associative mechanism or an inferential process interacting with memory. Either way, the findings are important because they show for the first time a blocking effect that cannot be the result of inferences made by participants about cue B.

This brief summary has included a number of experiments testing the idea that blocking in causal learning is, at least to some extent, the result of failures to encode stimuli and stimulus relationships in memory. Mitchell *et al.* (2006) showed that blocking can sometimes result in a failure to remember the outcome that was paired with the blocked cue. One explanation for this effect is that blocking is sometimes the consequence of the failure to encode a link in memory. However, Mitchell, *et al.* (2005, 2007) also showed that causal ratings are sometimes quite unrelated to the degree to which the cue–outcome relationship is encoded in memory. Griffiths and Mitchell (2008) showed that blocking training can result in the failure to encode the cue itself in memory. This implicates an attentional mechanism in blocking. Evidence presented by Griffiths and Mitchell (2009) is consistent with the idea that the attentional mechanism is non-inferential. That is, participants are not reasoning that cue B is non-causal. Rather, the simple presence of a predictive cue reduces the attention paid to the blocked cue.

I shall return to these issues in the conclusion to this chapter. First, however, I would like to describe some recent experiments that also suggest a role for attention and memory in perceptual learning. In fact, the attentional mechanism implicated by these perceptual learning experiments is very similar to that just described to explain blocking.

Perceptual learning

Very similar stimuli become easier to discriminate as they become more familiar. For example, identical twins are often, on first meeting, impossible to distinguish. However, after many meetings, they are easy to identify.

Laboratory experiments have demonstrated the reality of this effect under controlled conditions (e.g. Mackintosh, Kaye, and Bennett, 1991).

Two similar stimuli (such as identical twins) can be viewed as comprising a common element or feature, X, that is shared by both stimuli, and features specific to each stimulus, A and B. Thus, the two stimuli would be referred to as AX and BX. Gibson (1969) argued that mere exposure to two similar stimuli allows the participant (or subject in an animal experiment) to compare the stimuli, and therefore 'extract' the unique features A and B from the X background. Once extracted, these features can be more readily identified on test, and so AX and BX become more distinct. She termed this process 'differentiation'. However, Gibson did not explain how the organism might extract the unique features.

One straightforward account of the finding that familiar stimuli are more easily discriminated relates to the relative familiarity of the common and unique elements (see McLaren, Kaye, and Mackintosh, 1989; McLaren and Mackintosh, 2000). When the organism is exposed to AX and BX on a number of occasions, they receive twice as much exposure to X as to A or B. It is a common assumption in learning theory that familiar stimuli are less salient than novel stimuli. Thus, exposure to AX and BX should reduce the salience of X more than it does the salience of A or B. It is clear that if the salience of A and B increases *relative* to the salience of X, then AX and BX will become more distinct as a consequence of exposure. A simple attentional explanation for perceptual learning can, therefore, be provided in terms of the relative salience of the common and unique features.

There are, however, a number of findings that cannot be explained by recourse to this simple mechanism. A very good example, and the most studied phenomenon of this kind, is the intermixed-blocked effect seen in both animals (Honey, Bateson, and Horn, 1995; Symmonds and Hall, 1995; Blair and Hall, 2003) and humans (Lavis and Mitchell, 2006; Mitchell, Kadib, Nash, Lavis, and Hall, 2008; Mundy, Dwyer, and Honey, 2006). When AX and BX are presented on an 'intermixed' schedule (AX BX AX BX etc.), later discrimination is very good. However, equivalent exposures presented on a 'blocked' schedule, in which all AX presentations precede all BX presentations, are not so effective in increasing discrimination. On both schedules, X is twice as familiar as A or B, but discrimination is significantly better following the intermixed schedule. This result is, in fact, predicted by Gibson's differentiation account; the intermixed schedule allows more opportunity for 'stimulus comparison', one of the conditions suggested necessary for differentiation to occur.

Recent research in perceptual learning has focused closely on the intermixed-blocked effect, precisely because it cannot be explained in terms of relative familiarity and therefore salience of the features. Over the past decade, three accounts of this effect have been suggested. The first is an associative account proposed by McLaren and Mackintosh (2000). The second is an attentional account proposed by Hall (2003). The third is a recent elaboration of Gibson's differentiation theory proposed by Mitchell, Nash, and Hall (2008) (see Mundy, Honey and Dwyer, 2007, for a similar suggestion). All three approaches accept that the relative familiarity of common and unique features plays a role in perceptual learning, but the theories differ in the way they explain the intermixed-blocked effect.

McLaren and Mackintosh: associative inhibition between unique features

McLaren and Mackintosh's (2000) account of the intermixed-blocked effect is that on the intermixed, but not the blocked schedule, an inhibitory link forms between A and B. This theory relies on the idea that when AX and BX are presented, links will form between X and A, and between X and B, that allow X to activate the representations of A and B. These links render AX and BX more similar (on both the blocked and intermixed schedules). This is because presentation of AX will activate the representations not only of X and A, but also of B (via the X-B link). Presentations of BX will also activate X, A and B in a similar manner. Thus stimuli AX and BX are perceived to be largely equivalent. However, inhibition of B by A (and vice versa) develops when preexposure is intermixed because A predicts the absence of B on AX trials and B predicts the absence of A on BX trials. Inhibition will prevent activation of B on AX trials and A on BX trials and so render the two stimuli more distinct. The inhibitory link, it is argued, is more likely to form during intermixed than blocked preexposure (just as it does in standard conditioning; Yin, Barnet and Miller, 1994) and so inhibition between A and B can explain the intermixed-blocked effect.

This non-attentional mechanism has been placed under close scrutiny recently in studies of both humans and non-human animals. The results of these experiments present problems for the inhibition account. Firstly, intermixed exposure to AX and X produces better discrimination than does blocked preexposure in both rats (Rodriguez and Alonso, 2004) and humans (Mitchell, Kadib, *et al.*, 2008). It is not obvious how inhibition might develop when there is no second unique feature for A to inhibit.[2] Secondly, in humans,

[2] It has been suggested that inhibition might develop between A and the representation of the absence of A. This idea, however, rests on some rather tortuous logic. It is suggested that a stimulus might come to inhibit the (representation of) the absence of itself. It is not

simultaneous presentations of AX and BX produce better perceptual learning than do sequential presentations (Mundy *et al.*, 2007). Simultaneous presentations of AX and BX were also shown to foster excitatory, not inhibitory links between A and B. In a related result using rat subjects, preexposure on an intermixed schedule has been shown to increase the degree to which A and B can become associated with one another relative to blocked preexposure (Artigas, Sansa, Blair, Hall, and Prados, 2006; see also Lavis, 2009, for a similar result in humans). These latter results are precisely the opposite to that predicted by the idea that A and B inhibit one another. Recent focus, therefore, has been on attentional mechanisms of perceptual learning. The theory proposed by Hall (2003) and the recent reformulations of Gibson's differentiation theory can be classified as attentional theories.

Hall: reverse habituation

Just as in the case of inhibition, Hall's account relies on the formation of X–A and X–B links in preexposure. However, Hall argues that the important consequence of these links is not that inhibition forms between A and B on the intermixed schedule, but that A and B increase in salience. His theory is related to the idea of habituation. Habituation is thought to occur each time a stimulus is presented, with the consequence that the salience of that stimulus is reduced. That is, the stimulus is no longer able to elicit an orienting response, or is no longer able to capture attention. Hall proposed that the precise opposite of this process takes place ('reverse habituation') if the representation of a stimulus is activated associatively – in this case via the X–A or X–B link. Thus, on each AX trial, the representation of B is activated via the X–B link, and so B 'dishabituates' or increases in salience (the same is true of A on BX trials). This effect does not occur on the blocked schedule because on early AX trials, no X–B link has yet been formed, and on BX trials in the second half of the preexposure phase, the X–A link quickly extinguishes (it is not maintained by alternating AX exposures). Thus, Hall's mechanism explains the intermixed-blocked effect as being due to dishabituation (increases in salience) of A and B on the intermixed but not the blocked schedule. It is as if the novelty of the unique features is maintained on the intermixed schedule. This theory could be interpreted to predict, therefore, that the unique features of the stimuli preexposed on the intermixed schedule will feel less familiar (be less well remembered)

obvious how inhibition might improve discrimination here; the presence of A should already prevent activation of the representation of the absence of itself – no training is required.

than those presented on the blocked schedule.[3] Before turning to the evidence, the second attentional theory will be presented, which makes very different predictions about the relationship between perceptual learning and memory.

A mechanism for differentiation

Mitchell, Nash *et al.* (2008) suggested a mechanism for perceptual learning that is based on a principle of long-term memory encoding and which is closely related to Gibson's original differentiation theory. We suggested that AX and BX are only discriminable once the participant has encoded in memory representations of the unique features A and B. When the stimuli are later presented on a test that requires participants to tell AX and BX apart, the participant's search for unique features (A and B) is easier if those features are well encoded in memory. We also proposed a mechanism by which intermixed exposure will lead to better encoding of the unique features than will blocked exposure. This mechanism can be described in terms of an interaction between short- and long-term habituation processes.

On an AX trial, both A and X features suffer short-term habituation. When BX is presented on the following trial, the common feature X is habituated and therefore receives little attention. The B feature, therefore, receives all available processing resources. As a consequence of the greater processing resources devoted to the unique features A and B across intermixed exposure to AX and BX, more stable ('stronger') representations of these unique features are formed in long-term memory. In the blocked condition, most AX (and BX) trials will have been preceded by another AX (or BX) trial. Therefore, both the unique and common elements will have suffered short-term habituation and will be poorly processed. Overall, the unique features presented on an intermixed schedule will be better encoded in memory than those presented on a blocked schedule.

This same idea can also be expressed in terms of episodic memory. Jacoby (1978) suggested that when a stimulus is presented on more than one occasion, if prior presentations of a stimulus are remembered, then the resources

[3] In fact, the model proposed by McLaren and Mackintosh (2000) contains a mechanism (quite separate from the inhibitory mechanism described above) that can be seen as an associative account of Hall's dishabituation mechanism. They predict that when A is activated associatively on BX trials, the representation becomes deunitized. That is, the various links that go to form the representation of A will weaken. This version of the dishabutation mechanism more explicitly predicts that participants will view unique features presented on an intermixed schedule as novel stimuli, because they do not have a strong representation of the stimulus in memory.

devoted to encoding that stimulus in memory again will be reduced. Again, this suggests that the unique elements presented on an intermixed schedule will be especially well encoded in memory. On a BX trial following an AX trial, the common element X will receive few processing resources, because it is remembered from the previous trial. This will free up processing resources that can be focused on the unique feature B. This feature will, therefore, be especially well processed and especially well encoded in memory.

In summary, Hall (2003) suggests that intermixed preexposure maintains the novelty of the unique features A and B. This is because A and B are associatively activated on BX and AX trials respectively. In contrast, Mitchell, Nash *et al.* (2008) suggest that intermixed preexposure allows A and B to be especially well encoded in memory. One interpretation of Hall's view, then, is that participants should perceive the unique features to be quite unfamiliar following intermixed exposure (see also McLaren and Mackintosh, 2000). On Mitchell *et al.'s* view, the reverse should be true; unique features presented on an intermixed schedule should feel especially familiar.

We have recently tested this idea using multi-coloured checkerboard stimuli with common (X) and unique (A, B, C, and D) features (Lavis, Hall, Kadib and Mitchell, in preparation). The unique features A-D were shapes made up of a small number of squares of the same colour. These were placed on the multi-coloured checkerboard background (X) during preexposure. AX and BX were presented on an intermixed schedule, CX and DX presentations were in two separate blocks. On test, just the shape of each unique feature (one on each test trial) was shown with no checkerboard background and with the colour removed. Participants were required to match the shape of these features to the colours in which they had been presented in preexposure. An accurate shape-colour match was taken as evidence that a representation of the unique feature had been encoded in memory. As Mitchell *et al.* predicted, better colour matching was observed to unique features preexposed on the intermixed than on the blocked schedule.

Better memory for the unique features presented on the intermixed schedule seems at odds with Hall's idea that these features are dishabituated. Habituation implies that the stimuli become more familiar. Dishabituation, therefore, suggests that poorer performance should be seen on a memory test.[4] However, another interpretation of Hall's idea might be consistent with our memory data. Hall did not specify a mechanism by which the associatively activated features might dishabituate. Therefore, I may be accused of putting words in

[4] As noted above, this is the explicit prediction of the McLaren and Mackintosh (2000) account of salience modulation following intermixed preexposure

his mouth by assuming that dishabituation should necessarily be accompanied by poorer memory. Perhaps A and B are only dishabituated in the sense that they are more salient and attract greater attention. If this were the case, one might expect the increased attention to the unique features to result in better encoding of those features in memory, as was observed by Lavis *et al.* (in preparation).

On this interpretation, Hall's model has much in common with the memory model described by Mitchell, Nash *et al.* (2008). Both accounts now predict that unique features presented on an intermixed schedule will be both salient and well encoded in memory. However, Mitchell *et al.* suggest that these features are more salient *because* they are better encoded in memory; it is easier for participants to detect those well-encoded features on test. Hall (2003) suggests the opposite; in this case intermixed features are better encoded in memory because they are more salient.

In a final experiment, Lavis *et al.* (in preparation) tested Mitchell *et al.'s* (2008) account in a different way. We gave participants preexposure to AX, BX, CX, and DX, all intermixed with each other. In addition, we gave participants presentations of A and B alone. These additional presentations can be expected to produce habituation to A and B. According to Hall (2003), this will reduce the ease with which participants can distinguish AX from BX on test, because habituation will reduce the salience of A and B. In contrast, if strongly encoded unique features are necessary for perceptual learning to be observed (Mitchell, Nash *et al.*, 2008) then additional exposure to A and B should produce better discrimination of AX and BX. This is what was observed; in a same-different task, AX and BX were more easily discriminated than CX and DX.

Overall, the data from human participants tend to support the idea that intermixed preexposure to two similar stimuli AX and BX allows the unique features of those stimuli to be easily identified and then encoded in memory. Once encoded in memory, representations of the unique features A and B can then be easily detected and used to discriminate AX and BX on test. Both models of learning and models of memory (Jacoby, 1978) provide mechanisms by which intermixed preexposure will improve encoding of the unique features in memory. In terms of learning models, the competing X features suffer short-term habituation on each trial, and so compete less well with processing of the unique features A and B that appear only on alternate trials. Jacoby (1978) suggested a similar mechanism in the context of memory. Thus, on every trial of an intermixed preexposure schedule, the common X feature will be the most recently presented element. Therefore, the majority of processing resources will be taken up by the less recently presented, and so harder to process, unique features A and B. Both of these approaches provide a mechanism for Gibson's idea that the unique features of similar stimuli are 'extracted' from the background when the two stimuli are compared. Once extracted, the unique features can be used on test to discriminate AX from BX. Attention, therefore, plays an important role in encoding in perceptual learning. The unique features of stimuli presented on an intermixed schedule receive more of our limited attentional resources (because fewer resources are taken up in processing the recently presented common features). This attentional bias towards stimuli that demand processing resources allows those stimuli to be better encoded in memory.

The idea that unique features that are more familiar are more salient will seem quite counterintuitive to most learning theorists. One would naturally expect the opposite effect to be observed – novel stimuli are usually assumed to be more salient than familiar stimuli. And it is not only learning theorists who make this assumption. In visual search experiments (Strayer and Johnston, 2000; Wang, Cavanagh, and Green, 1994), participants easily detect a novel singleton in an array of familiar stimuli, but not a familiar stimulus from an array of novel stimuli. This asymmetry (a 'pop-out' effect for novel items) suggests that novel stimuli are more salient, or capture more attention, than familiar stimuli. If performance on the same-different task in our experiments were driven by salience in this way, the less well encoded (more 'novel') unique features from the blocked schedule should produce better performance. However, of course, participants in our experiments are probably not waiting for a feature to pop-out on test trials. It is more likely that they are deliberately searching for those unique features that they successfully detected during the intermixed preexposure phase. In fact, once the unique features have been detected in this task, participants might simply attend to the locations in which those features appeared. This alone would improve performance on a same-different task. Thus, quite different, deliberate (or endogenous) attentional mechanisms are implicated here from those involved in (exogenous) attentional capture, or pop-out effects (e.g. Posner, 1980).

In fact, endogenous attention (deliberate search) will likely play an important role during preexposure, as well as at test, in our procedure. Participants are told at the very beginning of the experiment to 'look for' the stimulus differences. Mackintosh (2009) has pointed out that, in contrast to our studies, subjects in animal experiments are not told to look for stimulus differences at the start of preexposure. As a consequence, he argued, the mechanisms responsible for ('unsupervised') perceptual learning in animals are likely to be quite different from those that underlie the perceptual learning seen in our experiments (but see Mitchell, 2009, for an alternative view). That is, the attentional mechanism suggested by Mitchell, Nash *et al.* (2008) may be restricted to humans who are given explicit instructions to look for stimulus differences at the start of training (although the engagement of deliberate search strategies does not, in itself, explain why some preexposure schedules are more effective than others). More specifically, unsupervised perceptual learning in humans may be determined by the mechanisms proposed by McLaren and Mackintosh (2000). This idea remains to be tested.

Conclusions

Memory and learning are clearly closely related areas of research. Indeed, many associative theorists assume that learning is determined by the degree to which links between stimulus representations are encoded in memory. However, learning theorists do not, generally, test this assumption. Rather, learning is measured by the degree to which a conditioned response is generated on test, or the degree to which a participant believes that a particular cue causes an outcome. In perceptual learning, the degree of generalization of a response from one stimulus to another is usually measured. To properly investigate the role of memory in learning, a more direct approach is needed.

In the experiments reviewed here, I hope to have provided some evidence for two kinds of cue competition in memory, both of which make contact with research on learning. My work with Oren Griffiths suggests that, in a blocking design (A+ followed by AB+ training), the presence of the pretrained cue A reduces the degree to which the added cue B is processed. That is, attention to B is reduced. This result seems consistent with the intuition at the heart of the model proposed by Mackintosh (1975); he suggested that a predictive cue will reduce attention to less predictive cues that are present. However, Mackintosh emphasized that he was not proposing a limited capacity attentional system in which the presence of a salient cue prevents the processing of a less salient cue (the 'inverse hypothesis'; Thomas, 1970). Rather, the reduction in attention to the blocked cue is learned across training trials. Thus, the Mackintosh (1975) theory would need some modification to account for the present data. As Quinlan (this volume) wonders, it may be time to reconsider the inverse hypothesis, as incorporated in the earlier Sutherland and Mackintosh (1971) model.

Indeed, probably the simplest account of Griffiths and Mitchell's data is that, on AB+ trials in Phase 2 of training, participants focused attention on A and, therefore, away from B, just as the inverse hypothesis predicts. Consequently, participants did not learn a B–outcome relationship and they did not remember having seen the individual exemplars of B that were presented. This account is entirely consistent with the evidence on the effects of divided attention in recognition memory experiments (e.g. Baddeley *et al.*, 1984). This mechanism would, of course, also account for the failure to remember the specific outcome paired with a blocked cue B in Mitchell *et al.'s* (2006) outcome memory task. Thus, in these experiments, although the failure to encode a B–outcome memory is consistent with an associative, or link-based, analysis of learning, an equally plausible alternative is that participants simply failed to encode a detailed episodic memory of the 'AB-outcome' event.

The perceptual learning data from my laboratory also permit an explanation in terms of competition between cues for attentional resources. In perceptual learning, it seems reasonable to assume that on each presentation of AX and BX, there is competition for attentional resources between the unique and common features. In intermixed preexposure, short-term habituation may reduce the degree to which X is able to compete for these resources. This will allow more thorough processing and better encoding of A and B in memory. Thus, the blocking effect in associative learning (Kamin, 1969) and the intermixed-blocked effect in perceptual learning (Honey *et al.*, 1995) may, at least to some extent, result from similar processes. In both cases, attention to a cue, and encoding of that cue in memory, is modulated by the salience of another cue simultaneously presented. In blocking, the competitor cue A is increased in salience through pairing with the outcome in Phase 1 (A+ trials). This results in reduced processing of the simultaneously presented B cue on AB+ trials in Phase 2. The opposite effect is seen in perceptual learning. On an intermixed prexposure schedule, the competitor X feature is low in salience on a BX trial because it was presented on the immediately preceding AX trial. This results in increased processing of the B feature, and better encoding of that feature in memory.

Whatever the merits of the analysis presented here (and I must admit that the bow being drawn is occasionally quite long), one thing is clear. Direct measurement of memory for both cues and cue–outcome relationships allows us to gain important insights into the mechanisms of learning. In particular, the data presented here raise the possibility that researchers of learning and memory are investigating different effects of the same attentional mechanism.

References

Artigas, A. A., Sansa, J., Blair, C. A. J., Hall, G., & Prados, J. (2006). Enhanced discrimination between flavor stimuli: Roles of salience modulation and inhibition. *Journal of Experimental Psychology: Animal Behavior Processes,* **32**, 173–177.

Baddeley, A. D. (1990). *Human memory: Theory and practice.* Hillsdale, NJ: Lawrence Erlbaum Associates.

Baddeley, A. D., Lewis, V., Eldridge, M., & Thomson, N. (1984). Attention and retrieval from long-term memory. *Journal of Experimental Psychology: General*, **113**, 518–540.

Batsell, W. R., Paschall, G. Y., Gleason, D. I., & Batson, J. D. (2001). Taste preconditioning augments odor-aversion learning. *Journal of Experimental Psychology: Animal Behavior Processes*, **27**, 30–47.

Beckers, T., De Houwer, J., Pineno, O., & Miller, R. R. (2005). Outcome additivity and outcome maximality influence cue competition in human causal learning. *Journal of Experimental Psychology: Learning, Memory and Cognition*, **31**, 238–249.

Bilodeau, I. M. & Schlosberg, H. (1951). Similarity in stimulating conditions as a variable in retroactive inhibition. *Journal of Experimental Psychology*, **41**, 199–204.

Blair, C. A. J. & Hall, G. (2003). Perceptual learning in flavor aversion: Evidence for learned changes in stimulus effectiveness. *Journal of Experimental Psychology: Animal Behavior Processes*, **29**, 39–48.

Bonardi, C., Graham, S., Hall, G., & Mitchell, C.J. (2005). Acquired distinctiveness and equivalence in human discrimination learning: Evidence for an attentional process. *Psychonomic Bulletin and Review*, **12**, 88–92.

Bouton, M. E. (1993). Context, time, and memory retrieval in the interference paradigms of Pavlovian learning. *Psychological Bulletin*, **114**, 80–99.

Chapman, G. B. & Robbins, S. J. (1990). Cue interaction in human contingency judgement. *Memory and Cognition*, **18**, 537–545.

Craik, F. I. M. & Lockhart, R. S. (1972). Levels of processing: A framework for memory research. *Journal of Verbal Learning and Verbal Behavior*, **11**, 671–684.

Craik, F. I. M. & Tulving, E. (1975). Depth of processing and the retention of words in episodic memory. *Journal of Experimental Psychology: General*, **104**, 268–294.

De Houwer, J., Beckers, T., & Glautier, S. (2002). Outcome and cue properties modulate blocking. *Quarterly Journal of Experimental Psychology*, **55A**, 965–985.

Dickinson, A. (2001). Causal learning: An associative analysis. *The Quarterly Journal of Experimental Psychology*, **54B**, 3–25.

Dickinson, A., Shanks, D., & Evenden, J. (1984). Judgement of act-outcome contingency: The role of selective attribution. *Quarterly Journal of Experimental Psychology*, **36A**, 29–50.

Escobar, M., Arcediano, F., & Miller, R. R. (2003). Latent inhibition in human adults without masking. *Journal of Experimental Psychology: Learning, Memory, and Cognition*, **29**, 1028–1040.

Gibson, E. J. (1969). *Principles of perceptual learning and development*. East Norwalk, CT: Appleton-Century-Crofts.

Griffiths, O. & Le Pelley, M. E. (2009). Attentional changes in blocking are not a consequence of lateral inhibition. *Learning and Behaviour*, **37**, 27–41.

Griffiths, O. & Mitchell, C. J. (2008). Selective attention in human associative learning and recognition memory. *Journal of Experimental Psychology: General*, **137**, 626–648.

Griffiths, O. & Mitchell, C. J. (in preparation). Outcome additivity does not increase blocking in a categorical causal learning task.

Hall, G. (2003). Learned changes in the sensitivity of stimulus representations: Associative and nonassociative mechanisms. *Quarterly Journal of Experimental Psychology*, **56B**, 43–55.

Hall, G. & Rodriguez, G. (2010). Attentional learning. In C. J. Mitchell and M. E. Le Pelley (Eds), *Attention and learning*. Oxford: Oxford University Press.

Holmes, N. & Harris, J. A. (2010). Latent inhibition. In C. J. Mitchell and M. E. Le Pelley (Eds), *Attention and Learning*. Oxford: Oxford University Press.

Honey, R. C., Bateson, P., & Horn, G. (1994). The role of stimulus comparison in perceptual learning. *Quarterly Journal of Experimental Psychology,* **47B**, 83–103.

Jacoby, L. L. (1978). On interpreting the effects of repetition: Solving a problem versus remembering a solution. *Journal of Verbal Learning and Verbal Behavior,* **17**, 649–667.

Kamin, L. J. (1969). Predictability, surprise, attention and conditioning. In B.A. Campbell and R.M. Church (Eds), *Punishment and aversive behavior* (pp. 279–296). New York: Appleton-Century-Crofts.

Konorski, J. (1967). *Integrative activity of the brain*. Chicago, IL: University of Chicago Press.

Lavis, Y. (2009). *An investigation into the mechnisms responsible for perceptual learning in humans.* Unpublished doctoral thesis.

Lavis, Y., Hall, G., Kadib, R., & Mitchell, C. J. (in preparation). Unitization of unique stimulus features in human perceptual learning.

Lavis, Y. & Mitchell, C. J. (2006). Effects of pre-exposure on stimulus discrimination: An investigation of the mechanisms responsible for human perceptual learning. *Quarterly Journal of Experimental Psychology,* **59**, 2083-2101.

Le Pelley, M. E. & McLaren, I. P. L. (2003). Learned associability and associative change in human causal learning. *Quarterly Journal of Experimental Psychology,* **56B**, 68–79.

Le Pelley, M. E., Oakeshott, S. M., & McLaren, I. P. L. (2005). Blocking and unblocking in human causal learning. *Journal of Experimental Psychology: Animal Behavior Processes,* **31**, 56–70.

Lovibond, P. F., Bean, S., Mitchell, C. J., Bouton, M. E., & Frohart, N. (2003). Forward and backward blocking of causal judgement is enhanced by additivity of effect magnitude. *Memory and Cognition,* **31**, 133–142.

Lubow, R. E. & Moore, A. U. (1959). Latent inhibition: The effect of nonreinforced pre-exposure to the conditional stimulus. *Journal of Comparative and Physiological Psychology,* **52**, 415–419.

Mackintosh, N. J. (1975). A theory of attention: Variation in the associability of stimuli with reinforcement. *Psychological Review,* **82**, 276–298.

Mackintosh, N.J. (2009). Varieties of perceptual learning. *Learning and Behavior,* **37**, 119–125.

Mackintosh, N. J., Kaye, H., & Bennett, C. (1991). Perceptual learning in flavour aversion conditioning. *Quarterly Journal of Experimental Psychology,* **43B**, 297–322.

McLaren, I. P. L., Kaye, H., & Mackintosh, N. J. (1989). An associative theory of the representation of stimuli: Applications to perceptual learning and latent inhibition. In R. G. M. Morris (Ed.), *Parallel distributed processing: Implications for psychology and neurobiology* (pp. 102–130). Oxford: Clarendon Press.

McLaren, I. P. L. & Mackintosh, N. J. (2000). An elemental model of associative learning: I. Latent inhibition and perceptual learning. *Animal Learning and Behavior*, **28**, 211–246.

Miller, R. R. & Matzel, L. D. (1988). The comparator hypothesis: A response rule for the expression of associations. In G.H. Bower (Ed.), *The psychology of learning and motivation,* Vol. 22 (pp. 51–92). Orlando, FL: Academic Press.

Mitchell, C. J. (2009). Human and animal perceptual learning: Some common and some unique features. *Learning and Behavior,* **37**, 154–160.

Mitchell, C. J., Harris, J. A., Westbrook, R. F., & Griffiths, O. (2008). Changes in cue associability across training in human causal learning. *Journal of Experimental Psychology: Animal Behavior Processes,* **34**, 423–436.

Mitchell, C. J., Kadib, R., Nash, S., Lavis, Y., & Hall, G. (2008). Analysis of the Role of Associative Inhibition in Perceptual Learning by Means of the Same-Different Task. *Journal of Experimental Psychology: Animal Behavior Processes,* **34**, 475–485.

Mitchell, C. J., Killedar, A., & Lovibond, P. F. (2005). Inference-based retrospective revaluation in human causal judgements requires knowledge of within-compound relationships. *Journal of Experimental Psychology: Animal Behavior Processes,* **31**, 418–424.

Mitchell, C. J., Livesey, E., & Lovibond, P. F. (2007). A dissociation between causal judgement and the ease with which a cause is categorised with its effect. *Quarterly Journal of Experimental Psychology,* **60**, 400–417.

Mitchell, C. J. & Lovibond, P. F. (2002). Backward and forward blocking in human electrodermal conditioning: Blocking requires an assumption of outcome additivity. *Quarterly Journal of Experimental Psychology,* **55B**, 311–329.

Mitchell, C. J., Lovibond, P. F., & Condoleon, M. (2005). Evidence for flexible rule use in blocking of causal judgements. *Learning and Motivation,* **36**, 77–87.

Mitchell, C. J., Lovibond, P. F., & Gan, C. (2005). A dissociation between memory and causal judgements. *Psychonomic Bulletin and Review,* **5**, 950–954.

Mitchell, C. J., Lovibond, P. F., Minard, E., & Lavis, Y. (2006). Forward blocking in human learning sometimes reflects the failure to encode a cue-outcome relationship. *Quarterly Journal of Experimental Psychology,* **59**, 830–844.

Mitchell, C. J., Nash, S., & Hall, G. (2008). The intermixed-blocked effect in human perceptual learning is not the consequence of trial spacing. *Journal of Experimental Psychology: Learning Memory and Cognition,* **34**, 237–242.

Mitchell, C. J. & Scully, A., (in preparation). Stimulus preexposure effects in learning and memory.

Mundy, M. E., Dwyer, D. M., & Honey, R. C. (2006). Inhibitory associations contribute to perceptual learning in humans. *Journal of Experimental Psychology: Animal Behavior Processes,* **32**, *178–184.*

Mundy, M. E., Honey, R. C., & Dwyer, D. M. (2007). Simultaneous presentation of similar stimuli produces perceptual learning in human picture processing. *Journal of Experimental Psychology: Animal Behavior Processes,* **33**, *124–138.*

Murdock, B. B. Jr. (1965). Effects of a subsidiary task on short-term memory. *British Journal of Psychology,* **56**, 413–419.

Pearce, J. M. & Hall, G. (1980). A model for Pavlovian learning: Variations in the effectiveness of conditioned but not unconditioned stimuli. *Psychological Review,* **87**, 532–552.

Posner, M. I. (1980). Orienting of attention. *Quarterly Journal of Experimental Psychology,* **32**, 3–25.

Quinlan, P. T. (2010). On the use of the term 'attention'. In C. J. Mitchell and M. E. Le Pelley (Eds), *Attention and learning.* Oxford: Oxford University Press.

Rescorla, R. A. & Cunningham, C. L. (1978). Withincompound flavor associations. *Journal of Experimental Psychology: Animal Behavior Processes,* **4**, 267–275.

Rescorla, R. A. & Wagner, A. R. (1972). A theory of Pavlovian conditioning: Variations in the effectiveness of reinforcement and non-reinforcement. In A.H. Black and W.F. Prokasy (Eds), *Classical Conditioning II* (pp. 64–99). New York: Appleton-Century-Crofts.

Rodriguez, G. & Alonso, G. (2004). Perceptual learning in flavor-aversion learning: Alternating and blocked exposure to a compound of flavors and to an element of that compound. *Learning and Motivation,* **35**, *208–220.*

Rosas, J. M. & Callejas-Aguilera, J. E. (2006). Context switch effects on acquisition and extinction in human predictive learning. *Journal of Experimental Psychology: Learning, Memory, and Cognition,* **32**, 461–474.

Scully, A. & Mitchell, C. J. (2008). Extinction in learning and memory. *Quarterly Journal of Experimental Psychology,* **61**, 1472–1478.

Shanks, D. R. (1985). Forward and backward blocking in human contingency judgements. *Quarterly Journal of Experimental Psychology,* **37B**, 1–21.

Shanks, D. R. & Darby, R. J. (1998). Feature- and rule-based generalization in human associative learning. *Journal of Experimental Psychology: Animal Behavior Processes,* **24**, 405–415.

Slamecka, N. J. & Ceraso, J. (1960). Retroactive and proactive inhibition of verbal learning. *Psychological Bulletin,* **57**, 449–475.

Strayer, D. L. & Johnston, W. A. (2000). Novel popout is an attention-based phenomenon: An ERP analysis. *Perception and Psychophysics*, **62**, 459–470.

Sutherland, N. S. & Mackintosh, N. J. (1971). *Mechanisms of animal discrimination learning.* New York: Academic Press.

Symonds, M. & Hall, G. (1995). Perceptual learning in flavor aversion learning: Roles of stimulus comparison and latent inhibition of common stimulus elements. *Learning and Motivation*, **26**, 203–219.

Thomas, D. R. (1970). Stimulus selection, attention and related matters. In J.H.Reynierse (Ed.), *Current issues in animal learning.* Lincoln, NJ: University of Nebraska Press.

Wagner, A. R. (1981) SOP: A model of automatic memory processing in animal behavior. In N.E. Spear and R.R. Miller (Eds), *Information processing in animals: Conditioned inhibition* (pp. 223–266). Hillsdale, NJ: Lawrence Erlbaum.

Wang, Q., Cavanagh, P., & Green, M. (1994). Familiarity and pop-out in visual search. *Perception and Psychophysics*, **56**, 495–500.

Yin, H., Barnet, R. C., & Miller, R. R. (1994). Second-order conditioning and Pavlovian conditioned inhibition: Operational similarities and differences. *Journal of Experimental Psychology: Animal Behavior Processes,* **20**, 419–428.

Chapter 11

Backward blocking of relevance-indicating cues: evidence for locally Bayesian learning

John K. Kruschke and Stephen E. Denton

The phenomenon in associative learning called 'blocking' has been a central target for theories that aim to explain learning and attention. The training phases of the blocking procedure, described in detail below, can be run in backward order, yet still produce the blocking effect (e.g., Shanks,1985; Dickinson and Burke,1996; Kruschke and Blair, 2000). Explaining forward and backward blocking, along with other associative learning phenomena, has proven to be challenging. Some accounts of forward blocking include an attentional mechanism that modulates the influence of the cues on learning and/or responding (e.g., Kruschke, 2001; Mackintosh, 1975). Some accounts of backward blocking employ a Bayesian framework in which different combinations of associative weights are considered simultaneously, with more belief allocated to the combination that is most consistent with training items (e.g., Dayan and Kakade, 2001; Tenenbaum and Griffths, 2003).

A theoretical framework that is able to combine the attentional and Bayesian approaches is called 'locally Bayesian learning' (Kruschke, 2006b). The framework is based on the idea that a learning system may consist of a sequence of subsystems in a feed-forward chain, each of which is a locally Bayesian learner. The argument for locally-learning layers was as follows. First, Bayesian learning is very attractive for explaining retrospective revaluation effects such as backward blocking, among many other phenomena (Chater, Tenenbaum, and Yuille, 2006). Second, globally Bayesian learning may also be unattractive for a number of reasons. In a large learning system, there are too many combinations of parameters to keep track of in a monolithic joint parameter space. Furthermore, many globally Bayesian models do not explain learning phenomena (such as 'highlighting', Kruschke, 2010) that depend on training order, because the models treat all training items as equally representative of the world to be learned, regardless of when the items occurred. Finally, the level of analysis for theories of learning is arbitrary: Learning occurs simultaneously at the levels of neurons, brain regions, functional components, individuals, committees, institutions, and societies, all of which may be modeled (in principle, if not accurately) as Bayesian learners. Therefore, a system of locally Bayesian learning components may retain some attractions of Bayesian models while also implementing Bayesian learning in smaller, tractable parameter spaces.

The general framework for locally Bayesian learning has been instantiated in a particular two-layer model, wherein one layer learns how to allocate attention to cues, and a second layer learns how to associate attended cues with outcomes (Kruschke, 2006b). The model showed retrospective revaluation effects such as backward blocking while also showing the order-sensitive phenomenon of highlighting. The two-layer model had locally Bayesian learning in both of its layers. Bayesian learning was needed in the upper, outcome layer to produce effects such as backward blocking. Attentional shifting was needed to produce effects such as highlighting. But there was no phenomenon that demanded Bayesian learning in the lower, attentional layer. Bayesian learning was conducted in the lower layer merely for mechanistic consistency and as a demonstration of the more general framework for locally Bayesian learning.

The purpose of the present chapter is to report a novel learning design, the results of which suggest the need for Bayesian learning in the lower, attentional layer. In essence, the results show backward blocking of cues to attentional allocation, as distinct from traditional designs that show backward blocking of cues to response allocation. This pattern of results can be accommodated by a model that has layers of locally Bayesian learning.

Background

Forward and backward blocking

In the standard forward blocking procedure, a learner is initially trained with cases of cue A leading to outcome X, denoted A→X. Subsequently, training continues with cases in which two cues, A and B, lead to the same outcome X, denoted A·B→X. It turns out that the strength of association from cue B to outcome X is weaker than if the initial training with A had not occurred. In other words, the learning of the association from B to X has been 'blocked', or attenuated, by the previous learning of the association from A to X. The phenomenon of blocking, first reported by Kamin (1968), challenges theories that base strength of association on merely the number of co-occurrences of cue and outcome (but cf. Miller and Matzel, 1988).

There are many types of explanations of blocking, but one family of explanations posits a role for attention. The intuition is that when learning cases of A · B→X, the learner re-allocates attention away from the redundant cue B because it is distracting resources away from the cue A that is already known to generate the correct outcome. In other words, the learner learns to ignore cue B. Some evidence for the attentional explanation comes from studies of learning about cue B after blocking. If learners have learned to ignore B, then subsequent learning about it should be retarded. This prediction has been confirmed (e.g., Kruschke and Blair, 2000; Kruschke, 2005; LePelley, Beesley, and Suret, 2007; Mackintosh and Turner, 1971; Mitchell, Harris, Westbrook, and Griffiths, 2008). Other evidence for reduced attention to the blocked cue comes from eye tracking experiments, in which it has been shown that gaze duration is reduced for blocked cues (Kruschke, Kappenman, and Hetrick, 2005; Wills, Lavric, Croft, and Hodgson, 2007).

Backward blocking, as a training procedure, simply reverses the phases of training in standard forward blocking. In other words, learners are first trained with cases of A · B→X, and subsequently trained with cases of A→X. It turns out that the strength of association from B to X is again weakened by the A→X training, even though it happened after the training with B, and even though B never appeared in the subsequent training (Shanks, 1985). Thus, cue B seems to have been retrospectively revalued in its absence. Backward blocking and other retrospective revaluations are especially challenging to theories of associative learning (for reviews see DeHouwer and Beckers, 2002; Dickinson, 2001).

The attentional theories that account for blocking do not account for backward blocking. This failure is caused by the fact that the theories rely on the presence of a cue to learn how much to attend to it. If a cue is absent, the models do not change its attention strength.

One class of theories that accommodates backward blocking is Bayesian models of association (e.g., Dayan and Kakade, 2001; Sobel, Tenenbaum, and Gopnik, 2004; Tenenbaum and Griffiths, 2003).[1] These Bayesian theories posit a set of associative hypotheses simultaneously entertained by the learner. For illustration, suppose that the learner considers three hypotheses: (1) A indicates X and B is irrelevant, (2) B indicates X and A is irrelevant, and

[1] A class of non-Bayesian theories of backward blocking asserts that absent-but-expected cues acquire reduced associations when the expected outcome is present. For absent-but-expected cues, either the learning rate or encoding of the absent-cue is negative, resulting in a loss of association (Dickinson and Burke,1996; Markman, 1989; Tassoni, 1995; Van Hamme and Wasserman, 1994).

(3) either A or B indicate X.The three hypotheses are mutually exclusive, and exhaust the space of possibilities for this particular learner. After seeing the initial cases of A · B→X, all three hypotheses have some credibility. But after seeing cases of A→X, the first and third hypotheses gain credibility, because they are both consistent with the additional training. Because the set of hypotheses are mutually exclusive and exhaustive, when the first and third hypotheses gain credibility, the second hypothesis loses credibility. Therefore, across all the hypotheses, there is reduced strength of belief that B indicates X. For a detailed tutorial, see the discussion of Bayesian associative models by Kruschke (2008).

Bayesian approaches to learning are attractive for a variety of other reasons. Bayesian models are not limited to associative formalisms, but can instead incorporate complex structural representations into the hypothesis space. Bayesian models merely assume that the learner executes normatively correct learning (i.e., uses Bayes' rule) on whatever formal hypothesis space is posited. This representational flexibility allows Bayesian models to be applied to situations from learning by neurons (Deneve, 2008) to learning of language (Xu and Tenenbaum, 2007).

Locally Bayesian learning

Bayesian formalisms are very attractive as theories of learning, but implementing them can be difficult because of their computational complexity. In principle, Bayesian systems need to keep track of the credibility of every possible hypothesis. In hypothesis spaces with many parameters, such as numerous associative weights, the system needs to keep track of the credibility of every possible combination of parameter values in a high-dimensionality joint parameter space. In some simple models, this can be done exactly and easily because the entire distribution across beliefs can be summarized by a simple function such as a multivariate normal distribution. In more complicated models, the infinite space of hypotheses can be represented by a large but finite random sample of representative hypotheses. In these 'particle filter' approximations, as new cue outcome cases are experienced, the representative hypotheses are resampled to reflect the new experience. These methods are not trivial, however, and Bayesian computation can be quite challenging in large hypothesis spaces.

One way to attack the problem is to recognize that learning happens at many levels of analysis simultaneously. Neurons learn, brain regions learn, functional components of mind learn, individual people learn, teams of people learn, and so on. Indeed, even more microscopic and macroscopic systems may learn. Any of those levels of analysis may be amenable to description as Bayesian learning.

Therefore, it is at least plausible that component processes of the mind may be describable as Bayesian learners, because the components have a tractable hypothesis space. Whether or not the system as a whole is Bayesian depends on how the components interact. A scheme for interaction of hierarchically organized, locally Bayesian learners was described by Kruschke (2006b).

The general framework for locally Bayesian learning assumes that there are component processes in a hierarchy from stimulus encoding to response generation. Each functional component in the hierarchical chain takes its local input representation, transforms it, and delivers its local output representation to the next component in the chain. The transformation is parameterized, meaning that the exact quantitative behaviour of the local transformation depends on its parameter values. As a simple example, consider a linear transformation $y = mx + b$, where x is the input and y is the output. The slope m and the intercept b are parameters that govern the quantitative value of the output for any given input. The parameters are learned as exemplary $\langle x, y \rangle$ values are experienced. The learning of parameters is Bayesian reallocation of credibility to combinations of parameter values that are most consistent with the incoming stimuli and the target response. For example, if the component system has experienced $\langle x, y \rangle$ pairs such as $\langle 1, 2.01 \rangle$, $\langle 2, 3.99 \rangle$, and $\langle 3, 6.01 \rangle$, then it will allocate strong credibility to $m = 2$ and $b = 0$, i.e., $y = 2x + 0$, and weaker credibility to other parameter values.

The challenge for such a framework is determining the target response for interior components, because the outside world only indicates the target response for the final component that generates an overt response. Formally, the world only supplies the exterior stimulus x and the exterior target response y. For a component buried in the interior of the hierarchy, the component's input can be computed by propagating the exterior stimulus x up through the transformations leading into the component. The component's target output, however, is not obvious, because the transformations feed forward from x to y, not the opposite direction.

A heuristic for determining interior targets is as follows. The target for a component should be whatever is the input to the next component that maximizes the probability of achieving the target of that next component. Start at the final component and determine the input to that component that would maximize the probability of achieving the known exterior target. Use that input as the target for the penultimate component. Given that target for the penultimate component, determine the input to the penultimate component that would maximize the probability of achieving its target. Use that input as the target for the preceding component. Continue this process down the hierarchy of components until every component has a target.

Notice that the targets selected in this manner are the inputs that are most consistent with the component's current beliefs. In other words, at any given time, the component gives strongest credibility to some particular combinations of parameter values. That component finds the candidate input that would be most consistent with the parameter values that the component currently believes. That best candidate input is declared to be the target for the preceding layer. In this way, each component is teaching the preceding component to 'tell me what I want to hear' based on its current beliefs.

A crucial consequence of choosing interior targets this way is that the temporal order of data has an effect on what is learned internally. The reason is that the interior targets are determined by the components' current beliefs, which depend on the set of data experienced so far. The interior targets generated for any particular exterior input-output pair depend on what has been previously learned.

When a component transformation has a target, along with its input, then the parameters of the component transformation are adjusted via Bayesian learning. Parameter values that are consistent with the input and target are deemed more credible. There are various temporal dynamics that could be used for interleaving parameter learning and target determination (Kruschke, 2006b, p. 683, footnote 2).

Attention in locally Bayesian learning

Locally Bayesian learning is a general framework for models. One particular application is to attention in associative learning. In this application, the first component learns how to allocate attention across cues. Attention is an interior value, and is not explicitly provided by exterior data. The second component learns how to associate attentionally-filtered cues to outcomes. Both the attentional allocations and the outcome associations are acquired via locally Bayesian learning.

Previous work demonstrated the usefulness of this architecture (Kruschke, 2006a, 2006b). In particular, locally Bayesian learning of the output associations allows the system to accommodate backward blocking and other retrospective revaluation phenomena. Figure 11.1 shows the basic elements of locally Bayesian learning applied to attentional learning. The lowest nodes encode the cues, the middle nodes represent the attentionally filtered cues, and the upper nodes represent the (anticipated) outcome. The left side of Figure 11.1 illustrates what happens when the system is trained in the backward blocking procedure. In this procedure, the model first experiences cases of A · B→X, and then experiences cases of A→X. The upper-left part of the figure shows a variety of output–weight combinations that the model finds

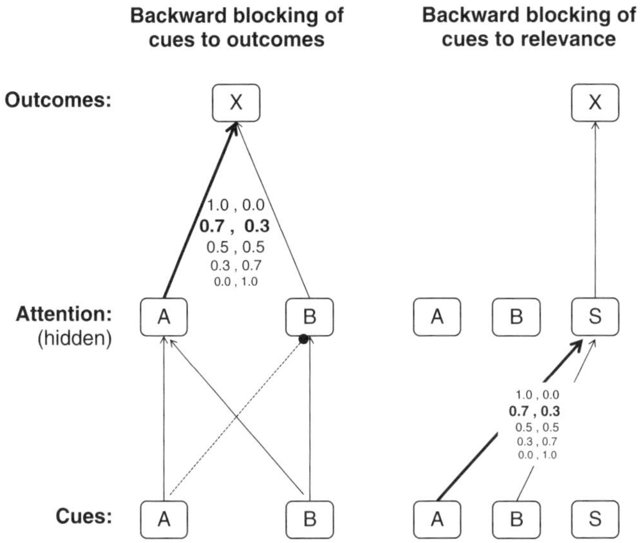

Fig. 11.1 Schematic of locally Bayesian learning applied to backward blocking. *Left*: Backward blocking of cues to outcomes. *Right*: Backward blocking of context cues to relevance. The pairs of numbers suggest some of the weight combinations that the model finds credible.

credible after training. The size of the font suggests how strongly the model believes in the weight combination. Thus, the model gives greatest credibility to an associative weight of 0.7 from A and an associative weight of 0.3 from B. But the model also gives some modest credibility to other weight combinations that are reasonably consistent with the training items. The layer of weights leading into the attentional gates also has a distribution of credibility across possible weight combinations.

Attentional shifting, and the temporal dependency of the scheme for selecting interior targets, also allows the system to accommodate the highlighting phenomenon (Kruschke, 2010). Highlighting is a trial-order effect that is particularly vexing for Bayesian models that treat all trials as equally representative of the world. The temporal dynamics of locally Bayesian learning also let the system show other trial-order effects, such as stronger forward blocking than backward blocking. A variety of other phenomena are addressed by the model.

The ability of the model to show backward blocking (and other effects) relied on Bayesian learning in the upper associative layer. But none of the phenomena considered by Kruschke (2006b) demanded Bayesian learning in the lower, attentional layer. In principle, the attentional layer could have been a non-Bayesian learner, and all the same effects could have been produced.

The primary goal of the present article is to report a phenomenon that does suggest the need for Bayesian learning of attentional allocation. The argument goes like this: Backward blocking is naturally accounted for by Bayesian learning. If it can be shown that there is backward blocking in the learning of attentional allocation, then one candidate explanation is that there is Bayesian learning of attentional allocation.

The right side of Figure 11.1 illustrates what is meant by backward blocking of attentional allocation. The complete design of the cue–outcome combinations will be described later, but the gist is provided here. Contrary to the standard design, cues A and B are not themselves diagnostic of the outcome: Across trials, the outcome occurs just as often when cues A and B are absent as when they are present. A different cue, labeled S in Figure 11.1, is perfectly predictive of the outcome, but only when cue A or cue B is present. When cues A and B are absent, cue S is not predictive. Thus, cues A and B do not indicate what outcome to anticipate, but they do indicate what other cue is relevant. In essence, cues A and B indicate what other cues should be attended.

The goal of the experiment reported below is demonstrate backward blocking of such cues to relevance. In the first part of training, cues A and B are both present whenever S is diagnostic. Therefore the model should learn to attend to S in the presence of A and B. Later in training, cue A is present without cue B whenever S is diagnostic. If there is backward blocking of B, then the association from B to S should be weakened. The weight pairs in the lower-right side of Figure 11.1 are intended to suggest the credible weight combinations after backward blocking of B as a cue to relevance.

The purpose of the experiment and modelling presented here is not to rule out other explanations or disconfirm other models. Instead, the goal is to bolster an assumption of locally Bayesian learning applied to attentional learning, a model which was already shown to address a spectrum of phenomena (Kruschke, 2006b). There are surely other models that can accommodate the data from the one new experiment presented here, but for a model to compete with locally Bayesian learning, the candidate model should also accommodate the spectrum of other phenomena addressed by locally Bayesian learning.

The new experiment presented here is offered merely as a suggestive proof of concept. Future experiments will be necessary to generalize the conditions under which the effects are observed, and to rule out alternative explanations. Nevertheless, it is hoped that the experiment and modeling may provoke interesting new ideas and research. In particular, the experiment presented here might not have been invented were it not for the implications of locally Bayesian learning applied to attentional learning.

Experiment: blocking and backward blocking of cues to relevance

Different cues can be relevant in different contexts. For example, when driving an automobile, the colour of the stoplight is relevant to the decision to stop or go, but when walking, the colour of the pedestrian signal is relevant to the decision to stop or go. In general, the cues in an environment can suggest which sources of information are relevant for determining a response. For example, the cue of having a steering wheel in your hands does not tell you whether to stop or go, but it does indicate that you should attend to stoplights, which will indicate whether you should stop or go.

Cues that are indirectly informative, such as the steering wheel in the previous example, are a type of context cue. The term 'context' has no generally accepted technical definition. Sometimes context refers to stimulus attributes that are spatially ambient (not focal) or temporally extended (i.e. tonic not phasic). Other times, context refers to cues that can be focal and phasic but that are not directly correlated with outcomes. This latter character is emphasized here. There has not been a vast amount of previous research into the role of context in learned attentional allocation, but several lines of work have indicated that people can learn about 'irrelevant' context as a cue to Attention (e.g., Chun, 2000; Nelson, 2002; Rosas, Callejas-Aguilera, Ramos-Alvarez, and Abad, 2006; Yang and Lewandowsky, 2003).

The present experiment is aimed at demonstrating forward and backward blocking of contextual cues to relevance. Continuing the example from driving discussed earlier, the idea is that people first experience steering wheels as a cue to attend to stoplights, and later people experience steering wheels along with a newly installed car stereo as a compound cue to attend to stoplights. The association from car stereo to attention may be blocked because of the previously learned association from steering wheel to attention.

To test this idea, we conducted a series of experiments in which all the cues were simple words on a computer screen, such as 'radio' and 'ocean'. Some words were perfectly correlated with the correct key to press. Other words had zero correlation with the correct response key, but were perfect indicators of which other words on the screen were relevant to the choice of response key. For example, suppose that people have learned that radio indicates key X and ocean indicates key Y. Subsequently, both 'radio' and 'ocean' appear simultaneously. Should the response be X or Y? The conflict is resolved by a third word on the screen, e.g., 'queen', which indicates to attend to 'radio'. Our experiments revealed that it was difficult for people to learn this sort of contextual dependency in a brief (< 20 min) experiment when the cues had no structural or semantic indicators of which were context cues and which were response cues. For the few people who could learn such structures quickly, we observed signs of blocking and backward blocking of cues to relevance. But it was unsatisfying to base conclusions on a small subset of participants. Presumably, all people could learn such structures if given enough practice, but before subjecting people to endurance training, we explored other stimulus arrangements.

In order to facilitate learning, and for purposes of an experiment that can act as a proof of concept, we set up a cue arrangement in which it was natural to think of some cues being indicators of responses, and other cues being indicators of which response cues to attend to. The learners were instructed that they were to diagnose the fictitious disease associated with symptoms, but only indirectly, by learning which medical specialist knew about which symptoms. For example, a patient might have the symptoms heartburn and myalgia, for which Specialist 1 says the patient has disease F, but Specialist 2 says the patient has disease J. After the learner makes a guess about the disease, corrective feedback indicates that it was disease J, thereby implying that Specialist 2 knows about these symptoms. The learner should therefore learn that when symptoms heartburn and myalgia occur, s/he should attend to Specialist 2, and give the response stated by Specialist 2. Importantly, there is no correlation between symptoms and diseases across trials. For example, half the time that heartburn and myalgia occur, the correct disease is F, but half the time the correct disease is J. Specialist 2 always indicates the correct diagnosis, however, for these symptoms.

The cues that indicate the correct overt response are here called 'response cues'. In the present scenario, the medical specialists are the response cues. Other cues that indicate which response cues to attend to are here called 'context cues'. In the present scenario, the symptoms are the context cues. These appellations, i.e., response cue versus context cue, are potentially misleading. On the one hand, the so-called context cues do indicate a response, but that response is an essentially covert re-allocation of attention (which may or may not have overt signatures such as eye movements or other orienting responses). On the other hand, the so-called response cues need not be known in advance to be indicators of overt responses; the response cues might serve as context to other cues. Despite these infelicities of nomenclature, a key aspect of intuitively contextual information *is* captured by the 'context' cues: They are not directly predictive of the correct overt response. The context cues only indicate which response cues to attend to, and the response cues, in turn, indicate which overt response to make.

Method

Design

Table 11.1 shows the design components of the experiment. Each phase has a different arrangement of context cues. In the Single Context phase, a single context cue is present with two Specialists who give conflicting diagnoses. For example, a trial might consist of $A_{S1}S1_FS2_J \rightarrow F$, which means that context cue A_{S1} occurred with specialists $S1_F$ and $S2_J$, with correct diagnosis F. The subscripts on the cues denote what the cue is intended to indicate. The notation A_{S1}, for example, means that cue A indicates specialist S1. This correspondence had to learned, however. Notice that across the eight cases of the Single Context phase, the context cue A occurs twice with outcome F and twice with outcome J. Hence the context cue is uncorrelated with the correct diagnosis. In all cases of the Single Context phase, only a single context cue occurs.

In the Redundant Context phase, some cases had two context cues. In particular, context cues A and B occurred together, and context cues C and D occurred together. As these context cues never occurred separately, they

Table 11.1 Components of the experiment design

Phase	Items	
Single Context	A_{S1} $S1_F$ $S2_J \rightarrow F$	A_{S1} $S1_F$ $S3_J \rightarrow F$
	A_{S1} $S1_J$ $S2_F \rightarrow J$	A_{S1} $S1_J$ $S3_F \rightarrow J$
	E_{S3} $S3_F$ $S2_J \rightarrow F$	E_{S3} $S3_F$ $S1_J \rightarrow F$
	E_{S3} $S3_J$ $S2_F \rightarrow J$	E_{S3} $S3_J$ $S1_F \rightarrow J$
Redundant Context	A_{S1} B_{S1} $S1_F$ $S2_J \rightarrow F$	$A_{S1}B_{S1}$ $S1_F$ $S3_J \rightarrow F$
	A_{S1} B_{S1} $S1_J$ $S2_F \rightarrow J$	A_{S1} B_{S1} $S1_J$ $S3_F \rightarrow J$
	$C_{S2}D_{S2}$ $S2_F$ $S1_J \rightarrow F$	$C_{S2}D_{S2}$ $S2_F$ $S3_J \rightarrow F$
	C_{S2} D_{S2} $S2_J$ $S1_F \rightarrow J$	$C_{S2}D_{S2}$ $S2_J$ $S3_F \rightarrow J$
	E_{S3} $S3_F$ $S2_J \rightarrow F$	E_{S3} $S3_F$ $S1_J \rightarrow F$
	E_{S3} $S3_J$ $S2_F \rightarrow J$	E_{S3} $S3_J$ $S1_F \rightarrow J$
Test: Conflicting Context	A_{S1} C_{S2} $S1_F$ $S2_J \rightarrow ?$	A_{S1} C_{S2} $S1_J$ $S2_F \rightarrow ?$
	A_{S1} D_{S2} $S1_F$ $S2_J \rightarrow ?$	A_{S1} D_{S2} $S1_J$ $S2_F \rightarrow ?$
	B_{S1} C_{S2} $S1_F$ $S2_J \rightarrow ?$	B_{S1} C_{S2} $S1_J$ $S2_F \rightarrow ?$
	B_{S1} D_{S2} $S1_F$ $S2_J \rightarrow ?$	B_{S1} D_{S2} $S1_J$ $S2_F \rightarrow ?$

Note: An item is shown in the format, Cues→Correct Response. The subscripts on the cues Indicate the design's intended correspondence from that cue. Cues A_{S1}, B_{S1}, C_{S2}, D_{S2}, and E_{S3} are symptoms. Cues $S1_F$, $S1_J$, $S2_F$, $S2_J$, $S3_F$, and $S3_J$ are specialists. Responses F and J are disease labels.

are called 'redundant'. As in the single-context phase, all context cues are uncorrelated with the correct diagnosis.

Notice that when the single-context phase occurs before the redundant-context phase, the context cues instantiate a standard blocking sequence. People learn first that context cue A indicates specialist 1, and then people see that context cue A with context cue B also indicate specialist 1. There may be blocking of learning about the redundant cue B. When the redundant-context phase occurs before the single-context phase, this constitutes a backward blocking design for the context cues.

Blocking is assessed in the test phase, wherein conflicting cues appear together. In particular, cue A_{S1} appears with either C_{S2} or D_{S2}, and cue B_{S1} appears with either C_{S2} or D_{S2}. If context cue B_{S1} is blocked, then when it is paired with either C_{S2} or D_{S2}, the response appropriate to Specialist 2 should be given, in preference over the response appropriate to Specialist 1. As a partial test that Specialist 2 is not favored generically whenever conflict occurs, the cases in which A_{S1} appears with either C_{S2} or D_{S2} should favor Specialist 1, or at least not Specialist 2. This issue is addressed further in the discussion after the results are reported.

There were three different 'epochs' of the experiment. Each epoch had the phases shown in Table 11.1, in different orderings or with different types of feedback. The first epoch was a backward blocking sequence (redundant-context phase before single-context phase), but with the correct specialist explicitly and directly indicated by corrective feedback. This design constituted a replication of the backward blocking design of Kruschke and Blair (2000, Experiment 3), except that the present procedure used a shorter-duration training to criterion(details of which are described below). The hope was that by replicating a previous design known to produce backward blocking, we would observe the effect here too.

The second epoch was a forward blocking sequence(single-context phase before redundant-context phase), with the correct specialist indicated only indirectly and implicitly via the correct diagnosis. In other words, this epoch was trained as shown in Table 11.1. New symptoms were used in all epochs, so that novel learning was involved. As forward blocking tends to be more robust than backward blocking (e.g., Kruschke and Blair, 2000; Shanks, 1985), it was hoped that we would be able to observe forward blocking even in this complex, indirect-feedback situation. This sort of procedure has never been reported before, as far as we know.

The third epoch was a backward blocking sequence (redundant context before single context), with the correct specialist indicated indirectly via the correct diagnosis. In other words, it was just like the second epoch, but with the phases of training reversed. This epoch constituted the main focus of the experiment. We hoped to observe backward blocking of context cues. Notice that the stimulus–outcome structure of Epoch 3 is identical to that of Epoch 1; only the response and feedback are different between the two epochs.

Procedure

Table 11.1 shows one 'block' of trials in each phase. Within each block, the cases were presented in a random order. Training continued in each phase until accuracy in a block exceeded 87% correct, meaning at least 7 correct in 8-trial blocks or at least 11 correct in 12-trial blocks. The maximum number of blocks allowed in each phase was 8, at which point training progressed seamlessly to the next phase. Each test block was repeated twice. The entire experiment took approximately 20 minutes or less.

All trials progressed in a seamless series. There were no pauses or markers between phases. When a new epoch began, the novel symptoms appeared. The response prompt for each trial indicated whether the learner was to guess the correct specialist (in epoch 1) or the correct diagnosis(in epochs 2 and 3).

Stimuli

Figures 11.2 and 11.3 show screen shots of the stimuli. Figure 11.2 shows a prompt and feedback screen from the first epoch, in which the correct specialist is explicitly and directly trained. The prompt asks the learner to press one of the keys 1, 2, or 3, and the feedback states the correct specialist and highlights the correct specialist with a heavy outline. The correct diagnosis is also indicated by a white (instead of grey) background. Figure 11.3 shows a prompt and feedback screen from the second and third epochs, in which the correct specialist is only indirectly trained via the diagnosis. Notice that the correct specialist is not indicated; only the correct diagnosis is shown. (It is only a random coincidence that Figures 2 and 3 both show Specialist 3 without a diagnosis. Across trials, the 'missing' specialist was counterbalanced, as indicated in the design of Table 11.1.)

Results

Participants

Participants volunteered for partial credit in introductory psychology courses at Indiana University. This subject pool has a median age of approximately 19 years, and is about 50–60% female. Procedures for protection of human subjects were approved by the local Institutional Review Board. There were 188 participants.

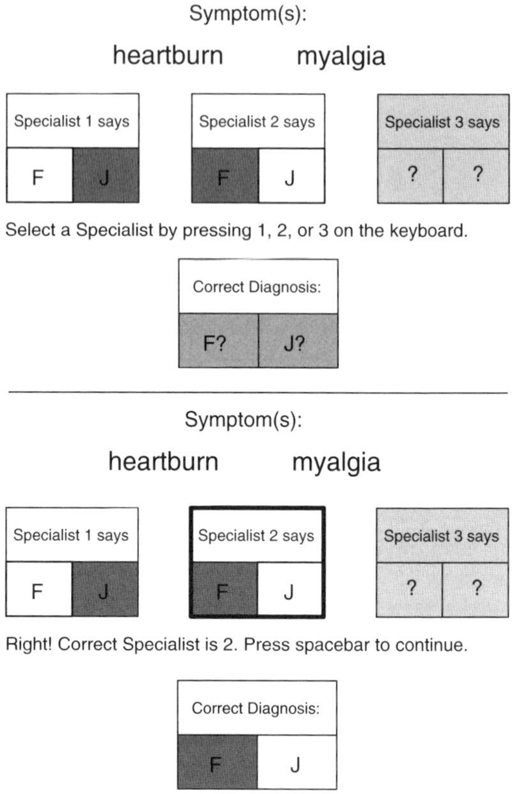

Fig. 11.2 For Epoch 1, involving explicit feedback about the correct specialist. *Upper*: Computer display for cues with response prompt. *Lower*: Computer display for cues with corrective feedback, after the correct response was made.

Learning criterion

For purposes of data analysis, epochs were excluded if accuracy did not achieve at least 58% in both training phases by the final block or training. The criterion was selected arbitrarily as a compromise between excluding too many subjects and including too many poor learners. Results did not change in any qualitative way with different criteria. The criterion resulted in 180, 122, and 131 subjects (out of 188) included in each of epochs 1, 2, and 3, respectively. Many or most of the excluded subjects appeared to have been unmotivated to learn, as their response times were on the order of 200 ms. or less, which indicates pressing a key as quickly as a stimulus appears without processing its attributes.

Choice in the test phase

Table 11.2 shows the choice preferences in the test phase, collapsed across participants. All three epochs show evidence of blocking, i.e., for the BC or BD tests, the response tends to be consistent with C or D more than with B.

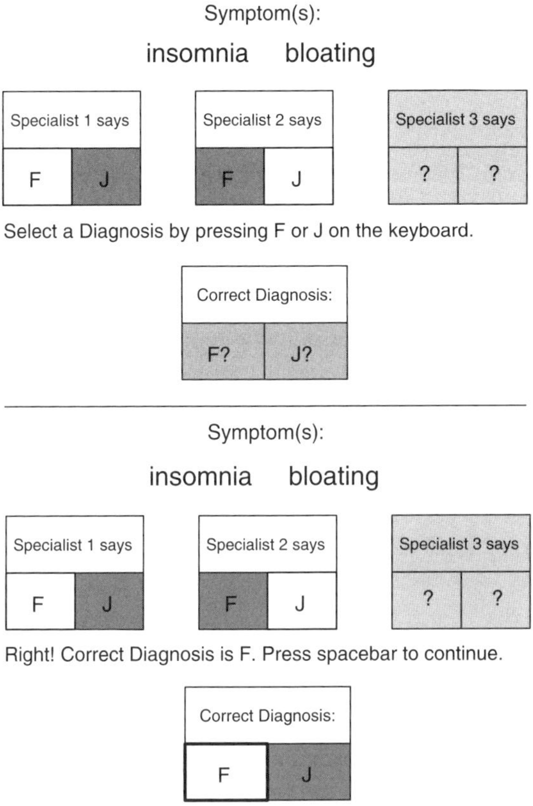

Fig. 11.3 For Epochs 2 and 3, involving feedback only about the correct diagnosis. *Upper*: Computer display for cues with response prompt. *Lower*: Computer display for cues with corrective feedback, after the correct response was made.

Table 11.2 Test phase response percentages, collapsed across subjects

	Response consistent with A/B or C/D					
	Epoch 1 Backward Blocking Explicit Specialist		**Epoch 2 Forward Blocking Indirect Feedback**		**Epoch 3 Backward Blocking Indirect Feedback**	
Test cues	A/B	C/D	A/B	C/D	A/B	C/D
AC or AD	54.5	45.5	59.8	40.2	52.3	47.8
BC or BD	42.1	57.9	44.5	55.5	45.3	54.7

The magnitude of the preference is weak, however. For example, the magnitude of backward blocking in Epoch 1 is notably weaker than that reported by Kruschke and Blair (2000).

We can only speculate as to why the blocking effect is so weak, but presumably it is because of the complex stimulus display and distraction by the disease diagnoses that were irrelevant in Epoch 1. Subsequent epochs also show weak magnitudes of blocking, presumably because of the difficulty of inferring the correct specialist indirectly from the diagnosis. We will say more about the magnitude of blocking in the discussion after the statistical analysis.

Bayesian statistical analysis

The data were analyzed using Bayesian methods. In a Bayesian analysis, a descriptive model of the data is defined, and the parameter values of the model are estimated. The Bayesian analysis yields an entire posterior distribution of parameter values, not merely a single best-fitting parameter value. One reason to prefer Bayesian methods over traditional null hypothesis significance testing (NHST) is that the Bayesian analysis yields an explicit distribution regarding the believability of various underlying choice probabilities, given the experiment data. Another reason to prefer a Bayesian approach is that individual differences are explicitly modelled and taken into account. In the following paragraphs, the model is first defined, followed by a description of how the posterior distribution was generated, followed, finally, by a description of the posterior distribution itself.

In the test phase of any epoch, each participant saw the two context types (i.e., either AC/AD or BC/BD) eight times, because there were two repetitions of the test block in Table 1. For each test type, the ith participant's 8 responses to that type were modeled as a random sample from a binomial distribution having underlying probability $\theta_{A/B,i}$ of selecting the response consistent with the A or B cue, and probability $\theta_{C/D,i} = 1 - \theta_{A/B,i}$ of selecting the response consistent with the C or D cue.

The individuals' probabilities, $\theta_{C/D,i}$, were modeled as a random selection from an overarching beta distribution that had (1) a parameter $\mu_{C/D}$ that specifies the central tendency of the group, and (2) a parameter κ that specifies how tightly the individuals were clustered around that central tendency. (In detail, the two 'shape parameters' of the beta distribution for $\mu_{C/D}$ were $a = \mu_{C/D}\kappa + 1$ and $b = (1 - \mu_{C/D})\kappa + 1$.)

The primary goal of the analysis is to generate a posterior estimate of the $\mu_{C/D}$ parameter for each test type. The $\mu_{C/D}$ parameter represents the overall response propensity for the type of context. The value of $\mu_{C/D}$ can range between 0 and 1, and can be thought of as the underlying probability of responding consistently with the C/D cues. When $\mu_{C/D} > 0.5$, the C/D cues are dominating the competing cues. When $\mu_{C/D} < 0.5$, the C/D cues are being dominated by the competing cues. If there is blocking, then the analysis should show that the credible values of $\mu_{C/D}$ are greater than 0.5, when the competing cue is B.

The hyperprior on $\mu_{C/D}$ was a uniform on the interval (0,1). This means that the prior was very noncommittal and gave the full range of $\mu_{C/D}$ values equal credibility. The hyperprior on κ was a gamma density with shape and rate parameter values of 0.01 (censored at 0.3 so that the random samples in the MCMC chain did not cause overflow errors in the beta density). This again means that the prior on κ was very noncommittal, allowing a huge range of possibilities, but emphasizing small values of κ that reflect large individual differences and a conservative estimate of $\mu_{C/D}$. The posterior distributions were robust to reasonable changes in the diffuse hyperpriors.

This hierarchical model allowed individual differences to be captured by variation in participant-level binomial probabilities, which in turn were mutually informed by being modeled as representative samples from the same higher level beta distribution. The higher level beta distribution captures across-subject response tendencies for each context type. The posterior certainty in the beta parameters depends on the consistency of response tendencies across subjects.

There is no general analytical solution for deriving the forms of the posterior distributions in hierarchical models. Nevertheless, the posteriors can be accurately estimated by generating large representative samples. The large samples include parameter values that are consistent with the data and the prior. The samples are generated by taking a random walk through the high-dimensional parameter space. Each step in the walk lands on a point for which the combination of parameter values is credible, given the data. Thus, after a large number of steps in the random walk, the sampled points provide an accurate reflection of the underlying continuous posterior distribution. The distribution of points also inherently reveals any correlations among credible parameter values.

The posterior distribution was determined by Markov chain Monte Carlo (MCMC) approximation. The program for generating the sample was written in the R language (Ihaka and Gentleman, 1996), using the BRugs interface (Thomas, 2004) to the OpenBUGS version (Thomas, O'Hara, Ligges, and Sturtz, 2006) of BUGS (Gilks,Thomas, and Spiegelhalter, 1994). Three parallel MCMC chains were simulated, using a burn-in of 10,000 steps and thinning of 200 steps. This burn-in and thinning produced well-mixed chains with small auto-correlation, so the posterior sample is very trustworthy. From each of the three chains, 1,000 steps were retained to represent the posterior, yielding 3,000 representative parameter values.

Figure 11.4 shows histograms of the believable values of the $\mu_{C/D}$ parameters. The upper three histograms indicate results from Epoch 1, i.e. backward

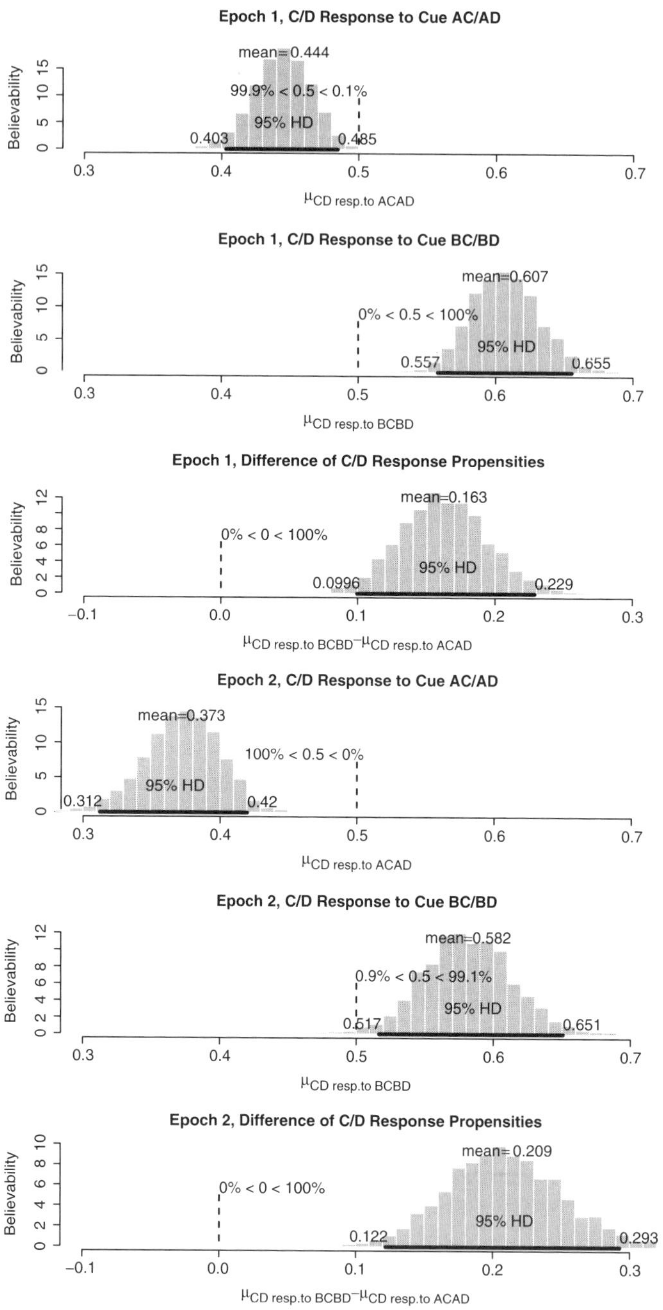

Fig. 11.4 Posterior distribution of C/D preference for the group. *Upper three histograms*: Epoch 1; backward blocking with direct feedback. *Middle three histograms*: Epoch 2; forward blocking with indirect feedback. *Lower three histograms (next page)*: Epoch 3; backward blocking with indirect feedback. The dark bar labeled '95% HD' spans the 95% highest density interval, such that all parameter values within the interval have higher believability than values outside the interval, and the interval covers 95% of the believable values.

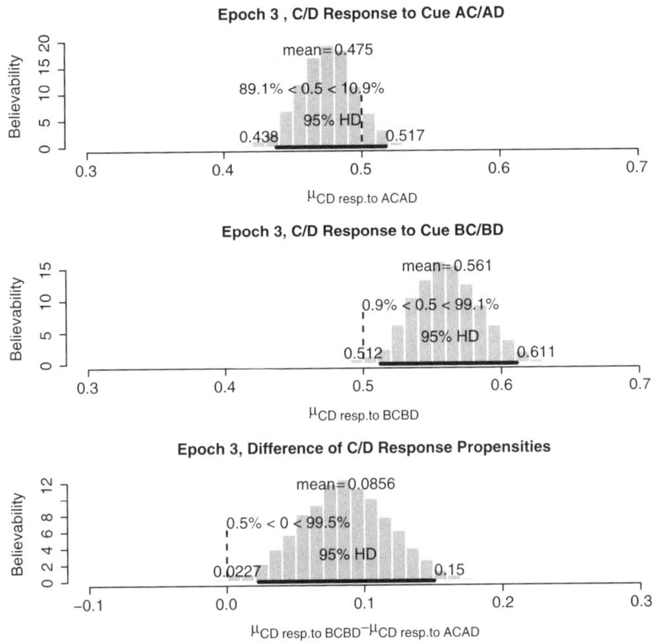

Fig. 11.4 (continued)

blocking with direct feedback regarding the relevant specialist. The upper histogram indicates that for the test probes AC or AD, the credible values of the response propensity are virtually all less than 0.5, i.e., people prefer the response consistent with cue A. The second histogram of the set indicates that for test probes BC or BD, the credible response propensities are all well above 0.5, indicating a robust backward blocking effect. The third histogram in the set indicates that the difference between the two types of probes is credibly different from zero.

The histograms in Figure 11.4 for Epoch 2 indicate that there was credible forward blocking of cues to relevance, even when there was only indirect feedback regarding the correspondence of context cues to response cues. In particular, virtually all the believable response propensities to BC or BD cues are in favor of the C/D consistent response.

Most important for our present purposes, the lower set of histograms in Figure 11.4 for Epoch 3 indicates that there was credible *backward* blocking of cues to relevance, even when there was only indirect feedback regarding the correspondence of context cues to response cues. Specifically, the distribution that estimates the C/D propensities for cues BC or BD falls mostly (99.1%)

above 0.5. The lowest histogram shows that the C/D propensity for BC or BD tests is larger than the C/D propensity for AC or AD tests, with nearly all the distribution falling above zero.

Summary and discussion of experiment results

The Bayesian analysis of the data incorporated a model of individual differences and yielded an explicit representation of credible response propensities. The analysis revealed that it is highly credible that there is forward and backward blocking of cues to relevance.

For devotees of the twentieth century ritual of null hypothesis significance testing, a chi-square analysis is hereby provided. In Table 11.2, for each epoch's 2×2 table, a chi-square test of independence was conducted on the raw frequencies. These three tests correspond to the lowest histogram in each of the three panels of Figure 11.4. For Epoch 1, $\chi^2(df = 1, N = 2880) = 44.55, p < 0.001$; for Epoch 2, $\chi^2(df = 1, N = 1952) = 46.19, p < 0.001$; for Epoch 3, $\chi^2(df = 1, N = 2096) = 9.90, p < 0.002$. A chi-square test can also be conducted on the the BD trials alone, i.e., the lower row of Table 11.2. These three tests correspond to the middle histogram in each of the three panels of Figure 11.4. For Epoch 1, $\chi^2(df = 1, N = 1440) = 36.10, p < 0.001$; for Epoch 2, $\chi^2(df = 1, N = 976) = 11.95, p < 0.001$; for Epoch 3, $\chi^2(df = 1, N = 1048) = 9.16, p < 0.003$. The implication from these tests is that there was highly significant backward blocking in all three Epochs. These standard analyses assume that all individuals have the same underlying magnitude of response preference. This is not a reasonable assumption; the Bayesian analysis does not make it. Furthermore, the standard computation of p values assumes that N was fixed in advance, and data collection was stopped when that N was reached. In fact, the data were collected for a set number of weeks during which participants volunteered, and data were excluded if learners did not reach the accuracy criterion. Bayesian analysis has no reliance on why data collection stopped. Notice also that the Bayesian analysis provides a complete distribution for credible values of the parameters (in Figure 11.4), while the chi-square analysis provides no interval estimate.

As mentioned earlier, the magnitudes of the forward and backward blocking effects were weak. We speculate that the small effects occurred because processing the corrective feedback was effortful and interfered with attentional re-allocation. For example, when the corrective feedback indicates disease F, the learner must first determine which specialist is consistent with that outcome, before then being able to determine which symptoms are relevant to selecting that specialist. If processing of the feedback interferes with allocation of attention to symptoms, and if blocking of symptoms depends in part on attentional allocation, then the extra processing of the feedback may impair learned inattention to the blocked cue.

The limited variety of test trials in this particular experiment admits a different explanation of the results. In this alternative explanation, there is no blocking during learning, but there is instead a response bias at test. On tests involving BC or BD cues, the preference for C/D-consistent responses is a result of a response bias to choose specialist S2 whenever two context cues appear. The response bias is an inference from the training phases, for which it is the case that only two-cue contexts occurred when specialist S2 was relevant. This general bias is overcome on tests involving AC or AD cues, because the association from A to S1 is very strong. Only future experiments will be able to distinguish the two explanations, perhaps by including tests involving single-cue contexts. For example, the two test items $B_{S1}\,S1_F\,S2_J$ and $D_{S2}\,S1_F\,S2_J$ involve a single context cue, and therefore would not suffer the hypothesized two-context-cue bias toward specialist S2, but blocking would predict a difference in response preferences across the two items. Until follow-up experiments are conducted, we must rest with the argument that structurally analogous previous experiments, involving blocking of cues to outcomes instead of cues to relevance, have shown less ambiguous blocking phenomena (e.g., Kruschke and Blair, 2000).

The current results at least indicate proof of concept: In principle, it is possible for people to learn which context cues indicate which response cues to attend to. And, most importantly, we have demonstrated data consistent with backward blocking of cues to relevance. Future experiments will attempt to use context and response cues that are not so blatantly distinct as symptoms and medical specialists. With enough training, people should be able to learn in those situations too, and presumably also show backward blocking.

Modelling

The experiment of the previous section showed results consistent with backward blocking of contextual cues to relevance. In this section we show that the behavior can be mimicked by a locally Bayesian learning model in which the first layer learns to allocate attention and the second layer learns to generate outcomes.

The architecture of the model is illustrated in Figure 11.5. Each node in the lower layer represents a cue that can be present or absent. Notice that the lower layer consists of 11 cues, including the symptoms and the specialist information. The symptoms and specialists were presented in the experiment

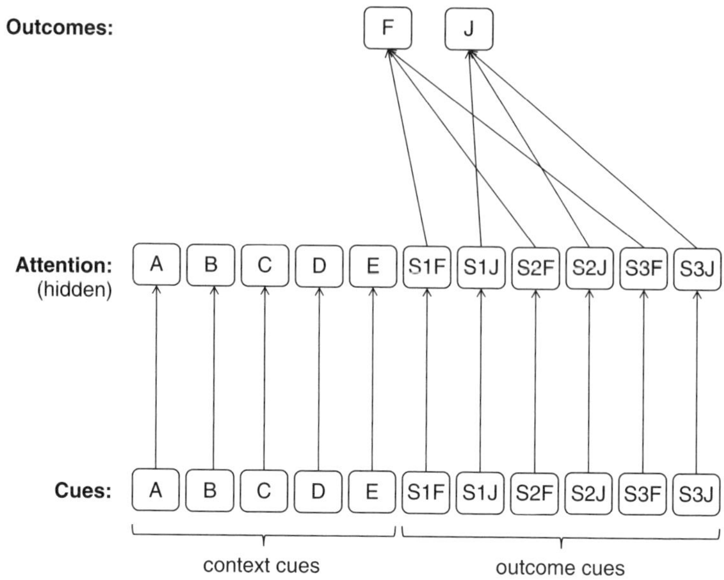

Fig. 11.5 Model architecture. Arrows denote the most credible associations at the beginning of training (i.e., the mean of the prior distribution). The cues are marked at the bottom as context or outcome cues, but this marking is purely for the benefit of the reader, as the model does not 'know' which cues are context cues and which cues are outcome cues.

as different types of cues, but in principle they are both just present/absent bits of information. For example, when stimulus A_{S1} $S1_F$ $S2_J$ is presented, input nodes A, S1F, and S2J are activated.

The middle layer, otherwise called the hidden layer, represents attentionally gated cue activations. Each input cue has a corresponding node in the hidden layer. By default, each cue calls attention to itself, indicated in Figure 11.5 by the 1-to-1 arrows. Learning can cause the magnitude of the 1-to-1 connection to change, and also generate 'lateral' connections between input cues and attentional nodes. In particular, when a cue is blocked, the 1-to-1 connection from that cue to its own attentional gate may be reduced, and the lateral connection to its attentional gate from the blocking cue may become negative. More accurately described, one would say that lower values of the 1-to-1 connection become more believable, and negative values from the blocking cue to the blocked attention node become more believable. (Griffiths and LePelley [2009] have shown that *forward* blocking of *response* cues is unlikely to produce strong negative lateral connections, in at least some situations. It is not yet known whether comparable experiments with backward blocking would lead to analogous conclusions. The present model can accommodate these results, at least in principle, by modulating the relative learnabilities of lateral and 1-to-1 weights.)

The upper layer represents outcomes, which are disease diagnoses in the present application. The associations from attentionally gated cues to outcomes must be learned. In principle, any of the cues could be indicative of any outcome. In the present application, only the cues corresponding to medical specialists happen to be correlated with the correct diagnoses. Moreover, the experiment presented the specialist cues in such a way that the corresponding diagnosis was explicitly indicated. In other words, the associative links from specialists to diagnoses were already suggested, and therefore the model has these links built in, as shown in Figure 11.5 by the arrows fanning into the outcome nodes. Through learning, these links can be altered, and other links from cues to outcomes can be established.

In locally Bayesian learning, multiple hypotheses about the associative weights are maintained, for both layers of weights. Learning consists of shifting credibility from unlikely hypothetical weights to likely hypothetical weights. The arrows in Figure 5 indicate the hypothetical weights with highest credibility at the beginning of the experiment, before training.

Intuitively, locally Bayesian learning proceeds in Epoch 3 as follows. The first phase, involving redundant-context cues, has cases of A_{S1} B_{S1} $S1_F$ $S2_J$→F, among others (see Table 11.1). This phase causes credibility to be enhanced on positive connections from cues A and B to attention on S1F and S1J, and perhaps also causes credibility to be enhanced on negative connections from cues A and B to attention on S2F and S2J. In other words, the model learns that when symptoms A or B are present, attend to specialist 1 and ignore specialist 2. Because the lower layer is a Bayesian system that keeps track of multiple candidate weight combinations, the system 'knows' that the training cases could be explained by either (1) A indicating S1 and B being irrelevant, or (2) B indicating S1 and A being irrelevant, or (3) A or B indicating S1. All of these plausible weight combinations retain some credibility. In the second phase, involving single-context cues, there are cases of A_{S1} $S1_F$ $S2_J$→F, among others (see Table 11.1). Of the weight combinations that remained credible after the first phase, the ones involving cue A gain increased credibility, thereby reducing the credibility of the ones involving cue B alone. In other words, locally Bayesian learning on the lower layer can account for backward blocking of contextual cues to relevance.

The remainder of this section is devoted to a detailed description of a particular instantiation of this approach. In this particular instantiation, the outcome and attention nodes are modeled as individual Kalman filters. Kalman filters have been previously used by Dayan and Kakade (2001) to model backward blocking, and the idea of using layers of locally learning Kalman filters was mentioned by Kruschke (2006a, 2006b). We do not intend to argue that Kalman filters are the best way to instantiate the components of locally Bayesian learning. Indeed, Kalman filters can only represent linear mappings, and are therefore quite limiting. We use Kalman filters merely because they are convenient for computational tractability. Presumably the model structure used by Kruschke (2006b), which did not involve Kalman filters, would show similar qualitative behavior.

One goal of the detailed modeling is to demonstrate by computer simulation that the intuitive argument provided in the previous paragraphs is actually correct. A second goal of the reporting the mathematical details is to present novel derivations that have not been previously presented elsewhere. There is not sufficient space here to provide an extensive tutorial on Kalman filters, but a tutorial regarding Kalman filters applied to associative learning has been previously provided by Kruschke (2008). The reader, who is not concerned at this time with the mathematical implementation of the model, is invited to skip ahead to the next subsection where the model results are reported.

Formal description of layers of Kalman filters

The Kalman filter assumes that the output to be predicted is a scalar metric value y. In our experiment, the outcome is dichotomous (present/absent), which is represented as $y=1$ or $y=0$. The Kalman filter assumes that y is a linear function of the input vector $\vec{x}$ (thought of as a column matrix), with normally distributed noise in the output. The variance of the noise is the scalar value v. The associative weights are denoted by the vector $\vec{w}$ (thought of as a column matrix). Formally, then, the probability of a value y is

$$p(y \mid \vec{x}, \vec{w}, v) = \frac{1}{\sqrt{v}\,(2\pi)^{1/2}} \exp\left(-.5 \frac{(y - \vec{w}^T \vec{x})^2}{v} \right) \qquad (11.1)$$

The value of v is considered to be a known constant, fixed by the modeler. Equation 11.1 is the likelihood function that specifies the probabilistic output of any node in the model. The normal distribution in Equation 1 is also denoted $N(y \mid \vec{w}^T \vec{x}, v)$.

Each outcome and attention node is a distinct Kalman filter. For example, the node for outcome F is a Kalman filter for which $y = 1$ means F is present, and $y = 0$ means F is absent. The input to that outcome node is the vector of attentional values from the hidden layer. The attentional values are the (means of the) output values of the attentional Kalman filter nodes. Each attentional node is also a Kalman filter. The input to each attentional node is the vector of cue values.

In each Kalman filter, the value of $\vec{w}$ has uncertainty, meaning that each possible combination of weights has a degree of belief, and beliefs are spread over a wide range of weight combinations. When the model learns, belief is shifted toward weight combinations that are consistent with the training items. The initial state of the network has beliefs spread out symmetrically and diffusely over a wide range of weight combinations. The initial state is called the prior distribution. It is assumed to be normal with mean $\vec{\mu}$ (a column matrix) and covariance matrix **C**. Thus, the prior on $\vec{w}$ is

$$p(\vec{w} \mid \vec{\mu}, \mathbf{C}) = \frac{1}{\sqrt{|\mathbf{C}|}(2\pi)^{d/2}} \exp\left(-.5(\vec{w} - \vec{\mu})^T \mathbf{C}^{-1} (\vec{w} - \vec{\mu})\right) \qquad (11.2)$$

where $|\mathbf{C}|$ is the determinant of **C**, and d is the dimensionality of $\vec{w}$, i.e., the number of input nodes. Equation 11.2 is merely the well-known formula for the multivariate normal distribution, and Equation 11.1 is merely the special case of that formula when $d = 1$ and $\mu = \vec{w}^T \vec{x}$. The normal distribution in Equation 11.2 is also denoted $N(\vec{w} \mid \vec{\mu}, \mathbf{C})$.

The mean vector for the weights was set to all zeros except for specific components that represented initial correspondences. The mean vector on weights fanning in to the outcome nodes was initialized to represent the explicit mappings indicated by the specialists. Therefore the mean weight to F from S1F was set to 1, as was the weight to F from S2F, and to J from S1J, and so forth. These mean connection weights of 1 are represented by the arrows in Figure 11.5. The mean vector on weights fanning in to the attention nodes was initialized to represent the 1-to-1 correspondence of cues to attention, but also to take into account only partial attention to any given cue. Therefore the 1-to-1 connections were initialized arbitrarily at a mean value of 0.1. These 1-to-1 connections are represented by the arrows in Figure 11.5.

The prior covariance matrix for each node specifies the prior certainty in the mean values. Because the specialists gave explicit diagnoses, the mean weights from specialists to outcome nodes had very small variances, i.e., very high certainties. But the weights to the outcome nodes from the context attention nodes had prior variances that were large, to reflect great initial uncertainty. The prior covariance matrices for the attention nodes were likewise set with small variances on the specialist cues and large variances on the context cues. This was because of the prior assumption that specialists do not inform each other, but the symptoms handled by each specialist must be learned.

Prediction by a Kalman-filter node

In propagating activation up a succession of Kalman filter nodes, the input to the upper layer is the mean output of the lower layer. The mean output of a Kalman filter is simply

$$\begin{aligned}\bar{y} &= \int d\vec{w}\, p(\vec{w} \mid \vec{\mu}, \mathrm{C}) \int dy\, y\, p(y \mid \vec{x}, \vec{w}, v) \\ &= \int d\vec{w}\, p(\vec{w} \mid \vec{\mu}, \mathrm{C})\, \vec{w}^T \vec{x} \\ &= \left(\int d\vec{w}\, p(\vec{w} \mid \vec{\mu}, \mathrm{C})\, \vec{w}\right)^T \vec{x} \\ &= \vec{\mu}^T \vec{x}\end{aligned} \tag{11.3}$$

In the architecture we use for expressing attentional gating, the attentional Kalman filter acts as a multiplier on the input cue. Formally, the hidden layer activation that acts as the input to the outcome nodes is the mean activation of the attentional Kalman filters times the corresponding input cue activations: $x_i^{hid} = \bar{y}_i x_i^{cue}$ where $\bar{y}_i$ is the mean output of the i-th attentional Kalman filter, as determined from Equation 11.3.

Learning by a Kalman-filter node

The values of $\vec{\mu}$ and C serve as the prior distribution for the trial's Bayesian updating. On a given trial, the input vector is $\vec{x}$ and the correct output value, a.k.a. the target, is denoted t (a scalar). It turns out (Meinhold and Singpurwalla, 1983) that the Bayesian updating formula simplifies to the following expressions:

$$\vec{\mu}' = \vec{\mu} + \mathrm{C}\,\vec{x}\left[v + \vec{x}^T \mathrm{C}\vec{x}\right]^{-1}\left(t - \vec{x}^T \vec{\mu}\right) \tag{11.4}$$

$$\mathrm{C}' = \mathrm{C} - \mathrm{C}\,\vec{x}\left[v + \vec{x}^T \mathrm{C}\,\vec{x}\right]^{-1} \vec{x}^T \mathrm{C} \tag{11.5}$$

Thus, for any given outcome node or attention node, Equations 11.4 and 11.5 are applied to update its beliefs. The computational simplicity of these updating equations is was makes the Kalman filter appealing as an implementation of Bayesian learning. The target for the outcome nodes is explicitly indicated by corrective feedback, and the input to the outcome nodes is the pattern of attentional activation as defined in the previous paragraph. For the attentional nodes, the input is the cue activation, but the target values for the attentional nodes will be defined in the next subsection.

In summary, at the beginning of a trial, the weight vector is distributed as in Equation 11.2. Then target and input for the trial are provided, and beliefs regarding credible weight combinations are adjusted by Bayes' rule. The posterior distribution of the weights conveniently turns out to be again normal, with mean and covariance given by Equations 11.4 and 11.5.[2]

Finding the attention that maximizes a desired output

To find a target for the attention nodes, we want to find the attentional input to the outcome nodes that would maximize the probability of the correct outcome. In other words, given the target outcome values, t_k of outcome k, we want to find the attention-node values $\vec{x}_t$ that maximize the joint probability of the outcome values:

$$\begin{aligned} \vec{x}_t &= \arg\max_{\vec{x}} \prod_k p\left(t_k \mid \vec{x}\right) \\ &= \arg\max_{\vec{x}} \prod_k \int d\vec{w}\; p(t_k \mid \vec{x}, \vec{w}, v)\, p(\vec{w} \mid \vec{\mu}, \mathrm{C}) \end{aligned} \tag{11.6}$$

A formal identity regarding the product of Gaussians states that

$$\begin{aligned} & N(\vec{w} \mid \vec{\mu}, \mathrm{C})\, N(\vec{x}^T \vec{w} \mid t, v) \\ &= N(t \mid \vec{x}^T \vec{\mu}, v + \vec{x}^T \mathrm{C} \vec{x})\, N(\vec{w} \mid \vec{m}, \mathrm{V}) \end{aligned}$$

where

$$\begin{aligned} \vec{m} &= \mathrm{V}\left(\mathrm{C}^{-1}\mu + \vec{x}t / v\right) \\ \mathrm{V} &= \left(\mathrm{C}^{-1} + \vec{x}\vec{x}^T / v\right)^{-1} \end{aligned}$$

[2] The full Kalman filter also assumes that the distribution of $\vec{w}$ changes in time, separately from and before any updating in beliefs inferred from observed data. This dynamic aspect of the weights is assumed to be linear at any given trial, so that the mean weights are dynamically changed into some linear transformation of the current mean weights. Dayan *et al.* (2000) used this mechanism to model unbiased diffusion of weights through time. Because afficianados of the Kalman filter may wonder what we did with the dynamic mechanism, it is summarized in this footnote. Denote the dynamic linear transformation by **D**. There is also assumed to be some additive change in the covariances of the weights; typically this is thought of as a constant increment in the uncertainty of the weights as time progresses. Denote the added uncertainty by **U**. Formally, then, at the beginning of each trial, the weight distribution is dynamically changed as follows: $\vec{\mu}^* = \mathbf{D}\vec{\mu}$ and $\mathrm{C}^* = \mathbf{D}\mathrm{C}\mathbf{D}^T + \mathbf{U}$. In all of our applications, we assume that **D** is the identity matrix and that $\mathbf{U} = 0$. That is, we assume that the weights are not systematically changing through time. This restriction implies that all the behavior of the model comes from Bayesian learning, not from additional dynamic assumption.

Hence the integral in Equation 11.6 can be rewritten as

$$\begin{aligned}
&\int d\vec{w}\; p(t_k|\vec{x},\vec{w},v)\; p(\vec{w}\,|\,\vec{\mu},\mathrm{C}) \\
&= \int d\vec{w}\;\; N\left(t_k\,|\,\vec{x}^T\vec{w},v\right) N\left(\vec{w}\,|\,\vec{\mu},\mathrm{C}\right) \\
&= \int d\vec{w}\;\; N\left(t_k\,|\,\vec{x}^T\vec{\mu},v+\vec{x}^T\mathrm{C}\vec{x}\right) N\left(\vec{w}\,|\,\vec{m},\mathbf{V}\right) \\
&= N\left(t_k\,|\,\vec{x}^T\vec{\mu},v+\vec{x}^T\mathrm{C}\vec{x}\right)\int d\vec{w}\; N\left(\vec{w}\,|\,\vec{m},\mathbf{V}\right) \\
&= N\left(t_k\,|\,\vec{x}^T\vec{\mu},v+\vec{x}^T\mathrm{C}\vec{x}\right)
\end{aligned} \qquad (11.7)$$

We used numerical approximation(specifically a Newton-Raphson method applied to the derivative) to find the $\vec{x}$ that maximizes Equations 11.6 and 11.7.

Model result: Single-layer Bayesian model fails

The experiment was designed such that no context cue is individually correlated with the correct diagnosis. Inspection of Table 11.1 reveals that every context cue occurs as often with outcome *F* and with outcome *J*. Therefore, a single-layer Kalman filter is unable to learn the correct responses in either the single-context phase or the redundant-context phase.

Because complex models have an uncanny way of confounding intuitions, especially when applied to complex designs, we simulated a single-layer Kalman filter to be sure that such a model truly was unable to learn the mapping. The results verified that the model could only produce 50–50 (i.e., chance) responding for Epochs 2 and 3.

Model result: Locally Bayesian learning succeeds

To fit the output of the model to the human response proportions in Table 11.2, we had to map the model output, expressed as $\bar{y}_k$, to response proportions. We did this via the often used softmax rule: $p(K) = \exp(\gamma\bar{y}_K)/\sum_k \exp(\gamma\bar{y}_k)$, where $\gamma > 0$ is a parameter called the 'decisiveness' of the choice. When γ is large, small differences in the outcome activations lead to large differences in choice proportion, but when γ is small, outcome activations must be very different to produce much difference in choice proportion. We arbitrarily set $\gamma = 1$.

The only free parameter was the noise variable v in Equation 11.1. The noise parameter acts much like a learning rate, as can be seen by its appearance in the update Equations 11.4 and 11.5. When v is larger, learning is slower.

The model was trained in each phase on the median number of blocks that human learners took. For successive phases in the three consecutive epochs, the median number of blocks was 3, 2, 4, 2, 3, and 2, respectively. The average of 40 simulated subjects, each with a different permutation of trials within

Table 11.3 Locally Bayesian model behavior

	Response consistent with A/B or C/D					
	Epoch 1 Backward Blocking Explicit Specialist		Epoch 2 Forward Blocking Indirect Feedback		Epoch 3 Backward Blocking Indirect Feedback	
Test cues	A/B	C/D	A/B	C/D	A/B	C/D
AC or AD	56.1	43.9	56.2	43.8	56.0	44.0
BC or BD	44.2	55.8	44.4	55.6	44.3	55.7

blocks, was used as the model prediction. The fit of the model was measured simply as sum-squared-deviation between the human response percentages in Table 11.2 and the corresponding model response percentages.

The best fit used $v = 0.047$, and the average model output is shown in Table 11.3. The model shows forward and backward blocking very similar to the human preferences in Table 11.2. The qualitative trend of the model is quite robust against changes in parameter values. The main point of the simulation is to demonstrate that the locally Bayesian model does indeed produce backward blocking of cues to relevance, as shown by the model behavior in Epoch 3. The magnitude of this backward blocking can be made larger with other parameter values. The magnitude is small in this simulation specifically to match the small magnitude shown by human learners.

The fit by the model is not 'spot on' the data, but the model uses only one free parameter and there are many aspects of the human procedure not directly imitated in the model procedure. For instance, all simulated subjects used exactly the median number of training blocks, but many human subjects took more blocks to learn. All simulated subjects used the same value of V, but presumably different human learners had different learning rates. The simulated model had a constant value of v throughout all three epochs, but human learners may have 'learned to learn' as they became familiar with the stimulus arrangement and task during training. And, perhaps most importantly, the simulation started the 1-to-1 attention links at the same neutral prior for every epoch, but people may have had progressively more certain priors in successive epochs. The purpose of the model simulation is to demonstrate that even with these simplifications, the locally Bayesian model shows robust backward blocking of cues to relevance.

Conclusion

We have provided some data that suggest that people exhibit backward blocking of cues to relevance. One way of modeling this behavior is with layers of locally Bayesian learning. The lower layer learns to allocate attention to cues, and the upper layer learns to produce outcomes based on the attended cues. Because there is Bayesian learning within each layer, the model can exhibit backward blocking of associations within each layer.

The novel contributions of this chapter are (1) the empirical suggestion of backward blocking of cues to relevance, and (2) the implementation of locally Bayesian learning as layers of Kalman filters. Backward blocking of cues to relevance may justify locally Bayesian learning in the attentional layer of Kruschke's (2006) model. The results of the new experiment reported here may have alternative interpretations, but we hope that this work may provoke interesting follow-up research to distinguish alternative accounts. Any competing model should also account for the spectrum of phenomena addressed by locally Bayesian learning applied to attentional learning (Kruschke, 2006b).

Acknowledgements

For help administering the experiments, thanks go to Kelsey Buckingham, Kevin Clemens, Alyssa Heggen, Kaitlyn Smith, Kari Vann, and Phaedra Willson. For providing pilot data and discussion, we thank Rima Hanania and Richard Hullinger. The editors, Chris Mitchell and Mike LePelley, provided helpful suggestions for clarification and discussion. Correspondence can be addressed to John K. Kruschke, Department of Psychological and Brain Sciences, Indiana University, 1101 E. 10th St., Bloomington IN 47405-7007, or via electronic mail to kruschke@indiana.edu. Supplementary information can be found at http://www.indiana.edu/~kruschke/

References

Chater, N., Tenenbaum, J. B., & Yuille, A. (Eds). (2006, July). Special issue: Probabilistic models of cognition. *Trends in Cognitive Sciences*, **10**(7), 287–344.

Chun, M. M. (2000). Contextual cueing of visual attention. *Trends in Cognitive Sciences*, **4**(5), 170–178.

Dayan, P., & Kakade, S. (2001). Explaining away in weight space. In T. Leen, T. Dietterich, & V. Tresp (Eds), *Advances in neural information processing systems* (Vol. 13, pp. 451–457). Cambridge, MA: MIT Press. Dayan, P., Kakade, S., & Montague, P. R. (2000). Learning and selective attention. *Nature Neuroscience*, **3**, 1218–1223.

De Houwer, J. & Beckers, T. (2002). A review of recent developments in research and theories on human contingency learning. *The Quartely Journal of Experimental Psychology*, **55B**, 289–310.

Deneve, S. (2008). Bayesian spiking neurons II: Learning. *Neural Computation*, **20**, 118–145.

Dickinson, A. (2001). Causal learning: Association versus computation. *Current Directions in Psychological Science*, **10**, 127–132.

Dickinson, A. & Burke, J. (1996). Within-compound associations mediate the retrospective revaluation of causality judgements. *Quarterly Journal of Experimental Psychology: Comparative and Physiological Psychology*, **49B**, 60–80.

Gilks, W. R., Thomas, A., & Spiegelhalter, D. J. (1994). A language and program for complex Bayesian modelling. *The Statistician*, **43**(1), 169–177.

Griffiths, O., & Le Pelley, M. E. (2009). Attentional changes in blocking are not a consequence of lateral inhibition. *Learning and Behavior*, **37**(1), 27–41.

Ihaka, R. & Gentleman, R. (1996). R: a language for data analysis and graphics. *Journal of Computational and Graphical Statistics*, **5**(3), 299–314. (With other contributors listed at http://www.r-project.org/)

Kamin, L. J. (1968). 'Attention-like' processes in classical conditioning. In M. R. Jones (Ed.), *Miami symposium on the prediction of behavior: Aversive stimulation* (pp. 9–33). Coral Gables, FL: University of Miami Press.

Kruschke, J. K. (2001). Toward a unified model of attention in associative learning. *Journal of Mathematical Psychology*, **45**, 812–863.

Kruschle, J. K. (2005). Learning involves attention. In G. Houghton (Ed.), *Connectionist models in cognitive psychology* (Ch 4, pp. 113–140). Hove, East Sussex: Psychology Press.

Kruschke, J. K. (2006a). Locally Bayesian learning. In Proceedings of the 28th Annual Conference of the Cognitive Science Society (pp. 453–458).

Kruschke, J. K. (2006b). Locally Bayesian learning with applications to retrospective revaluation and highlighting. *Psychological Review*, **113**(4), 677–699.

Kruschke, J. K. (2008). Bayesian approaches to associative learning: From passive to active learning. *Learning and Behavior*, **36**(3), 210–226.

Kruschke, J. K. (2009). Highlighting: A canonical experiment. In B. Ross (Ed.), *The psychology of learning and motivation* (Vol. 51, pp. 153–185). San Diego, CA: Academic Press.

Kruschke, J. K. & Blair, N. J. (2000). Blocking and backward blocking involve learned inattention. *Psychonomic Bulletin and Review*, **7**, 636–645.

Kruschke, J. K., Kappenman, E. S., & Hetrick, W. P. (2005). Eye gaze and individual differences consistent with learned attention in associative blocking and highlighting. *Journal of Experimental Psychology: Learning, Memory and Cognition*, **31**, 830–845.

Le Pelley, M. E., Beesley, T., & Suret, M. B. (2007). Blocking of human causal learning involves learned changes in stimulus processing. *The Quarterly Journal of Experimental Psychology*, **60**(11), 1468–1476.

Mackintosh, N. J. (1975). A theory of attention: Variations in the associability of stimuli with reinforcement. *Psychological Review*, **82**, 276–298.

Mackintosh, N. J., & Turner, C. (1971). Blocking as a function of novelty of CS and predictability of UCS. *Quarterly Journal of Experimental Psychology*, **23**, 359–366.

Markman, A. B. (1989). LMS rules and the inverse base-rate effect: Comment on Gluck and Bower (1988). *Journal of Experimental Psychology: General*, **118**, 417–421.

Meinhold, R. J., & Singpurwalla, N. D. (1983). Understanding the Kalman filter. *American Statistician*, **37**(2), 123–127.

Miller, R. R. & Matzel, L. D. (1988). The comparator hypothesis: A response rule for the expression of associations. In G.H. Bower (Ed.), *The psychology of learning and motivation: Advances in research and theory* (Vol. 22, pp. 51–92). San Diego, CA: Academic Press.

Mitchell, C. J., Harris, J. A., Westbrook, R. F., & Griffiths, O. (2008). Changes in cue associability across training in human causal learning. *Journal of Experimental Psychology: Animal Behavior Processes*, **34**(4), 423–436.

Nelson, J. B. (2002). Context specificity of excitation and inhibition in ambigous stimuli. *Learning and Motivation*, **33**, 284–310.

Rosas, J. M., Callejas-Aguilera, J. E., Ramos-Alvarez, M. M., & Abad, M. J. F. (2006). Revision of retrieval theory of forgetting: What does make information context-specific? *International Journal of Psychology and Psychological Therapy*, **6**(2), 147–166.

Shanks, D.R. (1985). Forward and backward blocking inhuman contingency judgement. *Quarterly Journal of Experimental Psychology: Comparative and Physiological Psychology*, **37B**, 1–21.

Sobel, D. M., Tenenbaum, J. B., & Gopnik, A. (2004). Children's causal inferences from indirect evidence: Backwards blocking and Bayesian reasoning in preschoolers. *Cognitive Science*, **28**, 303–333.

Tassoni, C. J. (1995). The least mean squares network with information coding: A model of cue learning. *Journal of Experimental Psychology: Learning, Memory, and Cognition*, **21**(1), 193–204.

Tenenbaum, J. B. & Griffiths, T. L. (2003). Theory-based causal inference. In S. Becker, S. Thrun, and K. Obermayer (Eds), *Advances in neural information processing systems* (Vol. 15, pp. 35–42). Cambridge, MA: MIT Press.

Thomas, A. (2004). *BRugs user manual (the R interface to BUGS).* http://mathstat.helsinki.fi/openbugs/data/Docu/ BRugs%20Manual.html.

Thomas, A., O'Hara, B., Ligges, U., & Sturtz, S. (2006, March). Making BUGS open. *R News*, **6**(1), 12–17.

Van Hamme,L.J.& Wasserman, E.A. (1994). Cue competition in causality judgments: The role of nonpresentation of compound stimulus elements. *Learning and Motivation*, **25**(3), 127–151.

Wills, A. J., Lavric, A., Croft, G. S., & Hodgson, T. L. (2007). Predictive learning, prediction errors, and attention: Evidence from event-related potentials and eye tracking. *Journal of Cognitive Neuroscience*, **19**(5), 843–854.

Xu, F. & Tenenbaum, J. B. (2007). Word learning as Bayesian inference. *Psychological Review*, **114**(2), 245–272.

Yang, L.-X., & Lewandowsky, S. (2003). Context-gated knowledge partitioning in categorization. *Learning, Memory*, **29**(4), 663–679.

Chapter 12

Brain systems of attention in associative learning

Peter C. Holland and Jean-Marie Maddux

Although attention has often been touted as the centre of psychology (e.g., Posner and Rothbart, 2007; Titchener, 1908), it remains a poorly specified construct. Everyone agrees that attention is an important component in the organization and control of behaviour, but what the term refers to varies from subfield to subfield and paradigm to paradigm. Most modern approaches stress that attention is not a monolithic construct, but instead a collection of processes that interact to guide behaviour according to current goals (Allport, 1989). Even within such a framework, in most of the literature, attention refers to processes that operate to control current actions. However, as many chapters in this volume attest, attention can also modulate information processing while learning about the stimuli in an environment, manifesting itself in behaviour only at some later time, when that learning is expressed. This role of attention in new learning seems nearly the exclusive domain of associative learning theorists; most recent reviews of both the psychology and neurobiology of human attention barely mention the possibility that modulation of attention might alter learning (e.g., Corbetta and Shulman, 2002; Knudsen, 2007; Posner and Rothbart, 2007; Raz and Buhle, 2006).

Much research from our laboratory has supported the assertion (Holland and Gallagher, 1999) that attentional processes that influence the acquisition of new learning and those that control current actions are often quite independent, being engaged under different circumstances and mediated by separate, but overlapping, brain systems (Maddux, 2008; Maddux *et al.*, 2007). In this chapter, we focus on brain systems involved in changes in processing of events that occur in simple associative learning procedures, that is, on what we have elsewhere called 'attention for learning'. However, this chapter is more about behavioural function than brain function. Our exploration of brain circuitry involved in basic attentional function in learning has revealed several interesting properties of associative learning, and has produced data relevant to the assumptions of a range of theories of associative learning.

In this chapter, we first outline a number of ways in which attention has been proposed to influence learning and action in the context of theories of associative learning. Next, we consider in more detail the relations between attention, outcome prediction, and prediction error ('surprise') by focusing on the Pearce-Hall (1980) model, which provides a framework for our study of brain systems involved in attentional processes in associative learning. In the main body of the chapter, we describe our studies and their implications for theories of associative learning. Finally, we briefly discuss the relation between these brain systems and those related to the control of action by learned cues.

Roles of attention in associative learning

Most associative learning theories include some explicit role for the direction of attention to conditioned stimuli. For example, the Rescorla-Wagner (1972) model includes a learning rate parameter (α) associated with each individual CS, which can be interpreted as the extent to which a CS engages attention. The greater a cue's α, the more rapid the learning about that cue. Similarly, in the presence of an array of CSs, the effects of any learning trial will be distributed among those CSs in proportion to their αs. Thus, such a model provides a simple mechanism for stimulus selection in learning, specifying, for each cue in an array, the proportion of the available associative strength that that cue will acquire. In addition, such a model also provides a means by which cues that grab more attention during learning are more likely to control behaviour later, at the time of action. Under most circumstances, cues with greater α's will have acquired stronger associations, and hence will be more likely to elicit learned behaviour later, often according to a winner-takes-all rule (e.g., Salzman and Newsome, 1994; Staddon, 2001). Notably, such stimulus selection at the time of action is not based on a performance rule for attention, but rather is the consequence of differences in attention at the time of learning.

Nevertheless, in the Rescorla-Wagner (1972) model, α is static and is solely a property of 'bottom up' aspects of attentional processing (Rescorla and Holland, 1982). That is, it is affected only by physical stimulus characteristics, and is not influenced by 'top-down' processing that depends on the subject's goals or expectations, typically based on prior learning. For example, as a cue is paired with a reinforcer more and more often, and becomes more 'meaningful' to the subject's goals, this view proposes that attention to that cue (i.e. α) remains unchanged. Although that cue is increasingly more likely to control behaviour than other cues, such increased control is not the consequence of increased attention to the cue but rather to its increased associative strength. Because α is unchanged, attention to that cue in some subsequent learning task, and hence new learning about that cue, will be unaffected by prior training except to the extent that its associations with the reinforcer complement or interfere with the demands of the new learning task.

By contrast, associative learning theories that are typically described as 'attentional' or 'CS processing' theories (Dickinson and Mackintosh, 1978; Le Pelley, 2004) endow learning rate and other CS-dependent parameters with dynamic properties. That is, attentional processing of CSs changes as a function of experience, especially exposure to the event contingencies that are responsible for the establishment of associations. For example, the values of learning rate parameters for cues (and cue dimensions in some cases) may increase when those cues or responding controlled by them are reinforced (e.g., Sutherland and Mackintosh, 1971), and/or decrease in the absence of such consequences (Mackintosh, 1975). In addition, within models that include the common assumption of limited attentional capacity, the presence of a highly attended stimulus may limit the attention that can be allocated to other cues. Thus, learning (and hence increased attention) to one cue might substantially alter attention to other simultaneously presented cues.

Dynamic attention theories vary as to whether attention influences the performance of learned responding directly, by the differential allocation of attention to various events at the time of action, or indirectly, by influencing the establishment of associative strength. For example, Mackintosh (1975, pp. 293–294) initially hesitated to assign a performance role for his dynamic, CS-dependent learning rate parameter. He argued that the more rapid accrual of associative strength to more-attended-to stimuli would guarantee that better-attended cues would control behaviour, even without a performance rule for attention. In Mackintosh's model, the 'associability' or learning rate parameter associated with an individual CS increased or decreased in learning episodes depending on the availability of better predictors of reinforcement. If a cue was the best available predictor of reinforcement, then its associability would increase, and if it was not, its associability would decrease. Better predictors would acquire associations more and more rapidly while poorer predictors would acquire them more and more slowly, guaranteeing a rapid divergence in the associative strengths of those cues. Thus, this model provides a positive feedback system that insures that the best predictors of reinforcement would come to control behaviour, without needing to assume commensurate differences in attention-grabbing power at the time of action.

However, as Mackintosh (1975, pp. 288–289, 293) noted, although this model allows for rapidly increasing associative strengths for the best predictors of reinforcement, it provides no mechanism by which associative strength might be lost once it is acquired by a poorer predictor. If α affects only learning, then even if α is subsequently driven to zero, any associations already acquired would remain capable of controlling behaviour. However, considerable evidence from redundant cue procedures (intermixed AB+ and A+ trials) indicates that a cue that is imperfectly correlated with reinforcement may first gain and then lose the ability to control responding as training proceeds, if it is accompanied by another more predictive cue. To deal with such evidence within his model, Mackintosh tentatively suggested that α might affect both learning and performance. In that case, as the α of a redundant cue is driven down, that cue will not only acquire associations more slowly but also be less able to control responding later in performance. More recently, several learning models (e.g., Kruschke, 2001; Schmajuk and Larrauri, 2006) have included formal roles for attention-related parameters in both learning and action.

By contrast, within another popular attention-based conditioning model, that of Pearce and Hall (1980), the role of the dynamic attention parameter (α) is explicitly limited to the acquisition of associations. This model provides a convenient frame of reference for much of our research, which led us to favour the view that modulation of attention in learning and in action are often influenced by different variables and engage different brain systems. Indeed, in some cases variables that enhance attention in action reduce attention for new learning. Although we comment briefly on parameters of attention in performance in the section 'Brain systems for control of attention for action in associative learning', the focus of this chapter is on attention in learning.

Prediction, prediction error, and attention: the Pearce-Hall (1980) model

Most modern associative learning theories assign an important role to prediction error, that is, the difference between predicted and actual outcomes. Our laboratory's research in associative learning is based on the notion that prediction error (which we will term 'surprise') has a range of consequences. The most commonly discussed consequence is what Schultz and Dickinson (2000) called the 'direct' effects of prediction error in determining reinforcement value. For example, within the Rescorla-Wagner (1972) model, the effectiveness of a given reinforcer is determined by the discrepancy ($\lambda - V\Sigma CS_{i \ldots k}$) between the intrinsic value of the reinforcer actually received (λ) and the expected value of that reinforcer. Importantly, the expected value is based on a composite of the associative strengths of all cues present on that trial, the so-called aggregate prediction. Thus, the more surprising a reinforcer, the more effective it is in establishing new learning on that trial. A notable feature of the Rescorla-Wagner (1972) model is that whereas the magnitude of the prediction error determines the momentary effective strength of the reinforcer, the sign of that error determines whether learning is excitatory or inhibitory. Thus, underexpectation of reward (positive prediction error) leads to excitatory learning and overexpectation (negative prediction error) leads to inhibitory learning.

Schultz and Dickinson (2000) also noted 'indirect' effects of prediction error on learning, whereby it alters learning by affecting some other learning parameter, that is, processing of events other than the surprising reinforcer itself. Pearce and Hall (1980) proposed that the absolute magnitude of the aggregate prediction error determines the associability of the available CSs, that is, their learning rate parameters (α's). Thus, $\alpha CS_A \approx |(\lambda - V\Sigma CS_{i...k}|$. As the US becomes better predicted on CS–US trials, associability of that CS declines, decreasing the amount of learning on subsequent trials, and generating the familiar negatively accelerated growth function. Therefore, as conditioning approaches asymptote, the associability of the CS will be driven low, making new learning about it relatively difficult. An implication of this simple rule is that the associability of such a predictive cue could be restored by degrading its predictive power. In support of this assertion, Hall and Pearce (1982) found that after extensive CS–US training, new learning about the CS, e.g., that is produced by pairing it with a new, larger US, was enhanced by first violating the well-established expectancy of the original US, by presenting the CS in the absence of any US. Within the model, this extinction trial would induce a prediction error and thus restore the CS's α, allowing rapid formation of an association when the CS was paired with the new US on the next trial.

The Pearce-Hall (1980) model can account for most simple conditioning phenomena without recourse to changes in the effectiveness of the US. Thus, their learning rule is $\Delta V_A = S_A \alpha_A \lambda$, whereby the change in the associative strength of CS_A is a product of the variable α_A and the constant US magnitude parameter, λ (S_A, not relevant to this discussion, is a constant also related to CS properties). However, to deal with overexpectation phenomena such as conditioned inhibition, Pearce and Hall (1980) introduced 'no-US' event representations and 'CS→no-US' associations, which counter CS→US associations. In most cases, this mechanism is formally comparable to assuming that negative prediction error produces inhibitory learning. Thus, in their model, prediction error produces both indirect and direct effects, with unsigned prediction error determining CS associability and negative prediction error determining inhibitory learning when reinforcers are overpredicted.

Our brain systems research suggests four broad conclusions about associability and prediction error in learning. First, mechanisms for increases and decreases in associability are separable, if not independent. Second, different brain systems are engaged by positive and negative prediction error. Third, the indirect effects of prediction error are not confined to changes in CS associability, but can also affect processing of reinforcers other than the surprising one. Thus, this research relates attention to reinforcement. Fourth, the direct and indirect consequences of prediction error, as described by Schulz and Dickinson (2000), may affect learning in very different ways.

Brain systems for changes in attention in associative learning

In this section, we first describe the basic observation that underlies all of our work: the amygdala central nucleus (CeA) is critically involved in surprise-induced enhancement of cue associability, but not expectancy-induced reductions in cue associability. Next, we describe a companion observation, that the hippocampus is critical to expectancy-induced decreases in cue associability but not surprise-induced enhancements of associability. Then, we discuss the results of experiments designed to trace the brain circuits involved in these changes, but which also have revealed interesting behavioural aspects of attention in associative learning. Finally, we discuss some recent evidence that leads to important limitations and extensions to our original conceptualization of these behavioural and brain systems. Most important, CeA's involvement in surprise-induced enhancement of event processing seems limited to cases of negative prediction error, but at the same time, CeA's involvement in such changes extends to enhancement of the effectiveness of reinforcers as well as the associability of signals.

Amygdala central nucleus is critical to surprise-induced enhancement of cue associability, but not expectancy-induced reductions in cue associability

The tasks we have used most frequently to examine changes in cue associability are a serial conditioning task first used by Wilson *et al.* (1992), and a combination of blocking, unblocking, and overshadowing procedures. These tasks permit assessing effects of brain manipulations on both increases and decreases in associability, although in somewhat different circumstances. Consider first the serial conditioning task (Table 12.1). In that task, two groups of rats are first given extensive training with a light→tone serial compound stimulus, which is reinforced with food on half the trials and nonreinforced on the other half. According to the Pearce-Hall (1980) model, because of the consistent relation between light and tone, the light's associability should be driven low as training continues. In a second phase, for the rats in the Shift condition, the

Table 12.1 Outline of design of serial prediction task

Group	Phase 1	Phase 2	Phase 3 (test)
Consistent	light→tone→food light→tone→nothing	light→tone→food light→**tone**→nothing	light→food
Shift	light→tone→food light→tone→nothing	light→tone→food light→**nothing**	light→food

The two treatment conditions differ only in the omission of the tone on nonreinforced trials in the Shift group in Phase 2. Enhanced associability of the light in that group is revealed by more rapid acquisition of learning in Phase 3. This design was first used by Wilson et al. (1992).

tone is omitted on nonreinforced trials, whereas rats in the Consistent condition continue to receive the same events as before. In the Shift condition, the unexpected omission of the tone should restore the light's associability. That associability is assessed in a final test phase by observing the acquisition of new learning to the light, typically involving trials in which the light is paired directly with food. Thus, the restored associability of the light after the surprising omission of the tone in Phase 2 should be reflected in more rapid light-food learning in test after the Shift treatment than in the Consistent condition. Intact rats and rats with sham lesions in a wide range of brain regions show this pattern of results (e.g., Figure 12.1a). In other experiments (e.g., Holland *et al.*, 2001; Wilson *et al.*, 1992), rats in the Shift condition have also shown faster

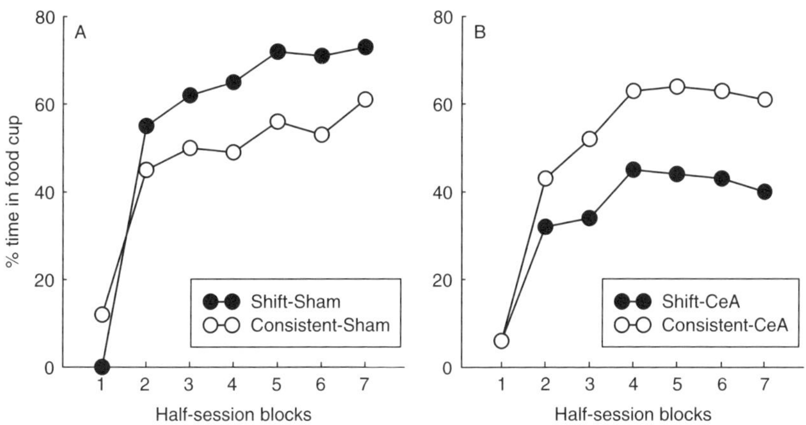

Fig. 12.1 Phase 3 test responding of rats with sham (A) or neurotoxic (B) lesions of the amygdala central nucleus (CeA) in a serial prediction task (Holland and Gallagher, 1993a). The lesions eliminated the normal shift-induced enhancement of the associability of the light.

acquisition of conditioned inhibition to the light when they are trained with a clicker→food, clicker+light→nothing discrimination in test. This observation of more rapid learning of both excitatory and inhibitory associations after exposure to the Shift condition further supports the claim that tone omission in this task enhances CS associability for subsequent learning rather than directly altering its associative strength at the time of the shift.

Holland and Gallagher (1993a) found that rats with excitotoxic lesions of the amygdala central nucleus (CeA) failed to show this more rapid acquisition of light-food learning in the Shift condition (Figure 12.1b). Indeed, such rats displayed significantly less responding than either the sham-lesioned rats in the Shift condition or the lesioned rats in the Consistent condition. Thus, we inferred that CeA was critical to some aspect of the enhancement or restoration of CS associability after surprise. At the same time, lesioned rats in the Consistent condition performed identically to sham-lesioned rats in that condition. From this observation, we inferred that CeA was not critical to the reduction of associability thought to occur with extensive confirmation of light-tone expectancies. Had these normal losses in associability been affected by the lesions, lesioned rats in the Consistent group would have shown more rapid light-food learning in the test than sham-lesioned rats trained in that condition.

The significantly lower responding of lesioned rats in the Shift condition than those in the Consistent condition deserves comment. In the absence of a mechanism by which the associability of inconsistent predictors is maintained at a higher level than that of events that consistently predict their consequences, there are reasons to expect more rapid learning in the test phase after the Consistent treatment than after the Shift treatment. Indeed, the serial conditioning task was devised in part to contrast the Pearce-Hall (1980) model with the Rescorla-Wagner (1972), Mackintosh (1975), and other models that do not assume such a mechanism. Note that in the Shift condition, whereas the light was accompanied by the tone on food-reinforced trials, the light was presented alone on nonreinforced trials. Thus, any direct light-food learning that may have occurred on light→tone→food trials would be extinguished in that group. By contrast, in the Consistent condition, the tone was also present on nonreinforced trials and thus might be expected to protect the light from extinction (e.g., Rescorla, 2003). Therefore, from the perspective of reinforcement theories such as the Rescorla-Wagner (1972) model, rats in the Consistent condition might enter the final test with greater conditioning to the light than rats in the Shift condition. Similarly, in latent inhibition procedures, many investigators have noted greater losses in the associability of a cue if it is presented alone than if it is presented in compound with another cue (e.g., Lubow *et al.*, 1982). Thus, from the perspective of attentional theories such as that of Mackintosh (1975), greater losses in the associability of the light might occur in the Shift than in the Consistent condition. From either of these perspectives, impairment of a Pearce-Hall (1980) enhancement mechanism might be anticipated to produce such a reversal, by revealing the normal operation of other learning processes.

A later experiment shed light on these possibilities. Holland *et al.* (2001) performed an experiment identical to the one just described, except that the associability of the light was assessed in a test of inhibitory rather than excitatory learning. After the Phase 2 Shift or maintained Consistent procedures, rats were trained on a clicker→food, light+clicker→ nothing discrimination. Among control rats, rats in the Shift condition showed more rapid acquisition of this discrimination than rats in the Consistent condition. Thus, coupled with Holland and Gallagher's (1993a) results, these results indicated that both inhibitory and excitatory learning about the light was enhanced by prior omission of the tone. Notably, as in Holland and Gallagher's (1993a) study, lesioned rats failed to show this Shift superiority in learning rate in test. Indeed, lesioned rats in the Shift condition showed poorer discrimination learning (although not significantly so) than lesioned rats in the Consistent condition. This latter observation is not consonant with the possibility that the Shift deficit relative to Consistent treatment among lesioned rats was due to greater extinction in the Shift procedure. In that case, a shift advantage in inhibitory learning would have been observed among lesioned rats as well as control rats. However, Holland *et al.'s* (2001) observations are consistent with the possibility that in the absence of a Pearce-Hall (1980) surprise mechanism, the Shift procedure results in greater *losses* in associability than the Consistent procedure (Lubow *et al.*, 1982). Thus, in normal rats, Pearce-Hall (1980) associability-enhancing mechanisms overcome Mackintosh (1975) associability-depressing mechanisms to produce a net Shift superiority in test.

Some additional observations lend further credence to these ideas. Evidence suggests that whereas surprise-induced enhancements in CS associability occur quickly, decreases in CS associability accrue more slowly and gradually. Using a between-subjects design, Holland, Bashaw, and Quinn (2002) found that extending the amount of Consistent training from 10 to 20 sessions further slowed the rate of learning about that light in the test phase, whereas variation in the number of Shift sessions from 5 to 20 had little effect on the enhancement of learning about the light observed in the test. Notably, when brief Shift training was used in rats with impaired function in CeA (e.g., Holland and Gallagher, 2006), those rats showed learning rates in test that were not significantly lower than those of Consistent rats. This observation is consistent with the notion that short Shift training, although sufficient to produce surprise-induced enhancements in normal rats, is insufficient to provide opportunities for additional losses in CS associability due to light-alone presentations that would normally be revealed.

We used a number of other training procedures to bolster our conclusions that CeA was critical for increases but not decreases in associability. First, rats with CeA lesions showed no deficits in latent inhibition (Holland and Gallagher, 1993a). Rats were preexposed to one visual cue (v1) and then given pairings of both that cue and of another visual cue (separately) with food (v1→food, v2→food). Within the Pearce-Hall (1980) model, because a preexposed cue becomes a reliable predictor of 'no event', that cue loses associability, and thus subsequent associative learning is slowed. Acquisition of conditioning to the preexposed cue (v1) was slower than that to the nonpreexposed cue (v2) in both CeA-lesioned and sham-lesioned rats. Thus, losses in associability found with simple preexposure were unaffected by CeA lesions. Second, blocking was unaffected by CeA lesions (Holland and Gallagher, 1993b). Light→food pairings were followed by pairings of a light+tone compound with food, followed by a final test of responding to the tone alone. Within the Pearce-Hall (1980) model, because the food is well-predicted by the light when the tone is introduced, the associability of that tone will decrease, and hence there will be little opportunity for the acquisition of tone–food associations. Both CeA- and sham-lesioned rats showed substantially less responding to the tone in test than control rats that received the same light+tone→food pairings without prior light→food training. Thus, to the extent that blocking is the result of such losses in associability, these results imply that CeA is uninvolved in associability losses.

By contrast, rats with CeA lesions failed to show enhanced associability after surprise in several other conditioning tasks that enhanced learning in sham-lesioned rats. First, we found that CeA lesions prevented the display of unblocking when the reinforcer was shifted down from a US1→US2 sequence to US1 alone (Holland and Gallagher, 1993b; Holland and Kenmuir, 2005). Rats in Unblocking and Blocking groups first received pairings of a light with a serial compound reinforcement that comprised the delivery of a food pellet followed 5 s later by more food. In a second phase, an auditory stimulus was added to the light and reinforced by either the same US1—US2 series in the Blocking group or by US1 alone in the Unblocking group. Within the Pearce-Hall (1980) model, although the associability of the added auditory cue should decrease in the Blocking group, the surprising omission of US2 should enhance or maintain the associability of that cue in the Unblocking group, permitting learning of excitatory associations between the added cue and US1. With sham-lesioned

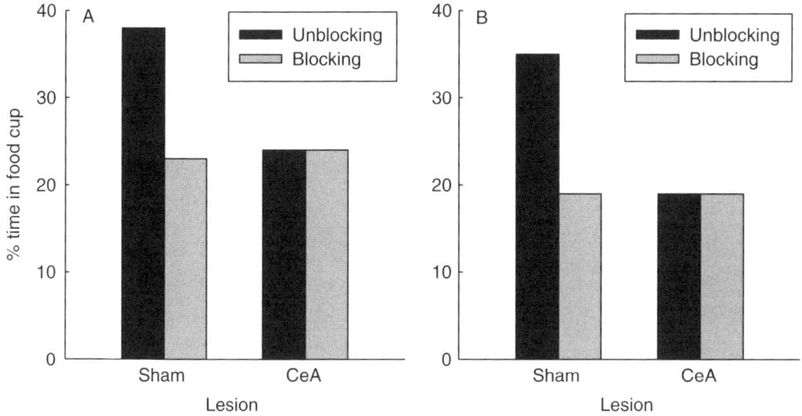

Fig. 12.2 Test responding of rats with sham or neurotoxic lesions of the amygdala central nucleus (CeA) to the added cue in the unblocking experiments of (A) Holland and Gallagher (1993b) and (B) Holland and Kenmuir (2005, Exp. 1). Lesioned rats failed to show unblocking.

rats, unblocking was observed (Figure 12.2): in both studies substantial conditioning to the auditory cue was observed in the Unblocking group but not in the Blocking group. However, rats with CeA lesions showed no evidence for unblocking.

Second, Holland *et al.* (2000b) showed that, unlike normal rats and pigeons (Rescorla, 1991), rats with CeA lesions failed to show enhanced learning of serial negative patterning discriminations relative to serial feature negative learning. Rats received either a noise→food, light→food, light→noise→nothing serial negative patterning or a noise→food, light→noise→nothing serial feature negative discrimination. Previous evidence suggested that both of these discriminations might be solved using 'occasion-setting' strategies, whereby the light set the occasion for the nonreinforcement of the noise (Ross and Holland, 1981). Given such a common solution strategy, the Pearce-Hall (1980) model somewhat paradoxically anticipates faster learning in the patterned discrimination condition because the ambiguous relation of the light with both the noise and the food maintains the light's associability in that group, whereas the consistent relation of the light with both the noise and 'no food' in the feature negative group would drive its associability down. Indeed, consistent with Rescorla's (1991) previous findings with pigeons, among sham-lesioned rats, learning was more rapid in the patterning group. However, rats with CeA lesions showed no such advantage, as would be expected if such lesions disabled an associability-enhancement mechanism (Fig. 12.3).

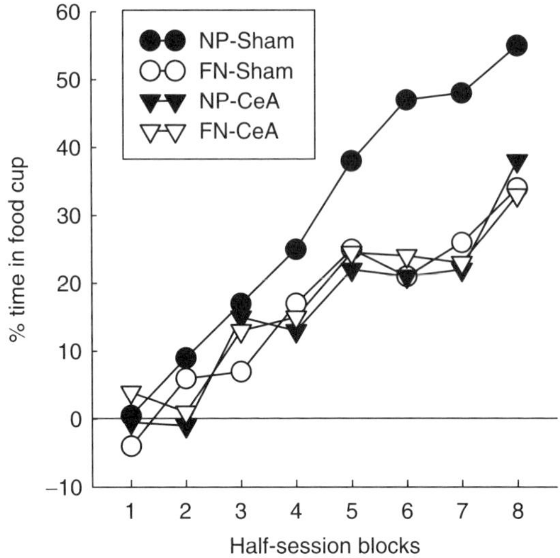

Fig. 12.3 Acquisition of negative patterning (NP; light→food, tone→food, light→tone→nothing) and feature negative (FN, tone→food, light→tone→nothing) discriminations by rats with sham or neurotoxic lesions of the amygdala central nucleus (CeA) (Holland et al., 2000b). The response measure is the difference in the time spent in the food cup during the tone on reinforced and nonreinforced trials. Lesioned rats failed to show the normal more rapid acquisition of NP than FN discriminations.

Hippocampus is critical to expectancy-induced decreases in cue associability but not surprise-induced enhancements of CS associability

Compared to the studies of rats with CeA lesions just described, the opposite patterns of results were observed in rats with lesions of the hippocampus. In experiments identical to those conducted by Holland and Gallagher (1993a), we found that rats with neurotoxic lesions of the entire hippocampus (Han *et al.*, 1995) and rats with cholinergic deafferentation of the hippocampus (accomplished by injections of 192IgG-saporin that targeted large cholinergic neurons in the medial septal area and vertical limb of the diagonal band; Baxter *et al.*, 1997) failed to show losses in CS associability but were unimpaired in surprise-induced enhancements of associability. First, those rats showed no evidence for latent inhibition, displaying learning about both preexposed and nonpreexposed cues that proceeded at the same rate as sham-lesioned rats' acquisition of learning about the nonpreexposed cue (Baxter *et al.*, 1997; Han *et al.*, 1995). Second, rats with hippocampal lesions showed no evidence for losses in associability to the light in the Consistent condition in the serial

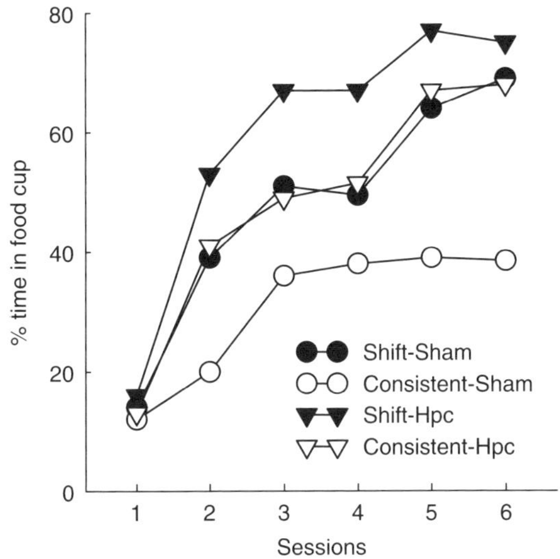

Fig. 12.4 Phase 3 test responding of rats with sham or neurotoxic lesions of the hippocampus (Hpc) in a serial prediction task (Han et al., 1995). Lesioned rats showed normal enhancement of the associability of the light after the omission of the tone, but failed to show losses in the associability of the light after consistent light→tone presentations.

prediction task (Han *et al.*, 1995). In testing, those rats learned light-food associations as rapidly as sham-lesioned rats in the Shift condition, and significantly more rapidly than sham-lesioned rats in the Consistent condition (Figure 12.4). Finally, rats with hippocampal lesions in the Shift condition showed even more rapid acquisition of learning in test than either the lesioned rats in the Consistent condition or the sham-lesioned rats in the Shift condition. Thus, although hippocampal lesions prevented losses in CS associability, they had no effects on surprise-induced enhancements in CS associability. Furthermore, the surprising omission of the tone enhanced the associability of the light even when no decrements in its associability had occurred as a result of its previous consistent pairings with the tone.

Similar conclusions can be drawn from a series of studies that used overshadowing, blocking, and unblocking procedures, although the methods were somewhat indirect at times. In the overshadowing experiment (Holland and Fox, 2003), responding acquired to a tone CS was evaluated after that cue was paired with food either alone (tone→food) or in compound with a light (light+tone→food). Normal rats showed considerably less responding to the tone after light+tone compound than after tone-only pairings with food. According to the Pearce-Hall (1980) model, because the food becomes expected more rapidly when trained with the compound cue, the associability of the light and tone are driven down more quickly than in the case of simple conditioning, preventing further increases in conditioning to either cue. If hippocampal lesions impair such losses in associability, then conditioning to the overshadowed cue should be greater in lesioned rats. Indeed, Holland and Fox (2003) found no evidence for overshadowing in hippocampally-lesioned rats (Fig. 12.5a).

In the blocking experiment, light→food pairings were followed by pairings of a light+tone compound with food, followed by a final test of responding to the tone alone. Within the Pearce-Hall model (1980), because the food is well-predicted by the light when the tone is introduced, the associability of that tone will decrease, and hence there will be little opportunity for the acquisition of tone–food associations. Thus, to the extent that blocking results from losses in the associability of the added cue, rats with hippocampal lesions should acquire conditioning to that cue, that is, fail to exhibit blocking. However, Holland and Fox (2003) found no evidence that blocking was affected by such lesions (Fig. 12.5a). Neither rats with hippocampal lesions nor rats with sham lesions displayed responding to the added tone in test. Nevertheless, other evidence from this experiment indicated that the lesions indeed impaired reductions in CS associability that occurred as a result of the blocking procedure in normal rats. After the test of responding to the tone, that cue was trained, in separate groups of rats, as either a conditioned excitor (tone→food) or a conditioned inhibitor (light2→food, tone+light2→nothing), where light2 was a second visual stimulus. The lesioned rats acquired both excitation (Fig. 12.5b) and inhibition (Fig. 12.5c) more rapidly than the sham-lesioned rats, consistent with the view that the blocking procedure reduced CS associability in normal rats but not in hippocampally-lesioned rats. Notably, we found an identical pattern of results after cholinergic deafferentation of the hippocampus (Baxter *et al.*, 1999b).

Why would these reductions in the tone's associability be revealed in tests of subsequent learning, but not in the blocking test itself? A simple answer is that although the blocking procedure indeed produces decrements in CS processing, as specified by Pearce and Hall (1980), the phenomenon of blocking itself is not produced by those mechanisms, but instead by Rescorla-Wagner (1972) reinforcement mechanisms. That is, from the first compound trial, prior training of the light rendered the food US expected and hence ineffective as a reinforcer. If the US was ineffective, any changes (or lack thereof) in CS associability would be irrelevant to the occurrence of blocking. Even if the tone maintained its associability at a high level, the lack of an effective US would prevent learning about that tone.

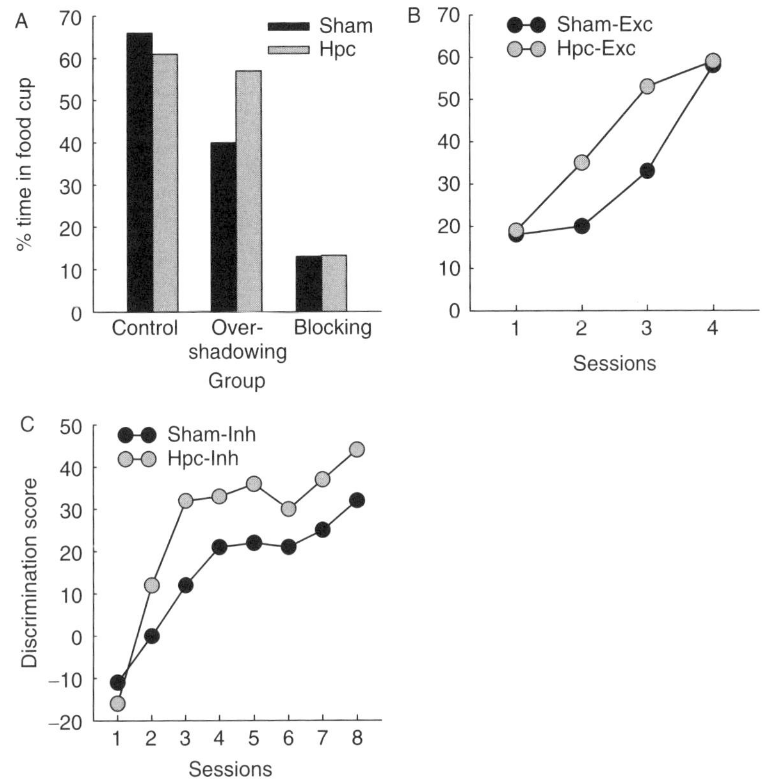

Fig. 12.5 Effects of hippocampal (Hpc) lesions on overshadowing and blocking (Holland and Fox, 2003). Panel A shows test responding to a tone that had been separately paired with food (Control), paired with food in compound with a novel light stimulus (Overshadowing) or paired with food in compound with a previously-trained light stimulus (Blocking). Overshadowing was impaired in lesioned rats, but both Blocking and simple conditioning in the behavioural Control group were unaffected. Panels B and C show the final acquisition of excitation (Exc) and inhibition (Inh) to the added tone cue in the rats previously exposed to the Blocking procedure. In both tests, lesioned rats showed more rapid acquisition than sham-lesioned rats, suggesting that the blocking procedure reduced the associability of the tone in sham-lesioned rats but not in lesioned rats.

Finally, Fox (1998) examined the effects of hippocampal lesions on unblocking. After initial conditioning in which a light was paired with the delivery of a serial US that comprised a single food pellet followed 5 s later by 2 more pellets, rats received presentations of a compound of that light and a tone with delivery of the first pellet alone. Next, responding to the tone was assessed. Compared to control groups of rats, which received either the single-pellet or pellet-series US in both phases, normal rats in the unblocking condition showed excitatory learning about the added tone. Rats with hippocampal lesions also showed unblocking, indeed significantly more responding than was observed in sham-lesioned rats. Thus, unlike with CeA lesions, hippocampal lesions did not impair surprise-induced enhancement of CS associability. Furthermore, the observation of greater unblocking in lesioned than in sham-lesioned rats is consistent with the observation of more rapid acquisition (relative to sham-lesioned rats) in the Shift condition in Han *et al.'s* (1995) experiment. These examples of enhancement beyond control levels suggest that surprise can go beyond restoring lost associability, and actually enhance it above original levels.

Circuit tracing for associability changes

Basal forebrain cholinergic system

Because of our interest in the role of prediction error in learning, we have performed an extensive series of experiments to determine the brain circuitry involved in surprise-induced enhancement of associability. Our starting point was observations by Kapp and colleagues (Kapp *et al.*, 1994; Whalen *et al.*, 1994) that conditioned activation of cortical EEG, which is tightly tied to the activity of neurons in the basal forebrain, is blocked by lesions of CeA, and elicited by electrical stimulation of CeA. To the extent that many aspects of attention are thought to be products of cortical processing of events (e.g., Posner and Petersen, 1990), it seemed reasonable to suspect that CeA might affect such processes by way of its interactions with the cholinergic basal forebrain (e.g., Everitt and Robbins, 1997; Sarter and Bruno, 1997). Initially, we found that 192IgG-saporin lesions of cholinergic neurons in the substantia innominata (SI) produced the same disruptions in performance in the serial prediction task as CeA lesions (Chiba *et al.*, 1995). That is, lesioned rats showed slower conditioning of the target light after the Shift than after the Consistent treatment. Also, as was the case after CeA lesions, SI lesions had no effect on performance in the Consistent condition, or on latent inhibition. Thus, SI lesions impaired surprise-induced enhancements of CS associability but had no effect on normal losses in CS associability produced when the expected and actual consequences matched.

A subsequent experiment demonstrated that CeA and SI act within a serial circuit in producing these effects, rather than each acting independently to enhance associability. This experiment took advantage of the fact that neural projections of these regions are almost exclusively ipsilateral and our observations that unilateral lesions of either of these regions have little or no effect on the phenomenon. In this experiment (Han *et al.*, 1999), we examined performance of rats in which CeA was lesioned in one hemisphere and SI was lesioned in the other. Because the projections of these regions are ipsilateral, communication between them is prevented in both hemispheres after this combination of lesions. However, each structure, and all of its connections with regions other than the other target region, is intact in one hemisphere. Thus, functions of the CeA and SI, other than those that require communication between them, should be available. Performance of rats in this 'disconnection' condition was compared primarily to the performance of rats that also had lesions to both CeA and SI, but in the same hemisphere. These rats had the same amount of damage to each structure in each hemisphere as the disconnection rats, but communication between these regions was possible in one hemisphere. Although performance of the rats in the Consistent training condition was similar in the disconnection and ipsilateral lesion conditions, rats with disconnection lesions failed to show surprise-induced enhancement of conditioning to the light in test. Thus, information must pass between CeA and SI at some point in the task for successful modulation of learning rate after surprise.

The results of disconnection experiments alone do not reveal either the direction of communication between the regions or whether that communication involves direct projections between the two regions or is mediated by additional brain structures. For example, although CeA sends light projections to the large cholinergic neurons in SI, SI has a heavier projection back to the amygdala. However, our supposition that the CeA modulated SI rather than the converse is supported by the observation that the SI neurons that project to CeA do not possess the receptor targeted by the selective toxin 192IgG-saporin. Although we did not perform anatomical tracing studies along with our lesions or count cells to confirm that this latter population of cells was relatively undamaged, it is notable that in a previous study (Chiba *et al.*, 1994) we used a less selective neurotoxin (AMPA) to lesion SI. That neurotoxin produced greater overall cell loss in SI but destroyed fewer of the neurons targeted by 192IgG-saporin. Interestingly, the behavioural effects of that neurotoxin were smaller, as would be anticipated if the cell population critical to the effect was that of large cholinergic cells, which do not project back to CeA.

Region-specific specialization of function

Several components of surprise-induced enhancement of learning might be identified. First, surprise must be detected. This detection requires a reinforcement signal, a prediction signal, and a computation of prediction error. Second, the surprise must alter the learning rate parameter associated with the relevant cues. Third, the altered learning rate parameter must be stored and then expressed in enhanced learning rate in test. Some of our research is designed to identify the nature and brain locus of these stages of analysis. A first step was simply to determine whether intact function of a particular brain region is needed at the time of surprise itself or at the time of expression of faster learning in test. Holland and Gallagher (2006) conducted four experiments using the serial prediction task (see Table 12.1) to examine the effects of transiently inactivating either the CeA or SI, at either the time of surprise or the time of test. Rats were first given unilateral lesions of either CeA or SI combined with implantation of a chronic cannula over the same region in the other hemisphere to permit infusion of an inactivating agent, NBQX. Delivery of NBQX, a potent AMPA antagonist, would temporarily disrupt function of the target region, whereas rats that received control deliveries of an artificial cerebrospinal fluid (ACSF) vehicle would be expected to be unimpaired because unilateral lesions of either area have little measurable effect on performance in this task. We adopted this combined lesion + inactivation procedure, rather than the more typical bilateral cannula placement, to provide better anatomical specification of the areas affected and to eliminate the need to insert multiple infusion cannulas in any individual rat.

After surgery, the rats were trained in Shift and Consistent training procedures as in our previous serial prediction experiments, except that the surprise phase comprised only three sessions, in an effort to reduce the total number of infusions that needed to be made. In each of the four experiments, all rats received infusions of ACSF 20 min before each of the last 4 sessions of Phase 1 Consistent training to adapt them to the infusion procedure. Two experiments were designed to test the effects of inactivating CeA or SI during the surprise sessions. In each of those experiments, some of the rats in each training (Shift or Consistent) condition received infusions of NBQX before each of the surprise sessions and some received ACSF infusions. These rats were then tested with ACSF infusions before each test session. Two other experiments were designed to test the effects of inactivating CeA or SI during the test sessions. In each of those experiments, all of the rats received ACSF infusions before each surprise session, and then half received test sessions after NBQX infusions and half were tested after ACSF infusions.

Figure 12.6 shows the results of these experiments. Inactivation of CeA during surprise sessions eliminated the shift advantage, whereas inactivation of SI during those sessions had no effect. By contrast, inactivation of CeA during test sessions had no effect, whereas inactivating SI in those sessions eliminated the shift advantage. Thus, CeA function was critical for the detection of surprise or the recalculation of CS associability, but not for the

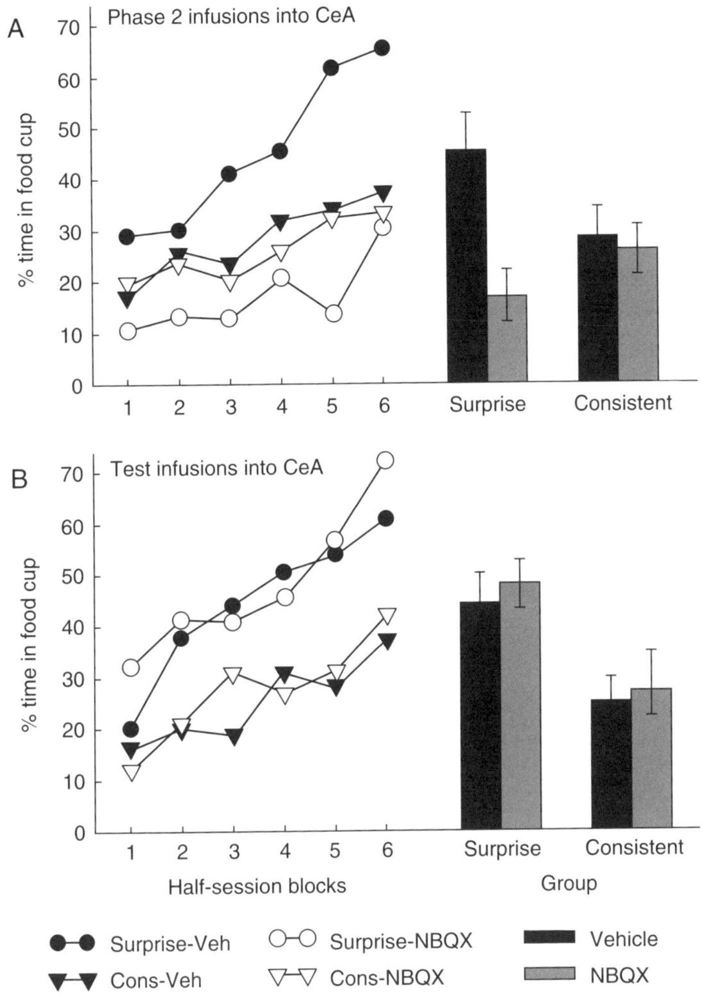

Fig. 12.6 Phase 3 test responding in a serial prediction task (Holland and Gallagher, 2006); the 'surprise' condition refers to the Shift procedure noted in Table 12.1. In four experiments, function of either the amygdala central nucleus (CeA) or the substantia innominata (SI/nBM) was disrupted temporarily by infusing an inactivating agent (NBQX) into that region prior to experimental sessions in either the surprise or test phases. The bar graphs summarize the data shown in the line graphs, which are similar in form to those dispayed in Figures 12.4 and 12.8. Rats that received infusions of an inert vehicle showed more rapid conditioning of the light after Surprise (shift) treatment than after Consistent treatment in all four experiments. These surprise-induced enhancements of associability were abolished by inactivation of CeA function during phase 2 surprise (panel A), but were unaffected by CeA inactivation during the test phase (panel B). The opposite pattern was observed with SI inactivation; surprise-induced associability enhancements were unaffected if SI was inactivated during Phase 2 surprise (panel C), but were abolished by SI inactivation during the test phase (panel D). Used by permission of the Society for Neuroscience.

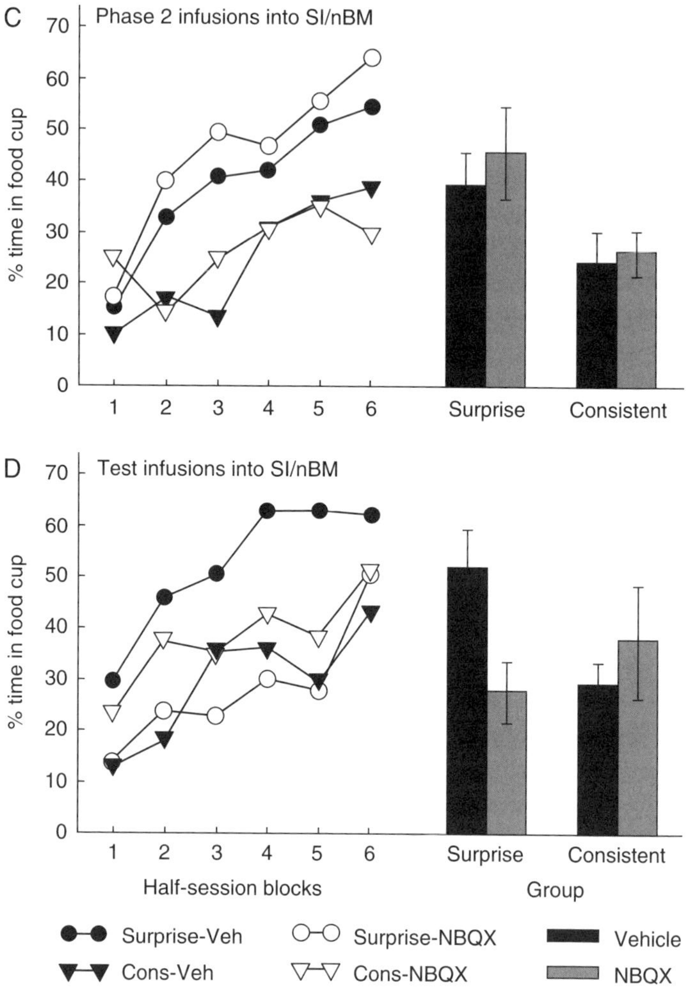

Fig. 12.6 (continued)

expression of that recalculated associability in subsequent learning. On the other hand, SI function was unnecessary for the detection of surprise or recalculation of alpha, but was critical for the expression of that recalculated alpha in new learning.

Role of neocortex in surprise-induced associability enhancements

The results of the previous studies supported the notion that CeA regulates the associability of CSs after surprise by modulating the subsequent responsiveness of SI cholinergic cells to those stimuli. These SI cells in turn project to most neocortical areas and are known to influence the responsiveness of neurons in those regions to external stimuli (Sarter *et al.*, 2005). Our first study focused on a cortical region, the posterior parietal cortex (PPC), which has frequently been implicated in processes of human attention (e.g., Bisley *et al.*, 2004; Buschman and Miller, 2007; Posner and Petersen, 1990).

Bucci *et al.* (1998) selectively lesioned SI cholinergic neurons that project to the PPC by infusing 192IgG-saporin into PPC. Those neurons express the 192IgG-responsive receptor on their axons as well as on their soma, and thus are destroyed when that 192IgG-saporin is injected near their terminal regions in PPC. Conversely, PPC neurons themselves do not express this receptor and thus are undamaged by this conjugate. After these lesions, PPC neurons remain intact but are relatively uninfluenced by the normal modulatory influences of SI cholinergic neurons. Bucci *et al.* (1998) found that rats with this PPC deafferentation failed to show surprise-induced enhancement of CS associability in either the serial prediction or unblocking tasks used in our previous studies (Fig. 12.7a,b). Similarly, Maddux *et al.* (2007) used an indirect test of CS associability based on cue competition in overshadowing to show that, unlike intact rats, rats with lesions like these failed to show greater cue associability after partial reinforcement training than after training with consistent reinforcement. In that study, rats' nose-poking to each of 4 illuminated ports was reinforced with food. Nose-pokes to two of the ports were consistently reinforced (CRF) whereas nose-pokes to the other two ports were reinforced only 50% of the time (PRF). Later, the rats received Pavlovian training in which two of those port cues were presented in compound with auditory cues, CRF+A1 and PRF+A2, and these compounds were paired with the delivery of another, more valuable reinforcer. In intact rats, tests of responding to the added auditory cues alone showed greater conditioning of A1, which had been trained in compound with the CRF port cue, than A2, which had been trained in compound with the PRF port cue. Thus, the PRF port cue overshadowed new learning of auditory CS–US associations more than the CRF port cue. PPC-lesioned rats (and also CeA-lesioned rats) failed to show this enhanced overshadowing by PRF cues (Fig. 12.7c).

At the same time, Bucci *et al.* (1998) found normal learning in PPC-lesioned rats after exposure to either the Consistent treatment in the serial prediction task or the blocking procedure (Fig. 12.7a,b). Similarly, Maddux *et al.* (2007) found no evidence for an effect of PPC cholinergic lesions on overshadowing by the port cue that had been associated with consistent reinforcement training (Fig. 12.7c). Thus, we concluded that cholinergic projections from SI to PPC were a critical part of the circuit responsible for surprise-induced enhancement of associability, but uninvolved in decrements in associability.

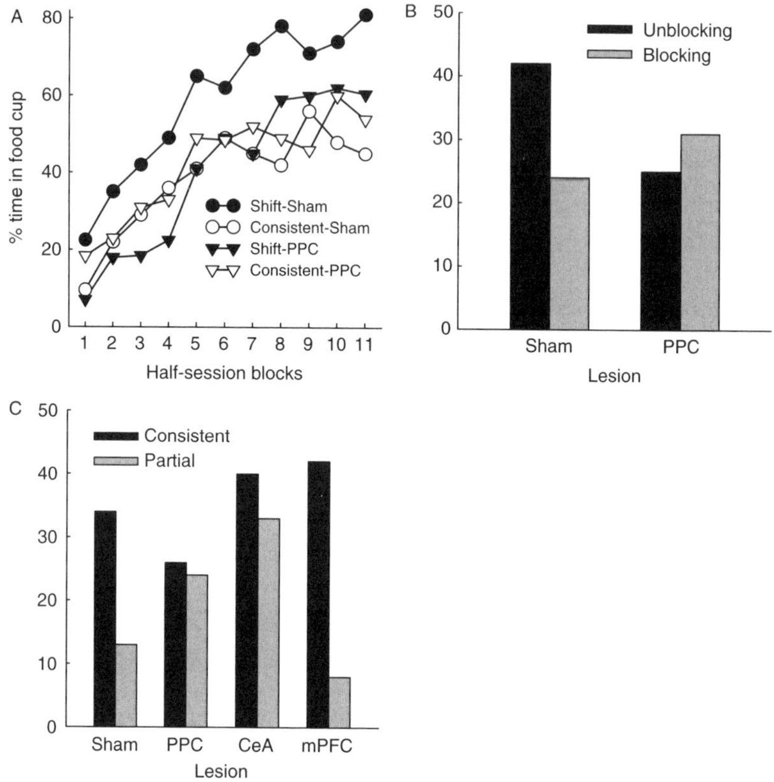

Fig. 12.7 Effects of cholinergic deafferentation of the posterior parietal cortex (PPC) on surprise-induced enhancements of associability. Panels A and B show Phase 3 test responding of rats with sham or PPC lesions in serial prediction and unblocking tasks (Bucci et al., 1998). The lesions eliminated the normal shift-induced enhancement of the associability of the light in the former study and prevented learning about the added tone in the latter study. Panel C shows test responding to an auditory cue after pairings of that cue with food in compound with a previously-trained visual cue. The visual cue had previously been trained with either a consistent (100%) or partial (50%) reinforcement schedule. Rats with sham lesions or with cholinergic deafferentation of the medial prefrontal cortex (mPFC) showed more overshadowing of conditioning to the auditory cue (less responding) if that cue had been conditioned in compound with a partially-reinforced visual cue, but rats with cholinergic deafferentation of PPC or neurotoxic lesions of the amygdala central nucleus (CeA) did not.

We have only recently begun investigations of the contributions of other neocortical regions to surprise-induced enhancement of associability. However, it is worth noting that in contrast to our observations with PPC, we have found little evidence for the involvement of another cortical region frequently implicated in attention, the medial prefrontal cortex (mPFC). Using the cue-competition (overshadowing) task just mentioned, Maddux *et al.* (2007) found no effect of cholinergic depletion in mPFC on surprise-induced learning enhancements (Fig. 12.7c), despite ample evidence for the efficacy of that lesion in disrupting other aspects of performance (see section 'Conjoint assessment of attention for learning and action'). Similarly, Maddux (2008; unpublished) found little effect of excitotoxic lesions of a number of mPFC subregions on the enhancement of cue associability.

Connectivity of amygdalo-cortical circuit with midbrain dopamine systems

The role of midbrain dopamine (DA) neurons in processing prediction error has long been recognized (e.g., Schultz and Dickinson, 2000). Although presentation of a food reward initially increases the spike firing rate of these neurons, as that food becomes well-predicted (for example, when consistently signaled by CSs), it becomes less able to provoke increased spiking. Instead, those neurons are increasingly activated by the predictive CS. However, if the food is presented unsignaled, the neuronal response is restored. Furthermore, omission of an expected reward (for example, by presenting the CS alone) typically decreases the firing rates of those neurons below basal levels. Thus, the spike activity of these midbrain DA neurons bears characteristics of prediction error signals. Most of these neurons have been found within the substantia nigra zona compacta (SNc) and the ventral tegmental area (VTA). Notably, these regions, especially SNc, are richly interconnected with CeA (Pitkänen, 2000). Indeed, we found that connections between CeA and SNc were critical for the acquisition and performance of conditioned orienting responses to auditory and visual stimuli paired with food (El-Amamy and Holland, 2006, 2007; Lee *et al.*, 2005). Thus, it seemed reasonable to determine if SNc dopamine neurons are part of a circuit responsible for surprise-induced enhancements in cue associability.

Lee *et al.* (2006b) found that lesions that disconnected SNc DA neurons from CeA eliminated the shift advantage in the serial prediction task. Using the same disconnection lesion logic as described in the section 'Basal forebrain cholinergic system', Lee *et al.* (2006b) performed ibotenic acid lesions of CeA in one hemisphere and 6-OHDA lesions of SNc in the other. Control rats received those lesions in the same hemisphere, leaving CeA-SNc communication intact in the other hemisphere. Rats with those ipsilateral lesions showed a normal shift advantage, whereas rats with disconnection lesions showed the same rate of acquisition after both Shift and Consistent training procedures as was shown by control rats in the Consistent condition (Fig. 12.8a). A subsequent study showed that the surprise-induced enhancements in CS associability depended critically on SNc function at the time of surprise, but not at the time of test, when that increased associability was expressed as faster light→food learning. Using a combined lesion/cannula procedure like that used by Holland and Gallagher (2006; section 'Region-specific specialization of function'), Lee *et al.* (2008) found that interruption of SNc function at the time of surprise eliminated subsequent associability enhancements, even when SNc function was restored in testing, when CS associability was assessed (Figure 12.8b). By contrast, although disrupting SNc function at the time of test impaired performance overall, it did not affect the magnitude of the shift advantage (not shown). Thus, as was found with CeA, SNc function seems critical at the time of surprise itself, but is apparently unnecessary to translate higher CS associability into faster learning.

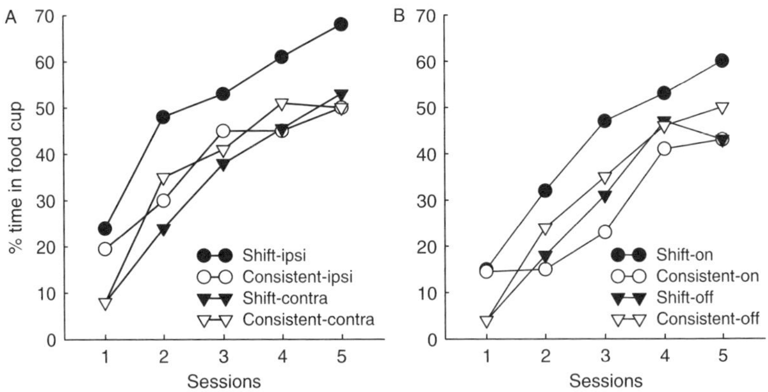

Fig. 12.8 Role of communication between amygdala central nucleus (CeA) and substantia nigra pars compacta (SNc) in surprise-induced cue associability. Panel A (Lee et al., 2006b) shows test responding of rats with lesions that disconnected those two brain regions (contra) or lesions that produced comparable damage to both structures but left communication intact in one hemisphere (ipsi). Panel B (Lee et al., 2008) shows test responding of rats in which CeA-SNc communication was disabled (off) during Phase 2 surprise but intact during the test phase, and rats in which that communication remained intact in one hemisphere during both phases (on). The results show that communication between CeA and SNc at the time of surprise is critical to surprise-induced enhancement of associability.

At this point, some speculation as to the nature of information exchange within this circuit is warranted. Evidence from simple conditioning experiments shows that populations of neurons in CeA that respond selectively to food cues project to SNc. Lee *et al.* (2005, 2006a, 2010) injected retrograde tracers into SNc, and then trained rats to expect either food or no food after a visual cue (CS+ or CS-, respectively). After testing with the visual cue, either alone or paired with food, the rats were sacrificed and their brains prepared for detection of the tracers and FOS, the protein product of the immediate early gene *c-fos*, which is often used as a marker of neural activity. A larger proportion of CeA neurons expressed FOS after presentation of the visual CS+ than after presentation of CS- alone. Thus, cued food predictions were represented in CeA neurons. Double-labelling for FOS and the tracers showed that most of the cue-activated neurons projected to SNc. Interestingly, these projecting neurons were more likely to be activated when CS+ was presented alone than when it was presented with food in test. Thus, these neurons were activated more when the food prediction was violated than when it was confirmed. Furthermore, these neurons were more likely to be activated when food was presented with CS- in test (and thus was surprising), than when it was presented with CS+ (and hence was expected). These data suggest that food prediction error information, rather than food prediction information alone, is represented in CeA neurons that project to SNc.

The observation (Lee *et al.*, 2008) that both CeA and SNc function must be intact at the time of surprise for increases in cue processing to occur is consistent with the idea that CeA and SNc work together to calculate prediction error. In CeA, this prediction error information might serve a reinforcement function for new learning or act by modulating SI processing, as described earlier. Alternatively, it is notable that SNc also has strong direct projections to SI. Thus, prediction error information in SNc might modulate SI function directly, rather than via CeA-SI projections. Because CeA-SNc communication may be critical to the computation of prediction error, this SNc-SI route is consistent with the prior observation of impairments after the contralateral CeA-SI disconnection lesions described in section 'Basal forebrain cholinergic system' (Han *et al.*, 1999): the intact SNc, which communicated with SI, would be unable to have properly computed prediction error because it had no input from CeA.

However, the further observation that neither CeA (Holland and Gallagher, 2006) nor SNc (Lee *et al.*, 2008) is critical at the time of expression of those associability increases as faster learning, suggests that this portion of the circuit alters the operating characteristics of another component. At first glance, that function seems servable by SI, which is known to enhance cortical activity, and which must be intact at the time of expression of associability enhancements in the serial prediction task (Holland and Gallagher, 2006). However, Holland and Gallagher (2006) also found that SI function was unnecessary at the time of surprise, when the CeA/SNc circuit was essential. Thus, SI characteristics could not have been altered by CeA/SNc at that time, and so surprise information must have been passed first to an additional brain area. We are exploring other candidate regions for this function.

Extensions and limitations

Positive prediction error and associability

Within the Pearce-Hall (1980) model, associability is based on the absolute value of prediction error. Thus, both overexpectation (negative prediction error) and underexpectation (positive prediction error) of outcomes are expected to maintain cues' associability. However, in an effort to contrast the predictions of the Pearce-Hall (1980) and Rescorla-Wagner (1972) models, most of the tasks used to reveal enhanced associability were those that involved overexpectation of events, for example the omission of an expected US, as in our unblocking studies, or an expected CS, as in our serial prediction task studies. Because the Rescorla-Wagner (1972) model predicts inhibitory learning when events are overexpected, the observation of enhanced excitatory learning in such cases would be difficult to explain within that model. By contrast, both models anticipate excitatory learning when reinforcers are underexpected. Thus, when Holland and Gallagher (1993b) found no evidence that CeA lesions affected the occurrence of unblocking when the reinforcer value was shifted upward (Fig. 12.9a), in experiments otherwise identical to their studies of unblocking with downshifts in reinforcer value (section 'Amygdala central nucleus is critical to surprise-induced enhancement of cue associability, but not expectancy-induced reductions in cue associability'), they argued that the unblocking they observed in the upshift case was due to Rescorla-Wagner (1972) reinforcement mechanisms, rather than CS associability changes, and hence not susceptible to CeA damage.

Recently, we reevaluated this claim by using an unblocking procedure that better distinguishes between upshifts produced by increased reinforcement and those produced by increases in CS associability (Holland, 2006). In this procedure, we shifted the US from a single food pellet to the delivery of the pellet followed 5 s later by delivery of a sucrose solution to a different location. A visual CS (V1) was first paired with food, and then a compound of V1 and a noise was paired with the food→sucrose US. Within the Rescorla-Wagner (1972) model, the sucrose is unexpected and hence should serve as an effective reinforcer for conditioning to the noise (and to V1 as well). However, the food

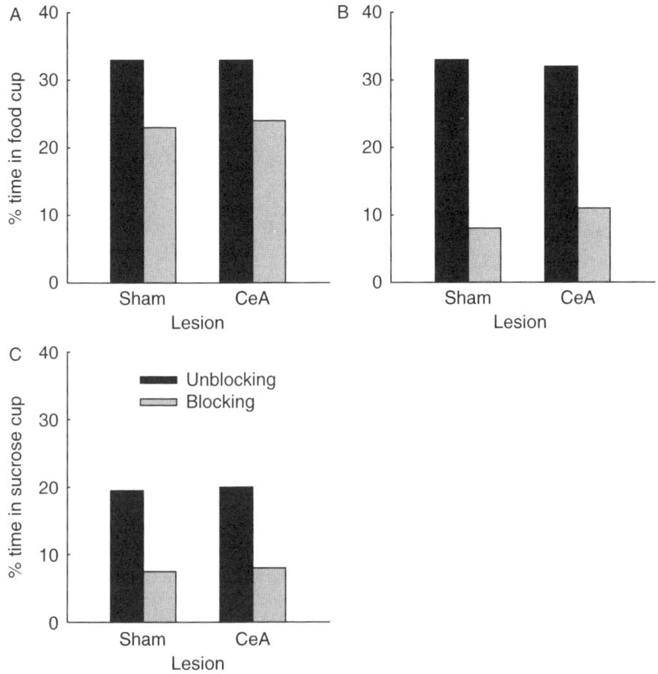

Fig. 12.9 No effects of lesions of the amygdala central nucleus (CeA) on unblocking when the value of the reinforcer was shifted upward when the compound was introduced (Panel A: Holland and Gallagher, 1993b; Panels B and C: Holland, 2006). See text for details.

US is expected by virtue of prior V1-food training, and hence would be ineffective as a reinforcer. Thus, unblocking of sucrose learning but not of food learning would be anticipated within the Rescorla-Wagner (1972) model, whereas both noise-sucrose and noise-food learning would be anticipated within the Pearce-Hall (1980) model. Because the two reinforcers were delivered to different food cups, these two types of learning could be readily distinguished.

In the blocking/unblocking phase of this experiment (Holland, 2006), two groups of rats received pairings of a compound stimulus that comprised a white noise and a visual cue (V1) with the delivery of a food pellet followed 5 s later by a sucrose solution. Rats in the Unblocking group had previously received extensive training with V1–food pairings, and rats in the Blocking control group had previously received parings of V1 with the food→sucrose reinforcer. To provide both groups with more comparable training to enter the sucrose cup, both groups also received pairings of a second visual stimulus

(V2) with sucrose intermixed with the other trials, throughout both phases of training.

At completion of the blocking/unblocking phase, acquisition of responding to the noise alone was assessed. Both rats with CeA lesions and rats with sham lesions showed unblocking of both noise–food (Fig. 12.9b) and noise–sucrose (Fig. 12.9c) learning. That is, regardless of lesion condition, rats in the Unblocking groups showed both more food cup responding and more sucrose cup responding than rats in the Blocking group.

Two conclusions can be drawn from this study. First, the addition of a second reinforcer in an unblocking experiment can produce learning about both the added reinforcer and the original, expected reinforcer. Although the Rescorla-Wagner (1972) model predicts only the former learning, the Pearce-Hall (1980) model predicts both, because the relatively greater associability of the noise should result in enhanced learning about any available reinforcer. Thus, Pearce and Hall's (1980) assertion that underexpectations of reward can enhance CS associability is supported. Second, because the lesion did not affect either the noise–food or noise–sucrose learning, it is possible that the role of CeA in surprise-induced enhancements of CS associability is limited to the case of surprising omissions of expected events.

Negative prediction error and enhancement of reinforcer value

The results of a recent series of experiments suggest that in some circumstances negative prediction error may enhance reinforcer value rather than CS associability. Consider the unblocking experiments described in section "Amygdala central nucleus is critical to surprise-induced enhancement of cue associability, but not expectancy-induced reductions in cue associability" (Holland and Gallagher, 1993b; Holland and Kenmuir, 2005). In those experiments, omission of the second of two pellet deliveries resulted in enhanced learning about a novel tone stimulus that was added when the US-omission unblocking phase began. We initially attributed those effects to surprise-induced enhancement of the associability of the tone, by which that cue was more readily associated with the remaining food pellet reinforcer. However, an alternative account attributes the rapid learning about the tone to a surprise-induced enhancement of the value of the remaining food pellet reinforcer (Holland, 1988), reminiscent of Kamin's (1968) notion of a backward scan of the contents of short term memory when surprise occurs. We evaluated this account in two ways.

First, we performed an unblocking experiment that permitted independent assessment of the formation of associations with the first (presented) and second (omitted) USs (Holland and Kenmuir, 2005, Experiment 2). If the associability of the added cue was increased by omission of the second US, then any kind of learning about that cue should be enhanced by omission of the second US, and all of those enhancements should be reduced by CeA lesions. Rats in an Unblocking group first received pairings of a visual cue (V1) with delivery of a food pellet followed 5 s later by sucrose to a different cup. Rats in a Blocking control group received pairings of V1 with only the first food pellet. Then both groups received pairings of a compound of a noise and V1 with the food alone. All rats also received pairings of a second visual cue (V2) with sucrose intermixed throughout Phases 1 and 2 of training, to provide more comparable experiences with both reinforcers in the two groups. A brief test of responding to the noise alone revealed food-based responding in sham-lesioned but not CeA-lesioned rats in the Unblocking condition (Fig. 12.10a). At the same time, rats with CeA lesions showed no deficit in sucrose cup responding based on second-order noise→V1 learning (not shown).

Next, the conditioned inhibitory powers of the added noise were assessed. According to the Rescorla-Wagner (1972) model, the surprising omission of the sucrose reinforcer in the Unblocking group should have established inhibitory noise–sucrose associations. To examine this possibility, after the conclusion of the noise-alone test, all rats were trained on a discrimination in which V2 was paired with sucrose when it was presented alone but nonreinforced when it was presented in compound with the noise. Both CeA-lesioned and sham-lesioned rats in the Unblocking group showed savings in the acquisition of this explicit conditioned inhibition discrimination relative to rats in the Blocking group, as would be expected from the Rescorla-Wagner (1972) model (Fig. 12.10b).

Because only the noise-food learning was impaired by the CeA lesion, it seems unlikely that the enhanced learning observed to the noise in the control rats was attributable to changes in its associability. In that case, all instances of learning about that cue, including second-order noise–V1 and inhibitory noise–sucrose learning, should have been impaired by the lesion. An alternative account (Holland and Kenmuir, 2005) is that omitting the sucrose enhanced the reinforcing value of the remaining food US, and that such a process also demands normal CeA function. Thus, noise–food learning would be impaired by the lesions, but not noise–V1 learning or inhibitory noise–sucrose learning.

In a second experiment, we examined whether omission of the second of two expected reinforcers would enhance the power of the first one in a procedure simpler than the blocking/unblocking procedure. Initially, we trained rats to expect a food→sucrose sequence, by pairing V1 with that serial

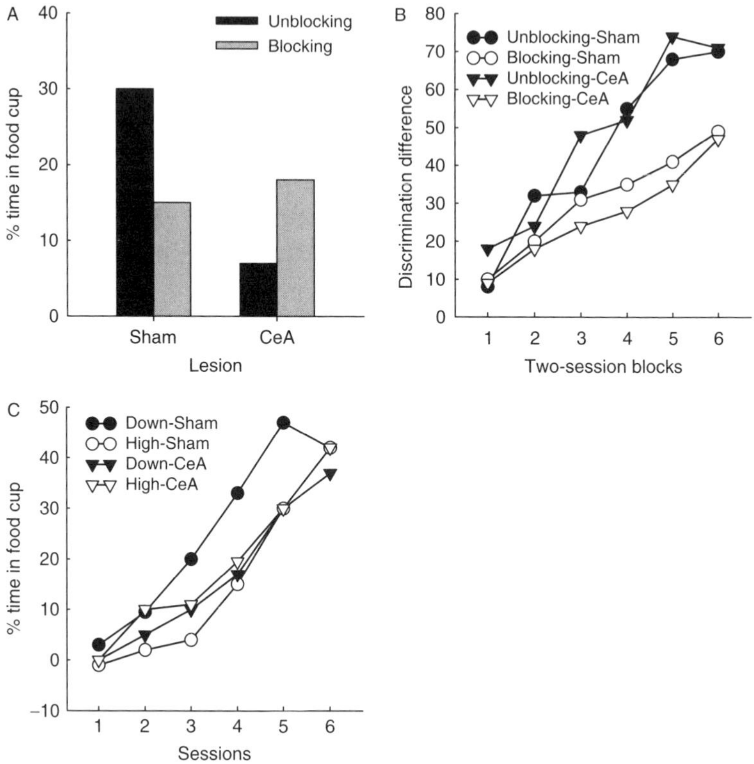

Fig. 12.10 Evidence for enhanced processing of one reinforcer after the surprising omission of another reinforcer (Holland and Kenmuir, 2005). Panel A shows responding of rats with sham or neurotoxic lesions of the amygdala central nucleus (CeA) to the added noise cue in an unblocking experiment in which a food→sucrose reinforcer was downshifted to food alone when the noise was added. Unlike sham-lesioned rats, rats with CeA lesions failed to show conditioning to the noise (unblocking). However, the CeA lesions had no effect on the rate of acquisition of inhibitory noise-sucrose associations (panel B), suggesting that the surprising omission of the sucrose in the Unblocking condition had enhanced processing of the remaining food reinforcer rather than of the added noise. The response measure shown is the difference between the time spent in the sucrose cup during reinforced presentations of a light cue paired with sucrose and during a nonreinforced compound of that light and the noise over the course of conditioned inhibition training. The same effects were observed if the effectiveness of the food reinforcer was evaluated by using it to reinforce learning to a novel cue (panel C) in the absence of any other cues. See text for details.

reinforcer. In the second phase, we presented the V1→food→sucrose sequence to the rats in Group High and a V1→food sequence to the rats in Group Down. If omitting the sucrose in Group Down enhanced the processing of the food US, then it should be more effective as a reinforcer later, even in the absence of V1. So, in the test phase we paired a novel noise with the food→sucrose reinforcer. Noise–food learning (Fig. 12.10c), but not noise–sucrose learning, was enhanced in Group Down, suggesting that the effectiveness of food as a reinforcer in test was enhanced by the surprising omission of sucrose in Phase 2. Notably, any changes in CS associability that might have occurred in Phase 2 could not have contributed to the test performance because the stimuli present in Phase 2 were absent in testing. Furthermore, rats with CeA lesions failed to show this enhancement, but otherwise did not differ from unlesioned rats. This last finding further supports our suggestion that the surprise-induced enhancement of US power, like that of CS associability, depends on CeA function.

Interestingly, in an upshift version of this experiment, Holland and Kenmuir (2005) found that presentation of an unexpected sucrose reinforcer after the usual food reinforcer also appeared to enhance the subsequent ability of the food to reinforce learning to a novel cue. However, in this case, the enhancement was not impaired by CeA lesions, consistent with Holland's (2006) suggestion that CeA may only be critical for enhanced event processing after overexpectation (negative prediction error).

Brain systems for control of attention for action in associative learning

In the introduction to this chapter, we distinguished between two adaptive functions of attentional processes: apportioning processing resources to control current actions and to enable new learning. Recent research in our laboratory suggests that separable but interacting brain circuits are involved in modulating attention for action and attention for new learning. The implication of these results for behavioural theories of attention is that changes in attention that occur as a result of learning do not necessarily produce across-the-board changes in event processing, but instead can have different consequences for the control of action and the establishment of new learning. This separation is consistent with the Pearce-Hall (1980) model, in which changes in associability do not contribute directly to performance. Our research has used two simple strategies. First, we have examined the effects of brain lesions identified as affecting associability on behaviour in tasks used by others to assess performance aspects of attention. Second, we have conducted experiments designed to separate the effects of attention in learning and action, by contrasting the roles of prediction and prediction error. Intuitively, action should be governed by the most accurate available predictor of the future. By contrast, within the Pearce-Hall (1980) model, cues whose consequences are poorly predicted maintain higher associability than those whose consequences are well predicted. Thus, control of action should be correlated with prediction accuracy whereas control of learning should be correlated with prediction error. In our experiments, we examined the effects of altering the predictive relations between cues and outcomes on attention in action and learning.

Assessment of attention in action

A wide range of behavioural tasks have been used to examine attention in action in rats (e.g., Bushnell, 1998). Most of these tasks establish a relatively difficult baseline performance that requires sustained attention to the task demands, and then present various challenges to that attention. The most commonly used tasks include a simple signal detection task, in which rats are asked to perform one response if a signal is presented in a trial and a different response if the signal is not presented (Sarter and McGaughey, 1998), and a multiple-cue task in which rats faced with an array of possible stimulus locations are asked to direct a response to the location of a briefly-presented cue (Robbins, 2002). Challenges to attention are mounted by degrading physical parameters of the cues (e.g., their duration or intensity), by introducing distracting events, or by altering established event relations within the task (e.g., by changing trial density or altering warning signals).

We have primarily used variants of the '5-choice serial reaction time' (5CSRT) design (Robbins, 2002). In our version of the task, rats are first trained to respond to a set of 3-7 nose-poke ports. After a 5-s warning signal, one of the ports is briefly (0.5–1.0 s) illuminated, and rats are given some interval (1–5 s) to respond. Correct responses (to the illuminated port) are reinforced with delivery of a food pellet, whereas errors have no scheduled consequences. A variety of performance measures are recorded, but we focus here on the probability, accuracy, and latency of responding to the ports. After performance is stabilized, various attentional challenges are introduced. These typically include reducing cue duration (to 0.10 or 0.25 s), introducing an auditory distractor cue during the trials, and varying the interval between warning signal onset and cue presentation. Finally, various brain lesions are made, the rats retrained, and the effects of attentional challenges again evaluated. Consistent with others' findings (e.g., Muir *et al.*, 1994, 1996), we found that disrupting function of the basal forebrain cholinergic system (SI) or of the mPFC, impaired probability, accuracy and latency of responding under conditions of attentional challenge, but rarely in the baseline task itself (Holland, 2007; Maddux *et al.*, 2007; Maddux, 2008). More novel was our observation that similar impairments were also observed after lesions of CeA (Holland *et al.*, 2000a; Maddux *et al.*, 2007).

In most of our experiments, we examined the effects of partial reinforcement on port responding. After standard training on the tasks, the probability of reinforcement after responses to two of the ports was reduced from 100% to 50% (PRF), while reinforcement probability was maintained at 100% (CRF) to two other ports. Unlike in our 'attention for learning' studies described in previous sections, in sham-lesioned rats, degrading the predictive cue-reinforcement relation from CRF to PRF impaired all measures of responding to the PRF cues. These response decrements were especially evident during attentional challenges. Furthermore, if presented with CRF and PRF port cues simultaneously, the rats consistently chose the CRF ports. Thus, a manipulation that would be expected to enhance cue associability within the Pearce-Hall (1980) model had the opposite effect on cues' ability to control attention in action.

Conjoint assessment of attention for learning and action

Importantly, in several of our studies, after the completion of the attentional challenge tests, we assessed the associability of those same cues in the overshadowing task described in the section 'Role of neocortex in surprise-induced associability enhancements' (Fig. 12.7c). In this task, the PRF cues grabbed more attention away from learning about an added tone than the CRF cues, despite their controlling less nose-poking (even during the overshadowing task itself) and being more susceptible to disruption by attentional challenges than CRF cues (Maddux *et al.*, 2007; Maddux, 2008).

This dissociation between contingency effects in learning and action was further revealed by examination of lesion effects in rats subjected to both tasks (Maddux *et al.*, 2007). First, although cholinergic deafferentation of mPFC especially impaired performance to PRF cues in the 5CSRT task after attentional challenges, those lesions had no effects on learning in the overshadowing task. That is, as with sham-lesioned rats, the PRF port cue interfered with learning about the tone more than the CRF port cue. Second, although cholinergic deafferentation of PPC had no effect on performance in the 5CSRT task, those lesions eliminated the enhanced overshadowing normally found after PRF training. Finally, in a separate study, Maddux (2008) found a comparable lesion dissociation within mPFC itself. Whereas neurotoxic lesions of dorsal mPFC reversed the normally greater overshadowing of learning by PRF cues than by CRF cues, they did not affect performance in 5CSRT challenges.

By contrast, larger mPFC lesions that also included ventral regions impaired 5CSRT challenge responding to PRF cues, but did not disrupt overshadowing by such cues. Thus, the abilities of PRF cues to control behaviour and to influence new learning clearly involve separable brain mechanisms.

Overt attention in action: learned orienting

Important events must be able to interrupt ongoing stimulus processing. Typically, novel stimuli with abrupt onsets (e.g., sudden sounds, appearance of an object in the visual field) trigger orienting responses (ORs), which often include movements directed towards the stimulus, autonomic responses, and neuronal activity characterized as vigilance. These behaviours suggest the apportionment of further processing to the eliciting event. We have examined the role of CeA in the acquisition and display of orienting behaviour in simple Pavlovian appetitive conditioning procedures with rats. Prior to training, discrete visual and auditory stimuli spontaneously elicit orienting behaviour including, for visual cues, rearing on the hind legs and other behaviours directed towards the light source (Holland, 1977), as well as autonomic responses, such as decreased heart rate (Hunt and Campbell, 1997). With repeated presentation of a stimulus with no other consequence, these unconditioned orienting behaviours (ORs) habituate. However, if the stimulus is repeatedly paired with food delivery, the ORs reemerge. Comparison with various control procedures shows that this potentiation of ORs is a product of Pavlovian conditioning (Holland, 1979). It seems likely that these learned responses both reflect and direct heightened attention to events that have acquired biological significance through associative learning.

Rats with neurotoxic lesions or transient pharmacological inactivation of CeA do not acquire these conditioned ORs to auditory and visual stimuli paired with food (Gallagher *et al.*, 1990; Groshek *et al.*, 2005; McDannald *et al.*, 2004). Nevertheless, such rats were unimpaired in their acquisition of food-cup directed conditioned responses, and showed normal unconditioned orienting prior to cue–food pairing. Thus, deficits in conditioned orienting were not likely due to general deficits in learning, motivation, motor control, nor orienting in general. Instead, CeA was selectively involved in learning to orient to a stimulus that reliably predicted food. Other research showed that the ascending projections of CeA also play critical roles in conditioned orienting. Disconnection of CeA from SNc (Lee *et al.*, 2005) or a major target of SNc dopamine neurons, the dorsolateral striatum (DLS; Han *et al.*, 1997), which is known to modulate cortical responsiveness to such stimuli, produced the same pattern of impairments as CeA lesions. Furthermore, the roles of the various portions of this system are specialized. Lesions or inactivation of CeA interfered with the acquisition of conditioned ORs, but not with the performance of such responses if they were previously learned while CeA function was intact (Groshek *et al.*, 2005; McDannald *et al.*, 2004). By contrast, DLS function was critical at the time of action, but not during learning (Han *et al.*, 1997), and SNc function was critical to both learning and performance of ORs (El-Amamy and Holland, 2006, 2007).

Although the acquisition of conditioned ORs thus demands the integrity of CeA–SNc communication, as does the surprise-induced enhancement of associability (section 'Connectivity of amygdalo-cortical circuit with midbrain dopamine systems'), brain processing of these two functions diverges. For example, although disconnections of CeA from SI or PPC eliminated surprise-induced increments in CS processing, they spared the acquisition of conditioned ORs (Bucci *et al.*, 1998; Chiba *et al.*, 1995). Furthermore, although El-Amamy and Holland (2006, 2007) found that SNc function was critical to both acquisition and expression of conditioned ORs, Lee *et al.* (2008) found no evidence for an SNc role in the expression of previously-acquired associability increases.

It is notable that Pearce and his colleagues (e.g., Kaye and Pearce, 1984) have described a behavioural OR that tracks a cue's associability (and hence prediction error) rather than its associative strength (and hence prediction). Although there have been attempts at reconciling these observations of ORs, we have not been successful at producing ORs that index associability. It would be of great interest to contrast the neural systems that mediate such responses and those that underlie the conditioned ORs we have studied.

A further note on brain dissociations in attention tasks

In this section we identify portions of brain circuitry tentatively designated as contributing to increments or decrements in cue associability and performance in simple learning tasks. However, these regions have much broader functions, and other brain regions are also likely to play major roles in attention in associative learning tasks. For example, in our investigations of basal forebrain modulation of cortical and hippocampal systems, we have emphasized the role of cholinergic systems. Although these systems are certainly the most thoroughly investigated, they are unlikely to be the only ones critical to attentional processes in associative learning. For example, Lin and Nicolelis (2008) showed that noncholinergic neurons in the basal forebrain also modulate neocortical activity in response to external stimuli, and that such modulation is altered by arranging associative relations between those stimuli and reinforcers.

Similarly, although we noted specialization of mPFC and PPC function, such that the former region contributed primarily to attention for action and the latter for attention in learning, there are clearly many exceptions to this double dissociation (Maddux, 2008). Notably, most descriptions of PPC function in attention in human and non-human primate studies emphasize its role in selecting behaviour in action, indeed, in many cases in bottom-up rather than top-down processing roles (e.g., Bisley *et al.*, 2004; Buschman and Miller, 2007).

Likewise, our identification of a role for hippocampal systems in decreases in cue associability and for amygdalo-cortical systems in associability increases does not fit simply within most modern concepts of the function of these systems. For example, although the hippocampus was once a popular substrate for modulations of attention (e.g., Moore and Stickney, 1980), most modern views emphasize its function in coding spatial information, performing pattern completion or pattern separation operations (Bakker *et al.*, 2008) or engaging associative or episodic memory processes (Fortin *et al.*, 2004). More to the point, our data suggest that the amygdalo-cortical system involved in enhancements in associability is fast-acting and the hippocampal system involved in associability decreases is slow-acting, the opposite temporal dynamics as are typically described for these brain regions (O'Reilly and Rudy, 2001). Nevertheless, models of attention in associative learning such as the Pearce-Hall (1980) model have provided a productive framework in which to view relations between these brain regions and behaviour. Expansion of that framework may help us better understand how these brain systems integrate multiple psychological and behavioural functions.

Implications for models of associative learning

Our brain systems research suggests five broad conclusions about the nature of attention in associative learning, all closely tied to the Pearce-Hall (1980) model. First, the roles of attention in learning and action are distinguishable. Several of our studies suggest distinctions in brain processing when rats are allocating attention for purposes of learning new information and for acting on the basis of previously acquired information. In addition, behavioural evidence from these experiments indicates that although attentional changes in learning follow Pearce-Hall (1980) model rules, attention in action does not. For example, in these experiments, compared to consistent predictors of reinforcement, inconsistent predictors control more attention in learning but less in action. Thus, these kinds of attentional changes occurring as a result of associative learning are unlikely to be limited to low-level modifications of sensory processing or to receptor orienting responses (Holland, 1977; Gallagher *et al.*, 1990), which would result in the enhancement (or depression) of all stimulus functions. Instead, these changes are likely to occur in a variety of neural systems, at multiple levels of processing. Thus, future models of associative learning, at both behavioural and brain systems levels, will need to include rules for determining changes in attention in both learning and action.

Second, mechanisms for increases and decreases in associability are independent. Although the Pearce-Hall (1980) model provides rules by which attention selects both for and against processing of particular cues, our data suggest a fast-acting neocortical system is critical to surprise-induced increases in CS associability, whereas a slower-acting hippocampal system is essential for more gradual losses in associability that occur when events are well-predicted. Thus, these changes differ in both the circumstances that generate them (prediction error versus prediction accuracy) and the speed at which they occur. Surprise is translated into increased associability in as few as 2–4 trials (e.g., Hall and Pearce, 1979, 1982; Holland, 2005), and may reach its maximum after a few sessions (Holland *et al.*, 2002). Curiously, extended exposure to surprise, defined as partial reinforcement contingencies, does not seem to reduce surprise-induced maintenance of CS associability (Holland *et al.*, 2002). One might imagine that extended exposure to inconsistent reinforcement would establish an expectation of uncertain reward (Yu and Dayan, 2005). Thus, associability seems to be more governed by local rather than more global surprise. By contrast, decreases in associability seem to take place gradually over many trial presentations (e.g., Holland *et al.*, 2002). Indeed, at least in our preparations, it is likely that these changes occur too slowly to be solely responsible for many instances of stimulus selection they are called on to explain within the Pearce-Hall (1980) model, such as blocking (e.g., Baxter *et al.*, 1999b; Holland and Fox, 2003).

Third, different brain mechanisms seem to be responsible for enhanced associability produced by negative and positive prediction error. Considerable evidence from our laboratory indicates that CeA is critical only for associability enhancements produced by negative prediction error. Nevertheless, our evidence suggests that at least in some circumstances, positive prediction error can produce indirect changes in event processing, as specified in the Pearce-Hall (1980) model, even though they are independent of CeA systems. These findings are also consistent with that model's more general contention that, despite their common consequences for CS associability, under- and over-expectations are processed differently. In the Pearce-Hall (1980) model, the effectiveness of underexpected USs is not altered by prediction error information, whereas the consequences of overexpectation are mediated by no-US representations, which vary in effectiveness depending on prediction error.

Fourth, indirect (Schultz and Dickinson, 2000) changes in event processing produced by over- or under-expectation of a reinforcer are not limited to changes in CS effectiveness or associability, but can also extend to processing of other reinforcers. In our studies, surprising omission of a second reinforcer in unblocking experiments enhanced the value of the remaining first reinforcer (Holland and Kenmuir, 2005). The observation that reward processing as well as CS associability can be influenced by the surprising omission of another event is novel, and may extend the domain of models like Pearce and Hall's (1980) in important ways. Surprising presentations or omissions of reinforcers may affect the extent to which attention is directed to other reinforcers as well as to signals. Furthermore, this observation relates changes in attention to changes in reward efficacy, a notion that is further supported by our observations of critical roles for midbrain dopamine neurons (often implicated in reward processing) in surprise-induced enhancements of CS associability (Lee *et al.*, 2006, 2008).

Finally, exposure to learning tasks is likely to have multiple consequences, including indirect changes in CS effectiveness, and both direct and indirect changes in US effectiveness. For example, we found that omitting an expected second US in an unblocking experiment simultaneously yielded excitatory associations between the added CS and the first US and inhibitory associations with the second US (Holland, 1988; Holland and Kenmuir, 2005). Although we found no evidence that this manipulation also enhanced processing of the added CS, as predicted by the Pearce-Hall (1980) model (Holland and Kenmuir, 2005), it seems likely that choice of different task parameters could encourage these changes as well. Casually speaking, in Holland and Kenmuir's (2005) study, processing of the first US may have been the primary beneficiary of the surprise induced by omission of the second US because it was both far more salient than the added auditory CS and closer in time to the surprise. Notably, in the serial prediction task (Wilson *et al.*, 1992), the surprise manipulation, omitting the anticipated tone, is unlikely to enhance US processing because the US is never present on surprise trials. In this task, we found ample evidence for enhanced CS processing (e.g., Holland *et al.*, 2001). Nevertheless, as we noted in the section'Amygdala central nucleus is critical to surprise-induced enhancement of cue associability, but not expectancy-induced reductions in cue associability', even that task has countervailing influences that may be revealed in the absence of Pearce-Hall (1980) associability change mechanisms. For example, obtaining the shift advantage in normal rats depends on these surprise-induced attention-enhancing mechanisms being more potent than extinction or latent inhibition. Indeed, Holland *et al.* (2002) found that by changing the relative salience of the elements of the serial compound to favor the occurrence of conditioning and extinction to the first element, the normal shift advantage could be replaced by a shift disadvantage, even in intact rats.

The use of 'reduced preparations' (Teitelbaum and Pellis, 1992), such as rats with brain lesions described in this chapter, provides one strategy for disentangling the influence of multiple processing changes in associative learning tasks. Rats with lesions to the amygdalo-cortical system shown to disrupt Pearce-Hall (1980) associability-enhancing processes could be used to more clearly reveal the operation of mechanisms that reduce CS associability or alter direct changes in US effectiveness. For example, Holland *et al.* (2000; section 'Amygdala central nucleus is critical to surprise-induced enhancement of cue associability, but not expectancy-induced reductions in cue associability') used such a strategy in evaluating behavioural explanations for the paradoxically more rapid acquisition of serial negative patterning discriminations than of serial feature negative discriminations. Similarly, use of this method might permit examination of a vexing question for the Pearce-Hall (1980) model. Although that model relates diminishing associability to diminishing prediction error, a simpler possibility is that decreases in associability are the consequence of mere stimulus presentation. Any associability increases produced by prediction error might then be superimposed on this steadily declining baseline. It would be interesting to use CeA-lesioned rats to examine the rates of decline in CS associability after constant numbers of CS presentations, but in the presence of different US prediction errors. If mere presentation was the critical determinant of associability decreases, then in the absence of an associability-enhancing mechanism, the CSs' predictive value would be irrelevant to the amount of associability loss.

In an analogous fashion, rats with hippocampal damage may more readily reveal event processing changes that occur apart from losses in CS associability. Furthermore, rats with damage to both amygdalo-cortical and hippocampal systems might serve as models for learning in the absence of indirect processing changes. For example, Baxter *et al.* (1999a) disrupted function of both of these systems by producing damage to neurons in both neocortical and hippocampal branches of the basal forebrain cholinergic system. These rats failed to show either surprise-induced increases in CS associability or losses with extended predictive exposure, but showed normal performance in simple acquisition and other tasks often attributed to Rescorla-Wagner (1972) US-processing mechanisms, such as blocking. Thus, these rats normally adjusted the effective value of USs based on prediction error, but were unable to adjust CS associability on the same basis.

Concluding comments

Attention is affected both by intrinsic stimulus characteristics and by the subject's goals and expectations, many of which are established through associative learning. This chapter is concerned with how outcome predictions and prediction errors alter processing of cues and perhaps reinforcers. But the boundaries between top-down, goal-directed attentional processes and bottom-up processes are fuzzy. For example, a hitherto unremarkable cue paired with food may take on the biological significance of that food, and be far more likely to capture attention. Does that enhanced capture exemplify top-down guidance of attention, or have the bottom-up processing characteristics of that stimulus been altered by learning? Some investigators of human attention have suggested that the automatic bottom-up filtering for 'innately relevant' or infrequent (e.g. 'oddball') salient stimuli extends to stimuli that have acquired their relevance through learning (e.g., Knudsen, 2007) or whose 'oddity' reflects violation of expectancies about their occurrence. Recent neuroscience research shows that even primary visual cortex (V1) represents reward information, including the timing of reward delivery (Shuler and Bear, 2006).

Nevertheless, it seems reasonable to speak of research like that described in this chapter as reflecting something akin to what Knudsen (2007) has described as 'top-down sensitivity control' by which the sensitivity of neural circuits that represent the information in many domains, including sensory, motor, internal state, and memory, is modulated. Our distinctions between attention in action and in learning may reflect such modulation at different levels of stimulus processing. Competitive selection processes that help eliminate distracting information and focus on the most salient and appropriate stimulus (Desimone and Duncan, 1995; Hampshire *et al.*, 2007) may follow somewhat different rules at these different processing levels. Thus, our observation that consistent pairing of events may enhance attention for action while at the same time decrease attention in new learning is not at all inconsistent with modern views of attention. Future research needs to specify these rules of operation within different neural systems that contribute to attention.

References

Allport, A. (1989). Visual attention. In M. Posner (Ed.), *Foundations of cognitive science* (pp. 631–682). Cambridge, MA: MIT Press.

Bakker, A., Kirwan, C.B., Miller, M., & Stark, C.E.L. (2008). Pattern separation in the human hippocampal CA3 and dentate gyrus. *Science*, **319**, 1640–1642.

Baxter, M., G., Holland, P. C., & Gallagher, M. (1997). Disruption of decrements in conditioned stimulus processing by selective removal of hippocampal cholinergic input. *Journal of Neuroscience*, **17**, 5230–5236.

Baxter, M., G., Bucci, D. J., Holland, P. C., & Gallagher, M. (1999a). Impairments in conditioned stimulus processing after combined selective removal of hippocampal and cortical cholinergic input. *Behavioral Neuroscience*, **113**, 486–495.

Baxter, M. G., Gallagher, M., & Holland, P. C. (1999b). Blocking can occur without losses in attention in rats with selective removal of hippocampal cholinergic input. *Behavioral Neuroscience*, **113**, 881–890.

Bisley, J.W., Krishna, B.S., & Goldberg, M.E. (2004). A rapid and precise on-response in posterior parietal cortex. *Journal of Neuroscience*, **24**, 1833–1838.

Bucci, D. J., Holland, P. C., & Gallagher, P. C. (1998). Removal of cholinergic input to rat posterior parietal cortex disrupts incremental processing of conditioned stimuli. *Journal of Neuroscience*, **18**, 8038–8046.

Buschman T.J. & Miller, E.K. (2007). Top-down versus bottom-up control of attention in the prefrontal and posterior parietal cortices. *Science*, **315**, 1860–1862.

Bushnell, P.J. (1998). Behavioral approaches to the assessment of attention in animals. *Psychopharmacology*, **138**, 231–259.

Chiba, A.A., Han, J-S., Holland, P.C., & Gallagher, M. (1994). Substantia innominata lesions impair incremental attentional processing in a Pavlovian conditioning paradigm. *Society for Neuroscience Abstracts*, **20**, 1215.

Chiba, A. A., Bucci, D. J., Holland, P. C., & Gallagher, M. (1995). Basal forebrain cholinergic lesions disrupt increments but not decrements in conditioned stimulus processing. *Journal of Neuroscience*, **15**, 7315–7322.

Corbetta, M. & Shulman, G.L. (2002). Control of goal-directed and stimulus-driven attention in the brain. *Nature Reviews Neuroscience*, **3**, 201–15.

Desimone, R., and Duncan, J. (1995) Neural mechanisms of selective visual attention. *Annual Review of Neuroscience*, **18**, 193–222.

Dickinson, A. & Mackintosh, N.J. (1978). Classical conditioning in animals. *Annual Review of Psychology*, **29**, 587–612.

El-Amamy, H. & Holland, P.C. (2006). Substantia nigra pars compacta is critical to both the acquisition and expression of learned orienting of rats. *European Journal of Neuroscience*, **24**, 270–276.

El-Amamy, H. & Holland, P.C. (2007). Dissociable effects of disconnecting amygdala central nucleus from the ventral tegmental area or substantia nigra on learned orienting and incentive motivation. *European Journal of Neuroscience*, 25, 1557–1567.

Everitt, B. J. & Robbins, T.W. (1997). Central cholinergic systems and cognition. *Annual Review of Psychology*, **48**, 649–684.

Fortin, N.J., Wright, S.P., & Eichenbaum, H. (2004). Recollection-like memory retrieval in rats is dependent on the hippocampus. *Nature*, **431**, 188–191.

Fox, G. D. (1998). *The hippocampus and stimulus selection*. Unpublished Ph.D. dissertation. University of North Carolina, Chapel Hill.

Gallagher, M., Graham, P. W., & Holland, P. C. (1990). The amygdala central nucleus and appetitive Pavlovian conditioning: Lesions impair one class of conditioned behavior. *Journal of Neuroscience*, **10**, 1906–1911.

Groshek, F., Kerfoot, E., McKenna, V., Polackwich, A.S., Gallagher, M., & Holland, P.C. (2005). Amygdala central nucleus function is necessary for learning, but not expression, of conditioned auditory orienting. *Behavioral Neuroscience*, **119**, 202–212.

Hall, G. & Pearce, J. M. (1979). Latent inhibition of a CS during CS-US pairings. *Journal of Experimental Psychology: Animal Behavior Processes*, **5**, 31–42.

Hall, G. & Pearce, J. M. (1982). Restoring the associability of a pre-exposed CS by a surprising event. *Quarterly Journal of Experimental Psychology*, **34B**, 127–140.

Hampshire, A., Duncan, J., & Owen, A.M. (2007). Selective tuning of the blood oxygenation level-dependent response during simple target detection dissociates human frontoparietal subregions. *Journal of Neuroscience*, **27**, 6219–6223.

Han, J. S., Gallagher, M., & Holland, P. C. (1995). Hippocampal lesions disrupt decrements but not increments in conditioned stimulus processing. *Journal of Neuroscience*, **11**, 7323–7329.

Han, J.S., McMahan, R. W., Holland, P. C., & Gallagher, M. (1997). The role of an amygdalo- nigrostriatal pathway in associative learning. *Journal of Neuroscience*, **17**, 3913–3919.

Han, J-S., Holland, P. C., & Gallagher, M. (1999). Disconnection of the amygdala central nucleus and substantia innominata/nucleus basalis disrupts increments in conditioned stimulus processing in rats. *Behavioral Neuroscience*, **113**, 143–151.

Holland, P. C. (1977). Conditioned stimulus as a determinant of the form of the Pavlovian conditioned response. *Journal of Experimental Psychology: Animal Behavior Processes*, **3**, 77–104.

Holland, P. C. (1979). Differential effects of omission contingencies on various components of Pavlovian appetitive conditioned behavior in rats. *Journal of Experimental Psychology: Animal Behavior Processes*, **5**, 178–193.

Holland, P. C. (1988). Excitation and inhibition in unblocking. *Journal of Experimental Psychology: Animal Behavior Processes*, **14**, 261–279.

Holland, P.C. (2005). Amount of training effects in representation-mediated food aversion learning: No evidence for a role for associability changes. *Learning and Behavior*, **33**, 464–478.

Holland, P.C. (2006). Enhanced conditioning produced by surprising increases in reinforcer value are unaffected by lesions of the amygdala central nucleus. *Neurobiology of Learning and Memory*, **85**, 30–35.

Holland, P.C. (2007). Disconnection of the amygdala central nucleus and the substantia innominata/nucleus basalis magnocellularis disrupts performance in a sustained attention task. *Behavioral Neuroscience*, **121**, 80–89.

Holland, P.C., Bashaw, M., & Quinn, J. (2002). Amount of training and stimulus salience affects associability changes in serial conditioning. *Behavioural Processes*, **59**, 169–183.

Holland, P.C., Chik, Y., and Zhang, Q. (2001). Inhibitory learning tests of conditioned stimulus associability in rats with lesions of the amygdala central nucleus. *Behavioral Neuroscience*, **115**, 1154–1158.

Holland, P.C. & Fox, G.D. (2003). Effects of hippocampal lesions in overshadowing and blocking procedures. *Behavioral Neuroscience*, **117**, 650–656.

Holland, P. C. & Gallagher, M. (1993a). Amygdala central nucleus lesions disrupt increments, but not decrements, in conditioned stimulus processing. *Behavioral Neuroscience*, **107**, 246–253.

Holland, P. C. & Gallagher, M. (1993b). Effects of amygdala central nucleus lesions on blocking and unblocking. *Behavioral Neuroscience*, **107**, 235–245.

Holland, P. C. & Gallagher, M. (1999). Amygdala circuitry in attentional and representational processes. *Trends in Cognitive Sciences*, **3**, 65–73.

Holland, P.C. & Gallagher, M. (2006). Different roles for amygdala central nucleus and substantia innominata in the surprise-induced enhancement of learning. *Journal of Neuroscience*, **26**, 3791–3797.

Holland, P. C., Han, J.-S., & Gallagher, M. (2000a). Lesions of the Amygdala central nucleus alter performance in a selective attention task. *Journal of Neuroscience*, **20**, 6701–6706.

Holland, P.C., and Kenmuir, C. (2005). Variations in unconditioned stimulus processing in unblocking. *Journal of Experimental Psychology: Animal Behavior Processes*, **31**, 155–171.

Holland, P. C., Thornton, J. A., & Ciali, L. (2000b). The influence of associability changes in negative patterning and other discriminations. *Journal of Experimental Psychology: Animal Behavior Processes*, **26**, 462–476.

Hunt, P. S. & Campbell, B. A. (1997). Autonomic and behavioral correlates of appetitive conditioning in rats. *Behavioral Neuroscience*, **111**, 494–502.

Kamin, L. J. (1968). Attention like processes in classical conditioning. In M. R. Jones (Ed.), *Miami Symposium on the Prediction of Behavior: Aversive Stimulation*, (pp. 9–32). Coral Gables, Florida: University of Miami Press.

Kapp, B.S., Supple, W. F. Jr., & Whalen, P. J. (1994). The effects of electrical stimulation of the amygdaloid central nucleus on neocortical arousal in the rabbit. *Behavioral Neuroscience*, **108**, 81–93.

Kaye, H. & Pearce, J. M. (1984). The strength of the orienting response during Pavlovian conditioning. *Journal of Experimental Psychology: Animal behavior Processes*, **10**, 90-109.

Kruschke, J. K. (2001). Toward a unified model of attention in associative learning. *Journal of Mathematical Psychology*, **45**, 812–863.

Knudsen, E. I. (2007). Fundamental components of attention. *Annual Review of Neuroscience*, **30**, 57–78.

Lee, H.J., Gallagher, M., & Holland, P.C. (2006a). The role of central amygdala connections to different midbrain dopamine systems for conditioned stimulus processing. Program No. 749.1. *2006 Neuroscience Meeting Planner*. Atlanta Georgia: Society for Neuroscience, Online.

Lee, H.J., Gallagher, M., & Holland, P.C. (2010). The central amygdala projection to the substantia nigra is important for processing prediction error information in appetitive conditioning. Submitted for publication.

Lee, H.J., Groshek, F., Petrovich, G.D., Cantalini, J.P., Gallagher, M., & Holland, P.C. (2005). Role of amygdalo-nigral circuitry in conditioning of a visual stimulus paired with food. *Journal of Neuroscience*, **25**, 3881-3888.

Lee, H.J., Youn, J.M., Gallagher, M., & Holland, P.C. (2008). Temporally-limited role of substantia nigra-central amygdala connections in surprise-induced enhancement of learning. *European Journal of Neuroscience*, **27**, 3043-3049.

Lee, H.J., Youn, J.M., O, M.J., Gallagher, M., & Holland, P.C. (2006b). Role of substantia nigra-amygdala connections in surprise-induced enhancement of attention. *Journal of Neuroscience*, **26**, 6077-6081.

Le Pelley, M. E. (2004). The role of associative history in models of associative learning: A selective review and a hybrid model. *Quarterly Journal of Experimental Psychology: Comparative and Physiological Psychology*, **57(B)**, 193–243

Lin, S.-C. & Nicolelis, M.A.L. (2008). Neuronal ensemble bursting in the basal forebrain encodes salience irrespective of valence. *Neuron*, **59**, 138–149.

Lubow, R. E., Wagner, M., & Weiner, I. (1982). The effects of compound stimulus preexposure of two elements differing in salience on the acquisition of conditioned suppression. *Animal Learning and Behavior*, **10**, 483–489.

Mackintosh, N. J. (1975). A theory of attention: Variations in the associability of stimuli with reinforcement. *Psychological Review*, **82**, 276–298.

Maddux, J.-M. (2008). *The roles of rat medial prefrontal cortex subregions in attention for action and attention for learning*. Ph.D. dissertation submitted to Johns Hopkins University.

Maddux, J.-M., Kerfoot, E.C., Chatterjee, S., & Holland, P.C. (2007). Dissociation of attention in learning and action: Effects of lesions of the amygdala central nucleus, medial prefrontal cortex, and posterior parietal cortex. *Behavioral Neuroscience*, **121**, 63–79.

McDannald, M., Kerfoot, E., Gallagher, M., & Holland, P.C. (2004). Amygdala central nucleus function is necessary for learning but not expression of conditioned visual orienting. *European Journal of Neuroscience*, **20**, 240–248.

Moore, J. W. & Stickney, K. J. (1980). Formation of attentional associative networks in real time role of the hippocampus and implications for conditioning. *Physiological Psychology*, **8**, 207- 217.

Muir, J.L., Everitt, B.J., & Robbins, T.W. (1994). AMPA-induced excitotoxic lesions of the basal forebrain: A significant role for the cortical cholinergic system in attentional function. *Journal of Neuroscience*, **14**, 2313–2326.

Muir, J.L., Everitt, B.J., & Robbins, T.W. (1996). The cerebral cortex of the rat and visual attentional function: Dissociable effects of mediofrontal, cingulate, anterior dorsolateral, and parietal cortex lesions on a five-choice serial reaction time task. *Cerebral Cortex*, **6**, 470–481.

O'Reilly, R.C. & Rudy, J.W. (2001). Conjunctive representations in learning and memory: Principles of cortical and hippocampal function. *Psychological Review*, **108**, 311–345.

Pearce, J. M. & Hall, G. (1980). A model for Pavlovian learning: variations in the effectiveness of conditioned but not of unconditioned stimuli. *Psychological Review*, **106**, 532–552

Pitkänen, A. (2000). Connectivity of the rat amygdaloid complex. In J. Aggleton (Ed.), *The Amygdala: A Functional Analysis*, pp. 31–115. Oxford: Oxford University Press.

Posner, M.I. & Petersen, S.E. (1990). The attention system of the human brain. *Annual Review of Neuroscience*, **13**, 25–42.

Posner, M.I. & Rothbart, M.K. (2007). Research on attention networks as a model for the integration of psychological science. *Annual Review of Psychology*, **58**, 1–23.

Raz, A. & Buhle, J. (2006). Typologies of attentional networks. *Nature Reviews Neuroscience*, **7**, 367–379.

Rescorla, R. A. (1991). Separate reinforcement can enhance the effectiveness of modulators. *Journal of Experimental Psychology: Animal Behavior Processes*, **17**, 259–269.

Rescorla, R.A. (2003). Protection from extinction. *Learning and Behavior*, **31**, 124–132.

Rescorla, R. A. & Holland, P. C. (1982). Behavioral studies of associative learning in animals. *Annual Review of Psychology*, **33**, 265–308.

Rescorla, R. A. & Wagner, A. R. (1972). A theory of Pavlovian conditioning: Variations in the effectiveness of reinforcement and nonreinforcement. In A. H. Black and W. F. Prokasy (Eds), *Classical Conditioning II* (pp. 64–99). New York: Appleton Century Crofts.

Robbins, T.W. (2002). The 5-choice serial reaction time task: behavioural pharmacology and functional neurochemistry. *Psychopharmacology*, **163**, 362–380.

Ross, R. T. & Holland, P. C. (1981). Conditioning of simultaneous and serial feature positive discriminations. *Animal Learning and Behavior*, **9**, 293–303.

Salzman, C.D., and Newsome, W.T. (1994). Neural mechanisms for forming a perceptual decision. *Science*, **264**, 231–237.

Sarter, M. & Bruno, J. P. (1997). Cognitive functions of cortical acetylcholine: toward a unifying hypothesis. *Brain Research Reviews*, **23**, 28–46.

Sarter, M., Hasselmo, M.E., Bruno, J.P., & Givens, B. (2005). Unraveling the attentional functions of cortical cholinergic inputs: interactions between signal-driven and cognitive nodulation of signal detection. *Brain Research Reviews*, **48**, 98–111.

Sarter, M. & McGaughy, J. (1998). Assessment of sustained and divided attention in rats: aspects of validity. *Psychopharmacology*, **138**, 260–262.

Schultz, W., and Dickinson, A. (2000). Neuronal coding of prediction errors. *Annual Review of Neuroscience*, **23**, 473–500.

Schmajuk, N.A. & Larrauri, J.A. (2006). Experimental challenges to theories of classical conditioning: Application of an attentional model of storage and retrieval. *Journal of Experimental Psychology: Animal Behavior Processes*, **32**, 1–20.

Shuler, M.G. & Bear, M.F. (2006). Reward timing in the primary visual cortex. *Science*, **311**, 1606–1609.

Staddon, J.E.R. (2001). *Adaptive dynamics: The theoretical analysis of behavior*. Cambridge, MA: MIT Press.

Sutherland, N. S. & Mackintosh, N. J. (1971). *Mechanisms of animal discrimination learning*. New York: Academic Press.

Teitelbaum, P. & Pellis, P. M. (1992). Toward a synthetic physiological psychology. *Psychological Science*, **3**, 4–20.

Titchener, E.B. (1908). *Lectures on the elementary psychology of feeling and attention*. New York: McMillan Company.

Whalen, P. J., Kapp, B. S., & Pascoe, J. P. (1994). Neuronal activity within the nucleus basalis and conditioned neocortical electroencephalographic activation. *Journal of Neuroscience*, **14**, 1623–1633.

Wilson, P. N., Boumphrey, P., & Pearce, J. M. (1992). Restoration of the orienting response to a light by a change in its predictive accuracy. *Quarterly Journal of Experimental Psychology*, **44B**, 17–36.

Yu, A.J. & Dayan, P. (2005). Uncertainty, neuromodulation, and attention. *Neuron*, **46**, 681–692.

Chapter 13

Neural correlates of attentional set

David N. George, Anaïs M. Duffaud, and Simon Killcross

Introduction

The first demonstration that stimuli may acquire or lose distinctiveness during the course of discrimination learning was provided by Lawrence (1949). Rats were initially trained on a simultaneous discrimination where they had to select one of two runways to locate a reward. The runways differed on several properties and variation on one of these properties (e.g. brightness) signalled the location of food, while the other properties (e.g. floor texture, width) were irrelevant to the solution of the discrimination. In a subsequent stage, animals solved a successive discrimination based on the previously relevant property more rapidly than one based on a previously irrelevant property. A similar effect has been shown a number of times in experiments using an intradimensional-extradimensional (IDED) shift design: animals learn more rapidly about novel stimuli belonging to a previously relevant dimension than they do about novel stimuli belonging to a previously irrelevant dimension (Shepp and Eimas, 1964; Mackintosh and Little, 1969; George and Pearce, 1999; Oswald *et al.*, 2001). These results are generally taken as evidence that, over the course of learning, animals come to attend more to relevant than to irrelevant stimuli, an idea that has been incorporated into a number of models of associative learning (e.g., Sutherland and Mackintosh, 1971; Mackintosh, 1975; Kruschke, 1992; Pearce *et al.*, 1998; Le Pelley, 2004). Indeed, Mackintosh (1974, p597) suggested that experiments using the IDED shift design may provide 'the best evidence that transfer between discrimination problems may be based partly on increases in attention to relevant dimensions and decreases in attention to irrelevant dimensions'.

Over the past two decades, the IDED shift design has been widely used as a tool to examine deficits in executive function in a number of patient populations and has been incorporated into the popular CANTAB cognitive testing battery. Lately, the use of rodent models to investigate the types of cognitive dysfunction observed in these human populations has led to considerable interest in the neural bases of performance on the IDED shift task. Here, we shall review some of the major findings in this area before turning to our recent development of an optional shift task that has allowed us to examine one aspect of IDED shift performance in more detail.

Set-shifting tasks in rodents

When animals learn a discrimination task, the presumed increase in attention to relevant stimuli and/or decrease in attention to irrelevant stimuli is often referred to as the acquisition of an attentional set. To the extent that attention generalizes between similar stimuli, or between values on a stimulus dimension, transfer to a novel discrimination problem where the same dimension is relevant involves an intradimensional shift (IDS), or shift within an attentional set. When stimuli that are irrelevant to the initial discrimination become relevant, the animal must perform an extradimensional shift (EDS)—a shift between attentional sets. In this latter case, it is necessary to ignore a previously relevant dimension (inhibit a previous attentional set) and attend to a previously irrelevant dimension (acquire a new attentional set). In the case of an IDS, it is necessary only to maintain the existing attentional set. Hence there may be multiple, separable processes involved in IDED shift learning: acquisition of a set which involves increase and/or decrease in attention to different stimuli, maintenance of that set, and disengagement from an attentional set.

Two tasks have been widely used to investigate the neural systems involved in set-shifting. The first of these utilizes a relatively conventional comparison of IDS and EDS learning and is based on the touchscreen CANTAB IDED task (Roberts *et al.* 1988) developed for use in humans and non-human primates (described in some detail by Hampshire and Owen 2010, this volume). The CANTAB task was adapted for use in rats by Birrell and Brown (2000) who retained the general task structure to allow some comparison to be drawn between their results and those of experiments involving primates. Birrell and Brown trained their rats to dig in bowls filled with sawdust to retrieve a food reward. The animals then progressed through a series of discrimination tasks in a set order (see Table 13.1). On each trial, the rat was given a choice between two bowls. One bowl contained half of a Honey Nut Loop, the other did not: the animal's task was to choose the baited bowl and avoid the unbaited one. If animals started to dig in the unbaited bowl, an error was recorded and the trial was terminated. The bowls were made distinct from each other by the odour and/or the nature of the digging medium that they contained. The first stage of the experiment involved a simple discrimination (SD) where the bowls

Table 13.1 Simplified design of the rodent intradimensional/extradimensional shift task used by Birrell and Brown (2000)

Phase	Exemplars		Relevant	Irrelevant
Simple discrimination (SD)	**O1**+	**O2**-	Odour	
Compound discrimination (CD)	**O1**/M1+ **O1**/M2+	**O2**/M2- **O2**/M1-	Odour	Medium
Reversal (Rev)	**O2**/M1+ **O2**/M2+	**O1**/M2- **O1**/M1-	Odour	Medium
Intradimensional shift (IDS)	**O3**/M3+ **O3**/M4+	**O4**/M4- **O4**/M3-	Odour	Medium
Reversal (IDR)	**O4**/M3+ **O4**/M4+	**O3**/M4- **O3**/M3-	Odour	Medium
Extradimensional shift (EDS)	O5/**M5**+ O6/**M5**+	O6/**M6**- O5/**M6**-	Medium	Odour
Reversal (EDR)	O5/**M6**+ O6/**M6**+	O6/**M5**- O5/**M5**-	Medium	Odour

Note: On each trial, rats were required to locate a food reward hidden in one of two bowls scented with different odours (O1 to O6) and/or containing different digging media (M1 to M6). In each stage, either odour or medium was relevant to the discrimination. + denotes that an exemplar was associated with reward, - that it was not. Relevant stimuli are shown in bold. Contingencies are shown for animals for whom odour was relevant during the initial stages of the task; for other animals medium was initially relevant and the extradimensional shift involved a transfer to a discrimination where odour was relevant.

differed in either odour or medium. Variation on the alterative dimension was introduced in the second, compound discrimination (CD) stage but was irrelevant to the discrimination. For example, in the SD stage, the odour of thyme might have been paired with food, and the odour of paprika with no food in a constant digging medium. In that case, during the CD stage an animal would experience trials where it was given a choice between thyme scented stone chips and paprika scented wood beads, or between thyme scented wood beads and paprika scented stone chips. In either case, the bowl containing the thyme scented digging medium contained the reward. The CD stage was followed by a reversal of this discrimination (REV): the same exemplars were presented, and the same dimension was relevant, but the food reward was located in the alternative bowl – that with the paprika scent. The animals then experienced an IDS (new odours and digging media were used but the same dimension was relevant as in the previous stages), a reversal of the IDS discrimination (IDR), an EDS (again, the bowls contained new odours and digging media, but the previously relevant dimension was irrelevant, and the previously irrelevant dimension was relevant), and finally a reversal of the EDS discrimination (EDR). As expected, rats learned to solve the IDS

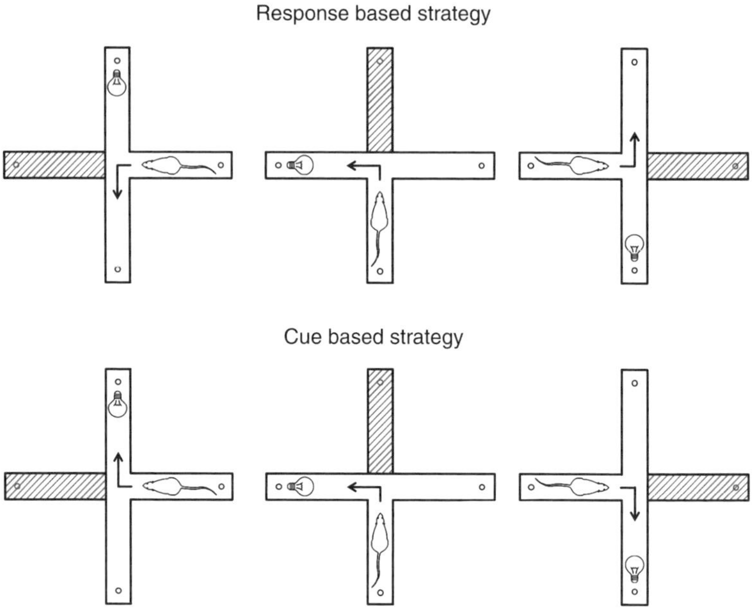

Fig. 13.1 Maze-based strategy set-shifting task. For the response version (upper panel), the baited arm is always in the same location relative to the start arm and the animal must always make the same response (turn 90° left) to retrieve the food reward. In the visual-cue version (lower panel), the arm containing a visual cue is always baited.

discrimination more rapidly than they learned to solve the EDS discrimination, suggesting that they had formed an attentional set during the initial stages of training.

The second commonly used set-shifting task involves a shift between different strategies. Strategy set-shifting experiments consist of just two stages – animals are trained consecutively on two discriminations which involve responding to different characteristics of the environment. In one version of the strategy set-shifting task, animals are trained in a plus-maze (see Figure 13.1; e.g., Ragozzino, Ragozzino *et al.* 2002; Floresco, Ghods-Sharifi *et al.*, 2006) and must shift between response- and visual cue-based strategies. On each trial, one arm of the maze serves as the start arm; the arm opposite the start arm is blocked off, and the rat must choose between making a 90° turn to the left or to the right. A visual cue is located in either one or other of the choice arms, and one of the choice arms is baited with a food reward. The food is always placed in the same position relative to the start arm for the response version of the task (see the top panel of Figure 13.1), and so the rat must always turn in the same direction to obtain the reward. In the visual cue version (see bottom panel of Figure 13.1), however, the arm containing the cue is baited on every trial. Animals are trained on one of tasks until they have achieved a performance criterion, and the following day they are transferred to the alternative task. Trials- or errors-to-criterion on this second, post-shift, task provide indices of shift performance.

Clear parallels may be drawn between strategy set-shifting and the EDS component of attentional set-shifting. In both cases, animals must learn to respond to a stimulus (location/cue) or stimulus dimension (odour/medium), which was previously irrelevant, and to inhibit responding to a previously relevant stimulus or dimension. There are important differences between the tasks too: strategy set-shifting designs involve a single shift; there is no equivalent to an IDS in these experiments, and hence they cannot be used to assess relative speed with which IDS and EDS discriminations are acquired. Also, the stimuli and apparatus used in the two stages of a strategy set-shifting experiment are the same. This raises the possibility that the shift involves a partial reversal of the initial discrimination. Consider, for example, a situation in which a rat has first learned to always turn left to gain reward. In a post-shift visual cue-based discrimination, there will be some trials on which the visual cue is located in the right arm of the maze and the animal must reverse its previously acquired tendency to turn left if it is to make a correct response. Hence, any manipulation that affects strategy set-shifting performance may be due to impaired reversal learning, rather than set-shifting ability. As we shall see in the next section, this consideration may not be terribly important. Lesions that produce specific effects on reversal learning whilst sparing EDS performance in an attentional set-shifting procedure have the same effects on strategy set-shifting. That is, they affect reversals of response- and visual cue-based discriminations but not shifting between these discriminations.

Use of the same stimuli in both stages of a strategy set-shifting experiment has some advantages: it allows a more detailed analysis of the types of errors made post-shift than is possible in attentional set-shifting. Let us return to the situation in which a rat is first trained to adopt a response strategy (e.g. always turn left) and is then shifted to the cue based task where reward is coincident with a visual stimulus. Post-shift trials can be either incongruent, where the visual cue is located in the previously nonreinforced (right) arm; or congruent, where the cue is located in the previously reinforced (left) arm. On incongruent trials, when the response- and cue-based strategies are in conflict, an error will be scored whenever an animal enters the arm that is consistent with the pre-shift rule. If, as might happen early in post-shift training, errors are made on more than 50% of incongruent trials it is likely that the animal is still using its pre-shift rule and the errors are classed as *perseverative* errors. The number of perseverative errors made is generally used as an index of an animal's ability to shift from a previously relevant strategy, since an animal making a large number of perseverative errors appears to be continuing to respond to the pre-shift rule. When errors are made on 50% or fewer of incongruent trials it is assumed that the animal is no longer using the pre-shift strategy. After this point, it is believed that errors on incongruent trials are not indicative of perseveration, but of a failure to acquire or maintain a new strategy and regression to the old strategy. Hence, these errors are characterized as *regressive*. Errors on congruent trials occur when the animal enters an arm that is consistent with neither the pre- or post-shift strategy: it makes a *never-reinforced* choice. Together, regressive and never-reinforced errors provide an index of the animal's ability to form and maintain a new strategy. A high rate of never-reinforced errors may also be indicative of a failure to inhibit inappropriate strategies: such errors in the absence of perseverative or regressive errors, for example, would mean that the animal is reliably choosing the right arm, consistent with a reversal of the pre-shift rule.

Throughout the following discussion of experiments using these two general procedures, we shall assume that strategy set-shifting and an EDS engage the same attentional processes since each involves learning about a previously irrelevant stimulus dimension. We shall also use the terms 'acquisition of a set' and 'set formation' interchangeably to refer to increases in attention to a relevant dimension and/or decreases in attention to an irrelevant dimension; and 'set shifting', unless otherwise qualified, to refer to the EDS components of both tasks.

Neural systems involved in set-shifting

Prefrontal cortex

There is considerable evidence that the frontal lobes are involved in the modulation of attentional set-shifting from studies involving humans and non-human primates. Almost half a century ago, Milner (1963, 1964) reported that patients with dorsolateral frontal lobe lesions, resulting from surgery performed to control seizures, were impaired on the EDS component of the Wisconsin Card Sorting Task[1] (WCST; Berg, 1948; Grant and Berg, 1948), but that those with orbital frontal lesions were not. Using a modified version of the

[1] In the WCST, participants are presented with stimulus cards showing different numbers of various shapes printed in different colours. Participants are required to sort these cards according to an undisclosed rule (i.e. shape, number, or colour) with corrective feedback given by an experimenter. Periodically over the course of the test there are unannounced

WCST designed to reduce stimulus ambiguity and refusal rates in patient populations, Nelson (1976) confirmed that the poorer performance seen in patients with frontal lobe damage was the result of perseverative responding. More recently, experiments using the CANTAB IDED task have also found impaired EDS performance in patients with frontal lobe damage (Owen *et al.*, 1991), as well as in a number of patient populations suffering from disorders associated to some degree with frontal dysfunction, such as schizophrenia (Elliott *et al.*, 1995), Parkinson's disease (Downes *et al.*, 1989), and Huntington's disease (Lawrence *et al.*, 1996).

Lesions of the lateral prefrontal cortex (lPFC) in marmosets also result in a selective impairment on the EDS component of the monkey version of the CANTAB IDED task (Dias *et al.*, 1996a, 1996b, 1997). Animals with these lesions show normal performance at all other stages of the IDED task (a series of IDS discriminations, and the reversal of the EDS discrimination). Dias *et al.*, (1997) found evidence of normal attentional set formation in these animals: IDS performance was significantly better than EDS performance, and performance improved over a series of IDS discriminations. Interestingly, there was no effect of lesion following a second EDS (reverting to the original assignment of relevant and irrelevant dimensions). It appears that lPFC lesions only produce a performance deficit when shifting from an existing attentional set to an entirely novel one. In contrast to the effects of lateral prefrontal lesions, lesions of the orbitofrontal cortex (OFC) selectively impaired performance on the reversal of the EDS discrimination. These findings imply that OFC and lPFC are involved in different aspects of performance on the IDED task. The OFC is implicated in shifting between responses to individual stimuli, whereas the lPFC supports shifting between entire stimulus dimensions or rules, suggesting a possible hierarchical organization of these structures (Robbins 2007).

Over the past decade, there has been a move towards investigating the neural bases of attentional set-shifting in rodents. Testing in rodents provides many practical advantages over using primates including, but not limited to: the speed at which animals acquire the tasks (in Birrell and Brown's IDED task, rats complete all stages of the experiment within a single day; Dias *et al.* trained their marmosets for a minimum of two or three days at each stage), purchase and housing costs, the ease with which some surgical and histological procedures may be performed on smaller brains, the availability of transgenic rodent models, and the ability to introduce additional stimulus modalities such as

shifts between these rules. Hence, the participants must shift between responding according to one perceptual dimension to another – an extradimensional shift.

texture to which the rodent vibrissae are highly sensitive. Although there has been some question as to whether rats possess a direct homologue of primate dorsolateral prefrontal cortex (dlPFC; e.g., Preuss, 1995), it has been suggested that functional homogeneity between primate and rodent PFC is sufficient to allow comparisons between species to be made (Kolb and Robbins, 2003). On this basis, there is evidence that rodent medial prefrontal cortex (mPFC) is related to primate dlPFC (Uylings *et al.*, 2003).

Both lesions to, and temporary inactivation of, the mPFC in rats result in impairment on a number of tasks involving shifting between rules. These include shifts between matching- and non matching-to-sample (Joel *et al.*, 1997), between spatial- and cue-based strategies in the Morris water maze (de Bruin *et al.*, 1994), or in a cheeseboard task (Ragozzino, Wilcox *et al.*, 1999), between response- and place-based strategies in a plus-maze (Ragozzino, Detrick, and Kesner, 1999), and between place and odour discriminations (Ragozzino *et al.*, 2003). When Birrell and Brown (2000) tested rats with mPFC lesions on their attentional set-shifting task, they observed a pattern of results consistent with the behaviour of marmosets with lesions to the lPFC. Their lesioned rats showed entirely normal performance at all stages of the task except for the EDS discrimination, where they took significantly more trials to reach a criterion of six consecutive correct choices compared to sham-operated control animals. Using the same task, McAlonan and Brown (2003; see also Kim and Ragozzino, 2004) found that lesions to the OFC resulted in a selective impairment on reversal learning while leaving EDS performance intact, consistent with the effects of OFC lesions in marmosets.

Temporarily inactivating structures by the infusion of local anaesthetics such as tetracaine or bupivacaine, or of the $GABA_A$ agonist muscimol, has allowed researchers to elucidate the involvement of structures at different stages of a set-shifting task. Ragozzino, Detrick, and Kesner (1999), for example, infused tetracaine or a saline vehicle directly into the prelimbic (PrL) and infralimbic (IL) subregions of the mPFC prior to either initial (pre-shift) learning, or post-shift learning in a strategy set-shifting procedure. Hence, some animals had functioning PrL and IL mPFC only during pre-shift learning, whereas for others these structures were functional only during post-shift learning. Ragozzino *et al.* found that inactivation of the PrL and IL mPFC had no impact on the rate of acquisition of either the response- or place-based discriminations during pre-shift learning, and inactivation during pre-shift learning had no effect on post-shift performance. The PrL and IL subregions of mPFC were, however, necessary for normal acquisition of a post-shift task: inactivation of these structures during learning of the post-shift task resulted in significantly impaired performance caused by an increase in perseverative errors. Floresco *et al.* (2008) found essentially the same pattern of results following temporary inactivation of PrL in an automated strategy set-shifting task in which rats were presented with two response levers each located below a stimulus light. The animals had to learn to respond either to one particular lever (response version) or to whichever lever was signalled by the illumination of the light above it (visual cue version). In these two studies, inactivation of PrL either in combination with IL or by itself had no effect on the acquisition of the reversal of a discrimination, suggesting that the strategy set-shifting deficits were not due to the partial reversal component of the set-shift. Further support for this contention is provided by observation that lesions to the OFC impair reversal learning but not strategy set-shifting (Ghods-Sharifi *et al.*, 2008).

Damage or inactivation of mPFC encompassing PrL consistently results in impaired set-shifting performance in both attentional and strategy set-shifting procedures. The results from inactivation studies suggest that PrL is involved in set-shifting, but not set formation/maintenance: if PrL was involved in the latter processes, one would expect inactivation during initial learning to influence set-shifting performance. Further evidence that PrL inactivation results in a set-shifting deficit comes from the analysis of post-shift error types. If the PrL is involved in inhibiting the pre-shift strategy, or in generating a new strategy, then inactivation should produce an increase in errors early in post-shift training consistent with utilization of the pre-shift strategy. An increase in these perseverative errors is exactly what is seen following PrL inactivation. If, alternatively, the PrL is involved in the acquisition of a new strategy once it has been selected, a different pattern of errors would be expected. In that case, inactivation might lead to regression to the pre-shift strategy, or generation of never-reinforced errors later in training (see Ragozzino, 2007). The evidence suggests that the PrL supports set-shifting by inhibiting a previously relevant strategy.

The results are not so clear, however, for other subregions of mPFC. Set-shifting deficits have been observed following combined inactivation or lesions of PrL and IL, and following more selective inactivation of PrL alone. The results of these experiments were broadly similar; there is no apparent effect of including IL in the manipulation. No studies have specifically looked at the effects of selective lesions or inactivation of IL on set-shifting performance except for our own experiments that are discussed later in this chapter. Hence, at this point we cannot make any firm comments on the structure's role in set-shifting behaviour. The area of mPFC dorsal to PrL has also received relatively little attention, and what little attention it has received has generated conflicting data. de Bruin *et al.* (1994) included a group with lesions to the dorsomedial PFC (dmPFC) in their study. The dmPFC lesioned animals sustained damage to the anterior cingulate cortex (ACC) and medial precentral cortex, and showed normal reversal learning but impaired set-shifting. Ragozzino, Wilcox *et al.* (1999), however, found no effect of ACC inactivation on set-shifting behaviour. To further complicate matters, Ng *et al.* (2007), observed a selective deficit on the IDS stage of an attentional set-shifting task following lesions to either anterior or posterior cingulate cortex. The authors claim that animals still formed attentional sets (that is, they increased attention to relevant cues) following cingulate lesions and that their results can be explained by an impaired ability to reduce attention to irrelevant cues. The evidence to support the former claim is weak – they cite the fact that lesioned animals show normal performance on a reversal of the IDS discrimination, but ignore the detail that they acquire the EDS discrimination in (numerically) fewer trials than the IDS discrimination. We shall discuss the involvement of ACC in set formation in more detail later in this chapter.

Medial striatum

The medial striatum is a major recipient of efferent projections from mPFC. The ACC projects to the dorsomedial striatum (dmS) and core of the nucleus accumbens (NAc); PrL also projects to dmS, the NAc core, and to a lesser extent the NAc shell; within the striatum, IL projects almost exclusively to the NAc shell (Heidbreder and Groenewegen, 2003). The area also appears to play a role in the formation and maintenance of attentional set. Temporary inactivation of the dmS results in a strategy set-shifting deficit (Ragozzino, Ragozzino *et al.*, 2002). dmS inactivation during acquisition of the pre-shift task has no effect on learning that task or the post-shift task; post-shift inactivation of dmS results in slower acquisition of the post-shift discrimination. The deficit does not, however, appear to be the same as that observed following PrL/IL inactivation: rather than seeing an increase in perseverative errors, Ragozzino, Ragozzino *et al.* found an increase in the number of regressive errors. Following a shift from one task to another, the animals were able to stop using the previously relevant strategy but then they later reverted to it. This pattern of errors suggests that inactivation of the dmS results in an impaired ability to maintain a new strategy or attentional set. Post-shift inactivation of the NAc core also disrupts set-shifting and results in increases in regressive and never-reinforced errors (Floresco, Ghods-Sharifi *et al.*, 2006). Inactivation of the NAc shell post-shift had no effect, but inactivation during acquisition of the pre-shift discrimination facilitated post-shift learning.

Several functions appear to be served by the medial striatum. Facilitation of a shift following inactivation of the NAc shell during initial learning suggests that the shell is involved in the formation of an attentional set. Without a functioning NAc shell, animals simply do not learn to ignore irrelevant stimuli and hence learn about them more rapidly than control animals when they are later relevant. A similar effect of NAc shell lesions is seen in latent inhibition: lesioned animals fail to show retarded acquisition of conditioned responding following nonreinforced preexposure to a stimulus (Weiner *et al.*, 1999). An increase in regressive and never-reinforced errors following inactivation of the NAc core suggests that it is involved in the maintenance of novel sets. That core inactivation does not result in an increase in perseverative errors suggests that it is not involved in disengaging from an established set. Increases in regressive and never-reinforced errors indicate that the role of the core is to maintain a novel set that conflicts with a previous strategy, and to inhibit inappropriate strategies such as reversal of the original discrimination. The dmS also supports the maintenance of novel sets.

Mediodorsal thalamic nucleus

Rose and Woolsey (1948) defined the prefrontal cortex as the cortical projection area of the mediodorsal thalamic nucleus (MD). The MD and mPFC have reciprocal connections, and the MD also projects to the NAc (Groenewegen, 1988). This pattern of connectivity led Floresco and colleagues (Block *et al.*, 2007) to propose that these three areas form a cortical-striatal-thalamic network that supports set-shifting behaviour. Block *et al.* found that inactivation of MD impaired set-shifting by increasing the number of perseverative and never-reinforced errors, suggesting that the structure is involved in disengagement from an established set, and inhibiting inappropriate sets. They then conducted a series of disconnection studies to examine the role of the pathways connecting the MD, mPFC, and NAc in shifting. In each case, two of the three structures were inactivated contralaterally.[2] Disconnection of the mPFC and MD, and of the mPFC and NAc resulted in impaired set-shifting performance and an increase in perseverate errors. Disconnection of the MD and NAc,

[2] The disconnections consisted of the unilateral inactivation of one structure and contralateral inactivation of a second structure. In a network where one structures projects to the other, contralateral inactivation removes the source of these projections in one hemisphere and their target in the other hemisphere, disrupting the flow of information between the structures. To control for any effects of unilateral inactivation of MD, mPFC or NAc, Block *et al.* included groups that received either unilateral inactivation of one of these structures or ipsilateral inactivation of two of them. Neither unilateral nor ipsilateral inactivation had any effect on behaviour relative to saline infused animals, suggesting that the effects of contralateral inactivation were due to the functional disconnection of structures.

however, did not cause a significant decrement in shifting performance, but was accompanied by an increase in never-reinforced errors. Since the MD shows increased activity following negative, but not positive, feedback in humans performing the WCST (Monchi *et al.* 2001), Block *et al.* suggest that the MD is involved in encoding information about changes in contingencies with reward. The MD-mPFC pathway relays this information to the mPFC, signalling a need to disengage from a previous strategy and shift to a new one. Once an animal has inhibited a previous strategy, the MD-NAc pathway suppresses inappropriate strategies, and when the appropriate strategy has been selected, the PFC-NAc pathway facilitates the maintenance of this new strategy.

Entorhinal cortex

Although the vast majority of research into the neural basis of set shifting has focused on frontal regions, other areas such as the entorhinal cortex are also implicated in attentional processes. The entorhinal cortex is of special interest because it is the main source of sensory input to the hippocampus and projects to the prefrontal cortex (Condé *et al.*, 1995). Lesions to the entorhinal cortex abolish latent inhibition (Coutureau *et al.*, 1999; Oswald *et al.*, 2002), an effect that can be explained by the reduction in attention to a preexposed stimulus (Mackintosh, 1975; Pearce and Hall, 1980; Lubow, 1989), and Oswald *et al.* (2001) found that these lesions also abolish the IDED effect.

Oswald *et al.* (2001) employed a modified version of an IDED design previously used in humans (Krushcke, 1996) and pigeons (George and Pearce, 1999). The design of their experiment is shown in Table 13.2, and while it is somewhat more complex than the IDED tasks we have so far considered, it is logically equivalent. Animals were trained on a Pavlovian discrimination in conditioning chambers where either one dimension (visual properties of the walls) or another (tactile properties of the floor) was relevant and the other was irrelevant. Following acquisition of this discrimination, novel wallpapers (white vs. black) and floors (warm vs. cool) were substituted and the animals were divided into two groups. For animals in the IDS group the dimension that was relevant during stage one remained relevant, whereas for animals in the EDS group the previously irrelevant dimension became relevant. Oswald *et al.* found that whereas sham-operated rats acquired the IDS discrimination more rapidly than the EDS discrimination, animals with lesions to the entorhinal cortex showed equivalent performance on the two tasks. There was no evidence that lesioned animals could learn to attend more to one stimulus dimension than to another.

Table 13.2 Simplified design of the intradimensional/extradimensional shift task used by Oswald et al. (2001)

Phase	Exemplars		Relevant	Irrelevant
Stage 1: Training	**check**/bumpy: T+ **check**/smooth: T+ **spot**/bumpy: C+ **spot**/smooth: C+	**check**/bumpy: C- **check**/smooth: C- **spot**/bumpy: T- **spot**/smooth: T-	wallpaper	Floor
Stage 2: IDS	**white**/warm: T+ **white**/cool: T+ **black**/warm: C+ **black**/cool: C+	**white**/warm: C- **white**/cool: C- **black**/warm: T- **black**/cool: T-	wallpaper	Floor
Stage 2: EDS	white/**warm**: T+ black/**warm**: T+ white/**cool**: C+ black/**cool**: C+	white/**warm**: C- black/**warm**: C- white/**cool**: T- black/**cool**: T-	floor	wallpaper

Note: Rats were trained in conditioning chambers that were made distinct from each other by the decoration of their walls and the tactile properties of their floor. Either the visual or tactile stimuli signalled the relationship between a tone (T) and a clicker (C) and food delivery. Following stage 1 training, animals were given either an IDS to a new discrimination where the same dimension was relevant, or an EDS to a discrimination where the previously irrelevant dimension was relevant. + denotes that a cue was paired with food, - that it was not. Relevant stimuli are shown in bold.

The authors submit that attentional modulation of stimuli by the entorhinal cortex results in them acquiring distinctiveness or equivalence. Stimuli that are relevant to the solution of a discrimination become less similar to each other, whereas stimuli that are irrelevant become more similar. This suggestion is consistent with the proposal that the entorhinal cortex is involved in a process of redundancy compression (increased generalization between cues that have signalled the same outcome; Gluck and Myers, 1993), and other evidence that it is implicated in predictive differentiation (reduced generalization between cues that have signalled different outcomes; Coutureau *et al.*, 2002). Honey *et al.* (2010, this volume) argue that these changes in similarity may be best explained in terms of simple associative principles rather than an additional, explicitly attentional, process. Whether this is true or not, acquired distinctiveness and equivalence may well play a role in IDED shift performance that is dissociable from that of the cortical-striatal-thalamic system described earlier.

Neurochemical modulation of set-shifting

Monoamines

Dopamine (DA), serotonin (5-HT), and noradrenalin (NA) are distributed throughout the rat mPFC and striatum. Although prefrontal DA dysfunction is implicated in cognitive impairments associated with a number of human disorders, its role in attentional set-shifting has not always been entirely clear. 6-Hydroxydopamine (6-OHDA) lesions of the prefrontal cortex result in marked prefrontal DA depletion, elevated levels of evoked DA in the striatum, and improved EDS performance in marmosets (Roberts *et al.*, 1994). Crofts *et al.* (2001) concluded that this improved EDS performance was due to an impaired ability to acquire an attentional set in the first place: when tested over a series of IDS discriminations, control animals showed accelerated learning whereas lesioned animals did not. In the rat, inhibition of the DA metabolism catalyst catechol-*O*-methyltransferase (COMT) by systemic administration of tolcapone has no effect on tonic levels of extracellular DA in the mPFC, but does elevate phasic increases in DA. COMT inhibition also improves EDS discrimination performance (Tunbridge *et al.*, 2004). It is possible that increases in mPFC DA facilitate shifts in attention from one dimension to another, but it is also possible that Tunbridge *et al.'s* results provide further support for the idea that increases in striatal DA impair set formation. There is some evidence that tolcapone can increase levels of DA in the striatum (Acquas *et al.*, 1992). If this is the case, then both 6-OHDA lesions of the mPFC and COMT inhibition may impair striatum-mediated set formation by increasing DA concentrations to supraoptimal levels.

Manipulation of different DA receptor subtypes by direct infusion of agonists and antagonists into the PrL has provided some more solid evidence that prefrontal DA is involved in set shifting. Ragozzino (2002) found that infusion of the DA D_1 receptor antagonist SCH23990 had no effect on the acquisition of either response- or cue-based tasks in a plus-maze, but impaired shifting from one to the other by increasing the number of perseverative errors. D_1 and D_2 agonists had no effect on set-shifting (Floresco, Magyar *et al.*, 2006). Floresco, Magyar *et al.* also reported that infusion of a D_2 antagonist or D_4 agonist impaired set-shifting by increasing perseverative errors, whereas a D_4 antagonist improved shifting performance. Following a shift from one task to another, DA D_1 and D_2 receptors appear to operate together to inhibit a previously relevant dimension. The opposing actions of D_4 receptor agonists and antagonists may be due to consequent changes in DA release or NMDA receptor activity. Overall it is fair to assume that mPFC DA is involved in set-shifting but, since changes in mPFC DA levels can affect DA in other parts of a cortical-striatal-thalamic circuit as well as activity in other neurotransmitter systems, manipulations that might be expected to impair set-shifting performance might actually enhance it.

The nature of the involvement of NA in extradimensional set-shifting is far more certain. Systemic administration of the α_2-adrenergic autoreceptor antagonist atipamezole improves performance on an EDS discrimination, and this improvement is reversed by local infusion of α_1-, but not β-, adrenergic receptor antagonists in the mPFC (Lapiz and Morilak, 2006). These results suggest that increasing prefrontal α_1 activity facilitates shifting between dimensions, as does increasing tonic NA levels in the mPFC through chronic treatment with the NA reuptake blocker desipramine (Lapiz *et al.*, 2007). Conversely, prefrontal NA-ergic deafferentation impairs EDS discrimination learning (McGaughy *et al.*, 2008), and this impairment is reversed by administration of an NA uptake blocker. A selective impairment on EDS performance has also been shown following lesions to the dorsal noradrenergic bundle through which the locus coeruleus provides the main NA input to the mPFC (Tait *et al.*, 2007).

The effect of selective 5-HT depletion on set-shifting has not been widely explored in the rat. Clarke *et al.* (2005) found that prefrontal 5-HT depletion did not affect IDS or EDS performance but did impair reversal learning, suggesting that 5-HT is not involved in attentional set-shifting. Hatcher *et al.* (2005) did observe improved performance at both the REV and EDS stages of an attentional set shifting task in rats that had received subchronic systemic pretreatment with 5-HT_6 receptor antagonists, but suggested that these effects might be due to the effects of the drugs on DA, NA, and acetylcholine (ACh) in the mPFC. It appears that 5-HT is not involved in set shifting, but is involved in reversal learning.

Acetylcholine

Cholinergic deafferentation of the mPFC has no effect on set-shifting (McGaughy *et al.*, 2008), but central blockade of muscarinic cholinergic receptors by systemic administration of scopolamine impairs both acquisition of an EDS discrimination and its reversal (Chen *et al.*, 2004). Because the scopolamine was administered systemically in the latter study, little can be concluded about the exact locus of the effect, but the authors suggested that it was likely to be the striatum. There may be some support for this position. 192-IgG-saporin lesions of the basal forebrain, which result in cortical ACh depletion, but do not affect striatal cholinergic neurons have no effect on set-shifting or reversal learning (Tait and Brown, 2008), whereas local infusion of scopolamine into the dmS impairs reversal learning (Ragozzino, Jih and Tzavos 2002) and ACh efflux in the dmS increases during reversal, but not acquisition, of place learning (Ragozzino *et al.*, 2009). Hence, it is probable that striatal ACh is involved in reversal learning, but there is still no clear evidence that it modulated EDS performance. It is interesting to note that although prefrontal ACh depletion does not significantly affect either IDS or EDS learning relative to control animals, the difference in the rate of acquisition of IDS and EDS discriminations is abolished, indicating that ACh depletion may impair attentional set formation (McGaughy *et al.*).

Glutamate

Blockade of NMDA or AMPA glutamate receptors in the mPFC by local infusion of antagonists into the PrL/IL region impairs strategy set-shifting performance, the former by increasing perseverative errors, and the latter by producing a more general increase across error types (Stefani *et al.*, 2003; Stefani and Moghaddam, 2005). Systemic administration of the NMDA antagonist phencyclidine (PCP) also impairs EDS performance when given as an acute (Egerton *et al.*, 2005), subchronic (Rodefer *et al.*, 2005; Rodefer *et al.*, 2008), chronic (Egerton *et al.*, 2008), or early postnatal treatment (Broberg *et al.*, 2008). While some of these deficits may be due to effects of PCP beyond NMDA glutamate receptors, Nicolle and Baxter (2003) found that in aged rats, which were impaired at an EDS discrimination compared to younger controls, EDS performance correlated with levels of Kainate binding in cingulate cortex and NMDA binding in the dmS. Hence, glutamate receptor activity throughout the rat mPFC and dmS is involved in shifting attention between dimensions.

Optional set-shifting

One limitation of the attentional set-shifting and the strategy set-shifting tasks discussed so far is that they do not always provide a direct assay of attentional set formation or maintenance. The effects of several manipulations have been attributed to modulation of these processes, but certain assumptions must often be made to support these attributions. Dias *et al.* (1997) claimed that set formation was unaffected in marmosets with lesions to either the lPFC or OFC, since these animals showed the same improvement in performance over a series of IDS discriminations: they assumed that this improvement indicated that the animals formed an attentional set. This assumption ignores, however, effects of habituation to the task and testing apparatus, or more general 'learning-to-learn' effects (learning-set formation; Harlow, 1949). Similarly, Crofts *et al.* (2001) interpreted the failure to show improved performance across a series of IDS discriminations by animals with 6-OHDA lesions to the frontal cortex as evidence of a failure to acquire an attentional set when it could reflect a failure to acquire a learning set.

The vast majority of experiments using Birrell and Brown's IDED task have revealed no effect of any sort on IDS performance. This may, of course, be because the manipulations that have been assessed with this task do not affect ID shifting. It is, however, also possible that the task is not especially sensitive to small changes in the ability to form or maintain attentional sets. In experiments using Birrell and Brown's procedure, it is quite normal to give the animals four 'discovery' trials at the start of each stage. In these trials, they are allowed to dig in both bowls and are therefore exposed to the reward contingencies. These four trials may also contribute to the criterion of six consecutive correct trials that defines the end-point for each discrimination. Animals typically solve the IDS discrimination is approximately nine or ten trials, meaning that their last error occurs, on average, no later than trial four – a discovery trial in which they are not penalized for making an initial incorrect choice. Given that rats clearly find this task very easy to solve, it is unlikely that any facilitation of set formation could result in improved performance, and it is possible that disruption of set formation would fail to cause a noticeable decrement in performance. That Ng *et al.* (2007) did observe impaired IDS learning following cingulate lesions does not negate this argument: it may reflect an especially profound effect of these lesions.

The strategy set-shifting task has no IDS stage. Rather, impairments to set formation or maintenance are inferred from a particular pattern of post-shift errors. Errors of the perseverative type made later in post-shift learning are termed regressive and are assumed to be symptomatic of a failure to maintain a set; whereas never-reinforced errors reflect an inability to inhibit inappropriate sets and, by extension, to acquire an appropriate novel set. Manipulations during initial learning that improve post-shift performance (e.g., Floresco, Ghods-Sharifi *et al.*, 2006) may also be attributed to failure to acquire a set. The strategy set-shifting task does not, however, allow one to assess generalization of attention between stimuli belonging to the same dimension—that is, the maintenance of attentional set following a shift from one set of stimuli to another—as is seen in a standard IDED procedure.

In an attempt to overcome some of these concerns, and to provide a more direct measure of attentional set formation and maintenance, we recently developed a novel, automated task to assess set formation and maintenance, based on an optional shift design (Duffaud *et al.*, 2007). Just like the attentional set-shifting task, in the classic optional shift task (e.g., Kendler *et al.*, 1964) rats are initially trained on a discrimination between pairs of stimuli which differ along two dimensions (see the left panel of Figure 13.2). One dimension (e.g., brightness) is relevant to the solution of the discrimination, whereas the second dimension (e.g., size) is irrelevant. For example, animals may be rewarded for selecting the darker of two squares, regardless of its size. Once this discrimination has been mastered, the contingencies associated with one pair of

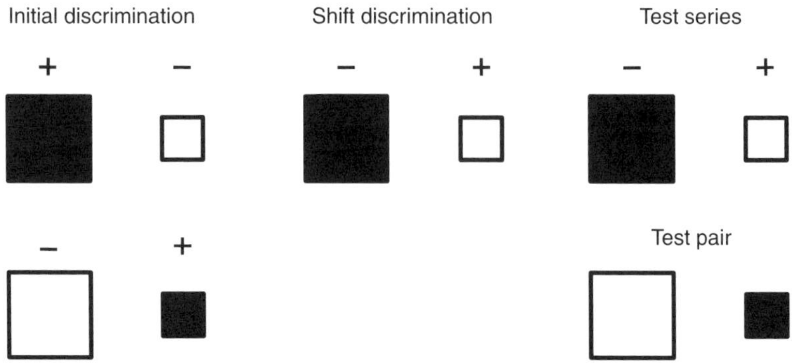

Fig. 13.2 The optional-shift task employed by Kendler et al. (1964).

the training stimuli are reversed (middle panel of Figure 13.2). Since the two stimuli used in this shift discrimination differ in both colour and size, the rule shift that has given rise to the change in contingency is ambiguous: it is consistent with both a full reversal of the original discrimination, where the lighter square is now associated with reward; or an extradimensional shift, where selecting the smaller square is rewarded. Animals' tendency to learn a reversal or extradimensional shift during the second phase of training is assessed during a test phase in which the shift discrimination is interleaved with nonreinforced test trials with the alternate pair of stimuli used in the initial discrimination. Responses to the lighter of these squares are consistent with a reversal shift, whereas responses to the smaller of these squares are consistent with an extradimensional shift.

Schwartz *et al.* (1971) adapted the optional shift design to assess rats' relative tendency to make optional intradimensional and extradimensional shifts by employing different sets of stimuli, which differed along the same two dimensions (in this case shape and location), in the initial discrimination and in the shift discrimination and subsequent test series. They found that rats made more IDS than EDS choices on test, and it was a version of this task that we used as an index of attentional set formation and maintenance.

The simplified design of our optional shift task is shown in Table 13.3. Rats were initially trained on a conditional instrumental discrimination in a standard operant conditioning chamber. On each trial, an audiovisual compound stimulus consisting of one of two auditory cues (A1 or A2) and one of two visual cues (V1 or V2) was presented for 4 min. Two response levers (R1 and R2) were inserted into the chamber throughout the experimental session, and during stimulus presentations responding on one of these levers was reinforced by the delivery of food pellets according to a variable interval schedule.

Table 13.3 Simplified design of the optional shift task used by Duffaud et al. (2007)

Phase	Exemplars		Relevant	Irrelevant
Stage 1: Initial discrimination	**A1**/V1: R1+ **A1**/V2: R1+ **A2**/V1: R2+ **A2**/V2: R2+	**A1**/V1: R2– **A1**/V2: R2– **A2**/V1: R1– **A2**/V2: R1–	Auditory	Visual
Stage 2: Shift discrimination	**A3/V3**: R1+ **A4/V4**: R2+	**A3/V3**: R2– **A4/V4**: R1–	Auditory and visual	
Optional shift test	**A3/V4**	**A4/V3**		

Note: Stimuli A1 to A4 were 500Hz, 8kHz, and 2kHz tones and a 10Hz train of clicks; V1 to V4 were a houselight, two panel lights, a magazine light and darkness. R1 and R2 were left and right levers. Both levers were extended at all times. + denotes that responses were reinforced, – that they were not. Responding on neither lever was reinforced on test trials. Contingencies are shown for animals for whom auditory cues were relevant during stage 1; for other animals, visual cues were relevant and auditory cues were irrelevant. Relevant stimuli are shown in bold.

Which lever was reinforced was determined, for each animal, by either the auditory or the visual component of the audiovisual compound. Contingencies were structured such that stimuli belonging to one modality were relevant and the other modality was irrelevant. For some rats the auditory cues were relevant and the visual cues irrelevant, whereas for others the visual cues were relevant and the auditory cues irrelevant. In the example shown in Table 13.3, the auditory cues were relevant: whenever A1 was present responses to R1 were reinforced regardless of whether it was accompanied by V1 or V2; whenever A2 was present responses to R2 were reinforced.

In a second phase of the experiment, rats were trained with different audiovisual compounds comprising novel auditory (A3 or A4) and visual (V3 or V4) components. During this shift discrimination, only two of the four combinations of these cues were presented, and hence both auditory and visual stimuli were relevant to the solution of the discrimination. Responses to lever R1 were reinforced during presentations of A3V3, and responses to R2 were reinforced during presentation of compound A4V4. On the final session of training, non-reinforced test trials were given with the unfamiliar compounds A3V4 and A4V3.

Each of the test compounds comprised elements that were associated with different reinforced responses during the shift discrimination: in the case of A3V4, A3 was associated with R1→food as part of the compound A3V3, whereas V4 was associated with R2→food as part of the compound A4V4; similarly, in the case of A4V3, A4 was paired with R2→food as part of A4V4, and V3 was paired with R1→food as part of A3V3. If animals did not form an attentional set during the initial discrimination, or an attentional set was not maintained throughout the shift discrimination, then during the shift discrimination they should learn about the relationship between each component of a compound and the reinforced response to an equal extent. They should also base their responses to test compounds on each of its components equally. As a result, we should have observed comparable levels of responding on both levers in the presence of both test compounds. Alternatively, if training on the initial discrimination had resulted in the formation of an attentional set, and this had persisted throughout the shift discrimination, we would expect to observe differences in the rates of responding to R1 and R2 during presentations of A3V4 and A4V3. This may be because animals learned more about stimuli from the previously relevant dimension than from the irrelevant dimension during the shift discrimination, or because stronger responses are elicited by relevant stimuli. In either case, we would expect animals to make more R1 responses than R2 responses during presentations of A3V4, and more R2 responses than R1 responses during presentation of A4V3. For ease of analysis, we labelled the response that we expected to be more frequent in the presence of each test compound as *correct*, and the alternative response as *incorrect*.

We found that rats made more correct than incorrect responses at test (Figure 13.3), suggesting that stage one discrimination training had been successful in establishing an attentional set, and that this set had transferred to the stimuli used in stage two. As a result, animals attended more to stimuli from the previously relevant dimension than to stimuli from the previously irrelevant dimension. When animals were presented, on test, with an audiovisual compound comprising stimuli that had been associated with different reinforced responses, they had a greater tendency to produce the response associated with the stimulus belonging to a dimension that was relevant during prior discrimination training than the alternative response. The magnitude of this *optional shift effect* may be used as an index of attentional set formation and maintenance.

We know that this optional shift effect is sensitive to large lesions of the mPFC that include damage to the PrL, IL, and ACC (George, Duffaud, and Killcross, 2007). Animals that have received these lesions before the beginning of training show no differential responding at test—the optional shift effect is abolished. This result may be somewhat unexpected given that such lesions are typically associated with deficits in shifting between sets which might, a priori, be expected to result in an enhanced optional shift effect relative to controls. The selective EDS impairment observed by Birrell and Brown, and the strategy set-shifting impairment reported by Ragozzino and colleagues, both suggest that rats with mPFC lesions are able to form attentional sets but have difficultly

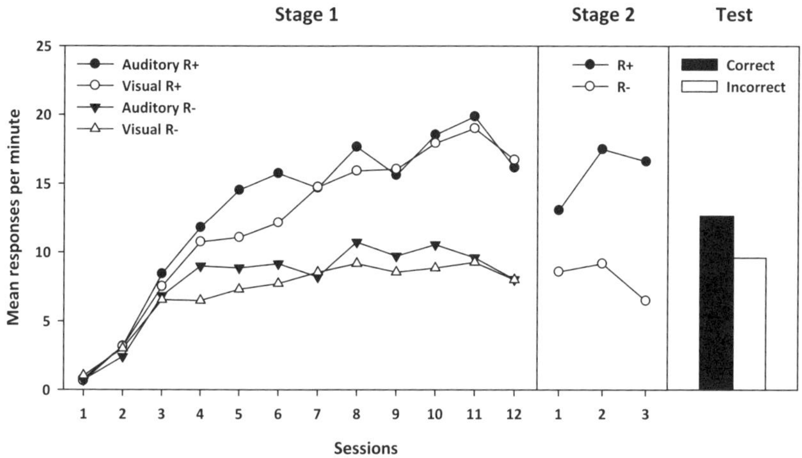

Fig. 13.3 The mean rates of lever-press responding during stage 1, stage 2, and test trials of an optional shift task. During stages 1 and 2, animals learned to respond more on the reinforced (R+) than on the nonreinforced (R–) lever during the presentation of various audiovisual compounds. During stage 1, there were no differences between animals for whom auditory or visual cues were relevant to the discrimination. At test, animals made more correct than incorrect responses, consistent with the successful formation and maintenance of attentional set throughout the previous stages (see Table 13.3 for the experimental design). Duffaud, A. M., Killcross, S., & George, D. N. (2007). Optional-shift behaviour in rats: a novel procedure for assessing attentional process in discrimination learning. *Quarterly Journal of Experimental Psychology*, **60**, 534–542. Printed with permission from Taylor & Francis Ltd. (http://www.informaworld.com).

disengaging from them. Ng *et al.* have, however, found that animals with ACC lesions have difficulty shifting between discriminations involving different stimuli from the same dimension. To elucidate the locus of our mPFC lesion effect, we conducted a series of experiments using our optional shift procedure in animals with discrete lesions to the PrL, ACC, or IL.

Effects of PrL lesions on optional shift behaviour

The PrL has often been manipulated in combination with the IL, or both the IL and ACC. In many of Ragozzino and Floresco's experiments where the authors describe cannulation of PrL/IL, cannula placement is, however, almost entirely confined to PrL (Ragozzino, Wilcox *et al.*, 1999; Ragozzino, 2002; Floresco, Ghods-Sharifi *et al.*, 2006; Floresco, Magyar *et al.*, 2006). Although it is likely that the infusate diffused to some degree into surrounding areas, including the IL and ACC, these experiments suggests that PrL is involved in shifting away from a previously relevant stimulus dimension rather than in

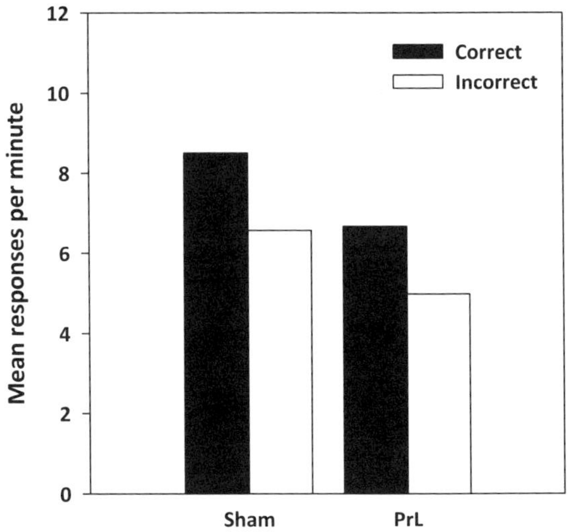

Fig. 13.4 The mean rates of correct and incorrect responding during the optional shift probe test trials for sham-operated animals and animals with neurotoxic lesions to the prelimbic cortex (PrL). Both groups of animals made significantly more correct than incorrect responses. The performance of lesioned animals did not differ from that of the controls.

the formation or maintenance of an attentional set (Ragozzino, 2007). Consequently, we did not expect excitotoxic lesions to the PrL, which spared the IL and ACC, to affect performance on the optional shift task which does not involve a shift in the relevance of a previously relevant stimulus dimension. Because the dimension that is relevant to the stage one discrimination is also relevant in stage two, there is no requirement to inhibit a previously learned set, and the PrL should not be involved. Our results (Figure 13.4) supported these predictions: animals with discrete lesions to the PrL, as well as sham-operated control animals, showed an optional shift effect—they responded more on the correct lever than they did on the incorrect lever.

Effects of ACC lesions on optional shift behaviour

Ng *et al.* (2007) reported impairments in intradimensional shift learning following lesions to ACC. They argued that the lesioned animals were not impaired at forming an attentional set (i.e. increasing attention to relevant stimuli), and that while it is possible that they have a problem transferring attention between similar cues belonging to the same dimension, this was not responsible for their IDS deficit. Rather, Ng *et al.* suggested that animals with ACC lesions cannot withdraw attention from irrelevant stimuli, allowing those stimuli to interfere with learning during an IDS discrimination.

Other authors have observed rather different effects of ACC lesions on set-shifting performance. de Bruin *et al.* (1994) found that animals with ACC lesions took longer to learn a shift between stimulus dimensions and Liston *et al.* (2006) reported that stress-induced retraction of apical dendritic arbors in the ACC was negatively correlated with performance on an EDS discrimination. Reduction in apical dendritic material was accompanied by an increase in the number of trials required to learn the discrimination. Both of these results suggest that animals have difficulty in ignoring previously relevant stimuli, rather than initially irrelevant ones. Finally, Ragozzino, Wilcox *et al.* (1999) found no effect of ACC inactivation on a strategy set-shifting task.

We observed no effect of ACC lesions at any stage of the optional shift task. At test, lesioned animals responded more on the correct lever than on the incorrect lever, suggesting that they had increased attention to relevant stimuli and/or decreased attention to irrelevant stimuli over the course of stage one training to the same extent as sham-operated control animals. If, as Ng *et al.* suggest, ACC lesioned animals find it harder to reduce attention to irrelevant stimuli than control animals do, one would expect stimuli from the previously irrelevant dimension to compete for learning during stage two and/or performance at test as a result. Hence, according to Ng *et al.'s* analysis, a smaller optional shift effect should be seen following ACC lesions. There was no indication that ACC lesions resulted in any reduction in the size of the optional shift effect. Rather, our results suggest that the ACC either has no involvement in set-shifting, or else is involved in shifting between dimensions.

It may be possible to reconcile these apparently conflicting results. The ACC lesions in Ng *et al.'s* experiment were more posterior than our lesions, de Bruin *et al.'s* lesions, Ragozzino *et al.'s* infusions, and the area of cortex sampled by Liston *et al.* In the former case, damage was sustained to cingulate area two and that part of area one caudal to the PrL. In all of the latter cases,

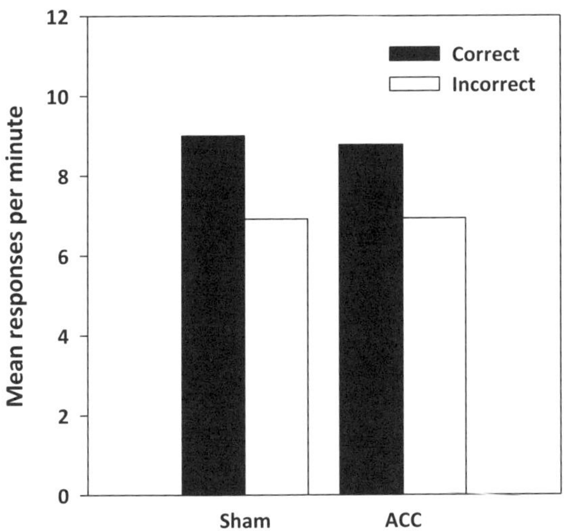

Fig. 13.5 The mean rates of correct and incorrect responding during the optional shift probe test trials for sham-operated animals and animals with neurotoxic lesions to the anterior cingulate cortex (ACC). Both groups of animals made significantly more correct than incorrect responses. The performance of lesioned animals did not differ from that of the controls.

damage or infusions were confined to the rostral portion of cingulate area one dorsal to the PrL. This rostral area of ACC, the PrL and the IL are strongly interconnected, with dorsal PrL projecting to rostral ACC, but are rather isolated from other cingulate areas including those lesioned by Ng *et al.* (Jones *et al.* 2005). Hence, the PrL and rostral ACC may both contribute to shifting attention between dimensions, whereas the remaining cingulate areas may be involved in learning to ignore irrelevant stimuli.

Effects of IL lesions on optional shift behaviour

The involvement of the IL in set-shifting behaviour is a topic that has been largely neglected. Although manipulations of the mPFC have often involved the IL, the effects of these manipulations have been attributed to their influence on the PrL. When we tested animals with lesion of the IL on the optional shift task, we found that the optional shift effect was abolished (Figure 13.6). Whereas sham-operated control animals responded more on the correct lever than on the incorrect lever, IL lesioned animals did not. These results suggest that the IL is involved in the formation and/or maintenance of attentional set.

What is the exact nature of the IL's role in set formation and maintenance? It can be very difficult to separate behavioural effects of these two processes. Impaired set formation has been inferred from a failure to observe improved performance over a series of IDS discriminations (Crofts *et al.*, 2001) or facilitated post-shift learning (Floresco, Ghods-Sharif *et al.*, 2006). The first of these effects, as we have already mentioned, can be explained in terms other than attentional set formation, and neither effect may be observed in our optional

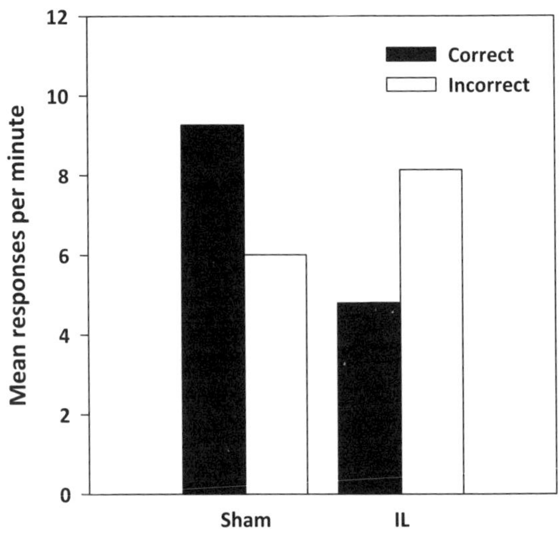

Fig. 13.6 The mean rates of correct and incorrect responding during the optional shift probe test trials for sham-operated animals and animals with neurotoxic lesions to the infralimbic cortex (IL). Control animals made more correct than incorrect responses. Lesioned animals made more incorrect than correct responses.

shift experiments where there are just two stages and no explicit shift between dimensions. Ng *et al.* (2007) suggest that deficits in set formation might lead to retarded conditioning in the initial stages of an IDED experiment, but it is wrong for them, and it would be wrong for us, to assume that the lack of a lesion effect on acquisition rates proves that lesioned animals acquire an attentional set as well as do normal animals. And there might be a reason to believe that IL is involved in set formation: the vast majority of the IL's projections to the striatum are to the NAc shell, inactivation of which disrupts set formation. The IL is clearly not necessary for set formation, however. Lesions to mPFC which include both PrL and IL (e.g. Birrell and Brown, 2000) disrupt set shifting which they could not do in the absence of set formation. Rather, lesions to the IL might retard the acquisition of attentional set sufficiently to abolish the optional shift effect, but not enough to affect learning of an IDS discrimination.

Impaired maintenance of an attentional set might also be expected to disrupt optional shift behaviour. Intact animals maintain attention to the previously relevant dimension during stage two learning and at test, resulting in stronger control of responding by stimuli from that dimension. Lesioned animals may, however, fail to transfer attention to novel cues from the previously relevant dimension leading to non-differential responding to the two dimensions at test.

We suggest that there is a third possibility—that there is a tendency for the PrL to disengage from a set and trigger the search for a new strategy when novel stimuli are introduced (or other changes occur such as negative feedback following a strategy shift), and that the IL exerts an inhibitory influence over the PrL, normally biasing the animal towards an established behavioural pattern (i.e. maintaining the current set). Hence, the intact IL promotes the maintenance of a set by inhibiting an inappropriate set shift. When the IL is lesioned, the PrL might disengage from a set acquired during initial discrimination learning when stimuli change, even if the same dimension is still relevant. This may result in a complete loss of attentional set or even a shift of attention to the previously irrelevant dimension. There is evidence that our IL lesioned animals did perform an EDS during stage two: they respond significantly more on the incorrect lever than on the correct lever which is consistent with them attending more to the previously irrelevant dimension.

If the role of the IL is to bias animals towards established or prepotent response patterns by exerting inhibitory control over the PrL, this may explain why inactivation of the PrL alone produces the same set shifting impairment as combined inactivation of the PrL and IL, or lesions of the mPFC encompassing both areas. Once the PrL is inactive or damaged, the IL involvement in set shifting is negated. Since the IL does not have a direct role in the formation or maintenance of set, we do not need to resort to conjecture about the relative sensitivity of the optional shift and IDED tasks to explain a failure to observe an effect of IL damage on an intradimensional shift. In the absence of both PrL and IL, the thalamic and striatal processes that modulate set formation and maintenance should still operate normally. Block *et al.* (2007) suggested that the MD-NAc pathway acts to inhibit inappropriate strategies during the acquisition of a novel set, but there is no reason to suppose that an EDS would be identified as an inappropriate strategy in stage two of an optional shift experiment. Both the previously relevant and previously irrelevant dimensions are relevant to the stage two discrimination, meaning that attending to either dimension is appropriate.

The IL projects to the PrL and ACC (Hurley *et al.*, 1991), two areas that have been implicated in shifting attention between perceptual dimensions. These pathways provide a possible anatomical substrate for the proposed modulatory influence of the IL on the set shifting apparatus of the dorsal mPFC. The insular cortex may provide additional support to this process through its reciprocal connections with both the PrL and IL (Gabbott *et al.*, 2003). Inactivation of the insular cortex has no effect on reversal learning in a set-shifting task but does reduce perseverative responding following a set shift (Stefani and Huff 2008). These results suggest that, following lesions of the IL or inactivation of the insular cortex, animals disengage from an established set more readily than intact animals.

There is also support for the idea that the PrL and IL may play complementary roles in other learning paradigms. Lesions of the PrL in rats lead to habit-based instrumental performance that is insensitive to goal devaluation after only minimal training. In contrast, lesions of the IL lead to performance that remains sensitive to goal devaluation even following extended training. That is, PrL lesions produce solely habit-based animals whereas IL lesions produce rats that are always goal-directed (Killcross and Coutureau, 2003). In addition, inactivation of the IL produces goal-directed responding in overtrained rats, relative to vehicle-infused control animals (Coutureau and Killcross, 2003). Moreover, the ability to use contextual cues to guide behaviour in the face of conflicting stimuli depends upon the integrity of the PrL (Haddon and Killcross 2006; Marquis *et al.*, 2007). In the same cue-based conflict task, a more extensively trained response will usually dominate a less well-trained, but context-appropriate, response (Haddon *et al.*, 2008). This effect is abolished by inactivation of the IL (Haddon, personal communication). Inactivation of the IL abolishes the ability of an overtrained stimulus-response association to dominate performance, indicating an analogous function in this cue-conflict task to the role the IL plays in the control of habit-based instrumental performance.

Concluding comments

The medial prefrontal cortex, medial striatum, and mediodorsal thalamic nucleus form a network of structures that together modulate the acquisition and maintenance of attentional sets, and shifting between sets. The entorhinal cortex is also involved in attentional set-shifting performance, altering the similarity of stimuli on the basis of their relevance to the solution of discriminations. The optional shift design provides a novel, automated operant conditioning task that can be used to assess animals' ability to maintain an attentional set. Our experiments have identified a functional dissociation between different subregions of the mPFC where IL is involved in maintenance of set, but PrL and ACC are not. We suggest that the IL contributes to maintenance of an attentional set by inhibiting the PrL set-shifting apparatus, and that lesions of the IL may result in an increased tendency to make unnecessary extradimensional shifts when the PrL remains intact.

Acknowledgements

Funded in part by the Royal Society, and by a studentship from the School of Psychology, Cardiff University and Eli Lilly and Company. The authors would like to thank Jo Haddon, Rob Honey, Mike Le Pelley and Chris Mitchell for comments on a draft of this chapter.

References

Acquas, E., Carboni, E., de Ree, R. H. A., Da Prada, M., & Di Chiara, G. (1992). Extracellular concentrations of dopamine and metabolites in the rat caudate after oral administration of a novel catechol-*O*-methyltransferase inhibitor Ro 40-7592. *Journal of Neurochemistry,* **59**, 326–330.

Berg, E. A. (1948). A simple objective technique for measuring flexibility in thinking. *Journal of General Psychology,* **39**, 15–22.

Birrell, J. M. & Brown, V. J. (2000). Medial frontal cortex mediates perceptual attentional set shifting in the rat. *Journal of Neuroscience,* **20**, 4320–4324.

Block, A. E., Dhanji, H., Thompson-Tardiff, S. F., & Floresco, S. B. (2007). Thalamic-prefrontal cortical-ventral striatal circuitry mediates dissociable components of strategy set shifting. *Cerebral Cortex,* **17**, 1625–1636.

Broberg, B. V., Dias, R., Glenthøj, B. Y., & Olsen, C. K. (2008). Evaluation of a neurodevelopmental model of schizophrenia — early postnatal PCP treatment in attentional set-shifting. *Behavioural Brain Research,* **190**, 160–163.

Chen, K. C., Baxter, M. G., & Rodefer, J. S. (2004). Central blockade of muscarinic cholinergic receptors disrupts affective and attentional set-shifting. *European Journal of Neuroscience,* **20**, 1081–1088.

Clarke, H. F., Walker, S. C., Crofts, H. S., Dalley, J. W., Robbins, T. W., & Roberts, A. C. (2005). Prefrontal serotonin depletion affects reversal learning but not attentional set shifting. *Journal of Neuroscience,* **25**, 532–538.

Condé, F., Maire-Lepoivre, E., Audinat., E., & Crépel, F. (1995). Afferent connections of the medial prefrontal cortex of the rat. II. Cortical and subcortical afferents. *Journal of Comparative Neurology,* **352**, 567–593.

Coutureau, E., Galani, R., Gosselin, O., Majchrzak, M., & Di Scala, G. (1999). Entorhinal but not hippocampal or subicular lesions disrupt latent inhibition in rats. *Neurobiology of Learning and Memory,* **72**, 143–157.

Coutureau, E., and Killcross, S. (2003). Inactivation of the infralimbic prefrontal cortex reinstates goal-directed responding in overtrained rats. *Behavioural Brain Research,* **146**, 167–174.

Coutureau, E., Killcross, A.S., Good, M., Marshall, V.J., Ward-Robinson, J., & Honey, R.C. (2002). Acquired equivalence and distinctiveness of cues: II. Neural manipulations and their implications. *Journal of Experimental Psychology: Animal Behavior Processes,* **28**, 388–396.

Crofts, H. S., Dalley, J. W., Collins, P. Van Denderen, J. C. M., Everitt, B. J., Robbins, T. W., & Roberts, A. C. (2001). Differential effects of 6-OHDA lesions of the frontal cortex and caudate nucleus on the ability to acquire an attentional set. *Cerebral Cortex,* **11**, 1015–1026.

de Bruin, J. P. C., Sànchez-Santed, F., Heinsbroek, R. P. W., Donker, A., & Postmes, P. (1994). A behavioural analysis of rats with damage to the medial prefrontal cortex using the Morris water maze: Evidence for behavioural flexibility, but not for impaired spatial navigation. *Brain Research,* **652**, 323–333.

Dias, R., Robbins, T. W., & Roberts, A. C. (1996a). Dissociation in prefrontal cortex of affective and attentional shifts. *Nature,* **380**, 69–72.

Dias, R., Robbins, T. W., & Roberts, A. C. (1996b) Primate analogue of the Wisconsin Card Sorting Test: Effects of excitotoxic lesions of the prefrontal cortex in the marmoset. *Behavioral Neuroscience,* **110**, 872–886.

Dias, R., Robbins, T. W., & Roberts, A. C. (1997). Dissociable forms of inhibitory control within prefrontal cortex with an analog of the Wisconsin Card Sorting Test: Restriction to novel situations and independence from 'on-line' processing. *Journal of Neuroscience,* **17**, 9285–9297.

Downes, J. J., Roberts, A. C., Sahakian, B. J., Evenden, J. L., Morris, R. G., & Robbins, T. W. (1989). Impaired extra-dimensional shift performance in medicated and unmedicated Parkinson's disease: Evidence for a specific attentional dysfunction. *Neuropsychologia,* **27**, 1329–1343.

Duffaud, A. M., Killcross. S., & George, D. N. (2007). Optional-shift behaviour in rats: A novel procedure for assessing attentional processes in discrimination learning. *Quarterly Journal of Experimental Psychology,* **60**, 534–542.

Egerton, A. Reid, L., McGregor, S., Cochran, S. M., Morris, B. J., & Pratt, J. A. (2008). Subchronic and chronic PCP treatment produces temporally distinct deficits in attentional set shifting and prepulse inhibition in rats. *Psychopharmacology,* **198**, 37–49.

Egerton, A., Reid, L., McKerchar, C. E., Morris, B. J., & Pratt, J. A. (2005). Impairment in perceptual attentional set-shifting following PCP administration: A rodent model of set-shifting deficits in schizophrenia. *Psychopharmacology,* **179**, 77–84.

Elliott, R., McKenna, P. J., Robbins, T. W., & Sahakian, B. J. (1995). Neuropsychological evidence for fronto-striatal dysfunction in schizophrenia. *Psychological Medicine,* **25**, 619–630.

Floresco, S. B., Block, A. E., and Tse, M. T. L. (2008). Inactivation of the medial prefrontal cortex of the rat impairs strategy set-shifting, but not reversal learning, using a novel, automated procedure. *Behavioural Brain Research,* **190**, 85–96.

Floresco, S. B., Ghods-Sharifi, S., Vexelman, C., & Magyar, O. (2006). Dissociable roles for the nucleus accumbens core and shell in regulating set shifting. *Journal of Neuroscience,* **26**, 2449–2457.

Floresco, S. B., Magyar, O., Ghods-Sharifi, S., Vexelman, C., & Tse, M. T. L. (2006). Multiple dopamine receptor subtypes in the medial prefrontal cortex of the rat regulate set-shifting. *Neuropsychopharmacology,* **31**, 297–309.

Gabbott, P. L. A., Warner, T. A., Jays, P. R. L., & Bacon, S. J. (2003). Areal and synaptic interconnectivity of prelimbic (area 32), infralimbic (area 25) and insular cortices in the rat. *Brain Research,* **993**, 59–71.

George, D. N., Duffaud, A. M., & Killcross, S. (2007). Excitotoxic lesions of the rat medial prefrontal cortex impair perceptual attentional set but result in an augmented latent inhibition effect. Program No. 741.10. *2007 Abstract Viewer/Itinerary Planner.* Washington, DC: Society for Neuroscience. Online.

George, D. N. & Pearce, J. M. (1999). Acquired distinctiveness is controlled by stimulus relevance not correlation with reward. *Journal of Experimental Psychology: Animal Behavior Processes,* **25**, 363–373.

Ghods-Sharifi, S., Haluk, D. M., & Floresco, S. B. (2008). Differential effects of inactivation of the orbitofrontal cortex on strategy set-shifting and reversal learning. *Neurobiology of Learning and Memory,* **89**, 567–573.

Gluck, M. A. & Myers, C. E. (1993). Hippocampal mediation of stimulus representation: A computational theory. *Hippocampus,* **3**, 491–516.

Grant, D. A. & Berg, E. A. (1948). A behavioral analysis of degree of reinforcement and ease of shifting to new responses in a Weigl-type card-sorting problem. *Journal of Experimental Psychology,* **38**, 404–411.

Groenewegen, H. J. (1988). Organization of the afferent connections of the mediodorsal thalamic nucleus in the rat, related to the mediodorsal-prefrontal topography. *Neuroscience,* **24**, 379–431.

Haddon, J. E., George, D. N., & Killcross, S. (2008). Contextual control of biconditional task performance: Evidence for cue and response competition in rats. *Quarterly Journal of Experimental Psychology,* **61**, 1307–1320.

Haddon, J. E. & Killcross, S. (2006). Prefrontal cortex lesions disrupt the contextual control of response conflict. *Journal of Neuroscience,* **26**, 2933–2940.

Hampshire, A. & Owen, A. M. (2010). Clinical studies of attention and learning. In C. J. Mitchell and M. E. Le Pelley (Eds) *Attention and associative learning.* Oxford: Oxford University Press.

Harlow, H. F. (1949). The formation of learning sets. *Psychological Review,* **56**, 51–65.

Hatcher, P. D., Brown, V. J., Tait, D. S., Bate, S., Overend, P., Hagan, J. J., & Jones, D. N. C. (2005). 5-HT6 receptor antagonists improve performance in an attentional set shifting task in rats. *Psychopharmacology,* **181**, 253–259.

Heidbreder, C. A. & Groenewegen, H. J. (2003). The medial prefrontal cortex in the rat: Evidence for a dorso-ventral distinction based upon function and anatomical haracteristics. *Neuroscience and Biobehavioral Reviews,* **27**, 555–579.

Honey, R. C., Close, J., & Lin, E. (2010). Acquired distinctiveness and equivalence: A synthesis. In C. J. Mitchell & M. E. Le Pelley (Eds) *Attention and associative learning*. Oxford: Oxford University Press.

Hurley, K. M., Herbert, H., Moga, M. M., & Saper, C. B. (1991). Efferent projections of the infralimbic cortex of the rat. *Journal of comparative neurology*, **308**, 249–276.

Joel D., Weiner I. & Feldon J. (1997) Electrolytic lesions of the medial prefrontal cortex in rats disrupt performance on an analog of the Wisconsin Card Sorting Test, but do not disrupt latent inhibition: Implications for animal models of schizophrenia. *Behavioural Brain Research*, **85**, 187–201.

Jones, B. F., Groenewegen, H. J., & Witter, M. P. (2005). Intrinsic connections of the cingulate cortex in the rat suggest the existence of multiple functionally segregated networks. *Neuroscience*, **133**, 193–207.

Kendler, T. S., Kendler, H. H., & Silfen, C. K. (1964). Optional shift behavior of albino rats. *Psychonomic Science*, **1**, 5–6.

Killcross, S. & Coutureau, E. (2003). Coordination of actions and habits in the medial prefrontal cortex of rats. *Cerebral Cortex*, **13**, 400–408.

Kim, J. & Ragozzino, M. E. (2005). The involvement of the orbitofrontal cortex in learning under changing task contingencies. *Neurobiology of Learning and Memory*, **83**, 125–133.

Kolb, B. & Robbins, T. W. (2003). The rodent prefrontal cortex. *Behavioural Brain Research*, **126**, 1–2.

Kruschke, J. K. (1992). ALCOVE: An exemplar-based connectionist model of category learning. *Psychological Review*, **99**, 22–44.

Kruschke, J. K. (1996). Dimensional relevance shifts in category learning. *Connection Science*, **8**, 225–247.

Lapiz, M. D. S., Bondi, C. O., & Morilak, D. A. (2007). Chronic treatment with desipramine improves cognitive performance of rats in an attentional set-shifting test. *Neuropsychopharmacology*, **32**, 1000–1010.

Lapiz, M. D. S. & Morilak, D. A. (2006) Noradrenergic modulation of cognitive function in rat medial prefrontal cortex as measured by attentional set shifting capability. *Neuroscience*, **137**, 1039–1049.

Lawrence, A. D., Sahakian, B. J., Hodges, J. R., Rosser, A. E., Lange, K. W., & Robbins, T. W. (1996). Executive and mnemonic functions in early Huntington's disease. *Brain*, **119**, 1633–1645.

Lawrence, D. H. (1949). Acquired distinctiveness of cues: I. Transfer between discriminations on the basis of familiarity with the stimulus. *Journal of Experimental Psychology*, **39**, 770–784.

Le Pelley, M. E. (2004). The role of associative history in models of associative learning; A selective review and a hybrid model. *Quarterly Journal of Experimental Psychology*, **57B**, 193–243.

Liston, C., Miller, M. M., Goldwater, D. S., Radley, J. J., Rocher, A. B., Hof, P. R., Morrison, J. H., & McEwen, B. S. (2006). Stress-induced alterations in prefrontal cortical dendritic morphology predict selective impairments in perceptual attentional set-shifting. *Journal of Neuroscience*, **26**, 7870–7874.

Lubow, R. E. (1989). *Latent inhibition and conditioned attention theory*. Cambridge: Cambridge University Press.

Mackintosh, N. J. (1974). *The psychology of animal learning.* London: Academic Press.

Mackintosh, N. J. (1975). A theory of attention: Variations in the associability of stimuli with reinforcement. *Psychological Review,* **82**, 276–298.

Mackintosh, N. J. & Little, L. (1969). Intradimensional and extradimensional shift learning by pigeons. *Psychonomic Science,* **14**, 5–6.

Marquis, J-P., Killcross, S., & Haddon, J. E. (2007). Inactivation of the prelimbic, but not the infralimbic, prefrontal cortex impairs the contextual control of response conflict in rats. *European Journal of Neuroscience,* **25**, 559–566.

McAlonan, K. & Brown, V. J. (2003). Orbital prefrontal cortex mediates reversal learning and not attentional set shifting in the rat. *Behavioural Brain Research,* **146**, 97–103.

McGaughy, J., Ross, R. S., & Eichenbaum, H. (2008). Noradrenergic, but not cholinergic, deafferentation of prefrontal cortex impairs attentional set-shifting. *Neuroscience,* **153**, 63–71.

Milner, B. (1963). Effects of different brain lesions on card sorting: The role of the frontal lobes. *Archives of Neurology,* **9**, 100–110.

Milner, B. (1964). Some effects of frontal lobectomy in man. In J. M. Warren and K. Akert (Eds) *The frontal granular cortex and behavior*. New-York: McGraw-Hill.

Monchi, O., Petrides, M. Petre, V., Worsley, K., & Dagher, A. (2001). Wisconsin card sorting revisited: Distinct neural circuits participating in different stages of the task identified by evern-related functional magnetic resonance imaging. *Journal of Neuroscience,* **21**, 7733–7741.

Nelson, H. E. (1976). A modified card sorting test sensitive to frontal lobe defects. *Cortex,* **12**, 313–324.

Ng, C-W., Noblejas, M. I., Rodefer, J. S., Smith, C. B., & Poremba, A. (2007). Double dissociation of attentional resources: Prefrontal versus cingulate cortices. *Journal of Neuroscience,* **27**, 12123–12131.

Nicolle, M. M. & Baxter, M. G., (2003). Glutamate receptor binding in the frontal cortex and dorsal striatum of aged rats with impaired attentional set-shifting. *European Journal of Neuroscience,* **18**, 3335–3342.

Oswald, C. J. P., Yee, B. K., Bannerman, D. B., Rawlins, J. N. P., Good, M., & Honey, R. C. (2001). Involvement of the entorhinal cortex in a process of attentional modulation: Evidence from a novel variant of an IDS/EDS procedure. *Behavioral Neuroscience,* **115**, 841–849.

Oswald, C. J. P., Yee, B. K., Rawlins, J. N. P., Bannerman, D. B., Good, M., & Honey, R. C. (2002). The influence of selective lesions to components of the hippocampal system on orienting response, habituation and latent inhibition. *European Journal of Neuroscience,* **15**, 1983–1990.

Owen, A. M., Roberts, A. C., Polkey, C. E., Sahakian, B. K., & Robbins, T. W. (1991). Extra-dimensional versus intra-dimensional set shifting performance following frontal love excisions, temporal lobe excisions or amygdalo-hippocampectomy in man. *Neuropsychologia,* **29**, 993–1006.

Pearce, J. M., George, D. N., & Redhead, E. S. (1998). The role of attention in the solution of conditional discriminations. In N. A. Schmajuk and P. C. Holland (Eds), *Occasion setting: Associative learning and cognition in animals* (pp. 249–275). Washington, DC: APA Press.

Pearce, J. M. & Hall, G. (1980). A model for Pavlovian learning: Variations in the effectiveness of conditioned but not of unconditioned stimuli. *Psychological Review,* **87,** 532–552.

Preuss, T. M. (1995). Do rats have prefrontal cortex? The Roe-Woolsey-Akert program reconsidered. *Journal of Cognitive Neuroscience,* 7, 1–24.

Ragozzino, M. E. (2002). The effects of dopamine D1 receptor blockade in the prelimbic-infralimbic areas on behavioural flexibility. *Learning and Memory,* **9,** 18–28.

Ragozzino, M. E. (2007). The contribution of the medial prefrontal cortex, orbitofrontal cortex, and dorsomedial striatum to behavioral flexibility. *Annals of the New York Academy of Sciences,* **1121,** 355–375.

Ragozzino, M. E., Detrick, S., & Kesner, R. P. (1999). Involvement of the prelimbic–infralimbic areas of the rodent prefrontal cortex in behavioral flexibility for place and response learning. *Journal of Neuroscience,* **19,** 4585–4594.

Ragozzino, M. E., Jih, J., & Tzavos, A. (2002). Involvement of the dorsomedial striatum in behavioral flexibility: Role of muscarinic cholinergic receptors. *Brain Research,* **953,** 205–214.

Ragozzino, M. E., Kim, J., Hassert, D., Minniti, N., & Kiang, C. (2003). The contribution of the rat prelimbic-infralimbic areas to different forms of task switching. *Behavioral Neuroscience,* **117,** 1054–1065.

Ragozzino, M. E., Mohler, E. G., Prior, M., Palencia, C. A. & Rozman, S. (2009). Acetylcholine activity in selective striatal regions supports behavioral flexibility. *Neurobiology of Learning and Memory,* **91,** 13–22.

Ragozzino, M. E., Ragozzino, K. E., Mizumori, S. J. Y., & Kesner, R. P. (2002). Role of the dorsomedial striatum in behavioral flexibility for response and visual cue discrimination learning. *Behavioral Neuroscience,* **116,** 105–115.

Ragozzino, M. E., Wilcox, C. Raso, M., & Kesner, R. P. (1999). Involvement of rodent prefrontal cortex subregions in strategy shifting. *Behavioral Neuroscience,* **113,** 32–41.

Robbins, T. W. (2007). Shifting and stopping: fronto-striatal substrates, Neurochemical modulation and clinical implications. *Philosophical Transactions of the Royal Society B,* **362,** 917–932.

Roberts, A. C., De Salvia, M. A., Wilkinson, L. S., Collins, P., Muir, J. L., Everitt, B. J., & Robbins, T. W. (1994). 6-Hydroxydopamine lesions of the prefrontal cortex in monkeys enhance performance on an analog of the Wisconsin Card Sorting Test: Possible interactions with subcortical dopamine. *Journal of Neuroscience,* **14,** 2531–2544.

Roberts, A. C., Robbins, T. W., & Everitt, B. J. (1988). The effects of intradimensional and extradimensional shifts on visual discrimination learning in humans and non-human primates. *Quarterly Journal of Experimental Psychology,* **40B,** 321–341.

Rodefer, J. S., Murphy, E. R., & Baxter, M. G. (2005). PDE10A inhibition reverses subchronic PCP-induced deficits in attentional set-shifting in rats. *European Journal of Neuroscience,* **21,** 1070–1076.

Rodefer, J. S., Nguyen, T. N., Karlsson, J-J., & Arnt, J. (2008). Reversal of subchronic PCP-induced deficits in attentional set shifting in rats by sertindole and a 5-HT_6 receptor antagonist: Comparison among antipsychotics. *Neuropsychopharmacology,* **33,** 2657–2666.

Rose, J. E. & Woolsey, C. N. (1948). The orbitofrontal cortex and its connections with the mediodorsal nucleus in rabbit, sheep and cat. *Research Publications – Association for Research in Nervous and Mental Disease,* **27**, 210–232.

Schwartz, R. M., Schwartz, M., & Tees, R. C. (1971). Optional intradimensional and extradimensional shifts in the rat. *Journal of Comparative and Physiological Psychology,* **77**, 470–475.

Shepp, E. M. & Eimas, P. D. (1964). Intradimensional and extradimensional shifts in the rat. *Journal of Comparative and Physiological Psychology,* **57**, 357–361

Stefani, M. R., Groth, K., & Moghaddam, B. (2003). Glutamate receptors in the rat medial prefrontal cortex regulate set-shifting ability. *Behavioral Neuroscience,* **117**, 728–737.

Stefani, M. R. & Huff, M. M. (2008). Transient inactivation of rat insular cortex affects extradimensional set-shifting but not reversal learning. Program No. 875.9. *2008 Neuroscience Meeting Planner*. Washington, DC: Society for Neuroscience. Online.

Stefani, M. R. & Moghaddam, B. (2005). Systemic and prefrontal cortical NMDA receptor blockade differentially affect discrimination learning and set-shifting ability in rats. *Behavioral Neuroscience,* **119**, 420–428.

Sutherland, N. S. & Mackintosh, N. J. (1971). *Mechanisms of animal discrimination learning.* New York: Academic Press.

Tait, D., S. & Brown, V. J. (2008). Lesions of the basal forebrain impair reversal learning but not shifting of attentional set in rats. *Behavioural Brain Research,* **187**, 100–108.

Tait, D. S., Brown, V. J., Farovik, A., Theobald, D. E., Dalley, J. W., & Robbins, T. W. (2007). Lesions of the dorsal noradrenergic bundle impair attentional set-shifting in the rat. *European Journal of Neuroscience,* **25**, 3719–3724.

Tunbridge, E. M., Bannerman, D. M., & Harrison, P. J. (2004). Catechol-*O*-methyltransferase inhibition improves set-shifting performance and elevates stimulated dopamine release in the rat prefrontal cortex. *Journal of Neuroscience,* **24**, 5331–5335.

Uylings, H. B. M., Groenewegen, H. J., & Kolb, B. (2003). Do rats have a prefrontal cortex? *Behavioural Brain Research,* **146**, 3–17.

Weiner, I., Gal, G., & Feldon, J. (1999). Disrupted and undisrupted latent inhibition following shell and core lesions. *Annals of the New York Academy of Sciences,* **877**, 723–727.

Chapter 14

Clinical studies of attention and learning

Adam Hampshire and Adrian M. Owen

Introduction

Clinical research and basic science exist and proceed synergistically; experimental manipulations that are developed to tease apart different cognitive and neural circuits within the healthy population become useful tools for quantifying the cognitive and neural basis of impairments within different clinical populations. Conversely, examination of how behaviour changes when specific neural circuits are impaired within those clinical populations feeds back into our understanding of what those circuits contribute to healthy cognition, leading to further refinement of neuroscientific methods and models. Tasks developed in this context also provide useful tools for examining how effective different pharmacological and psychological interventions are, both in cognitive and neural terms. In addition, they provide metrics by which individual differences within clinical populations may be examined, i.e. the mechanisms by which genetic, neural, and psychological factors interact with disease and treatment. This process yields information that has the potential to inform the development of interventions that are more targeted, not just to one disease or another, but also tailored to each individual in terms of their genetic makeup and the likely time-course that various discrete aspects of their disease are likely to follow. Whilst much of this potential is only just being realized, where attention and learning are concerned, clear progress has already been made; in particular, in understanding rule learning deficits and the impact that this has on various clinical populations in terms of poor adaptive behaviour, or 'executive dysfunction'.

Rule learning and the intradimensional/extradimensional set-shifting task

Humans are remarkably adept at adapting rapidly when environmental conditions change. This behavioural flexibility is commonly described as being under 'executive control'; that is to say, driven by conscious, wilful decision-making processes that guide the temporal organization of behaviour. There are, however, a number of phenomenologically distinct aspects to executive processing. One of the most important of these is the ability to identify and focus attention on just those types of object or feature that are of the most relevance to the task at hand, with deficits in this ability leading to an inflexible 'attentional set', i.e. the inability to switch the locus of attention away from previously relevant stimulus dimensions (e.g. Owen *et al.*, 1991; Roberts *et al.*, 1988; Dias *et al.*, 1996). Another is the ability to override habitual behaviours when feedback from the environment signals that the desired outcomes are no longer being achieved, with deficits in this ability leading to 'perseveration', i.e. the repetition of sub-optimal behaviours (e.g. Bechara *et al.*, 1994; Anderson *et al.*, 1999). Experimentally, perhaps the most influential tool that has been used to examine these two aspects of executive control is the CANTAB attentional set-shifting task (Roberts *et al.*, 1988) which assesses, at various points during the test, intra- and extra-dimensional set-shifting ability. An 'intra-dimensional shift' (ID) occurs when a participant is required to cease responding to one exemplar of a particular stimulus dimension (e.g. 'blue' from the dimension 'colour') and must begin responding to a new exemplar of that same dimension (e.g. 'red'). An 'extra-dimensional shift' (ED) occurs when a participant is required to switch responding to a novel exemplar of a previously irrelevant dimension (e.g. from 'blue' to 'squares' from the dimension 'shape'). When undertaking the CANTAB attentional set-shifting task, participants are required to select between one of two compound stimuli that are displayed on the screen. The compound stimuli each comprise two dimensions (in the original form of the task, these dimensions were 'stick' figures and solid shapes, although in subsequent versions 'colour', 'number', and 'shape' have also all been used. In the illustrative example below, the dimensions 'colour' and 'shape', which have been used in later versions of the task, will be used for clarity). For example, a participant may have to choose between a red square and a blue circle, but on the next trial the choice may be between a red circle and a blue square. During any given block of the task, there is a 'rule' and the participant has to discover it by a process of trial and error. Each 'rule' relates to just one exemplar of one of the two dimensions (thus, in the above example, 'blue' may be the current rule) and this rule determines which of the two compound stimuli is currently the 'correct' selection (in this case, the blue stimulus, regardless of whether that is a square or a circle). Therefore, at any point during the task, there is both a relevant (e.g. colour) and an irrelevant (e.g. shape) visual dimension. After every response, feedback is given to indicate whether the last selection was correct or incorrect and the participant has to learn to apply the rule by a process of trial and error. Once the participant reaches a predefined criterion of a certain number of consecutive correct responses, the task moves on to a new block with a new rule. The participant is only made aware of this change of rule when he/she begins to receive negative feedback for making choices according to the previous rule. At the time of the rule change, one of a number of task manipulations may occur. In the simplest case, an entirely new stimulus set is displayed, using the same two familiar dimensions but with different exemplars from those dimensions (e.g. yellow triangles and orange hexagons, to continue the illustrative example above). If the rule defining which dimension is now correct does not change (i.e. it still relates to an exemplar from the previously relevant dimension – colour, in the example above) then this manipulation is termed an intra-dimensional shift. The participant is simply required to learn which of the two new exemplars from the previously relevant dimension is now 'correct'. By contrast, if the new rule relates to the previously irrelevant dimension (shape, in the example above), then the participant must also learn, not only that the rule has changed to a new exemplar, but also that the previously attended dimension (colour) is now no longer relevant. This manipulation is termed an extra-dimensional shift and requires the participant to adapt their entire 'attentional set' by switching the focus of their search away from the previously relevant dimension (colour) and towards the previously irrelevant dimension (shape). In a third type of manipulation, the compound stimuli may not change at all, but the current rule may reverse within the previously relevant dimension (e.g. from blue to red). This manipulation is termed a 'reversal' and the participant is required to stop responding to the previously correct exemplar and to 'reverse' their response to the other exemplar from within the same general dimension. The CANTAB attentional set-shifting task has made a number of important contributions to our understanding of attention and learning through its application in non-human primate studies and through investigations in human patients with frontal-lobe lesions. This research has demonstrated that ED switching and reversal learning are selectively impaired by lesions within the lateral prefrontal cortex (LPFC) and the orbitofrontal cortex (OFC), respectively (Dias *et al.*, 1996; Hornak *et al.*, 2004).

In terms of clinical applications, the IDED task has been a popular marker of executive dysfunction in various patient populations. In particular, the ED stage of the task (which requires a dimensional shift) has proven sensitive to cognitive impairments in schizophrenia (Pantelis *et al.*, 1997), ageing (Robbins *et al.*, 1998), Huntington's disease (Lawrence *et al.*, 1996), obsessive compulsive disorder (Veale *et al.*, 1996), and Parkinson disease (Downes *et al.*, 1989; Owen *et al.*, 1992), to name but a few. As a consequence, this manipulation has been used extensively, both to assess executive dysfunction per se and to measure pharmacological efficacy in patients and healthy controls.

To some extent, the CANTAB task is limited by its own success, as the many clinical populations that are impaired on the task undoubtedly have quite diverse pathology and it seems unlikely, therefore, that they all suffer from the same basic impairment. In this respect, performance on the task should be considered to be a relatively non-specific marker of executive dysfunction, as it does not generally differentiate between the cognitive and neural circuits that are degraded in these different clinical populations (although for a counter example, see Owen *et al.*, 1993). The reason for this non-specificity becomes clear when the demands placed on the participant during the ED manipulation are considered in detail. The CANTAB attentional set-shifting task only examines the first (novel) ED shift to a previously irrelevant visual dimension (e.g. the first time that you shift from a colour such as 'blue' to a shape such as 'squares'), and this manipulation has multiple discrete cognitive components. For example, because only one dimension (e.g. colour) is relevant during the task *prior* to the ED switch (and therefore, the participant may never even have considered the alternative dimension—e.g. shape—as being a possibility), they must first identify it as being an option at all. Second, the participants must also work out that switching attention across object dimensions may be a relevant operation in the task. This difficulty in dimension identification is exacerbated further, because at the same time, they have to overcome the learning that has occurred during the previous stages of the task indicating that the dimension that they now have to switch to ('shape') was (previously) irrelevant. This type of prior learning, known as 'learned irrelevance', is well documented as biasing an individual's subsequent choices (Mackintosh, 1973). Finally, if the participant fails at this stage by responding continuously to exemplars from the previously rewarded dimension (as is typically the case), then picking an incorrect exemplar after an ED switch will lead to a partial, rather than a total, reward contingency. That is to say, because the stimuli are 'compound' (each made up of an exemplar from the two dimensions), half of the time, the participant's selection will lead incidentally to positive feedback. Thus, if a participant makes selections according to the rule 'blue', when the rule is in fact 'square', half of the time the blue shape that is selected will be a square and will result in a positive feedback. This is in direct contrast to both the ID shift and the reversal manipulation, where selecting an exemplar from the previously relevant dimension will *always* lead to an absolute reward contingency, i.e. only positive feedback (if the correct stimulus is chosen) or only negative feedback (if the incorrect stimulus is chosen). This means that after an ED shift, the participant not only has to process the task feedback correctly, but they also have to make the more difficult judgement that a switch of attention is required because, depending on their disposition, positive feedback 50% of the time may be considered to be a quite reasonable reward. Given these difficulties of interpretation, it might be better to describe the CANTAB attentional set-shifting test as measuring general problem-solving ability, rather than set-shifting ability in particular. Moreover, whilst this task is sensitive to executive dysfunction across a broad range of clinical populations, the reasons why those populations show a deficit may differ and this may, in turn, relate to the exact pathology—i.e. which neural circuits are degraded and which cognitive processes are consequently impaired.

Notwithstanding these problems of cognitive heterogeneity, the CANTAB attentional set-shifting task is also not an ideal tool for delineating the neural circuits underlying cognitive flexibility on the basis of human neuroimaging data. This is because the task is built around just one instance of an ED switch and just a few instances of reversals. Although it is possible to examine changes in activity using fMRI or PET by comparing different stages of the task, there are too few 'events' to make the results meaningful. This is because the key processes (e.g. shifting attentional set) are likely to be transient and occur at only one point in time when attention is switched from one dimension to another (Konishi *et al.*, 1998; Nagahama *et al.*, 1999; Dove *et al.*, 2000; Cools *et al.*, 2002; Nakahara *et al.*, 2002; Monsell, 2003). For imaging studies, these transient events need to occur multiple times in order to be estimated separately from the noisy background of other task-related events. As an example, consider the comparison between imaging data acquired during the ED and ID blocks of the original task. The ED block will tend to involve more responses (because it is more difficult and takes longer to arrive at the correct solution) and, therefore, more feedback and a larger overall proportion of negative compared with positive feedback. A cross block comparison (ED vs. ID) would be most likely, therefore, to activate circuitry involved in (primarily negative) feedback processing as opposed to that specifically related to the switching of attention between (as compared with within) the different stimulus dimensions.

The behavioural effects of extradimensional switching beyond novelty

We have recently adapted the CANTAB attentional set-shifting task to make it more suitable for use in event-related fMRI studies (Hampshire and Owen, 2006). As a first step, it was necessary to demonstrate that the behavioural costs of ED switching existed beyond the first (novel) instance of a switch. To this end, an attentional switching experiment was designed based upon the original CANTAB attentional set-shifting task (Roberts *et al.*, 1988), with similar visual dimensions—'stick' figures and solid abstract shapes—but using an extended stimulus set that allowed multiple occurrences of each of the key manipulations. In common with the original task, participants were required to optimize their behaviour by learning the rule that defined which of the two available compound stimuli was correct and the rule always related to just one visual dimension. Participants had to complete as many blocks as they could within the space of 20 min.

When the rule that defined which stimulus was correct switched between exemplars from the same visual dimension (e.g. from one 'stick' to another 'stick'), this was termed an 'intra-dimensional' rule change, whereas when the target switched between exemplars drawn from different visual dimensions (e.g. from a 'stick' to a solid abstract shape), this was termed an 'extra-dimensional' rule change. If the stimulus set *remained the same* between blocks, but the rule changed (e.g. from one 'stick' to another 'stick' or from one 'stick' to an abstract solid shape), this was termed a 'reversal'. If the stimulus set changed between blocks (for either ID or ED rule changes), this was termed a 'shift'. There were, therefore, four types of rule change, intradimensional shifts (ID; stimuli all change, shift required to one stimulus from the previously relevant dimension), intra-dimensional reversals (IDR; stimuli stay the same, shift required to the alternate stimulus from the previously relevant dimension), extra-dimensional shifts (ED; stimuli all change, shift required to one stimulus from the previously irrelevant dimension), and extra-dimensional reversals (EDR; stimuli stay the same, shift required to one stimulus from the previously irrelevant dimension), and these could all be examined, both at the first novel instance, and beyond novelty, when the visual dimensions and task manipulations were all familiar and the participant knew that they were relevant to the task.

The results showed that the ED shift effect was indeed robust beyond the very first shift, such that significantly more errors were made before the rule was derived when the target changed between the two visual dimensions, than when it changed within one visual dimension. A second analysis compared the first novel instances of the four types of rule change to those that occurred subsequently. The results demonstrated a significant effect of novelty, with participants making far more errors during the first occurrences of the four conditions than those subsequently. These findings demonstrate how important it is to consider the issue of novelty in these attentional set-shifting tasks—the first instances of the different task manipulations are behaviourally far more difficult than those required later on because the various visual dimensions and task manipulations that make up the overarching schema required for optimal performance have to be initially acquired. This is particularly relevant to studies that take repeated measures from the same participant, as is often the case in drug trials. However, the results of this study also demonstrate that the ED effect is robust beyond novelty, confirming that this new variant of the task is likely to be of use for repeated measures designs, as well as fMRI studies.

IDED switching examined with fMRI

A further complexity of the CANTAB attentional set-shifting task design concerns how the experimenter knows exactly when the participant switches their attention between, or within, the two visual dimensions. This ambiguity exists because of the compound nature of the stimuli (e.g. each stimulus is made up of two components and either one of those components can be the reason that the stimulus is selected). Although it is possible to be certain that the participant is selecting one particular exemplar from one dimension after a number of repeated responses, it is not possible to determine which of the two component exemplars was actually the focus of attention (and selection) on the basis of any individual response. Whilst unimportant for behavioural studies, this uncertainty makes it impossible to synchronize the blood oxygenation level-dependent (BOLD) response with the attentional switch events in fMRI studies. The solution to this problem was to swap the two exemplars from which the compound stimulus pairs were composed after each and every response, whilst only giving feedback after every second response. This effectively forces the participants to make two (identical) selections of the same type before deciding to shift or stay on the basis of feedback (which only occurs after the second response). On the basis of these two responses, it is possible to determine exactly which exemplar has been selected (for details, see Hampshire and Owen, 2006). For the fMRI version of the task the visual dimensions were also changed from 'sticks' and abstract solid shapes to faces and buildings. This adaptation allows the posterior brain regions that are involved in processing the different exemplar dimensions to be examined (Kanwisher *et al.*, 1997; Epstein and Kanwisher, 1998) for attentional effects (as it turns out, 'sticks' and abstract solid shapes do not appear to be represented by anatomically distinct posterior regions, at least not at a level that is discernable with current fMRI methods).

Analyses of the behavioural data from 16 healthy young participants who undertook the fMRI task again demonstrated that the ED effect was robust beyond the first (novel) instance of the switch.

An important difference between these results and the original CANTAB attentional set-shifting task was that the fMRI analysis was focused on discrete events (i.e. individual trials) as opposed to whole task blocks (which comprise many trials). Thus, the design of the task allowed these event types to be defined very specifically according to the current and previous foci of attention.

As in all of these attentional set-shifting tasks, the participant's behaviour varies between periods of trying to solve the current rule (when many mistakes are made) and periods of repeated responding according to the rule in order to reach the criterion for successfully demonstrating that they have acquired the rule successfully (when, typically, no mistakes are made). Once this criterion is reached, the next rule change occurs and the participant again begins trying to derive the new rule. Two types of event were contrasted during the period of time when the current rule was being derived. One was termed 'extra-dimensional' because the focus of attention switched between stimuli of different types (for example, from a face to a building) and the other 'intra-dimensional', because the focus of attention switched between stimuli of the same type (for example, from one face to another face). Whilst each of these events involved multiple switch components (for example, response suppression and attended stimulus change), unlike in the original CANTAB attentional set-shifting task, the only way in which they differed from one another was with respect to the allocation of attention between, or within, visual dimensions. Thus, the comparison of one with the other effectively isolated this extra-dimensional switching component in a way that is entirely impossible with any previous version of this task. This contrast activated a network of brain areas, including a region of the inferior frontal gyrus (IFG) spreading back into the anterior insula bilaterally and the pre-supplementary motor area (preSMA). This result both accords with, and extends, the findings of Dias *et al.* (1996) who reported that lesions of the lateral prefrontal cortex impaired attentional set-shifting in marmosets, whilst undertaking the primate version of the CANTAB attentional set-shifting task.

Two additional events were contrasted from the period immediately after the volunteer had passed the criterion of six consecutive correct responses and the rule changed. One of these events corresponded to the point in time that the stimulus set was changed and the volunteer selected a novel exemplar – effectively removing any response suppression component (because the previously relevant stimulus was no longer present to respond to). The other event was the reversal, modelled as the point in time when the participant first made a new selection within the same stimulus set on the basis of a change in the current rule. Whilst these two events had multiple components, subtraction of reversal minus stimulus set change allowed examination of the reversal aspect of attentional shifting specifically. That is to say, although both events involve a shift of response from one stimulus to another, in only one case did this also require the inhibition of response to a previously available stimulus (note: although, arguably, these two condition also differ—unavoidably—in that one involves new stimuli and in the other the stimuli remain the same, since two faces and two houses remain present in all cases, the differences observed are unlikely to relate to any basic changes in the perceptual scene). A second quite distinct executive circuit was associated with reversal; this included the anterior portion of the lateral OFC, the posterior extent of the dorsolateral prefrontal cortex (DLPFC) and the posterior parietal cortices (see Figure 14.1). These results again confirm and extend those of Dias *et al.* (1996) who reported that lesions of the orbitofrontal cortex lead to perseveration (or a failure of 'reversals') in non-human primates.

In addition, comparing neural activity during the reception of positive feedback with that observed during negative feedback identified a positive feedback related change in the medial OFC and the medial frontal wall, in line with previous reports of a role for this region in the processing of rewarding external feedback (Figure 14.1).

Interestingly, the anterior portion of the DLPFC, which has been widely implicated in attentional set-shifting, was active throughout the period of time when the rule was being derived, but this activity did not correlate disproportionately with any individual event type, suggesting that this region may play a more general (i.e. abstract) role in rule acquisition (Figure 14.1).

On the basis of these findings and previous research, we have suggested that at least four distinct neural circuits are active during, and contribute to performance of, this attentional set-shifting task. Thus, a 'ventrolateral frontal-lobe circuit' is centrally involved in disengaging attention from one dimension and refocusing attention on another. A 'medial orbitofrontal circuit' plays a key role in processing reward and presumably guiding responses made on the basis of that reward. A 'dorsolateral frontal-lobe circuit' is involved in problem solving at the most abstract level—perhaps maintaining the dimensions and manipulations that form the overarching task schema. Finally, a 'lateral orbitofrontal circuit' that also includes the posterior extent of the DLPFC and the posterior parietal cortices is crucial for suppressing previously learned but now inappropriate responses, as required by reversals.

The question that arises, therefore, is whether any of these circuits can be delineated in the various clinical populations that have been shown to be impaired at attentional set-shifting tasks, including the original CANTAB attentional set-shifting test. In addition, to what extent can disruption of one or more of these circuits be shown to be responsible for the pattern of deficits observed in any given population of patients? We now consider these questions in the context of recent data from obsessive compulsive disorder, healthy aging and Parkinson disease.

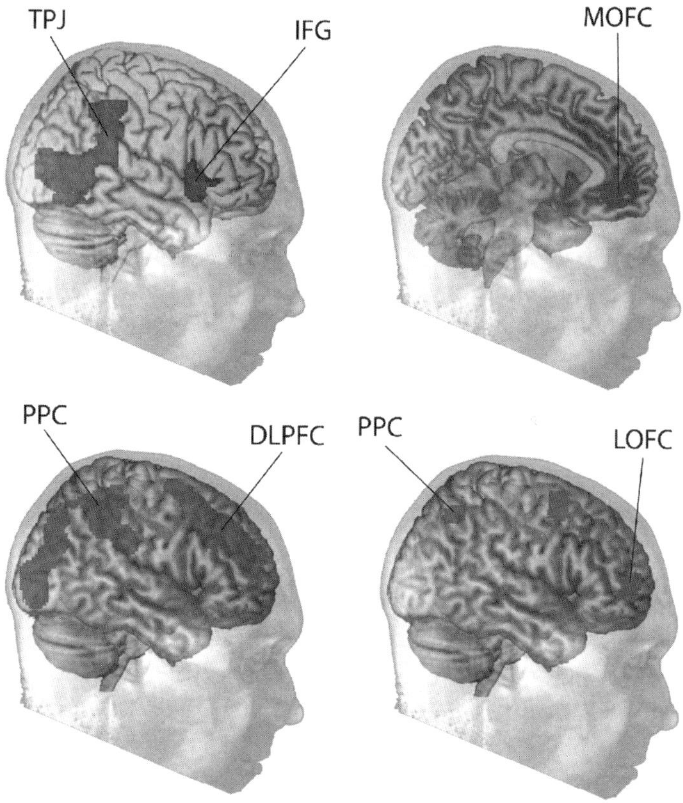

Fig. 14.1 Four cortical circuits that have been functionally dissociated in recent fMRI studies on attention and learning. Top left: activity during target detection in the posterior inferior frontal gyrus (IFG) and in a swathe of cortex centred on the temporal parietal junction (TPJ). Top right: medial orbitofrontal cortex (MOFC) activity during the reception of positive feedback. Bottom left: activity during rule learning. A dorsal network is recruited including the dorsolateral prefrontal cortex (DLPFC) and a swathe of posterior cortex spreading along the dorsal visual stream to the parietal cortex. Bottom right: activity during reversal learning. The lateral orbitofrontal cortex (OFC) posterior parietal cortex (PPC) and a region at the posterior extent of the middle frontal gyrus are all activated at the point of reversal.

The IDED task and obsessive compulsive disorder

Obsessive-compulsive disorder (OCD) is a 'dysexecutive syndrome' that is characterized by repetitive thoughts and behaviours. Previous research has implicated the OFC as being central to OCD (Hollander *et al.* 1996), although the causal relationship between OFC function and OCD is poorly understood. Initial pilot data, in which a group of patients and matched controls undertook the adapted IDED task described above (Hampshire and Owen, 2006), indicated that OCD patients were disproportionately impaired during reversal learning *beyond novelty*. This result accords well with the findings of the fMRI validation study in healthy volunteers (Hampshire and Owen, 2006), which showed that the lateral OFC was recruited when a reversal was performed. On this basis, it seemed likely that the fMRI task described above would be a suitable tool for investigating the causal relationship between the lateral OFC circuit and the set-shifting deficits that have been reported previously in OCD. This was recently confirmed by Chamberlain *et al.* (2008) who used the task developed by Hampshire and Owen (2006) to demonstrate that not only OCD patients, but also their unaffected first degree relatives have abnormally reduced activation within the lateral OFC circuit during reversal learning.

The implications of this finding are that reduced activity within the lateral OFC circuit can be considered to be an endophenotype (Gottesman and Gould, 2003) of OCD, i.e. a neurological marker of the unknown genetic factors that predispose an individual towards developing OCD. The nature of the OCD deficit also refines our understanding of the contribution made by this circuit, not only to rule learning per se, but to adaptive behaviour in general, i.e. it appears to be the case that hypoactivity within the lateral OFC circuit is associated with a form of cognitive inflexibility that is characterized by repetitive thoughts and behaviours. For future research, activation within the OFC circuit during reversal learning may be a useful clinical marker, both for disease susceptibility and treatment efficacy. An interesting related question is what the difference is between the OCD patients and their first degree relatives that leads to the (behavioural) executive deficit only being expressed in the former group? One clue is evident from the response time data; the first degree relatives were slower to respond during the stage of the task when the rule was being derived compared with both controls and patients, suggesting perhaps that they deliberated more when choosing which response to make. Further research is required, however, to fully elucidate the cognitive and neural basis of the factors which modulate the expression of OCD.

Self-organized attentional switching in (healthy) aging

As people progress from adulthood into old age there are changes throughout the brain at the molecular, cellular, and structural level, with concomitant changes in cognitive ability. The brain undergoes a global decline in terms of thinning of the cerebral cortex (Uylings and de Brabander, 2002; Salat *et al.*, 2005), reduction in grey matter (Good *et al.*, 2001), sulcal depth (Rettmann *et al.*, 2006), increased ventricular volume (Resnick *et al.*, 2000), dysmorphology of neurons, and loss of dendritic spines (Raz and Rodrigue, 2006).

However, not all regions in the brain show similar levels of age-related decline. Studies of the ageing brain have demonstrated that areas of the frontal cortex, along with their associated top down executive control processes, are particularly prone to the neurodegenerative effects of age.

It has previously been demonstrated that, in terms of executive deficits, the largest difference between old and young participants is in their ability to carry out the ED switch stage of the original CANTAB attentional set-shifting task (Robbins *et al.*, 1998). On this basis, it seems likely that switching attention between object dimensions may be one of the most vulnerable aspects of age-related degeneration, manifesting itself as impaired cognitive flexibility in older participants. Furthermore, it seems likely that this cognitive impairment relates to the disproportionate degeneration of frontal-lobe systems. It is not clear, however, which frontal-lobe circuits are responsible for age-related deficits on this task and which of the various cognitive processes that have been shown to be recruited during ED shifting are (relatively speaking) conserved or impaired.

Behaviourally, when the effects of ageing on performance of the fMRI task described above (Hampshire and Owen, 2006), were examined, older participants showed no increase in *perseverative behaviour*, either to the recently rewarded objects (i.e. at the stimulus level) or to the recently relevant visual dimension (i.e. at the dimensional level) (Hampshire *et al.*, 2008b). This fails to confirm previous suggestions that the effects of ageing on attentional set-switching ability reflect a specific deficit in switching attention between dimensions, as indexed by *perseveration* to the previously relevant dimension at the point of shift (Robbins *et al.*, 1998). In line with the observed lack of perseveration in the elderly participants, lateral and medial regions of the orbitofrontal cortex, which have previously been shown to activate during inhibitory control and reward processing, respectively (Hampshire and Owen, 2006), appeared to be functionally intact in the elderly participants.

However, these older participants did show a deficit of a more general kind; specifically, a global loss of efficient problem solving strategy (used while trying to derive the rules) was apparent (as indexed by a disordered search between possible rules) and there was a concomitant decrease of neural activity in the IFG and the preSMA. Interestingly, comparison of ID switches with non-switches also revealed an age-related decrease in this circuit. The dorsolateral prefrontal cortex circuit was also impaired during problem solving.

These results demonstrate that the executive impairment observed within the normal ageing population differs both in behavioural and neural terms to that observed in the OCD group. Such dissociations are not possible using the standard (behavioural) form of this task. The lowered activity within the

IFG-preSMA circuit in the older group was concomitant with a general decrease in efficient strategy during the solution search phase of the task. More specifically, when trying to acquire the rules guiding the shifts, older participants tended to repeatedly check those exemplars that had already been eliminated. This deficit did not reflect a total loss of strategy, however, (that is to say, it did not reflect a complete failure to understand the basic task requirements) as older participants still showed an overall cost of ED switching which would only be evident if the basic task instructions are being followed (as opposed to truly random responding). The IFG has been implicated in attentional control, responding selectively to task relevant and attentionally demanding inputs (Rao *et al.*, 1997; Freedman *et al.*, 2001; Everling *et al.*, 2002; Duncan, 2006; Hampshire *et al.*, 2007; Hampshire *et al.*, 2008a). On the basis of these results, we have proposed, therefore, that the primary age-related deficit in these tasks reflects a failure to bias or 'tune' attentional processing between competing representations in modality-specific posterior regions in order to maintain their relevance to current behavioural goals (Hampshire *et al.* 2008b). Interestingly, in the original CANTAB attentional set-shifting task—where the ED shift only occurs once in the entire test—such a deficit would most likely manifest as an inefficient approach to the identification and elimination of those parameters and dimensions that could be relevant during the forthcoming novel ED shift. This would result in an overall reduction in cognitive flexibility which is indeed what has been observed in that task (Robbins *et al.* 1998).

Rule learning and Parkinson disease

In recent years, increasing emphasis has been placed on the cognitive and behavioural symptoms that often accompany the primary motor deficits in Parkinson's disease (PD). Executive dysfunction is often particularly prominent in early PD (Foltynie *et al.*, 2004; Muslimovic *et al.*, 2005) and has important implications for treatment and quality of life (Aarsland *et al.*, 2000; Schrag *et al.*, 2000). PD patients as a group are impaired on the CANTAB attentional set-shifting task (Downes *et al.*, 1989; Owen *et al.*, 1992) and it has proved to be a useful tool for both characterizing patient deficits and for assessing treatment efficacy (e.g. Lange *et al.*, 1992; Owen *et al.*, 1992; 1993; 1995).

In a recent study, we compared PD patients and age-matched controls while undertaking the fMRI task involving faces and houses described above. Behaviourally, the most notable deficit was in terms of the rate at which the PD patients acquired the task. Specifically, they found it difficult to learn how to approach the task at the most general level, took longer during the training phase outside the scanner and still performed poorly in the first of the two blocks of the scanning acquisition itself, despite extensive pre-training. In contrast, by the second block of scanning acquisition, the patients and the age-matched controls were performing at the same level. In contrast to previous studies that have suggested a specific ED shifting deficit in PD (e.g. Downes *et al.*, 1989; Owen *et al*, 1993), these results—using a version of the tasks that involves multiple ED and ID shifts—suggest a rather general 'task-level' learning deficit in the PD group. When the fMRI data from the two groups was compared, an abnormal decrease in activity was observed in the patients in the right DLPFC and the anterior cingulate cortex, concomitant with a role for this circuitry in the problem solving processes that are intrinsic to learning any task of this sort.

PD is a heterogeneous disorder, however, with marked variability in individual susceptibility to executive dysfunction (Lewis *et al.*, 2003). The neurological basis of PD lies in dopamine (DA) depletion, and frontostriatal circuits are known to be modulated by levels of DA (Lange *et al.*, 1992; Owen *et al.*, 1995). On this basis, it seems likely that executive deficits, where they are observed, are also caused by abnormal DA levels, a suggestion supported by the observation that dopaminergic medication modulates both executive behaviour and DLPFC function in PD (Lange *et al.*, 1992; Cools *et al.*, 2001). One gene that is likely to account for some of the variability in susceptibility to executive dysfunction in PD is the COMT val^{158}met polymorphism. The COMT gene plays a particularly important role in metabolizing DA within the frontal lobes and the two commonly occurring polymorphisms produce marked differences in frontal-lobe DA levels (Karoum *et al.*, 1994; Gogos *et al.*, 1998; Lewis *et al.*, 2001; Mazei *et al.*, 2002; Chen *et al.*, 2004).

In a recent study (Williams-Gray *et al.* 2008), PD patients in the two COMT val^{158}met homozygous groups were scanned while performing the fMRI attentional set-shifting task described above (Hampshire and Owen, 2006). The behavioural results revealed a novel dissociation between the strategies adopted by the two patient groups. As described above, typically, healthy participants preferentially shift attention within, rather than between, stimulus dimensions, and consequently identify the correct target with fewer errors when an ID shift is required rather than when an ED shift is required. Amongst the PD patients, a similar (i.e. normal) pattern was observed in the val/val homozygote group. However, the met/met homozygote group performed equivalently in terms of number of errors whether an ID or ED shift was required, indicating that they had not formed an attentional 'set' to the previously relevant stimulus dimension, but rather treated each new stage of the task as though it were an entirely independent problem. This alternative strategy, although 'abnormal', was not detrimental in terms of the overall number of errors;

however, it was associated with increased response time when the rule was being derived. Moreover, this poorly formed ‘attentional set’ in the met/met group was concomitant with under-activation within the dorsolateral frontal cortex and the posterior parietal cortex, regions that have been shown previously to be necessary for rule acquisition.

Finally, examination of the effects of L-Dopa medication revealed an interaction between dose and COMT genotype, both in terms of task performance and BOLD response. Thus, in the val/val group, increasing levels of L-Dopa medication had a detrimental effect on performance by increasing the number of errors made whilst searching for the target stimulus. In contrast, in the met/met group, there was no significant effect of L-Dopa dose on performance. The imaging data revealed similar results; there was a significant interaction between genotype and the relationship between L-Dopa dose and BOLD activation in frontal and parietal areas, such that higher L-Dopa doses had a greater negative impact on activation in val/val than in met/met homozygotes.

This study demonstrates that executive function (and dysfunction) in PD is critically determined by a combination of both genetic and pharmacological influences on dopaminergic levels within the frontal lobes. These data can be accommodated by the well-established hypothesis of an ‘inverted U-shaped relationship’ between dopamine levels and prefrontal function (e.g. either too little or too much dopamine is bad for prefrontal functioning; for discussion, see Williams-Gray *et al.* 2008). According to this model, in healthy controls, an increasing number of met alleles is associated with improved prefrontal function as predicted by the left-hand side of the inverted U-shaped curve. The findings in PD suggest that they are, conversely, on the right hand side of the curve where an increasing number of met alleles is associated with impaired prefrontal function. It is well known that in the early stages of PD, the prefrontal cortex is in ‘hyperdopaminergic state’ providing a pathophysiological mechanism for this shift rightwards on this hypothesized inverted U-shaped curve. The inverted U model also suggests that the effect of dopaminergic medication (L-Dopa) will differ according to an individual’s pre-existing position on the curve. In line with this, we observed a greater detrimental effect of L-Dopa medication in PD val homozygotes who are expected to be nearer the peak of the curve than in PD methomozygotes who are already near the base of the curve, suggesting a floor effect in the latter group. These findings have important implications for understanding the neurobiological basis of attentional control, and highlights the risk of medication-induced cognitive dysfunction in certain genotypic groups of PD patients, which may ultimately impact on clinical practice.

Conclusions

Using fMRI and a task that can independently measure the effects of various different cognitive demands, it has been possible to functionally define several of the anatomical components which underpin human executive processing (see Figure 14.1). These circuits facilitate different aspects of performance during tests of attention and learning. When differentially degraded, dissociable forms of executive dysfunction are observed, yielding clinically-specific patterns of impairment within different pathological conditions and abnormal BOLD activity. In this way, a number of distinct executive circuits have been delineated including a ventral prefrontal circuit that appears to be involved in disengaging and refocusing attention (e.g. between different stimulus dimensions in an attentional set-shifting task) a DLPFC/posterior parietal circuit that appears to be involved in learning and maintaining the overarching task schema, a lateral OFC circuit, that appears to enable behaviour to adapt when response-outcome contingencies change and a medial OFC circuit that processes reward.

Using this framework, we have begun to dissociate the neural correlates of attention and learning deficits in PD patients, OCD patients, and in the healthy aging population. In the latter case, the findings suggest that a re-evaluation is required regarding the underlying basis of age-related cognitive inflexibility—dimensional perseveration and an associated ED shifting deficit do not provide an adequate explanation for the deficits observed. In the case of OCD, neuroimaging analysis has allowed a 'vulnerability marker' to be identified, for the first time, in first degree relatives. This endophenotype lends insight into the causal relationship between OFC function and OCD pathogenesis and could form a useful neurological marker for the efficacy of pharmacological interventions in this population. Finally, in the case of PD, it has been possible to begin to unravel the complex relationship between activity within the affected executive circuit, inheritable (genetic) factors, and medication—raising the real possibility of generating individually tailored interventions that take each patient's genetic vulnerability to both disease- and drug-related executive dysfunction into account.

Importantly, the results of this clinical work feed back into the basic science by allowing new hypotheses to be generated and tested about how these various cortical circuits—and their pharmacological and genetic influences—operate during healthy cognitive functioning. For example, by studying genetic sub-groups of patients with PD, we have shown that an increasing number of met alleles is detrimental to performance on set-shifting tasks and is associated with impaired prefrontal function (Williams-Gray *et al.* 2008). If, as we have argued, these results reflect the relative positions of these two sub-groups on the hypothesized inverted U-shaped curve, then a direct prediction that follows about the general population is that healthy met homozygotes will be *better* at attentional set-shifting than healthy val homozygotes (i.e. the exact opposite to the pattern observed in PD). That is to say, because the genetic predisposition of healthy met homozygotes generates more optimal operating levels of dopamine within the prefrontal cortex and because the prefrontal cortex is crucial for set-shifting performance, their baseline performance should be better. Our recent results in healthy volunteers suggest that this is indeed the case (Fallon, Hampshire, Owen *et al.* in preparation). By extension, a hypothesis that remains to be tested is that healthy val homozygotes would benefit more on such tasks from dopaminergic intervention (because they are improving from a lower baseline) than healthy met homozygotes (who would be 'pushed' beyond their point of optimal performance on the inverted U-shaped curve).

In summary, we have tried to illustrate, through example, how the relationship between basic science and clinical research is synergistic—the cognitive and neural circuits that have been defined through studies of attention and learning in the healthy population become tools for understanding how and why performance breaks down in various pathological conditions. In contrast, the impaired performance of well-studied clinical populations with known genetic, pharmacological or neurological disorders can be used to generate and test new hypotheses about how attention and learning are instantiated in the healthy brain, leading to advances in cognitive models, as well as the tools that are developed to test those models.

Abbreviations

ED	Extra-dimensional shift
ID	Intra-dimensional shift
EDR	Extra-dimensional reversal
IDR	Intra-dimensional reversal
PD	Parkinson disease
OCD	Obsessive-compulsive disorder
DA	Dopamine
LPFC	Lateral prefrontal cortex
OFC	Orbitofrontal cortex
MOGC	Medial orbitofrontal cortex
LOFG	Lateral orbitofrontal cortex
TPJ	Temporal parietal junction

PPC	Posterior parietal cortex
preSMA	Pre-supplementary motor area
IFG	Inferior frontal gyrus
DLPFC	Dorsolateral prefrontal cortex
fMRI	Functional magnetic resonance imaging
BOLD	Blood oxygenation level dependent
PET	Positron emission tomography

References

Aarsland, D., Larsen, J.P., Tandberg, E. et al. (2000). Predictors of nursing home placement in Parkinson's disease: a population-based-prospective study. *J Am Geriatr Soc*, **48**, 938–942.

Anderson, S.W., Bechara, A., Damasio, H., Tranel, D., & Damasio, A.R. (1999). Impairment of social and moral behavior related to early damage in human prefrontal cortex. *Nat Neurosci* **2**, 1032–1037.

Bechara, A., Damasio, A.R., Damasio, H., & Anderson, S.W. (1994). Insensitivity to future consequences following damage to human prefrontal cortex. *Cognition* **50**, 7–15.

Chamberlain, S.R., Menzies, L., Hampshire, A. et al. (2008). Orbitofrontal dysfunction in patients with obsessive-compulsive disorder and their unaffected relatives. *Science*, **321**, 421–422.

Chen, J., Lipska, B.K., Halim, N. (2004). Functional analysis of genetic variation in catechol-O-methyltransferase (COMT), effects on mRNA, protein, and enzyme activity in postmortem human brain. *Am J Hum Genet*, **75**,807–821.

Cools, R., Barker, R.A., Sahakian, B.J. et al (2001). Enhanced or impaired cognitive function in Parkinson's disease as a function of dopaminergic medication and task demands. *Cerebral Cortex*, **11**,1136–1143.

Cools, R., Clark, L., Owen, A.M., & Robbins, T.W. (2002). Defining the neural mechanisms of probabilistic reversal learning using event-related functional magnetic resonance imaging. *J* Neurosci, **22**, 4563–4567.

Dias, R., Robbins, T.W., & Roberts, A.C. (1996). Dissociation in prefrontal cortex of affective and attentional shifts. *Nature*, **380**, 69–72.

Dove, A., Pollmann, S., Schubert, T., Wiggins, C.J., & von Cramon, D.Y. (2000). Prefrontal cortex activation in task switching: an event-related fMRI study. *Cogn Brain Res*, **9**, 103–109.

Downes, J.J., Roberts, A.C., Sahakian, B.J., Evenden, J.L., Morris, R.G., & Robbins, T.W. (1989). Impaired extra-dimensional shift performance in medicated and unmedicated Parkinson's disease: evidence for a specific attentional dysfunction. *Neuropsychologia*, **27**, 1329–1343.

Duncan, J. (2006). EPS Mid-Career Award 2004: brain mechanisms of attention. *Q J Exp Psychol* (Colchester), **59**, 2–27.

Epstein, R. & Kanwisher, N. (1998). A cortical representation of the local visual environment. *Nature* **392**, 598–601.

Everling, S., Tinsley, C.J., Gaffan, D., & Duncan, J. (2002). Filtering of neural signals by focused attention in the monkey prefrontal cortex. *Nat Neurosci*, **5**, 671–676.

Foltynie, T., Brayne, C.E., Robbins, T.W., & Barker, R.A. (2004). The cognitive ability of an incident cohort of Parkinson's patients in the UK. The CamPaIGN study. *Brain*, **127**, 550–560.

Freedman, D.J., Riesenhuber, M., Poggio, T., & Miller, E.K. (2001). Categorical representation of visual stimuli in the primate prefrontal cortex. *Science*, **291**, 312–316.

Gogos, J.A., Morgan, M., Luine, V. et al. (1998). Catechol-O-methyltransferase-deficient mice exhibit sexually dimorphic changes in catecholamine levels and behavior. *Proc Natl Acad Sci U S A*, **95**, 9991–9996.

Good, C.D., Johnsrude, I.S., Ashburner, J., Henson, R.N., Friston, K.J., & Frackowiak, R.S. (2001). A voxel-based morphometric study of ageing in 465 normal adult human brains. *Neuroimage*, **14**, 21–36.

Gottesman, II, Gould TD (2003). The endophenotype concept in psychiatry: Etymology and strategic intentions. *Am J Psychiatry*, **160**, 636–645.

Hampshire, A. & Owen, A.M. (2006). Fractionating attentional control using event-related fMRI. *Cerebral Cortex*, **16**, 1679–1689.

Hampshire, A., Duncan, J., & Owen, A.M. (2007). Selective tuning of the blood oxygenation level-dependent response during simple target detection dissociates human frontoparietal subregions. *J Neurosci*, **27**, 6219–6223.

Hampshire, A., Thompson, R., Duncan, J., & Owen, A.M. (2008a). The target selective neural response – similarity, ambiguity, and learning effects. *PLoS ONE*, **3**(6), e2520.

Hampshire, A., Gruszka, A., Fallon, S.J., & Owen, A.M. (2008b). Inefficiency in self-organized attentional switching in the normal aging population is associated with decreased activity in the ventrolateral prefrontal cortex. *J Cogn Neurosci*, **20**, 1670–1686.

Hollander, E., Kwon, J.H., Stein, D.J., Broatch, J., Rowland, C.T., & Himelein, C.A. (1996). Obsessive-compulsive and spectrum disorders: overview and quality of life issues. *J Clin Psychiatry*, **57** (Suppl 8), 3–6.

Hornak, J., O'Doherty, J., Bramham, J. et al. (2004). Reward-related reversal learning after surgical excisions in orbito-frontal or dorsolateral prefrontal cortex in humans. Journal of *Cogn* Neurosci, **16**, 463–478.

Kanwishe, N., McDermott, J., & Chun, M.M. (1997). The fusiform face area: a module in human extrastriate cortex specialized for face perception. *J Neurosci*, **17**, 4302–4311.

Karoum, F., Chrapusta, S.J., & Egan, M.F. (1994). 3-Methoxytyramine is the major metabolite of released dopamine in the rat frontal cortex: reassessment of the effects of antipsychotics on the dynamics of dopamine release and metabolism in the frontal cortex, nucleus accumbens, and striatum by a simple two pool model. *J Neurochem*, **63**, 972–979.

Konishi, S., Nakajima, K., Uchida, I. et al. (1998). Transient activation of inferior prefrontal cortex during cognitive set shifting. *Nat* Neurosci, **1**, 80–84.

Lange, K.W., Robbins, T.W., Marsden, C.D. et al. (1992). L-dopa withdrawal in Parkinson's disease selectively impairs cognitive performance in tests sensitive to frontal lobe dysfunction. *Psychopharmacology*, **107**, 394–404.

Lawrence, A.D., Sahakian, B.J., Hodges, J.R., Rosser, A.E., Lange, K.W., & Robbins, T.W. (1996). Executive and mnemonic functions in early Huntington's disease. *Brain*, **119**, 1633–1645.

Lewis, D.A., Melchitzky, D.S., Sesack, S.R., Whitehead, R.E., Auh, S., & Sampson, A. (2001). Dopamine transporter immunoreactivity in monkey cerebral cortex: regional, laminar, and ultrastructural localization. *J Comp Neurol*, **432**, 119–136.

Lewis, S.J., Cools, R., Robbins, T.W., Dove, A., Barker, R.A., & Owen, A.M. (2003). Using executive heterogeneity to explore the nature of working memory deficits in Parkinson's disease. *Neuropsychologia*, **41**, 645–654.

Mackinto, N.J. (1973). Inhibition and Learning – Boakes, RA and Halliday, MS. *Quarterly Journal of Experimental Psychology*, **25**, 281–283.

Mazei, M.S., Pluto, C.P., Kirkbride, B., & Pehek, E.A. (2002). Effects of catecholamine uptake blockers in the caudate-putamen and subregions of the medial prefrontal cortex of the rat. *Brain Res*, **936**, 58–67.

Monsell, S. (2003). Task switching. *Trends Cognitive* Sci, **7**, 134–140.

Muslimovic, D., Post, B., Speelman, J.D., & Schmand, B. (2005). Cognitive profile of patients with newly diagnosed Parkinson disease. *Neurology*, **65**, 1239–1245.

Nagahama, Y., Okada, T., Katsumi, Y. et al. (1999). Transient neural activity in the medial superior frontal gyrus and precuneus time locked with attention shift between object features. *Neuroimage*, **10**, 193–199.

Nakahara, K., Hayashi, T., Konishi, S., & Miyashita, Y. (2002). Functional MRI of macaque monkeys performing a cognitive set-shifting task. *Science*, **295**, 1532–1536.

Owen, A.M. Roberts, A.C. Polkey, C.E. Sahakian, B.J. & Robbins, T.W. (1991). Extra-dimensional versus intra-dimensional set shifting performance following frontal lobe excisions, temporal lobe excisions or amygdalo-hippocampectomy in Man. *Neuropsychologia*, **29**(10), 993–1006.

Owen A.M., Roberts, A.C., Hodges, J.R., Summers, B.A., Polkey, C.E., & Robbins T.W. (1993). Contrasting mechanisms of impaired attentional set-shifting in patients with frontal lobe damage or Parkinson's disease. *Brain*, **116** (Pte 5), 1159–1179.

Owen, A.M., Sahakian, B.J., Hodges, J.R., Summers, B.A., Polkey, C.E., & Robbins, T.W. (1995). Dopamine-dependent frontostriatal planning deficits in early Parkinson's disease. *Neuropsychology*, **9**, 126–140.

Owen, A.M., James, M., Leigh, P.N. et al. (1992). Fronto-striatal cognitive deficits at different stages of Parkinson's disease. *Brain*, **115** (Pt 6), 1727–1751.

Pantelis, C., Barnes, T.R., Nelson, H.E. et al. (1997). Frontal-striatal cognitive deficits in patients with chronic schizophrenia. *Brain* **120** (Pt 10), 1823–1843.

Rao, S.C., Rainer, G., & Miller, E.K. (1997). Integration of what and where in the primate prefrontal cortex. *Science*, **276**, 821-824.

Raz, N. & Rodrigue, K.M. (2006). Differential aging of the brain: patterns, cognitive correlates and modifiers. *Neurosci Biobehav Rev*, **30**, 730–748.

Resnick, S.M., Goldszal, A.F., Davatzikos, C. et al. (2000). One-year age changes in MRI brain volumes in older adults. *Cereb Cortex*, **10**, 464–472.

Rettmann, M.E., Kraut, M.A., Prince, J.L., & Resnick, S.M. (2006). Cross-sectional and longitudinal analyses of anatomical sulcal changes associated with aging. *Cereb Cortex*, **16**, 1584–1594.

Robbins, T.W., James, M., Owen, A.M. et al. (1998). A study of performance on tests from the CANTAB battery sensitive to frontal lobe dysfunction in a large sample of normal volunteers: Implications for theories of executive functioning and cognitive aging. *J Int Neuropsychol* Soc, **4**, 474–490.

Roberts, A.C., Robbins, T.W., & Everitt, B.J. (1988). The effects of intradimensional and extradimensional shifts on visual discrimination learning in humans and non-human primates. *Q J Exp Psychol* **B 40**, 321–341.

Salat, D.H., Tuch, D.S., Greve, D.N. et al. (2005). Age-related alterations in white matter microstructure measured by diffusion tensor imaging. *Neurobiol Aging*, **26**,1215–1227.

Schrag, A., Jahanshahi, M., & Quinn, N. (2000). What contributes to quality of life in patients with Parkinson's disease? *J Neurol Neurosurg Psychiatry*, **69**, 308–312.

Uylings, H.B. & de Brabander, J.M. (2002). Neuronal changes in normal human aging and Alzheimer's disease. *Brain Cogn*, **49**, 268–276.

Veale, D.M., Sahakian, B.J., Owen, A.M., & Marks, I.M .(1996). Specific cognitive deficits in tests sensitive to frontal lobe dysfunction in obsessive-compulsive disorder. *Psychol* Med, **26**, 1261–1269.

Williams-Gray, C.H., Hampshire, A., Barker, R.A., & Owen, A.M. (2008). Attentional control in Parkinson's disease is dependent on COMT val 158 met genotype. *Brain*, **131**, 397–408.

Index